DEBATING NEW APPROACHES TO HISTORY

DEBATING NEW APPROACHES TO HISTORY

Edited by Marek Tamm and Peter Burke

BLOOMSBURY ACADEMIC
LONDON · NEW YORK · OXFORD · NEW DELHI · SYDNEY

BLOOMSBURY ACADEMIC
Bloomsbury Publishing Plc
50 Bedford Square, London, WC1B 3DP, UK
1385 Broadway, New York, NY 10018, USA
29 Earlsfort Terrace, Dublin 2, Ireland

BLOOMSBURY, BLOOMSBURY ACADEMIC and the Diana logo are trademarks of
Bloomsbury Publishing Plc

First published in Great Britain 2019
Reprinted by Bloomsbury Academic 2019 (twice), 2020, 2021, 2023

Cover design by Catherine Wood

Cover image: *Resultative Tug-of-War 2*, Acrylic on canvas, 100 x 120 cm, 2012,
by August Künnapu (augustkunnapu.epifanio.eu). Private collection.

A catalogue record for this book is available from the British Library.

Names: Tamm, Marek, editor. | Burke, Peter, 1937- editor.
Title: Debating new approaches to history / edited by Marek Tamm and Peter Burke.
Description: London, UK : Bloomsbury Academic, 2019. | Includes bibliographical
references and index.
Identifiers: LCCN 2018014157 (print) | LCCN 2018040759 (ebook) |
ISBN 9781474281942 (ePDF) | ISBN 9781474281935 (ePUB) |
ISBN 9781474281911 (hardback) | ISBN 9781474281928 (pbk.)
Subjects: LCSH: Historiography. | History–Methodology. | History–Philosophy.
Classification: LCC D13 (ebook) | LCC D13 .D389 2019 (print) | DDC 907.2–dc23
LC record available at https://lccn.loc.gov/2018014157

ISBN: HB: 978-1-4742-8191-1
PB: 978-1-4742-8192-8
ePDF: 978-1-4742-8194-2
eBook: 978-1-4742-8193-5

Typeset by Deanta Global Publishing Services, Chennai, India
Printed and bound in Great Britain

To find out more about our authors and books visit www.bloomsbury.com and
sign up for our newsletters.

CONTENTS

Contents

LIST OF FIGURES

LIST OF CONTRIBUTORS

Steve F. Anderson is Professor of Digital Media in the School of Theatre, Film and Television at the University of California, Los Angeles, working at the intersection of media, history, technology, and culture. He is the founder/principal investigator of the public media archive and fair use advocacy network Critical Commons. Along with Tara McPherson, he is co-editor of the interdisciplinary electronic journal *Vectors* and co-principal investigator of the Alliance for Networking Visual Culture, developers of the open source electronic publishing platform Scalar. He is the author of *Technologies of History: Visual Media and the Eccentricity of the Past* (Dartmouth College Press, 2011) and *Technologies of Vision: The War Between Data and Images* (MIT Press, 2017).

Gil Bartholeyns is an associate professor at the University of Lille, where he is in charge of the MA and PhD programmes in visual humanities. His recent research is focused on domestic cultures, miraculous images from the Middle Ages to today, and on visual experiences of the past in contemporary societies. He is the author of *Image et transgression au Moyen Age* with P.O. Dittmar and V. Jolivet (PUF, 2008), and the editor of *Adam et l'astragale. Essais d'anthropologie et d'histoire sur les limites de l'humain*, with P.O. Dittmar et al. (Editions de la MSH, 2009); *La performance des images*, with A. Dierkens and T. Golsenne (Brussels University Press, 2010); *Culture matérielles: anthologie raisonnée*, with N. Govoroff and F. Joulian (Editions de la MSH, 2011); *Politiques visuelles* (Les Presses du réel, 2016) as well as *Images de soi dans l'univers domestique* (with M. Bourin and P-O. Dittmar, PUR, 2018).

Rob Boddice is Marie-Curie Global Fellow at the Friedrich-Meinecke-Institut, Freie Universität Berlin, and at McGill University, Montreal. His research is focused on the history of pain, sympathy, cruelty, disease, and evolution, with particular emphasis on the moral status of human beings and other animals. His recent book publications include *The Science of Sympathy: Morality, Evolution and Victorian Civilization* (Illinois University Press, 2016); *Pain: A Very Short Introduction* (Oxford University Press, 2017); *The History of Emotions* (Manchester University Press, 2018); and *A History of Feelings* (Reaktion, forthcoming).

Peter Burke is Professor Emeritus of Cultural History and Life Fellow of Emmanuel College, University of Cambridge. He is also a fellow of the British Academy and member of the Academia Europea. He is a specialist in the social and cultural history of early modern Europe as well as in theoretical and methodological questions of historical research. His most recent books include *What Is the History of Knowledge?* (Polity, 2015); *Secret History and Historical Consciousness from Renaissance to Romanticism* (Edward Everett Root, 2016); and *Exiles and Expatriates in the History of Knowledge, 1500–2000* (Brandeis University Press, 2017).

Geoffrey Cubitt is a reader in the Department of History, and Director of the Institute for the Public Understanding of the Past (IPUP) at the University of York. His recent research focuses on social memory, commemoration, museum representations of history, and the political and cultural uses of the past in modern and contemporary societies. He is the author of *The Jesuit Myth: Conspiracy Theory and Politics in Nineteenth-Century France* (Oxford University Press, 1993) and *History and Memory* (Manchester University Press, 2007) and editor of *Imaging Nations* (Manchester University Press, 1998); *Heroic Reputations and Exemplary Lives* (with A. Warren, Manchester University Press, 2000); and *Representing Enslavement and Abolition in Museums: Ambiguous Engagements* (with L. Smith, R. Wilson, and K. Fouseki, Routledge, 2011).

Lorraine Daston is Director of the Max Planck Institute for the History of Science in Berlin and Visiting Professor in the Committee on Social Thought at the University of Chicago. She has published on a wide range of topics in the history of science, including the history of probability and statistics, wonders in early modern science, the emergence of the scientific fact, scientific models, objects of scientific inquiry, the moral authority of nature, and the history of scientific objectivity. Her recent books include (with Paul Erikson et al.) *How Reason Almost Lost Its Mind: The Strange Career of Cold War Rationality* (Chicago University Press, 2014) and *Histories of Scientific Observation*, ed. with Elizabeth Lunbeck (Chicago University Press, 2011).

Ewa Domanska is Professor of Human Sciences in the Department of History, Adam Mickiewicz University in Poznań, Poland, and Visiting Associate Professor in the Department of Anthropology, Stanford University. Her teaching and research interests include the comparative theory of the human and social sciences, the history and theory of historiography, ecological humanities, genocide and ecocide studies. Her more recent publications include *Re-Figuring Hayden White* (ed. with Frank Ankersmit and Hans Kellner, Stanford University Press, 2009); *Existential History: A Critical Approach to Narrativism and Emancipatory Humanities* (in Polish, 2012); and *Necros: An Introduction to the Ontology of Human Corpses and Remains* (in Polish, 2017).

Laura Lee Downs is Professor of History at the European University Institute, Florence, where she holds the chair in gender history, and is Directrice d'Études at the École des Hautes Études en Sciences Sociales, Paris, where she holds a chair in the comparative history of social management. She has published extensively on issues of gender and labour in twentieth-century Europe, on working-class childhood, and on the comparative history of social protection in Europe. She has also published widely on gender analysis and historical method, most notably in her *Writing Gender History* (2nd edn, Bloomsbury, 2010). Her publications also include *Childhood in the Promised Land: Working-Class Movements and the Colonies de Vacances in France, 1880–1960* (Duke University Press, 2002), and *Why France? American Historians Reflect on an Enduring Fascination*, ed. with Stéphane Gerson (Cornell University Press, 2007).

Prasenjit Duara is the Oscar L. Tang Family Professor of East Asian Studies at Duke University, and previously worked as the Raffles Professor of Humanities at the National University of Singapore where he was also director of the Asian Research Institute and Research in Humanities and Social Sciences (2008–15). In addition to Chinese history, he works more broadly on Asia in the twentieth century, and on historical thought and historiography. Among his recent books are *The Global and Regional in China's Nation-Formation* (Routledge, 2009) and *The Crisis of Global Modernity: Asian Traditions and a Sustainable Future* (Cambridge University Press, 2014). He has recently co-edited *A Companion to Global Historical Thought* (John Wiley, 2014).

Ute Frevert is Director at the Max Planck Institute for Human Development and a scientific member of the Max Planck Society. From 2003 to 2007 she was Professor of German History at Yale University and previously taught history at the University of Konstanz, Bielefeld University, and the Free University in Berlin. Her research interests include the social and cultural history of the modern period, the history of emotions, gender history, and political history. Her recent publications include *Emotions in History: Lost and Found* (Central European University Press, 2011); *Gefühlspolitik: Friedrich II. als Herr über die Herzen?* (Wallstein, 2012); *Learning How to Feel: Children's Literature and the History of Emotional Socialization, 1870-1970* (Oxford University Press, 2014); and *Die Politik der Demütigung: Schauplätze von Macht und Ohnmacht* (Fischer, 2017).

Ivan Gaskell is Professor of Cultural History and Museum Studies, and Head of the Focus Project at Bard Graduate Center, New York City, having taught and curated at Harvard University between 1991 and 2011. His areas of special interests are the material culture of North America and Europe from the sixteenth through twentieth centuries, and philosophy of museums and material culture. Recently he has published *Tangible Things: Making History through Objects*, with Laurel Thatcher Ulrich, Sara J. Schechner, Sarah Anne Carter, and photographs by Samantha S. B. van Gerbig (Oxford University Press 2015), *Sturm der Bilder: Bürger, Moral und Politik in den Niederlanden, 1515–1616*, with Martin van Gelderen (Kunst, 2016), and *The Oxford Handbook of History and Material Culture*, ed. with Sarah Anne Carter (Oxford University Press, forthcoming).

Dominick LaCapra is Bryce and Edith M. Bowmar Professor Emeritus of Humanistic Studies at Cornell University. His scholarly interests range widely in the areas of modern European intellectual and cultural history, historiography, trauma studies, history and literature, and critical theory. He is the author or editor of many books, including most recently *History in Transit: Experience, Identity, Critical Theory* (Cornell University Press, 2004); *History and Its Limits: Human, Animal, Violence* (Cornell University Press, 2009) and *History, Literature, Critical Theory* (Cornell University Press, 2013).

Rochona Majumdar is Associate Professor in the Departments of Cinema and Media Studies, and South Asian Languages and Civilizations at the University of Chicago. She is a historian of modern India and her interests span the histories of Indian cinema, gender, and marriage in colonial India, and Indian intellectual thought in the nineteenth and twentieth centuries. She has published *Marriage and Modernity: Family Values in Colonial Bengal* (Duke University Press, 2009); *Writing Postcolonial History* (Bloomsbury, 2010); and *From the Colonial to the Postcolonial: India and Pakistan in Transition*, ed. with Dipesh Chakrabarty and Andrew Sartori (Oxford University Press, 2007).

Martin Mulsow is Professor of Cultures of Knowledge in Early Modern Europe and Director of the Gotha Research Centre at the University of Erfurt. He previously worked as professor of history at Rutgers University in New Brunswick (2005–08), specializing in the history of early modern Europe, with research interests located between the history of philosophy, the history of ideas, historical anthropology, and cultural history. Among his recent book publications are *Prekäres Wissen. Eine andere Ideengeschichte der Frühen Neuzeit* (Suhrkamp, 2012); *Enlightenment Underground: Radical Germany, 1680–1720* (Virginia University Press, 2015); and *Decorum and Disorder: The Republic of Letters 1550–1750* (Michigan University Press, forthcoming).

Piroska Nagy is Professor of Medieval History at the Université du Québec à Montréal. Her research explores the relation between collective religious emotions, events, and change in the Middle Ages and medieval affective anthropology, especially embodied religious emotions, experience, and charismas. She is author of *Le don des larmes au Moyen Age: Un instrument spirituel en quête d'institution, Ve–XIIIe siècle* (Albin Michel, 2000) and co-author, with Damien Boquet, of *Medieval Sensibilities: A History of Emotions in the Middle Ages* (Polity, 2018). Recently she has also edited with N. Cohen-Hanegbi the volume *Pleasure in the Middle Ages* (Brepols, 2018).

Bjørnar Olsen is Professor of Archaeology at the University of Tromsø – the Arctic University of Norway. He has worked with northern and Sámi archaeology as well with theoretical issues in archaeology. His research interests also include contemporary archaeology, modern ruins, material memory, and thing theory. His latest books are *In Defence of Things: Archaeology and the Ontology of Objects* (AltaMira Press, 2010); *Persistent Memories: Pyramiden – a Soviet Mining Town in the High Arctic* (with E. Andreassen and H. Bjerck, Tapir Academic Press, 2010); *Archaeology: The Discipline of Things* (with M. Shanks, T. Webmoor, and C. Witmore, California University Press, 2012); *Hunters in Transition: An Outline of Early Sámi History* (with L.I. Hansen, Brill, 2014); and *Ruin Memories: Materialities, Aesthetics and the Archaeology of the Recent Past*, ed. with Þ. Pétursdóttir (Routledge, 2014).

Jürgen Osterhammel is Professor Emeritus of Modern and Contemporary History at the University of Konstanz. He works on European and Asian history from the eighteenth century. He has also published widely on history and theory of historiography, and is currently preparing a study of Jacob Burckhardt as a world historian. His recent publications include *The Transformation of the World: A Global History of the Nineteenth Century* (Princeton University Press, 2014); *Die Flughöhe der Adler: Historische Essays zur globalen Gegenwart* (Beck, 2017); *Decolonization: A Short History* (with Jan C. Jansen, Princeton University Press, 2017), and *Unfabling the East: The Enlightenment's Encounter* *with Asia* (Princeton University Press, 2018). With Akira Iriye, he is the editor-in-chief of *A History of the World* in six volumes (Harvard University Press, since 2012).

Grégory Quenet is Professor of Environmental History at the University of Versailles-Saint-Quentin-en-Yvelines. He has worked on the intellectual history of environmental history (*Qu'est-ce que l'histoire environnementale?*, Champ Vallon, 2014) and case studies such as natural disasters (*Les tremblements de terre en France aux XVIIe et XVIIIe siècles*, Champ Vallon, 2005) and iconic national places revisited (*Versailles, histoire naturelle*, La Découverte, 2015). His current research deals with a global history of Paradise islands and historical regimes of nature.

Ann Rigney is Professor of Comparative Literature at Utrecht University. Her research is located at the intersections between narrative, cultural memory, and contestations of the past. She has published widely in the field of modern memory cultures, with projects both on the nineteenth century and on contemporary developments, including most recently *The Afterlives of Walter Scott: Memory on the Move* (Oxford University Press, 2012; 2017); *Transnational Memory: Circulation, Articulation, Scales*, ed. with Chiara de Cesari (De Gruyter, 2014); and *Commemorating Writers in Nineteenth-Century Europe*, ed. with Joep Leerssen (Palgrave Macmillan, 2014).

Miri Rubin is Professor of Medieval and Early Modern History at the School of History, Queen Mary University of London. Her research has ranged across the period 1100–1600, through the exploration of themes in the religious cultures of Europe, with a special interest in social and community relations, Jewish-Christian relations, gender, identity and the body, and visual and material expressions of ideas and practices. She has recently published *Mother of God: A History of the Virgin Mary* (Allen Lane, 2009); *Emotion and Devotion: The Meaning of Mary in Medieval Religious Cultures* (Central European University Press, 2009); *The Cambridge History of Christianity, vol. 4*, ed. with Walter Simons (Cambridge University Press, 2009); and *A Very Short Introduction to the Middle Ages* (Oxford University Press, 2014). She has also edited and translated *The Life and Passion of William of Norwich* (Penguin, 2014).

Pierre-Yves Saunier is Professor of European History at Université Laval, Québec, Canada. His research interests lie in modern history of Europe, with a focus on urban history, history of international organizations, nursing history, and transnational history. His previous publications include *The Palgrave Dictionary of Transnational History*, ed. with Akira Iriye (Palgrave Macmillan, 2009); *The Other Global City: Explorations into the Transnational Municipal Moment 1850–2000*, ed. with Shane Ewen (Palgrave Macmillan, 2009); and *Transnational History* (Palgrave Macmillan, 2013).

Jean-Claude Schmitt is Directeur d'Études at the École des Hautes Études en Sciences Sociales, Paris, where he directed from 1992 to 2014 the Groupe d'Anthropologie Historique de l'Occident Médiéval. He has published extensively on the socio-cultural aspects of medieval history in Western Europe and has made important contributions in using anthropological and art historical methods to interpret history. His recent books include *The Conversion of Herman the Jew* (Pennsylvania University Press, 2010); *L'invention de l'anniversaire* (Arkhe, 2012, new edn 2017); *Les rythmes au Moyen Âge* (Gallimard, 2016); and *Rêver de soi: Les songes autobiographiques au Moyen Age*, ed. with Gisèle Besson (Anacharsis, 2017).

Daniel Lord Smail is Frank B. Baird, Jr. Professor of History at Harvard University, where he works on the history and anthropology of Mediterranean societies between 1100 and 1600 and on deep human history. In medieval history, his work has explored the social and cultural history of the cities of Mediterranean Europe, with a focus on Marseille in the later Middle Ages. His work in deep history and neurohistory has addressed some of the methodological and theoretical underpinnings of these approaches to the human past. His recent publications include *On Deep History and the Brain* (University of California Press, 2008) and, with Andrew Shryock and others, *Deep History: The Architecture of Past and Present* (University of California Press, 2011), as well as *Legal Plunder: Households and Debt Collection in Late Medieval Europe* (Harvard University Press, 2016).

Sverker Sörlin is Professor of Environmental History at the Division of History of Science, Technology and Environment at the Royal Institute of Technology (KTH) in Stockholm. He has published in the fields of history of science, environmental history, the history of forestry, human ecology, environmental humanities, innovations studies, and the history and politics of higher education. Among his recent book publications are *Science, Geopolitics and Culture in the Polar Region* (2013); *The Future of Nature: Documents of Global Change*, ed. with Libby Robin and Paul Warde (Yale University Press, 2013); *Northscapes: History, Technology, and the Making of Northern Environments*, ed. with Dolly Jørgensen (University of British Columbia Press, 2014); and *The Environment: A History*, with Libby Robin and Paul Warde (Johns Hopkins University Press, 2018).

Marek Tamm is Professor of Cultural History and Senior Research Fellow in Medieval Studies at the School of Humanities, Tallinn University. He is also Head of Tallinn University Centre of Excellence in Intercultural Studies and of the Estonian Graduate School of Culture Studies and Arts. His primary research fields are the cultural history of medieval Europe, the theory and history of historiography as well as cultural memory studies. He has recently published *Crusading and Chronicle Writing on the Medieval Baltic Frontier*, ed. with Linda Kaljundi and Carsten Selch Jensen (Ashgate, 2011); *Afterlife of Events: Perspectives on Mnemohistory* (Palgrave Macmillan, 2015); and *How to Study Culture? Methodology of Culture Studies* (in Estonian, Tallinn University Press, 2016).

Jane Winters is Professor of Digital Humanities at the School of Advanced Study, University of London. Her research interests include digital history, web archives, big data for humanities research, peer review in the digital environment, text editing, and open access publishing. She has led or co-directed a range of digital projects, including Big UK Domain Data for the Arts and Humanities; Digging into Linked Parliamentary Metadata; Traces through Time: Prosopography in Practice across Big Data; the Thesaurus of British and Irish History as SKOS; and Born Digital Big Data and Approaches for History and the Humanities. She has published *The Creighton Century, 1907–2007*, ed. with David Bates and Jennifer Wallis (Institute of Historical Research, 2009).

INTRODUCTION
A FRAMEWORK FOR DEBATING NEW APPROACHES TO HISTORY
Marek Tamm

The one duty we owe to history is to rewrite it.

Oscar Wilde, *The Critic as Artist* (1891)

'History is the intellectual form in which a culture gives account of its past' was the memorable way for defining history proposed in 1929 by the Dutch historian Johan Huizinga (1929: 166). In fact, this is rather similar to another definition articulated by Huizinga's great predecessor, the Swiss historian Jakob Burckhardt (2007: 179), at the end of the nineteenth century; in his view, history is 'the record of what one age finds worthy of note in another'. We need not conclude from these definitions that the study of the past could be reduced to the requirements of the present, or to a social demand – certainly the internal explorations of the academic world must be taken into account; yet it seems clear that developments in history writing cannot be discussed in isolation from major social, technological, cultural, and other changes. Thus, in order to understand the new approaches and major debates in history of recent decades – that being the main aim of the present volume – we must first pay attention to some deeper tendencies prevalent in the modern (Western) world: to changes in the culture's fundamental principles, technological opportunities, and in our attitudes to the environment.

Alternative spatialities

Time and space, the two fundamental categories of Western culture, have undergone important shifts over the past decades. The modernist time regime dating back to the eighteenth century (with academic historiography as one of its fruits) as well as the Eurocentric hierarchically articulated conception of space (with its close link between history and nation) have crumbled or at least lost their air of self-evidence, by now. In recent times, we have witnessed the emergence of a number of alternative ideas of spatiality and temporality which, of course, have exercised retroactive influence on how we conceptualize historical space and time

I don't think it is any longer necessary to adopt any ideological position in order to regard 'globalization' as the focal byword of our times – a concept so polyvalent as to be well fit for the role of a common denominator for various processes often only weakly linked to each other. Although the term goes back right to the 1930s and was first taken into use in the context of education and international relations, its true breakthrough took place in the 1990s (James and Steger 2014; see also Osterhammel and Petersson 2005). In its most general sense, globalization refers to the ever-greater interconnectedness, entanglement of the world – its 'compression', as it were. Although driven mostly by market forces, globalization undoubtedly is far more than just an economic phenomenon; instead, its political, cultural, ecological, and ideological dimensions must be taken into account (Steger 2017).

It is fair to say that globalization has forced or inspired historians to search for spatial alternatives in making sense of the past, to pay more attention to supranational connections and networks. These searches have given rise to a number of approaches that, under various names such as transnational history, connected history, entangled history, or global history, share the same desire to move beyond conventional geopolitical articulations and discrete civilizations, to turn the concept of space again into a significant theoretical category. Unlike traditional universal or world history, the new trends (which we could, for convenience' sake, group under the name of global history) do not tell a story about everything that has come to pass in the world – 'global' does not refer so much to the object of study but to a perspective that focuses on connections, entanglements, and integration (see Chapter 1). As Sebastian Conrad (2016: 90) has happily summed it up: 'Global history as a distinct approach explores alternative spatialities, is fundamentally relational, and is self-reflective on the issue of Eurocentrism. … It means that global history takes structured integration as a context, even when it is not the main topic.'

Global history sets store by what Jacques Revel (1996) has called 'scale shifts' (*jeux d'échelles*) – a study of past phenomena on different scales so as to bring to light unexpected associations, link seemingly isolated phenomena, map overlapping spaces. It becomes ever more important in the study of history not to set out from a given spatial framework but to follow the ideas, people, and things selected for study, no matter where they may lead. Thus, history becomes a multilayered and intertwined process wherein the different layers are characterized by a different logic, a different tempo, and a different geographical extension. In the eyes of a global historian, the world is indeed an integrated phenomenon, yet it is also internally heterogeneous. Therefore, the triumph of the global perspective of history does not imply the loss of the local dimension; instead, it becomes important to discuss local and global, micro- and macro-history conjointly, even to the extent of developing a 'global microhistory' – an effort for which there have, in recent times, already been calls (Andrade 2010; Trivellato 2011; Medick 2016).

Globalization has been paralleled by the ebbing importance of the West in the world – what Dipesh Chakrabarty (2000) has memorably called 'provincializing Europe', or what can, in turn, be linked to the phenomenon known as 'empire writes back' (Ashcroft, Griffiths and Tiffin 1989). The crumbling of empires and the process of decolonization have called into question many historiographical tenets that had taken root over more than a century, linked either to teleological narratives, West-centred periodizations or a progressivist notion of time that doomed non-European colonized regions to a place in an 'imaginary waiting room of history' (Chakrabarty 2000: 8). Over the last decades, postcolonialist history (see Chapter 2) has successfully contributed to a revision of West-centred history writing (Majumdar 2010), while a 'new imperial history' has helped place the history of colonies and the metropolis into one and the same framework and show that both are understandable only in the general context of imperialism (Wilson 2004; Howe 2010).

It is well known that academic history writing and nation-building have been closely related from the start; nationalism has been a major factor feeding interest in history, and history has provided important material for nation- and national identity-building (Berger and Conrad 2015). From the nineteenth century on, the nation state has been taken for granted as the primary unit of history writing. Global history in its diverse aspects is, indeed, first and foremost unified by a desire to leave behind 'methodological nationalism', an approach that naturalizes the nation state and follows the implicit conviction 'that a particular nation would provide the constant unit of observation through all historical transformations, the "thing" whose change history was supposed to describe' (Wimmer and Glick Schiller 2002: 305). Recent research has clearly demonstrated that even for the heyday of nationalism it is useful not to think of the nation as a given and isolated 'container' but rather to regard it in a broader systemic context, in terms of the connected influences of various transnational factors (see Tamm 2016).

Even though global history has become possible primarily due to the globalization of present-day spatial experience – 'global spatiality implies global history', as Prasenjit Duara and his colleagues have observed (Duara, Murthy, and Sartori 2014: 1) – this does not necessarily mean it is a temporary phenomenon that will again disappear as new trends arise. Rather, one can agree with those who may not foresee a long life for 'global history' or related notions, but also consider it highly unlikely that the world could cease to be seen as a more or less integrated phenomenon so that traditional spatial categories could be revived (Sachsenmaier 2011: 245; Conrad 2016: 235).

Alternative temporalities

The 'compression of space' accompanying globalization is related to a phenomenon that has with increasing frequency come to be called 'acceleration of time' (Rosa 2013; Wajcman 2015). In fact, the metaphor seems to remain somewhat constrained, particularly in the context of the study of history, and it would be more to the point to speak about a pluralization and expansion of the perception of time, about the crumbling of a progressivist and linear notion of time. This shift can be presented as a downturn of the modernist time regime (Assmann 2013) that saw time as a 'necessary agent of change' and presumed 'an asymmetry between the past as a circumscribed space of experience and the future as an open horizon of expectations' (Gumbrecht 1998: 420; cf. Gumbrecht 2014). Nowadays, a notion succinctly articulated by Michel Serres is gaining ground: 'every historical era is likewise multitemporal, simultaneously drawing from the obsolete, the contemporary, and the futuristic' (Serres and Latour 1995: 60; for an earlier history of this idea, see Landwehr 2012). Historians are ever more eager to 'break with the idea of the fully contemporaneous present' (Bevernage 2015: 351) and 'embrace the richness and variability of different forms of time that exist throughout our lives' (Tanaka 2015: 161). Whereas the traditional, historicist history writing valued coherence, kept the past clearly apart from the present, and strove to gloss over temporal discontinuities, the contemporary non-linear history writing 'allows for a pluralisation of times and to conceive of the present, past and future as multidimensional and purely relational categories' (Lorenz 2014: 46). As in the case of space, the new attitude to (historical) time has also partially been shaped by a postcolonialist perspective, demonstrating a clear connection between historicist and colonialist notions of time and emphasizing that 'the writing of history must implicitly assume a plurality of times existing together, a disjuncture of the present with itself' (Chakrabarty 2000: 108).

In modern history writing, the alternative notion of historical time that we may try to capture in the concept of 'multiple temporalities' (Jordheim 2012; 2014) has taken very varied shapes. By way of example, I am going to present here two most characteristic extremes. 'In many realms of historical writing, big is back', David Armitage (2012: 493) wrote some years ago, with a certain amount of euphoria. In the same article, he proposed a new concept, 'transtemporal history', that, taking its cue from 'transnational history', intends 'to stress elements of linkage and comparison across time, much as transnational history deals with such connections across space'. Yet he immediately considers it necessary to specify that 'transtemporal history is not transhistorical: it is time-bound not timeless' (2012: 498). 'Transtemporal history' would appear to be a convenient umbrella term capable of covering the various opportunities for expanding the historians' temporal horizons that have been proposed over the past few years: big history, deep history, evolutionary history, history of *longue durée*, and so on.

'Big history', in all likelihood, is the best known and most ambitious of them, even if also the most criticized in the context of academic history writing. Tracing its origins back to the 1990s, big history wishes to take the beginnings of history back to the Big Bang, identifying universal history with the history of the universe. At the same time, the focus still remains on man: big history is 'an account of human history written with the Earthrise view in mind' (Spier 2015: 179). David Christian, a foremost advocate of this line of thought, opens his book *Maps of Time: An Introduction to Big History* (2004) with the origins of the universe and winds it up with a survey of the 'modern era'. Big history draws the majority of its data not from the conventional historical disciplines but from cosmology, astronomy, geology, and evolutionary biology.

'Deep history' is the younger brother of big history, with an even clearer focus on the past of humanity, but in as long a temporal perspective as possible, proposing 'a new architecture for human history' (Shryock and Smail 2011). Deep history relevantly reminds us of the fact that of the entire past history of humankind, conventional historiography covers but a trifling part – just a few seconds, if we were to liken the history of humanity to a clock with a twenty-four-hour display: 'If we imagine the 5 million years of human evolutionary time as a 24-hour period, the entire 300,000 years of modern humanity comprises about an hour and a half, the 60,000 years since modern humans left Africa comprise about 17 minutes, and the 12,000 years since the end of the Pleistocene comprise slightly more than 4 minutes' (Brooke 2014: 114). Daniel Lord Smail and other proponents of 'deep history' argue that historians still write within 'the grip of sacred history' (Smail 2008: 12–39), according to which the sources of human culture can go back no further than 4000 BC. Yet the definition of history should not be based on the invention of writing, but upon the evolution of anatomically modern humans. That is, 'paleohistorians', as the representatives of 'deep history' have called themselves, rely on anthropology, archaeology, genetics, neurophysiology, and evolutionary biology: 'Histories can be written from every type of trace, from the memoir to the bone fragment and the blood type' (Shryock and Smail 2011: 13).

The temporal scope of the 'evolutionary history' proposed by Edmund Russell, 'that studies the ways populations of human beings and other species have shaped each other's traits over time and the significance of those changes for all those populations' (Russell 2011: 5), places it in the same series with the previous two approaches. This would, of course, mean stretching the historians' perspective to include the temporal scale of human evolution as a whole, and addressing evidence completely different from the one that historians have been habituated to work with.

The same desire to broaden the historians' time horizon is well expressed in the much-vaunted *The History Manifesto* (2014) by Jo Guldi and David Armitage. Tending slightly towards exaggeration they state that contemporary history is haunted by the spectre of the short term, whereas 'long-term thinking about the past and the future proliferates outside the discipline of history' (Guldi and Armitage 2014: 61). Thus, their book urges historians to return to the perspective of *longue durée* that, according to the authors, characterized the study of history as recently as a couple of academic generations ago. This return, Guldi and Armitage believe, is propelled by technological development, by which they mean first and foremost the massive digitization of sources and the new opportunities for quantitative analysis provided by it (Armitage and Guldi 2015: 290).

But the alternative temporality of our days is also characterized by another tendency, contrasting with the former, that has been called the emergence of 'presentism' as a new 'regime of historicity' by François Hartog (2015). While over the last couple of centuries, a future-oriented 'regime of historicity' dominated in the West, future as a means of interpreting our historical experience has, over the past decades, clearly been receding and giving ground to a focus on the present. 'After "1990" both the past and the future seem to have collapsed as points of orientation, so to speak – and as a consequence academic history is stuck in the present' (Lorenz 2010: 93). In Hartog's view, this shift is exemplified by the rapid growth of the importance of heritage, museums, memories, commemorations, witnesses, victims, and so on, with the extensive popularity of memory studies being one of the most significant among them. From the perspective of presentism or memory, the past is far from final or irreversible but lives on in many ways; the past has become part of the present. In relation to this, Berber Bevernage (2011: 5) has made the important observation: 'A persisting "past" does not simply deconstruct the notions of absence and distance; rather, it blurs the strict delineation between past and present and thereby even questions the existence of these temporal dimensions as separate entities.' The treatment of history not as something that 'is irremediably gone', but 'as ongoing process' (Runia 2014: 57), has enabled historians to ask new questions, no longer about the original meaning of past phenomena but rather about how these have later been carried on, supplied with new meanings, appropriated and actualized; about their perpetuation in time and their spectral energy (Tamm 2013; Kleinberg 2017). Jan Assmann has called this new approach 'mnemohistory' (*Gedächtnisgeschichte*, in German) which 'is concerned not with the past as such, but only with the past as it is remembered. … It concentrates exclusively on those aspects of significance and relevance which are the product of memory – that is, of a recourse to a past – and which appear only in the light of later readings' (Assmann 1997: 9; see also Tamm 2015). The introduction of memory into the study of history, the rise of the history of memory (see Chapter 5), has thus significantly transformed the traditional linear concept of time in history. All in all, the two general trends described above – increased attention both to 'deep past' and to 'persistent past' – mark a considerably broader understanding of temporality than those that used to characterize history writing for a long time.

Anthropocene and more-than-human history

The growing interest in 'transtemporal history' is symptomatic of another radical change that is redefining our relations with the environment and thereby also our relation to the past. Among representatives of different disciplines, there has been growing recognition that the evolution of planet Earth has reached a phase where humankind has become one of the major factors shaping its destiny. This has been the inspiration for coining the term 'Anthropocene', to signify a new, post-Holocene epoch in the geological history of the Earth. Although the name has not yet been officially confirmed by the relevant organizations and its precise definition is still being debated, it has by now spread virally in natural as well as human and social sciences. More generally, 'Anthropocene' refers to the notable human impact on the Earth's ecological systems and geology, an impact that has grown particularly weighty over the last half century (the so-called Great Acceleration) and is revealed most clearly by climate change, the extinction of species, and various environmental problems. Bruno Latour (2017: 60) has recently summed this new unexpected situation up very succinctly: 'Today, the decorations, the props, the backstage, the whole edifice have mounted onto the stage and are contesting the actors for the main role. This changes all the scripts, suggests completely new outcomes. Humans are no longer the only actors, even as they find they have been entrusted a role much too important for them.'

Thus, the Anthropocene is radically de-centring humans and has led to the placing of human activity in deep co-evolutionary time – or, as Chakrabarty (2015: 181) states, 'We have fallen into "deep" history, into deep, geological time. This falling into "deep" history carries a certain shock of recognition – recognition of the otherness of the planet and its very large-scale spatial and temporal processes of which we have, unintentionally, become a part.' Chakrabarty was among the first to raise the issue of how the Anthropocene would influence our understanding of history, underscoring most importantly the conclusion that the new situation would mark the 'collapse of the age-old humanist distinction between natural history and human history' (Chakrabarty 2009: 201) and that historians must discuss humans and their history within a much broader context, to 'think of humans as a form of life and look on human history as part of the history of life on this planet' (Chakrabarty 2009: 213). Thus, the Anthropocene not only implies the recognition of human responsibility for major environmental and climate changes, but is more fundamentally part of a readjustment of the relationship between the human and the natural world. It has afforded an opportunity to conceptualize history in a completely new and unexpected manner, to give up the traditional view of 'human exceptionalism' and to integrate the environment and other forms of life into history writing, but no longer as passive objects or external decorations, but as active agents in their own rights.

The hypothesis of the Anthropocene has called for a revision and surpassing of various deeply rooted distinctions in historical epistemology, such as, for instance, between natural history and human history, written history and deep history, human history and multispecies history, national history and planetary history. More generally, the Anthropocene may indeed be discussed, from the perspective of history, as 'the reunion of human (historical) time and Earth (geological) time, between human agency and non-human agency', which 'gives the lie to this – temporal, ontological, epistemological and institutional – great divide between nature and society that widened in the nineteenth and twentieth centuries' (Bonneuil and Fressoz 2016: 38). The Anthropocene has enabled us to understand the anthropocentric character of traditional history, creating a mistaken impression of humankind as the only main protagonist on the stage of history. In the light of the new situation, it is ever more significant to ask what would history be like if it were regarded from the perspective not of humans, but of non-human species. This question has been most forcefully phrased by advocates of animal history who desire to study not only the relations between humans and animals in the past, but wish to study history 'from the viewpoint of animals' (Baratay 2012). Such an approach obviously calls for a reconsidering of the fundamentals of history as a discipline, or, as justly pointed out by Ewa Domanska (2017: 271), the animal-historical perspective demands 'a different way of knowing the past from the one offered by historical epistemology with its specific understanding of time, space, change, rationality, and causality'.

Side by side with animal history, another variant of 'more-than-human history', namely 'multispecies history', has made its presence felt in the most recent times, inspired by the 'multispecies ethnography' proposed by anthropologists (Kirksey and Helmreich 2010; see also Pilaar Birch 2018 for 'multispecies archaeology'). Multispecies history is interested in how humans have become commingled in the past with small organisms – microfauna and -flora – and how they form within temporally as well as spatially dynamic 'webs of interspecies dependence' (Tsing 2012: 144; see also O'Gorman 2017). Such an approach, of course, challenges the historians' habitual way of using their sources, demanding that attention be paid also 'to the tracks and traces of nonhumans' since, even though non-human organisms 'tell no tales', 'they contribute to the overlapping tracks and traces that we grasp as history'. 'History, then', Anna Tsing (2015: 168) concludes, 'is the record of many trajectories of world making, human and not human'.

The trends described here can be linked to the general 'posthuman turn' in contemporary humanities. 'Posthumanism', as it has recently been written, 'rejects that humans are the only species capable of producing knowledge and instead creates openings for other forms/things/objects/beings/phenomena to know. It also problematizes distinctions that are drawn between and among species. This is significant because when humans are decentred as the only possible knowers, a wealth of research possibilities emerge' (Ulmer 2017: 834). One of the trends that has emerged from among these possibilities, is 'posthumanist history' (see Chapter 12) that will probably evolve into an important new approach to history at the time of the Anthropocene.

But in the age of the Anthropocene, new importance and significance have become attached to the environmental history that already evolved in the United States in the 1970s (see Chapter 3). Having first emerged as a sub-branch of history, this trend has in recent years spread all over the world and considerably expanded its grasp, becoming regarded as a necessary part of the study of history as a whole. A few years ago, Kenneth Pomeranz (2014: 351) could ask, 'Is the principal goal [of environmental history] establishing a separate, focused subfield (e.g. women's history, ethnic histories, the histories of science and technology) or integrating the new topic into "mainstream" narratives?'. Today, the answer clearly seems to fall in favour of the latter. In the contemporary study of history, it is no longer possible to discuss the environment as one of many other subject-matters or as a mere neutral backdrop of human activities; instead, it must be regarded as a central protagonist of the historical process which no historical study of any ambition can afford to neglect.

History in the digital age

While in ecological terms, we live in the age of Man, in technological terms we are inhabitants of the digital age. The changed attitudes to time and space reviewed above, as well as the rapid growth of man's ecological footprint, are indeed all, in one way or another, linked to the rapid development of digital technology. Globalization would never have acquired its present importance, had it not been supported by technological advances, primarily the rapid dissemination of digital means of communication. Manuel Castells (2008: 24–5) has plausibly written that 'the forces driving globalization could only be effectuated because they have at their disposal the global networking capacity provided by digital communication technologies and information systems, including computerized, long-haul, fast, transportation networks'.

In more than one sense, the World Wide Web is a symbol of our age, and without much exaggeration it can be said that 'mass adoption of the Internet is driving one of the most exciting social, cultural, and political transformations in history, and unlike earlier periods of change, this time the effects are fully global' (Schmidt and Cohen 2013: 4). The rise of the internet and digital communication has also marked an important change in our knowledge system, the third major revolution since the invention of writing and printing. This has brought along new debates about the birth of a 'knowledge society' or 'information age', which, in turn, have encouraged an historical approach to the topic – the emergence of the history of knowledge (Burke 2016: 4–5; see Chapter 6).

The development of technology and media has always influenced cultural attitudes and shaped our relations with the past (Kittler 1999; Anderson 2011). Having spread extensively all over the world in but a few decades, digital technology has forcefully reshaped our relationship with the past, as well as the ways and means of studying the past; and it is quite safe to say that these developments will only intensify in the future (Weller 2013). The ever more extensive digitization of source materials, coupled with new and increasingly web-based tools and methods to process and analyse these materials, have opened completely new prospects to historians and forced them to rethink the fundamentals of their profession (see Chapter 10).

In the interest of clarity, however, a distinction must be made between two phenomena: history in a digital age and digital history. In a sense, all historians are digital historians nowadays, since we all use the means supplied by digital technology, be it the internet or programmes for text processing. Let alone the general digitization of historical culture: from history-themed computer games to historical virtual reality experiences (Fogu 2009). Digital history in the narrower sense, however, should still be taken to signify an approach to history that uses digital technology in researching and representing the past. In an online discussion hosted by the *Journal of American History*, Douglas Seefeldt and William G. Thomas (2009) have offered a definition of digital history that still seems to be the most suitable:

> Digital history might be understood broadly as an approach to examining and representing the past that works with the new communication technologies of the computer, the internet network, and software systems. On one level, digital history is an open arena of scholarly production and communication, encompassing the development of new course materials and scholarly data collection efforts. On another level, digital history is a methodological approach framed by the hypertextual power of these technologies to make, define, query, and annotate associations in the human record of the past.

Thus, digital history is to be conceived not as history's new ancillary, but as a new way of studying and writing history. From the viewpoint of research work, historians must get used to a new situation described by Roy Rosenzweig (2011: 7) as 'a fundamental paradigm shift from a culture of scarcity to a culture of abundance'. The massive digitization of sources and the ever new opportunities offered by quantitative analysis confront historians with the question of how the new situation will modify the current understanding of a 'historical source'. What are the consequences of 'sources' becoming '(big) data'? If the nature of historical sources changes, how does that affect our methods of analysis? In what ways does the balance between researcher and machine shift, and how can we integrate, for instance, close and distant reading? (Zaagzma 2013: 19). Like the general evolution of digital humanities (Berry and Fagerjord 2017), digital history has passed from stage 1.0 to that of 2.0 over the last years. While digital history 1.0, carried away by a general enthusiasm for computers and digital technology, was oriented mostly to the creation of data bases and to quantitative analysis, digital history 2.0 places increasingly greater emphasis on the need for a qualitative and critical analysis, as well as a more active involvement of users (Noiret 2013). As the initial technological enthusiasm died down, new techniques of visualization and data analysis have begun to emerge, allowing again for more attention to be paid to the conventional methodological strengths of humanitarian research: 'attention to complexity, medium specificity, historical context, analytical depth, critique and interpretation' (Schnapp and Presner 2009).

The 'digital turn' challenges not only the study of the past, but also the ways of representing it. Digital environment liberates historians from the obligation of using a linear narrative, online historical writing enables them to create intermedial hypertexts and virtual historical realities, with every user choosing the path suited for him/her. Chiel Van den Akker (2013: 111) recently proposed a convenient typology to distinguish between the historians' narratives in the analogue versus the digital age:

Old narrative	New (online) narrative
Book, article, review	Enriched publication, wiki, blog, exhibition
Monographic	Collaborative, participatory, interactive
Linear	Non-linear, hypertextual
Panoramic	Collage
Writing and reading	Direct communication

Online history writing supports the users' active participation in the creation of knowledge, it enables historians to develop collaborative and participatory projects of historical research on the internet, which in the future will certainly have an impact on how history writing will be conceived. This participatory online culture, as Ann Rigney (2010: 111) has justly underscored, 'is not only creating new conditions for the production of narratives about the past but also new challenges for conceptualization'.

True enough, online history narratives are nothing unheard of, and their future is not all sunny. Almost twenty years ago Edward Ayers (1999: 1) wrote that 'the new technologies seem tailor-made for history, a match for the growing bulk and complexity of our ever more self-conscious practice, efficient vehicles to connect with larger and more diverse audiences'. From that period, likewise come the first more original attempts at online historical writing, such as Robert Darnton's (2000) electronic essay on the information networks of eighteenth-century Paris which integrated different media (texts, images, sounds). As president of the American Historical Association, Darnton also belonged among the historians who, in the early 2000s, contributed enthusiastically to the development of the electronic publishing of historical research yet realized, only a few years later, that 'the triumphalist enthusiasm from the early stages of experimentation with electronic publishing has evaporated, and we now are dealing with workable projects' (Tamm 2004). The Achilles' heel of electronic publishing and online history writing is still the problem of preservation. Just as Darnton's electronic essay of 2000 has disappeared from the internet, so many other innovative digital history projects of the 2000s have also gone down the drain. Whereas the traditional medium of printing has been able to support scientific communication successfully for several centuries, the digital medium as yet remains ephemeral, and as long as it is impossible to guarantee its longevity, there is no reason to think that digital history writing could replace earlier forms of historiography. Thus, 'digital history' should first and foremost be conceived of as a transitional term that has helped raise new important questions and led historians to acquire new technical skills. In a longer perspective, however, it is likely that 'there will be no more talk of "digital history" as all history is somehow "digital" in terms of incorporation of new types of sources, methods and ways of dissemination (just as all humanities will be inherently "digital")' (Zaagsma 2013: 16).

Beyond words

An important part of the historical innovation of the last decades of the last century had, as their starting point, the 'linguistic turn' – a realization that language not merely reflects the reality but actively creates it. In the present century, on the contrary, historians have rather desired to escape from 'the prison-house of language', to move beyond discourse, out of the labyrinths of text. Explanations are expected to come forth from things rather than words. This desire found its clearest expression in the new and growing interest for materiality, visuality, and corporeality, which in turn has been influenced by deeper social and cultural trends. The French philosopher Tristan Garcia (2014: 1) has recently observed that 'our time is perhaps the time of an epidemic of things'. In his view, it is not so much our relations with things that need to be rethought, as the nature of things themselves and their impact on us.

It is a generally accepted fact that Western culture has grown increasingly visual over the last decades, but it is equally important to notice the transformation of the role that images play in culture: images are no longer seen as abstract and passive but concrete and performative, they are characterized by a certain agency, which is why the central question of visual studies is no longer what the images mean, but what the images want (Mitchell 2005). Bruno Latour (1993) and Alfred Gell (1998) were among the first to begin to speak about the agency of things and images; by now, however, the notion that 'objects not only are the product of history, they are also active agents in history' (Auslander 2005: 1017) has taken root ever more extensively among historians, too, particularly in the sphere of the history of things (see Chapter 8) and visual culture (see Chapter 9).

The return of the body into humanitarian debates goes back to the 1970s, and 'the history of the body' has been an important avenue in historical studies (e.g. Porter 1991; 2001; Corbin, Courtine, and Vigarello 2004–2006). Nevertheless, up to very recent times, the body has been a metaphor rather than matter for historians; a cultural rather than physical phenomenon. Under the rubric of history of the body, various discourses about or perspectives on the body have usually been studied; it is rather the semantics than the pragmatics of the body that have been highlighted. 'For by entering the realm of meaning, the body's physical reality is still left out' was the critical observation of Annemarie Mol (2002: 11), who has proposed a new approach that she calls 'praxiography', focusing on the historical study of body practices. Bodies, things, and techniques are no longer treated as silent objects but as important actors. 'In this way, praxiography might offer historians of the body an interesting method to study the physical body as an actor in history, by analysing the "actions" of bodies, techniques, materials, and sites in practice instead of historical representations' (Clever and Ruberg 2014: 554).

Behind that new approach there is a broader trend that could be called a new meeting of history and biology. While the 'linguistic turn' preferred mind over matter, soul over body, and culture over nature, by now these distinctions are fading and the world is increasingly seen as a hybrid phenomenon, in terms of assemblage rather than of antagonism. 'There is not much culture without biology', Daniel Lord Smail (2008: 154) laconically states, seconded by Julia Adeney Thomas (2014: 1587): 'in the age of the Anthropocene, history and biology seem to converge'. The nature/culture debate has been supplanted in recent years by bioculture (Davis and Morris 2007; McGrath 2017) and the mind/body dilemma redefined by the 'extended mind' and 'embodied cognition' (Menary 2010; Shapiro 2014). Yet in their introduction to the round table 'History Meets Biology' in the *American Historical Review*, the authors justly point out that the collaboration of history and biology (and, in fact, of other sciences) is not a one-way street and that historians need to preserve their critical attitude:

> The challenge for historians is to come to grips with these biological discoveries while recognizing that historians have an ever more important role to play in an era when biology holds sway: as critics of the tendency of science to universalize and decontextualize human behavior; as discoverers of patterns in human behavior and changes in human bodies that can reshape scientific thought and redirect scientific research; and as champions of history as a humanistic mode of inquiry. (AHR Roundtable 2014: 1499)

While in the evolution of the history of the body, the contribution of women and gender history played a key role, the novel interest in the 'real' bodies and things has made it possible to expand the 'questionnaire' of gender history (see Chapter 4), but also challenged its main distinctions (including sex and gender) (Downs 2010). The 'material turn' has helped us understand the great importance of things in shaping and constructing gender identities; even though gender roles are undoubtedly also defined by language use, it is important to notice how gender relations operate through material objects (Kirkham 1996; Greig, Hamlett, and Hannan 2016). In the long history of humankind, gender identities have been expressed not just through speech acts and conceptual categories, but through textiles, timber, metal, images, rituals, dance, music, and so on. Leora Auslander (2005: 1019) has written, rising to a suggestive level of generalization:

Human beings need things to individuate, differentiate, and identify; human beings need things to express and communicate the unsaid and the unsayable; human beings need things to situate themselves in space and time, as extensions of the body (and to compensate for the body's limits), as well as for sensory pleasure; human beings need objects to effectively remember and forget; and we need objects to cope with absence, with loss, and with death.

The addressing of things and matter has, at the same time, meant moving away from anthropocentrism; things do not necessarily acquire their meaning through humans, just like the impact of things on humans may be no less than that of humans on things. More radical thinkers have, in connection with this, spoken about 'object-oriented democracy', in which 'subaltern things will be liberated from the humanist rule of subject-centered discourse' (Trentmann 2009: 284). This philosophical trend, that has won renown under the name of new materialism, emphasizes that humans and things are fundamentally co-constitutive, to the point that distinctions between them have not only become blurred but actually can no longer be sustained at all (LeCain 2017). 'New materialists further suggest', writes Sonia Hazard (2013: 67), 'that we, as ostensible humans, are protean assemblages of things, human and non-human, as well. The mass of matter that is the human body – its brain and nervous system, bones and organs – is never sealed off from the external world, but continually intermingles with food, air, metal plates, microbes, and other things without which it could not live.'

Thus, the materialist perspective goes hand in hand with a reassessment of corporeality. Our perceptions and feelings have a material background and involve both human and non-human actors. 'Sounds, for example, are external vibrations resounding in the ear. Smells are nonhuman particles entering the nose. Emotions like sadness or joy are inextricable from their porous physiology, relating to chemicals in the blood and excitations of the nerves' (Hazard 2013: 68). Integrated with neurosciences, this approach has opened new prospects for studying the history of emotions (see Chapter 7), as well as laid the foundations for the research field of neurohistory (see Chapter 11). It is no longer the classical problem of 'how it really was' that is put forward, but also 'what it was like' in the past (Hunt 2009). Whereas only a few decades ago, one of the influential bywords in historical studies said 'history from below', it is now 'history from within' that has risen to the status of the new catchphrase (Burman 2012). Even though collaboration with neurosciences is complicated for historians, with these sciences being in constant flux and the ideas held at any one point rapidly getting discarded a few years later, cooperation should nevertheless not be avoided; instead, the ideas of neuroscientists ought to be taken as inspiring input, not as categorical arguments (Mandressi 2011; Becker 2012; cf. Kleinberg 2016).

Debating history today: The rationale of the volume

The study of history has undergone several changes in the present century; new research fields, new subjects, new epistemological platforms have emerged. While the 1990s were still dominated by talk about a 'crisis' of history (Scott 1989; Noiriel 1996; Fahrmeir 2003), the new century has seen a return of optimism, with more and more opportunities looming on the horizon. When the French historian and publisher Pierre Nora founded a new intellectual journal called *Le Débat*, in 1980, he justified its name in the first issue with the words, 'Le débat, parce qu'il n'y en a pas' ('The debate, because there no longer is any'). The present volume also partly owes its inception to the realization that debating the new developments might be more interesting than presenting a triumphant narrative of the consecutive conquests achieved by the study of history in the new century. We are convinced that in any field of academic study, the boldness and intensity of debate over the foundations and perspectives of research bears witness to the vitality of the field.

Starting from this realization, we as the editors compiled a list of some novel approaches to history that we wished to include in our volume (there is hopefully no need to emphasize that the list makes no pretence at being exhaustive) and asked each contributor to tackle the key problems and challenges he or she was willing to address within that particular field of history. However, the aim of the enterprise was not just to provide a useful overview of the new approaches to history, but also to offer insights into current historical debates, into the process of historical method in the making. Therefore, each chapter is followed by critical comments written by another specialist in the same field, offering some alternative and/or complementary perspectives to the topic. The chapter is concluded, in turn, by the author's short reply to the commentator. Though this certainly doesn't result in an all-encompassing portrait of the current approaches to history and the controversies that surround these, we believe that it does help to clarify key points of tension and multiple visions of a rapidly changing historiographical landscape.

We hope that the innovative format of the book, somewhat inspired by the collaborative volume *Key Debates in Anthropology* edited by Tim Ingold (1996) will, better than any other, help the readers get an idea of the main themes dominating contemporary historical thought and enable them to understand the problems currently at the top of the theoretical and methodological agenda in historical studies. While our goal has been to provide a comprehensive companion to contemporary history writing, we have deliberately set some important limits to the temporal and spatial reach of the volume. In temporal terms, we decided to focus on the developments in historical research since about the 1990s (taking also into account the fact that the previous enterprise of a similar kind, *New Perspectives on Historical Writing*, edited by Peter Burke, was published in 1991). In spatial terms, we opted to focus mostly on the new approaches in Western history writing, while encouraging our contributors to include as much comparative and global perspective in their texts as possible. We are very happy to have been able to bring together a truly international collective of authors, from more than ten countries and several generations, allowing us to hope that our volume will be able to offer a sufficiently representative cross-section of all the various traditions of history writing in the modern Western world.[1]

Note

1. *Acknowledgements*: I am grateful to Peter Burke for his careful reading of the first version of the introduction. Work on this chapter as well as on the volume was supported by the Estonian Research Council grant IUT18-8.

References

AHR Roundtable (2014), 'Introduction: History Meets Biology', *American Historical Review*, 119 (5): 1587–607.

Anderson, S. F. (2011), *Technologies of History: Visual Media and the Eccentricity of the Past*, Hanover, New Hampshire: Dartmouth College Press.

Andrade, T. (2010), 'A Chinese Farmer, Two African Boys, and a Warlord: Toward a Global Microhistory', *Journal of World History*, 21 (4): 573–91.

Armitage, D. (2012), 'What's the Big Idea? Intellectual History and the Longue Durée', *History of European Ideas*, 38 (4): 493–507.

Armitage, D. and Guldi, J. (2015), 'Le retour de la longue durée: une perspective anglo-américaine', *Annales. Histoire, Sciences Sociales*, 70 (2): 289–318.

Ashcroft, B., Griffiths, G. and Tiffin, H. (1989), *The Empire Writes Back: Theory and Practice in Post-Colonial Literature*, London and New York: Routledge.

Assmann, A. (2013), *Ist die Zeit aus den Fugen? Aufstieg und Fall des Zeitregimes der Moderne*, Munich: Hanser.

Assmann, J. (1997), *Moses the Egyptian: The Memory of Egypt in Western Monotheism*, Cambridge, MA: Harvard University Press.

Auslander, L. (2005), 'Beyond Words', *American Historical Review*, 110 (4): 1015–45.

Ayers, E. L. (1999), 'The Pasts and Futures of Digital History', available online: http://www.vcdh.virginia.edu/PastsFutures.html (accessed 20 December 2017).

Baratay, É. (2012), *Le point de vue animal. Une autre version de l'histoire*, Paris: Seuil.

Becker, P. (2012), 'History and the Neurocentric Age', in E. Russell (ed.), 'Environment, Culture, and the Brain: New Explorations in Neurohistory', 69–73, *RCC Perspectives*, 6.

Berger, S., with Conrad, C. (2015), *The Past as History: National Identity and Historical Consciousness in Modern Europe*, Basingstoke: Palgrave Macmillan.

Berry, D. and Fagerjord, A. (2017), *Digital Humanities: Knowledge and Critique in a Digital Age*, Cambridge: Polity Press.

Bevernage, B. (2011), *History, Memory, and State-Sponsored Violence: Time and Justice*, New York and London: Routledge.

Bevernage, B. (2015), 'The Past Is Evil/Evil Is Past: On Retrospective Politics, Philosophy of History, and Temporal Manichaeism', *History and Theory*, 54: 333–52.

Bonneuil, C. and Fressoz, J.-B. (2016), *The Shock of the Anthropocene: The Earth, History and Us*, London: Verso.

Brooke, J. L. (2014), *Climate Change and the Course of Global History: A Rough Journey*, Cambridge: Cambridge University Press.

Burckhardt, J. (2007), *Judgements on History and Historians*, London and New York: Routledge.

Burke, P., ed. (1991), *New Perspectives on Historical Writing*, Cambridge: Polity Press.

Burke, P. (2016), *What is the History of Knowledge?*, Cambridge: Polity Press.

Burman, J. T. (2012), 'History From Within? Contextualizing the New Neurohistory and Seeking Its Methods', *History of Psychology*, 15 (1): 84–99.

Castells, M. (2008), *Communication Power*, Oxford: Oxford University Press.

Chakrabarty, D. (2000), *Provincializing Europe: Postcolonial Thought and Historical Difference*, Princeton, NJ: Princeton University Press.

Chakrabarty, D. (2009), 'The Climate of History: Four Theses', *Critical Inquiry*, 35: 197–222.

Chakrabarty, D. (2015), 'The Human Condition in the Anthropocene: The Tanner Lectures in Human Values, delivered at Yale University, February 18–19, 2015', available online: https://tannerlectures.utah.edu/Chakrabarty%20manuscript.pdf) (accessed 20 December 2017).

Christian, D. (2004), *Maps of Time: An Introduction to Big History*, Berkeley and Los Angeles: University of California Press.

Clever, I. and Ruberg, W. (2014), 'Beyond Cultural History? The Material Turn, Praxiography, and Body History', *Humanities*, 3: 546–66.

Conrad, S. (2016), *What is Global History?*, Princeton and Oxford: Princeton University Press.

Corbin, A., Courtine, J.-J. and Vigarello, G., eds (2004–2006), *Histoire du corps*, 3 vols, Paris: Seuil.

Dartnon, R. (2000), 'An Early Information Society: News and the Media in Eighteenth-Century Paris', *American Historical Review*, 105 (1): 1–35. (A much expanded electronic version of this essay was published online at www.indiana.edu/~ahr/darnton, but is not available anymore.)

Davis, L. J. and Morris, D. B. (2007), 'Biocultures Manifesto', *New Literary History*, 38: 411–8.

Domanska, E. (2017), 'Animal History', *History and Theory*, 56 (2): 267–87.

Downs, L. L. (2010), *Writing Gender History*, 2nd edn, London: Bloomsbury.

Duara, P., Murthy, V. and Sartori, A. (2014), 'Introduction', in P. Duara, V. Murthy and A. Sartori (eds), *A Companion to Global Historical Thought*, 1–18, Malden, MA and Oxford: Blackwell.

Fahrmeir, A. (2003), 'Zur "Krise" der Geschichte. Anmerkungen zu einer aktuellen Diskussion', *Historische Zeitschrift*, 276 (3): 561–79.

Fogu, C. (2009), 'Digitalizing Historical Consciousness', *History and Theory*, Theme Issue 47: 103–21.

Garcia, T. (2014), *Form and Object: A Treatise on Things*, Edinburgh: Edinburgh University Press.

Gell, A. (1998), *Art and Agency: An Anthropological Theory*, Oxford: Clarendon Press.

Greig, H., Hamlett, J. and Hannan, L., eds (2016), *Gender and Material Culture in Britain since 1600*, London: Palgrave.

Guldi, J. and Armitage, D. (2014), *The History Manifesto*, Cambridge: Cambridge University Press.

Gumbrecht, H. U (1998), *In 1926: On the Edge of Time*, Cambridge, MA: Harvard University Press.

Gumbrecht, H. U. (2014), *Our Broad Present: Time and Contemporary Culture*, New York: Columbia University Press.

Hartog, F. (2015), *Regimes of Historicity: Presentism and Experiences of Time*, New York: Columbia University Press.

Hazard, S. (2013), 'The Material Turn in the Study of Religion', *Religion and Society: Advances in Research*, 4: 58–78.

Howe, S., ed. (2010), *The New Imperial Histories Reader*, London and New York: Routledge.

Huizinga, J (1929), 'Over een definitie van het begrip geschiedenis', in J. Huizinga, *Cultuurhistorische verkenningen*, 156–68, Haarlem: H. D. Tjeenk Willimk & Zoon N. V.

Hunt, L. (2009), 'The Experience of Revolution', *French Historical Studies*, 32: 671–78.

Ingold, T., ed. (1996), *Key Debates in Anthropology*, London and New York: Routledge.

James, P. and Steger, M. B. (2014), 'A Genealogy of "Globalization": The Career of a Concept', *Globalizations*, 11 (4): 417–34.

Jordheim, H. (2012), 'Against Periodization: Koselleck's Theory of Multiple Temporalities', *History and Theory*, 51: 151–71.

Jordheim, H. (2014), 'Multiple Times and the Work of Synchronization', *History and Theory* 53 (4): 498–518.

Kirkham, P., ed. (1996), *The Gendered Object*, Manchester and New York: Manchester University Press.

Kirksey, S. E. and Helmreich, S. (2010), 'The Emergence of Multispecies Ethnography', *Cultural Anthropology*, 25 (4): 545–76.

Kittler, F. A. (1999), *Gramophone, Film, Typewriter*, Stanford: Stanford University Press.

Kleinberg, E. (2016), 'Just the Facts: The Fantasy of a Historical Science', *History of the Present*, 6 (1): 87–103.

Kleinberg, E. (2017), *Haunting History: For a Deconstructive Approach to the Past*, Stanford: Stanford University Press.

Landwehr, A. (2012), 'Von der "Gleichzeitigkeit des Ungleichzeitigen"', *Historische Zeitschrift*, 295 (1): 1–34.

Latour, B. (1993), *We Have Never Been Modern*, Cambridge, MA: Harvard University Press.

Latour, B. (2017), *Où atterrir? Comment s'orienter en politique*, Paris: La Découverte.

LeCain, T. J. (2017), *The Matter of History: How Things Create the Past*, New York: Cambridge University Press.

Lorenz, C. (2010), 'Unstuck in Time. Or: The Sudden Presence of the Past', in K. Tilmans, F. van Vree and J. M. Winter (eds), *Performing the Past: Memory, History and Identity in Modern Europe*, 67–105, Amsterdam: Amsterdam University Press.

Lorenz, C. (2014), 'Blurred Lines: History, Memory and the Experience of Time', *International Journal for History, Culture and Modernity*, 2 (1): 43–62.

Majumdar, R. (2010), *Writing Postcolonial History*, London: Bloomsbury.

Mandressi, R. (2011), 'Le temps profond et le temps perdu. Usages des neurosciences et des sciences cognitives en histoire', *Revue d'histoire des sciences humaines*, 25: 165–202.

McGrath, L. S. (2017), 'History, Affect, and the Neurosciences', *History of Psychology*, 20 (2): 129–47.

Medick, H. (2016), 'Turning Global? Microhistory in Extension', *Historische Anthropologie*, 24 (2): 241–52.

Menary, R., ed. (2010), *The Extended Mind*, Cambridge, MA and London: The MIT Press.

Mitchell, W. J. T. (2005), *What do Pictures Want? The Lives and Loves of Images*, Chicago and London: University of Chicago Press.

Mol, A. (2002), *The Body Multiple: Ontology in Medical Practice*, Durham: Duke University Press.

Noiret, S. (2013), 'Digital history 2.0', in F. Clavert and S. Noiret (eds), *L'histoire contemporaine à l'ère numérique. Contemporary history in the digital age*, 155–90, Berlin et al.: Peter Lang.

Noiriel, G. (1996), *Sur la "crise" de l'histoire*, Paris: Belin.

O'Gorman, E. (2017), 'Imagined Ecologies: A More-Than-Human History of Malaria in the Murrumbidgee Irrigation Area, New South Wales, Australia 1919–45', *Environmental History*, 22: 486–514.

Osterhammel, J. and Petersson, N. P. (2005), *Globalization: A Short History*, trans. Dona Geyer, Princeton, NJ: Princeton University Press.

Pilaar Birch, S. E., ed. (2018), *Multispecies Archaeology*, London and New York: Routledge.

Pomeranz, K. (2014), 'Environmental History and World History: Parallels, Intersections, and Tensions', in P. Duara, V. Murthy and A. Sartori (eds), *A Companion to Global Historical Thought*, 351–68, Malden, MA and Oxford: Blackwell.

Porter, R. (1991), 'History of the Body', in P. Burke (ed.), *New Perspectives on Historical Writing*, 206–32, Cambridge: Polity Press.

Porter, R. (2001), 'History of the Body Reconsidered', P. Burke (ed.), *New Perspectives on Historical Writing*, 232–60, 2nd rev. edn, Cambridge: Polity Press.

Revel, J., ed. (1996), *Jeux d'échelles. La micro-analyse à l'expérience*, Paris: Gallimard and Seuil.

Rigney, A. (2010), 'When the Monograph Is No Longer the Medium: Historical Narrative in the Online Age', *History and Theory*, Theme Issue 49: 100–17.

Rosa, H. (2013), *Social Acceleration: A New Theory of Modernity*, New York: Columbia University Press.

Rosenzweig, R. (2011), *Clio Wired: The Future of the Past in the Digital Age*, New York: Columbia University Press.

Runia, E. (2014), *Moved by the Past: Discontinuity and Historical Mutation*, New York: Columbia University Press.

Russell, E. (2011), *Evolutionary History: Uniting History and Biology to Understand Life on Earth*, New York: Cambridge University Press.

Sachsenmaier, D. (2011), *Global Perspectives on Global History: Theories and Approaches in a Connected World*, Cambridge: Cambridge University Press.

Schmidt, E. and Cohen, J. (2013), *The New Digital Age: Reshaping the Future of People, Nations and Business*, London: John Murray.

Schnapp, J. and Presner, T. (2009), 'Digital Humanities Manifesto 2.0', available online: http://manifesto.humanities.ucla.edu/2009/05/29/the-digital-humanities-manifesto-20/ (accessed 20 December 2017).

Scott, J. W. (1989), 'History in Crisis? The Others' Side of the Story', *American Historical Review*, 94 (3): 680–92.

Shapiro, L., ed. (2014), *The Routledge Handbook of Embodied Cognition*, London and New York: Routledge.

Shryock, A. and Smail, D. L. (2011), 'Introduction', in A. Shryock and D. L. Smail (eds), *Deep History: The Architecture of Past and Present*, 3–20, Berkeley: University of California Press.

Seefeldt, D. and Thomas, W. G. (2009), 'What is Digital History?', in *Perspectives on History: The Newsmagazine of the American Historical Association*, available online: https://www.historians.org/publications-and-directories/perspectives-on-history/may-2009/intersections-history-and-new-media/what-is-digital-history (accessed on 20 December 2017).

Serres, M. with Latour, B (1995), *Conversations on Science, Culture, and Time*, Ann Arbor: The University of Michigan Press.

Smail, D. L. (2008), *On Deep History and the Brain*, Berkeley: University of California Press.

Spier, F. (2015) *Big History and the Future of Humanity*, 2nd edn, Malden, MA and Oxford: Blackwell.

Steger, M. B. (2017), *Globalization: A Very Short Introduction*, 4th edn, Oxford: Oxford University Press.

Tamm, M. (2004), 'Interview with Robert Darnton', *Eurozine*, 21 June, available online: http://www.eurozine.com/interview-with-robert-darnton/ (accessed 20 December 2017).

Tamm, M. (2013), 'Beyond History and Memory: New Perspectives in Memory Studies', *History Compass*, 11 (6): 458–73.

Tamm, M., ed. (2015), *Afterlife of Events: Perspectives on Mnemohistory*, Basingstoke: Palgrave Macmillan.

Tamm, M. (2016), 'Writing Histories, Making Nations: A Review Essay', *Storicamente*, 12: 1–29, available online: http://storicamente.org/tamm_writing_histories_making_nations (accessed 20 December 2017).

Tanaka, S. (2015), 'History without Chronology', *Public Culture*, 28 (1): 161–86.

Thomas, J. A. (2014), 'History and Biology in the Anthropocene: Problems of Scale, Problems of Value', *American Historical Review*, 119 (5): 1587–607.

Trentmann, F. (2009), 'Materiality in the Future of History: Things, Practices, and Politics', *Journal of British Studies*, 48 (2): 283–307.

Trivellato, F. (2011), 'Is there a Future for Italian Microhistory in the Age of Global History?' *California Italian Studies*, 2 (1), available online: http://scholarship.org/uc/item/Oz94n9hq (accessed 20 December 2017).

Tsing, A. (2012), 'Unruly Edges: Mushrooms as Companion Species for Donna Haraway', *Environmental Humanities*, 1 (1): 141–54.

Tsing, A. L. (2015), *The Mushroom at the End of the World: On the Possibility of Life in Capitalist Ruins*, Princeton and Oxford: Princeton University Press.

Ulmer, J. B. (2017), 'Posthumanism as Research Methodology: Inquiry in the Anthropocene', *International Journal of Qualitative Studies in Education*, 30 (9), 832–48.

Van den Akker, C. (2013), 'History as Dialogue: On Online Narrativity', *BMGN – Low Countries Historical Review*, 128 (4): 103–17.

Wajcman, J. (2015), *Pressed for Time: the Acceleration of Life in Digital Capitalism*, Chicago: Chicago University Press.

Weller, T., ed. (2013), *History in the Digital Age*, London and New York: Routledge.

Wilson, K., ed. (2004), *A New Imperial History: Culture, Identity and Modernity in Britain and the Empire, 1660–1840*, Cambridge: Cambridge University Press.

Wimmer, A. and Glick Schiller, N. (2002), 'Methodological Nationalism and Beyond: Nation-state Building, Migration and the Social Sciences', *Global Networks*, 2 (4): 301–34.

Zaagsma, G. (2013), 'On Digital History', *BMGN – Low Countries Historical Review*, 128 (4): 3–29.

CHAPTER 1
GLOBAL HISTORY
Jürgen Osterhammel

There was a time when programmatic reflections on what global history was supposed to be seemed to outnumber attempts to put all those ambitious recipes into historiographical practice. Today the situation has changed. A solid body of work is available not only to demonstrate the strengths and virtues of global history but also to expose its difficulties and its fragility. The present stage of semi-consolidation of the field is a propitious time to attempt a survey, with special emphasis on debates and open questions.

Yet the dramatic expansion of global history does not really facilitate such a task. At the moment, the most diverse kinds of historical writing dress up as 'global', sharing nothing but a vague resolve to overcome national history and Eurocentrism – two bogeys whose despicability is too often taken for granted. Adopting a strictly nominalist view and abstaining from any kind of value judgement, one might austerely catalogue and classify these practices. In this sense, global history is what people choose to call by that name. While pursuing, up to a certain point, such a track of historicization, the present chapter will not entirely avoid normative issues. An intellectual field loses shape and coherence when it abandons the quest for a consensual minimum of shared methodological requirements. Debates, apart from their usual side-purpose of jockeying for academic power and influence, ought to serve a search for such common standards.

Success and its perils

The extraordinary ambition to practice history writing on a grander scale than usual invests the rise and future fate of global history with uncommon drama. Can this ambition be sustained? Are wide-ranging programmatic visions matched by historical analyses that convince the experts as well as a wider public? Is it possible to embed rare virtuoso performances by experienced historians within broader routines of research carried out in monographic projects by scholars in the early stages of their careers? How closely does global history reflect ongoing 'globalisation' in the real world? Do crises in that real-world globalization – the resilience and re-emergence of nationalist politics and mentalities, the upsurge of inter-religious conflict, a partial disintegration of the world economy – weaken the intellectual foundations and the credibility of global history?

The present chapter does not offer answers to all these questions. It starts out from the premise that global history, so far, has proved an ambivalent success. While it has attracted much attention and enthusiasm and has produced an impressive library of outstanding work, in many ways it remains a field in search of itself. It would be premature to celebrate global history as the one historiographical perspective most suitable for our time and the global historian as the avatar of the present age. Such naive and self-serving avantgardism seems to be out of place. The primacy of a global approach in academic historiography, in school curricula, and in the public marketplace is far from assured, and global historians should take seriously the warning by one of the greatest of world historians, the late Sir Christopher Bayly (2011: 13), 'that evolutionary nationalist historicism remains, at the beginning of the twenty-first century, the dominant form of historical understanding across much of the world'.

Global history emerged, along with a more modestly conceived 'transnational' history, in the 1990s as one among several new fields that arose in a general atmosphere of an epochal break. This was the heyday of 'post'-discourses: postmodernism, post-structuralism, and postcolonialism. Still, global history, by its very nature, occupied a special place and evolved under unique circumstances. Other sub-disciplines of historical studies emerged in the course of the differentiation and division of labour that is to be expected from expanding fields of scientific knowledge. Some of them were launched through carefully orchestrated 'turns'. Sometimes emergent fields caught on and solidified into self-sustaining discourses, in other cases they failed to develop the way their proponents envisaged.

Global history evokes a more complex and contradictory image. In the shape of 'world history', understood as a trans-tribal reflection on the past that reaches out beyond one's own polity, social group, or religious community, it has an old pedigree going back to the beginnings of historiography (Subrahmanyam 2014). At the same time, global history represents a mere intra-academic development to a lesser degree than other sub-disciplines. World histories have always appealed to a wider public and have exuded an aura of grandeur and importance. With the rise of scientifically minded historical studies since the time of Barthold Georg Niebuhr and Leopold von Ranke they lost their academic reputation and were banished to a shadowy world of irresponsible speculation, nevertheless continuing to cater to a considerable public demand. Such a bifurcation between popularity and respectability was still evident in the worldwide fame of Arnold J. Toynbee who, towards the end of his life, was probably the best-known historian on the planet while few academic historians – for several reasons, not all of them justified – took him seriously any more.

It is one of the major achievements of the 'new' global history to have bridged the gap between the narrowly specializing professional and the generalist amateur. But the gap has not entirely disappeared, and global historians, more than anyone else, continue to be torn between the expectations of different audiences and constituencies. The recent rise of global history cannot be explained by reference to its intrinsic merits alone. It would have been impossible without the active support and commercial interest of publishers who opened their lists for monographs, textbooks, multi-volume works, book series, and new journals that only a few years before would have kindled much less enthusiasm. Popular and academic global history and world history have grown in a kind of interactive co-evolution within the parameters of academia and the culture industry.

This solid and sustained growth cannot disguise the fact that global/world history always verges on the impossible. Although global historians almost unanimously reject the view that they are in charge of everything, this is exactly what the public demands of them. And, indeed, in a media-conscious age the temptation can be hard to resist – and not entirely without reason. Even if it would be a vulgar misunderstanding to think that world historians aim at knowing everything, they still have to know an extraordinary amount. Since they always have to keep a great number of people, places, periods, and systematic aspects in mind, they are often condemned to patchy and superficial coverage. It is easy for any regional specialist to fault the world historian on points of detail. Not even the greatest masters of world history are exempt from Edward Gibbon's verdict on Gottfried Wilhelm Leibniz, the outstanding polymath of early modern Europe: 'Even *his* powers were dissipated by the multiplicity of his pursuits' (Gibbon 1972: 401). No other sub-discipline of historiography is to a similar degree endangered by hubris. None has a greater responsibility towards a non-expert reading public. The larger the generalizations offered by historians, the more these generalizations have to be taken on trust.

The rise of global history has been geographically uneven. Focusing exclusively on historiographical developments in the English-speaking world tends to distort the picture and to undermine the cosmopolitan credentials and aspirations of global history. If its subject matter is 'globality' in all its many facets, then its inherent universality deserves to be taken seriously. It is undoubtedly true that historians in Britain and the United States have been at the forefront of the new global history and that English is the only common language shared by the global history community. Many global historians in non-Anglophone countries prefer to publish in English; everywhere in the world a book under contract with one of the most prestigious university presses or trade publishers in the United Kingdom or the United States is regarded as the pinnacle of a global historian's achievement.

Even so, there are considerable communities of world historians in a number of non-Anglophone countries, and rich literatures in languages such as Japanese, Chinese, Spanish, French, and German deserve a place in the overall picture. One of the best surveys of world and global history has never been translated from its original Italian (Di Fiore and Meriggi 2011). The enormous influence of a small number of canonical British, US-American or Indian authors whose works have been translated into numerous languages does not mean that writings in a global history mode form a discourse of seamless universality. Locally specific traditions of world history writing have not been completely erased just as the particular kind and degree of institutionalization of global history varies enormously (Stuchtey and Fuchs 2003; Sachsenmaier 2011; Inglebert 2014).

Is it the rule or rather the exception for history departments to include at least one position in global history? Is global history merely regarded as a pedagogical necessity or does it include a research perspective? Do universities offer the broad range of supporting area studies and language tuition facilities that is indispensable for providing global history with a firm empirical basis? Do young scholars receive career incentives to take up global history topics? Is global history taught at secondary schools and colleges and are universities involved in training the respective teachers? For many countries the answers to these questions are likely to be in the negative or carefully hedged. Only a precise mapping of global history activities around the globe would provide clear answers and identify trends over time. Such a mapping is likely to reveal highly uneven development, distinctions between centres and peripheries and sometimes stagnation and reversal.

Paths towards global history

There are three different narratives to account for the growth of global history. All three are basically plausible or even accurate but they have to be combined in making sense of specific trajectories.

Story number one sees the new global history of the 1990s and after as just the latest among several universalist episodes in the history of historical thought and writing. According to this view, global history continues a long tradition of world history or general history which can be found, above all, in Europe, China, and the Islamicate civilization. Before the discovery and early colonial settlement of Australia in the late eighteenth century, such world history did not encompass the entire globe. Rather, the intermittent resurgences of world history should be seen as attempts to arrive at the largest picture possible under the practical and cognitive constraints of a given time. In this sense, it is legitimate to speak of Herodotus, Sima Qian, or Ibn Khaldūn as world historians within the paradigm of their respective epochs. Following this line of reasoning the new global history builds on precursors in the eighteenth century (Voltaire in France, William Robertson in Scotland, or August Ludwig Schlözer in Germany) and also stands in some sort of uneasy genealogical relationship to universalist approaches in the early twentieth century as diverse as Max Weber's cross-cultural comparisons, Eduard Meyer's comprehensive history of the ancient world, or Marxist theories of imperialism. Chinese world history, to give a second example, could build on the historiography of the eighteenth-century Qing empire that was diverse enough to include a plurality of historical experiences within a vast multi-ethnic imperial system. Global history, on this reading, belongs to a longer development of 'transnational challenges to national history writing' (Middell and Roura 2013). Formally speaking, the entire history of historiography might be construed on the model of the antagonism between Thucydides and Herodotus, as a see-saw between the local and the universal, the micro view and the macro perspective: a tension that will never disappear but is now being eased in scholarly practice by a new global microhistory (e.g., Andrade 2010; Ghobrial 2014).

Story number one sounds somewhat antiquarian: It establishes an impressive pedigree for global history but one that is of limited consequence for the practice of global historians today. Story two, by contrast, is set within a radically shorter time span: it sees global history as the third step in a progressive sequence of historiography's advance since the 1960s. Social history was the dominant and most exciting tendency in the 1960s and 1970s, followed by cultural history in the 1980s and 1990s which in turn was succeeded and superseded by global history from the late 1990s onwards. If served without the necessary pinch of salt, this self-historicization easily takes on the flavour of a teleological 'Whig history' of unbroken progress. Social and cultural history serve as mere forerunners of a triumphant global history.

Thinking in terms of such neatly demarcated 'paradigms' imposes welcome order on an extremely complex historiographical landscape and energizes the frontier spirit of those who see themselves in the vanguard on the march towards intellectual hegemony. At the same time, it may occlude the extent to which global history profits from those earlier innovations and inherits their methodological achievements. In contrast to story number one, this alternative narrative considers global history resolutely as a stage – certainly not the ultimate one – in the post-1945 modernization of historical studies. It gains in persuasiveness when it also acknowledges semi-autonomous developments in the various regional historiographies. Until around 1950 or even 1960 empirical world histories – as distinct from philosophical constructions of history – were condemned to some sort of Eurocentric bias. Not enough was known about many parts of the world. Only a huge burst of effort and creativity since about 1960, documented above all in the numerous *Cambridge Histories* (including the *Cambridge World History* of 2015) that now cover virtually every corner of the globe, laid the foundations for the work that has since been accomplished by global historians. The structural antagonism between area studies and global history, probably more pronounced in the United States than anywhere else, should not conceal the fact that global history is greatly indebted to region-based research and in more than one way dependent on it.

Finally, story number three connects the rise of global history to that of globalization studies in the social sciences. Not counting a few early swallows, these studies really took off in the early 1990s: after the collapse of the Soviet Bloc and the Soviet Union, after the invasion of everyday life – and the working habits of scholars – by the internet, and after the incipient emergence of parts of Asia, above all China, from Third World poverty and economic stagnation (Selchow 2017). The optimistic 1990s, when visions of a glorious 'global age' proliferated, were the decade when the foundational texts of globalization theory were written by sociologists, economists, anthropologists, and cultural theorists. Global history, this narrative maintains, was the large-scale application of this kind of theory to the past: network theories, world society theory, world system theory (dating back already to the 1970s), theories of communication, of identity, hybridity, and cultural encounter, of motion, flows and circulation, and so on. The crucial point about this interpretation is the contention that the new global history signifies a deep break with the historiographical past. It owed its existence to the theoretical innovations of the 1990s from Anthony Giddens via Arjun Appadurai to Manuel Castells and thus has no filiations back to older traditions. But it is derivative and dependent on theoretical inputs from outside the discipline. Since globalization theory has engendered a huge literature and has passed through numerous fashions and metamorphoses that historians rarely have the time and energy to study with the necessary comprehensiveness and care, global history has relaxed its ties to social theory and has developed its own somewhat simplified idiom (Osterhammel 2016). According to this narrative, global history is not necessarily identical with the history of 'globalisation' but owes its intellectual foundations to theories of globalization, even if their practical relevance for historians may have declined in recent years.

The third story is intuitively perhaps the most convincing of the three. Just as sociologists and political scientists reacted to experiences of the end of international bipolarity, the annihilation of time and space through digital communication, or the explosive rise of China, so did historians. But in placing developments in historiography squarely in the context of present-day concerns, story number three misses something important. Global history has, in an eclectic way that is fully legitimate, absorbed impulses not just from the social sciences but also from the innovative social and cultural history of the post-war decades. It can also fruitfully be seen as a revitalization of Enlightenment thinking that highlighted cultural relativity, tolerance, and the moral unity of the human species. Thus, each of the three narratives contains a kernel of truth.

Varieties of large-scale history

So far, it has been left deliberately vague what global history is after all. This vagueness reflects common practice. Numerous suggestions have been made to distinguish between various forms of large-scale history. It is astonishing that they have not caught on. There is plenty of evidence of a semantic confusion to which very few people seem to object. Especially in the English-speaking literature 'world history' and 'global history' are often treated as synonyms. The *Journal of World History* and the *Journal of Global History* carry the same type of article without any visible attempt at mutual differentiation. Multi-volume series such as the *Cambridge World History* (Wiesner-Hanks 2015) or *A History of the World* published by Harvard University Press (Iriye and Osterhammel 2012) commit themselves to 'world history' as the more comprehensive concept, basically meaning a 'general' history of socially organized human life on earth since the beginnings of archaeological evidence. Many chapters in those works, however, employ a decidedly 'global' perspective that looks for lateral connections.

The picture is further confused by the intrusion of 'Big History' into the realm of world history (Christian 2004; Hesketh 2014); it is sometimes even seen as identical with global history (Clavin 2005: 436). Popular audiences these days expect speakers who are being introduced as 'global historians' to be knowledgeable about the Big Bang and anything that resulted from it. Big History evidently satisfies a need for the largest possible picture that used to be traditionally met by religion and theology. Made popular by the French priest and scientist Pierre Teilhard de Chardin long before the term 'Big History' was coined and rose to prominence in the United States, the issue of the position of life in the long-term evolution of the cosmos has long since fascinated reading audiences. It stretches the competence of conventionally trained historians who lack sufficient expertise in astrophysics and the theory of biological evolution. Big History is an interdisciplinary subfield of its own and will not be considered further in this chapter. Still, its obvious popularity cannot be ignored. When professional global historians prefer to leave it to a small group of devotees the reason is only partly a lack of competence and a distrust of generalizations that are not based on sources. In addition, such a quasi-metaphysical approach distracts from the mundane concerns of the politically conscious citizen and is liable to lead to a de-politicization of history. What kind of relevant insight do we gain from a contemplation of billions of years?

In spite of early initiatives by Bruce Mazlish and others (Mazlish and Buultjens 1993), there has hardly ever been a true debate among world historians about finer points of the internal classification and mapping of the field. While this neglect has blurred the contours of the historiographical landscape and allowed anyone with the necessary self-confidence to claim credentials as a global historian, it may have contributed to the new sub-discipline's success. Struggles for and against old and new orthodoxies have been avoided, in-fighting has been reduced to an unusual minimum. The policing of the epistemic boundaries has been laissez-faire and almost negligent, sparing us discussion about the purity and contamination of doctrine. Everybody can claim to be a world historian. This comes at the price of indeterminate criteria of judgement. To this day, there is no widely shared consensus about the standards for successful world history writing. This absence is not just a problem for intra-academic tasks such as assessing students, reviewing books, and evaluating manuscripts or applications. Criteria are also needed for keeping a distance from a kind of popular world history that may be deeply influential in society but often shades off into unsupported speculation and fantasy.

A simple attempt to circumscribe, or even define, the terms most commonly used might look like this:

Universal history is a philosophically or theologically informed and vaguely fact-based reflection on major dynamic patterns and regularities in the development of humanity over extended periods of time (Inglebert 2014). It is often based on the assumption that history is a unified, though internally differentiated process with a clear origin and a discernible goal. For the twentieth century, Karl Jaspers's book title *The Origin and Goal of History* (German original: 1949) expresses this programme succinctly (Jaspers 1953). It is closely connected to theories of long-term societal evolution (Sanderson 2014). This kind of discourse is the domain of philosophers and sociologists (Gellner 1988); professional historians tend to avoid it (but see Cook 2003).

World history is the study of human communities – often but not exclusively conceptualized as large-scale 'civilizations' integrated by religious belief systems and basic social practices (Eisenstadt 2001) – and their social and cultural creativity in different ecological settings, putting additional emphasis on contacts between those communities (an excellent example is Vanhaute 2013). It is usually based on the – more or less implicit – assumption that 'globality' is not constituted by real cross-boundary activities of a 'networking' type but through the existence of a limited number of general challenges to which the various communities find answers varying in space, time, and societal framing. These answers can be meaningfully compared to each other, making comparison – at various levels of explication and formality of design – a preferred tool of world historians. In contrast to universal history, world history puts a premium on difference and rejects holistic concepts such as 'mankind', 'humanity', 'world society', or 'world system'. Whereas global history treats mobility and boundary-transgressing connectivity as primordial phenomena, world history focuses on the internal dynamics of communities and societies. During the nineteenth century and at least up to Arnold J. Toynbee's deliberately ecumenical work of the 1930s, world history used to follow the master trope of the 'rise of the West'. This Eurocentrism lingers on but is now widely considered a problem and seldom defended on grounds of principle.

Transnational history has not evolved from traditions of world history and is not predicated on any notion of 'globality' or a closed world system. It rather is a refining extension of the insight that territorial states (with the modern nation state as a special articulation of the territorial state) are embedded in wider contexts. This embedding takes place at different levels. Where the leading actors are governments wielding the tools of diplomacy, military force, and managed economic relations ('mercantilism'), we are at the level of *international* relations revolving around power, war, and peace. Whenever societal actors are involved, relations are *transnational*. They assume the form of 'entanglements' of varying intensity and stability. Entanglement frequently occurs between spatially contiguous societies but also between imperial metropoles and their distant colonies (Margolin and Markovits 2015; Lowe 2015). A more attenuated form than a dense *histoire croisée* (Werner and Zimmermann 2006) is the *histoire connectée* that also looks for first traces of emerging contacts (Subrahmanyam 1997; Gruzinski 2012). Transnational history exposes myths of purity and autonomy while emphasizing the persistent relevance of borders and boundaries. It aims at 'a history with nations that is not a history of nations' (Saunier 2013: 8).

Global history is a perspective for considering all kinds of cross-border mobilities and their consequences, especially within vast and multicultural spaces; it focuses on connections and connectivity (or connectedness), with special attention to empirical connections that are uneven and have a transformative impact on the interconnected social and cultural units (Belich, Darwin, and Wickham 2016). From the point of view of a given social or political unit, global history is less interested in endogenous dynamics (as world history is) than in forces impacting from the outside. At a systemic level (which is absent from transnational history) it makes two assumptions. Firstly, it ascribes separate agency to actors operating at that level and 'causal relevance' to 'factors that do not lie within the purview of individuals, nations, and civilisations' (Conrad 2016: 89). Secondly, even if most global historians do not invoke and need such a strong assumption in their daily practice, leading theorists of global history assert a long-term world historical process that bundles and aligns the colourful chaos of relations and connections in the direction of increasing global integration (Conrad 2016: 102). In this sense, global history shows a closer affinity to universal history with its inbuilt teleology than do world history and transnational history.

My own preference, though not supported by a broad consensus among scholars, would be to leave global history more loosely defined as a history of transformative connections and reserve the pointed requirement of integration for the *history of globalisation*. This should be seen as a subfield of global history concerned with the construction of institutionalized and robust networks of planetary extension that jointly, though not without contradictions, contribute to a progressive integration of societies, states, and cultural arenas on the globe, especially since the technological advances of the mid-nineteenth century (Conrad 2016: 92–100; for a critical position see Lang 2014).

This typology helps to gain a contrastive understanding of the characteristic features of global history. Global history, as the term is used here in a fairly narrow way, is one among several types of large-scale history. It presupposes a direction in history that is vaguely described with terms such as 'integration', 'convergence', and 'homogenization', moving in a dialectical rather than a continuous and steady way. Additional *a priori* assumptions about the overall shape of history are not required. Whereas *universal* history – and, even more so, Big History – has long time spans in view, *world* history is a history of human societies since the earliest palaeontological and archaeological evidence, and *transnational* history limits itself to the last 200 to 250 years, *global* history does not have to be long-term history. The temporalities used by global historians do not derive from a given epistemological programme but are freely chosen according to specific purposes of investigation. Few global historians are likely to go further back than c. 1500, although exciting new work has been done on the global significance of that caesura (Gruzinski 2004; Boucheron 2009). However, very few research-based studies cover several centuries. Analyses of complex connections such as migrations, commodity chains or the transfer of ideas between different civilizational contexts have been most effective whenever they have dealt with shorter periods.

Since its key feature is the focus on connections, global history, in contrast to simplistic but widespread forms of world history, is never merely additive and mosaic-like. It is never content with the collection of anecdotes, isolated data, and distinct regional case studies. Global history has been most persuasive when it managed to discover hidden or unexpected connections that presented familiar phenomena in a new light. Typically, aspects of a national history, sometimes graced by claims to uniqueness and exceptionality, were shown to be influenced by external factors or to form part of larger historical trends (here global history overlaps with comparative world history). These detective-like qualities have contributed strongly to the attractiveness of a global approach. It does not just 'widen' the picture, as is usually thought, but deepens it by uncovering background factors. Seeing familiar things in a new light and understanding the constructed nature and variability of temporal horizons and spatial framings is the central pedagogical purpose of global history (Pomeranz 2014: 19; Grataloup 2011: 131–74). In this sense it is always analytical and never encyclopaedic as world history tends to become.

The 'thought-style' or cognitive habitus of global history works against exceptionalism and special paths. It rejects the privileging of particular historical normalities or yardsticks – like 'the West' or 'the transition from feudalism to capitalism' – against which different trajectories are profiled as aberrations or manifestations of backwardness. It prefers 'externalist' to 'internalist' explanations and ideally combines them both. Methodologically speaking, global history is not defined by its object of study or its subject matter in the way that economic history is about the economy and legal history is an investigation into law and its practice. Global history is not about 'the globe'. Rather, it should be seen as a particular mode of inquiry: the search for lateral and boundary-crossing connectivity, preferably over long distances. Thus, most kinds of conventional historical research are suitable for being reframed in a global way. 'Global' as an adjective can be added to nearly all existing fields. Economic history becomes global economic history when it addresses planetary flows of goods and money or discusses the distribution of income, wealth, and productivity between different world regions. Legal history, conceived of as global legal history, studies the entanglement, and mutual impact of various legal traditions in conditions of colonialism and intercultural encounter. A 'globalized' history of music establishes connections between the study of the Western 'great tradition', ethnomusicology, and a media-based approach to the worldwide dissemination and modification of popular musical idioms. Other examples of such 'double hyphenation' come readily to mind: global intellectual history, global social history, a global history of consumption, and so on. Many sub-disciplines of historiography lend themselves to this kind of 'globalification' (Osterhammel 2015). It does not render established approaches obsolete but adds a new perspective to them.

Non-debates

International relations theory knows the model of 'hegemonic war': a rising power challenges the incumbent hegemon who in turn struggles to defend his position. Several episodes in the history of historiography more or less conform to that model. The rise of social history in the 1960s was accompanied by vehement polemics against political, diplomatic, and military history and also against a history of ideas that was deemed old-fashioned at the time. Two decades later, the victorious social historians found themselves provoked by similarly vitriolic and dismissive cultural historians who celebrated their own successful toppling of the reigning paradigm.

Compared to those stormy quarrels, the ascent of global history took place under much more irenic auspices. Widely respected historians of an older generation, foremost among them William H. McNeill and Fernand Braudel, lent respectability to the parvenu field. The general zeitgeist of the 1990s was globalist and allowed global history to look like the obvious and natural way for historians to respond to the demands of a new age. Whereas in the 1950s Toynbee had been attacked as a megalomaniac dilettante by leading lights of the historical profession, hardly any major historian denied the legitimacy and feasibility of global history. Those who may have remained sceptical kept their reservations to themselves. Many leading journals opened their pages to global topics. The fact that an increasing number of manuscripts with some kind of global thematic passed the acid test of peer reviewing testified to the viability of the emerging trend.

How can this low level of conflict be explained? In addition to the generally supportive atmosphere of the time, it should be noted that everywhere national history was so deeply entrenched as not to be unsettled by the newcomer. The writing and teaching of history within the framework of the nation state has remained indispensable for civic education even in those countries – certainly a minority – where shaping a national outlook and a national memory did *not* explicitly belong to the duties of historians paid by the state.

Archives continue to be organized on a national basis. Most historians in the world prefer to express themselves in their mother tongue. Moreover, only with a little effort could national history be expanded to accommodate 'global' issues such as migration, colonialism, and intercultural exchange (Bender 2002, 2006; Boucheron 2017; Conrad and Osterhammel 2004; for China: Osterhammel 1989). In practice, global history was not necessarily seen as a fundamental threat to national history. Openly nationalist attacks on the cosmopolitan thinking of globally oriented historians were very rare, at least in academia.

Criticism was mainly voiced by those who were doubtful whether global history would meet the general methodological standards of the historical profession. The questions of sources and of language skills were raised time and again. They could not be resolved in a general way. A growing number of convincing monographs and articles put many of those doubts to rest. A kind of unspoken consensus emerged to the effect that topical research in global history should be based on sources in all the languages indispensable for the project at hand.

Surprisingly, one major issue was largely left undiscussed. It touched the basic legitimacy of global history. The new tendency had prospered, generally speaking, in a postmodernist atmosphere. It took on board certain tenets of the postmodernist and postcolonial critique, for instance a strong aversion to 'essentialism' and 'othering' and a sensibility for the precariousness of language and meaning. In other words, it shared a constructivist epistemology. Where global historians parted ways with other adherents of postmodernism is in the question of master narratives. Classical postmodernism, especially in its French incarnation, had radically rejected any kind of *grand récit*. Global history, however, even if it emphasizes the specificity of locality, place, and individual voices and identities, can never entirely avoid making the kind of general statement that had been roundly condemned by influential theorists of postmodernism. This inherent contradiction at the heart of global history has never been sufficiently discussed.

Debates: Explanation, comparison, and circulation analysis

Another debate that did not really unfold was that about description and explanation. The historiographical mainstream of the 1980s and 1990s celebrated the boundless plurality of identities and individual voices and achieved impressive feats of colourful description. At the same time, issues of explanation, so important for Marxist or Weberian social history, retreated into the background. Foucault-inspired epistemologies of 'archaeology' and 'genealogy', immensely influential as they were on both sides of the Atlantic, were difficult to reconcile with conventional notions of explanation. Still, advancing from questions of 'how?' to questions of 'why?' remains at the core of any scientific inquiry and forms the strongest bridge between the humanities and the natural sciences. If the 'widest possible horizon' is not seen as an incontestable value in itself, then a global approach requires justification in terms of its analytical or explanatory surplus. It has to be shown in specific cases how a global re-contextualization of a given issue improves historical understanding.

To give an obvious example, our insight into the 'Age of Revolution' in the decades around 1800 has been immensely enriched by adding the Haitian Revolution to the canonical pair of the American and French revolutions and placing the events into the context of a vast Atlantic arena of interaction (Canny and Morgan 2011; Klooster 2009; Polasky 2015). It has gained even more by extending the gaze farther to encompass the revolutionary struggles for Latin American independence and turmoil in Africa and Asia from Egypt to the Qing empire (Bayly 1989, 1998; Armitage and Subrahmanyam 2010; Wills 2014). But does this shed new light on standard topics of history? Does it, for instance, deepen our understanding of the French Revolution? Drawing attention to developments that occurred simultaneously with the revolutionary events in France is not the same as establishing causal connections which show in what way external factors helped to trigger the revolutionary cataclysm in Paris. Fortunately, longer chains of causation have now been suggested and conventional explanations of the revolution have been refined to combine endogenous and exogenous elements (Campbell 2013; Hunt 2013). These attempts have to be discussed individually and on their own merit.

A *general* debate should address the question of the significance of explanation in the overall methodology of global history. A concomitant question concerns the relation between cause and effect which is best discussed in economic or ecological terms (Parker 2013). A local event can have distant or general – in other words 'global' – causes; in the early modern period, to give just one example, certain crises in purportedly closed Asian economies can be traced back to changes in the supply of American silver (Flynn and Giráldez 2002). Inversely, the ramifications of a local event may affect faraway parts of the globe. The eruption of the Indonesian volcano Tambora on 10 April 1815 is a dramatic case in point (Wood 2014). In many other instances, effects made themselves felt much more slowly. A global approach is probably of little relevance in accounting for the July Crisis of 1914. Yet the war that began on 4 August very quickly evolved into a true world war. Intra-European causes set free global effects. This cannot be shown by simply stringing together chapters on the different theatres of war (Jeffery 2015). It requires precise analyses of concrete interactions combined with a sense of the multi-locational escalation of the conflict (Winter 2014).

One of the debates that was relevant for global history, without being conducted afresh within the new framework, was about comparative history (Kaelble and Schriewer 2003; Haupt and Kocka 2009; Berg 2013; Olstein 2015: 59–97). It is closely related to the question of explanation since comparison is one of the most powerful explanatory tools available to historians. By the early 1990s, the methodology of historical comparison, pioneered by classical authors like Max Weber, Otto Hintze, or Marc Bloch and elaborated by the historical sociologists of the 1960s and 1970s, had taken account of 'cross-cultural' comparison in the social sciences and had started to reflect on comparisons between cases from markedly different cultural contexts. The debate centred on questions of comparability and on the difficult issue of nomenclature: is it justifiable to impose a unified social science terminology of Western origin on historical situations outside Western modernity? If not, how do 'emic' and 'etic' vocabularies relate to one another? Would a strictly 'emic' language, that is one grounded in the self-perception and self-expression of the historical actors, leave any room for the semantic commonalities that are a precondition for comparison?

The next stage in the debate juxtaposed comparison with the study of relations and transfers, or, to put it differently, the comparative assessment of 'pure' cases with the assumption of ubiquitous entanglement, hybridity, and *métissage*. Everyone agreed that at least from the late eighteenth century onwards, pristine, uncontaminated, and unrelated cases – such as Marc Bloch's distinct feudalisms in Western Europe and Japan – have been the exception rather than the rule. Comparison must always take into account the possibility of external influences on the units of comparison – sometimes mutual influences, in other cases determinants from a third position. A radical position, probably endorsed only by a minority of scholars participating in the debate, claimed that comparison was artificial, ignored the realities of ever-increasing connectivity and should therefore be abandoned altogether (Werner and Zimmermann 2006; Cohen 2001; Cohen and O'Connor 2004). There is probably a tacit consensus among global historians that comparison is not entirely useless but has a somewhat old-fashioned feel and is associated with an old-style world history of 'great civilisations' as it nowadays survives in historical sociology rather than in historiography proper. In any case, the analysis of relations, movements, and connections has gained unchallenged precedence.

Thus, an anti-comparativist stance chimes in with the principles of global history. Yet paradoxically, one of the most spectacular success stories of global or world history is quintessentially comparative: the debate about the Great Divergence (surveyed in Vries 2013). It is impossible to summarize this debate in a few sentences. It was conducted mainly among economic historians from the early 1980s onwards but has to be seen within the even wider context of the world historical role of Western modernity and, if one accepts the premise of the theorem of 'multiple modernities', of analogous developments elsewhere. The results have not been conclusive, but the debate was conducted at a very high level of sophistication and methodological awareness and has proved the fruitfulness of 'intercultural' comparison, in this case especially a comparison between Europe and China.

Significantly (and seldom remarked on in the discussion), connectivity and flows – the hallmarks of global history – played only a marginal role in the various explanations put forward for Europe's and North America's exceptional economic success since the late eighteenth century. Very few discussants invoked imperialism, colonialism, and a politically engineered 'development of underdevelopment' as the principal causes of the economic backwardness of the Global South – factors that had been prominent in world system theory and Latin American *dependencia* theories of the 1960s and 1970s. Thus, in terms of the typology suggested above, the debate about the Great Divergence falls under the category of comparative world history rather than that of global history understood as the study of transformative connectivity. The original reasons for the Great Divergence were usually seen in endogenous factors such as geographical opportunities and ecological constraints, state structures, or culture and mentality. Only the further widening of the gap between rich and poor countries that took place during the nineteenth century was widely attributed to some kind of malign connectivity: the colonial exploitation of the South by the North.

A track still to be taken in the international debate refers to a different sense of comparison: comparison as 'a process of relational self-definition' (Seigel 2005: 64; Epple and Erhart 2015). Individuals, communities, and entire nation states form mental connections by comparing themselves with others. Europeans of the eighteenth century compared themselves with Asia. In the nineteenth century, Asian countries from the Ottoman Empire to Japan took Western Europe (and increasingly the United States) as a model to be emulated. 'World society' as a 'real' social formation of worldwide classes and strata has never come into being, but as an 'imagined community' it began to be created in the nineteenth century through mutual observation and recognition in a mode of comparison and competition, adaptation, and rejection (Wittmann 2014). Conceptualizing comparison as a cognitive activity of historical actors easily incorporates the global level since during the nineteenth and twentieth centuries global standards – from 'world power' to 'world championships' – increasingly served as benchmarks of reference. Another way to bring in the global is to take a more dialectical view of integration and homogenization at a world level (as pioneered by Bayly 2004). Spinning the 'human web' (McNeill and McNeill 2003; Northrup 2015) ever more densely does not mean that everything on earth is getting continuously more similar and, thereby, less suitable for comparison; economists are now coming up with more nuanced concepts of convergence (Baldwin 2016). As Nile Green has argued, it is precisely the method of comparison that helps 'to demonstrate how common forces and parallel processes operating at a global level can lead to distinct cultural outcomes at a local and regional level' (Green 2013: 519).

Whereas the uses of comparison will always be controversial, 'connectivity' and 'circulation' enjoy a secure position as the twin master concepts of global history. Much of the enthusiasm surrounding global history derives from a fascination with fluidity, unimpeded mobility, and endless opportunities for 'hybrid' re-combination. However, it would mean an abdication of intellectual responsibility if the perceived shapelessness of a dynamic reality were to be reflected in a deliberate fuzziness of analytical categories. Frederick Cooper's well-founded warning against the false contrast between 'a rhetoric of containers and a rhetoric of flows' has had little impact, and his question whether it is possible to 'develop a differentiated vocabulary that encourages thinking about connections and their limits' has largely been left unanswered, at least at the general level of methodology (Cooper 2005: 112).

The virtues and charms of a semantics of motion are obvious. An impressive array of studies has shown how spaces of interaction and widely dispersed communities have been created through the movement of people, commodities, and knowledge (Sood 2011, 2016). Yet the observation of realities in the early twenty-first century makes it difficult to ignore the fact that mobility stops at fences, walls, and border security desks, that economic flows produce winners as well as losers, and that ideas and information can get distorted and manipulated in their passage through less-than-transparent circuits. The mirage of a world of flat barriers and limitless permeability deserves serious reconsideration. Global historians are likely to engage with the critique of their own 'mobility bias' that has been voiced by anthropologists (Rockefeller 2011; Sedgewick

2014) as well as in two recent thoughtful articles by Monika Dommann (Dommann 2016) and Stefanie Gänger (Gänger 2017). This may also lead to the debate, suggested by Frederick Cooper in the early 2000s, on how to arrive at a better understanding of various forms of connectivity within their historical settings. Such a debate will link up with the problem of causation: connections differ in their impact and transformative power. They also operate within different framings of space and time. Global history has been most successful in a synchronic mode that limits the field of observation to relatively short time spans. Incorporating long-term dynamics without jeopardizing source-based precision is one of the greatest challenges ahead.[1]

Comment

Pierre-Yves Saunier

'Nobody expects the Spanish Inquisition', and this is why neither three men in purple robes, nor I, will wittingly spoil this section by putting Jürgen Osterhammel to the question about specific aspects of his chapter, or being redundant by making points he covers. I would rather use this space to raise one, two, or even three additional points that he mentioned briefly, or may have decided to leave out for lack of space. I invite Jürgen Osterhammel to pick one of these, and to leave the other two for a day when we have a chance to get acquainted. All of them, I feel, address the capacity of global history to hold its place in the universe of historical writing in the years to come, and as such they seem appropriate topics for my comments. Or rather, the capacity of 'global/world/ transnational/connected history' – as Jürgen Osterhammel rightly explains these terms – are often swapped for one another, despite their differences in scope and angle, and this is why I will use 'global' as the sign post for that compact in the rest of this text.

My first entry point deals with the currency of global history, and possible absence thereof. Here, I will build on two clues provided by the author: on the one hand, he wonders about the possible backlash of current 'crises in real globalisation' on global history, and on the other he underlines the mostly 'irenic' auspices under which global history has found a place in the sun. Let me start with the latter: During their emergence and semi-consolidation, did the different propositions for global, connected, transnational, or transcultural perspectives meet with unanimous assent? I rather feel that vigorous counter arguments have never ceased to be raised, but initially with limited traction among academics. Speaking of critical accounts, I do not point to recent expressions of academic fatigue like David Bell's (2013) 'no networks no vast spaces' slimming diet. I rather think of the low-intensity but constant academic exchanges that pitted global approaches against national history regarding performance, perspectives, and interpretation, not unlike previous discussions about world history in the 1940s and 1960s. Instances of such exchanges are familiar to US and German historians, but they also took place in several other instances such as the reception of Sanjay Subrahmanyam's biography of Vasco da Gama, a key figure of the Portuguese national imaginary, by some

Portuguese historians (McGerr 1991; Johnson 2006; Wehler 2006; Xavier and Santos 2007). The defence of the national framework, as an object of specific or comparative study, and as a basis for the national narrative, was the key here and there.

There were other mild appraisals on similar grounds elsewhere, but none gave way to a controversy like the ones that have left their mark in nineteenth- and twentieth-century historiography. First, because the challenge was often modestly worded and developed in niches. Secondly, because of momentum: globalization processes were the talk of the town, from the economy to migrations to terrorism. It was hard to be against perspectives that chimed in with the general atmosphere and which could place history in debates and discussions where sociologists, economists, and anthropologists had featured prominently without much of a contribution by historians. Third, the new perspectives were sociologically compatible with changes at work in the profession regarding the ways one became and operated as a historian, especially through the increased familiarity with other historical milieus, historiographies, and histories than one's national.

Jürgen Osterhammel then seems to be right when he states that 'openly nationalist attacks on the cosmopolitan thinking of globally oriented historians were very rare, at least in academia'. Yet, such attacks were not rare in the public sphere, especially around redefinitions of school curricula. In the United States, the College Board's plan to revamp its framework for the US history advanced placement course raised hell in 2012–15, while in France the new curricula for history at the secondary school level never ceased to be disputed from 2008 to 2013. In both countries, individuals and movements identified with conservatism denounced anti-national narratives and identified global/transnational perspectives as one of the culprits, propelled by a leftist hostility to the nation.

With recent events such as Brexit in Europe, the election of Donald Trump in the United States, and a series of major elections in 2017 Europe, from the Netherlands to Germany, some in the North Atlantic world feel that we have reached a pivotal moment – although those events and their exact consequences remain to unfold. The cleavage between 'patriots and globalists' would now be the new fault line within societies and polities, and more generally the *Zeitgeist* would turn against global/world/transnational/connected history. Early in 2017, a book and its reception seemed to materialize this possibility (see Wikipedia 2017 for a round up). Published a few months before the French presidential election, *L'histoire mondiale de la France*, mentioned by Jürgen Osterhammel, is an edited collection of vignettes that each starts from a specific date/event to showcase what French history owes to the world out there, with contributions by 122 historians. The introduction is explicit that the book aims at providing a contrapuntal timeline to that of the 'national legend', using the insights provided by global and connected history. The public has embraced the volume with unexpected enthusiasm for an edited collection written by academic historians, but its publication also unleashed scathing comments from columnists and essayists who qualified the book as an attempt to 'dissolve France', its contributors as 'gravediggers of the great French heritage', and the global perspective as the silver bullet to 'make France disappear'. Pierre Nora, a major

French intellectual and historian of international fame as the anchor for the *Lieux de mémoire* series, added his voice to the choir and stated the book was nothing but a political statement. This was in line with previous interventions he had made, especially during the 2008–13 curriculum debate where he stressed how global or world history approaches were used to oust the teaching of national history. Other historians have also expressed critical views and crossed swords with the volume's editor, and the quarrel is certainly not finished.

Like the debate around *L'histoire mondiale de la France*, the discussion around curricula and the low-intensity academic skirmishes surrounding the growth of global history build on trends, arguments, and positions that have long been shaping the relationship between the teaching and writing of history and the social and political struggles to define the spine of the French and US nations. This is why I ask Jürgen Osterhammel to return to his evaluation of the conflictual situations around global history: when we move beyond the polite world of scientific journals and conferences, how extensive have been the conflicts surrounding the development of such perspectives? If the elephant has been in the room much before Brexit and the 2016–17 'year of living dangerously', what is the potential of this moment to renew or reshape the debate, and is there any reason to think that global history 'has had its moment' and will lose its currency? How shall global history continue its investigations of past impactful connections in a present that would discredit such connections?

Jeremy Adelman's recent intervention will allow me to segue into my next point, whose keyword would be 'timeliness'. The director of the Global History Lab at Princeton University confesses to the original sin that global history has forgotten the 'power of place', something which real-world events of 2016–17 would remind us of with a vengeance (Adelman 2017). He also identifies global history with the project of making the world safe for cosmopolitanism through a celebration of border-crossing. He has a point here: the contribution to an appeased world, freed from the scourge of confronting nations and cultures thanks to a better understanding of its interdependences, has been part and parcel of the motivations of many global historians. It was and is a frequent rationale for convincing reviewers, readers, funding agencies, and university committees of the worthiness of their approach (global history for a global present and a better future). Moreover, it is clear that not enough attention has been paid to the strikingly similar use and value current historians append to the very same terms and phrases that were used by historical protagonists who conducted or observed world-making projects over time, such as 'connections', 'networks', 'links', 'interdependence', 'cosmopolitanism', or 'space compression' (Sivasundaram 2017). But, unlike what Adelman suggests in his final paragraph, possibly in a cunning rhetorical double flip, this did not prevent global history to write stories of disintegration, chart the interruption of circulations, analyze the severance or rejection of connections, identify cross-border individuals, ideas, and situations that did not aim at or work at the welfare of humankind and to provide critical assessments of views that the world was becoming flat, homogenous, and irenic. Likewise, global history has not boiled down to macro-narratives forgetful of place, and its obvious mobility tropism did not drum out what stays put and contained.

Studies of communication and transportation have enhanced the role of immobile infrastructures, anchored into specific sites, work about migrations has woven together the stories of those who left and those who remained to see if and how the latter were affected, historians of commodities and their chains have anchored stories that moved in specific sites where values and usages build up. The concern about the effectiveness of circulations and connections is not foreign to global/world/transnational/connected historians: it is an element of their question list, side by side with their commitment to work across spatial levels (and to be critical of the definition and hierarchy of the latter). That leads me to the question I submit to Jürgen Osterhammel: if there have been several guiding scripts motivating global historians, what has been the place of the study of 'transformative dis-connections', and does it constitute a promising horizon for global history?

My third point, which bears the tag of possibilities, has to do with the ongoing digitization process and the way it affects historians: digitization of sources, digitization of documentation and research practices, digitization of methods, digitization of publication. This is not the right place, nor the right author, to assess the process and pronounce on its final outcome, a big revolution or a great illusion – in either case it will involve major consequences for all branches of knowledge production. At this moment, I would rather invite Jürgen Osterhammel to ponder the relationship between digital history and global history through a few configurations, and to tease out the possibilities in front of us.

The first configuration takes shape at the intersection of the banal digitization of global historians' daily practices and of the prospects of big data for global history. Lara Putnam has explored how the amount of digital resources has, incrementally and without that much self-reflection, affected the way we build our reference apparatus and bibliography as much as the way we identify and obtain our primary sources (Putnam 2016). What has been gained in the process of becoming digitized historians is especially clear to those who stretch across the usual territorial units of historical understanding to create courses and course materials, or to imagine and conduct research projects: the cost, speed, scope, and effectiveness of 'lateral glances' were dramatically redefined, as stressed by Putnam. But she also puts her finger on the 'disintermediated' sort of relationship that emerges from the fact that algorithms and processors have substituted our eyes, ears, fingers, brain, and bodies. The material we process, or the places we study, may now remain at arm's length without visible damage. Knowability, though, is affected by what this is making redundant: the familiarization with search tools and what they have 'under their hood'; a capacity for self-reflection on the research strategies that we elaborate; the heuristic input from on location discussions and disputes with librarians, archivists, and scholars in and from places we are not conversant with, and so on. These consequences of a yet under acknowledged dependent relationship with the digital 'search box', probably the most frequently used historians' tools by now, shape the first leg of my argument. The second leg, about the prospects of big data for global history, stems from the different undertakings led by Patrick Manning at the University of Pittsburgh around the World History Center/Collaborative for Historical Information and Analysis

(Manning 2013, 2017). Through a number of initiatives and consortia, Manning and his team are proposing a combination that should be able to reshape history as we know it. Based on the collection, aggregation, and analysis of world historical data on a global scale for the post-1500 era, the agenda is to tackle issues that humanity is grappling with at the planetary level – beginning with inequality. Generally, the treatment of the data to be aggregated will provide a picture 'of global social patterns and interactions' (Manning 2012: 1). Regarding inequality, analysis of the interaction between variables and confrontation with social theories 'will seek to identify the sources, scale, and effects of inequality, with an effort to disaggregate its various economic, social, and natural dimensions' (Manning 2017: 17). The establishment and treatment of that huge amount of data will be based on massive collaborative work among historians and with social scientists, and its results would bring historians and history together with the social sciences to bear on policy formulation and implementation, thus giving the discipline a new purchase.

If I connect these two legs, the disintermediation of ordinary practices and the hypervitaminated global quantitative historical sociology approach, I find a version of the historical episteme that seems at odds with some points recently made by Sebastian Conrad in his overview of global history (Conrad 2016, esp. chaps. 8, 9, and 10). Here, Conrad insists on the need for global historians not to 'flatten the world' by seeing it at a distance and through abstract terminology, categories, and notions of which universality is not questioned as the product of specific local histories. In his text, Jürgen Osterhammel criticizes 'big history' à la David Christian or Fred Spier for delivering generalizations that are not based on sources and for being too distant from mundane concerns. His concluding sentence returns to that point when he suggests that 'incorporating long term dynamics without jeopardizing source-based precision is one of the greatest challenges ahead'. What does he think of the possibilities that the digitization of history and digital history offer to global history in terms of sources, their abundance, and distance thereof, both in access and in analysis?

This not being a state-of-the-art survey of digital history and the way global historians have responded to it, I will add just another aspect that I feel to be of special interest here. Because of its interest in circulations, connections, and relations as they have been made, not made, and unmade, and in consequence of its need to work across scales, global history faces a narrative challenge. Mobile or not, the processes, factors, living and non-living organisms that these stories deal with have to be located and followed in space and across time. Such stories have been told with talent by means of the book and the article, and we have certainly not exhausted the capacity of the codex format. Yet, the digital is presenting global history with additional options for telling a story and presenting a thick argument: mapping, visualization techniques, hyperlinked writing, non-linear organization are some of the features that can match form and content, bringing readers and users to engage differently with historians' arguments, stories, and source material. Being hindered from boasting about my ignorance by the briefness of these comments, I will offer out two instances among the many publications that can be used to discuss the relationship between global history and digital narration. One of these is the now defunct but still suggestive HyperCities platform, which was built to create and publish 'geotemporal narratives' (HyperCities 2017; Presner, Shepard, and Kawano 2014). HyperCities offered the capacity to geolocalize points of narration and to enrich these with text and multimedia material. This provided authors with the capacity to 'write time in space', which seems congenial to what global/world/transnational/connected historians are doing. Let me just add that HyperCities did not disappear from lack of users or interest, but because Google discontinued its Earth browser Application Programming Interface in February 2017: without this indispensable cog, the platform stopped working, an additional clue of the durability challenge in digital humanities.[2] The other is the web site that has been created to pair with Nicole Starosielski's book about the historical and present condition of undersea cable systems in the Pacific (Starosielski 2015; Starosielski, Loyer, and Brennan 2016). Here, stories are told sequentially and can be read along paths or hops along the cables themselves. They are organized by place and themes to convey both the enclosure and extent, vulnerability and capacity, homogeneity and differentiation of these systems as an infrastructure with technological, environmental, human, and economic coordinates. My final question then invites Jürgen Osterhammel to examine if he feels there are special opportunities for global history in such formats, genres, and modes of digital narrative, and how they can combine with, supplement, replace the ones we are using now. By and large, this should be more enticing than the rack and cushion treatments.

Response

Jürgen Osterhammel

Since I was cautious enough not to tout my own preferred version of global history Pierre-Yves Saunier did not feel obliged to demolish an edifice of axioms, key concepts, value judgements, and unspoken assumptions. A sterner critic might have taken issue with my reconstruction of actual and virtual debates and pointed out, for example, a lack of engagement with discussions in national or regional history communities outside the Anglophone, Francophone, and German-speaking worlds (but now see Beckert and Sachsenmaier 2018). It is indeed a striking paradox that global history writing, while united in a shared mood of barrier-free cosmopolitanism, is not on the way to becoming monochrome and monolingual. Fortunately, I should add.

Pierre-Yves Saunier agrees with my emphasis on the role and special responsibility of global history in the public sphere and he encourages us to go even further than I did in my remarks and confront scepticism and even hostility, as he puts it, 'beyond the polite world of scientific journals and conferences'. On this kind of well-groomed home turf global historians have, as a rule, been treated kindly. For their part, they have refrained from the iconoclastic vehemence, sometimes verging on verbal patricide, that helped the young social historians of the 1960s and 1970s – my own academic teachers – to clear away what they believed to be the debris of woolly-minded political and intellectual

TRANSACTION RECORD

ANTIGONISH STN MAIN
133 CHURCH ST
ANTIGONISH, NS B2G OAO

TYPE: PURCHASE
ACCT: VISA
AMOUNT: $ 28.14

CARD NUMBER: ***********5017
DATE/TIME: 2023-11-20 13:47:23
REFERENCE #:   0010018860 H
AUTH #:   084589
Visa Credit
A0000000031010
INVOICE NUMBER   1097161

01 Approved - Thank You 027

FF / DT   20

IMPORTANT - retain this copy for
your records

CUSTOMER COPY

TRANSACTION RECORD

ANTIGONISH 5TH MAIN
133 CHURCH ST
ANTIGONISH, NS B2G 0A0

TYPE: PURCHASE
ACCT: VISA
AMOUNT: $ 28.14

CARD NUMBER: ************5017
DATE/TIME: 2023-11-20 13:47:23
REFERENCE #:   00100188S0 H
AUTH #:   084589
Visa Credit
A0000000031010
INVOICE NUMBER   1057151

01 Approved - Thank You 027

FF / DT   20

IMPORTANT - retain this copy for
your records

CUSTOMER COPY

history. In contrast to social history, global history has not been a one-generation project. It also did not come along with a fully articulated methodology similar to that of a Neo-Weberian *Historische Sozialwissenschaft* as represented by Hans-Ulrich Wehler and Jürgen Kocka in Germany. In a word that I was reluctant to use in my chapter: It was, and still is, the methodological and theoretical *eclecticism* of global history that blunted the edge of its bursting onto the scene and that guaranteed its respectability. Had this been otherwise and had, for example, all global history nailed orthodox postcolonialism to its mast, the threshold of acceptance would have been much higher.

Resistance outside 'the polite world' comes from parliamentary politics and ministries of science and education, from funding agencies, university managements, and the media, sometimes from censorship bodies. Nationalist backlashes, invariably linked to restrictions of free speech, are today in evidence in many important countries from China and India through Poland and Turkey to the United States, though least of all in Germany where not even conservative historians celebrate the glory of the nation. There are no general recipes what global historians can do to move – or keep – their own concerns close to the top of any list of political and academic priorities. My own experiences are limited to the small – and hardly representative – world of German academia (Osterhammel 2009). As far as the university is concerned, they would suggest that not all energies should be invested in the constructing of a neat and autonomous sub-discipline at the expense of keeping boundaries permeable and striking alliances with neighbouring fields and 'enlightened' representatives of national history and area studies. Young scholars in countries where the job market does not offer a steady stream of attractive options for global historians would be well advised not to put all their academic eggs into the global basket but cultivate a sideline interest in at least one more modest and mundane topic that is compatible with the average sensibilities in smallish history departments.

In the public realm, and provided individual access to media is secured, historians should feel called upon to oppose historical misrepresentations and perversions of history of *any* kind, even, if necessary, doubtful accounts of global constellations – think only of one-sided and triumphalist interpretations of the Cold War. The question is who seeks when and with what purpose the advice of the world historian. Sometimes, the temptation is considerable. Media crave for the biggest picture in the roughest possible outline, and nobody seems more willing and able to offer it than the seemingly omnicompetent and prophetically gifted globalist. This is a big chance for the right word at the right moment. Yet, and this partly explains my reservation towards certain kinds of Big History, the much-vaunted global perspective may sometimes lack the necessary acuity and sense of proportion. Then climate change is not a real problem because we already had it millions of years ago, mass migration is a 'normal' feature of history (correct, but what does that mean for the pressing problems in today's Mediterranean?), or active head of states evoke entertaining but hardly instructive parallels to some of the more colourful tyrants in the global past. The very large picture can obfuscate things and create an atmosphere of specious profundity. In other words, global historians should never sacrifice a commitment to the outmost precision and clarity – a cardinal virtue of all kinds of historical argument. This is why I am seldom impressed by the plain assertion *that* something is connected. The rewarding question rather is why things are connected, with what effects on whom, and who made them connect in the first place.

This leads immediately to the second issue raised by my benevolent commentator. The observation that some connections look inevitable, flowing, as it were, with the stream of history, while upon closer inspection they appear to be highly improbable and almost a source of wonder, has always been a starting point for the kind of global history I am trying to practice and, with some hesitation, to advocate. Niels Petersson and I made that idea a cornerstone of a small book on globalization that we published in 2003, at a time when the topic was just being discovered by historians and the globalization euphoria among social scientists was reaching unprecedented heights (English version, Osterhammel and Petersson 2005). Perhaps this scepticism, too, owes something to a generational experience. My generation saw two progressivist kinds of 'Whiggism' collapse and disappear: modernization theory (with its offshoots in 'end of history' fantasies) and Marxism of the Soviet type, while we were raised on various less sanguine antidotes: a 'sober' realism in Max Weber's footsteps, the more dialectical manifestations of Marxism (including Frankfurt-style critical theory) and a postmodernist sense of ambiguity and precariousness. This is why Pierre-Yves Saunier's injunction, as I understand him, to develop a rich repertoire of 'guiding scripts' far beyond the blatantly obvious master narratives of integration, connectedness, entanglement, hybridization, and cosmopolitan harmony is very well taken.

Global history still holds an enormous potential for experiments with literary forms and modes of presentation. Current practice ranges from the short essay via the solid monograph to the textbook and the sprawling 'synthesis'. But guiding – and not so guiding – scripts may come in many more shapes and guises, a great number of them still unexplored or unknown. These include stories of failure, loss, and regression; stories about groups and individuals; stories not just with active globalizers as their heroes but also about the passively globalized or the simply forgotten. Once again, this is a plea for the specific and for its inclusion into wider horizons. I am not proposing that global historians limit themselves to studies of diasporas or biographies of globetrotters, the more obscure the better. The task ahead is to come up with more refined forms of writing that combine life-stories with the larger tendencies and more comprehensive contexts that historians are trained to identify and analyse.

This detour to problems of narration should, finally, serve as an excuse when Pierre-Yves Saunier invites me to comment on global history's digital future about which he writes so persuasively. Whoever cares for telling a tale is likely to keep a distance from numbers. To be sure, methods of digitization have an apparent affinity with my insistence on precision. That I harbour a certain suspicion when it comes to more or less intelligent estimates, especially for premodern times, dressed up as 'data', is probably born out of ignorance. Still, I am inclined to skirt the issue. Why? For the last time, let me invoke the generational factor. Internationally speaking, digital humanities are less than twenty years old. They came to the attention of the ordinary German historian just a few years ago. Most members of the profession still lack a sufficient understanding of the new world of possibilities, let alone an adequate technical training. As a retired professor, cut off from funding for costly digitization projects, I revel in the simplicity of pen and paper, occasional use of a personal computer not entirely ruled out.

Notes

1. *Acknowledgements*: This article has benefited enormously from comments by the members of the Konstanz-based Leibnizpreis Research Group 'Global Processes', funded by the Deutsche Forschungsgemeinschaft (DFG).
2. Communication with Todd Presner, March 2017.

References

Adelman, J. (2017), 'What is Global History Now?', *Aeon*, 2 March 2017, available online: https://aeon.co/essays/is-global-history-still-possible-or-has-it-had-its-moment (accessed 16 April 2017).

Andrade, T. (2010), 'A Chinese Farmer, Two African Boys, and a Warlord: Toward a Global Microhistory', *Journal of WorldHistory*, 21 (4): 573–91.

Armitage, D. and Subrahmanyam, S., eds (2010), *The Age of Revolutions in Global Context, c. 1760–1840*, Basingstoke: Palgrave Macmillan.

Baldwin, R. (2016), *The Great Convergence: Information Technology and the New Globalization*, Cambridge, MA and London: Belknap Press of Harvard University Press.

Bayly, C. A. (1989), *Imperial Meridian: The British Empire and the World 1780-1830*, London and New York: Longman.

Bayly, C. A. (1998), 'The First Age of Global Imperialism, c. 1760–1830', *Journal of Imperial and Commonwealth History*, 26 (2): 28–47.

Bayly, C. A. (2004), *The Birth of the Modern World 1780–1914: Global Connections and Comparisons*, Oxford: Blackwell.

Bayly, C. A. (2011), 'History and World History', in U. Rublack (ed.), *A Concise Companion to History*, 3–25, Oxford: Oxford University Press.

Beckert, S. and Sachsenmaier, D., eds (2018), *Global History, Globally: Research and Practice around the World*, London: Bloomsbury.

Belich, J., Darwin, J. and Wickham, C. (2016), 'Introduction: The Prospect of Global History', in J. Belich, J. Darwin, M. Frenz and C. Wickham (eds), *The Prospect of Global History*, 3–22, Oxford: Oxford University Press.

Bell, D. A. (2013), 'This Is What Happens When Historians Overuse the Idea of the Network', *New Republic*, 25 October, available online: https://newrepublic.com/article/114709/world-connecting-reviewed-historians-overuse-network-metaphor (accessed 14 April 2017).

Bender, T., ed. (2002), *Rethinking American History in a Global Age*, Berkeley, CA, Los Angeles and London: University of California Press.

Bender, T. (2006), *A Nation among Nations: America's Place in World History*, New York: Hill and Wang.

Berg, M., ed. (2013), *Writing the History of the Global: Challenges for the Twenty-first Century*, Oxford: Oxford University Press.

Boucheron, P., ed. (2009), *Histoire du monde au XVe siècle*, 2 vols, Paris: Fayard.

Boucheron, P., ed. (2017), *Histoire mondiale de la France*, Paris: Seuil.

Campbell, P. (2013), 'Rethinking the Origins of the French Revolution', in P. McPhee (ed.), *A Companion to the French Revolution*, 3–23, Malden, MA, Oxford and Chichester: Wiley-Blackwell.

Canny, N. and Morgan, P., eds (2011), *The Oxford Handbook of the Atlantic World*, Oxford: Oxford University Press.

Christian, D. (2004), *Maps of Time: An Introduction to Big History*, Berkeley, CA, Los Angeles and London: University of California Press.

Clavin, P. (2005), 'Defining Transnationalism', *Contemporary European History*, 14 (4): 421–39.

Cohen, D. (2001), 'Comparative History: Buyer Beware', *German Historical Institute Bulletin*, 29: 23–33.

Cohen, D. and O'Connor, M., eds (2004), *Comparison and History: Europe in Cross-national Perspective*, London and New York: Routledge.

Conrad, S. (2016), *What Is Global History?* Princeton, NJ and Oxford: Princeton University Press.

Conrad, S. and Osterhammel, J., eds (2004), *Das Kaiserreich transnational: Deutschland in der Welt, 1871–1914*, Göttingen: Vandenhoeck & Ruprecht.

Cook, M. (2003), *A Brief History of the Human Race*, New York and London: Norton.

Cooper, F. (2005), *Colonialism in Question: Theory, Knowledge, History*, Berkeley, CA, Los Angeles and London: University of California Press.

Di Fiore, L. and Meriggi, M. (2011), *World History: Le nuove rotte della storia*, Rome and Bari: Laterza.

Dommann, M. (2016), 'Alles fließt: Soll die Geschichte nomadischer werden?', *Geschichte und Gesellschaft*, 42 (3): 516–34.

Eisenstadt, S. N. (2001), 'Civilizations', in N. J. Smelser and P. B. Baltes (eds), *International Encyclopedia of the Social and Behavioral Sciences*, vol. 3, 1915–21, Amsterdam: Elsevier.

Epple, A. and Erhart, W., eds (2015), *Die Welt beobachten: Praktiken des Vergleichens*, Frankfurt am Main and New York: Campus.

Flynn, D. O. and Giráldez, A. (2002), 'Cycles of Silver: Global Economic Unity through the Mid-eighteenth Century', *Journal of World History*, 13 (2): 391–427.

Gänger, S. (2017), 'Circulation: Reflections on Circularity, Entity, and Liquidity in the Language of Global History', *Journal of Global History*, 12 (3): 303–18.

Gellner, E. (1988), *Plough, Sword and Book: The Structure of Human History*, London: Collins Harvill.

Ghobrial, J.-P. A. (2014), 'The Secret Life of Elias of Babylon and the Uses of Global Microhistory', *Past and Present*, 222: 51–93.

Gibbon, E. (1972), 'Antiquities of the House of Brunswick', in P. B. Craddock (ed.), *The English Essays of Edward Gibbon*, 398–531, Oxford: Clarendon Press.

Grataloup, C. (2011), *Faut-il penser autrement l'histoire du monde?*, Paris: Armand Colin.

Green, N. (2013), 'Maritime Worlds and Global History: Comparing the Mediterranean and Indian Ocean through Barcelona and Bombay', *History Compass*, 11 (7): 513–23.

Gruzinski, S. (2004), *Les quatre parties du monde: Histoire d'une mondialisation*, Paris: Éditions de La Martinière.

Gruzinski, S. (2012), *L'aigle et le dragon: Démesure européenne et mondialisation au XVIe siècle*, Paris: Fayard.

Haupt, H.-G. and Kocka, J., eds (2009), *Comparative and Transnational History: Central European Approaches and New Perspectives*, New York and Oxford: Berghahn.

Hesketh, I. (2014), 'The Story of Big History', *History of the Present: A Journal of Critical History*, 4 (2): 171–202.

Hunt, L. (2013), 'The Global Financial Origins of 1789', in S. Desan, L. Hunt and W. M. Nelson (eds), *The French Revolution in Global Perspective*, 32–43, Ithaca, NY and London: Cornell University Press.

HyperCities (2017), available online: http://www.hypercities.com/ (accessed 14 April 2017).

Inglebert, H. (2014), *Le monde, l'histoire: Essai sur les histoires universelles*, Paris: PUF.

Iriye, A. and Osterhammel, J., general eds (2012–), *A History of the World*, Cambridge, MA and London: Belknap Press of Harvard University Press.

Jaspers, K. (1953), *The Origin and Goal of History*, trans. M. Bullock, New Haven, CT: Yale University Press.

Jeffery, K. (2015), *1916: A Global History*, London: Bloomsbury.

Johnson, R. D. (2006), 'Transnational Trojan Horse', *Historically Speaking*, 8 (2): 26–7.

Kaelble, H. and Schriewer, J., eds (2003), *Vergleich und Transfer: Komparatistik in den Sozial-, Geschichts- und Kulturwissenschaften*, Frankfurt am Main and New York: Campus.

Klooster, W. (2009), *Revolutions in the Atlantic World: A Comparative History*, New York and London: New York University Press.

Lang, M. (2014), 'Histories of Globalization(s)', in P. Duara, V. Murthy and A. Sartori (eds), *A Companion to Global Historical Thought*, 399–411, Malden, MA, Oxford and Chicester: Wiley-Blackwell.

Lowe, L. (2015), *The Intimacies of Four Continents*, Durham, NC and London: Duke University Press.

Manning, P. (2012), 'Big Data in History: A World-Historical Archive Version 1.1,' 27 September 2012, available online: http://www.dataverse.pitt.edu/announcements/documents/BigData. History.Manning.pdf (accessed 19 April 2017).

Manning, P. (2013), *Big Data in History*, Basingstoke: Palgrave Macmillan.

Manning, P. (2017), 'AHA Presidential Address. Inequality: Historical and Disciplinary Approaches', *American Historical Review*, 122 (1): 1–23.

Margolin, J.-L. and Markovits, C. (2015), *Les Indes et l'Europe: Histoires connectées, XVe-XXIe siècle*, Paris: Gallimard.

Mazlish B. and Buultjens, R., eds (1993), *Conceptualizing Global History*, Boulder, CO: Westview Press.

McGerr, M. (1991), 'The Price of the "New Transnational History"', *The American Historical Review*, 96 (4): 1056–67.

McNeill, J. R. and McNeill, W. H. (2003), *The Human Web: A Bird's-eye View of World History*, New York and London: Norton.

Middell, M. and Roura, L., eds (2013), *Transnational Challenges to National History Writing*, Basingstoke: Palgrave Macmillan.

Northrup, D. (2015), 'From Divergence to Convergence: Centrifugal and Centripetal Forces in History', in M. Wiesner-Hanks (ed.), *The Cambridge World History*, vol. 1, 110–31, Cambridge: Cambridge University Press.

Olstein, D. (2015), *Thinking History Globally*, Basingstoke: Palgrave Macmillan.

Osterhammel, J. (1989), *China und die Weltgesellschaft: Vom 18. Jahrhundert bis in unsere Zeit*, Munich: C.H. Beck.

Osterhammel, J. (2009), 'Global History in a National Context: The Case of Germany', *Österreichische Zeitschrift für Geschichtswissenschaft*, 20 (2): 40–58.

Osterhammel, J. (2015), 'Globalifizierung: Denkfiguren der neuen Welt', *Zeitschrift für Ideengeschichte*, 9 (1): 5–16.

Osterhammel, J. (2016), 'Global History and Historical Sociology', in J. Belich, J. Darwin, M. Frenz and C. Wickham (eds), *The Prospect of Global History*, 23–43, Oxford: Oxford University Press.

Osterhammel, J. and Petersson, N. P. (2005), *Globalization: A Short History*, trans. Dona Geyer, Princeton, NJ: Princeton University Press.

Parker, G. (2013), *Global Crisis: War, Climate Change and Catastrophe in the Seventeenth Century*, New Haven, CT and London: Yale University Press.

Polasky, J. L. (2015), *Revolutions without Borders: The Call to Liberty in the Atlantic World*, New Haven, CT and London: Yale University Press.

Pomeranz, K. (2014), 'Histories for a Less National Age', *American Historical Review*, 119 (1): 1–22.

Presner, T., Shepard, D. and Kawano, Y. (2014), *Thick Mapping in the Digital Humanities*, Cambridge, MA: Harvard University Press.

Putnam, L. (2016), 'The Transnational and the Text-Searchable: Digitized Sources and the Shadows They Cast', *American Historical Review*, 121 (2): 377–402.

Rockefeller, S. A. (2011), 'Flow', *Current Anthropology*, 52 (4): 557–78.

Sachsenmaier, D. (2011), *Global Perspectives on Global History: Theories and Approaches in a Connected World*, Cambridge: Cambridge University Press.

Sanderson, S. K. (2014), *Human Nature and the Evolution of Society*, Boulder, CO: Westview Press.

Saunier, P.-Y. (2013), *Transnational History*, Basingstoke: Palgrave Macmillan.

Sedgewick, A. (2014), 'Against Flows', *History of the Present*, 4 (2): 143–70.

Seigel, M. (2005), 'Beyond Compare: Historical Method after the Transnational Turn', *Radical History Review*, 91: 62–90.

Selchow, S. (2017), *Negotiations of the 'New World': The Omnipresence of 'Global' as a Political Phenomenon*, Bielefeld: Transcript.

Sivasundaram, S. (2017), 'Towards a Critical History of Connection: The Port of Colombo, the Geographical Circuit, and the Visual Politics of New Imperialism, ca. 1880–1914', *Comparative Studies in Society and History*, 59 (2): 346–84.

Sood, G. D. S. (2011), 'Circulation and Exchange in Islamicate Eurasia: A Regional Approach to the Early Modern World', *Past and Present*, 212: 113–62.

Sood, G. D. S. (2016), *India and the Islamic Heartlands: An Eighteenth-Century World of Circulation and Exchange*, Cambridge: Cambridge University Press.

Starosielski, N. (2015), *The Undersea Network*, Durham: Duke University Press.

Starosielski, N., Loyer, E. and Brennan, S. (2016), *Surfacing*, available online: http://www.surfacing.in (accessed 20 April 2017).

Stuchtey, B. and Fuchs, E., eds (2003), *Writing World History 1800–2000*, Oxford: Oxford University Press.

Subrahmanyam, S. (1997), 'Connected Histories: Notes towards a Reconfiguration of Early Modern Eurasia', *Modern Asian Studies*, 31 (3): 735–62.

Subrahmanyam, S. (2014), *Aux origines de l'histoire globale*, Paris: Collège de France and Fayard.

Vanhaute, E. (2013), *World History: An Introduction*, trans. L. Weix, London and New York: Routledge.

Vries, P. H. H. (2013), *Escaping Poverty: The Origins of Modern Economic Growth*, Göttingen: Vandenhoeck & Ruprecht.

Wehler H. U. (2006), 'Transnationale Geschichte – der neue Königsweg historischer Forschung?', in G. Budde, S. Conrad and O. Janz (eds), *Transnationale Geschichte. Themen, Tendenzen und Theorien*, 161–74, Göttingen: Vandenhoeck & Ruprecht.

Werner, M. and Zimmermann, B. (2006), 'Beyond Comparison: "Histoire croisée" and the Challenge of Reflexivity', *History and Theory*, 45 (1): 30–50.

Wiesner-Hanks, M. E., general ed. (2015), *The Cambridge World History*, 7 vols. in 9 parts, Cambridge: Cambridge University Press.

Wikipedia (2017), "Histoire mondiale de la France", https://fr.wikipedia.org/wiki/Histoire_mondiale_de_la_France (accessed 20 April 2017).

Wills, Jr., J. E. (2014), 'What's New? Studies of Revolutions and Divergences, 1770–1840', *Journal of World History*, 25 (1): 127–86.

Winter, J., ed. (2014), *The Cambridge History of the First World War*, 3 vols, Cambridge: Cambridge University Press.

Wittmann, V. (2014), *Weltgesellschaft: Rekonstruktion eines wissenschaftlichen Diskurses*, Baden-Baden: Nomos.

Wood, G. D. (2014), *Tambora: The Eruption That Changed the World*, New York and Oxford: Princeton University Press.

Xavier, Â. B. and Santos, C. M. (2007), 'Entrevista a Sanjay Subrahmanyam', *Cultura*, 24, available online: http://cultura.revues.org/904 (accessed 15 April 2017).

CHAPTER 2
POSTCOLONIAL HISTORY
Rochona Majumdar

A search for postcolonialism's intellectual genealogy will no doubt lead us to literature and cultural studies departments of Anglo-American universities where this body of ideas found their earliest articulation and nurturance. Stuart Hall, Gayatri Spivak, Edward Said, and others' call to change the canon of literary studies issued in the wake of the publication of such novels as Salman Rushdie's *Midnight's Children* (1981) was a prominent aspect of postcolonial theory's complex past. The focus on its literary background, however, obscures the ways in which postcolonial thought has shaped such humanistically oriented social science disciplines as history. Fundamental interventions by historians have produced significant shifts in postcolonial theory, so much so that a new subfield 'postcolonial history' is now well established within the discipline. This new sub-discipline of history, by no means homogenous, is nonetheless characterized by some common themes. In what follows, I lay out the conceptual foundations of postcolonial history. Following that, I consider the widespread influence of the postcolonial outlook by analysing some examples from domains as further afield from one another as medieval history, new imperial history, and histories of gender and race. I close this chapter by identifying some new directions in which postcolonial historians appear to be headed.

Beginnings

As with any complex set of ideas, it would be a mistake to seek a single point of origin of postcolonial history writing. But there is no doubt that certain events and themes that became popular during the era of decolonization in the mid-twentieth century contributed to the making of this oeuvre. The Bandung conference of 1955, described by the postcolonial theorist Homi Bhabha as 'that daunting quest for a nonaligned postcolonial world', was one such event (Bhabha 2004: ix). Twenty-nine free nations of Asia and Africa, represented by some 600 delegates, came together from 18 to 24 April 1955 in Bandung, Indonesia, to mark their commitment to a post-imperial world. Another contributing factor, alongside the anti-imperial euphoria on display at Bandung, was also the disappointment of many decolonized peoples at the failure of their respective nation states to deliver on the promises of modernization, alleviation of poverty, forms of inequality, and varieties of prejudice. By the late 1960s, several countries – South Africa, Palestine, India, Pakistan, Vietnam, Hungary, and Poland to name but a few – were convulsed by people's struggles that challenged the legitimacy of their respective governments, if not their nations as well. Both decolonization and strident critiques of the newly independent nation states marked the beginning of what later came to be described as the postcolonial outlook. The postcolonial stance, while sharing with anti-colonial movements their criticisms of imperialism, was also different in that it incorporated a critique of the nation state, something that anti-colonial thought took for granted.

The process is captured well in the African writer Ngugi wa Thiong'o's remembrance of his time during 1964–67 at the University of Leeds where he witnessed the global character of postcolonial protests:

> The political struggles to move the centre, the vast decolonization process changing the political map of the post-war world, had also a radicalizing effect in the West particularly among the young and this was best symbolized by the support the Vietnamese struggle was enjoying among the youth. This radical tradition had in turn an impact on the African students at Leeds making them look even more critically at the content rather than the form of the decolonization process, taking their cue from Fanon's critique in the rightly celebrated chapter in *The Wretched of the Earth* entitled 'the Pitfalls of National Consciousness'. (Thiong'o wa 1993: 3)

If the nation state idealized as a form lost some legitimacy in the ex-colony by the late 1960s, the former metropolitan countries too became sites of post-imperial upheaval. Indigenous groups and minorities in the United States, Canada, Australia, and New Zealand grew vocal in their demands for rights and compensation from their respective states while second-wave feminism asserted women's rights to their bodies, their sexual being, and against gender stereotypes. Anti-colonial thinkers were rediscovered anew in these turbulent times: Gandhi by Martin Luther King in the United States and Frantz Fanon by indigenous and anti-race activists in Australia and Britain. But the racism they fought, as postcolonial historian Dipesh Chakrabarty (2009: 14) noted, was 'itself of post-imperial origins: it was born of cultural adjustments necessitated by the loss of empire and rise in migration of colored peoples'.

This brief rehearsal of its genealogy clarifies two aspects of postcolonial historical thought. The first is a suggestion about periodization built into the expression postcolonial. Leela Gandhi alluded to this when she remarked, 'Whereas some critics invoke the hyphenated form "post-colonialism" as a decisive temporal marker of the decolonizing process', there were others who queried 'the implied separation between colonialism and its aftermath on the grounds that the postcolonial condition is inaugurated with the onset rather than the end of colonial occupation' (Gandhi 1998: 3). Scholars of the latter dispensation prefer the unbroken term 'postcolonialism' as a more accurate approximation of conditions that ensued with colonial rule. More recently, David Armitage offered an analysis of postcolonialism that resonates with Gandhi's gloss on the term. A 'strong version' of the term postcolonial Armitage proposed 'assumes the continuity of colonialism beyond independence or decolonisation but avoids the disabling narratives of inclusion and exclusion, inferiority and superiority, achievement and potential, which informed the ideology of colonialism itself' (Armitage 2007: 251). Robert Young gave postcolonialism's genealogy a different twist when he insisted on a distinction between 'anticolonial' ideas of the periphery and those that developed in the heart of the former metropolitan societies. The label 'postcolonial', in his opinion, was more apposite to the latter. Postcolonial writings, he noted, argue for the equality of the 'cultures of the decolonized nations' by taking 'the struggle into the heartland of the former colonial powers' (Young 2001: 57–65).

Related to the issue of periodization is also a limitation of postcolonial histories. As is clear from the aforementioned statements, postcolonial theory emerged late in the second half of the twentieth century in the wake of the second wave of anti-colonial liberation movements in Asia, Africa, the Pacific, and the Caribbean. Since its conception, it left out of reckoning the 'first wave' of independence movements that took place in Latin America in the early nineteenth century, a shortcoming pointed out by Fernando Coronil among others. Any project that attempts to seriously revise the claims of postcolonial theory will have to engage with the ideas contained in the works of Latin American critics, thinkers, and historians such as Enrico Dussel, Anibal Quijano, Walter Mignolo, Fernando Coronil, José Rabasa, Florencia Mallon, Barbara Weinstein, and others. However, the emergence of independent nations in Latin America in the nineteenth century, as argued by Benedict Anderson's celebrated book *Imagined Communities*, belonged to the story of the rise of nation states and not their later critiques. It was the era of decolonization of the mid-twentieth century that created the condition for the rise of postcolonial theory. Latin American nations gained independence from colonial rule in the nineteenth century, an age that witnessed a tide of nationalisms. Postcolonial history and theory could not have arisen under those conditions.

These upheavals in the political sphere did not leave undisturbed the sanctum of the university. The challenge to the legitimacy of imperialism and colonialism gave rise to critical questions among left-leaning intellectuals about the efficacy of Marxist and other structuralist theories in understanding global change and their representation. One sign of this shift was the popularity of Frantz Fanon's text *The Wretched of the Earth* in the 1980s. Popular mobilization in rural hinterlands, beginning with the Cultural Revolution in 1966 and climaxing with the Vietnam War, brought to the fore the role of the peasant as an agent of revolutionary social change, a theme that inspired academic efforts such as the *Journal of Peasant Studies* and later on *Subaltern Studies*. Postcolonial studies emerged in the academe during this critical conjuncture of global events. Situating its emergence thus, it should come as no surprise that the field is 'marked by a dialectic between Marxism on the one hand, and poststructuralism/postmodernism, on the other' (Gandhi 1998: viii). Given this background, it is also not hard to fathom why the field is rife with 'debates between the competing claims of nationalism and internationalism, strategic essentialism and hybridity, solidarity and dispersal, the politics of structure/totality and the politics of the fragment' (Gandhi 1998: ix).

Informed by this theoretical outlook, postcolonial historians, though sympathetic to the works done by the British Marxist 'histories from below', were also critical of the Marxist teleology of development that marked the works of Eric Hobsbawm or E. P.

Thompson. Likewise, debates about high and low cultures led them to renew attention to literary texts as historical sources. While a serious questioning of the canon became the mainstay of postcolonial studies in literature departments, in the field of history the privileged position of the nation as a predominant theme of research and received litanies about a unified nationalism came to be questioned as scholars began to think of identities not as a Manichean separation between black and white or colonizer and colonized but as interstitial or in-between. Likewise, mainstream nationalism was perceived as unrepresentative of the different peoples who constituted any particular nation state. These moves shared some overlaps with parallel developments in writing the history of everyday life and oral history such as *Alltagsgeschichte* in Germany and *microstoria* in Italy. What distinguished postcolonial historiography from these bodies of scholarship was its sympathy with certain ideas gleaned from poststructuralist and other continental philosophy that inspired, among other things, critiques of notions of an unified subjectivity, teleological thinking, and attention to cultural and discursive aspects of colonialism.

Conceptual foundations

Many of the foundational ideas of postcolonial history writing were first enunciated in historical scholarship focused on South and East Asia, respectively. In the interest of space, and acutely conscious of the risks that attend simplifying a considerable and complex body of ideas, let me attempt a summary of postcolonial history's conceptual core. Crucial to this mode of history writing is a demonstration of the legacy of the colonial past in many insoluble problems faced by nation states following decolonization (Guha 1997: ix). This in turn, as demonstrated by scholars such as Partha Chatterjee, Gyanendra Pandey, and others, is due to the complicated genealogy of both nationalist movements and nationalist thought. Nationalism, as a political project could only be successful if it challenged the 'alleged inferiority' of the colonized, thereby calling into question the legitimacy of colonial rule. It had then to follow up that challenge by promising modernization and development whilst also maintaining a sense of cultural authenticity. Notwithstanding the huge achievement of nationalisms that accomplished these tasks, there remained a contradiction at the heart of the nationalist project. Namely, that even as such thought challenged the colonial claim to political domination, it also accepted the intellectual premises of 'modernity' on which colonial domination was based. Building on the notion of the 'fragment', defined by Gyanendra Pandey as that which resisted 'the drive for a shallow homogenisation', and favouring instead potentially richer definitions of the 'nation' and the future political community, postcolonial historians turned their attention to groups whose fit with official narratives of nationalism was always uneasy (Pandey 1997: 3). Documenting the histories of women, lower castes, peasants, the vernacular press, and the theatre, Partha Chatterjee evolved a theory of cultural sovereignty that accounted for the claims that Third World nationalisms made about the colonial-nationalist subject being 'modern' while maintaining an autonomy of consciousness vis-à-vis the colonizer.

In an argument that has gained wide currency among historians globally, Chatterjee claimed 'anticolonial nationalism creates its own domain of sovereignty well before it begins its political battle with imperial power' (Chatterjee 1993: 6). A binary division between the inner and the outer, the spiritual and the material, and the private and public realms of life marks the history of nationalism and of the postcolonial state that followed, he argued. The inner/spiritual/private domains corresponded to the realms where the colonized felt capable of resisting the thrall of the colonizer and staked their sovereignty vis-à-vis the West. In sharp contrast were the outer/material/public realms that included the arena of official politics and professional life where the colonized succumbed to political will and ideological power of the West. Nationalism's success in holding the colonizer at bay from the inner domain did not mean that this realm was sequestered from change. Rather, as Chatterjee argued, 'here nationalism launches a "modern" national culture that is nevertheless not Western. If the nation is an imagined community, then it is brought into being in the inner/ spiritual/ private realms. Here, its true and essential domain, the nation is already sovereign, even when the state is in the hands of the colonial power' (Chatterjee 1993: 6).

Chatterjee's analysis of the nationalist separation inner/outer or material/spiritual division has not gone unchallenged. It has been justifiably argued that these binaries mapped too neatly on to a classical liberal separation between church and state, home and the world, and therefore remained a modular variant of the metropolitan model. Feminist critics, in particular, argued that the equation of women with the inner/spiritual/ private realm underplayed late-nineteenth- and early twentieth-century critiques of patriarchy and of women's increasing participation in professional and political life.

Chatterjee's analysis of nationalism has to be placed alongside Prasenjit Duara's critique of Hegelian teleology and a specific understanding of the 'people'. The latter, he demonstrated was a formation both 'ancient and pristine' as well as a 'new and modern'. The 'people' was 'the basis of the nation's sovereignty', an entity that was acknowledged by nationalist leaders and intellectuals alike as 'old', and yet requiring a rebirth so as 'to partake of the new world' (Duara 1995: 31). A telling example Duara discusses in this connection was the post-1948 debate around the emblem of the menorah and the seven stars on the Israeli flag. The former a symbol of the ancient rootedness of the Jewish people in the land and the latter a sign of the modern work-week. The cumulative thrust of these critiques was a questioning of the quasi-Hegelian idea of linear progression in history and the periodization of modernity as a post-Enlightenment phenomenon. Bringing this critique to bear on writings in the People's Republic of China that regarded the emergence of the Chinese state as a modernization story, Duara showed it instead, to be a repository of contested subjectivities, where older forms of community tangled with newer imaginings that arose in conversation with Western Europe and other emerging nations of the world.

No discussion of the conceptual arsenal of postcolonial history is complete without reference to the idea of 'provincializing Europe' (Chakrabarty 2007). If a demonstration of the limitations of mainstream nationalism and the failure of totalizing national histories in representing the reality of subaltern lives is a critical aspect of postcolonial history's conceptual arsenal, so too is a critical reappraisal of narratives of transition to capitalism, otherwise known as developmentalism. Dipesh Chakrabarty's 2000 book *Provincializing Europe* offers the clearest articulation of this aspect of postcolonial history writing. The book issues challenge to Eurocentric thought even as it acknowledges the importance of this body of thinking to the historian's enterprise. Described as at once 'indispensable' and 'inadequate', a cluster of ideas that became global is subjected to interrogation in this book. One such important idea is the developmental sense of history that Chakrabarty calls 'historicism'. 'Historicism', he argues, refers to a mode of thinking that 'tells us that in order to understand the nature of anything in this world we must see it as an historically evolving entity, that is, first as an individual and unique whole – as some kind of unity in potential – and second, as something that develops over time' (Chakrabarty 2008: 89–90). Marxist histories abound in references to historical phases described as the pre-capitalist, feudal, or pre-bourgeois. The assumption undergirding such categories is that as societies move from the pre-capitalist to the capitalist, or from feudal to modern, they eventually converge on the global stage. Until they do so, non-Western societies must strive to follow the model set by those ahead of them in the developmental race.

The political implications of this type of developmental thought are not hard to deduce. Until they were schooled in protocols of Western politics and civility – in other words 'political modernity' – non-Western societies were deemed incapable of self-rule. 'Historicism', Chakrabarty (2007: 7) posits, 'is what made modernity or capitalism look not simply global but rather as something that became global *over time*, by originating in one place (Europe) and then spreading outside it'. The vehicle of this spread was colonial rule and its central message of the superiority of the West. As a schema, this message denied what Johannes Fabian called 'coevalness' to colonized peoples (Fabian 2014). In what has become an influential shorthand of the idea of *Provincializing Europe*, historicism is the means by which large sections of the world's populations are relegated to an imaginary 'waiting room' of history where they are told that they are 'not yet' ready for rights that are in principle considered universal. Most anti-colonial nationalisms asserted that the colonized were always already fit for self-rule, regardless of their level of education or political consciousness measured by the yardsticks of Western, classical, liberal thought. They substituted the colonial injunction of the 'not yet' with the nationalist assertion of the 'now' (Chakrabarty 2007: 8–9).

By conceptualizing the history of capitalism and ideas of progress associated with it in this manner, the postcolonial critique embodied in *Provincialing Europe* holds up in clear relief the problems of Eurocentrism. To provincialize Europe is not to reject European ideas. It is rather to demonstrate the inadequacies of European thought to the task of understanding the 'plural normative horizons' specific to the lives and existence of different populations in the world. Crucially, it establishes that postcolonial historiography is not a nativist turn that demanded an outright rejection of European categories; a crude or simple-minded project of 'bashing the Enlightenment and modernity' that the historian Frederick Cooper (2005: 6) alleges it to be. Chakrabarty's move of acknowledging the crucial importance of European thought in shaping the intellectual world of the colonized also incorporated a point made central to postcolonial criticism by the writings of Homi Bhabha in particular: that postcolonial criticism actually rejects a binary divide separating the colonizer from the colonized.

Postcolonial historiographies

The aforementioned ideas that constitute the core of postcolonial historiography's intellectual agenda have profoundly shaped works by historians working in other subfields of history. Let me offer a few snapshots of the most remarkable instances of synergy between postcolonial and other histories that I have analysed at length elsewhere (Majumdar 2010).

Medieval postcolonialism

Even though it might initially appear oxymoronic, postcolonial histories of the Middle Ages have emerged as a thriving area of historical scholarship. Despite the caution sounded by some that a 'postcolonial society has a historical specificity and density that is not easily translated into premodern worlds' (Spiegel 2000: 250), others have proceeded to illustrate the rich dividends that postcolonial approaches bring to the study of the Middle Ages.

Three related areas best illustrate the synergy between postcoloniality and medieval history. First, medieval historians, most prominently Kathleen Biddick and Kathleen Davis, have drawn upon postcolonial theories of temporality to interrogate the practice of periodization that is so central to the historian's craft. Periodization, they have argued, was never an innocent gesture and was always inextricably related to questions of politics. Thus, the consigning of the medieval period to the 'dark ages' of European history, neatly boxed in the millennium stretching from the fall of the Roman Empire to the Renaissance and Reformation, was tied with questions of European imperialism, colonialism, and sovereignty. The insights drawn from this body of medieval historical work make us aware of the ideological power wielded by those (peoples, institutions, nation states) who deploy the category of the medieval to critique certain social formations. Second, infused with a postcolonial temper many revisionist works demonstrate the myriad ways in which the Middle Ages haunt debates about modernity from the late eighteenth to the twentieth centuries. Rather than regard the medieval and modern as hermetically sealed units of time and culture, scholars have demonstrated how ideas of the medieval were constitutive of the modern. As well, the presence of medieval traces in the modern signal certain recalcitrant and critical currents within modernity. Finally, medievalists like Ananya Kabir, Nicholas Howe, and Louise D'Arcens have drawn upon postcolonial critiques of Eurocentrism, calling into question the spatial conception of the Middle Ages as a purely European phenomenon. By tracking the histories of empire, nationalism, and imperialism, they have shown the heterogeneous territorial spread of medieval histories. While Howe treats England as a postcolony of the Roman imperium, Kabir analyses the ways in which notions of medievalism guided the educational or land reform works of British administrators, Henry Maine, and Thomas Macaulay. D'Arcens extends the scope of Victorian medievalism to a settler colonial context, through her analysis of John Woolley and George Arnold Wood, both professors of Sydney University from the 1850s onward. Engaging Woolley's reading of Alfred Tennyson's *Idylls*, D'Arcens demonstrates the nineteenth-century scholarly recasting of Tennyson's literary rendering of the Arthurian past to make it relevant to the conditions on the ground in Australia. Likewise, Wood used another important medieval figure, St. Francis of Assisi, to oppose Australia's involvement in the 'immoral' Boer War of 1899–1902 (D'Arcens 2010). While installing the European medieval as a resource in modern narratives of the nation, medievalisms such as Woolley's or Wood's effaced another medieval – that of the Australian Aboriginal's from the national narrative.

In sum, it may be argued that the traffic between medieval and postcolonial studies takes many routes. For some scholars, it is not so much a question of describing the so-called Middle Ages in their own terms as asking what contemporary purpose such a periodizing device served. For others, the project is to deploy some of the tools of postcolonial theory to describe and analyse the so-called medieval period.

Postcolonial histories and empire

Over the last three decades, the historical subfield, new imperial history, has consolidated itself in the academy. Not all the work conducted in this field would fall under the rubric of postcolonial history. But contributions by Catherine Hall, Kathleen Wilson, Antoinette Burton, Ann Stoler, and Nicholas Dirks speak to the close linkages between postcolonial history writing and new imperial history.

According to Antoinette Burton, a leading practitioner in both fields, new imperial history developed as a response to 'the imperial turn' that she defined as 'the accelerated attention to the impact of histories of imperialism on metropolitan societies in the wake of decolonisation, pre- and post-1968 racial struggle and feminism in the last quarter century' (Burton 2003: 2). The similarity in the intellectual genealogies of new imperial and postcolonial histories, evident in Burton's statement, was clarified further by Kathleen Wilson when she observed that 'Energized by the political and imaginative wakes of postcolonial and cross-disciplinary scholarship, … "new imperial history" … has at its heart the importance of difference … that supports and extends the pluralities of historical interpretation' (Wilson 2004: 2–3). Difference was central to imperial projects and policies; it was one of the central justifications for European domination of the backward races.

New imperial historians analysed the historical deployment of difference as a hierarchical category that separated colonizer from colonized. They were also committed to analysing the ways in which empires led to the circulation of European peoples, institutions, customs, laws, religions, around the globe and the 'contribution of these extended territories and peoples' to the formation of 'national' cultures within Europe. Such an orientation produces a critical stance among new imperial historians towards other practitioners of imperial history. For example, new imperial historians of the British Empire are critical of projects such as the five-volume *Oxford History of the British Empire*. The latter regarded the British empire as a 'series of discrete components of limited relevance to the study of Britain, rather than … a permeable web or network shaped by global and regional currents, that impacted metropolitan as much as colonial culture' (cited in Wilson 2004: 14). Finally, new imperial historians are particularly committed to studying the internal difference between imperial projects. For example, eighteenth-century accounts abounded in references to 'the empire of the seas', 'the empire of the east', and to the 'New World Dominions'. These 'empires' were by no means identical, even though there were points of commonality, and all of them profoundly shaped the formation of British or other metropolitan imperial identities.

Readers will recall that the question of historical difference – both its existence and blurring – is central to the project of postcolonial history writing. Postcolonial historians do not treat the difference between the colonizer and colonized as a Manichean separation. Related to this is a deep investment in understanding the processes of translation of universal categories in particular locales and languages across different historical time periods. Colonialism, as both postcolonial and new imperial historians demonstrate, was far from being a monolithic entity. The emphasis of both types of revisionist scholarship is to explore the tensions of empire, rather than its triumphs alone.

Before turning to a more detailed analysis of some postcolonial approaches to histories of empire, let me point out a slight difference in emphasis between new imperial historians and their postcolonial counterparts. For the new imperial historian the main focus of attention is the imperial formation(s), a term used first by Mrinalini Sinha – a model that allows for the different trajectories of metropole and colony while insisting that both were constituted by a history of imperialism, a point that has since then also been made by Frederick Cooper and Ann Stoler (Sinha 1995; Cooper and Stoler 1997). The historians in question strenuously argue in favour of shifting analytical focus away from the nation form – both colonizing and colonized – to empire seen as an organic (if uneven) relationship between metropole and colony. They are critical of notions of splendid isolation of any colonizing nation state, and are committed to demonstrating the close linkages, indeed the mutually constitutive role, between ideas of empire/colony and nation/empire.

Postcolonial historians in turn take colonialism, decolonization, and neo-colonial practices as their object of study. But their fundamental unit of analysis is the nation state, not so much as an entity they celebrate, but as an apparatus that often fails to live up to its promises due to endemic historical reasons. As they illustrate the links between colony and postcolony, postcolonial historians focus on the ways in which colonial categories were operationalized on the ground by the natives, often described by the colonizers as uncivilized or backward. But at that moment of encounter 'colonial oppositions were crossed and hybridized' (Prakash 1995: 3). Thus every colonial category has written into its history the story of the native's appropriation, resistance, and translation. The task of postcolonial history is to read these hybrid pasts for a richer understanding of the present. And it is in their mutual commitment to analysing the history of colonialism as one of encounter that brings together postcolonial and new imperial histories.

As Edward Said remarked, the work of postcolonial criticism was fuelled by the recognition 'that even though a hard and fast line separated colonizer from colonized in matters of rule and authority (a native could never aspire to the condition of the white man), the experiences of ruler and ruled were not so easily disentangled. On both sides of the imperial divide men and women shared experiences – though differently inflected experiences – through education, civic life, memory, war' (Said 2000). Said's argument, I propose, is equally applicable to new imperial histories. It comes as no surprise therefore that many postcolonial and new imperial historians are critical of viewpoints articulated by imperial historians Peter Marshall, Niall Ferguson, Linda Colley, and David Cannadine whose writings, they would argue, add up to supporting the following propositions: (i) developments in the empire were not that relevant to the trajectory of British history at home; (ii) there prevailed among many – both historians and the public – a belief in the beneficial effects of empire. Issuing a strong critique of the historians in question Edward Said noted, 'A generation ago the influence of Fanon's typology of empire ensured that one could only be either very much for or very much against the great imperial structures'. Writing in 2003, from the vantage of American imperial mis(adventures), Said observed with some irony that 'the empires that ruled Africa and Asia don't seem quite as bad'. The 'perplexingly affirmative work of Niall Ferguson and David Armitage scants', he wrote, 'if it doesn't actually trivialise, the suffering and dispossession brought by empire to its victims. More is said now about the modernising advantages the empires brought, and about the security and order they maintained. A crucial tactic of this revisionism is to read present-day American imperial power as enlightened and even altruistic, and to project that enlightenment back into the past' (Said 2000).

Postcolonial histories, migration, and settler societies

New imperial history does not exhaust histories of imperialism and post-imperialism written from a postcolonial vantage. Andrea Smith's edited volume *Europe's Invisible Migrants* analyses European returnees from Indonesia, Algeria, Angola, and Mozambique after the collapse of colonial empires in these countries (Smith 2003). These groups numbering some 5–7 million were not repatriates but ex-settlers for whom 'return' to Europe was not a choice. Frederick Cooper explained the lack of scholarly interest in these groups to their postcolonial status. 'The very distinctiveness that the Indonesian Dutch, Angolan Portuguese, or Algerian French had asserted', writes Cooper, 'no longer had legitimacy in a decolonizing world: they were people who had no right to exist'. Their return to France, the Netherlands, and Portugal was not due to any 'profound sentiment' associated with life in these places but on more 'abstract affinities of race and citizenship' (Cooper 2003: 169–70).

Postcolonial thought has influenced the writing of revisionist history of countries considered marginal to Europe, such as Turkey or what in some diplomatic circles is cynically referred to as PIGS (Europe's 'south', consisting of Portugal, Italy, Greece, and Spain). Much of this work is a postcolonial, intellectual/ literary history that interrogates

Eurocentrism through revisionist readings of European literary and philosophical traditions from the vantage point of Europe's borders or margins (Chabal 2003).

By way of concluding this discussion on postcolonial and imperial histories, we must acknowledge the work of historians of white settler colonies, namely Canada, Australia, and New Zealand. Even though these countries did not go through a political decolonization movement, settler culture in the three aforementioned countries has been seriously called into question by a process of, what the historian Miranda Johnson has described as, 'ethical' decolonization – a sustained and continuing process of questioning the past assumptions of white supremacy by dialogue between and across different socio-cultural communities. Historians such as Bain Attwood, Fiona Magowan, Marilyn Lake, and others have combined a postcolonial outlook with an awareness promoted by pioneering figures like Henry Reynolds to turn the history of these settler societies 'not upside down, but inside out' (Reynolds 2006: 199). Thanks to the efforts of historians like Reynolds and others 'History has become a matter of fierce public debate in the three settler states of Australia, Canada, and New Zealand' (Johnson 2008: 97). Aspects of indigenous-settler relations are often the subject of public debate in the media, documentary, and feature films. The case of the so-called 'stolen generations', Aboriginal children forcibly removed from their parents and raised by settlers, is a telling example of a subject that has most recently fuelled 'history wars' in Australia. These efforts have undoubtedly gone a long way towards transforming these settler states into postcolonial states by helping raise public awareness of colonial/Aboriginal issues.

No discussion of postcolonial history's impact is complete without referencing histories of gender. The Martinique-born anti-colonial intellectual Frantz Fanon's scathing indictment of French colonialism in *A Dying Colonialism* begins with a discussion of the role of women, in particular the veiled Algerian Muslim woman, in the armed struggle for Algerian liberation. The veil, (and by implication the woman under the veil), argued Fanon, constituted the ideological battleground between the colonizer and colonized, the former claiming to stand for progress and depicting the latter as representing stasis. Questions of tradition, modernity, patriarchy, racialism, agency, and oppression are all intimately bound up with the colonial discourse about gender.

The problem of the veiled woman appears like a microcosm that contained many of the themes that postcolonial historians of gender continue to grapple with. On the one hand, the category of the 'veiled woman' raises questions about representation and the particular condition of subalternity for the 'Third World Woman' which in turn folds back into the problem of empire. On the other hand, historians critical of the stereotype of the veiled or Third World woman have expended their energies in search for the 'real' woman (behind the veil/or unveiled). These efforts have produced a whole raft of possibilities for thinking through postcolonial modernities. Despite their differences, the many approaches to the history of gender signal that this has been an area in which postcolonial historians have had a noticeable imprint. Briefly, these may be summarized as the question of the Third World woman; the role of gender in the so-called civilizing mission; gender in nationalist discourse; gender as the site for a 'clash of civilisations'.

Postcolonial history now

Europe

Having outlined some of areas in which postcolonial historiography has been most productive, it is important to ask if the field continues to be relevant in our times. Or, has postcolonial history been overshadowed by theories of globalization? In this context, it is useful to remind ourselves of the French theorist Etienne Balibar's call, issued in the context of debates about a 'fortress Europe', for a global recognition of our postcolonial condition (Balibar 2003). '[W]hat has truly unified the planet', argued Balibar, 'is not just colonial expansion, but the revolts, the liberation struggles that put into question the notion of "different natures" that separate peoples of the "metropoli" from those of the colonies, producing a dialectic between these two demographic groups that results in a reversal of roles, a "particularizing" of the old metropolis and a "universalisation" of the former colonies'. By 'universalisation' of former colonies, Balibar alludes to the waves of migration of people from the global South and ex-colonies, people belonging to diverse cultures, with varied family and religious values, into post-Maastricht Europe (Balibar 2003).

For scholars such as Etienne Balibar, Sandro Mezzadra, Brett Nielson, Joan Scott, and Naomi Davidson the critical historical knots that need unravelling in the context of the 'new' Europe are notions of borders, migration, and citizenship. During the colonial ventures of the nineteenth and twentieth centuries, Europe distinguished itself physically and culturally from the rest of the world by drawing political borders. This was an attempt to 'appoint itself the center of the world' as well as a strategy to 'divide up the earth' into nation states modelled after the European pattern (Balibar 2004: 7). Colonialism, writes Balibar, 'was at once a way to organize the world's exploitation and to export the "border form" to the periphery, in an attempt to transform the whole universe into an extension of Europe'. The process continued into decolonization and formed the basis for a new international order. Yet, 'in a certain sense it was never completely achieved' (Balibar 2004: 7) for the new nation states were not homogenous, sovereign states but agglomerates of diverse populations – Israel, India, West and East Pakistan (which later became Bangladesh) as well as several eastern European states.

The demographic and cultural diversity of European populations many of whom are 'postcolonial' – a result of immigration, repatriation of displaced peoples, and colonial returnees – reflect a projection of 'global diversity' within Europe. The different modes by which European residents from 'other' countries are designated in the context of different European states – ethnic minorities, *immigrés*, *extracommunatari*, *Ausländer* – show the fragility of the European Union (EU). The EU appears unresolved on the question of the outsider, the 'less than white (*sous blanc*), … neither white, nor secular, nor Christian' (Balibar 2004: 44). If the EU were to remain, it needs to reconcile the question of how certain 'fundamental anthropological differences' (those of sexuality, culture, and religion) will be respected in tandem with the universal rights of citizenship. The challenge facing Europe is one that Frantz Fanon had written about in a slightly different register in *The Wretched of the Earth*: to seek a fulfilment of its destiny as the bearer of universal values by taking lessons from postcolonial developments both within its borders as well as from other parts of the ex-colonized world.

The uneven regression of the welfare state, migration from ex-colonized countries, war-torn states in the Middle East, Eastern and Southern Europe, deindustrialization that has accompanied economic globalization, rising unemployment, and the fear of a global Islamic terrorism have contributed to the rise of racist and xenophobic politics in many European nation states, making the question of membership to the EU a vexed one. Policing of borders has intensified along with the expansion of zones of 'nonrights' in the suburbs of many great European cities. This context makes clear why the quintessential postcolonial question, one harking back to the days of decolonization, about how we reconcile ideas about the universal rights of man with cross-cultural diversity looms large in these global times. Gayatri Spivak argued that the 'universal' political subject of modernity, whose institutional expression is the citizen, is always geopolitically differentiated. Scholars are now documenting the histories of scores of nationals from 'third countries' who have lived for one or several generations on European soil, and who are indispensable to European conceptions of well-being, culture, tolerance, and civility (Balibar 2004; Scott 2004). The plight of displaced peoples in the ex-metropole and the interference of the ex-metropole in the politics and economies of the ex-colonies signal 'the extreme ambivalence of (Europe's) relationship with the colonial past'. This makes Europe 'the postcolonial locus par excellence' whose future depends, in large measure, on how its leaders recognize and grapple with these political realities.

Asia

Borders, migration, and traffic in human beings are also emergent issues in historical discussions on Asia. Practitioners of postcolonial and connected histories have broached the question of 'Asian' regionalism, but with significant differences in emphases. In a provocatively titled essay, 'One Asia or Many?', Sanjay Subrahmanyam demolishes notions of an Asian unity. A pioneer of 'connected history', Subrahmanyam (2016: 34) tracks networks and the circulation of texts and peoples, from the sixteenth century onwards, only to conclude that

if there were some extraordinarily powerful networks and circuits that crossed early modern political boundaries in Asia, whether for political, military, or commercial reasons, we must also be aware of the limits of these networks and circuits. Not everything was connected, and not all of the time.

Any notion of a unified Asia evaporates in the heat of 'Islamophobia and barely mitigated racist and patronizing stereotypes regarding the Central Asian peoples'. In thinking thus, Subrahmanyam shares common ground with scholars Wang Hui and John Steadman who argue against 'any attempt to characterize Asia as a unitary culture' (Subrahmanyam 2016: 40).

Postcolonial historians share in this interest of an Asian region, but they approach the problem from a different vantage. Asian unity or its absence is less of a concern for them than are the meanings that inhere in proclamations of an Asian regionalism or in those of India and China as future superpowers of the twenty-first century. In contrast to a formation such as the EU, writes Prasenjit Duara (2010: 981), 'region formation in Asia is a multipath, uneven, and pluralistic development'. It is marked, on the one hand, by an imagination of certain national identities such as Indian or Chinese assuming global scope transcending, as it were, the territorial limits of their nation states. He cites chauvinistic articles in contemporary media as evidence of such imaginations. Invocations of the *'pravasi bharatiya'* (non-resident Indians) or *huaren, haigui* (global Chinese) signal 'a neoliberal model of globalisation' that coincides with 'state withdrawal in many areas of provisioning public goods, such as education and health care' (Duara 2010: 979). By contrast, the fate of less-qualified peoples who migrate as seasonal or domestic workers, Malayalis to the Gulf states of West Asia, Rohingyas to Thailand, or Bangladeshis to India, are precarious. True, their wages help in shoring up family fortunes in their home countries. But these (often undocumented) populations are subject to untold brutality in the hands of labour contractors, local police, and political groups.

Prasenjit Duara and Sangita Gopal have also commented on the creation of an Asian cultural consumption zone through media. The wide popularity of Korean television serials in East Asian countries, Korean action films adapted by Bollywood, and the large Indian and Bangladeshi following of Pakistani soap operas are cited as cases as also the wide popularity of manga, anime, and other mediatized commodities (Gopal 2016). These together with 'extraterritorial' metropolises constituted by the flow of labour, capital, and knowledge make up new 'intra-Asian' zones such as Bipolis and Fusionopolis in Singapore (Duara 2010: 978). Instead of reading these flows as culminating in the creation of a new, unified Asian identity, Duara (2010: 982) prefers Gayatri Spivak's refusal to name an entity, thereby resisting demarcation, preferring instead 'to deal with "Asia" as the instrument of altered citation: an iteration'.

Coda: Looking ahead

To be sure, the circulation of peoples, ideas, and goods is not unique to the twenty-first century. The histories of Hinduism, Buddhism, Confucianism, Daoism, and Islam bear ample testimony to the spread and circulation of people, texts, ideas, and faiths. The question facing historians today is how to analyse present-day Asian cultural identities that are shaped by 'circulations of culture, knowledge, technology, goods, services, and finance that are dizzying in their velocity while also … deeply commodified or consumerist' (Duara 2010: 983). Put differently, what if any will be the normative contributions to global political thought of a putative Asian century?

Citing the example of the anti-colonial Indian intellectuals who internalized elements of Western political thought and humanism so deeply that they would deploy those same ideas to critique the excesses of British imperialism, Dipesh Chakrabarty (2012a: 141) asks if India and China, as ascendant nation states today, have the capacity to generate 'new visions of humanity'. The contemporary moment, racked as it is 'by problems of planetary proportions: climate change, food security, global refugees and asylum seekers, failed states, and terrors of various kinds', urgently requires projects of justice and fairness that are global in scope (Chakrabarty 2012a: 151). We live in times when the hegemony of the nation state form is such that statelessness is almost a new form of being 'savage' (Chakrabarty 2012b: 7). In these conditions, the urgent question facing postcolonial scholars is whether the new global powers and their intelligentsias – Indian, Chinese, or any other – will continue to pursue the American model of domination while their normative visions remain those that became 'global during the era of European ascendancy' (Chakrabarty 2012a: 151).

In writing thus, however, we also reach a limit point of postcolonial history writing. The subject of this history is unremittingly focused on humans who live in an international world divided into nation states. Jeremy Bentham, it is widely accepted, coined the word 'international' in 1780. Disputing the view that Bentham's coinage was a translation of the Roman '*ius gentium*', Hidemi Suganami (1978: 231) argues that Bentham 'reserves the term international for relations between sovereigns as such, maintaining that transactions between private individuals belonging to different states, or those between the sovereign of one state and a private individual of another, are concerns not of international, but of internal jurisprudence'. Bentham himself argued that a new word was necessary to 'express, in a more significant way, the branch of law which goes commonly under the name of law of nations'. The latter was 'an appellation so uncharacteristic', that, were it 'not for the force of custom, it would seem rather to refer to internal jurisprudence' (Suganami 1978). Bentham came up with the expression international in the era of empires at a time when the first wave of colonialisms was ending in Latin America and North America, and the British, French, Dutch, and Portuguese were spreading their political and commercial tentacles into Asia. The concept of international, in this coinage, was thus inseparable from ideas of both empires and nation states. And sovereignty was the mediating link between these ideas.

Does it, however, make sense to speak of the international in these Benthamite terms in today's context? If the international only makes sense in a conversation between sovereigns, then what of those who have been rendered stateless by failed states, national governments, climate crises, and myriad other forms acting singly or in combination? Postcolonial history's salutary lesson has been to remind us that it is not nation states alone, but a deeper predicament produced by the conflicting forces of neoliberal capitalism, failed states, demography, and environmental crises that have pushed to the brink not only stateless peoples, illegal migrants, guest workers, and asylum seekers – 'today's subalterns' who 'embody the human condition negatively, as an image of privation' but also plants, birds, fish, animals, and other forms of life, in a word, the worlds of the non-human (Chakrabarty 2012b: 7; Duara 2015). While postcolonial historiography helps us make sense of the privations borne by human beings it has yet to come up with an adequate vocabulary for speaking about the non-human. The task that awaits the next generation of postcolonial historians is to put the history of nation states into a dialogue with the problems that are of planetary proportions, to bring into the ambit of its analysis both the human being as subject and the human being as a member of a nexus of biological species whose activities have precipitated environmental and other crises on a planetary scale.

Comment

Prasenjit Duara

Rochona Majumdar has written an admirable and comprehensive analysis of postcolonial historical writing, admirable particularly because there are no easy ways of defining or even delimiting the scope of 'postcolonial' historiography. Yet she has succeeded in addressing the roots, the affinities with poststructuralism and mutual influences between it and the histories of everyday life, the subaltern (including in Latin America), Marxism, gender, environment, medieval history, new imperial history, global history, and more. Furthermore, she demonstrates the principal tenets of postcolonial history through the writings about gender. In her essay, she poses a 4-D cross-section of global perspectives on the figure of woman that can best be grasped by a postcolonial understanding of modernity: gender in the civilizing mission; gender in nationalist patriarchal discourse; and gender as the site for the clash of civilizations (white men and women saving brown women from brown men). To understand this figure, we need a layered analysis of legacies of empire and colonialism connecting different parts of the world over the last couple of centuries.

At its most basic level, postcolonial history reveals that the contemporary world, including most especially, the de-colonized nation states, still operates within the mental and often the material framework (institutions and laws) of the colonial masters they strove so hard to expel in the mid-twentieth century. Much of this legacy derives from Enlightenment ideals both in its liberatory rhetoric and its dark underbelly linked to the imperatives of capitalism. By sanctioning property rights, economic individualism, legal rights as a measure of civilization and sovereignty and not least, the untrammelled conquest of nature, it facilitated the exploitation of other people, lands, and nature. In several ways, postcolonial thought refers to this hitherto underexplored or even unthought nexus, especially as postcolonial nation states adopt it in its alluring rhetorical package.

Yet few of the historians described by Majumdar and others, including myself, will readily assume the self-description as postcolonial historians, particularly during the early period of its emergence in the 1990s. Thus, Gayatri Spivak in an interview famously declared that postcolonial theory is 'bogus' (Spivak 1999: 358). Others, such as Michael Dutton, Leela Gandhi, and Sanjay Seth have described it simply as a 'toolbox' to explore perspectives alternative to hegemonic modernity (Dutton, Gandhi, and Seth 1999: 121–2). My late colleague from the University of Chicago, Professor Bernard Cohn, once likened these scholars in a conversation to the cat that has climbed (been chased?) up a tree and does not know how to come down. I have often tried to reflect on this curious disavowal. In the rest of this comment, I will probe the reasons for it, the scope and status of postcolonial history and my own effort to grasp its relevance to contemporary life.

The most important reason for the reticence regarding postcolonialism is that it is not a theory; it is a perspective pointing to another cosmology. A theory, in the contemporary sense, is a mid-level epistemic statement – by which I mean that it accepts the axioms of secular rationality. This statement not only explains the structure and dynamics of a phenomenal cluster, it also presents solutions or ways of resolving the problems encountered therein – a way for the cat to climb out. On the other hand, it is very difficult – though by no means impossible – to find alternative solutions drawn from the vanquished and delegitimated cosmologies from the past. In some ways, postcolonialism is similar to Derridean deconstructive poststructuralism which does not seek to provide resolutions in any ordinary or causal sense, although, to be sure, not all poststructuralisms share this quality.

Postcolonial histories function more like cosmological pathways. The critique of modern practices reveals the highly damaging and exorbitant effects of modernization particularly upon the lower orders of society. Take the case of the 'anti-superstition and build schools' movement that took place in China from the beginning of the twentieth century through the Communist revolution. The smashing of idols and temples and their replacement by modern schools and police in Republican and Communist China entailed very high costs for the peasants. They were deprived of their temple market fairs, community life, social networks, and religious anchors. Besides, they had to pay exorbitant new taxes for the additional bureaucracy even while the schools and police did not necessarily benefit ordinary peasants. In these and other ways, regarding women for instance, as suggested by Majumdar, a pathway is opened up that leads to the critique of the modern complex. But a critique is only a critique.

In some formulations of the critique, tools for reconstruction are drawn from other theoretical models. Thus, a left-wing postcolonial historian may suggest that if the modernizers had been attuned to class issues, the education of peasants need not have been so dysfunctional. Or that it may have been an aspect of primitive capital accumulation necessary for all modern societies. Others may argue that with more resources available – after all Western imperialism did bankrupt the late Qing state – modernization could have been more painless. Yet others like the twentieth-century Confucian-Buddhist thinker and rural reformer, Liang Shuming, urged that while some reform was necessary, it was more important to restore the rural order so that peasants could live more organically with their built environment (He 2002: 11–2). It is in these ways that postcolonialism is also thought of as a 'toolbox'.

But postcolonialism is not merely a critique of the gap between the ideals and practices of modernity. It suggests a deeper cosmological critique – which can suggest that the gap itself is part of the package of modernity – and its pathways point to a different cosmology. As Dipesh Chakrabarty (2007: 71) has suggested, postcolonialism evokes modes of apprehending the world that are at considerable distance from the logics of modern society and Enlightenment rationality. To use social science etic categories to grasp this universe of meaning and practice is at best to distance oneself from its meaning and experience, and at worst, an epistemic violence whereby these modes of knowing are denigrated and/or become opportunities for their elimination.

Perhaps the academic discipline most sensitive to the problem of epistemic violence – and hence closest to postcolonial studies – is the school of cultural anthropology that may be traced to Franz Boas's move from Germany to the US academia in the early twentieth century. Boaz developed the Herderian tradition of 'culture' as a human phenomenon that is not reducible to civilizational notions of evolution and progress. The more recent history of this tendency may be found in the movement among cultural anthropologists of the 1990s towards the 'reflexive turn' when the scholar turned the lens back on herself to grasp her ways of knowing the society to be studied. This movement tended to lapse into a solipsistic stance. The present trend towards the 'ontological turn', particularly in the work of Bruno Latour and his colleagues, may be seen as the inheritor of this effort to apprehend if not understand the radically other in its own mode of existence.

There are two significant novelties in this position. First, the 'other' includes not only people, but things, plants (e.g. trees), and animals. These anthropologists and science and technology studies' scholars seek to show how in non-modern societies, the culture/nature, subject/object, and human/non-human divisions of what Latour (2013: 7–11) calls the Modern ideology are non-existent (in the same ways). These relations are fluid and relational and the human is seen as a part of the complex world of nature and artifice. Unlike modern man who is creator (after God) and controller, the shaman and the chief, for instance, are conduits for these wider forces.

Second, the emphasis is not on some unified cultural system of 'other' peoples, but how their actions are conditioned by their *reality* viewed through their material and practical circumstances. The ethnographer who is charged with a high degree of critical self-reflexivity regarding his own modernist assumptions seeks to probe this alternative reality complex and hopes for the best kind of understanding. While this represents advances in understanding the 'other', yet the effort among some of these researchers to root the understanding in reality/ontology that escapes human subjective formatting of this reality is deeply *unrealistic*. What Latour calls modern ideology that divides reality into the subject-object binary itself plays a role in the process of the real.

It may well be that ethnography can approach the reality of the radically Other better than other disciplines – certainly not many disciplines are committed to this task. But the professional discipline of history has no such privilege nor does it easily preserve the voices and actions of different worlds in the archive. While historians have done remarkable work in the history of the environment in recent years, this history remains physical and institutional. How the historical 'other' has perceived and understood their relation to the natural and social environment is much harder to access. These are methodological problems which subaltern historians in South Asia and elsewhere, particularly Latin America, have striven to overcome. But the weight of interpretation in reading these materials against the grain is necessarily great.

In recent decades, the fundamental critique embedded in postcolonial thought has revealed itself as a yawning maw that has the capacity to swallow the world as we know it. I refer here to the environmental and climate crisis of our time which some of the deepest critics of colonial modernity – such as Rabindranath Tagore and Mahatma Gandhi – predicted almost a century ago. Their critique was as much about colonialism as it was about the logics of capitalist modernity: a rapidly accelerating transformation of nature and society driven by fossil fuels and unconstrained greed. To be sure many in the West, particularly the Romantics and American Transcendentalists, were also moved by similar insights. But the perspective from the colonized side of the world arguably produced a more comprehensive vision of the massive disruptions to a more nature-based order of the old society.

I believe that postcolonial historical writing would do well to align itself with this most powerful critique of modernity that may be found in its repertoire. At the simplest level, few non-modern cultures and cosmologies were grounded in the hubris that humans were free to conquer nature. Doubtless this idea which spread in the modern West had to do with the disenchantment of the world which was an important condition for the emergence of modernity, but some have argued that it also had to do with the Abrahamic conception of an absolute God who makes nature available to man for his purposes. Indeed, one might argue that the disenchanted vision replaced God with the human, particularly the scientific, rational human. Gilles Deleuze (2001: 71) puts this well: 'But did we kill God when we put man in his place and kept the most important thing, which is the place?'

The idea that humans and natural beings were part of one interfluent and processual activity was true not only for pantheistic or animistic communities, they were also central to cosmologies in premodern China and India. In Chinese cosmology, nature represented the greatest of all living organisms and its governing principles had to be understood so human life could live in harmony with it (*tianren heyi*). The process of self-formation was inseparable from nature. In most Indic cosmologies, the social and moral order was seen as a correlate of the natural order, and both reflected the unity of an inner order.

To be sure cosmological ideas of revering nature do not necessarily translate into reverential practices on the ground. Population pressure and state-driven imperatives to open more and more natural spaces for human settlement in imperial China and other parts of Asia, for instance, led to periodic ecological crises with Malthusian consequences. Moreover, with the advent of modernization in these societies, postcolonial leaders were among the most enthusiastic advocates of exploiting nature and transforming the commons for the purposes of national wealth and power. But in many parts of the developing world where marginal populations most often feel the brunt of the devastation of the environment, these cosmological and religious ideas are often the only resource they possess to protect their livelihoods. In many parts of the world, communities are resisting efforts to exploit or industrialize their natural resources by appealing to the sacrality of these commons. Daoism, animism, Buddhism, Christianity, and Hinduism are utilized to protect resources of community by using terminology of sacred homeland, community forests, holy waters to oppose local environmental ravaging.

Across Asia, folk religion, lineages, *fengshui*, indigenous traditions, symbols, and rituals (Catholic mass, parades, funerals, ritual theatre, martial arts performances that can turn into real resistance) have played a significant role in framing, empowering, and enhancing the solidarity of local environmental movements since the 1980s. Cambodia and Thailand's forest monks led grass-roots movement of robing and sacralizing trees. Today this has emerged as a community movement among forest dwellers across several parts of Indochina. In Sri Lanka, Buddhist monks have evolved a philosophy of development geared to meeting local needs through appropriate technology. In India where the environment movement is probably the strongest among developing countries, local communities and activists build closely upon sacred geography – 'a living landscape in which mountains, rivers, forests and villages are elaborately linked to the stories of the gods and heroes' (Eck 2012: 4–5). Here also many Hindu groups have refashioned themselves as environmental protection groups. In several cases, these movements converge with the strong Gandhian movement for rural and environmental recovery. Taiwan is witnessing the most progressive environmental movement in Asia led by its various new or resurgent Buddhist societies. The hugely popular groups with millions of followers such as the Ciji, Fagu, and Foguan, which have also extended their activities into mainland China and elsewhere, have developed robust environmental agendas known as *huanbao* (protect the environment) that have become one of the most important planks and new spaces of sacrality for the Buddhist movement.

How does history enter the picture? Through my recent work, I have learnt that the historical is not something that simply happened in the past. The idea of the past as dead and subject to clinical analysis is perhaps a necessary aspect of our scientific endeavour, but it does not capture the way the past enters the present (Certeau 1988: 56–60). The past represents a cultural and practical repertoire that is always emergent (or re-emergent). The philosophy of emergence, central to complexity theory, has been developed in science studies by scientists and philosophers of science greatly inspired by the work of Alfred North Whitehead (1861–1947), the mathematician and philosopher of science. To simplify drastically, Whitehead's ideas belong to the minor Western tradition of process philosophy that rejects the stable subject–object dichotomy. Whitehead reveals that emergent complexity is not necessarily a directional process with a *telos*. His ideas probably did more to reverse the (one-way) subject-to-object vector so dominant since Kantian philosophy. Indeed, the purposive subject is understood to *emerge* from the past activity of the universe just as the objective universe is the product of creative subjects (Stengers 2011).

Not unexpectedly, process philosophy dominates most Asian philosophical thought, particularly that of early Buddhist philosophers, the Buddha and Nagarjuna (second century CE). Without immersing the reader in this track, suffice it to say that the Buddhist doctrines of conditioned and interdependent *arising* represent parallel methodologies and are useful for thinking of the past as the repertoire of emergence. Yet of course, the emergent entity or event is always novel because it is diverse 'from the "many" which it unifies' (Whitehead). The historical lesson we take here is not that there is always a conditioning past from which new events arise, but that the conditioning includes a selective projection of the past to address the present and future.

Projective histories necessarily carry a strong subjective or emic element in their representation of the past. But they also have powerful reality effects that shape future histories. All the same, we as historians cannot avoid our own conditioning by the profession of history which has helped us chart the way in our time. It is difficult to always keep projective histories apart from the professional historian's more objective treatment of the past, but the two tend towards opposite poles of the spectrum. Professional history is a valid enterprise which can be judged by professional standards. It is the business of the historian to also assess the different goals of the historical project and its capacity for appropriation.

Let me close with a simple instance taken from recent research. The Prey Lang forests of northern Cambodia is a vast evergreen forest zone of 3,600 square kilometre with 200,000 people that is being ravaged by logging and dam building. Its communities have organized a decade-long agenda of protest and protection. The agenda includes frequent performances of ritual theatre in Phnom Penh's main public square drawn from their own traditions as well as organizing forest protection squads that, among other things, robe the giant trees with Buddhist saffron garments to sacralize them. These communities are critically assisted by a multi-scale assemblage of civil society organizations ranging from the local to the global which has brought public – even global – attention and considerable success to their cause. Not least interesting is that these communities call themselves Cambodia's Avatars. Avatar of course is a Hindu-Buddhist term familiar to them meaning re-incarnated being, but in their ritual performances they refer as much to James Cameron's blockbuster film about environmental resistance called Avatar. In such ways, they hope to widen the meaning of their movement to a global audience without losing their historical inspiration.

Response

Rochona Majumdar

Prasenjit Duara raises a series of thoughtful and important issues in his response to my chapter in his brief, but lucid intervention. Instead of responding to his thoughts serially, let me take up a few themes that I regard as most important in a spirit of discussion.

Duara asks whether or not scholars I have identified as such would regard themselves as postcolonial. This is followed by a set of key remarks about postcolonialism constituting 'not a theory' but 'a perspective pointing to another cosmology'. To argue about whether or not a group of practitioners self-identify by a particular moniker is always tricky, and ultimately futile. For example, in India the category 'art cinema' became widely used in critical and mainstream writing on film ever since Satyajit Ray (1921–92) sailed into the world with his debut feature film *Pather Panchali* ('Song of the Little Road', 1955). But most art cinema directors strenuously resisted calling themselves by that name. Likewise, many regard the epithet feminist as problematic and limited, preferring to be called womanist, third wave, global-humanist through a variety of arguments that gesture towards intersectionality and queerness instead. Their resistance, however, does not detract from the value of the work done for women and minorities.[1]

Duara asks if postcolonialism constitutes a body of 'theory' as such. As I have used it in my chapter, and as it informs the scholarship, postcolonialism is a particular vantage point from which to apprehend the world. In this context, I find film theorist D. N. Rodowick's discussion of theory and its salience to the New Humanities instructive. Rodowick traces the origins of theory to 'the Greek sense of *theoria* as viewing, speculation, or the contemplative life'. Elaborating on it further, he explains that 'for Plato, it is the highest form of human activity; in Aristotle, the chief activity of the Prime Mover. For the Greeks, theory was not only an activity, but also an *ethos* that associated the love of wisdom with a style of life or mode of existence' (Rodowick 2007: 92). Moving towards the contemporary period, he invokes Raymond Williams who noted that by the seventeenth century four 'primary senses' came to be associated with the term: spectacle, a contemplated sight, a scheme of ideas, and an explanatory scheme. 'A contemporary commonsensical notion', argues Rodowick (2007: 93), follows from the last two meanings. Postcolonialism, and the histories written from this perspective, I submit, retains all four aspects of the term.

The second issue that I want to touch on has to do with Duara's observations on the relation between postcolonial history and critiques of modernity. Duara urges postcolonial historians to align themselves with critical takes on modernity, such as those articulated by the likes of Rabindranath Tagore and M. K. Gandhi. There were Western exemplars too, he writes, such as the Romantics and Transcendentalists who were 'moved by similar insights'. The 'West', however, Duara clarifies, fell far short of most 'non-modern cultures' when it came to being critical of a world view governed by ideas about the ultimate perfectibility of man who could subjugate nature. The distinction that Duara draws here between the 'West' and 'non-modern cultures' is too sharp. Figures such as Tagore and Gandhi from India, or Frantz Fanon from Martinique, have been analysed by postcolonial thinkers and historians because of the ways in which putative distinctions between the West and non-West blur and fraternize in their thought.

Leela Gandhi's *Affective Communities* offers an important corrective to the anti-Western stance of postcolonial history by bringing to light the lives and careers of individuals and groups in the West who 'renounced the privileges of imperialism' and sought alliance with those who were 'victims of their own expansionist cultures' (Gandhi 2006: 1). She focuses in particular on a group of fin-de-siècle individuals, who were not known to each other, but forged, sometimes real and at other times only intellectual, affinities with kindred souls in the colony. Thus M. K. Gandhi and Edward Carpenter, Aurobindo Ghose and Mira Alfassa, Manmohan Ghose and Oscar Wilde constitute, in her work, a postcolonial vision of 'anti-communitarian communitarianism' (Gandhi 2006: 26). Intellectuals and leaders as varied as Friedrich Engels, Robert Blantchford, V. I. Lenin, Max Nordau, George Orwell wrote off these examples of fin-de-siècle utopian thought as too 'immature' to ever constitute a model for a productive and transformative political praxis. Orwell's dismissive description of these ways of being in the world is worth citing at length for the bitterness of his invective. Late nineteenth-century utopianism, he wrote, was a 'magnetic field' that drew towards itself 'every fruit-juice drinker, nudist, sandal-wearer, sex-maniac, Quaker, "Nature Cure" quack, pacifist, and feminist in England' (Gandhi 2006: 178).

Recently, Vicky Albritton and Fredrik Albritton Jonsson have drawn attention to another set of 'non-players' they call the 'green Victorians'. In the same spirit as that of Gandhi, Tagore, and many lesser-known colonial-era individuals, John Ruskin inspired a community of students and followers, including one, William Gershom Collingwood, father of the renowned philosopher of history, Robin George Collingwood, to develop what they call 'a culture of sufficiency' (Albritton and Jonsson 2016: 8). In a historical epoch that is being identified as one of anthropogenic climate change, that is to say when human beings are acknowledged as agents wielding geological force, Albritton and Jonsson recover histories of figures such as Ruskin and Collingwood as models for a future where we might buy 'less' and consume 'wisely' for a healthier society and planet.

Reading Ruskin and Robert Somervell's criticisms of railways as corrupting the 'moral character' of Cumbrians, or their rant against industrial society more generally, reminds one of M. K. Gandhi's strident critique of railways, doctors, and lawyers in his 1909 tract, *Hind Swaraj*. A sentence from Somervell 'the frenzy of avarice is daily drowning our sailors, suffocating our miners, poisoning our children, and blasting the cultivable surface of England into a treeless waste of ashes' could easily be replaced with Gandhi's about the 'evils' of 'civilization' epitomized by the railways that spread the bubonic plague and famine in many parts of India (Albritton and Jonsson 2016: 97).

These views might indeed be a 'cosmology' in Duara's words. But, such a cosmology can only be properly understood by taking seriously postcolonial historiography's mandate that there were values that many among the colonizer and colonized shared, in spite of the harsh and cruel power relations that separated them. Postcolonial history gives us visions of a world imagined by Frantz Fanon – 'There is no Negro Mission, there is no white burden' – even as other histories teach us about a globe geopolitically divided into West and non-West, European, African, and Asian (Fanon 1967: 228).

Postcolonial theory and history emerged as important themes in the academy in the last two decades of the twentieth century. Historians influenced by the postcolonial optic have made fundamental interventions in histories of nationalism, colonialism, gender, and minority histories, as well as histories of race, caste, and community. As we progress into the twenty-first century, the exigencies of our times dictate that historians, like practitioners of other disciplines, calibrate their views. Duara's singling out of histories of climate and environment is important in this regard.

I wish to conclude by recalling the 1997 Kyoto Protocol's missive to developed nations of the world to undertake 'common but differentiated responsibilities' as they tackle the challenge of greenhouse gas emissions. To comprehend what the idea of 'common' but 'differentiated' might look like on the ground brings us once more into the domain of postcolonial history and theory. As I have argued, postcolonial historians and theorists are committed to understanding what we share in our past and present even as they take full account of the fissures that have divided us, sometimes irremediably. As we face shared crises, whose proportions have spilled from the global into the planetary, it is postcolonial history's burden once more to guide scholars into understanding the full complexity of that which the Kyoto Protocol described as our 'common' responsibility as we negotiate our teeming differences.

Note

1. The debate around feminism is one that roils the academy and the wider public sphere. Catherine MacKinnon's writings brought to the centre of academic and policy debates the question of women's rights as human rights. For a summary of positions, see Evans and Bobel 2007, and also Kaminer 1993.

References

Albritton, V. and Jonsson, F. A. (2016), *Green Victorians: The Simple Life in John Ruskin's Lake District*, Chicago: University of Chicago Press.

Armitage, D. (2007), 'From Colonial History to Postcolonial History: A Turn Too Far?', *William and Mary Quarterly*, 64 (2): 251–4.

Balibar, E. (2003), 'Europe: An "Unimagined" Frontier of Democracy', *Diacritics*, 33 (3/4): 36–44.

Balibar, E. (2004), *We, The People of Europe? Reflections on Transnational Community*, Princeton, NY: Princeton University Press.

Bhabha, H. (2004), 'Foreword', in F. Fanon (ed.), *The Wretched of the Earth*, vii–xli, New York: Grove Press.

Biddick, K. (1998), *The Shock of Medievalism*, Durham: Duke University Press.

Burton, A., ed. (2003), *After the Imperial Turn: Thinking with and Through the Nation*, Durham: Duke University Press.

Certeau, M. de (1988), *The Writing of History*, transl. T. Conley, New York: Columbia University Press.

Chabal, P., ed. (2003), *A History of Postcolonial Lusophone Africa*, Bloomington, IN: Indiana University Press.

Chakrabarty, D. (2007), *Provincializing Europe: Postcolonial Thought and Historical Difference*, 2nd edn, Princeton, NJ: Princeton University Press.

Chakrabarty, D. (2008), 'In Defense of Provincializing Europe: A Response to Carola Dietze', *History and Theory*, 47: 85–96.

Chakrabarty, D. (2009), 'An Anti-Colonial History of the Postcolonial Turn', *Melbourne Historical Journal*, 37: 1–23.

Chakrabarty, D. (2012a), 'From Civilization to Globalization: The "West" as a Shifting Signifier in Indian Modernity', *Inter-Asia Cultural Studies*, 13 (1): 138–52.

Chakrabarty, D. (2012b), 'Postcolonial Studies and the Challenge of Climate Change', *New Literary History*, 43 (1): 1–18.

Chatterjee, P. (1986), *Nationalist Thought and the Colonial World*, New York: Zed.

Chatterjee, P. (1993), *The Nation and Its Fragments: Colonial and Postcolonial Histories*, Princeton, NJ: Princeton University Press.

Cohen, J. J., ed. (2000), *The Postcolonial Middle Ages*, New York: St. Martin's Press.

Cooper, F. (2003), 'Postcolonial Peoples: A Commentary', in A. L. Smith (ed.), *Europe's Invisible Migrants*, 169–83, Amsterdam: Amsterdam University Press.

Cooper, F. (2005), *Colonialism in Question: Theory, Knowledge, History*, Berkeley and Los Angeles: University of California Press.

Cooper, F. and Stoler, A., eds (1997). *Tensions of Empire*, Berkeley: University of California Press.

Davis, K. (2008), *Periodization and Sovereignty: How Ideas of Feudalism and Secularization Govern the Politics of Time*, Philadelphia: University of Pennsylvania Press.

D'Arcens, L. (2010), '"Most Gentle Indeed, But Most Virile": The Medievalist Pacifism of George Arnold Wood', in K. Davis and N. Altschul (eds), *Medievalisms in the Postcolonial World: The Idea of 'the Middle Ages' Outside Europe*, 80–108, Baltimore, MD: Johns Hopkins University Press.

Deleuze, G. (2001), *Pure Immanence: Essays on a Life*, transl. A. Boyman, New York: Zone Books.

Duara, P. (1995), *Rescuing History from the Nation: Questioning Narratives of Modern China*, Chicago: University of Chicago Press.

Duara, P. (2010), 'Asia Redux: Conceptualizing a Region for our Times', *Journal of Asian Studies*, 69 (4): 963–83.

Duara, P. (2015), *The Crisis of Global Modernity: Asian Traditions and a Sustainable Future*, Cambridge: Cambridge University Press.

Dutton, M., Gandhi, L. and Seth, S. (1999), 'The Toolbox of Postcolonialism', *Postcolonial Studies*, 2 (2): 122–4.

Eck, D. L. (2012), *India: A Sacred Geography*, New York: Harmony Books.

Evans, M. and Bobel, C. (2007), 'I am a Contradiction: Feminism and Feminist Identity in the Third Wave', *New England Journal of Public Policy*, 22 (1): 207–22.

Fabian, J. (2014), *Time and the Other*, New York: Columbia University Press.

Fanon, F. (1967), *Black Skins White Masks*, New York: Grove Press.

Gandhi, L. (1998), *Postcolonial Theory: A Critical Introduction*, New South Wales: Allen and Unwin.

Gandhi, L. (2006), *Affective Communities: Anticolonial Thought, Fin-de-Siècle Radicalism, and the Politics of Friendship*, Durham: Duke University Press.

Gopal, S. (2016), 'Bourgeois Extreme: Cultural Flows and the Micro Import' (unpublished paper).

Guha, R., ed. (1997), *A Subaltern Studies Reader 1986-1995*, Minneapolis and London: University of Minnesota Press.

He, P. (2002), *China's Search for Modernity: Cultural Discourse in the Late 20th Century*, Basingstoke: Palgrave Macmillan.

Ingham, P. C. and Warren, M. R., eds (2003), *Postcolonial Moves: Medieval Through Modern*, New York: Palgrave Macmillan.

Johnson, M. (2008), 'Making History Public: Indigenous Claims to Settler States', *Public Culture*, 20 (1): 97–117.

Kabir, A. and Williams, D., eds (2005), *Postcolonial Approaches to the European Middle Ages: Translating Cultures*, Cambridge: Cambridge University Press.

Kaminer, W. (1993), 'Feminism's Identity Crisis' *The Atlantic*, October, available online: https://www.theatlantic.com/magazine/archive/1993/10/feminisms-identity-crisis/304921/ (accessed 22 July 2017).

Latour, B. (1993), *We Have Never Been Modern*, transl. C. Porter, Cambridge, MA: Harvard University Press.

Latour, B. (2013), *An Inquiry into Modes of Existence: An Anthropology of the Moderns*, transl. C. Porter, Cambridge, MA: Harvard University Press.

Majumdar, R. (2010), *Writing Postcolonial History*, London: Bloomsbury.

Pandey, G. (1997), 'In Defense of the Fragment: Writing About Hindu-Muslim Riots in India Today', in R. Guha (ed.), *A Subaltern Studies Reader, 1986–1995*, 1–33, Minneapolis: University of Minnesota Press.

Prakash, G. (1995), *After Colonialism: Imperial Histories and Postcolonial Displacements*, Princeton, NJ: Princeton University Press.

Reynolds, H. (2006), *The Other Side of the Frontier*, new edn, Sydney: University of New South Wales Press.

Rodowick, D. (2007), 'An Elegy for Theory', *October*, 122: 91–109.

Said, E. (2000), 'Always on Top', *The London Review of Books*, 20 March.

Scott, J. (2004), *The Politics of the Veil*, Princeton, NJ: Princeton University Press.

Sinha, M. (1995), *Colonial Masculinity: The 'Manly Englishman' and the 'Effeminate Bengali' in the Late Nineteenth Century*, Manchester: Manchester University Press.

Smith, A. L., ed. (2003), *Europe's Invisible Migrants*, Amsterdam: Amsterdam University Press.

Spiegel, G. M. (2000), 'Epater Les Médiévistes', *History and Theory*, 39 (2): 243–50.

Spivak, G. C. (1999), *A Critique of Postcolonial Reason: Toward a History of the Vanishing Present*, Cambridge, MA: Harvard University Press.

Stengers, I. (2011), *Thinking with Whitehead: A Free and Wild Creation of Concepts*, transl. M. Chase, Cambridge, MA: Harvard University Press.

Subrahmanyam, S. (2016), 'One Asia or Many: Reflections from Connected History', *Modern Asian Studies*, 50 (1): 5–43.

Suganami, H. (1978), 'A Note on the Origin of the Word "International"', *British Journal of International Studies*, 4 (3): 226–32.

Thiong'o wa, N. (1993), *Moving the Centre: The Struggle for Cultural Freedoms*, London: James Curry.

Wilson, K. (2004), *A New Imperial History: Culture, Identity and Modernity in Britain and the Empire, 1660-1840*, Cambridge: Cambridge University Press.

Young, R. (2001) *Postcolonialism: An Historical Introduction*, Oxford: Blackwell.

CHAPTER 3
ENVIRONMENTAL HISTORY
Grégory Quenet

Environmental history (EH) as a self-identified field was born in the United States at the beginning of the 1970s.[1] Before the end of the 1990s, it had little influence on historical analysis and remained underground.[2] However, since the end of the 1990s, there has been a surge of interest. This new approach to history can be seen in a large part of the world, even if in some countries permanent positions for environmental historians are still very recent or limited. Academic recognition and internationalization raised new questions about the unity and definition of EH. Beyond the auto-referential concern of a professional community, a more fundamental question emerged about how the discipline had taken and should take into account environmental issues and non-human beings. Owing to global climate and environmental change, this debate is now vibrant both in and outside of the realm of EH, among historians and non-historians alike. 'Anthropocene', 'Capitalocene', 'Plantationocene', and 'Chtulucene' enriched the vocabulary of the humanities and social sciences, and put environmental perspectives at the top of the theoretical and methodological agenda (Quenet 2017). Did we, as historians, neglect these issues because of our anthropocentric point of view? Was history built as a humanist knowledge on the bedrocks of the divide between the history of humans and the history of nature? Are the humanities and the social sciences able to integrate non-humans without destabilizing all their theoretical architecture, or should they call for a re-foundation? All these relevant questions must be precisely contextualized while remaining respectful of existing attempts to analyse societies in relation to their environment.[3]

Environmental history, although non-exhaustive, is a good point from which to evaluate how empirical studies could deal with the non-human part of history. The initial assumption of environmental historians was to consider non-human beings, in a large sense, as actors in history, rather than as merely inert things manipulated by human actors. This symmetrical perspective revealed an asymmetry of relations because societies had a strong impact on their environment, which in turn influenced the course of history. This Copernican turn, from static nature to environmental dynamics, opened up the way for innovative empirical research on pollution and management, animals and fish, landscapes and territories, environmental and gender inequalities, capitalism and the commodification of nature. The subject of this chapter is not to introduce and summarize this very large set of works but to go deeper, to a more idiosyncratic understanding of EH. While there are many sophisticated monographs in the field, there exist few firm theoretical discussions. Moreover, state-of-the-art papers developed generally a normative approach about the strengths and weaknesses of EH oversimplifying the sedimentation of intellectual and methodological contexts that shaped the historical question of nature. The empirical productivity of EH was originally based on disciplinary borders that compensated for imprecise theoretical baselines, but this conceptual vagueness is no longer sustainable in light of current awareness of global climate and environmental change that redefined the debate about nature in the humanities and social sciences. This new context requires a rigorous definition of EH to be established from the patterns of its existing practice.

Writing the history of non-humans: Between theory and observation

With the growth of visibility in the 1990s came a set of critiques from inside and outside EH underlining its lack of coherence and significance. Environmental historians remarked that expansion, both thematically and geographically, highlighted divisions between researchers who, at the beginning of the field, were unified neither by a common definition of nature and environment, nor by a clear methodology (Weiner 2005). Geographers, among others, have criticized the manner in which different disciplines used to analyse the relations between people and their environment (Williams 1994). If the first generation of environmental historians quoted anthropologists, geographers, ecologists, and historians, the subsequent generations did not often refer to the vast literature on nature and culture available in other disciplines.[4] Environmental historians in general did not produce many conceptual and methodological texts capable of establishing the foundations of the new field. In order to answer the question of 'what is environmental history?' many took recourse to intellectual mapping rather than theoretical perspective.[5] In spite of sharing a common idea of history from below, EH was very different from other new fields of the 1970s and 1980s, such as cultural, gender, and science studies.

The usual introduction to EH for readers is very broad and considers diversity: 'like every other subset of history, EH represents different things to different people. Our preferred definition of the field is the study of the relationship between human societies and the rest of nature on which they depended' (McNeill and Mauldin 2015: xvi). This level of generality didn't help to situate these perspectives inside historiography. There exist many works, prior or parallel to EH, that can lay claim to such an analytical approach. In terms of methodology, geography, anthropology, and cultural ecology are very close to EH. Among historians, the 'ecological history' of Robert Delort and François Walter proposed exactly the same definition, whereas the content of US ecological history is quite different (Beck and Delort 1991; Walter 1994; Delort and Walter 2001). In the former edition of Peter Burke's volume on new perspectives in history, Richard Grove (2001) used that definition to include in EH all former attempts to study the relationships between people and nature from the end of the eighteenth century onwards. A more elaborate and contextualized definition of EH would have reduced ambiguity at the price of a less inclusive academic umbrella. If William Cronon's Western history looked like EH, his cultural approach was difficult to appropriate for those working on historical variations of the physical world, especially with methodology coming from the natural sciences: 'The story of human beings working with changing tools to transform the resources of the land, struggling over how that land should be owned and understood, and defining their notions of political and cultural community, all within a context of shifting environmental and economic constraints' (Cronon 1987: 172).

To counterbalance this vague generality, a thematic definition was usually added, distinguishing the different aspects of the relationship between human societies and nature. EH combines the study of material environment as modified by human action, the influence of environmental factors on human history, and the history of human thought about the environment (Hughes 2006: 3). This exhaustive and vast description of what environmental historians are doing left room for diversity, depending on which segment was being focused on. However, such a tripartite view should not be considered as purely descriptive, and is not theoretically neutral – the devil is in the structures. Donald Worster was the first, in a 1988 paper, to propose a triptych for EH, distinguishing 'natural environments of the past', from 'human modes of production', and 'perception, ideology and value' (Worster 1988). Even if Worster did not refer to Maurice Godelier, the dialogue with Marxism and the debate about materialism in anthropology was the intellectual context (Godelier 1977, 1988). This agenda has since weakened, and the vocabulary has shifted to a more descriptive meaning, such as three 'clusters' or 'themes'; this, however, merely confused the issue. Are these three relationships only themes that circumscribe the perimeter of EH, or are they three levels that develop a structural and hierarchized understanding of societies? Does the material environment introduce the idea of a reality that human beings did not create, or a physical and cultural point of view that weakened the idea of nature per se? Despite a general consensus, environmental historians find themselves situated at different positions along these graduated theoretical lines.

The key problem of EH is situated at the crossroads of this thematic approach used as a definition; the main theoretical and methodological debates about the environment[6] in the social sciences come together at the articulation and intersection of each cluster. The idea of three main fields of inquiry – material, institutional, and symbolic – is an attempt to avoid the main conceptual problem. What is the relation between, on one side, the material order, and, on the other side, the institutional and symbolic orders? All environmental historians agree that these segments are not disconnected, but they do not necessarily agree on the nature of this connection. The problem is usually resolved practically, through the writing of history and case studies that elucidate an entangled narrative of interwoven levels or realities (Cronon 1992a). The story of the material world is always mediated by cultural and intellectual categories carried out by actors who describe and transform their environment, as well as by historical sources. However, the existing environment does not determine human institutions. A current of anthropology, coming from Julian Steward, Marvin Harris, and Roy Rappaport, influenced Worster's paper. At different degrees of causality and sophistication, they developed the idea of adaptation and cultural ecology, a perspective criticized by a large part of anthropology (Descola 2013b). The dispute between the natural sciences and the social sciences was never resolved, and an argument for or from the two cultures of environmental historian – ecological science and the humanities – was never methodologically established from sources and archives.

Nevertheless, this theoretical appraisal of EH underestimates the manner in which the new field is already self-defined by its distinction from existing fields. Historiography is an essential part of reflexivity, and not only a methodology.[7] EH was born out of critiques of the intellectual and political history that dominated US historiography in the 1960s, and found some inspiration in the *histoire totale* of the Annales school, the human geography of Carl Sauer, and cultural ecology as a compromise between ethnology and ecology. However, none of these references were satisfying, and EH created its own space between disciplines, a space which was not well identified before the 1990s.

In placing itself between disciplines, EH was able to avoid at least five of the conceptual traps about nature that embarrassed scholars at the time: theory, harmony, relativism, naturalization, and objectivity (Quenet 2014: 14–97). Environmentalism partly explained the lack of theoretical elaboration about the environment. Knowing from advocacy that something outside of societies existed and had to be protected, environmental historians did not lose time with the aporetic concept of nature. It was environmental historians who introduced the idea of power relations between human and non-human beings. This was the main difference between environmental historians and the French historians of the Annales school who placed real importance on the physical and natural world but who were less attentive to such asymmetries. It was close to new contemporary fields of the 1970s in that its view from below challenged the view of dominating actors, but it differed in regard to social construction and situated perspectives. The idea that there existed something that human beings did not create that could be analysed both as a fact and as a construction kept EH, at least until the end of the 1990s, far from postmodernism and the linguistic turn. EH helped elaborate an original methodological approach through the invention of new historical objects and the reinterpretation of existing case studies. The institutional difficulties of the first two decades led EH to confine itself to a narrower orientation than its original ambition of writing a world EH on the *longue durée* (Worster 1982; Hughes 1984, 2001). The US identification of the field provided a firm academic foundation while, paradoxically, avoiding any naturalization of history, as the US definition of 'nature' was, more and more, just one definition among the plurality of definitions found across human societies. The idiosyncratic narrative form of EH permitted both the use of data coming from the natural sciences and the development of a comprehensive view of the relations between human and non-human beings. John Opie, the forgotten founder of the field, defined EH as a dialectical relation between the two cultures of the natural sciences and the social sciences (Opie 1983).

This identity gradually weakened. At the end of the 1990s, EH underwent a cultural turn, followed by a global turn – both represent different ways of dealing with the contradiction between the universality of physical nature and the diversity of human societies. The evolution of the environmental movement was part of this divided process too. Strongly coherent from the US origin of the conservation and park movement, global environmental mobilization became more and more diverse and contradictory, between top and down perspectives, Western urban movement and Third World environmentalism of the poor (Radkau 2014). In the 2000s, three important articles were published to address the problem. Ted Steinberg (2002) proposed viewing environment in terms of the same model as race, class, and gender. Following Anthony Giddens and William Sewell, he placed ecological factors among structures that constrain human action and that are reproduced by social institutions. More than a specific type of power, environment is a way to analyse places and landscapes. Ellen Stroud (2003) rejected this perspective on the grounds that the generality of power relations implicated in the definition dissolves the specificity of nature. The word 'dirt', for example, is emphasized in order to accentuate the non-human, material dimensions of EH, the ones that legitimate the environmental ethics of historians. The divide between nature and culture is, according to Sverker Sörlin and Paul Warde (2007), 'the problem of the problem of environmental history': that is an ontological organization that is supposed to be given and real, rather than being socially constructed, as is taught by the social sciences. They encouraged environmental historians to take more inspiration from new social theory, especially that of Anthony Giddens, Ulrich Beck, Bruno Latour, and Sheila Jasanoff, as well as everything related to the history of science and knowledge regimes in general. Thanks to these debates, EH is more reflexive today than it used to be. But the theoretical definition is still neither clear nor sustainable. Global climate and environmental change created a new intellectual context that put pressure on historians to consider the history of non-humans.

Historians under pressure: The challenge of climate and global environmental change

With the start of the new millennium a new intellectual and political context arose, one dominated by global environmental issues and philosophical and anthropological debates.

The radical critique of the division between nature and culture by the French anthropologists Philippe Descola and, better known internationally, Bruno Latour, had paradoxical effects on environmental historians.[8] On the one hand, their radical critique of the divide between nature and culture provided philosophical foundations for the overall history of environmental historians. On the other hand, the habitual definitions of the relationships between societies and nature collapsed with the categories themselves. Nature and environment are no longer more than provincial ideas belonging to modern Western societies, ideas that are unable to describe the common world of non-human and human beings.[9] Environmental historians explored three partial escapes from this philosophical trap.[10] Firstly, they historicized the production of discontinuities between nature and culture, and elaborated a set of micro divides, contextualized and specific to different periods and territories. However, this sophisticated empirical approach did not provide an exit from a Western naturalist perspective. Only non-Western ontologies, such as that of Amerindians, or perhaps those elaborated prior to the Renaissance, could do that. But EH was mainly devoted to contemporary times and the impact of modernity on nature. Secondly, the history of science allowed environmental historians to be more reflexive about knowledge regimes at the price of an ambiguous appraisal of materiality, that is the under-estimation of the environmental dynamics dear to environmental historians. The double language of the natural sciences and the social sciences did not become more coherent. Thirdly, an internal perspective that uses its own vocabulary of historical sources and archives is a respectful way of analysing the diversity of relationships between humans and non-humans. However, applying the notion of 'environment' to periods that did not use the word reinforces the naturalistic viewpoint of modern societies and weakens the category of environment.

Global climate and environmental change recomposed the disciplinary and intellectual frontiers of EH. Environmental historians such as Richard Grove, who inspired Christopher Bayly and Kenneth Pomeranz (Grove 1995; Bayly 2004: 450; Pomeranz 2000), contributed to the elaboration of a global historical perspective. This precursor role masked at least three contradictory ways of considering the global. Firstly, that world history is the study of historical processes of integration through economy, culture, and ecology. The expansion of trade and capitalism from the seventeenth and eighteenth centuries accelerated environmental changes, and the discovery of the New World was an ecological shock (Braudel 1981: 69–70; Crosby 1986). Secondly, this approach is related to a global point of view that highlights historical phenomena that are not visible at the local, regional, and national scales, especially environmental and climatic processes. Richard Grove and Mike Davis established new connections between different parts of the world through the ENSO variation, challenging the interpretation of social phenomenon such as famine and crisis (Davis 2001; Grove 1998, 2002). Thirdly, connected history placed different European knowledges and non-European epistemologies of nature in relation to one another. This new chapter of EH and the history of science differed from the first model of ecological imperialism in that it was more symmetrical; it also differed from the diffusionist model (Drayton 2000; Bonneuil 2000; Anker 2001; Livingstone and Withers 2011). Moreover, connecting different spaces opened up room for at least three different hypotheses, provided that culture was not reduced to the laws of biology and evolution (Bertrand 2012; Chartier 2006). The first is related to an anthropological universal that relies on the diversity of cultures and contexts to explain formal homologies. The second hypothesis concerns forgotten direct contacts between different spaces, and studies exchanges and reciprocal appropriations (McNeill 2010). Some works used mainly European sources, whereas others are closer to connected history. The third hypothesis, ecological polygenesis, assumes that an identical environmental context will produce identical processes of social and cultural transformation. In short, global EH is heterogeneous and has not yet stabilized its definition of 'global'. In the context of global climate and environmental change, such ambiguities are no longer sustainable.

At first glance, the Anthropocene hypothesis should be in favour of EH. The idea of a geological epoch in which humanity exerts a geological force able to modify the climate of the planet put environment at the core of human history, examining the impact of humans on the Earth and the impact of climate on societies. However, this hypothesis moved EH's centre of gravity towards Deep History and Big History (Christian 2011; Smail and Shyrock 2013). It weakened the comprehensive dimension that was present at the field's debut, and that was reinforced during the cultural turn of the 1990s.[11] The pre-Anthropocene of Paul Crutzen, Will Steffen, and John McNeill began before agriculture, with hunter-gatherers, the evolution of the size of the human brain, and the extinction of the Pleistocene megafauna (Steffen, Crutzen, and McNeill 2007). Considerations of the history of evolution and *Homo sapiens* also form part of the historical agenda of Dipesh Chakrabarty, despite his (not entirely convincing) attempts to keep his distance from Big History (Chakrabarty 2014: 1, 2016b).[12] In proposing to zoom in and out of human history in order to combine human inequality and suffering with geological and evolutionary times, he fails to articulate the relation between the two. This hiatus is one of the reasons that David Armitage and Jo Guldi are uncomfortable with the concept of the Anthropocene when the plea is for closer collaborations between history, the natural sciences, and the cognitive sciences: the Anthropocene is too narrow for Big History and Deep History, and too large for the usual practice of history (Guldi and Armitage 2014: 65–6, 69–70, 84, 86).

This shift upset the narrative standards that marked the identity of environmental historians. Local and regional history was now reduced to an effect of global dynamics (Heise 2008; Hornborg 2010). Primary sources, especially archives, were central to renewing old historical objects and being reflexive about the effects of printed and narrative sources. Is a history written from second-hand sources and bibliographical synthesis a desirable future (Sörlin and Warde 2007: 116)? Historical depth was the way to answer past challenges to EH without falling into the trap of established patterns. How is it possible to avoid anachronism if climate change is the gateway to understanding past societies? The narrative dimension of history was the tool used to include human and non-human beings in a common history. How could a dominant quantitative point of view, constructed from ecological balance and natural science data, avoid reducing non-human beings to an anthropocentric perspective? Manipulating scales helped environmental historians be attentive to situated experiences and suffering. What is the place of dominated peoples in a history reduced to a planetary level?

Last but not least, the sudden interest of non-historians in the environment and climate through time may bring a larger audience and promote debate, but it could also result in unexpected secondary effects, something like a kiss of death. Bruno Latour brought a nuanced approach to nature and non-human beings that was missing in EH. His arguments about the new climatic regime provided a lens to show how the present was specific and different from the past. Nevertheless, Latour's use of time is ambiguous, and one should be wary about any attempt to import his approach into history. For Latour, time is more of a heuristic tool, one that can be used to change perspectives, than a social phenomenon to analyse. At least four different temporal regimes are present in Latour's thought. The first one concerns the feedback loops of Gaia that abolish the distinction between past and future. This movement establishes 'a new and dramatic connection between powers of action that have until now been unknown, taking place at increasingly vast scales, and according to an increasingly frenetic rhythm' (Latour 2015: 182). The second is ahistorical, as the naturalism of the Moderns was an illusion, a historical parenthesis to be closed. Analogism and animism survived through art and images (Heinz and Latour 2012); this permanent coexistence of different ontologies put an end to the naturalist project of the scientific revolution. The third is a proposition to reset a technological system. The exhibition and book 'Reset Modernity' proposed to equip the people of Earth with new tools. Literally speaking, the proposition is to return to the beginning of the sixteenth century, before the triumph of Western Naturalism and the expansion of European territories in the New World (Latour 2016: 405–9).[13] The fourth is apocalyptical and prophetic, although the *telos,* or kingdom to come, is neither clear nor certain (Hartog 2014). All these perspectives are far from the experience of time as lived by past societies and the analysis of the temporal structures of the social world familiar to historians. This context pressures historians to answer as historians, with their own tools and with a clear definition of EH.

The patterns of environmental history

Beyond the specific, shared objectives that define the community of EH, the debate about nature and history is addressed to all historians. In a famous article, Dipesh Chakrabarty (2009) challenged the concept of history with four theses: one, that anthropogenic explanations of climate change spell the collapse of the distinction between natural history and human history; two, that the idea of the Anthropocene severely qualifies humanist histories of modernity and globalization; three, that this geological hypothesis requires historians to put global histories of capital in conversation with the species history of humans; and four, that the cross-hatching of species history and the history of capital is a process of probing the limits of historical understanding (see also Chakrabarty 2012; 2016a, b). The reason for which one of the most famous representatives of subaltern studies unsettled the local and comprehensive dimension of history remained unintelligible for many scholars (Vincent 2012). A close study of the Indian context that gave birth to the first version of this paper, written initially in Bengali, highlights a more coherent intellectual trajectory than that which appears at first glance. The fossil-oriented understanding of history in the Anthropocene returned the Western world, especially England and the United States, to the centre of the process of modernity. For Chakrabarty, assuming the demographic impact of emergent countries on the planet's climate was a way of maintaining a certain idea of provincializing Europe, and the species concept was a means to avoid a regressive comeback of nations in the writing of history. The use of this Voltairian tactic of shifting attention away from a weak point to a new controversy was a success, and the Indian debate was overshadowed by the impact of the geological turn proposed to the social sciences and to history.

Rather than making previous works obsolete, the rise of the concept of the Anthropocene should be seen as an opportunity to create a dialogue between EH and different perspectives about the history of the physical world beyond the limits of the Anglophone version. Chakrabarty himself insisted that his statement about the historiographical hiatus between natural history and human history would require a deeper analysis than a few references to Giambattista Vico, Benedetto Croce, and Robin Collingwood (Chakrabarty 2009: 201–7). First trained in India, he is familiar with the Annales school, the geohistory of Fernand Braudel, and the climate history of Emmanuel Le Roy Ladurie. The first EH of India, written by Ramachandra Guha and Madhav Gadgil, began by taking inspiration from Marc Bloch and his 'great study of agriculture – itself a model of ecological analysis' (Gadgil and Guha 1992: 7). Historical geography has a long tradition and is very active today in many countries such as Canada, the UK, Brazil, and China (Powell and Wilson 2015). The dialogue between history, archaeology, and ecological history gave birth to many works in Italy around the School of Genova, which unfortunately have not been translated into English (Moreno 1990). Rural history, dealing with the land and the landscape (many references exist in Spanish and Portuguese from Uertaga 1987 to Pádua 2002 and Cabral 2014), produced an impressive number of studies in nearly every country in the world, while many seminal texts written by anthropologists and sociologists about societies and their environment have so far only been published in Danish, Norwegian, German, Chinese, Vietnamese, and so on.

The debate between the core of history as a discipline and EH did not occur in the 1970s nor in the 1980s, because the original perspective brought by environmental historians was not very visible at a time when different questions animated the agenda of the social sciences. Now is the time to open the floor for debates about nature, materiality, and environmental and climate dynamics. The issue is no longer about the different subfields of history but about the concept of history itself, since, by reinterpreting temporal processes and discontinuities, non-historians are unsettling history as a specific mode of knowledge. More fundamentally, the current question of nature is also the question of the nature of history. Environmental historians should take the initiative to reread the evolution of the discipline of history in the light of the question of nature, by investigating the way in which relations between natural history and human history have been formulated in different contexts and in relation to other disciplines. The debate about organicism in sociology at the end of the nineteenth century was about the dangers of conflating organisms with societies (Mucchielli 1998: 269–76). Prominent scholars such as Gabriel Tarde and newcomers such as the Durkheimians pointed out the risk that the use of metaphors posed in confusing the two orders. Human beings are different from the elements that compose an organism; they can belong to multiple social groups simultaneously, groups which have no defined dates of birth and death, and which neither feed nor breed (Tarde 1895, 1896). Analogy is not a scientific method and a firm social science can only consider the identities between two facts and two relations of comparison (Simiand 1897: 498). In the second half of the nineteenth century, Wilhelm Dilthey pushed for a science of the mind (*Geisteswissenschaft*) separate from that of the natural sciences. This position was representative of German historicism but was based on epistemological arguments rather than metaphysical ones. According to Dilthey, reality is not divided into two different ontological domains. However, subjective and objective points of view must be separated in order to implement knowledge (Mesure

1988: 7–12). Even during older periods, the question of nature and history formed part of a debate among scholars. When Jean Bodin (1530–96) differentiated between divine history, human history, and natural history, he included the distinction in a meditation on the decline of political eschatology and the capacity of European states to maintain peace (Koselleck 2004: 15–6).

How can EH contribute to the Anthropocene forum? Certainly not in elaborating a sophisticated concept of something beyond human societies, at a time when the divide between nature and culture is being unsettled by disciplines better equipped than history for this purpose, but rather in going back to the fundamentals, the understanding of societies through time. The processual definition of EH was central at the beginning of the field, before the thematic and interactionist approach became consensual. To introduce his monograph about Island County, Richard White (1980: 6) wrote: 'it is the history of changes wrought in the natural environment by both Indian and white occupation and use of the land, and the consequences of these changes for the people who made them'. The major contribution of EH is that it has enriched the understanding of historical change in connecting environmental changes with social and cultural changes. Three different types of articulation shape the historical thresholds of the appropriation of nature.

Social processes are limited by 'field forces', a concept coined by Emmanuel Le Roy Ladurie. The complete version of his doctoral dissertation – *The Peasants of Languedoc* – begun with this mysterious title, which unfolded in three different chapters: 'Climate Suggestions', 'Plants and Technics from the South', and 'Migrations and Temptations from the North' (Le Roy Ladurie 1966).[14] Le Roy Ladurie did not elaborate on this programme but opened up a history, inextricably biological and human, that was fed by exchanges and flows, and that included material constraints without reducing environment to a static geographical framework. In *The Writing of History*, Michel de Certeau (1988: 70–2, 106) highlighted this original approach, especially the chapter about the 'vegetal civilisation', drawing a parallel with what Michel Foucault wrote about sexuality, bodies, and diseases. These historical approaches considered materiality at once as a given and as a construction crossing the border between nature and culture. The concept of field forces proposes to historicize the physical constraints that frame social changes. Limits are both a given and a social construction, because they are inseparable from the technical and economic system used to exploit resources, and from representations that shaped the categories to describe nature and fostered environmental awareness. From Scotland's case study, Fredrik Jonsson studied how the dream of richness and nature without limit – that is cornucopia – emerged at the crossroads of political economy and financial mathematics, of debates about imperialism and conservation of local societies. When coal proposed an alternative to organic economy at the end of the eighteenth century, mineral cornucopia did not end the fear of nature being exhausted until the 1850s (Jonsson 2013, 2014).

The modes of exchange and circulation between human beings and non-human beings opens up a new field for research, since societies are no longer created exclusively by human beings. This hypothesis of hybrid collectives, originally proposed by Latour

(2004: 238) and Descola (2013a: 247–80), but with a different meaning, had not been given in-depth consideration by historians.[15] In counterpoint to the anthropocentric vision of resources in neo-classic economy that refused to include the agency of nature in the production of wealth, the Italian historian Piero Bevilacqua (1996) proposed to consider the agency and productivity of nature, rehabilitated as a full partner of human history. This agency can be caught and measured through the flux of material and energy that is metabolism. The process of history is conjointly made by the creative force of nature and the transformative force of human beings (Armiero and Barca 2004). Far from the planetary framework of geology that subsumes societies, processuality is then analysed from the diversity of places and territories where it is at work. This approach is based on the manipulation of different scales, from micro to macro (Trivellato 2011). The different types of exchanges are situated along the large set of different ways of appropriating the Earth, from symmetrical, non-naturalist ontologies to predation as forced and unequal exchange. My work about the EH of Versailles was an attempt to analyse this territory from a narrowly defined point of departure as a confrontation between three different ecologies, each interrogating the relations between human beings and nature in a different way, whether organized by technique, by mode of living, or by heritage (Quenet 2015). When the technical networks of water extended all around the castle without internal limits, the practices of living beings inside the hunting park proposed a new government of nature that was impossible to assume in the political context of the Old Regime. This organic and metabolic Versailles, full of fluxes and energy, disappeared when the king and the court left. The mineral figure of cultural heritage was born out of the death of the palace as an inhabited place. Extended to include global and imperial scales, this perspective would allow one to follow the variations of the gradients of ecological forces.

The differential game of temporalities constitutes the third analytical tool. From a linguistic point of view, the asymmetry of exchanges between human beings and non-human beings is difficult to completely erase, as human beings speak in the place of non-human beings. Anthropological hypotheses are only beginning to explore alternative paths to this anthropocentric road (Kohn 2013). Nevertheless, the process of social and environmental dynamics establishes a common time by writing history through the lens of different temporalities. Even the most asymmetric form of predation and exploitation provokes feedback from nature in society. Environmental issues and the destruction of the material basis of human communities demonstrate the ways in which human history is full of non-linguistic signs. The decline of fish is a classic example. The near extinction of salmon in California in the 1970s is one chapter in the history of the global pressure exercised upon ecosystems, a result of the discrepancy between the temporal regime of oceans and that of the exploitation of marine resources. Whereas the population of fish saw tipping points (the sudden collapse of catch when biomass was overexploited), the political schedule of environmental issues followed different temporalities. In 1976, the *Federal Fishery Conservation and Management Act,* the result of increasing green social movements (McEvoy 1986), arrived too late to have a positive effect on the salmon population. The landscape becomes more and more complex if, rather than focusing only on fish catch, the full networks of hybrid collectives are opened up. Unstable environmental dynamics, such as that of ENSO and floods, the temporal technologies of the market, the impact of the Gold Rush on rivers, the exploitation of woods for settlers and cities, and the rise of agriculture, breeding, and mills are all part of the story (Taylor 1999). A critical sociology of time based on manipulating temporal scales would help historians escape from Scylla and Charybdis, from the reductionism of the global and from the trap of the local.[16]

The environmental and climate question probes the limits of the professional organization of historians in world academia. Specialization in different subfields is inevitable, due to the necessary scientific interactions around specific objectives and the sheer fact that the immense number of publications makes it impossible for an individual to read everything, even in their own subfield. But some debates are transversal and call for a common forum; the distinction between human and natural history is one of these. Calls for interdisciplinarity are not able to tackle the theoretical foundations of disciplines, as they work at the borders of scientific knowledge, and not at the core. A firm definition of EH must be embedded in historical writing and epistemology.

Comment

Sverker Sörlin

It is rare in the recurring discussions of the point and purpose of EH to read an essay with so much sophisticated erudition, subtle verve, theoretical awareness, and generous, yet critical reflexivity as Grégory Quenet's contribution to this volume. I will side with many of Quenet's ambitions while distancing myself from some of his reformative impulses, including his request for a defining theoretical core of the discipline. If Quenet's scepticism of the ability of the field to assert itself theoretically is undisputable it is truly surprising that EH has become so attractive to so many historians, and scholars from neighbouring fields including the natural sciences. My sense is that both claims can be true at the same time. Yes, Quenet is right that there are certain fundamental dimensions of EH that weren't well thought through as the field emerged and grew.[17] Yes, there must be some reason why EH has worked out despite these shortcomings. I will try and use this comment to demonstrate why these seemingly contradictory positions can both be valid.

Quenet is probably right in assuming that with the growth and increasing centrality of the field, and its many vibrant contact zones with neighbouring subfields, such as agricultural history, forest history, water history, climate history, economic history, history of science, and history of technology, the curiosity and interest in what environmental historians are up to have intensified. With this follows some responsibility and perhaps a duty to be able to articulate a raison d'être more clearly than when the enterprise had a more colloquial nature restricted largely to the United States.

Quenet, being French and with a broad training, has his own rendering of the trajectory of EH, an 'idiosyncratic understanding' in his own words. He is in fact not much interested in the multiple dimensions of growth within EH. His concern is climate change appearing and Anthropocene debates raging, features that he thinks will turn the table of disciplinary development profoundly. This may or may not be the case; it remains hard to know how deeply the posthumanities and geo-humanities streaks will affect history, a discipline in which there tends to always be an element of caution towards prediction, what Reinhart Koselleck once called the *Postulat der Prognosenkontrolle* (cited in Müller 2014: 80). For the sake of the argument, I will assume that Quenet's critique has a point and that practitioners of EH in the past were too limited. Quenet reads our predecessors as by and large a group of well-meaning and conventional fellow travellers pleading loyalty to humanist virtues, keeping agency among the humans and steering away from any questioning of the dualist orthodoxy. History 'was built … on the bedrocks of the divide between the history of humans and the history of nature'. All that EH talk of distributed agency, of nature as an actor in history was never really serious. But the 'conceptual vagueness' could be forgiven; it was after all compensated for by magnificent empirical works that also Quenet admires.

EH, unfortunately, has positioned itself in the old, sturdy, Western, neutralist middle-ground and is mute and numb in the face of both climate change and the posthumanities. This is the main point of Quenet's critique and from it also derives his recommendation for EH research in the future. It needs to depart from its mainstream of human–nature relations and address the most central point, that of dualistic separation of humans and nature. In that regard the challenges from the posthumanities, the post-dualist anthropology (Philippe Descola, Eduardo Kohn), climate change, and Anthropocene thinking are more than stress factors, they provide the entry to the kind of agenda that will transform EH from a subfield of endless tolerance and diversity to one of theoretical rigour.

Most scholars in EH would probably agree with Quenet in some of his critique. Even after the several post-millennium internal critiques[18] it is true that EH remains a broad church, a polyphonic conversation. The level of theoretical presence and sophistication has gone up considerably, partly by the new coverage of more theoretically oriented European, Australian, and Latin American scholars. Most would think this is good, but if it isn't yet on the level of other post-1970 subfields such as gender history or science and technology studies it is also true that many environmental historians aren't extremely worried about that. Should they be?

Quenet's critique presupposes an understanding of historical sub-disciplines as ring fenced areas of deep inquiry that may, at this point in time, not be the most interesting alternative. His ideal is a group of scholars assembled around a set of ideas (theory) and a set of analytical problems (agenda). The archetypical ideal of this kind of approach is the list of twenty-three most important unsolved problems in mathematics that Hilbert presented in the beginning of the twentieth century, of which some are still unsolved (Hilbert 1902). History doesn't work that way. If a certain set of issues seems absolutely essential in the 1950s (social history, for example) another seems just as essential in the 1960s (Cliometrics) and yet another one in the 1970s (microhistory or history from below). These meta-themes are not replaced by new ones because the problems were 'solved'. History doesn't often 'solve' problems and, needless to say, EH is more like history than it is like mathematics which is why environmental historians have moved from national parks and conservation in the 1970s to urban EH, pollution, and green imperialism in the 1980s, to social constructions of nature in the 1990s, to situated, place-based studies à la Haraway and Latour in the 2000s.

The themes were temporarily exhausted (and probably their scholars as well) even if their specific questions were not fully answered. Some themes also ran across several decades (natural resources, environmental politics). Anthropocene and posthumanities are just the most recent of these meta-themes, flourishing in the 2010s, likely to be superseded, or supplemented during the 2020s or 2030s by some new meta-theme, it may come from the digital world, from medicine, from extractive industries; it will almost certainly not be anything we can foresee.

That is the most serious concern I have with Quenet's quest for theoretical rigour: that it would require so much energy if it was to become core business of EH that there wouldn't be enough space and resources for more mundane work. I don't think the risk is very high though. Because, just like history, EH will probably allow for both to happen. EH is in reality an archipelago of islands, even atolls, where specialized work is done by groups, networks, or even larger multinational clusters. There are climate historians, forming a special group. There is work on the boundary between technology and environment, in an ad hoc organization called Envirotech. There are forest historians, adding to the diversity, with their own journals and societies. This list could go on. But most aren't even organized, they do their work anyway, in agriculture, gender, environmental visual culture, disaster history, and so on. Any EH conference programme can attest to this complex hybridity, and the days of theoretical frugality or indifference are, happily, part of the past.

Quenet has, however, identified a trade-off that should be much more discussed. Is there a point when the church is becoming too broad? Is groundbreaking work sacrificed because of the innate, unruly pluralism of EH? Hard to say in any precise way, but I am inclined to say no. To begin with, it was not better when the field was small and geographically most active in the United States. That was certainly no guarantee of theoretical rigour nor was there any particular concentration on big issues, on the contrary (with individual exceptions of course). Theoretical work has come with more scholars entering the field, exposing it to influences from other fields of history (labour history, migration history, educational history, diplomatic history, history of visual culture, climate history) and even more often from entirely different disciplines including the social sciences and the natural sciences (the surge of historical work on the Anthropocene is a case in point). The volume and diversity of the community is a way of balancing the risk of inertia. The back side of growth, on the other hand, is fragmentation and lack of coherence.

Quenet's suggestions seem to me to serve as perfect assembly points for those who wish to take on long-term big issues. Writing a species history, as suggested by Dipesh Chakrabarty (2009), is such an undertaking.[19] It seems extremely valid for environmental historians, probably with significant support from, for example, biologists, archaeologists, historical ecologists, anthropologists including those physical anthropologists working on genetic analysis of the human phylogenetic tree.[20] Colonizing the Anthropocene seems like another equally inspiring EH mega-project. As Quenet observes, environmental historians have been very active in these debates, with J. R. McNeill serving on the Anthropocene Working Group of the Stratigraphic Committee. On a more general level EH has developed a growing interest in geophysical issues and the fate of 'the planetary' as an extension of the human–nature relationship, and inspired by the same strand of earth systems science that has produced the Anthropocene (Crutzen 2002; Höhler 2015; Bonneuil and Fressoz 2016). This has also meant that new hybrid relationships have been opened up with the history of science and studies of the history of the geosciences.

Some of this work may indeed lead some EH scholars to come up with new ways of understanding the human–nature divide and to question the divide. It is an exciting thought and an attractive prospect, if successful it would be truly groundbreaking. But already now we could say that we have learned enough in our hybridizing collaborations with the sciences that we can claim with some confidence that R.G. Collingwood's (1994 [1946]) definition of history as the result of human intentionality is questioned. If nature has agency, as EH has claimed for a long time now that it has (albeit mostly indirectly as the effects of previous human intervention), then the separation of acts (human) and events (nature) cannot be upheld. The posthumanities would add even more critical mass to the ontological issue of the place of the human.

I even find it plausible that Quenet might have identified some of the issues for EH work in the next decade or two. If so, it would, just as meta-themes of the past half century, ultimately reflect societal change, widely taken. We are likely to enter an era of profound post-fossil fuel transformations. Some of the changes are likely to be comprehensive enough to justify the period from say 1950 to 2050 to be called a new *Sattelzeit* ('saddle period'), on a par with the arrival of modernity in the period 1750 to 1850 (Koselleck 1988). Concepts such as the Environment, Anthropocene, the Great Acceleration, climate, posthuman, and many others have already changed their meaning considerably as compared to classical Enlightenment modernity before 1950, or didn't even exist then (Steffen et al. 2015; Warde, Robin, and Sörlin 2018). They belong in the vocabulary of such change and to theorize it and rethink history and historiography using these concepts seems in fact almost inevitable. Interestingly, they all revolve around the man–nature relationship and drawing them into the analysis will become a significant contribution to the core issue that Quenet has identified.

We may recall that Koselleck (1997: 18) himself thought of the Enlightenment as a period when history could finally be separated from nature. What Quenet argues is that, after two centuries in separation from nature it is the mission of the presently emerging *Sattelzeit* to re-join the two. This would surely be an undertaking major enough to attract many more than environmental historians, but EH should appropriately feel a duty to be part of its very core. If this work is done radically and thoroughly enough it may measure up to the challenge that Quenet also raises for 'the concept of history itself' and about the 'nature of history'. This is a grand idea and one that is very timely. He suggests a wealth of literature that is already renegotiating the place of nature in history, to which he could have added work on 'toxic bodies' by Stacy Alaimo (2010) and Nancy Langston (2010).

He outlines what is essentially the contours of a revolution in historiography on a par with shifts happening previously with the introduction of secular temporalities by Jean Bodin in the sixteenth century and early work on periodization by Giambattista Vico, taking place in Koselleck's *Sattelzeit*. Quenet makes a very important point when he argues that this could also provide a way of differentiating planetary history which has in its current incarnation become overly dominated by geological scales, partly as a result of the Anthropocene debates on periodization which in turn have sparked a historiographical discussion about the relative contributions of past and present societies to stratigraphy and given new life to old ghosts of environmental determinism.[21] It remains the task of historians to make sure that the scales on which human societies act are part of an 'integrated history', a concept so far mostly applied in science-led attempts to connect natural and human histories.[22]

Quenet rightly emphasizes the need to understand temporalities as a much more complex phenomenon than periodizations. Again, new work is appearing in a number of disciplines, from philosophy to religious studies to anthropology which suggests the emergence of an age of multi-temporalities that may also be part of the new *Sattelzeit*. It is for example possible to see the work of the earth system sciences and climatology as an act of what Helge Jordheim (2014) has called 'work of synchronisation', which is also an instance of the 'scaling' that is necessary to translate natural processes to times and places where they intersect with the human enterprise. How do genes and micro-organisms 'from below' or geophysical teleconnections 'from above' become integrated parts of the kind of complex narratives of change, and the attempts to explain change, that we call 'the writing of history'? It is truly inspiring to think of EH in this visionary light.

My small caveat in the prospect of such an exciting and even revolutionary progression of historiography would be not to recommend this to be elevated to *the* (only) 'rigorous definition of environmental history'. Why should we? I would see it as a welcome, perhaps even expected enlargement of intellectual energies drawn to new core topics. I wouldn't even be extremely nervous about whether the bulk of this work is undertaken by environmental historians or by anthropologists or sociologists or critical geographers or, indeed, other kinds of historians, although I would be surprised if EH presence isn't very high. But even in such exciting times there will be scholars who wish to study extinctions, pollution, and Arctic sea ice or tropical disease and the prairies of the American West. They would be using methods and theory that may not always be groundbreaking, and I would think that is all right, regardless of its relationship to the rigorous definition.

Quenet's argument that the siren's call for interdisciplinarity doesn't relieve EH from being precise of its own core mission is valid, but only because it is obvious. If he means that a disciplinary identity can't include interdisciplinary ambitions I disagree. The future discipline of history that he so enticingly lays out for us is, by his own example, perfectly interdisciplinary, borrowing gracefully from wherever something useful is to be found. It is inclusive, integrative, receptive, interactive, it absorbs information from much wider sources than before, including data provided by the natural sciences. The *differentia specifica* of the historiographical enterprise we should be discussing are rather to do with the capacity to manage radical pluralism of sources and methodologies, of ingenuity in interpretation. Here, I think, is where we need to keep our minds cool. The basic virtues of the profession still prevail. We are already experts in multilayered analysis and we are already dealing with 'supercomplexity' (Barnett 2000). We will expand in many directions and we will go to places where we never went before, but we will not cease to be who we are.

Inspired by creative propositions and visionary calls, just like Quenet's own, there will possibly be many who will join this enterprise. Some have already started the interdisciplinary work under the banner of 'environmental humanities', where EH looms large (Sörlin 2012; Emmett and Nye 2017). It is hard to see this taking shape under a master plan. I can't perceive EH as an enterprise where some board decides what is core business and streamlines the organization to address the most major challenges. Nor would I recommend anything like that in any subfield of history, or in the whole discipline called history. We can entice and promote, foster and stimulate, recognize and award in order to make sure that the right conditions occur for things we find important, including major theoretical issues. This may, for example, imply the mainstreaming of EH and nature-culture thinking into broader, traditional history programmes on all levels.

Response

Grégory Quenet

Sverker Sörlin has developed an elaborate argument about the two dimensions of EH, a soft theory and a diversity of practices that he opposes to my idealistic call for theory. This vision, based on a deep and long knowledge of the field, is however not exempt from an idealized description of the daily life of environmental historians, especially young ones. Sörlin reminded us in his generous and acute manner that history is a conversation between scholars; nevertheless, this conversation is becoming more and more fragmented and difficult owing to the increasing demands on our time, the reorganization of universities on business models, and the growing number of researchers. We should have more collective discussions about the professional conditions and its evolution among different countries. Besides, climate change puts increasing pressure on environmental historians, since the dialogue about past natures is no longer confined to this community but is now open to all the urgent winds of environmental challenges.

In reality, our discussion of problems and solutions is more important than deciding which organizational model is the best for EH. Needless to say, we share the same enthusiasm for thematic diversity, a broad church, and experimentation, and the same scepticism about any rigid model imposed by any board. Our divergence is mainly about how differently we interpret the seminal metaphor used by Sörlin himself: 'environmental history is in reality an archipelago of islands, even atolls'. This sentence evokes for Sörlin a set of different communities of environmental historians, happy to gather around some themes and objects, whereas only a few adventurous travellers are able to work at the theoretical margins of the sub-discipline.

Why not go further? EH is now mature enough to bring the question of nature back to the centre of history. When the debate is about history itself, all environmental historians and historians are affected. The point is not about discipline and border police but is fundamental: Why is knowledge of change over time so essential when we are confronted with environmental issues? The answer is anything but obvious and the question subsumes that of analysing past environments or that of time as a social structure.

Climate change has set in movement the relations between past, present, and future that were blocked in the last few decades by the end of ideological promises about the future and the inflation of memory and commemoration. But, time is now disoriented and its heuristic value contested. For some scholars, the distinction between past and future has no more sense because of the loops of climate (Latour 2017). For other scholars, a hiatus able to break the continuity of time is a serious hypothesis (Chakrabarty 2009). It's where islands and atolls can help us: more than a trope, it's a filigree twisted and plaited into the design of EH and even history.

If EH as a dedicated field began in the United States, it was partly due to the New World being a laboratory of environmental degradations, and of national identities shaped by this intensive human action on nature, both practically and culturally (Nash 1967). Richard Grove (1995) established later that the historical matrix of this approach was situated in the Atlantic and the Indian Ocean islands under the impact of European expansion since the end of the fifteenth century. This spatio-temporal model of human beings into the Garden of Eden influenced the most famous EH monographs. As a consequence, EH is full of encounter narratives, which diverged from the Braudelian spatio-temporal model based on sedimentation and the coexistence of different times. This narrative model of encounters perpetuated the acheiropoïetic temptation of EH without the intervention of humans, despite all the conceptual and empirical critiques of that idea. In fact, the deconstruction of the concepts of wilderness and nature didn't cancel the idea of something that human beings didn't create (Cronon 1995). There is always a garden and a beginning somewhere. Climate change amplified this schema at a planetary level when the Anthropocene debate focused on the opening date of this new geological period. It brought back into history the 'idol of chronology' mocked by François Simiand (1960 [1903]) more than a century ago.

The narrative model of the archipelago of islands had both positive and negative consequences. On the one hand, I agree with Sörlin that, thanks to it, the field included a set of brilliant case studies exploring the relations between human beings and their environment on a dedicated territory. On the other hand, the model contributed to the fragmentation of EH and its difficulties in offering general perspectives, such as national history revisited or global studies that would recognize the complexity of societies. Islands and atolls once again, but 'no island is an island'.[23] The metaphor also offers a way to escape from the trap of fragmentation, and to define the theoretical core of the discipline, provided that the centre of gravity of the model is moved from space to time.

Two different options exist for this reconnection. The first is to make visible the temporal model that informs sources and archives about place-based studies and to reconnect it with the history of history. Environmental historians didn't refer that much to the work of the famous anthropologist Marshall Sahlins, and more precisely missed his great book *Islands of History* (1985).[24] Certainly, Sahlins didn't consider the natural environment of Hawaii, Tahiti of Fiji, but he established that there is no experience of islands and encounters without culture being altered in action, system and event, structure and history. The core of EH should be to propose a new paradigm for historical changes, from processes that are not only human-made but result from exchanges between all beings and even between human beings and inanimate forms.

The second option is to re-examine how the concept of history was inhabited by tensions since the conquest of the New World. Some minority voices were conscious of its disastrous impact, on non-European societies, including their environment. Jean de Léry and Michel de Montaigne were at the origins of the ecological pessimism of Claude Lévi-Strauss; Denis Diderot wrote strong pages in the *Histoire des deux Indes* by Raynal and gave a voice to the old Tahitian in the *Supplément au voyage de Bougainville*; in Cuba and Latin America, Alexander von Humboldt associated the natural history of humans and the human history of nature. Certainly, all centuries didn't manifest the same degree of anxiety, and the eighteenth century was more conscious of its own fragility than the nineteenth century (see Lilti 2011).

Having said that, I agree with Sörlin's argument about seemingly contradictory positions that can be both valid about what EH is and should be. On one side, the field is diverse, vibrant, open to everybody interested in environmental issues. On another side, all these voices should be part of the general and theoretical debate on history and the social sciences, where very different options exist, far from any irenic vision of science. How can environmental historians contribute to this debate? Sörlin is sceptical because he refers to the endless and exhausting debate about the social construction of nature. The theoretical turn I suggested, however, is not related to cosmologies beyond the idea of nature but based on the concept of history, considered as the weak point of the climate change debate.

The ontological critique of the Western idea of nature was very fruitful for opening new conceptual perspectives, and as an alternative to an exhaustive appropriation of the Earth. Nevertheless, this approach was less relevant to assessing the historical and geographical diversity among naturalism, and the complexity of environmental and social changes. It offers only a few alternatives for Westerners other than the utopia of becoming Amerindian or erasing modernity. Moreover, the call for new cosmologies contrasts with the global expansion of dualism, especially today when the new leaders of the South – China, India, Brazil, and tomorrow some African countries – are more and more fuelling the Anthropocene. If it's partly too late – and that's certainly unfortunate – to have a common world between human and non-human beings, is it possible to have a common time? The duty of EH should be to elaborate history both as a theoretical and practical tool able to analyse and discriminate between the diversity of entanglements between human and non-human beings through time. This programme is not limited to a subfield of history, but aims to re-materialize history itself and pluralize natural history at the risk of the dissolution of EH into history.

Notes

1. The birth of environmental history is usually identified with a special issue of the *Pacific Historical Review* published in 1972 (Nash 1972). The term is, in fact, a bit older (Nash 1970).

2. In 1990, for the first time, a leading historical review devoted a special issue to environmental history (*Journal of American History*, 76, 4). In 1995, Alfred Crosby described environmental history as a 'sect' with scholars who 'write for and talk to each other exclusively' (Crosby 1995: 1188). The 1990s also marked the beginning of the dialogue between US environmental history and Indian subaltern studies dedicated to environmental issues (Guha 1989; Sutter 2009).

3. In this volume, Ewa Domanska (Chapter 12) examines these questions from outside of environmental history: post-anthropocentric humanities call for posthumanist history that is a shift from classic environmental history.

4. Many references would be necessary to make this point. I refer here, as in other parts of this chapter, to the results of my intellectual history of environmental history, that contains the basic bibliography (Quenet 2014).

5. The mapping of new territories of environmental history is at the core of the classical paper by John McNeill (2003).

6. Alice Ingold (2011) elaborated this point, arguing that environmental history seems to ignore a large part of the tradition of the social sciences.

7. It is only recently that environmental history started to look back to its origins and its own history without avoiding the corporate history of its precursors. In 2008 the 'ASEH Founders – Oral histories' (http://www.aseh.net/about-aseh/history-of-aseh) began, along with a series of interviews published by *Environmental History*. These projects focused on the US side of environmental history.

8. In the US *Journal of Environmental History*, thirty-eight papers referred to Bruno Latour up until the first issue of 2017, twenty-nine of which appeared since 2005, but none referred to Descola's individual work. The English translation of Descola's magnum opus will certainly increase the use of his ideas by environmental historians (Descola 2013a).

9. The definition of environment as a second nature, or as nature as modified by human beings by distinction with nature per se, is not relevant from Descola's and Latour's perspective. Artificialization does not account for the philosophical problem of object and subject (Latour 2015: 92–3).

10. So many works should be quoted to illustrate this point, that I will only quote one firm and synthetic analysis by Castonguay (2006).

11. 'The environment is taken for what is not universal but at a particular point in history' (Opie 1983: 15). The cultural turn of environmental history started with the controversy about wilderness (Cronon 1995).

12. This scepticism is largely shared by the participants of the workshop organized by the University of South Carolina and the Rachel Carson Center (Emmett and Lekan 2016: 66–7, 89–90, 92–4, 107, 111).

13. Exposition 'Reset Modernity!', curated by Bruno Latour, Martin Guinard-Terrin, Christophe Leclercq, and Donato Ricci, ZKM (Zentrum für Kunst und Medientechnologie), Karlsruhe, 17 April–21 August 2016.

14. This first part was nearly forgotten when the popular paperback version fell out of circulation (Le Roy Ladurie 1969) along with the English translation (Le Roy Ladurie 1974). Anglophone readers had access to the climate chapter – thanks to Le Roy Ladurie 1971 – but in a context isolated from its initial framework.

15. For Latour, a collective is a procedure for collecting humans and non-humans, whereas for Descola it is an existing social form to be studied by anthropologists.

16. In that sense, this hypothesis is different from the total history of local places developed by William Cronon, confronted both by the difficulties of rising in generality and of limiting an analysis which is, by definition, without any limit (Cronon 1992b).

17. In an essay co-authored with Paul Warde I made a similar claim about a decade ago, see Sörlin and Warde (2007).

18. Of these Quenet mentions Steinberg (2002), Stroud (2003), Sörlin, and Warde (2007), but one could just as well add others, for example Asdal (2003) (discussing mostly Haraway and Latour).

19. Among many counter voices to species history we find Emmett and Lekan (2016) and Cooper (2014).

20. Like the Max Planck Institute in Leipzig, where such work has been conducted and changed the way we perceive human evolution and diffusion over hundreds of thousands of years.

21. *The Anthropocene Review* has carried a range of articles on these themes, for example, Lowenthal (2015) and Paglia (2015). See also Pálsson et al. (2013); Swanson (2016); and Pálsson and Swanson (2016).

22. The role of natural scientists for the debates on temporalities is underarticulated by Quenet, and several contributions in recent years have argued that there is an 'integrated history' possible that link nature and humans and with capacity to make predictions, see Cornell et al. (2010) and Costanza et al. (2012).

23. The sentence 'no island is an island' refers to Carlo Ginzburg (2000) revisiting English (literary) history.

24. I found no reference to *Islands of History* neither in the journal *Environmental History* nor in *Environment and History*, despite the violent dispute with Gananath Obeyesekere that made this book famous.

References

Alaimo, S. (2010), *Bodily Natures: Science, Environment, and the Material Self*, Bloomington, IN: University of Indiana Press.

Anker, P. (2001), *Imperial Ecology: Environmental Order in the British Empire, 1895–1945*, Cambridge, MA: Harvard University Press.

Armiero, M. and Barca, S. (2004), *Dell'ambiente. Una introduzione*, Rome: Carocci.

Asdal, K. (2003), 'The Problematic Nature of Nature: The Post-constructivist Challenge to Environmental History', *History and Theory*, 42: 60–74.

Barnett, R. (2000), *Realizing the University in an Age of Supercomplexity*, Milton Keynes: Open University Press.

Bayly, C. A. (2004), *The Birth of the Modern World, 1780–1914*, Oxford: Blackwell.

Beck, C. and Delort, R., eds (1991), *Pour une histoire de l'environnement*, Paris: CNRS Editions.

Bertrand, R. (2012), 'La tentation du monde: "histoire globale" et "récit symétrique"', in C. Granger (ed.), *À quoi pensent les historiens? Faire de l'histoire au XXIe siècle*, 181–96, Paris: Autrement.

Bevilacqua, P. (1996), *Tra nature e storia*, Rome: Donzelli.

Bonneuil, C. (2000), 'Development as Experiment: Science and State Building in Late Colonial and Postcolonial Africa, 1930–1970', *Osiris*, 15: 258–81.

Bonneuil, C. and Fressoz, J.-B. (2016), *The Shock of the Anthropocene: The Earth, History and Us*, London: Verso.

Braudel, F. (1981), *Civilization and Capitalism*, vol. 1, transl. S. Reynolds, London: Collins.

Cabral, D. de C. (2014), *Na presença da floresta. Mata Atlântica e história colonial*, Rio de Janeiro: Garamond/FAPERJ.

Castonguay, S. (2006), 'Les rapports sociaux à la nature: l'histoire environnementale de l'Amérique française', *Revue d'histoire de l'Amérique française*, 60 (1–2): 5–9.

de Certeau, M. (1988), *The Writing of History*, transl. T. Conley, New York: Columbia University Press.

Chakrabarty, D. (2009), 'The Climate of History: Four Theses', *Critical Inquiry*, 35: 197–222.

Chakrabarty, D. (2012), 'Postcolonial Studies and the Challenge of Climate Change', *New Literary History*, 43: 1–18.

Chakrabarty, D. (2014), 'Climate and Capital: On Conjoined Histories', *Critical Inquiry*, 41 (1): 1–23.

Chakrabarty, D. (2016a), 'The Human Significance of the Anthropocene', in B. Latour (ed.), *Reset Modernity!*, 189–99, Cambridge, MA: MIT Press.

Chakrabarty, D. (2016b), 'Whose Anthropocene? A response', in R. Emmett and T. Lekan (eds), 'Whose Anthropocene? Revisiting Dipesh Chakrabarty's Four theses', 103–15, *RCC Perspectives, Transformations in Environment and Society*, 2.

Chartier, R. (2006), 'La conscience de la globalité (commentaires)', *Annales. Histoire, Sciences Sociales*, 56 (1): 119–23.

Christian, D. (2011), *Maps of Time: An Introduction to Big History*, Berkeley: University of California Press.

Collingwood, R. G. (1994), *The Idea of History*, revised edn, with an introduction by J. van der Dussen, Oxford: Oxford University Press.

Cooper, T. (2014), 'Why we Still Need a Human History in the Anthropocene' (blogpost 6 February), History, Environment, Future: critical perspectives on environmental history, available online: https://blogs.exeter.ac.uk/historyenvironmentfuture/ (accessed 5 August 2017).

Cornell, S., Costanza, R., Sörlin, S. and van der Leeuw, S. E. (2010), 'Developing a systematic "science of the past" to create our future', *Global Environmental Change*, 20 (3): 423–5.

Costanza, R., van der Leeuw, S., Hibbard, K., Aulenbach, S., Brewer, S., Burek, M., Cornell, S., Crumley, C., Dearing, J., Folke, C., Graumlich, L., Hegmon, M., Heckbert, S., Jackson, S. T., Kubiszewski, I., Scarborough, V., Sinclair, P., Sörlin, S. and Steffen, W. 2012. 'Developing an Integrated History and future of People on Earth (IHOPE)', *Current Opinion in Environmental Sustainability*, 4 (1): 106–14.

Cronon, W. (1987), 'Revisiting the Vanishing Frontier: The Legacy of Frederick Jackson Turner', *The Western Historical Quarterly*, 18 (2): 157–76.

Cronon, W. (1992a), 'A Place for Stories: Nature, History, and Narrative', *Journal of American History*, 78 (4): 1347–76.

Cronon, W. (1992b), 'Kennecott Journey: The Paths Out of Town', in G. Miles, J. Gitlin and W. Cronon (eds), *Under an Open Sky: Rethinking America's Western Past*, 28–51, New York: W. W. Norton & Co.

Cronon, W. (1995), 'The Trouble with Wilderness: Or, Getting Back to the Wrong Nature', in W. Cronon (ed.), *Uncommon Ground: Toward Reinventing Nature*, 69–90, New York: Norton.

Crosby, A. (1986), *Ecological Imperialism: The Biological Expansion of Europe, 900–1900*, New York: Cambridge University Press.

Crosby, A. (1995), 'The Past and Present of Environmental History', *American Historical Review*, 100 (4): 1177–88.

Crutzen, P. J. (2002), 'Geology of Mankind', *Nature*, 415: 23.

Davis, M. (2001), *Late Victorian Holocausts: El Niño Famines and the Making of the Third World*, London: Verso.

Delort, R. and Walter, F. (2001), *Histoire de l'environnement européen*, Paris: PUF.

Descola, P. (2013a), *Beyond nature and culture*, transl. J. Lloyd, Chicago: University of Chicago Press.

Descola, P. (2013b), *The Ecology of Others*, transl. G. Godbout and B. P. Luley, Chicago: Prickly Paradigm Press.

Drayton, R. (2000), *Nature's Government: Science, Imperial Britain, and the 'Improvement' of the World*, New Haven: Yale University Press.

Emmett, R. and Lekan, T., eds (2016), 'Whose Anthropocene? Revisiting Dipesh Chakrabarty's Four theses', *RCC Perspectives, Transformations in Environment and Society*, 2.

Emmett, R. S. and Nye, D. E. (2017), *The Environmental Humanities: A Critical Introduction*, Cambridge, MA: MIT Press.

Gadgil, M. and Guha, R. (1992), *This Fissured Land: An Ecological History of India*, Berkeley: University of California Press.

Ginzburg, C. (2000), *No Island is an Island*, New York: Columbia University Press.

Godelier, M. (1977), *Perspectives in Marxist Anthropology*, transl. R. Brain, Cambridge, Cambridge University Press.

Godelier, M. (1988), *The Mental and the Material: Thought, Economy, and Society*, transl. M. Thom, London: Verso.

Grove, R. (1995), *Green Imperialism. Colonial Expansion, Tropical Island Edens and the Origins of Environmentalism, 1600–1860*, New York: Cambridge University Press.

Grove, R. (1998), 'Global Impact of the 1789–93 El Niño', *Nature*, 393: 318–9.

Grove, R. (2001), 'Environmental History', in P. Burke (ed.), *New Perspectives on Historical Writing*, 2nd edn, 261–82, Pennsylvania: The Pennsylvania State University Press.

Grove, R. (2002), 'El Niño Chronology and the History of Socio-Economic and Agrarian Crisis in South and Southeast Asia, 1250–1900', in Y. P. Abrol, S. Sangwan and M. K. Tiwari (eds), *Land Use – Historical Perspectives: Focus on Indo-Gangetic Plains*, 147–57, New Delhi: Allied Publishers.

Guha, R. (1989), 'Radical American Environmentalism and Wilderness Preservation: A Third World Critique', *Environmental Ethics*, 11: 71–83.

Guldi, J. and Armitage, D. (2014), *The History Manifesto*, Cambridge: Cambridge University Press.

Hartog, F. (2014), 'L'apocalypse, une philosophie de l'histoire', *Esprit*, 6: 22–32.

Heinz, D. and Latour, B. (2012), 'Bücherschau: Wiedergelesen II', in H. Bredekamp (ed.), *Bildwelten des Wissens, Vol. 9,1: Präparate*, 99–102, Berlin: Akademie Verlag.

Heise, U. (2008), *Sense of Place and Sense of Planet: The Environmental Imagination of the Global*, New York: Oxford University Press.

Hilbert, D. (1902), 'Mathematical Problems', *Bulletin of the American Mathematical Society*, 8 (10): 437–79.

Höhler, S. (2015), *Spaceship Earth in the Environmental Age, 1960–1990*, London: Chatto & Windus.

Hornborg A. (2010), 'Toward a Truly Global Environmental History: A Review Article', *Review: Fernand Braudel Center*, 33 (4): 295–323.

Hughes, D. J. (1984), 'Introduction', *Environmental Review*, 8 (3): 213.

Hughes, D. J. (2001), 'Global Dimensions of Environmental History', *The Pacific Historical Review*, 70 (1): 91–101.

Hughes, D. J. (2006), *What is Environmental History?* Cambridge: Polity Press.

Ingold, A. (2011), 'Écrire la nature: de l'histoire sociale à la question environnementale?', *Annales: Histoire, Sciences Sociales*, 66 (1): 1–29.

Jonsson, F. A. (2013), *Enlightenment's Frontier: The Scottish Highlands and the Origins of Environmentalism*, New Haven: Yale University Press.

Jonsson, F. A. (2014), 'The Origins of Cornucopianism: a Preliminary Genealogy', *Critical Historical Studies*, 1 (1): 151–68.

Jordheim, H. (2014), 'Introduction: Multiple Times and the Work of Synchronization', *History and Theory*, 53 (4): 498–518.

Kohn, E. (2013), *How Forests Think: Toward an Anthropology Beyond the Human*, Berkeley: University of California Press.

Koselleck, R. (1988), *Critique and Crisis: Enlightenment and the Pathogenesis of Modern Society*, Cambridge, MA: MIT Press.

Koselleck, R. (1997), 'The Temporalization of Concepts', *Finnish Yearbook of Political Thought*, 1: 16–24.

Koselleck, R. (2004), *Futures Past: On the Semantics of Historical Time*, transl. K. Tribe, New York: Columbia University Press.

Langston, N. (2010), *Toxic Bodies: Hormone Disruptors and the Legacy of DES*, New Haven, CN: Yale University Press.

Latour, B. (2004), *Politics of Nature: How to Bring the Sciences to Democracy*, transl. C. Porter, Cambridge, MA: Harvard University Press.

Latour, B. (2015), *Face à Gaïa: Huit conférences sur le nouveau régime climatique*, Paris: La Découverte.

Latour, B., ed. (2016), *Reset Modernity! Field Book*, Karlsruhe: ZKM.

Latour, B. (2017), *Facing Gaia: Eight Lectures on the New Climatic Regime*, Cambridge: Polity Press.

Le Roy Ladurie, E. (1966), *Les paysans de Languedoc*, Paris: SEVPEN.

Le Roy Ladurie, E. (1969), *Les paysans de Languedoc*, Paris: Flammarion.

Le Roy Ladurie, E. (1971), *Times of Feast, Times of Famine: A History of climate since the Year 1000*, transl. B. Bray, New York, Doubleday.

Le Roy Ladurie, E. (1974), *The Peasants of Languedoc*, transl. J. Day, Urbana: University of Illinois Press.

Lilti, A. (2011), '"Et la civilisation deviendra générale": L'Europe de Volney ou l'orientalisme à l'épreuve de la Révolution', *La Révolution française* 4, available online: http://lrf.revues.org/290 (accessed 4 November 2017).

Livingstone, D. N. and Withers, C. W.J., eds (2011), *Geographies of Nineteenth-Century Science*, Chicago: University of Chicago Press.

Lowenthal, D. (2015), 'Origins of Anthropocene Awareness', *Anthropocene Review*, 2 (2): 102–7.

McEvoy, A. (1986), *The Fisherman's Problem: Ecology and Law in the California Fisheries, 1850–1980*, New York: Cambridge University Press.

McNeill, J. R. (2003), 'Observations on the Nature and Culture of Environmental History', *History and Theory*, 42: 5–43

McNeill, J. R. (2010), *Mosquito Empires: Ecology and War in the Greater Caribbean, 1620–1914*, Cambridge: Cambridge University Press.

McNeill, J. R. and Mauldin, E. S. (2015), 'Global Environmental History: An Introduction', in J. R. McNeill and E. S. Mauldin (eds), *A Companion to Global Environmental History*, xvi–xviii, Oxford and Chichester: Wiley Blackwell.

Mesure, S. (1988), 'Présentation', in W. Dilthey, *L'édification du monde historique dans les sciences de l'esprit*, transl. S. Mesure, 5–28, Paris: Éditions du Cerf.

Moreno, D. (1990), *Dal documento al terreno: Storia e archeologia dei sistemi agro-silvo-pastorali*, Bologne: Il Mulino.

Mucchielli, L. (1998), *La découverte du social: Naissance de la sociologie en France*, Paris: La Découverte.

Müller, J.-W. (2014), 'On Conceptual History', in D. M. McMahon and S. Moyn (eds), *Rethinking Modern Intellectual History*, 74–93, Oxford: Oxford University Press.

Nash, R. (1967), *Wilderness and the American Mind*, New Haven: Yale University Press.

Nash, R. (1970), 'The State of Environmental History', in H. J. Bass (ed.), *The State of American History*, 249–60, Chicago: Quadrangle Books.

Nash, R. (1972), 'American Environmental History: A New Teaching Frontier', *Pacific Historical Review*, 41 (3): 362–72.

Opie, J. (1983), 'Environmental History: Pitfalls and Opportunities', *Environmental Review*, 7 (1): 8–16.

Pádua, J. A. (2002), *Um Sopro de Destruição: Pensamento político e crítica ambiental no Brasil escravista (1786–1888)*, Rio de Janeiro: Jorge Zahar.

Paglia, E. (2015), 'Not a Proper Crisis', *The Anthropocene Review*, 2 (3): 247–61.

Pálsson, G., Szerszynski, B., Sörlin, S., Marks, J., Avril, B., Crumley, C., Hackmann, H., Holm, P., Ingram, J., Kirman, A., Pardo Buendía, M., and Weehuizen, R. (2013), 'Reconceptualizing the "Anthropos" in the Anthropocene: Integrating the Social Sciences and Humanities in Global Environmental Change Research', *Environmental Science and Policy*, 28: 3–13.

Pálsson, G. and Swanson, H. (2016), 'Down to Earth: Geosocialities and Geopolitics', *Environmental Humanities*, 8 (2): 149–71.

Pomeranz, K. (2000), *The Great Divergence: China, Europe and the Making of the Modern World Economy*, Princeton: Princeton University Press.

Powell, R. and Wilson, R. (2015), 'Conference Report. What Futures for the Pillar of Geography? A Report on the 16th International Conference of Historical Geographers, London', *Historical Geography*, 43: 1–4.

Quenet, G. (2014), *Qu'est-ce que l'histoire environnementale?* Seyssel: Champ Vallon.

Quenet, G. (2015), *Versailles, histoire naturelle*, Paris: La Découverte.

Quenet, G. (2017), 'L'Anthropocène et le temps des historiens', *Annales. Histoire, sciences sociales*, 72 (2): 267–99.

Radkau, J. (2014), *The Age of Ecology: A Global History*, Cambridge: Polity Press.

Sahlins, M. (1985), *Islands of History. Ethnology and History*, Chicago: The University of Chicago Press.

Simiand, F. (1897), 'L'année sociologique française 1896', *Revue de métaphysique et de morale*, 5: 489–519.

Simiand, F. (1960), 'Méthode historique et science sociale', *Annales. Économies, Sociétés, Civilisations*, 15: 83–119.

Smail, D. L. and Shyrock, A. (2013), 'History and the Pre', *American Historical Review*, 118: 709–37.

Sörlin, S. (2012), 'Environmental Humanities: Why Should Biologists Interested in the Environment Take the Humanities Seriously?', *BioScience*, 62 (9): 788–9.

Sörlin, S. and Warde, P. (2007), 'The Problem of the Problem of Environmental History: A Re-reading of the Field', *Environmental History*, 12 (1): 107–30.

Steffen, W., Broadgate, W., Deutsch, L., Gaffney, O. and Ludwig, C. (2015), 'The Trajectory of the Anthropocene: The Great Acceleration', *The Anthropocene Review*, 2: 81–98.

Steffen, W., Crutzen, P. and McNeill, J. R. (2007), 'The Anthropocene: Are Humans Now Overwhelming the Great Forces of Nature?', *Ambio*, 36 (8): 614–21.

Steinberg, T. (2002), 'Down to Earth: Nature, Agency, and Power in History', *American Historical Review*, 107 (3): 798–820.

Stroud, E. (2003), 'Does Nature Always Matter? Following Dirt Through History', *History and Theory*, 42 (4): 75–81.

Sutter, P. (2009), 'When Environmental Traditions Collide: Ramachandra Guha's *The Unquiet Woods* and U.S. Environmental History', *Environmental History*, 14 (2): 543–50.

Swanson, H. (2016), 'Anthropocene as Political Geology: Current Debates over How to Tell Time', *Science as Culture*, 25 (1): 157–63.

Tarde, G. (1895), 'Le transformisme social', *Revue philosophique de la France et de l'étranger*, 40: 26–40.

Tarde, G. (1896), 'L'idée de l'organisme social', *Revue philosophique de la France et de l'étranger*, 41: 637–46.

Taylor, J. III (1999), *Making Salmon: An Environmental History of the Northwest Fisheries Crisis*, Seattle: University of Washington Press.

Trivellato, F. (2011), 'Is there a Future for Italian Microhistory in the Age of Global History?', *California Italian Studies* 2 (1), available online: http://escholarship.org/uc/item/0z94n9hq (accessed 20 August 2017).

Urteaga, L. (1987), *La tierra esquilmada*. Barcelona: Serbal, CSIC.

Vincent, J. (2012), 'Le climat de l'histoire et l'histoire du climat: à propos des 'quatre thèses' de Dipesh Chakrabarty', *RdL – La revue des livres*, 3: 28–35.

Walter, F. (1994), 'L'historien et l'environnement', *Nature, Science, Sociétés*, 2 (1): 31–9.

Warde, P.; Robin, L. and Sörlin, S. (2018), *The Environment. A History of the Idea*, Baltimore, MD: Johns Hopkins University Press.

Weiner, D. R. (2005), 'A Death-defying Attempt to Articulate a Coherent Definition of Environmental History', *Environmental History*, 10 (3): 404–20.

White, R. (1980), *Land Use, Environment and Social Change: The Shaping of Island County*, Washington: Seattle, University of Washington Press.

Williams, M. (1994), 'The Relations of Environmental History and Historical Geography', *Journal of Historical Geography*, 20 (1): 3–21.

Worster, D. (1982), 'World Without Borders: The Internationalizing of Environmental History', *Environmental Review*, 6 (2): 8–13.

Worster, D. (1988), 'Doing Environmental History', in D. Worster (ed.), *The Ends of the Earth: Perspectives on Modern Environmental History*, 289–307, Cambridge: Cambridge University Press.

CHAPTER 4
GENDER HISTORY
Laura Lee Downs

Is there any place more suited to an article on gender history than a volume whose focus is debates in history? For the fields of women's and gender history have been shaped through an evolving series of debates since these two deeply connected fields first began to emerge in the wake of 1968 social movements: Debates about the personal and political significance of identity, debates over what the term 'identity' actually means, debates about poststructuralist versus more 'traditional' approaches. While constant debate may not seem like the most efficient way to build a new field of scholarship, it is a sign of the intellectual and democratic vitality that characterizes scholarly exchange in a field whose analytic tools are still being developed and refined.

The same may be said of the history of sexuality, which emerged just a few years later, also in the company of a social movement. The penchant for debate placed both gender history and the history of sexuality at the cutting edge of theoretical developments in the historical discipline more broadly, especially during the 1980s and 1990s. For the debates that traversed the entire discipline over poststructuralist and postmodern understandings of identity posed themselves with particular acuity in the study of women, gender, and sexuality, where the often tense relationship between identities, politics, and scholarship formed an essential layer in the foundation on which these fields were built.

The study of gender and sexuality is thus bound up, historically, with the emergence of second-wave feminism and of sexual liberation movements in the postwar era. These activist origins produced one of the key elements that has marked the fields of gender and sexuality ever since: their highly productive proximity to social and political movements. Moreover, the political urgency of the theoretical tasks activists set for themselves has encouraged forms of interdisciplinary encounter from the very start; encounters that continue to mark both fields in distinctive ways.

But pursuing political aims through academic engagement has also posed specific challenges, especially with regard to the scientific construction of one's object of study and the need to establish the kind of analytic distance that good scholarship demands. When the object of scholarly investigation is also connected in some way to one's politics and/or identity, both of these tasks become immensely more complicated, as the scholar must be aware of and resist the temptation to identify overly closely with her or his object of study. The opportunities and challenges that have been posed by the connection between politics and scholarship in the history of gender and sexuality is something that distinguishes them both from other fields in the discipline such as diplomatic history or the history of ideas. As such, this connection and its evolution over the past fifty years will be an important theme in this chapter, winding through it like a red thread.

Gender history: A very short introduction

Gender history does not define a field, per se. Unlike women's history, which focuses on women as a social group, gender history focuses on the shifting constellation of relations between men and women, and on the ways that ideas about masculinity and femininity have changed over time. But gender as an analytic tool does not define a single approach or method of doing history. It is rather a perspective that focuses on the ways that relationships between women and men have been constructed through language (discourses, stereotypes, etc.) but also through the social practices within which those discourses are embedded and take living shape.

The term 'gender' itself is based on the idea that there are both biological and social components to the sexual identities of women and men, and that much of how we understand what it means to be a woman or a man is shaped by particular cultural, legal, and social practices that determine the behaviours, hopes, and expectations of individual women and men. By the same token, the frontiers that shape and reshape the categories 'women' and 'men' as social and political entities are similarly understood to be grounded in social and discursive practices, rather than in the immutable dictates of nature/biology. As such, these gendered roles, categories, and identities are open to change, and indeed, can be seen to have evolved in multiple directions across time and in different societies.

But of course, women and men do not form unified categories. They are, rather, divided by such things as social class, religion, and race/ethnicity (to name but a few). Good scholarship in gender history is therefore grounded in the practice of intersectionality, that is, in the idea that one must understand women and men as individuals who stand at the confluence of multiple social forces. Their identities are therefore shaped in variable ways by the forces of class difference, religious conviction, understandings of race or ethnicity as well as by their social positioning as women or men.

Gender history emerged rather quickly from the field of women's history, which was itself the product of second-wave feminist militancy (1960s to 1970s) as it expressed itself in the academy. Central to this approach was the distinction that women's historians were already starting to draw between biological sex, understood as the material and unchanging ground of one's identity, and the infinitely malleable carapace of gender – a socially constructed series of behaviours that code one as male or female, but that vary across time and space in such a way as to reveal their constructed nature. Women (and men, for that matter) were thus made and not born, and much productive research proceeded on the ground of the sex/gender distinction, as feminist historians smoked out the various ways that gender, understood as a socially constructed system of difference, had operated to shape social relations and understandings of self in societies past.

The notion that individual identities as well as the social categories within which they are embedded could be social constructions rather than the inevitable outcome of hard and fast biological 'realities' was to have a great future in the fields of women's and gender history. Soon, scholars of both sexes began working on masculinity as well, exploring the various ways that manhood has been understood and enacted over time and the consequences this has had for social organization. Think of the different ways that men's military service has been organized and understood in relation to the state, or the various ways that fatherhood has been understood in relation to both family and society.

The sex/gender distinction and the concept of social construction it gave rise to also inspired scholars who were working on histories of homosexuality and of sexuality more broadly. Beginning at the turn of 1990s, with the publication of such key works as David Halperin's *One Hundred Years of Homosexuality* (1990), or Judith Butler's *Gender Trouble* (1990), the history of sexuality began to take off as a field in its own right. A number of scholars (including Halperin) had already been working on the history of sexuality well before this take-off, often in connection with the social movements around gay liberation that erupted in the late 1960s (Boswell 1980; Vance 1984). These scholars followed a parallel trajectory to that being followed by feminist scholars in the wake of second-wave feminism.

Interestingly enough, the turn of the 1990s take-off in the study of sexuality was based on an important critique of the very sex/gender distinction that had allowed the field to blossom in the first place. This critique was voiced by a number of scholars who began to question the idea that biology and bodies are as fixed and immobile a ground for sexual identity as the earlier formulations of this distinction would have it. These critiques were framed in different ways depending on the critic's disciplinary perspective – history, anthropology, biology, psychoanalysis (Alexander 1984; Fausto-Sterling 2000). But what they all shared was a radical calling into question of the biological determinism implicit in previous formulations of the sex/gender distinction.

Successive waves of critical reflection, conducted in greater or lesser proximity to political movements, have thus shaped these fields since their inception, and continue to shape them in less obvious ways as they make their way through the academy. The text that follows traces a few of these debates while always keeping to the fore the central question of what it is that gender, as a way of analysing institutions and social relations, can offer. For like any pertinent analytic perspective, gender offers a way of catching things you might not otherwise see.

So what does a gender approach offer to historical research and writing, you may ask?

The answer is, many things, starting with an awareness of what the world looks like from a perspective other than that of dominant white males. But the reward goes well beyond this crucial harvest of new knowledge, as a quick glance at Leonore Davidoff and Catherine Hall's classic study of the formation of the middle classes during England's industrial revolution, *Family Fortunes* (1987), reveals. Conceived at a time when the concept of gender was beginning to take shape as an analytic tool of great power, *Family Fortunes* takes as its point of departure the crucial insight that class formation is an inherently gendered process. Hall and Davidoff were writing in dialogue with other feminist historians who in the 1980s were pushing against the limits of a women's history – or 'herstory' – focused solely on the project of restoring women to history. By placing the focus on women *and* men, masculinity and femininity and the way these two categories are mutually constructed, scholars such as Caroline Bynum (1987), Christiane Klapisch-Zuber (1990), and Jacqueline Jones (1985) (to name but a few) were, together, forging the idea of gender as a *relational* concept. The force of this idea would find powerful expression in Hall and Davidoff's book.

But Hall and Davidoff were also writing in dialogue with Marxist historians and sociologists who were concerned with understanding the social processes through which classes are made. As the opening lines of the book concisely announce: '*Family Fortunes* is a book about the ideologies, institutions and practices of the English middle class from the end of the eighteenth to the middle of the nineteenth centuries. It concerns both men and women [and] the principal argument rests on the assumption that gender and class always operate together, that consciousness of class always takes a gendered form' (Davidoff and Hall 1987: 13). The resonance with E. P. Thompson's seminal *Making of the English Working Class* (1963) is no accident; on the contrary, it signals *Family Fortunes'* grounding in the 'new' social history, ushered in twenty years earlier by Thompson's neo-Marxist approach, with its strong emphasis on the role of culture in working-class formation.

It is worth underscoring the depth of Hall and Davidoff's ambition, which looked beyond the project of restoring women to history and sought instead to transform through the lens of gender analysis the very tools with which historians were working at the time. Chief among these was that large social process known as class formation, which was one of the fundamental *problématiques* underpinning the new social history: 'We wanted not just to put the women back into a history from which they had been left out, but to rewrite that history so that proper recognition would be given to the ways in which gender, as a key axis of power in society, provides a crucial understanding of how any society is structured and organized', wrote Catherine Hall some five years after the publication of *Family Fortunes*. 'What was the specific relation of women to class structures and how should women's class position be defined? How was class *gendered* …? Do men and women have different class identities? Are their forms of class consciousness and class solidarity the same? … D[o] women have an identity as women which cuts across forms of class belonging?' (Hall 1992: 12–3)

Predictably enough, Hall and Davidoff's bold and innovative analysis was received with suspicion by the more conservative social historians (i.e. non- or anti-Marxist) who guarded the gates at the temples of wisdom against any possible incursion by scholars whose militant feminist purpose and 'tenacious devotion to preconceived dogma' menaced the notionally pure objectivity of historical research (McCord 1988: 996). Defending the alleged 'neutrality' of what was, in fact, a history focused solely on men, scholars like Norman McCord or Harold Perkin put scant effort into trying to understand what Hall and Davidoff were actually saying and simply dismissed them as prisoners of a 'narrow feminist agenda' that rendered them incapable of understanding the feelings of 'contented wives and mothers' (Perkin 1988: 309).

But Hall and Davidoff's real interlocutors – feminist, Marxist, and Marxist-feminist historians – gave *Family Fortunes* the serious and critically engaged reception it deserved.

Miriam Slater (1989: 733) praised the authors' abandonment of the then standard analytic frame that privileged a strict separation of public and private in favour of a more nuanced and fluid understanding of their interconnection, while Theodore Koditschek (1989: 179) hailed as a 'breakthrough' the authors' cogently argued and abundantly documented demonstration that class formation is a gendered phenomenon. John Gillis (1989: 171), for his part, announced that *Family Fortunes* 'transforms' our understanding of the early industrial era, offering historians and sociologists alike a 'model' for studying the family in other periods and places.

The bases of this enthusiastic reception were fourfold. Firstly, the authors placed at the heart of their argument the proposition that identities are deeply gendered and that the organization of sexual difference is central to social organization; an idea that, as John Gillis underscored, opened out broad new avenues for research on family history and the study of class formation. Secondly, Hall and Davidoff set about demonstrating this proposition via a form of gender analysis that was highly innovative at the time, namely, an approach that treats gendered categories as inherently unstable because perpetually caught up in processes of construction, contestation, and reconfiguration. As a consequence, there are at any given moment multiple, even competing views of what gender divisions are, what they mean and how they should express themselves in social life. This plurality of meaning creates spaces for negotiation and change within institutions and in social practices. Yet there is always a seemingly unified 'common sense' to gender divisions that arches over and above these diverse interpretations, papering them over with an apparently unified structure and significance. As a result, visions that are in fact shot through with contradiction prevail nonetheless in a dialectic of (hidden) movement, on the one hand, and (overt) hegemony, on the other. (The term 'common sense' is Gramsci's, see Hoare and Nowell Smith 1971: 625.)

Hall and Davidoff's Gramscian approach to the instability of social categories led them to further postulate that the frontiers between public and private are mobile and porous, and that the family, as an institution that links the market to the domestic sphere, acts as a mediator between the notionally separate domains of public and private. Finally, their decision to focus on both men and women made of their book a pioneering work in the study of masculinity – or at least, of one form of masculinity, that of the bourgeois, heteronormative family man. Indeed, some of the book's most striking passages focus on the ways that middle-class men bought into a domestic ideology intended to tame not only women but also some of the wilder aspects associated with manhood.

A book as ambitious as *Family Fortunes* was bound to attract plenty of criticism as well, and *Family Fortunes* certainly had its share. Amanda Vickery (1993) questioned the usefulness of the separate spheres optic for understanding developments in this period, pointing out that, *pace* Hall and Davidoff's implication that middle-class women were retreating into the private realm after the French Revolution, such women were in fact increasingly involved in the public sphere during these years. Several years later, Carolyn Steedman (1994) remarked that, for all the distance they take from separate spheres ideology, Hall and Davidoff seem nonetheless partially ensnared in its functionalist logic, at least in the portrayal they give of provincial middle-class life:

'Men would deal with the formal, women with the informal. Men would be decisive, women would be supportive. Men would take their proper place in the world, women would remain associated with the home', conclude the authors in a discussion of local associational life that blurs the distinction between separate spheres as ideology and separate spheres as a description of social life. At such moments, Hall and Davidoff abolish the critical distance from separate spheres ideology that they work so carefully to establish at other points in the narrative (Davidoff and Hall 1987: 143). And indeed, there is something disturbing in the peaceful harmony with which the tale of the complementary division of public and private unfolds. It is a tale in which the political problem of male domination tends to fade behind the comfortable harmonies of gender complementarity. It is a tale that, in Carolyn Steedman's (1994: 65) ironic formulation, 'repeats the imperative of the *Bildungsroman*, which, in its many forms, typically symbolizes the process of socialisation, and makes its characters and its readers really want to do what it is that they have to do anyway (be married, have children, clean the stairs)'.

Yet the separate spheres model, rendered more supple and nuanced in the hands of Hall and Davidoff, remained seductive: a structure of binary classification that allowed feminist researchers to integrate women and gender into social and economic histories while looking beyond towards their integration into political histories as well, notably studies of the gendered contours of social and political citizenship. Indeed, the ongoing pertinence of separate spheres would emerge quite forcefully after the collapse of the Berlin Wall, as scholars turned their concerted attention to understanding the very different ways these two realms of existence had been gendered under state socialism (Gal and Kligman 2000; Penn and Massino 2009; Drakulić 1992).

Despite some important critiques, *Family Fortunes* was widely understood to be clearing new ground. For this reason it had great impact: not only was it widely taught in women's history classes, but across the historical discipline more broadly. One of the most telling demonstrations of *Family Fortunes'* impact is the fact that their approach, with its stress on the instability of gender categories as well as the constant imbrication of public with private – widely hailed as innovative, even path-breaking at the time – now seems utterly evident to any historian, whether she or he works primarily on gender or some other topic. In the fall of 1987, however, the insights on which Hall and Davidoff built their argument were anything but obvious. A scant ten months earlier, Joan Scott (1986) had published her famous essay 'Gender: A Useful Category of Historical Analysis', which argues powerfully for a poststructuralist approach to women's and gender history based on the idea that sexual categories are constructed through representations and discourse rather than at the level of social practice. *Family Fortunes* proposes an alternative route that requires a demanding mobilization of techniques and approaches drawn from the social historian's toolkit. During the wrenching 'theory wars' that followed (in the late 1980s through the mid-1990s), the route marked out by Hall and Davidoff, which treats gender as a *social* category, would continue to inspire a new generation of historians for whom structures and practices count for as much as discourses and representations.

Identity/subjectivity after the linguistic and cultural turns

Historians have spilled much ink in an effort to come to grips with the linguistic and cultural turns in history, and I do not intend to reproduce those debates here. Suffice it to say that the very productive idea that gender identities are social/ideological constructs led some scholars to pursue a more philosophical/discursive approach to the question of where such identities come from in the first place. This line of inquiry helped to pose more sharply the question of whether identities are essential, unitary, in-born, and inwardly felt – and therefore the biological and cultural base on which a solid identity politics may be built – or whether awareness of their social and discursive construction might open up spaces of freedom for imagining individual and collective identities in more fluid ways.

For many years, debate between essentialists and non-essentialists/constructivists raged on among historians of gender and sexuality, polarizing both fields in a struggle for pre-eminence between two warring conceptions of identity that are in fact incompatible because grounded in opposed ontologies of the human being. The one thus understands identity as an essential, inner core to which the experiences of life contribute additional layers of individual subjectivity, while the other sees identity as a 'subject position' that arises at the convergence of various discursive vectors. In this latter, poststructuralist view, individual subjects are constructed from the outside inwards, as it were, through discourses and representations that make certain subject positions available while closing off others.

Despite the occasional violence of debate between proponents of essentialist versus anti-essentialist understandings of identity, the two warring conceptions continued their uneasy coexistence within many departments and programmes of women's and gender history long after the mid-1990s, when the mutual sniping of the 'theory wars' gradually gave way to an uneasy ceasefire. At that moment, the notion of intersectionality came progressively to assume primacy of place in many historians' toolkits. This is perhaps not entirely surprising. For with its stress on the idea that individual identities are made up of multiple and shifting identifications – of class, ethnicity, religion, or gender – along with its silence on the question of where identities come from or how they are made, intersectionality was a way to navigate between essentialist and non-essentialist understandings of individual identity and its complex relationship to social/collective identities (Crenshaw 1991; Davis 2008). At the same time, it is worth recalling that intersectionality is less a tool of analysis than a declaration of good practice. For affirming that individual identities are multiple and mutable, while an important step forward, tells us nothing about the ways that different shards of identity, such as race, gender, or ethnicity, articulate with class to form structures that are simultaneously classed, raced, and gendered. Only detailed historical or sociological research can lay bare the particular shape assumed by those articulations at any given place or moment in time.

During this same period, scholars began questioning many of the fundamental elements of foundational approaches in the history of gender and sexuality, such as the links that 1970s-style identity politics assumed between individual identity, social identity, and politics, or even the very concept of identity itself. Hence, the 'new' social history was anchored in the idea that individual identity leads unproblematically to collective identity, which later forms the indispensable ground of political consciousness/ action. The epistemological chain binding individual to social identity and leading therefrom to politics formed a powerful legacy that 1970s social movements and the new social history had bequeathed to early feminist scholarship on women, gender, and sexuality. In the wake of the theory wars, these connections no longer seemed so obvious or automatic, and sustained reflection on this fact helped to loosen the ties between politics and identity (Cerutti 1997). At the same time, the notion of identity as an analytic concept, whether individual or collective, essentialist or anti-essentialist, came in for some hard scrutiny (Brubaker and Cooper 2000).

These years of debate and reflection over the tools and concepts of history in general, and of gender history more specifically allowed some new and very interesting questions and analytic objects to emerge. These included a focus on individual subjectivity and its material and bodily contexts, agency, and the role of emotions in shaping both. These are areas to which gender history and the history of sexuality have made a decisive contribution. I would therefore like to conclude this chapter with a look at two texts that offer distinct yet complementary views on these new objects of inquiry: Michael Roper's (2005) manifesto 'Slipping Out of View', which makes a powerful plea for exploring subjectivity and emotion in gender history, and Garthine Walker's (2016) article on infanticide and emotion in sixteenth- to eighteenth-century England and Wales. By emphasizing the body as a site of emotion and subjective experience, Roper and Walker seek to move beyond the oddly detached and disembodied feel that characterizes so much cultural history, with its focus on linguistic and cultural codes and concomitant marginalization of subjective experience. Both authors also privilege the search for traces of evanescent feelings on the part of actors' past, and for the clues that textual sources might give us to the subjective dimensions of their experience. Finally, both allow us to consider how the concepts of subjectivity and agency may or may not be doing some of the work that scholars were asking of 'identity' some forty years ago.

I choose these two texts in part because they allow us to see how Roper and Walker engage with the possibilities and limitations of earlier British scholarship on gender, sexuality, and subjectivity. By remaining within the British social and cultural context within which Hall and Davidoff produced *Family Fortunes*, I hope to give this brief overview of developments in gender history greater coherence. For if the transnational circulation of ideas, concepts, and key texts, from Simone de Beauvoir to Michel Foucault, Joan Scott, or Judith Butler, has played a crucial role in shaping the study of gender and sexuality across borders, historical research always unfolds in particular places and spaces. The dialectic between the local and particular (in this case, early modern and modern Britain, and the debates that have shaped its historiography) and wider, transnational currents of thought has been decisive in shaping historical research in both gender history and the history of sexuality.

Michael Roper's 'Slipping Out of View' offers an eloquent and searching point of entry into some of the fundamental problematics that have traversed the fields of British social and cultural history for at least twenty years now, including questions of subjectivity, agency, the materiality of lived experience and the effort to grasp that experience as at once social and psychic. It also offers a compelling analysis of what John Tosh (2004: 52) has called the 'curiously detached' feel of so much cultural history vis-à-vis its human subjects. For in the wake of the cultural and linguistic turns, notes Roper (who is a historian of male subjectivity), 'masculinity [or, for that matter, femininity – L.L.D.], is still viewed, by and large, as more as a matter of social or cultural construction than as an aspect of personality' (Roper 2005: 57). Cultural historians have thus tended to analyse masculinity and femininity through studying discourses and socio-cultural codes rather than exploring sexual identity as lived experience. But as Roper astutely observes, this way of thinking about subjectivity 'elides' the psychic into the cultural, treating the subject as if she or he were 'a blank page onto which cultural processes are then inscribed' rather than an active, thinking, feeling being who is engaged in constant negotiation with and selective appropriation of cultural norms (Roper 2005: 58, 66). Why this 'flattening' of complex and varied individual emotional experiences into a version of collective consciousness or *mentalité*? How is it that subjectivity gets 'placed' on the agenda, only to slip away from view? Have earlier visions of masculinity and femininity as 'bridging concepts' between the social and the psychic failed?

Roper attributes these limitations to the particular way that Joan Scott defined gender as a tool of historical analysis in her widely read 'Gender: A Useful Category of Historical Analysis', which famously argues that gender is a key aspect of how power is structured and symbolized. On the one hand, this way of conceiving gender gave Scott's formulation 'imperial reach', allowing her to argue that gender is present even when women are not. On the other hand, it did so by prising gender from the realm of human experience and applying it to relations of power. Scott thus redirected historians' attention from the familiar terrains of gender/sexual identity like the family, or kinship structures, to more public and institutional sources of such identity: labour markets, education, the polity, all of which, Scott argues persuasively, are structured by sexual difference.

It is easy to understand why Scott might have privileged focusing on the wider social, political, and institutional bases of sexual identity. For in the mid-1980s, when women's history had trouble liberating itself from the history of the family, such an approach promised to give gender a broader purchase on historical analysis in its many guises – political, social, intellectual, and economic. But this has come at a cost, argues Roper, for Scott's way of defining gender has tended to produce work that 'looks down from political discourse' and through to a subject who is understood to be constituted by cultural representations, as they operate through institutions. Subjectivity is thus reduced to an 'after-effect of political discourse', and subjective experience pushed to the 'edge' of historical analysis (Roper 2005: 61–2).

In his own research, which explores different dimensions of male subjectivity during the First World War, Roper takes as his point of departure the idea that personality is formed through lived experiences. By focusing on the 'vicissitudes' of masculinity – by which he means the fact that sexual identities are often felt to be in danger of unravelling – Roper seeks to grasp the 'precariousness' of masculinity; the ways in which it is felt to be an uncertain acquisition, forever in need of shoring up. He does this in part through a close reading of letters between mothers and their sons at the front; a reading that views writing as a psychological activity, and the letter as a source of 'clues' about emotional states. Within this optic, the inability to write holds as much meaning as a letter filled with graphic detail: 'Just a line to say I'm quite safe, although I've been through, I've been through a rather trying experience', wrote a soldier known simply as 'Hall' after a brutal, and tragic experience of battle. 'Several of my friends have been killed in the business, which is sad. I feel so tired today I cannot write anymore. Please send socks as soon as possible'. Roper pauses over Hall's 'calculated understatement' ('a rather trying experience') and abrupt change of topic ('please send socks'); signs that Hall was struggling to wrench his thoughts away from the unbearable horror of his recent experience of battle and re-establish 'normal', comforting domestic routines. In Roper's reading, signs such as these point to the moments at which social codes of masculinity falter, or are, 'by the sheer force of emotional experience, broken through' (Roper 2005: 65).

If Scott's discursive notion of gender, with its implicit orientation of historical research towards political and cultural history, has anchored gender history solidly within the discipline, this conceptualization has nonetheless left historians who are interested in subjectivity faced with a new challenge: that of finding ways to write about bodily and emotional experiences that do not treat such experiences as wholly composed by ideological formations. As Michael Roper's own work suggests, this means going back to analyse in new ways the very family structures that Scott recommended we flee in favour of broader, cultural and political sources of identity, so that we might explore those 'primitive emotional investments' that underpin the 'social scripts' of gender. For at the end of the day, 'familial relationships might have a more foundational significance for subjectivity than others – such as political discourse'. After all, as Leonore Davidoff (1995: 229) has pointed out, it is within the family – 'however it has been constituted – that formation of both body and psyche, literally and symbolically, first takes place'. To persist in conceiving of subjectivity primarily in terms of representation is to endorse a 'profoundly lifeless notion of human existence', concludes Roper in words that remind us that much of the current dissatisfaction with the cultural and political/ discursive understanding of gender stems from its inability to do what E. P. Thompson did so beautifully for the notion of class, that is, to capture its profound anchoring in human relationships.

Garthine Walker's fascinating essay 'Child-Killing and Emotion in Early Modern England and Wales' explores the complex and variable emotional responses to child killing in sixteenth- to eighteenth-century Britain through a close reading of legal testimonies which offer some access (however fleeting) to the subjectivities of accused women. These testimonies were accumulated under the aegis of Britain's 1624 Concealment [of pregnancy] Act, which was based on the fear that unmarried women who concealed their pregnancies, murdered their newborns, and secretly disposed of their bodies were avoiding conviction by claiming stillbirth. Concealment of death rather than homicide thus became the fact to be determined by law. This widened the dragnet, creating a rich archive of testimonies from the accused and from various witnesses, which has drawn the attention of scholars in early modern legal and social history.

Walker opens her article with one of these testimonies: the tale of one Jane Williams, who in the winter of 1734 gave birth, alone and unassisted in a corridor of the house where she worked as a domestic servant. 'Alone during her labor, she afterwards buried the child in an "aisle in said dwelling house, without acquainting any person about it"' (Walker 2016: 152). So, reads Jane Williams' laconic testimony before the magistrates. 'Any modern scholar is likely to fashion from Jane's brief confession a variant of a generic story constructed in the shadow of the 1624 Concealment Act', writes Walker in an insightful reflection on scholars' desire to comprehend and connect with subjectivities past. She then spins out a brief example of how such a 'generic' story of Jane Williams' sad fate as might be elaborated by present-day scholars.

> Whether the child had been stillborn, survived for minutes or hours, or died by neglect or her own hand, she secretly disposed of its body. The discovery of the corpse precipitated a search for the mother, who was identified by material signs of childbirth on bed-linen or elsewhere, by visible changes in her body or by other incriminating behavior. The woman was interrogated by magistrates who took sworn statements from witnesses, and thereafter tried at the Assizes or Great Sessions, where she was convicted, effectively, of murder. She died on the gallows, or narrowly escaped with her life, a victim of patriarchal society in which the shame of bearing an illegitimate child compelled her to murder her newborn babe or allow it to die. So the story goes. (Walker 2016: 152–3)

But what can we really know of the subjectivities of those involved, asks Walker, pointing to the large gaps in Jane Williams' terribly fragmented story, which was transmitted via a brief transcript that says 'literally nothing' about her subjective experience of pregnancy, labour, the dead child, or what she did with its body. These are gaps that can all-too-easily be filled by present-day scholars' desire to immediately understand (and perhaps identify with) Jane Williams' terrible predicament and the never-expressed, but easily imagined feelings that must have accompanied it: the shame, isolation, and fear of the presumably infanticidal mother, and the disapproval and contempt of the neighbours and legal officials she faced.

This presentist perspective is embedded in an emotion-laden narrative of the infanticidal mother as both guilty and blameless: 'Compelled' to murder her newborn babe by the 'shame' of bearing an illegitimate child, she is, ultimately 'a victim' of patriarchal society. It is a narrative that is over-determined by present-day political stances – and emotional reactions – to the presumably 'impossible' predicament that illegitimate pregnancy posed for women in early modern Britain (Francus 2012: 21). But, Walter asks, what if we were to replace Jane Williams' story in the social, cultural, and demographic context of early modern Britain, where the 'problem' of illegitimacy was understood quite differently, then re-read her story in relation to that context? What other kinds of sense might we make of it? For early modern people did not see infanticide as the inevitable, or even common, outcome of illegitimate pregnancy. Indeed, in a society where long-term demographic growth had led to declining opportunities to marry and form households 'bastardy was commonplace and infanticide was not'. Moreover, persistently high infant mortality rates meant that the unexplained death of a newborn child was not necessarily seen as suspicious, even when the mother was unmarried (Walker 2016: 154).

Under these circumstances, neonaticide was clearly not a 'default path' for unmarried pregnant women, and the statistics on criminal conviction would seem to uphold this proposition. Hence, though the Concealment Act dragged many women into its net, the acquittal rate was also quite high, indicating that, in the absence of positive evidence that an infant had been murdered, juries were reluctant to deliver a conviction of homicide on the sole basis of proof of concealment. Finally, Walker cites ample evidence of sympathy for the unmarried women concerned, much of which was expressed through public concern over the problem of the men responsible, each of whom, via promises of matrimony had seduced, betrayed, and then abandoned a young woman, leaving her to deal with the consequences herself.

By assembling these elements of historical context, Garthine Walker makes possible an alternative reading of the evidence; one that, moreover, allows glimpses into the subjectivity of the women accused. In order to do this, she musters a number of intellectual resources, including Michael Roper's telling critique of cultural history's inability to grasp the 'deep, complex and varied individual emotional experiences', in this case, of suspected women and girls. Crucially, Walker also draws from oral historians' long-standing challenge to the idea of a single, isolated subject (or a singular subject position) and asks instead that we be alert to the multiple subject positions that might be assumed by one individual.

The story of domestic servant Gwen Foulk, who, in 1716 gave birth near a stile on a common footpath leading to the highway, allows Walker to develop this perspective. A neighbour, Dorothy Williams, who happened on Gwen, 'uneasy and groaning' on the footpath, suspected her condition and offered help, which, according to her testimony, Gwen 'obstinately refused'. Lingering nearby, Dorothy and another neighbour, Elizabeth Salesbury, watched Gwen 'throw something from her' and leave. When they returned to see what she had left there, they found 'a child (as they took it) covered with the attendants of nature lying in the ditch'. In these depositions, we see Gwen from Dorothy's perspective; 'an obstinate denier of pregnancy and a concealer of childbirth and we may imagine how desperate she might have felt. ... Here, the 'typical' infanticidal mother of the historiography may be seen'.

The account given by Gwen's employer, Mary Jones, is rather different. Arriving home that evening, she found Gwen sitting in the dark by the fire, speaking in a 'feeble distressed voice' and crying. Jones later heard the story from Dorothy Williams, and then asked Gwen why she had left the child there. Gwen claimed simply 'that she had not known what it was'. 'This Gwen is abject, isolated, distressed', observes Walker.

Yet a third subject position emerges in Gwen's own testimony, that of a 'feisty, intelligent girl who is able to deflect the accusations against her'. Hence, the reason she had not provided linens for the child was that she had only recently suspected that she might be pregnant. Further, she would not have concealed her condition from Dorothy except that a manservant was present as well as Elizabeth Salesbury, 'a person whom her master and mistress had no good opinion of'. Had Dorothy been alone, she would have told her. Gwen then 'denied the child to have any life in him' and pointed out that had she sought to conceal the pregnancy, surely she would have used her mistress's house (which was empty at the time) and not a 'common public field that had so many footpaths in it' in order to deliver the child (Williams, Jones, and Foulks depositions, cited in Walker 2016: 163–4).

The 'multiple selves' that emerge in the depositions surrounding Gwen Foulk's case are not coherent narratives from which we can construct 'fixed, authentic subjectivities', writes Walker. Rather, these sources suggest '*something* of subjectivity in very particular contexts'. Is the subjectivity we encounter in Gwen's testimony transcribed by a clerk who was not obliged to produce a verbatim account but only as much as was 'legally relevant' more 'authentic' than that which we see in Dorothy's and Mary's accounts? Not necessarily, states Walker, if we reject the notion of the self as a 'pre-existing entity', waiting to be uncovered by a historian's analysis. For Gwen's experience of giving birth in a field was affected by all who were present at one moment or another: Dorothy, the manservant, Elizabeth Salesbury. 'If they had been absent, her experience would have been different', affirms Walker. The 'self' we may discern in these sources was thus 'co-produced' in the moment where the parties met, 'with all the contextual weight that implies' (Walker 2016: 164–5).

A specialist of crime and violence in early modern England and Wales, Garthine Walker has found herself wrestling with the ongoing legacy of those overtly militant forms of gender history which are nourished more by an imagined proximity to early modern victims of male violence and oppression than by careful historical contextualization of that same violence. In this respect, Walker is not alone, as the work of Farid Azfar (among others) testifies (Azfar 2012). The tension between militancy and scholarship thus continues to play itself out in histories of gender and sexuality, as scholars who assert a militant proximity to victims past duel with those who, like Walker or Azfar, express their commitment to people in the past (whether victims or otherwise) through a careful mobilization of analytic tools whose deployment rests above all on the understanding that the past is a 'foreign country', and that good scholarship demands that we respect the distance between then and now, them and us (Hartley 1953: 1).

It is worth underscoring, moreover, that militant histories based on proximity to victims' past tend to work with notions of identity that are based on the idea of a fixed subject who is constructed through interaction with the social scripts and cultural codes of their era. In other words, they are working precisely with those 'lifeless' forms of identity of which Michael Roper and John Tosh are so critical. This is perhaps because such forms, made up of abstract cultural and linguistic codes, lend themselves more easily to the retrospective projection of present-day concerns and identifications onto the past than do approaches that emphasize the individuality, even unrecognizability of subjectivities past.

Walker thus concludes her article with a brief return to the story of Jane Williams, on the theory that, in the end, even a 'mere fragment' of testimony 'might provide us with some sense of emotion that does not rely on our discovering a conscious, fixed subject. Alternative subject positions might be simultaneously occupied'. In support of this hypothesis Walker cites two seemingly incompatible forms of material evidence that stand at the heart of Williams' case. On the one hand, there were 'observed marks of violence' on the baby's throat and neck. On the other, there is the way that Jane chose to deal with the body, 'which speaks not just of the extraordinary but of the everyday, not only of violence but also possibly of nurturing, not just of death but also, in a way, of life'. For Jane laid her dead baby 'under a stone under the hen's nest in a [passageway] in her dwelling house'. Whether this was a pragmatic, calculated, panicky, or unthinking act, 'placing the body there in that specific spot may have had some emotional meaning'. For the baby was not abandoned on a hillside or thrown into a dung-heap; rather, its mother placed it carefully under a stone, 'which was under a nest, which was under an egg, which was under a hen. This baby, whom Jane had secretly carried in her womb, but whose birth, whose death she had not acknowledged to a soul, was now perpetually like an egg, kept safe and warm by a surrogate mother ... in a way, it was as if the baby had never been and never would be born, but would always be in a state of becoming'. (Walker 2016: 165–6)

From identity to subjectivity

If concepts of identity continue to be deployed in historical research, it would seem, nonetheless, that the centre of gravity is shifting towards the notion of subjectivity. What are the implications of this shift? Is subjectivity doing the same kind of analytic work that was asked of identity some forty years ago? I think the answer to this question must be both yes and no. In order to see why, we must look more closely at how each of these two concepts functions in order to take stock of the analytic distance that separates them. In this vein, it is worth underscoring the extent to which the keywords that structure much present-day scholarship – intersectionality, subjectivity, agency – put the emphasis on the individual: The individual and her multiple, shifting sources of identity, in the case of intersectionality; the individual and how she experiences particular events, in the case of subjectivity; the individual and her capacity for action, shaped as it is by her resources, but also by the larger socio-economic and political frameworks which limit that capacity, in the case of agency.

One striking consequence of this focus on the individual is that the notion of collective identity, so central to the 'new' social history (and the new social movements) of the 1970s, has faded from sight. This is no minor matter, given the centrality of collective identity to the understanding of political consciousness that underpinned both social movements and social history in this era. For collective identities were the crucial switching point in the new social history's epistemological chain that bound (essentialized) individual identities to collective ones, and led from there to political consciousness (and action).

Much current scholarship, by contrast is anchored in a new dyad that links subjectivity with agency. These two are then sometimes linked to politics, other times, not. If the earlier formulation was unidirectional, moving from individual consciousness outwards to its more collective and political manifestations, the subjectivity-agency-politics triad allows for more circular relationships among these three terms, with shaping influences that move in both directions, creating circular flows that allow for a constant evolution in all three.

As we have seen, the concept of subjectivity has been developed in opposition to the essentialism on which identity politics rests, and to the linear and unidirectional nature of the ties that bind those fixed and 'authentic' identities to society and then politics. But this does not mean that politics has completely fallen out of the equation. Rather, the focus on intersectionality, subjectivity, and agency is meant to illuminate the individual as an actor and give us a more fine-grained and less deterministic understanding of the alliances and more temporary collectivities that can emerge in the course of a political mobilization.

Perhaps the best answer to the question 'is subjectivity doing the same kind of analytic work that was asked of identity?' is that the new social history – including all the dissatisfactions its underlying presumptions provoked, clearly inspired the turn to subjectivity and the attendant shift from more sociologically informed tools of analysis to more psychoanalytically informed ones. (Oral history, with its focus on the intersubjective relationship between interviewer and interviewee, may also have played an important role in this shift.) As Leonore Davidoff (1995) observed, this analytic shift entails placing the emphasis on far smaller collectivities like the family, and on the psychic dimensions of various dyadic and triadic relations within that context. But as Garthine Walker's work reminds us, such psychoanalytically informed approaches are not incompatible with methods inspired by the linguistic turn. Intersectionality in the form of multiple subject positions thus stands at the heart of Walker's notion of subjectivity/the self, which is always seen as shaped by particular contexts rather than as something that is fixed and 'authentic'.

If the concept of subjectivity is not doing precisely the same work we asked of the notion of identity, there are nonetheless clear connections between the concerns that the two concepts seek to illuminate. In the end, the distance between them may illuminate most sharply the very different political conjuncture in which we are now living, and the consequently different shape that identity-cum-subjectivity is taking.

Comment

Miri Rubin

Around mid-point in Laura Lee Downs' stimulating chapter, she introduces the call for the history of sexuality and gender to open itself up to the history of the emotions. Michael Roper's call of 2005 clearly captured a moment, a mark of the coming of age in the history of gender (Roper 2005). For to study the emotions is to delve into bodies, with all their personal idiosyncrasy and variation. To study the emotions is to accept bafflement, as well as the limitations of the sources at the historian's disposal. Roper went on, of course, to do important work, not least his recent exploration of soldiers in the battles of the First World War through their letters. Masculinity appears front and centre in this research, thus taking the history of sexuality into new domains too (Roper 2009). In this work historians of the periods usually described as medieval and early modern can find inspiration, even while knowing that they could not quite emulate it. For when scholars of earlier centuries approach gender and sexuality, they often have to do so in oblique ways, and through the use of sources often removed from – and hostile to – the people whose subjectivity is in question.

Another important contributor to the exploration of emotions, mentioned in Downs' essay, is Garthine Walker. Her distinctive approach is in exploring the gendered language of emotion as this arises from the rich court records of early modern England. Testimonies, confessions, answers to interrogation, provide not only insights into the gendered arena of the law, but also into life-worlds reported – sometimes even decades after the event – by participants called to remember specific events (Walker 2016). The gendered work of memory is opened up in such sensitive work, just as it has been revealed in work on ecclesiastical court records in late medieval England, by Bronach Kane (2008, 2018), and on those of the city of Marseille, by Daniel Lord Smail (2016). More recently, Walker has turned her attention to the material objects invoked, presented, or remembered by those involved in litigation. The historian is called to tease out very carefully the meanings of such objects from the fraught arena that is the court, but objects – documents, keepsakes, torn, or bloody garments – all offer pathways into emotional worlds, worlds we are unable to explore otherwise, since ego-documents are so sparse in the earlier centuries.

Such interesting and testing work on the emotions was made possible – as well as prompted – by the foundations laid down over decades in the work of social historians, like Catherine Hall and Leonore Davidoff, discussed in Downs' essay. This is not to say that there is a hierarchy of more or less determining factors, first the social and economic, then the cultural, last the emotional. Rather, it is to suggest that when the history of women, in whose wake the history of gender was born, was closely aligned with and linked to the new social history, a history from below above all, which energized history making since the 1960s and 1970s. Historians of more recent centuries have been able to use census material and tax records to discern structures of family life and demographic trends, but also to revel in written sources and objects emanating from the rhythms of household life – letters, accounts, clothes – and to situate these in a fabric, both rural and urban, which helped situate the lives emerging into historical view.

Once the sense of social organization in households and other social groups – villages, factories, neighbourhoods, trade unions – emerged ever clearer, the sheer variety of women's ways of living faced historians, and caused them to reflect on the historical variations and cultural making of the category woman. Hence gender, and the correlated reflection on masculinity, not only in its own variations, but also in its dialectical relation to the category of female. So, the history of gender arises out of the manifest contradictions and variations which troubled historical explanation once a rich and multifaceted historical project of women's history and social history of families and communities raised new, and sometimes, challenging questions.

The contradictions and phenomena begging explanation were those that defied the rationalizing, 'sensible' expectations of the history of women in its more social scientific mode. An interesting example arises from Lyndal Roper's work on witchcraft. Roper pioneered the gendered history of the Reformation in her book on the reformed urban family, *The Holy Household: Women and Morals in Reformation Augsburg* (1991). Although the title says 'women', it is in fact a gendered analysis of marriage and household work, within communities recently reformed and hard at work at scrutinizing the moral behaviour of neighbours. She powerfully countered the prevailing historical understanding, that the Reformation brought women greater freedom with the removal of clerical scrutiny, and a traditional brand of clerical misogyny. She showed how persistent was the gendered order in the reformed household, and the ways in which patriarchy was reinforced with the passage of some religious/pedagogic tasks from priests to the male head of household. This analysis built on the procedures of previous analyses of household work, marriage, and family life, but its gendered approach saw the roles of men and women in conjunctions, defining – and sometimes defying – each other.

Next, Roper studied such German women as they became involved in witchcraft trials. As we have seen above, court records offer great riches, and so Roper inquired into the confessions some women made of their nocturnal activities as witches. Even without torture, even when other avenues were open to them, some women elaborated powerful fantasies: of sexual adventure, of revenge, and of super-natural powers. Roper brought to bear psychoanalytic concepts to the analysis of the relationships between women accused of witchcraft and their interrogators, in *Witch Craze: Terror and Fantasy in Baroque Germany* (2004). In the course of these exchanges an occasion to speak fantasy arose, out of the relationship to interrogators which combined discipline, fear, arousal, and paternal care, too. Here are added to the gendered analysis of what appeared to be a legal exchange, considerations of subjectivity, the manifestation of repressed feelings. It showed women desiring and taking pleasure in transgression, even at a great cost to themselves. We are here far from the 'rational' subject of social analysis, but we are closer to the rich physicality of life in moments of particular pressure and dislocation.

This is not to say that we can easily discern feelings and desires in the past, but we can identify clusters of preoccupation which troubled men and women, and which went unnoticed until historians of gender and sexuality became involved. An interesting area where historians and literary scholars have interacted fruitfully is that of humanism and its pedagogy. Here again the trail of inquiry passes through women's history, leading to the history of gender and sexuality, and on to the emotions. From the bringing of women and girls into the classroom by Lisa Jardine, to the exploration of sodomy in humanistic writings (Stewart 1997), and on to the history of the emotions among scholars bound by gift giving, book sharing, and learning from each other (Enterline

2012; Essary 2016). For the world of humanism was a world of schools and courts, diplomacy and scholarship, worlds usually closed to women. This is not to say that elite women did not benefit from humanistic education, nor that women were not important and discerning patrons of endeavours in art and letters in the various regions touched by the new learning between 1300 and 1600. It is rather to appreciate how normatively male was the idea of learning and how gendered the mental world of school, university, college. Humanistic pedagogues emphasized the importance of diverting the boy from mother to schoolmaster,[1] and similarly from the vernacular to Latin.[2] School exercises were associated with pain and exertion, where the hand inflicting pain was also the one comforting. Translation and grammar exercises imbued the classroom or private study with desire; even the simplest lesson in conjugation cast the teacher at the centre: 'Amo magistrum'. And relationships between teacher and pupil marked by pain were long remembered, and felt on the body (Wootton 2000). When we consider relations between men, we do so now with a high awareness of the role femininity – desire for it, fear of it, aversion to it – plays in the making of the masculine subject. And in all these sophisticated exercises, the body is to the fore.

I am an historian of the medieval centuries of the second millennium, and I usually deal with religious ideas and practices. Here the work of women's history has been intense and innovative; we know far more about the religious experience of exceptional female nuns than we do about most other categories of experience. Best known are those women who wrote – or dictated – texts in description of their spiritual world: visions, journeys, conversations with God. In the case of the twelfth-century Rhenish abbess Hildegard of Bingen, we even possess a repertoire of liturgical music, composed for the use of the nuns under her care (Hildegard of Bingen 1988). Much of this work has been inspired by the inquiry into bodily experience and religious imagery, based on accounts of the lives of tens of religious women, Caroline W. Bynum's *Holy Feast and Holy Fast: The Religious Significance of Food to Medieval Women* (1987).

While the discovery and treatment of writings by female religious are welcome additions to the history of women and gender, historians have had to confront the question of women's voice. So many of the accounts of women's lives and experiences – be they hagiographical *vitae* or books of visions and revelations – were written about them, for them, making the ascription of *voice* an extremely challenging issue, just as it was for Roper, when dealing with court records written by male interrogators. So many layers of mediation, translation, editing, interposed between women's experience and the source we study in search for subjectivity. The more ambitious we are in our search for historical experiences, the more acute becomes our awareness of the opacity of mediation. For historians are no longer innocents trespassing in the world of textuality and its performances, we are knowing inhabitants of that land.

After decades of preoccupation with textuality historians have now turned to inquire into the human agency involved in the making and use of material objects. And where there are things there are the spaces they inhabit and define. Gender and sexuality are mobilized in these inquiries, and religion has been a rich terrain for research. Following objects, it has been possible to recover domestic religious practices, often associated with women and children, like those captured in the recent exhibition *Madonnas and Miracles*, curated by Mary Laven.[3]

The interest in gender and sexuality and their performance in space and time have drawn scholars to the abundant field of liturgy with new and fascinating results. Liturgy – the texts and procedures of worship – has traditionally been the domain of specialists – many in religious orders – who treated it apart from the mainstream of historical studies. Yet the search for religious experience through the body and its senses – the fruit of feminist and sexuality scholarship – has identified in liturgy the script of rituals which touched the many, lay women and men, alike. In liturgical performance men sang the voices of women – think of renditions of the Magnificat, Mary's song – and performed dressed as women, as in the Easter Play *Quem Quaeritis*, playing the women approaching Christ's empty tomb. A religion of incarnation which also taught that Christ's body was still available from the hands of the priest at every altar was bound to inspire fantasies of transgression, and feelings of longing and union. Historians of gender and sexuality – among them Bynum – empowered by the insights of literary scholars, have made sense of words and images of great complexity, complex because they are gendered. Like the image of the *Lactation of St. Bernard*, inspired by a story told about Bernard a century after his death (Berlioz 1988; Dupeux 1991). Here the twelfth-century mystic, a man known for his devotion to the Virgin Mary, was imagined as receiving a special gift from Mary, alive in a statue on the altar – of the milk of her breast. A gendered reading discovers layers of meaning, and relates them to trends in Marian devotion, which make sense of the memory of holy men, and the pressure to humanize them, making them owners of experiences and rewards which those who remembered them could only imagine in delight. Work with liturgical and devotional materials, I suggest, mobilizes religious images and texts and reads them with the insights of the history of gender and sexuality (Rubin 2016).

Out of the debates within the history of women emerged the acknowledgement of difference and variation which led scholars – and then publics – to think through gender and the historical – and cultural – nature of sexual identities. Historians, who must seek out these identities and their realization in past times, and depend in their tasks on always incomplete, and sometimes frustratingly scanty, sets of evidence, have sought to refine their procedures – in dealing with texts, images, objects – so as to understand these sources as best as possible. Historians have thus added attention to agency and experience mediated by gender, and have done so with the desire to understand subjectivity, and in ages when religious cultures prevailed, this meant paying a great deal of attention to devotional behaviour and religious participation.

It may appear that some of the political energy, which Laura Downs delineated in her essay, is missing in this historical landscape, that historians labour over their procedures rather than their commitments to the vexed issues associated in our public arenas with gender and sexuality. In that sense, the 'detachment' about which John Tosh (2004: 52) warned us over a decade ago, as Downs reminds us in her essay, may have been transformed into something more robust. I suggest that if this is the case, it is not to be lamented. For it is a mark of the coming of age of the fledgling new histories begun half a century ago, and with the aim of including half of humanity in our historical record. However more perfect we can make that history, it has left an indelible mark on history making. No serious historian can any longer maintain that gender is anything but an essential category in historical study, even if its prominence varies in different social locations, and can be more or less central to particular historical situations. Yet this is not to say that gender work is done. As the history of gender and sexuality becomes less polemical on the pages of journals and in conference halls, it has entered a phase of urgent political activism in most parts of the world. For it pours light on debates over imperilled reproductive rights, over the right of people to inhabit bodies whose sexuality they recognize, and on the right of girls to live in bodies which elders have not mutilated into an imagined sexual docility. The exquisite work of historians of gender and sexuality continues to inform urgent discussions on gendered pay gaps and hyper-sexualized domains of consumption and entertainment. This is important work, and a tribute to an academic field ripe in its political resonance.

Response

Laura Lee Downs

Miri Rubin's thoughtful and wide-ranging reflection on my chapter offers an invigorating set of observations on subjectivity and the performance of gender and sexuality from the necessarily different perspective of a medieval historian. Her comment thus takes us on an informative tour of several key lenses through which medievalists have sought to access and write about subjectivities in a far more distant past: religious ideas and practices, humanism and pedagogy, material history, the history of the body. Miri Rubin then closes on a cautiously optimistic note, hailing the 'coming of age' of a gender history that has left behind the searing theory wars of the early 1990s in favour of a broad eclecticism, turning away from polemics around the politics of history and towards a serious concentration on sources and method, in a scholarly context in which gender's status as an essential category of analysis is no longer frontally contested.

The ultimately successful struggle to establish gender as a category of analysis has won for historians of gender and sexuality the intellectual space and freedom to work like any other historian on the issues that bind all historians in a common quest. But if political battles in the shape of internecine polemics no longer leap off the pages of discussions within the domains of gender and sexuality, real-world battles continue to be fought on a daily basis around these issues. Moreover, as Miri Rubin rightly reminds us, the work of historians of gender and sexuality continues to inform these struggles: around gender pay gaps, the hyper-sexualized realms of consumption and entertainment, the rights of gay and transsexual people (to name but a few).

I heartily concur with this analysis and, indeed, would go one step further: if discussion among historians of gender and sexuality is no longer fraught with conflict, the world in which female and male academics labour is still constructed in such a way that the moral and sexual harassment of younger scholars by their elders, the less powerful by the entrenched, remains a rampant issue. If such harassment is not peculiar to the academy (far from it), there are structural issues around the way that universities work that make the enduring problem of harassment a particularly complicated one to address. For the model of knowledge transmission in academia is an apprenticeship model, structured by hierarchies of power/knowledge. Opportunities for harassment are thus entwined in the very socio-pedagogical hierarchies that shape the university as a place of teaching, research, and learning.

I do not mean to say by this that universities are *more* haunted by moral and sexual harassment than are other work spaces. On the contrary, the problems that women confront within the university are continuous with those they confront outside its walls: unequal pay, more difficult access to stable employment, careers that slow down (or stagnate altogether) if the woman in question chooses to have children. This is in sharp contradistinction to men, whose careers tend to take off the very moment they become fathers, marking their entry into the statute of stable paterfamilias at a crucial moment (age 25–40) in career development. Finally, women are routinely subjected to forms of moral and sexual harassment that are specific to their status as women, from denigration of their intellectual capacities, to pressure to sleep with their professors, to threats – and acts – of sexual violence.[4]

So far, this sounds an awful lot like the problems women grapple with in the society at large. What is distinctive about the academy, therefore, are not the problems women face, but rather the particular kind of social and work contexts within which these problems and abuses unfold. Within universities, those contexts are shaped by a socio-pedagogical structure that is grounded in steep hierarchies of knowledge/power.

These formal hierarchies are, moreover, flanked by informal networks which reinforce the reproduction of a university that privileges white, male, heterosexual men from the middle and upper classes. The imbrication of official hierarchy and unofficial networks has produced what Marieke van den Brink has called 'vertical hiring structures' that reproduce the current social profile of the professoriate from the very bottom rungs of the hierarchy upward.[5]

The problem of informal networks is a difficult, though not intractable one, and considerable attention has been paid in recent years to undermining their power via rules for greater transparency in procedures, so as to give women and other non-traditional candidates a more equal chance at fellowships, post-docs, entry-level positions, and promotion. The creation and strengthening of counter-networks linking feminist scholars of both sexes is another, constructive approach that creates platforms for the exchange of information, experiences, and moral support while providing an additional source of pressure for rendering more transparent procedures around evaluation and selection.

But the problem of the vertical order of knowledge transmission is a much thornier one. Why? Because university teaching is, by its very nature, a transmission that occurs in the context of a hierarchical relationship of age, training, and experience, that is to say, inside of a power relationship. Moreover, this hierarchical relationship is undergirded by notions of 'excellence' which aspiring young scholars share with those who are already installed in powerful and prestigious positions.

The vulnerability of the younger partner in this pedagogical relationship reaches its most extreme point in the context of graduate, and especially doctoral, training. For preparing a doctorate engenders a very real and narrow dependency on the director, who exercises extensive power over whether the student will advance and prosper with grants, publication opportunities, and proper access to a good job. The vertical transmission of knowledge and skills from the 'master' to the apprentice thus makes of this relationship a fertile terrain for abuses of all sorts, from theft of students' work to various forms of verbal violence and denigration, to pressure for sexual favours. As much as one might (and should) work for a greater democratization of the university, with a more important role for student organizations and instances of appeal in case of conflict between student and thesis supervisor, it is less easy to see how one might restructure the pedagogical relationship itself, as countless experiments over the past 150 years with 'student-centered learning' and less authoritarian teacher–student relationships have shown. Which doesn't mean that it's not worth trying.

Of course, we are no longer in the world that US Supreme Court Justice Ruth Bader Ginsburg describes when speaking of her own experiences as a law student in the 1950s at Harvard University (and here I paraphrase liberally the story she told me during her visit to the European University Institute in February 2016): 'Yes indeed, you are without a doubt the most brilliant student in the class. But we cannot give you a scholarship because that would be like pouring money down the drain. For that money, which could have been awarded to a worthy, if less gifted male student, will have been wasted the day that you decide to have children.'

Such explicit and legitimized forms of discrimination would be among the first to fall in the face of second-wave feminism's determined assault on legally enshrined inequalities between women and men. Thanks to this hard-won success, the problems women face today have more to do with what has been aptly called a culture of everyday sexism; a culture that expresses itself daily in the practices, gestures, and jokes that shape and reflect the everyday work environment. To offer a modest, but telling example: In November 2015, during a post-seminar cocktail at one of Oxford's renowned colleges, a respected older don regaled a circle of younger male colleagues and post-docs with tales of his exploits and adventures. The happy discourse concluded on a theme to which said don believed all could subscribe: 'Having pretty young graduate students is one of the perks of the job'. Whether the titters that rose from the circle of eager young men around him were genuine expressions of approval or mere polite noise is of course, unknowable. What we can say is that the hierarchical rules of the game dictated some kind of response that signalled readiness to join the pack. In a world where good jobs are scarce, standing apart in protest could seem too risky a gesture.

These days one hears a great deal about 'changing the culture', as if such a thing could be achieved via mere incantation or sheer good will. What I would like to suggest here is that 'the culture' is not easily dissociated from the socio-pedagogical structures that underwrite it. And so perhaps the place that we should be looking is at those very structures, with an eye towards imagining how they might be reshaped.

Here is where we run up against a difficult fact of human life: to those who carry privilege, the arrival of equality feels like oppression. For privilege is carried lightly, unconsciously; it is part of the everyday landscape, of the order of the world as they (and we) know it. Rather than screaming 'you are privileged', the roots of this practical knowledge plunge deep into people's everyday sense of how the world is, and should be. Any movement towards equality must perforce feel like a loss. This is why the long, patient, and unrelenting struggle against everyday sexism is where our struggle must live right now.

Notes

1. On the representation of parental involvement in the education of sons, see Potter (2002). See also Bushnell (1996), esp. pp. 26–44.

2. On the tension between English to Latin proficiency, see Nicholson (2013), especially chapter 1.

3. http://www.fitzmuseum.cam.ac.uk/madonnasandmiracles, Fitzwilliam Museum, Cambridge, 7 March–4 June 2017.

4. For the sake of simplicity, I have spoken solely about the situation of women, although the problems confronted by trans and gay people (or anyone whose sexuality is understood as 'atypical') are no less thorny. But they are different.

5. Marieke van den Brinke, Channah Herschberg, and Yvonne Benschop, 'La construction genrée de l'excellence dans les pratiques de recrutement et de sélection des chercheur.e.s en début de carrière', paper in the 9th Conférence européenne sur l'égalité entre les femmes et les hommes dans l'enseignement supérieur et la recherche, Paris, 12–14 September 2016.

References

Alexander, S. (1984), 'Women, Class and Sexual Differences in the 1830s and 1840s', *History Workshop Journal*, 17: 125–49.

Azfar, F. (2012), 'Geneology of an Execution: The Sodomite, the Bishop and the Anomaly of 1726', *Journal of British Studies*, 51 (3): 568–93.

Berlioz, J. (1988), 'La *Lactation* de saint Bernard dans un *exemplum* et une miniature du "Ci Nous Dit"', *Cîteaux*, 39: 270–84.

Boswell, J. (1980), *Christianity, Social Tolerance and Homosexuality: Gay People in Western Europe from the Beginning of the Christian Era Till the Fourteenth Century*, Chicago: The University of Chicago Press.

Brubaker, R. and Cooper, F. (2000), 'Beyond "identity"', *Theory and Society*, 29: 1–47.

Bushnell, R. W. (1996), *A Culture of Teaching: Early Modern Humanism in Theory and Practice*, Ithaca, NY: Cornell University Press.

Butler, J. (1990), *Gender Trouble: Feminism and the Subversion of Identity*, New York: Routledge.

Bynum, C. W. (1987), *Holy Feast and Holy Fast: The Religious Significance of Food to Medieval Women*, Berkeley, CA: University of California Press.

Cerutti, S. (1997), 'Le linguistic turn en Angleterre: Notes sur un débat et ses censures', *Enquête*, 5: 125–40.

Crenshaw, K. (1991), 'Mapping the Margins: Intersectionality, Identity Politics and Violence against Women of Color', *Stanford Law Review*, 43 (6): 1241–99.

Davidoff, L. (1995), *Worlds Between: Historical Perspectives on Gender and Class*, New York: Routledge.

Davidoff, L. and Hall, C. (1987), *Family Fortunes: Men and Women of the English Middle Class, 1780–1850*, Chicago: The University of Chicago Press.

Davis, K. (2008), 'Intersectionality as Buzzword: A Sociology of Science Perspective on What Makes a Feminist Theory Successful', *Feminist Theory*, 9 (1): 67–85.

Drakulić, S. (1992), *How We Survived Communism and Even Laughed*, New York: W. W. Norton & Company.

Dupeux, C. (1991), 'La lactation de saint Bernard, genèse et évolution d'une image', in F. Dunant, J.-M. Spieser and J. Wirth (eds), *L'image et la production du sacré*, 165–93, Paris: Méridiens Klincksieck.

Enterline, L. (2012), *Shakespeare's Classroom: Rhetoric, Discipline, Emotion*, Philadelphia, PA: University of Pennsylvania Press.

Essary, K. (2016), 'Fiery Heat and Fiery Tongue: Emotion in Erasmus' *Ecclesiastes*', *Erasmus Studies*, 36: 5–34.

Fausto-Sterling, A. (2000), *Sexing the Body: Gender Politics and the Construction of Sexuality*, New York: Basic Books.

Francus, M. (2012), *Monstrous Motherhood: Eighteenth Century Culture and the Ideology of Domesticity*, Baltimore, MD: Johns Hopkins University Press.

Gal, S. and Kligman, G. (2000), *The Politics of Gender after Socialism: A Comparative Historical Essay*, Princeton, NJ: Princeton University Press.

Gillis, J. (1989), 'Review of *Family Fortunes*', *American Journal of Sociology*, 94 (1): 170–2.

Hall, C. (1992), *White, Male and Middle-class: Explorations in Feminism and History*, New York: Routledge.

Halperin, D. (1990), *One Hundred Years of Homosexuality: And Other Essays on Greek Love*, New York: Routledge.

Hartley, L. P. (1953), *The Go-Between*, London: H. Hamilton.

Hildegard of Bingen (1988), *Symphonia: A Critical Edition of the 'Symphonia Armonie Celestium Revelationum' (Symphony of the Harmony of Celestial Revelations)*, ed. B. Newman, Ithaca, NY: Cornell University Press.

Hoare, Q. and Nowell Smith, G., eds (1971), *Selections from the Prison Notebooks of Antonio Gramsci*, London: Lawrence & Wishart.

Jones, J. (1985), *Labor of Love, Labor of Sorrow: Black Women, Work and the Family from Slavery to the Present*, New York: Basic Books.

Kane, B. (2008), *Impotence and Virginity in the Late Medieval Ecclesiastical Court of York*, York: Borthwick Papers.

Kane, B. (2018), *Popular Memory and Gender in Medieval England: Men, Women and Testimony in the English Church Courts, c.1200–1500*, Woodbridge: Boydell.

Klapisch-Zuber, C. (1990), *La maison et le nom: Stratégies et rituels dans l'Italie de la Renaissance*, Paris: Éditions de l'École des Hautes Études en Sciences Sociales.

Koditschek, T. (1989), 'Review of *Family Fortunes*', *Contemporary Sociology*, 18: 179.

McCord, N. (1988), 'Review of *Family Fortunes*', *English Historical Review*, 103: 994–6.

Nicholson, C. (2013), *Uncommon Tongues: Eloquence and Eccentricity in the English Renaissance*, Philadelphia, PA: University of Pennsylvania Press.

Penn, S. and Massino, J., eds, (2009), *Gender Politics and Everyday Life in State Socialist Eastern and Central Europe*, New York: Palgrave Macmillan.

Perkin, H. (1988), 'Review of *Family Fortunes*', *Economic History Review*, 41: 309.

Potter, U. (2002), 'Cockering Mothers and Humanist Pedagogy in Two Tudor School Plays', in K. B. McBride (ed.), *Domestic Arrangements in Early Modern England*, 244–78, Pittsburgh, PA: Duquesne University Press.

Roper, L. (1991), *The Holy Household: Women and Morals in Reformation Augsburg*, Oxford: Oxford University Press.

Roper, L. (2004), *Witch Craze: Terror and Fantasy in Baroque Germany*, New Haven, CN: Yale University Press.

Roper, M. (2005), 'Slipping in and out of View: Subjectivity and Emotion in Gender History', *History Workshop Journal*, 59: 57–72.

Roper, M. (2009), *The Secret Battle: Emotional Survival in the Great War*, Manchester: Manchester University Press.

Rubin, M. (2016), 'Liturgy's Present: How Historians are Animating a "New" History of Liturgy', in T. Berger and B. D. Spinks (eds), *Liturgy's Past/s. Methodologies and Materials in the Writing of Liturgical History*, 19–35, Collegeville, MN: Liturgical Press.

Scott, J. W. (1986), 'Gender: A Useful Category of Historical Analysis', *American Historical Review*, 91: 1053–75.

Slater, M. (1989), 'Review of *Family Fortunes*', *Journal of Economic History*, 49: 733.

Smail, D. L. (2016), *Legal Plunder: Households and Debt Collection in Late Medieval Europe*, Cambridge, MA: Harvard University Press.

Steedman, C. (1994), 'Bimbos from Hell', *Social History*, 19 (1): 57–66.

Stewart, A. (1997), *Close Readers: Humanism and Sodomy in Early Modern England*, Princeton, NJ: Princeton University Press.

Tosh, J. (2004), 'Hegemonic masculinity and the history of gender', in S. Dudink, K. Hagemann and J. Tosh (eds), *Masculinities in Politics and War: Gendering Modern History*, 41–58, Manchester: Manchester University Press.

Vance, C. S., ed., (1984), *Pleasure and Danger, Exploring Female Sexuality*, Boston and London: Routledge & Kegan Paul.

Vickery, A. (1993), 'Golden Age to Separate Spheres? A Review of the Categories and Chronology of English Women's History', *Historical Journal*, 36 (2): 383–414.

Walker, G. (2016), 'Child Killing and Emotion in Early Modern England and Wales', in K. Barclay, K. Reynolds and C. Rawnsley (eds), *Death, Emotion and Childhood in Premodern Europe*, 151–71, Basingstoke: Palgrave Macmillan.

Wootton, D. (2000), 'Unhappy Voltaire, or "I Shall Never Get Over it as Long as I Live"', *History Workshop Journal*, 50: 137–55.

CHAPTER 5
HISTORY OF MEMORY
Geoffrey Cubitt

The last three decades have witnessed a spectacular and widely noted 'turn to memory' in historical studies. The scope and significance of this development were still uncertain when Peter Burke published *New Perspectives on Historical Writing* in 1991: that volume's limited attention to memory, either as analytical category or as field of study, is reflected in an index entry narrowed to 'memory, selective', directing attention to a small section of the article on oral history. But Burke himself had already, in an article on 'History as social memory' two years earlier, indicated how an engagement with memory begun in the 1960s with the work of oral historians had broadened in the late 1970s, when other practitioners had begun to explore 'the social history of remembering' (Burke 1989: 99–100). Since Burke's article, the turn to memory among historians has proceeded apace, to the point where it has recently been suggested that memory is now 'as familiar a category for historians as politics, war or empire' (Tumblety 2013: 1). To be sure, the 'emergence of memory in historical discourse' has had its critics (Klein 2000; Gedi and Elam 1996). It has been suggested that the term 'memory' is in danger of being 'depreciated through surplus use' (Confino 1997a: 1397), and that the idea of 'collective memory' in particular 'has been stretched far beyond the boundaries of validity' (Green 2011: 106). It is now, however, seventeen years since Jay Winter (2001: 65–6) spoke of 'memory' as the 'historical signature of our own generation': another generation has followed, without the appetite among historians for studies of memory noticeably abating.

This chapter will explore some of the ideas and approaches involved in historians' engagements with memory over recent decades.[1] It must be recognized, however, that history's turn to memory has been part of a much broader movement: a major part of its significance has lain, indeed, in the opportunities it has created for exchanges with other disciplines on the broad terrain of memory studies.[2] As it has taken shape over the last two or three decades, memory studies has drawn ideas, methods, and practitioners from multiple disciplinary directions, and has produced a proliferation of jostling subfields.

A recent overview (Kattago 2015: 2) lists the following foci – 'collective memory, mentalities, cultural memory, *lieux de mémoire*, monuments, museums, tradition, trauma, nostalgia, historical consciousness, forgetting, silence, commemoration, cosmopolitanism, narrative, mnemohistory, myth, event, modernity and hauntology'; others – for example, oral history, heritage, landscape, mediation, transcultural memory, multidirectionality, everyday memory, usable pasts, organizational memory – could easily be added. Not surprisingly, despite progress towards a more integrated interdisciplinary approach in some areas (see Cubitt 2014), even sympathetic commentators on memory studies are apt to see a 'swag-bag multidisciplinarity' (Pickering and Keightley 2013: 3) as characteristic of the field's development: it remains a loosely structured domain, traversed by diverse currents and traditions.

Determining history's relationship to this field is not easy. Of the many historical studies of memory that have been produced (not all of them by historians), some have circulated widely in the memory studies arena, others less so. Some historians have been active and influential participants in transdisciplinary debates, and others (particularly in oral history) have been important in developing particular approaches. Some have explicitly reflected on how a focus on memory connects to earlier movements in historical studies (Hutton 1993, 2016; Confino 1997a). But it is not easy, at present, to see these various contributions as adding up to a clear collective contribution of historians steering memory studies in a specific direction. It is clear, on the other hand, that many strands in interdisciplinary memory studies creatively interpenetrate the thought and research of historians. In what follows, then, the aim is less to chart a separate disciplinary achievement than to elucidate some of the currents of thought and practice that historians studying memory are caught up in and contribute to. Some of these relate specifically to history as a discipline; others apply to memory studies more generally. First part of this chapter will introduce some of the basic notions underpinning the interest shown in memory by historians, some of its implications for history's disciplinary identity, and some of the contexts and conditions that have shaped the way it has developed; the second part will then explore some of the key themes, issues, and strands in historical memory scholarship in greater detail.

Introducing history's memory turn

Meanings and assumptions

'Memory' as a term has multiple applications, both in scholarly and in common usage. Considered in one dimension, it refers both to actions of recollection (looking backwards at past experiences) and to actions of mnemonic commitment (setting things up to be remembered in the future). Considered in another, it refers both to personal and to societal or collective manifestations of past-related awareness. Sophisticated memory scholarship respects conceptual distinctions between these applications but is also attentive to their interconnections. The term's breadth of reference ensures, however, that historical memory scholarship has many different emphases in practice. Three broad assumptions do, however, seem to have informed and motivated the interest in memory among historians in recent decades.

The first assumption is that what is 'made of the past' – meaning both 'making sense' and 'making use' – is a vital element of human culture. How a given society, and groups and individuals within that society, relate to the past – interpret it, refer to it, evoke it, represent it, manage it, deploy it, instrumentalize it – is a key aspect of that society's cultural make-up, integrally connected to many other features of its activity and organization. Historians studying that society should be concerned to analyse this aspect – which concepts of social memory broadly denote – just as they are to analyse, for example, its political institutions, economic relationships, or religious systems.

The second assumption ties the notion of memory to notions of experience and identity. Memory, in this understanding, does not consist simply of facts or stories or images about a past reality, but of structures of consciousness, binding these things together, that purport to speak, not just of 'what happened', but of how what happened was experienced, and of the mark this experience leaves in subsequent being and self-understanding, whether of individuals or of societies. In looking to memory, historians articulate a sense of the importance of this subjective, experiential, identity-forming dimension of the relationship to the past, often seen as wrongly neglected in conventional historical accounts.

The third assumption is that memory processes, both in the individual and in society, are fundamentally selective and reconstructive. Remembering does not resuscitate or recapture a past reality, or even a past perception of reality, but reconstructs and reconfigures the past through the application of current mental templates and connections, which themselves are always evolving. The past, in short, is not a static source of meaning, to which memory merely gives us access, but is always being reworked through memory, taking on fresh meanings as individuals, groups, and societies adjust to new experiences and conditions. This continuous reprocessing of the past in memory is itself an integral part of the historical process.

The turn to memory and disciplinary identity

Turning to memory has implications for disciplinary identity among historians not paralleled in most other disciplines. History 'deals with the past': it shares memory's referential terrain. The question of its relationship to memory has, therefore, long been central to debates over history's credentials as a form of knowledge (Cubitt 2007: 26–65). Up until the Enlightenment, memory and historical knowledge were not clearly distinguished, but the emergence of history as an assertive intellectual discipline in the nineteenth century altered the picture. Initially, practitioners of this discipline often understood it as a higher form of memory – a memory purged of particularism, refined through scholarly study, and narratively focused on the emergent destiny of the organic national community. But as history's positivist pretensions deepened, the relationship was reframed: memory came to be regarded as history's defining other – partial, subjective, traditional, where history was objective, scientific, and universal. This dichotomy was central to thinking on the historical discipline for most of the twentieth century.

For late twentieth-century historians to start referring to 'history as social memory' (Burke 1989) or as 'an art of memory' (Hutton 1993) thus involved a significant rethinking of disciplinary perspectives. 'Displac[ing] history onto the larger field of memory' (Healey 1997: 5) implied a measure of acceptance, first, that history as practised by professional historians has no natural monopoly or enforceable monitorial authority over the production and circulation of knowledge of the past within society; second, that it is therefore incumbent on historians to engage in a critical but also open and exploratory spirit with other forms and sources of this knowledge; and third, that such an engagement is not best advanced by taking a polarized history-memory dichotomy as axiomatic. Perhaps not surprisingly, many of the first moves in this direction were among self-consciously dissident historians, seeking to undo the conventional complicity of historical studies with established structures of power. Oral historians (Frisch 1990; Thomson, Frisch, and Hamilton 1994), radical theorists of 'popular memory' (Popular Memory Group 1982), proponents of subaltern studies reversed the usual reading of the history-memory relationship, looking not to history for the means of correcting memory, but to the memories of the previously marginalized and excluded for the means of refashioning history itself as a radical instrument, reimagining it as 'a social form of knowledge' (Samuel 1994: 8), and opening it to new community-focused or 'public history' encounters. Later developments have created a questionable boundary between oral history and public history movements on the one hand and more theoretically defined memory studies practices on the other, leading to repeated calls to bring them closer together (Hamilton and Shopes 2008; Pickering and Keightley 2013: 4). Oral history in particular remains, however, an important contributor to history's engagements with memory, both through its powerful insistence on an individual perspective, and through its developing methodological engagement with issues of subjectivity and narrativity and the constructive character of remembering (Thomson 2007).

Another path towards memory ran first through the *histoire des mentalités*, with its challenge to historians to analyse collective attitudes and structures of feeling, and then through the emphasis on meaning and representation associated with the 'new cultural history' of the 1980s. Aligning themselves with approaches in anthropology, literary studies, and art history, new cultural historians shifted the focus of historical inquiry from questions of structure and causation to grasping the discursively constructed character of reality, through the analysis of cultural representations (e.g. Hunt 1989). Though 'memory' was not initially a prominent term in the new cultural historians' repertoire, extending this thinking to encompass representations of the past was a further prospect, which constructivist understandings of memory encouraged historians to explore. Bringing culture and memory together gave cultural history a new focus, and turned historians' interests in memory towards the analysis of cultural forms and mediations.

If radical historical practices and cultural history interests were instrumental in opening the minds of many historians to memory as a field of investigation, the radical challenge posed by postmodernism to history's traditional disciplinary credentials was also important in calling its rigid separation from memory into question. Understanding history itself not as a self-evidently 'objective' form of knowledge, but as a positioned discursive construction, prompted historians to develop a more flexible understanding of how this construction intersects and interacts with others, including those which memory offers. While some historians have held fast to a view of history as 'precisely non-memory' (Bentley 1999: 155), more would nowadays probably agree with Joanna Bourke's (2004: 484–5) contention that, while history and memory 'work with different rules, as different genres', they are also interactive and interdependent, making the 'chasm' between them 'not only narrow', but 'wholly imaginary in places'. The idea that history's value lies in its ability to insulate itself from memory has receded.

Turning to memory: Contexts and conditions

Efforts to contextualize the memory movement in contemporary scholarship often refer, on the one hand, to a general 'crisis of memory' in modernity, and on the other, to a more focused 'memory boom' affecting (or afflicting) contemporary societies, of which the memory turn in scholarship is presumed itself to be an outgrowth. Accounts of the longer-term crisis evoke an 'acceleration of history' (Nora 1996: 1–2), linked to the interwoven effects of political revolution, urbanization, industrialization, and evolving communications technologies in the period following the French Revolution. The sustained shock of these developments shattered assumptions of continuity between past, present, and future, inducing a melancholic sense of loss on the one hand and a restless compensatory quest for new ways of connecting to past histories on the other (Fritzsche 2004: 5–7). For a time, the grand narratives of nationalist, liberal, socialist, and scientific progress woven by historians and others held mnemonic unease in check, but faith in these narratives was itself brutally disrupted by the twentieth century's experiences of war and genocide and menacing threats of nuclear and environmental catastrophe, leaving contemporary societies existentially stranded once again between a forbiddingly uncertain future and a painfully receding past, clutching at memory in a doomed bid for security.

In general outline, this is a serviceable narrative. It gives a clear framework for understanding how memory practices are tied up with broader historical experiences, cultural patterns, and ideological structures, and has helped to give memory studies a sense of contributing to investigation of key aspects of the modern condition. Its principal disadvantage, from the historian's standpoint especially, lies in the impression sometimes created that issues of memory are somehow only significant – or only interesting – in modernity. Students of memory are often too ready to follow Nora in assuming that memory in premodern societies was entirely tied up in the traditional lifeways of stable, territorially defined, pre-industrial communities, or in an 'art of memory' basically geared to the retention and reproduction of pragmatically useful information. It is as well to be reminded not just that theorizing about memory itself has a long intellectual history (e.g. Carruthers 1990), and that the political (and religious) uses of the past have been contentious in many past societies, but also that fluctuations in the cultural presence of the past are not confined to the modern era. Daniel Woolf (2003: 12), for example, detects a 'progressive saturation of public and private discourses, oral and written, by historical references' in early modern England, manifest both in political rituals and in cultural habits like collecting and local history. Nor, finally, as Marita Sturken (1997: 17) observes, is the sense of a memory crisis peculiar to modernity: 'Throughout history, the most prominent characterization of memory has been the idea that it is in crisis'.

The idea of a 'memory boom' in contemporary society likewise requires scrutiny. 'Boom' is not a neutral term: it implies a movement carried to excess and thus in the end inherently unsustainable: boom leads to bust. The literature on contemporary memory abounds in pathologizing descriptions: 'surfeit of memory', 'memorial mania', 'commemorative bulimia', and so on. Denunciations of memorial excess or obsession are seldom, however, supported by an offer of clear criteria for deciding how much memory or commemoration would be enough, or what kinds of memory practice would be regarded as well-balanced, and seem often to overlook the possibility that 'backward-looking' cultural practices may also have 'forward-looking' implications. The 'memory boom' is a 'lumping' construction, which imposes a presumption of common significance on a great diversity of practices. Commentators vary in how they describe it. For many, the key lies in Nora's (1998) account of the present as an 'era of commemoration', but Nora himself (1996: 8–9) saw 'the obsession with the archive' as equally characteristic. Others highlight the prevalence of a grievance-based politics of identity (Maier 1993), or catalogue an escalating series of cultural appetites – for genealogy, antiques, retrochic, historical re-enactment, historical novels – or explore the ubiquity of history in media scheduling, or the commercialization of the past more generally. There are no doubt important connections to be discovered between different kinds and levels of past-related activity, but binding such a variety of activities and experiences up as a single phenomenon, to which pathologizing labels are then sweepingly attached, may not be the best way of exploring them. If the notion of a memory boom is to avoid being unhelpfully reductive, subtler distinctions are needed between (for example) the presence of the past in public political discourse and in private conversation; between researching the past and rhetorically evoking it; between use of the past for recreation and use for political legitimation, between clinging to a past that is in living memory and recalling or reviving a more ancient history, and between historical consumerism and a participatory historical culture. It is also important not to limit memory studies too exclusively to the analysis of contemporary conditions: historians have an obvious role to play in maintaining a broader focus.

While the desire to analyse the temporal insecurities of modernity has been a general influence, developments in memory studies have also been influenced by more specific historical occurrences. The Holocaust is a frequent point of reference. Reflecting on Nazi genocide and its postwar legacy has trained our culture and our scholarship in the idea of the unmasterable traumatic past, applied both to the mental condition of those directly affected by atrocities and – under the more controversial heading of 'collective' or 'cultural trauma' (Alexander et al. 2004) – to the case of post-atrocity societies struggling to deal with issues of guilt and responsibility and their implications for national identity. Notions like trauma, repression, witness, neurosis, and working through have lodged in the core lexicon of memory studies, migrating outwards from the original case of Nazi genocide to encompass other national cases (Rousso 1991), other genocidal experiences, and a widening range of 'difficult' histories: North American slavery (Eyerman 2001), Latin American state repression (Jelin 2003: 71–5), the Irish Troubles (Dawson 2007), even the Norman Conquest of England (Van Houts 1999: 123–42). The significance of all this lies not just in the central place that the notion of trauma has come to hold in many accounts of social memory, but also in the critical reflections this has sometimes given rise to. Critics have argued, for example, that applying the quasi-psychiatric language of trauma to the case of entire societies obscures the extent to which it is political and social factors rather than mental neuroses or inhibitions that determine whether, how, and when difficult or divisive histories are publicly confronted (Kansteiner 2002: 187; Bourke 2004: 473–4). The Holocaust retains, however, its significance as a paradigmatic case for memory studies, which indeed has recently been extended through work which uses Holocaust memory as a primary example for exploring memory's increasingly global and transcultural articulations (Levy and Sznaider 2001; Assmann, A. 2010).

If the Holocaust has been a spectre from recent history haunting memory studies, the dramatic political changes associated with the overthrow of communist regimes in Eastern Europe from the end of the 1980s (and the roughly contemporaneous upheavals in Southern Africa and Latin America) have been a more immediate backdrop to the field's development. These developments brought the politics of regime change and the politics of memory into simultaneous focus and close conjunction. Previously suppressed or 'frozen' memories resurfaced (sometimes very violently), old regimes of memory were sharply interrogated, national histories were rewritten, insecurities generated multiple forms of nostalgic longing. Memory, both personal and collective, became both a value and a stake in processes of lustration, purges, truth commissions, the opening of police archives, the rediscovery of old atrocities, museums, and symbolic conflicts over monuments. Internationally, too, the complexities of memory politics were brought into focus, as former Soviet states whose populations harboured painful memories of Soviet invasion and occupation sought room for these memories within a European Community accustomed to taking the Holocaust as its foundational atrocity, or negotiated uneasy relationships to a Russia still wedded to a triumphalist vision of the wartime Soviet achievement (see, for example Mälksoo 2009; Onken 2007). The attention of scholars was directed both to reconsidering the memory politics of the period after 1945 – now widely viewed as a period of carefully cultivated amnesia (Judt 2000) – and to studying, often within a comparative framework, the complex entanglements of memory, politics, and identity currently unfolding (e.g. Bernhard and Kubik 2014). Studies of this kind – increasingly replicated in scholarship on other global regions – have helped to refine the conceptual apparatus available to historians and political scientists for analysing the stakes and strategies of memory politics in different settings.

Themes, issues, and strands in memory scholarship

The contextual factors so far evoked have helped to shape the lines along which interest in memory among historians has developed: it is time now to explore these lines in greater detail. Though memory studies have always adopted a multiplicity of approaches, from a height a general pattern of evolution is apparent. The drift is from fixity to flux. We have moved, over twenty or thirty years, from a mnemonic arena imaginatively organized into more or less stable and bounded objects or containers – individuals, mnemonic communities, textual representations, static images, locatable memory places – to one where memory is increasingly regarded as palimpsestic, multidirectional, transnational, transcultural, travelling or nomadic, unsettled, entangled, and connective. Unravelling some of the different strands of thought that have contributed to this complex conceptual evolution is the task for the next section of this chapter. Two often intersecting dimensions of memory thinking will be distinguished, the first relating to power and social identity, the second to communication and mediation.

Memory, power, collective identity

One persistent area of discussion concerns the relationship of individual remembering to collective or social frameworks. With rare exceptions like Maurice Halbwachs (1994 [1925], 1997 [1950]), who insisted on the fundamental role of group-specific mnemonic frameworks, earlier twentieth-century scholarship on memory took the individual as its field of study. The late twentieth-century turn to memory, by contrast, was for most practitioners also a movement towards a more socialized understanding. The term 'collective memory', inherited from Halbwachs, became for a time the embattled flagship of this movement. While some scholars rejected the term as misguidedly blurring distinctions between psychological processes in the individual and collective structures of knowledge, and some used it simply as a convenient metaphor, others found it helpful in articulating the idea that memory movements in society are not reducible to multiple acts of individual recollection, but also involve 'shared communications about the meaning of the past', which make use of cultural resources and are grounded in collective experience (Kansteiner 2002: 188).

Over time, moves have been made to soften the once sharp dichotomy of individual and collective. 'Collective memory' remains in use, but reservations about its reifying and homogenizing implications limit its currency. 'Social memory' and 'cultural memory' have gained ground, as have more bespoke coinages like 'collected memory' (Young 1993: 11; Olick 2000), or 'collective remembrance' (Winter and Sivan 1999: 9). There has been movement on the one hand to 'socialize the individual', by recognizing that remembering is something we learn and practice in social situations, and on the other to 'write the individual back into collective memory' (Crane 1997), by showing how individual recollection draws on and feeds back into social memory structures. Frederick Corney (2003) has shown, for example, how the Bolshevik authorities in Russia in the 1920s orchestrated the production of personal narratives cumulatively establishing the status of the October Revolution as a defining moment in popular experience, while Bain Attwood (2001) has traced in detail the processes by which initially dispersed individual memories of the enforced removal of Aboriginal children were brought together as constituents of a 'stolen generations narrative' demanding political and historical recognition. Increasingly, it is the interplay and interdependence of individual and collective that scholars seek to explore.

Early work in social memory studies, largely influenced by Halbwachs, linked memory to group identity. Groups were taken to be the possessors of largely stable and homogeneous mnemonic cultures, through which information pertaining to the group's collective life was transmitted, and individual recollection by group members channelled along lines supportive of the collectivity. The Halbwachsian notion of a 'group' is flexible and variable: scholars working along roughly these lines have fruitfully explored the workings of social memory within, for example, families, villages, businesses, research institutes, monastic communities, and generations.

The most influential collective 'container' for memory studies, has, however, undoubtedly been the imagined community of the nation. A host of studies posit the nation both as primary frame and as principal object – and the institutions of the nation state as key promoters and coordinators – of social or collective memory. Pierre Nora's multi-authored survey of French *lieux de mémoire* (1984–92), despite the diffuseness of its central concept, set an example in compendious compiling of a nation's symbolic places, texts, images, ideas, and institutions that was swiftly imitated and adapted for other countries (Majerus 2014), while the title of Gillis's influential essay collection *Commemorations: The Politics of National Identity* (1994) likewise set the tone for now extensive literatures on monuments and memorials, calendars, anniversaries and days of celebration, and the 'afterlives' or 'mnemohistories' of famous events or individuals.

It is also chiefly in the context of nationally framed studies that students of social memory have conceptualized its social and political dynamics. Central to discussion here is the presumed relationship of memory to social and political unity and thus to power. According to one reading, shared memory is a constituent of unity, and hence a source of power for the united community. According to another, power within a potentially divided society comes from the ability to define or dictate the terms of collective memory, and thus to impose one vision of unity at the expense of others.

Building on the notion of a community bonded by a shared content and joint experience of remembering, one important strand in social memory scholarship analyses the production, codification, preservation, and transmission of memory as a form of collective property. Where Halbwachs concentrated on the short-term workings of social memory in the consciousness of individuals and groups of contemporaries, the influential work of Jan and Aleida Assmann uses the term 'cultural memory' to describe the long-term 'concretion of identity' that arises within societies from the encapsulation of selected memories in durable cultural form – in 'that body of reusable texts, images, and rituals specific to each society in each epoch, whose "cultivation" seems to stabilize and convey that society's self-image' (Assmann, J. 1995: 130–2). The model is refined further by distinguishing between the 'canon' (or 'cultural working memory') – the elements that are continually publicly articulated and that symbolically capture the society's self-image at any given moment – and the 'archive' (or 'cultural reference memory') – the elements that are stored away, out of mind but retrievable for future use (Assmann, A. 2008; see also Cubitt 2007: 144–6).

Work of this kind valuably focuses attention on the need for memory scholarship to analyse long-term transmissions and structurations, but there is a risk of abstraction if we overlook the operations of power that may be involved in determining what is remembered or forgotten, what is archived or canonized, when and how the canon is revised, and how and by whom the meanings of that canon are interpreted. A different approach to social memory analysis treats mnemonic unity as an ideological construct masking realities of contestation and exclusion. Historians have shown, for example, how the analysis of American Civil War monuments reveals 'a story of systematic cultural repression, carried out in the guise of reconciliation and harmony' (Savage 1994: 143), how the politics of commemoration in early twentieth-century Spain 'served to disrupt rather than to forge bonds of social and political solidarity' (Boyd 2002: 40), or how mythicized mnemonic structures applied to Caribbean history (Trouillot 1995) or to France's Second World War experience (Rousso 1991) promote certain memories while obfuscating others.

Accounts of memory conflict have often utilized a basic conceptual opposition between 'official' or 'elite' memory on the one hand, usually envisaged as unitary, hegemonic, and institutionalized (often through state structures), and 'popular', 'vernacular', or 'subaltern' memories, or 'counter-memory' on the other, generally understood as plural, diffuse, grounded in grass-roots non-elite experiences, and resisting assimilation (Popular Memory Group 1982; Zerubavel 1995; Marschall 2010). Recent scholarship, without abandoning an interest in underlying issues of power, has however often sought to develop a more fluid understanding of the relationships involved. Sometimes this has come through refinements of the 'elite versus popular' model, positing 'public memory', for example as an intermediate realm of negotiation and accommodation between unitary official and plural vernacular cultures (Bodnar 1991), or simply stressing that 'polarized confrontations' between official and unofficial memory cultures are less common than 'a messy, uneven, dynamic, creative *interplay*' between them (Wood 2013: 21). Other scholars focus less on the categories of elite and popular than on the plural dynamics of civil society and its relationship to state agency. In Winter and Sivan's influential 'social agency' interpretation of First World War commemoration, the state is only one participant in a commemorative process thrashed out 'through exchanges among members of social networks' within civil society (Winter and Sivan 1999: 30, 17), while Franziska Seraphim (2006: 5) sees public memory in postwar Japan as fashioned on a 'middle level of the political process' occupied by 'groups of ordinary citizens communicating their interpretations of the war and the postwar to their own constituents, to the state and to the larger public as well'.

A more radical conceptual challenge to conventional understandings of memory conflict comes from the literary scholar Michael Rothberg's recently influential theorization of memory as 'multidirectional'. Rothberg challenges two assumptions which he sees as fundamental to previous thinking: first, the idea that groups and memories are essentially connected (so that each group owns a particular set of memories, and each set of memories belongs to a particular group); and second, the idea that memories are engaged in a 'zero-sum' competition, in which the flourishing of some is automatically to the detriment of others. Rather than conceiving of the public sphere as 'a pregiven, limited space in which already-established groups engage in a life-and-death struggle', with memories as stakes and weapons, Rothberg argues, we should see it as 'a malleable discursive space', in which group identities are continually produced and adjusted through 'dialogical interactions with others', of which memory interactions are an essential medium (Rothberg 2009: 5). While Rothberg does not deny that power differentials affect outcomes in this fluid discursive realm, he creatively prompts students of memory to develop a more complex exploration of memory's relationships to power and identity.

By querying the adequacy of 'containerised' understandings of memory in general, the notion of memory as multidirectional adds a fresh dimension to movements which, while recognizing nationhood as a key mnemonic domain in modern societies, have investigated the intersections and interactions of that domain with other mnemonic framings. Moving 'inwards' from the nation, studies have questioned the once assumed zero-sum relationship between national and local constructions of community, exploring the ways in which national and local identifications are jointly expressed through pageants and civic ritual, local history and archaeology, folklore and the 'sense of place' or Heimat (Bodnar 1991; Confino 1997; Glassberg 2001; Gerson 2003).

Moving 'outwards' from single-nation studies, investigations have been launched which, in various ways, spread the study of memory across national boundaries. Comparisons of commemorative practice in different national settings expose important differences, but also sometimes the extent to which different countries draw on and contribute to shared repertoires of symbolic practice, even when pursuing nationalist commemorative agendas – as, for example, when different combatant nations adopted the commemorative cult of the Unknown Soldier (Inglis 1993), or when the nineteenth-century commemorative cult of great literary figures 'fan[ned] out from Shakespeare' to the literary heroes of other nations (Rigney and Leerssen 2014). Comparing commemoration of the 1848 Revolutions in different countries (Brubaker and Feischmidt 2002), or foundational anniversaries in the United States and Australia (Spillman 1997), or memories of transatlantic slavery around the Atlantic (Araujo 2014), also reminds us how often ostensibly 'national' memories relate to historical experiences – of war, revolution, imperialism, decolonization, slavery – that were international or transnational in character. Nationalized memories of (for example) the French Revolutionary and Napoleonic Wars coexist and intersect with ways of remembering these experiences that resonate transnationally, contributing in some cases to wider – in this case European – conceptions of identity (François 2012). Migrations, exiles, and diasporic movements also generate flows of memory that cut across national memories, complicating memory politics with competing, ambivalent, or hybridized identity constructions (Gilroy 1995; Halstead 2014). The memory cultures of medieval Christendom, of the Reformation or of the international Enlightenment offer earlier evidence of memory's geographically extensive propensities.

Recent scholarship uses the terminology of 'transnational' or 'transcultural' memory to explore these issues (De Cesari and Rigney 2014; Bond and Rapson 2014). 'Transnational' and 'transcultural' are not coterminous (since cultures can be transnational and nations transcultural), but the distinction between them is often blurred in practice. Both convey an emphasis on what Astrid Erll (2011: 9) calls the 'travelling' character of memory. Importantly, however, the travelling focused on is not just around the world in ever widening global memory circuits, but backwards and forwards between experiences and expressions of mnemonic community pitched at local and national as well as transnational or global levels. Globalized memories (like that of the Holocaust) are 'prismatic and heterogeneous rather than holistic and universal' (Huyssen 2003: 26), while local memories are constantly impinged on and remodelled through encounters with nationalizing, globalizing, or transnationalizing constructions (Beyen and Deseure, 2015) – as for example when Jamaican Maroon communities, traditionally self-protectively averse to sharing local memories with outsiders, are forced to reckon with appropriations of their history by the assimilationist postcolonial state and by pan-Africanist interests intent on building Maroon resistance into a larger African heroic history (Bilby 2005: xiv, 26).

Memory, communication, mediation

Thinking about memory's relationship to the social dynamics of power and identity runs repeatedly into thinking about its practices and processes of transmission: memory can achieve no effect outside the heads of isolated individuals unless it is communicated. In an influential article, Olick and Robbins (1998) registered and promoted a shift of attention in memory studies 'from "collective memory" to the historical sociology of mnemonic practices'. What was described was really a shift on two related levels: away from viewing collective memory as a reified group-specific collective property towards understanding it as a dynamic process; and away from a methodology based on representational analysis towards a social analysis of practice. Analysis, here, may be focused at a number of interconnecting levels: at a societal level, on understanding how memory processes are affected by systemic social and economic features (Connerton 2009); at an intermediate level, on how memory practices are fitted to the requirements and social rhythms of particular groups or organizations; at a more intimate level, finally, on the social dynamics of particular memory practices.

Mnemonic practices are extremely varied: the term can cover anything from the complex organization of national anniversaries to practices of genealogy or collecting, from the erection of memorials to the use of photo albums or the medieval cult of relics, from informal fireside story-telling practices to the preservation of historical monuments or – since the organization of forgetting is itself an element of mnemonic strategy (Connerton 2008; Passerini 2003) – political procedures of *damnatio memoriae*. Scholarly attention focuses on practices that become part of a familiar repertoire of practice within a given group or society. Culturally embedded, regularized and sometimes institutionalized, such practices may become in themselves objects as well as vehicles of recollection: thus, for example, the meanings of a war may effectively be filtered for future generations through the repetitive memory of annual commemorative ceremonial. In such cases, mnemonic practices are not merely technical instruments for transmitting memory messages but are themselves active constituents in a social memory process.

Analysis, in this practice-focused approach, is directed at how memory becomes 'embedded in social action' (Confino and Fritzsche 2002: 4–5) – how the activities that develop it also build, mobilize, or modify social relationships, both real and imagined.

By understanding how memory practices are socially organized – how they connect to roles, routines, and relationships, including those of gender (e.g. Van Houts 1999; Leydesdorff, Passerini, and Thompson 1996; Jelin 2003: 76–88), class and generation, and how they intersect with other social activities, we gain a deepened understanding of memory as a social resource. The approach also helps to 'write the individual back into collective memory', by showing how the practices which develop these individuals as remembering subjects also socialize their frames of mnemonic reference and contribute to memory's social circulation.

Representations, in the form of texts or images or monuments or rituals, still have a place in a practice-focused analysis but are not automatically central: they appear less as privileged containers of mnemonic meaning than as points around and through which different, often interconnecting, kinds of practice are organized. Understanding the mnemonic resonances of a text, for example, requires analysis not just of its content, but of its relationships and processes of production, circulation, reception, use, and interpretation. A war memorial, similarly, may be the outcome of complex and conflicted intersecting processes of planning, funding, and artistic production, and is then put to use in practices of collective remembrance, in which the same or different social forces may be enlisted (King 1998). For some recent students of commemoration, indeed, memorials are interesting less in themselves than for the debates and negotiations that they occasion both before and after their production: their significance is 'dialogic' and therefore always evolving, rather than material, static, and definitive (Carrier 2005: 3–9).

If a practice-focused approach displaces attention from culture as a discrete realm of autonomously embodied meanings, it redirects it to culture as the medium of mnemonic exchanges. As Erll and Rigney (2009a: 1) put it, the concept of cultural memory is 'premised on the idea that memory can only become collective as part of a continuous process whereby memories are shared with the help of symbolic artefacts that mediate between individuals and, in the process, create communality across both space and time'. The term 'mediation' has become central to many discussions of how cultural memory operates, often combining two different though related notions – that cultural devices 'mediate' communicatively between individuals (thus allowing memory to be 'shared' or 'transmitted'); and that this communicative process also 'mediates' (in the sense of (re)configuring or (re)encoding) the meanings that are conveyed. Whether applied to the use of narrative templates in journalism or historical writing (Wertsch 2002: 5; Hoskins 2009: 37) or to the articulation of memory through ritual or material culture, the idea of mediation works with a doubled account of memory's operations: scripts or templates or generic conventions charged with a certain cultural resonance are retained and transmitted in social memory, which are then used over time to assimilate fresh data to familiar structures of mnemonic meaning: 9/11 is read through the memory of Pearl Harbor, the Columbine High School massacre linked in to an age-old discourse of Christian martyrdom (Castelli 2004: 172–96).

Recent work by literary scholars has extended this thinking further via the notion of 'remediation'. Particular enactments of memory in text or image or ritual serve as 'relay stations' (Rigney 2008: 350–1), picking up and recycling and redirecting figurations of memory from a variety of sources. Over time, memories relating to particular events or personalities pass through a series (and often a simultaneous multiplicity) of mediating encounters, involving different media and cultural genres, each remediation bringing adjusted meanings and fresh connections, as well as new audiences for the memory in question. The result, typically, is a situation in which 'what is known about a war, a revolution or any other event which has been turned into a site of memory ... seems to refer not so much to what one might cautiously call the "actual events", but instead to a canon of existent medial constructions, to the narratives and images circulating in a media culture' (Erll 2008: 392). But mediatory processes also, by forging new connections, gradually modify the imaginative templates that then – in a further extension of terminology – work to 'premediate' fresh assimilations of data. Through multiple remediations and premediations along these lines, palimpsestic layerings, transfers, and entanglements of meaning are built up within memory culture: references to Ancient Rome or to the Holocaust become touchstones for understanding later republican or imperial experiences or human rights abuses; memories of England's seventeenth-century experiences of revolution and restoration pass, through readings of Clarendon and Hume and Walter Scott, into the memory repertoire drawn on by nineteenth-century Frenchmen struggling to navigate their own post-Revolutionary history (Cubitt 2007a).

Thinking about *mediation* leads us to *mediatization*. Where the former refers to the effects of passing particular sets of memories through particular cultural artefacts, the latter extends the concept to embrace the systemic effects on memory in general of particular media 'regimes' or 'ecologies' – terms used to designate the cultures and conditions, both technological and social, associated either with the dominance of particular media (orality, written script, print, the newspaper press, broadcast media, digital media, etc.) or with the interplay of different media within a given society (Neiger et al. 2011; Garde-Hansen 2011). In a general descriptive sense, 'mediatization' is an aspect of memory in any society, including ones heavily dependent on oral communication (since orality is itself a medium of communication which imposes a certain shape on memory and its social uses). The term is also, however, used in some scholarly contexts to refer more specifically to an *escalating* dependence of memory on media (meaning in this case the modern 'mass' media) which is perceived by scholars to be a characteristic tendency of contemporary societies (Garde-Hansen 2011: 1, 6; Hoskins 2009: 29). Under either usage, analyses of mediatization impart two additional emphases to discussions of how memory is culturally mediated. First, by shifting attention from specific instances of mediation to systems-level analysis, such analyses bring issues of consumption and commodification into the foreground: under most media regimes, the majority of individuals appear more as consumers than as generators of the memory content put into circulation. Second, focusing on the structural and systemic features of media ecologies heightens awareness of systemic contrasts, and thus directs attention to the effects of major changes in media technology on the way memory is formed and circulated, and on its social and cultural significance.

Historians, anthropologists, and others have long explored the mnemonic effects of, for example, transitions from orality to literacy and contemporary memory studies has engaged avidly with the rapid revolutionary changes in media technologies and cultures that have been a continuous backdrop to its own development. Critical debates have arisen over the kind of historical consciousness – and more specifically of ethical engagement with the past – that contemporary media-driven culture supports. Are we in contemporary society merely 'tourists of history', enjoying the specious pleasures of a mediated connection to the past within a 'consumer culture of comfort' which protects us from any assumption of responsibility? (Sturken 2007: 9–12). Or are the 'prosthetic memories' (Landsberg 2004) that modern media allow contemporary citizens to acquire by connecting them vicariously to the historical experiences of others a genuine potential basis – notwithstanding the commercial impulses that underpin them – for new historically grounded forms of ethical community? Another strand of research focuses more specifically on the 'new memory ecology' – relentlessly interactive, hyper-connective, and convergent – which digital media, the internet, and social media are deemed to be introducing (Garde-Hansen, Hoskins, and Reading 2009; Reading 2011). 'Digital memory', as analysed in this literature, blurs temporal distinctions, accelerates communication, by-passes conventional authority, hybridizes public and private, replaces top-down dissemination and containerized mnemonic community with peer-to-peer interaction and viral diffusion, adding yet further levels of fluidity to the transcultural, multidirectional, transactional modalities of contemporary memory already referred to. As well as stimulating longer-term reflections on memory's and media's interconnecting evolutions, work along these lines directs the attention of historians in particular to the altered conditions under which history's own relationship to social memory has now to be negotiated.

Conclusion

From the initial mental linkages of memory to 'experience' on the one hand and 'cultural representation' on the other, historical investigations of memory have radiated outwards, drawing sustenance from contacts with other disciplines, across a vast and varied territory of inquiry. Memory is no longer best understood as a subfield of historical study; rather it is a perspective, drawn on in multiple branches of historical investigation, and applicable in principle to almost any. Historical memory studies have many different emphases and directions (only some of which have been explored in this chapter), but the conceptual space they take shape in is broadly triangular: power, cultural meaning, and communication are the coordinates, which scholars bring together in different combinations. The movement of memory studies from fixity and discreteness to flux and interdependence has called once taken-for-granted boundaries and distinctions into question, and in so doing, has drawn historians into increasingly subtle and multidimensional reflections. In these memory appears less as a stable cultural property than as a circulatory medium of appropriation and interaction, through which individuals, cultures, and societies negotiate shifting relationships both to each other and to a past whose forms and connotations are themselves continually mutating.

Memory is important to historians, not just because it is part of how history is experienced, but because as a crucial factor in human perception, it is part of the causal matrix that influences human action. Writing history with memory left out impoverishes our historical understanding, but building 'histories of memory' adjacent to mainstream structures of historical analysis is at best a partial solution: the ultimate challenge is to integrate the two more fully. The challenge is twofold. First, there is a need to reflect on how an awareness of memory as an important historical dimension may refresh or reform the conventional toolkit of historical analysis: how does it affect how we think about the status of 'events', the role of structures, periodization, continuity, and rupture, and causality in general? The second task is to develop methodologies that will allow the questions memory scholars are used to asking about how memories are formed, articulated, contested, mediated, and circulated to nourish a deeper investigation of how they are operationalized, how they motivate, mobilize, enable, or inhibit individual or collective action – how, in short, memory does not simply reflect on but actively contributes to shaping human history.[3]

Furthering a response to these challenges runs beyond the remit of this chapter. A starting point might, however, be to consider how bringing memory into the forefront of historical studies transforms conventional historical understandings of temporality. Traditionally, historical analysis has played in two temporal registers – the linear chronological register that allows historical happenings to be dated and related to each other synchronically or diachronically; and the narrative register in which collections of happenings are gathered together into stories that connect them thematically and causally and endow them with collective cultural significance. Conventionally in historical scholarship, these registers work in tandem: narrative constructions, especially when they involve causal relationships, run beyond but are understood as constrained by 'the order in which things happened'. Introducing memory complicates the picture, since memory as a medium of perception disrupts temporal linearity and only intermittently concurs with the kinds of narrative ordering historians are used to imposing. Events and experiences that are remembered are not contained within their moment of occurrence, but take on 'spectral energy' (Tamm 2015: 4), lingering in consciousness for greater or lesser periods, submerging and re-emerging, acquiring and shedding meanings and connections. Memories of events that are chronologically separate, mediated through different channels, and circulating in different circuits, get brought together in shifting and unpredictable combinations.

All of this imparts to the historical process, as we imaginatively experience it, 'a texture not of orderly sequence but of tangled simultaneity' (Cubitt 2007: 22), which conventionally framed historical narratives struggle to capture. Notions of 'haunting' capture aspects of it in a fanciful language and recent theorizations of 'mnemohistory' provide a conceptual approach to exploring it. Mnemohistory 'is concerned not with the past as such, but only with the past as it is remembered', less with the 'factuality' of a given memory (whether it corresponds to what actually happened) than with its 'actuality' – the meanings it takes on in 'an ever-changing present in which these events are remembered as facts of importance' (Assmann J. 1997: 9–10). It would be misleading, however, to read this as affirming a flatly 'presentist' understanding of memory, in which each successive age or generation simply configures a past to fit its present needs and conditions: there is commonly a degree of path-dependency in mnemonic practice, so that 'part of the context for any new commemoration is the residue of earlier commemorations' (Olick 2007: 57). Nor should we assume too rigid a conceptual separation of events 'as such' from the way those events are remembered. The remembering of an event generally starts with the event itself – with the sense made of that event by participants and observers, which may itself be 'premediated' by 'deep memory' (Beiner 2007) of earlier experiences, and which may also be embodied in conscious and even formal efforts to influence or predetermine the way the event will be remembered in future. Indeed, events themselves – as supposedly discrete 'moments' of concentrated historical action, locatable in time and possessed of discernible causes and effects – are not primal realities, but complex mental constructions, pulled into shape over time through complex social memory processes (Cubitt 2014: 37–9). Memory is not posterior to eventuality – something that kicks in once 'things have happened': making history, experiencing it, remembering it, and working it up into shared understandings of how past and present are related are activities whose intimate interconnections historians are called on to investigate.

Comment

Ann Rigney

Geoffrey Cubitt has given us a magisterial overview of the evolution of memory as topic of study and analytic concept within the discipline of history. Written within the framework of a handbook for historians, his chapter bears eloquent testimony to a sea change in conceptualizations of the relationship between 'history' and 'memory' that has taken place over the last decades as a result of shifting positions within the field of history, on the one hand, and the emergence of memory studies as an academic field of inquiry, on the other. Three decades ago 'history' stood across from memory as close relations but also as rivals. In its most neutral version, the opposition between 'history' and 'memory' represented two different modes of relating to past experience. In its more contentious form, the distinction served to underscore and reassert the epistemological authority of the disciplined historian or, alternatively, the claim on the part of those who challenged that authority to speak on behalf of groups who had been left out of dominant models of history. Luckily this either-or approach is largely a thing of the past.

This is because there have been significant developments within the field of history, as Cubitt shows, including a rethinking of temporality and the concept of the event. This rethinking can be seen as one of the broader offshoots of historians' exposure to theorizations of memory and its non-linear temporalities (see also Hartog 2015; Bevernage 2012). Even more important in the present context, however, is the fact that memory no longer needs defending as a legitimate object of scholarly concern. As a result of sustained scholarly engagement over a period of three decades, memory has become conceptualized in more sophisticated and discriminating ways (compared for example to Klein 2000 which critically decried the use of the concept of memory for its purported essentialism). To be sure, there is some variation in terminology: literary and media scholars, like myself, use the term 'cultural memory' as a leading concept in order to capture the cultural constituents of memory and its mediated transmission; sociologists in contrast use collective memory as a leading concept in order to capture the social relations shaped and sustained through shared memory. But by now, there is a general consensus in the literature summarized by Cubitt that cultural/collective memory should be viewed as the shared understanding of the presence of the past; that this shared understanding is the outcome of a historically contingent social-cultural dynamic; that it involves a complex and multidirectional transfer of meaning and affect between the individual and the community; that it is the outcome of mediated acts of recollection which are informed by and in turn help to shape ideas of belonging; that while the nation has been a key social framework in the production of memory and identity in the last 200 years, memory also circulates in communication networks outside the framework of the nation; that memory is subject to processes of canonization but also to contestation on the parts of groups jostling for recognition or power within particular contexts; and finally, that cultural practices of memory and the importance attached to memory as a basis for identity may differ from one period to another.

As the study of such a socio-cultural dynamic, memory studies could only emerge at the intersection of multiple disciplines from across the humanities and social sciences: cognitive science, literary and cultural studies, cultural history, political science, sociology, anthropology, and human rights law. Each of these disciplines has inflected the slowly institutionalizing field of memory studies in specific ways. The exchanges between them, albeit limited and always falling short, have certainly helped advance understanding of the complex interplay between culture, social relations, and politics in the evolution of memory in particular contexts. The next few years will be crucial for consolidating these gains and advancing further cross-disciplinary exchanges. Suffice it to note here that 'history' is only one among many within this multidisciplinary constellation, rather than the only significant 'other'. By now, a quarter century or so after the foundation of the journal *History and Memory* (1989), the publication of Pierre Nora's *Lieux de mémoire* (1984–92), and Jan Assmann's *Das kulturelle Gedächtnis* (1992), bringing 'history' and 'memory' into conversation no longer presupposes a territorial battle or a hostile takeover in which you have to privilege one term or field of inquiry above another.

Exemplifying this change, a recent survey article by historian Alon Confino marks a milestone recognition of the significance of memory studies: 'the enduring contribution of memory studies has been to document in wholly new ways the fundamental importance of the presence of the past in human society' (2011: 46). Where Confino is concerned with what memory studies can add to history, I would like to ponder instead what the specific expertise of historians can *add* to the interdisciplinary field of memory studies. I take Cubitt's coining of the term 'historical memory studies' to be indicative in this regard, but also an invitation to think more about how memory studies could in turn benefit from the contribution of historians. Cubitt has already indicated how research is called for into the long-term interaction between memory and politics if we are ever to grasp the agency of memory ('how it not only reflects on, but actively contributes to shaping human history'). In what follows, I shall expand briefly on some of the topics raised by Cubitt in what is already a very comprehensive essay and, in doing so, reflect further on how historicization could significantly contribute to the further advancement of memory studies, working with its agenda rather than opposing it. With the bulk of work in memory studies concentrating on the post-Second World War period and even on contemporary memory practices, historians have a particular task in examining longer-term dynamics and providing a counter-weight to presentism.

Changing memory and the dynamics of (un)forgetting

It is a truth universally acknowledged in contemporary memory studies that remembering is inseparable from forgetting. The complex dynamic whereby certain narratives become canonized can also be turned inside out so as to uncover the mechanisms whereby alternative narratives are overlooked or actively erased. As Cubitt mentions 'the organisation of forgetting is itself an element of mnemonic strategy'. To this observation can be added another: namely, that forgetting is not a simple operation and that, as Paul Connerton (2008) and Aleida Assmann (2016) among others have pointed out, there are varieties and modes of forgetting. These range from the active erasure of all traces to the conscious decision to remain silent (Ben-Ze'ev at al. 2010; Passerini 2003; Weinrich 1997), to the inability to remember, or to what Ann Laura Stoler (2011) has called, with reference to the memory of colonialism, 'aphasia'. Originally a term referring to the loss of linguistic ability, aphasia in this case means a cognitive and affective inability to make sense of signs: to see what is before one's eyes. Some of the most interesting work in recent years has sought to explain why certain events or episodes, which people now find important, could have been overlooked in the past. Using Stoler's concept of aphasia, Paul Bijl (2015) has shown with detailed reference to photographs of atrocities committed under Dutch colonial rule in Atjeh how these photographs were present in the public sphere for decades but were structurally overlooked because they contradicted the dominant national narrative; it took repeated 'discoveries' of the photographs in changing cultural contexts before their significance registered. A similar story of the slow emergence of a memory narrative and the concomitant overcoming of aphasia has been told by Susanne Knittel (2014) with reference to the memory of the victims of Nazi euthanasia policies.

Studies outlining such resistance to the memory of 'difficult' pasts that challenge dominant identity narratives mark an important counterpoint to earlier studies of traumatic events that continue to haunt victims because of their inability to fit them into schemes of knowledge (Caruth 1995). Research especially in the field of colonialism has shown that it is not enough for things to be experienced or even recorded for them to be remembered; cultural memory only emerges in conjunction with the availability of the languages, schemata, and frames that are needed to make a story stick by making collective sense. This is also one of the key insights of Michael Rothberg's *Multidirectional Memory: Remembering the Holocaust in the Age of Decolonization* (2009): that the memory of one set of events can help another memory to emerge by providing a model for its articulation. More historical research is needed into the long-term emergence of new memories in this way, including the role of the arts in helping provide languages with which to overcome the aphasia associated with difficult pasts. As Cubitt reminds us, research into intra-national struggles about the meaning of the collective past has long been important in memory studies. Recent years have seen an additional concern with the challenges posed by migration to the very idea of a unitary national memory associated with a particular territory. This has led to a growing body of research into diasporic memory as well as into the impact of migrants on local traditions of commemoration (Rothberg 2014; Glyn and Kleist 2012). Understanding better how groups can change their memories and not just defend them, and providing historical evidence to show such changes in the past, is a matter not just of scholarly but also of societal urgency at a time when memory is being used as a bulwark against the integration of migrants in Europe.

Historicizing trauma

Different historical accounts have been given of the emergence of memory in society and in scholarship. Although a strong case can be made for the centrality of memory to nineteenth-century nation-building, and for the importance of the First World War in inaugurating a culture of mourning (Winter 1995), there is no doubt that the Holocaust marked a watershed in the emergence of the concept of memory as such. It generated a new repertoire of mnemonic practices, including the genre of testimony (Wieviorka 2006), and a new set of scholarly concerns relating to the ethics of remembrance and the comparability of suffering (Margalit 2002; Rothberg 2011). As the decades passed, it also focused attention on transgenerational transmission, secondary trauma, and the dynamics of family remembrance (Hirsch 2008; Welzer, Moller, and Tschuggnall 2002). Even more fundamentally, Holocaust memorial culture put trauma, victimhood, and suffering at the centre of memory. To be sure: memory cultures and politics continue to transform and enter into new alignments and new critical tools are being developed to capture them: recent studies of perpetratorship (Critchell et al. 2017) and of 'implicated subjects' (Rothberg 2013) have challenged the exclusive focus on victimhood. But they remain within the same logic of grievance and a 'politics of regret' (Olick 2007), with memory continuing to be conceptualized in terms of hurt and, in the context of transitional justice, as something to be 'worked through'.

By now, however, questions are being raised about the historical and theoretical limits of trauma in the study of memory. Does cultural memory by definition relate only to painful things and things that are not to be repeated, as summed up in the phrase *nie wieder* or *nunca más*? Cubitt rightly challenges the standard narrative in which cultures of memory are linked to a modernity set in opposition to traditional or ancien régime societies where, it is claimed, a relatively stable world made the need to remember less urgent: the past was not experienced as such, so great was its continuity with the present (see also Terdiman 1993; Nora 1984–92; Koselleck 1979). As Cubitt reminds us, studies of memory cultures in the periods prior to the French Revolution have provided evidence with which to bridge the modern-premodern fault line and open perspectives on alternative cultures of remembrance. However, Cubitt's nuancing of the modernity-memory nexus can be taken even a step further, by not just taking the variable intensity of mnemonic activity into account, but also the modes of remembrance that characterize different periods. Even within the post-1800 period, there are differences: the celebratory memory cultures predominant in the nineteenth century involved festivals, parties, and parades (Rigney 2012; Leerssen and Rigney 2014) rather than memorials to the dead and the emphasis on mourning familiar today.

Historicizing contemporary cultures and conceptualizations of memory is necessary for a fuller picture of the politics-memory nexus and its varieties. It provides a theoretical impulse to think beyond trauma in the study of memory and to recognize alternative traditions that have been occluded. Reflecting a larger unease with the predominance of the traumatic, there have been recent calls to study the cultural remembrance of non-violent struggle (Hamilton 2010; Katriel and Reading 2015) as well as commemorative cultures within social movements (Rigney 2016) and utopian traditions (Traverso 2016). More historical research along these lines into the alternative modes of remembrance practised by activist groups is set to bring to light a broader range of mnemonic possibilities than those offered by war and genocide. In expanding the very notion of memory beyond the transfer and working through of trauma, it may open the way for a better understanding of how pride and hope are also conveyed across generations.

Parallel to these calls to historicize the traumatic, there have been calls to open the field of research to consideration of non-European cultures of memory. If this has involved extending the notion of trauma to the colonial experience (Craps 2013), it has more often meant challenging the assumption that Western post-Holocaust models of memory are automatically transferable to non-European situations (Fassin and Rechtman 2009) and that indigenous cultures of memory fit into the models developed in the global north (Cole 2001).

The productive tension between memory and history

As work in the field of cultural memory studies has shown, memory is not constituted on any one occasion or at any single site. Instead, it is continuously being produced, reproduced, and contested as it is reiterated across different media and cultural practices, and transferred across groups and generations (see Erll and Rigney 2009). This multi-sited and multidirectional model affords a new perspective on the role of historians, which both relativizes their authority and enhances their importance. It is helpful at this point to recall Paul Ricœur's presentation of the relationship between historical inquiry and memory practices in terms of a dialectic. History (as the disciplined knowledge of the past) provides society with documented evidence and well-informed judgements on what actually happened, while collective memory consists of narratives that provide a sense of collective purpose, value, and identity in the present. History and memory both need each other, Ricœur insisted, since each helps keep the other in check. Historical research does this by challenging collective memories that in being repeated too often have acquired the character of a myth resistant to change (Ricœur 2000, 2006). People's commitment to memory, on the other hand, continuously generates a demand for historians to look for knowledge that is not only true but also meaningful and relevant to present-day concerns.

The availability of archival evidence is not enough for an event to become a part of cultural memory. Something can be true and still not be meaningful, as we have seen. Equally, something can be very meaningful (as in strongly held beliefs about the origin and homogeneity of the nation) but untrue and unfounded. Within the larger social-cultural dynamics of memory, then, history has a particular role to play in providing and validating evidence that may work against mythmaking and help produce a counter-memory. While Ricœur emphasized above all the critical role of historians in deconstructing unfounded beliefs, historians are arguably more effective when they bring new materials into circulation that counter amnesia by providing the basis for new narratives. One of the premises of cultural memory studies is that popular media and cultural practices are key sites in the production and circulation of shared narratives. The challenge for historians, then, is to be heard in today's highly mediatized society with its new channels of communication but also its welter of unsubstantiated claims and alternative facts.

Response

Geoffrey Cubitt

Ann Rigney's judicious comments tend to confirm rather than to call in question the suggestions of my inevitably broad-brush account of history's recent engagements with memory and memory studies. Certain points are accentuated, others insightfully glossed, and readers will be grateful for Rigney's elegantly efficient summary of the emergent features which she and I broadly agree in finding characteristic of a field to which we have come from somewhat different intellectual directions. I am thus, to my relief, not called on here to improvise defence for an analysis under attack, or to challenge contrary interpretations. Instead, I shall follow Rigney in addressing the question that she rightly proposes should be explored further: given that the project of memory studies has opened historians to new intellectual experiences, and brought them into productive contact with other disciplines, what kind of contribution might we expect historians to be involved in making to the further development of the field?

Both in Rigney's account and in my own, the breaking-down of the once conventional rigid opposition between memory on the one hand and the working habits and professional knowledge of historians on the other marks a significant moment, challenging historians to develop more flexible intellectual interactions and working partnerships, and forcing memory studies more generally to reconsider what was often a rather lazy habit of conceptualizing memory through this supposedly fundamental opposition. This is not to say that the defining project of the historian – the 'reasoned reconstruction of the past rooted in research' (Blight 2002) – and the critical and analytical tools developed for the pursuit of that project have now become redundant: they remain important both for social memory and for memory studies. A society with a vigorous and widespread culture of historical investigation is still likely to be better protected than a society lacking such a culture from the efforts of power to use the past as an instrument of control, oppression, or exclusion. Abandoning the excessively prestigious forms of cultural authority that professional history once laid claim to, and reinterpreting its relationship to the general play of social memory, should not mean relinquishing this benefit. Bringing the skills and aptitudes of historians to bear, conjunctively with those of other disciplines, in refining and developing the approaches and conceptual horizons of memory studies is equally important. I shall suggest that historians can contribute usefully in three particular ways.

First, as already suggested, historical studies focused on different periods and historical societies can help to safeguard memory studies against a sometimes excessive tendency to privilege the insecurities of modernity, and to see these as somehow fundamentally constitutive of memory's call on us as an object of study. Appreciating the profoundly important ways in which modern and postmodern conditions and experiences have inflected – and continue to transform – our understandings and experiences of memory, framing them around trauma, loss, temporal anxiety, crises of identity, encroaching hyperconnectivity, and the multiple disjunctures and fluidities of a world in perpetual mobility, is obviously an important task for memory studies, but should not obscure the fact that many of the ingredients we can trace in modern or postmodern memory cultures also have longer histories. Concepts of collective trauma can be used to explore the impact in memory of events like the Norman Conquest (Brownlie 2013) or the Portuguese defeat at Alcácer Quibir (Valensi 1992); memories of the Fall of Constantinople or the Saint Bartholomew massacre have circulated over centuries transnationally and transculturally; the politics of political amnesty was known to ancient Greece (Loraux 2001) long before it became an issue of contemporary transitional politics. The relationships that societies and their members have to the past are never things that can simply be read off from some generalized schematic model of cultural transition. The political uses of history, and the memory's relationships to collective identity, to communicative media, to the physical environment, and to ritual performance – these and many other aspects of memory are present, in some way or other, in more or less any historical society, and require detailed and discriminating analysis, which in turn can open the way to comparison and to longer evolutionary studies.

Second, as Rigney herself suggests, historically informed studies can also help us to interrogate the too readily assumed 'predominance of the traumatic' in memory studies, by refurbishing other – perhaps occluded – frames of investigation. A personal note may be in order here. As a fledgling historian of nineteenth-century France in the later decades of the twentieth century, my own fascination with issues of memory drew inspiration from various sources – partly from broader reading on the Holocaust and the First World War, certainly, and partly from exposure to innovative work in oral history, as well as from readings of Benedict Anderson, Hobsbawm and Ranger, and others – including Halbwachs, eventually. But it was driven, probably more than anything, by my own efforts (e.g. Cubitt 1993, 2000), and those of a stream of more distinguished scholars (Joutard 1977; Agulhon 1979; Amalvi 1988; Martin 1989 among them) to analyse the mythologies and symbolic repertoires of French politics on both the Right and the Left, to understand their modes of transmission, and to grasp the ways in which they were informed by, referred back to, and reworked the memories of earlier political and religious conflicts. (It was in the context of this investigation, rather than of a broader critical theorization, that Nora's work on *lieux de mémoire* first impinged on me.) Memories of traumatic experiences like the Revolutionary Terror and the massacres of the Vendée were not irrelevant here, and the larger historical rupture of the French Revolution was a key reference in the political cultures I was examining, but understanding the workings of memory in tradition, and the ways in which these connected to the political uses of history, were fundamental challenges. Rigney encouragingly highlights the attention recently paid by memory scholars to the remembrance of less violent histories and to the memory cultures of social movements, and there is much scope for further work by social historians (among others) to uncover the routine workings of social memory in different social or corporate settings – within families, local communities, businesses, professions, political parties, educational institutions, military formations, or religious bodies – and the contribution of these cultures to larger patterns of social recollection. Without by any means jettisoning trauma as a vital (if also debatable) conceptual reference, it is appropriate to balance it with Wulf Kansteiner's suggestion (2002: 189–90) that it may be 'low intensity memories' – 'rituals and representations of the past that are produced and consumed routinely without causing much disagreement' – that supply 'the backbone of collective memories' for most purposes.

Third, historians have a role to play in developing more sophisticated ways of analysing the temporal structurations that give memory a crucial role in orienting human consciousness and motivating action, and thus make it an active element in the historical process. The notion of scalarity, usually applied laterally to frame investigations into the complex interplay between different spatialized constructions of memory (local, regional, national, transnational, global, etc.), has recently begun to be applied also to investigating transfers and interconnections between different temporal extensions (Kennedy and Nugent 2016) – between, for example, the time of living memory and the time of written history, or the ancient time whose traces are borne in landscape, or the 'dream time' of indigenous Australian cosmology, or the deep times of myth or sacred history evoked in other traditions. Thinking along these lines invites us to consider how experiences in one time draw meanings from another, how memories referring to one historical event become part of an interpretative matrix conditioning how later events are experienced, but also how memory can draw meanings in the other direction, refashioning inherited readings of earlier experiences through the interpretation of new ones. As already seen, literary scholars have supplied a range of concepts – palimpsestic remembering, multidirectionality, and memory remediation in its broader applications – for analysing these transactions. Ann Rigney's efforts (2005, 2016) further to conceptualize the process of cultural memory in terms of a principle of 'scarcity', which operates to produce not just selectivity, but convergence or coalescence, recursivity, and transfers of symbolic meaning between memories drawn from different sources, concentrating mnemonic resonance in certain associative clusters, adds a further level to understanding. But there is room to push our thinking further. Guy Beiner, in a recent discussion (2014: 304–6), suggests that historians may be less inclined than cultural studies scholars to focus solely on a 'regenerative' model of memory as 'an open-ended series of recycled representations': their attention to the concrete conditions of historical experience may impel them to seek ways of analysing the affective charges – hopes, fears, frustrations, 'yearnings and trepidations' – that attach to memory at particular historical moments. The opening of such a perspective in itself brings us closer to understanding how memory becomes entangled with motivation, and with the conflicts, manoeuvres, and stand-offs that shape the ebb and flow of historical contingency and possibility. Doing so more fully will involve also paying new kinds of attention to the social and institutional settings within which, and to the interactive experiences through which, memories are continually formulated, disseminated, received, socially embedded, and woven into structures of behaviour.

Notes

1. Some of the issues introduced here are explored more fully in Cubitt (2007). For other discussions of recent historical approaches to memory, see Tumblety (2013); Berger and Niven (2014); and Hutton (2016).

2. For general introductions to the field, see Radstone and Schwarz (2010); and Olick et al. (2011).

3. A number of scholars have moved in this direction by exploring in greater detail the expectations attached to memory, and the complex layerings of hope and fear wound up in its invocation and evocation in different contexts or traditions: notable examples include Eyal (2004) and Beiner (2007).

References

Agulhon, M. (1979), *Marianne au combat: l'imagerie et la symbolique républicaines de 1789 à 1880*, Paris: Flammarion.

Alexander, J. C., Eyerman, R., Giesen, B., Smelser, N. J. and Sztompa, P. (2004), *Cultural Trauma and Collective Identity*, Berkeley: University of California Press.

Amalvi, C. (1988), *De l'art et de la manière d'accomoder les héros de l'histoire de France*, Paris: Albin Michel.

Araujo, A. L. (2014), *Shadows of the Slave Past: Memory, Heritage, and Slavery*, New York: Routledge.

Assmann, A. (2008), 'Canon and Archive', in A. Erll and A. Nünning (eds), *Cultural Memory Studies: An International and Interdisciplinary Handbook*, 97–107, Berlin and New York: De Gruyter.

Assmann, A. (2010), 'The Holocaust – A Global Memory? Extensions and Limits of a New Memory Community', in A. Assmann and S. Conrad (eds), *Memory in a Global Age: Discourses, Practices and Trajectories*, 97–117, Basingstoke: Palgrave Macmillan.

Assmann, A. (2016), *Formen des Vergessens*, Göttingen: Wallstein.

Assmann, J. (1992), *Das kulturelle Gedächtnis: Schrift, Erinnerung und politische Identität in frühen Hochkulturen*, Munich: Beck.

Assmann, J. (1995), 'Collective Memory and Cultural Identity', *New German Critique*, 65: 125–33.

Assmann, J. (1997), *Moses the Egyptian: The Memory of Egypt in Western Monotheism*, Cambridge, MA: Harvard University Press.

Attwood, B. (2001), 'Learning about the Truth: The Stolen Generations Narrative', in B. Attwood and F. Magowan (eds), *Telling Stories: Indigenous History and Memory in Australia and New Zealand*, 183–212, Crows Nest: Allen and Unwin.

Beiner, G. (2007), 'Between Trauma and Triumphalism: The Easter Rising, the Somme, and the Crux of Deep Memory in Modern Ireland', *Journal of British Studies*, 46 (2): 366–89.

Beiner, G. (2014), 'Probing the Boundaries of Irish Memory: From Postmemory to Prememory and Back', *Irish Historical Studies*, 39 (154): 296–307.

Ben-Ze'ev, E., Ginio, R. and Winter, J., eds (2010), *Shadows of War: A Social History of Silence in the Twentieth Century*, Cambridge: Cambridge University Press.

Bentley, M. (1999), *Modern Historiography: An Introduction*, Abingdon: Routledge.

Berger, S. and Niven, B., eds (2014), *Writing the History of Memory*, London: Bloomsbury.

Bernhard, M. and Kubik, J., eds (2014), *Twenty Years After Communism: The Politics of Memory and Commemoration*, Oxford: Oxford University Press.

Bevernage, B. (2012), *History, Memory, and State-Sponsored Violence: Time and Justice*, London and New York: Routledge.

Beyen, M. and Deseure, B., eds (2015), *Local Memories in a Nationalizing and Globalizing World*, Basingstoke: Palgrave Macmillan.

Bijl, P. (2015), *Emerging Memory: Photographs of Colonial Atrocity in Dutch Cultural Remembrance*, Amsterdam: Amsterdam University Press.

Bilby, K. M. (2005), *True-Born Maroons*, Gainesville: University Press of Florida.

Blight, D. (2002), 'Historians and "Memory"', *Common-Place*, 2 (3): available online: www.common-place-archives.org/vol-02/no-03/author/ (accessed 5 September 2017).

Bodnar, J. (1991), *Remaking America: Public Memory, Commemoration and Patriotism in the Twentieth Century*, Princeton: Princeton University Press.

Bond, L. and Rapson, J., eds (2014), *The Transcultural Turn: Interrogating Memory Between and Beyond Borders*, Berlin: De Gruyter.

Bourke, J. (2004), 'Introduction: "Remembering" War', *Journal of Contemporary History*, 39 (4): 473–85.

Boyd, C. (2002), 'The Second Battle of Covadonga: The Politics of Commemoration in Modern Spain', *History & Memory*, 14 (1/2): 37–64.

Brownlie, S. (2013), *Memory and Myths of the Norman Conquest*, Woodbridge: Boydell.

Brubaker, R. and Feischmidt, M. (2002), '1848 in 1998: The Politics of Commemoration in Hungary, Romania and Slovakia', *Comparative Studies in Society and History*, 44 (4): 700–44.

Burke, P. (1989), 'History as Social Memory', in T. Butler (ed.), *Memory: History, Culture and the Mind*, 97–113, Oxford: Blackwell.

Burke, P., ed. (1991), *New Perspectives in Historical Writing*, Cambridge: Polity.

Carrier, P. (2005), *Holocaust Monuments and National Memory Cultures in France and Germany Since 1989*, New York and Oxford: Berghahn.

Carruthers, M. (1990), *The Book of Memory: A Study of Memory in European Culture*, Cambridge: Cambridge University Press.

Caruth, C., ed. (1995), *Trauma: Explorations in Memory*, Baltimore, MD: Johns Hopkins University Press.

Castelli, E. A. (2004), *Martyrdom and Memory: Early Christian Culture Making*, New York: Columbia University Press.

Cole, J. (2001), *Forget Colonialism? Sacrifice and the Art of Memory in Madagascar*, Berkeley, CA: University of California Press.

Confino, A. (1997), *The Nation as a Local Metaphor: Württemberg, Imperial Germany and National Memory, 1871–1918*, Chapel Hill: University of North Carolina Press.

Confino, A. (1997a), 'Collective Memory and Cultural History: Problems of Method', *American Historical Review*, 102: 1386–403.

Confino, A. (2011), 'History and Memory', in A. Schneider and D. Woolf (eds), *The Oxford History of Historical Writing*, vol. 5: *Historical Writing since 1945*, 36–51, Oxford: Oxford University Press.

Confino, A. and Fritzsche, P. (2002), 'Introduction: Noises of the Past', in A. Confino and P. Fritzsche (eds), *The Work of Memory: New Directions in the Study of German Society and Culture*, 1–21, Urbana & Chicago: University of Illinois Press.

Connerton, P. (2008), 'Seven Types of Forgetting', *Memory Studies*, 1 (1): 59–71.

Connerton, P. (2009), *How Modernity Forgets*, Cambridge: Cambridge University Press.

Corney, F. C. (2003), 'Rethinking a Great Event: The October Revolution as Memory Project', in J. K. Olick (ed.), *States of Memory: Continuities, Conflicts, and Transformations in National Retrospection*, 17–42, Durham and London: Duke University Press.

Crane, S. A. (1997), 'Writing the Individual Back into Collective Memory', *American Historical Review*, 105 (5): 1372–85.

Craps, S. (2013), *Postcolonial Witnessing: Trauma out of Bounds*, Basingstoke: Palgrave Macmillan.

Critchell, K., Knittel, S., Perra, E. and Üngör, U. (2017), 'Editors' Introduction', *Journal of Perpetrator Research*, 1 (1): 1–27.

Cubitt, G. (1993), *The Jesuit Myth: Conspiracy Theory and Politics in Nineteenth-Century France*, Oxford: Oxford University Press.

Cubitt, G. (2000), 'Memory and Fidelity in French legitimism: Crétineau-Joly and the Vendée', *Nineteenth-Century Contexts*, 21 (4): 593–610.

Cubitt, G. (2007), *History and Memory*, Manchester: Manchester University Press.

Cubitt, G. (2007a), 'The Political Uses of Seventeenth-Century English History in Bourbon Restoration France', *Historical Journal*, 50 (1): 73–95.

Cubitt, G. (2014), 'History, Psychology and Social Memory', in C. Tileagă and J. Byford (eds), *Psychology and History: Interdisciplinary Explorations*, 15–39, Cambridge: Cambridge University Press.

Dawson, G. (2007), *Making Peace with the Past? Memory, Trauma and the Irish Troubles*, Manchester: Manchester University Press.

De Cesari, C. and Rigney, A., eds (2014), *Transnational Memory: Circulation, Articulation, Scales*, Berlin: De Gruyter.

Erll, A. (2008), 'Literature, Film, and the Mediality of Cultural History', in A. Erll and A. Nünning (eds), *Cultural Memory Studies: An International and Interdisciplinary Handbook*, 389–98, Berlin and New York: De Gruyter.

Erll, A. (2011), 'Travelling Memory', *Parallax*, 61: 4–18.

Erll, A. and Rigney, A., eds (2009), *Mediation, Remediation and the Dynamics of Cultural Memory*, Berlin: De Gruyter.

Erll, A. and Rigney, A. (2009a), 'Introduction: Cultural Memory and its Dynamics', in A. Erll and A. Rigney (eds), *Mediation, Remediation, and the Dynamics of Cultural Memory*, 1–14, Berlin and New York: De Gruyter.

Eyal, G. (2004), 'Identity and Trauma: Two Forms of the Will to Memory', *History and Memory*, 16 (1): 5–36.

Eyerman, R. (2001), *Cultural Trauma: Slavery and the Formation of African American Identity*, Cambridge: Cambridge University Press.

Fassin, D. and Rechtman, R. (2009), *The Empire of Trauma: An Inquiry into the Condition of Victimhood*, Princeton, NJ: Princeton University Press.

François, É. (2012), 'Conclusion: The Revolutionary and Napoleonic Wars as a Shared and Entangled European *lieu de mémoire*', in A. Forrest, É. François and K. Hagemann (eds), *War Memories: The Revolutionary and Napoleonic Wars in Modern European Culture*, 386–402, Basingstoke: Palgrave Macmillan.

Frisch, M. (1990), *A Shared Authority: Essays on the Craft and Meaning of Oral and Public History*, Albany: SUNY University Press.

Fritzsche, P. (2004), *Stranded in the Present: Modern Time and the Melancholy of History*, Cambridge, MA: Harvard University Press.

Garde-Hansen, J. (2011), *Media and Memory*, Edinburgh: Edinburgh University Press.

Garde-Hansen, J., Hoskins, A. and Reading, A., eds (2009), *Save As… Digital Memories*, Basingstoke: Palgrave Macmillan.

Gedi, N. and Elam, Y. (1996), 'Collective Memory – What is It?', *History and Memory*, 8 (1): 30–50.

Gerson, S. (2003), *The Pride of Place: Local Memories and Political Culture in Nineteenth-Century France*, Ithaca and London: Cornell University Press.

Gillis, J. R., ed (1994), *Commemorations: The Politics of National Identity*, Princeton: University of Princeton Press.

Gilroy, P. (1995), *The Black Atlantic: Modernity and Double-Consciousness*, Cambridge, MA: Harvard University Press.

Glassberg, D. (2001), *Sense of History: The Place of the Past in American History*, Amherst: University of Massachusetts Press.

Glynn, I. and Kleist, J., eds (2012), *History, Memory and Migration: Perceptions of the Past and the Politics of Incorporation*, Basingstoke: Palgrave Macmillan.

Green, A. (2011), 'Can Memory be Collective?', in D. A. Ritchie (ed.), *The Oxford Handbook of Oral History*, 96–111, Oxford: Oxford University Press.

Halbwachs, M. (1994), *Les cadres sociaux de la mémoire*, Paris: Albin Michel.

Halbwachs, M. (1997), *La mémoire collective*, Paris: Albin Michel.

Halstead, H. (2014), 'Heirs to Byzantium: Identity and the Hellenic-Romaic Dichotomy Amongst the Istanbul Greek Migrant Community in Greece', *Byzantine and Modern Greek Studies*, 38 (2): 265–84.

Hamilton, C. (2010), 'Activist Memories: Politics, Trauma, Pleasure', in R. Crownshaw, J. Kilby and A. Rowland (eds), *The Future of Memory*, 265–78, Oxford and New York: Berghahn Books.

Hamilton, P. and Shopes, L. (2008), 'Introduction: Building Partnerships Between Oral History and Memory Studies' in P. Hamilton and L. Shopes (eds), *Oral History and Public Memories*, vii–xvii, Philadelphia: Temple University Press.

Hartog, F. (2015), *Regimes of Historicity: Presentism and Experiences of Time*, transl. S. Brown, New York: Columbia University Press.

Healey, C. (1997), *From the Ruins of Colonialism: History as Social Memory*, Melbourne: Cambridge University Press.

Hirsch, M. (2008), 'The Generation of Postmemory', *Poetics Today*, 29 (1): 103–28.

Hoskins, A. (2009), 'The Mediatisation of Memory', in J. Garde-Hansen, A. Hoskins and A. Reading (eds), *Save As… Digital Memories*, 27–43, Basingstoke: Palgrave Macmillan.

Hunt, L., ed. (1989), *The New Cultural History*, Berkeley, CA: University of California Press.

Hutton, P. H. (1993), *History as an Art of Memory*, Hanover: University Press of New England.

Hutton, P. H. (2016), *The Memory Phenomenon in Contemporary Historical Writing: How the Interest in Memory Has Influenced Our Understanding of History*, Basingstoke: Macmillan.

Huyssen, A. (2003), *Present Pasts: Urban Palimpsests and the Politics of Memory*, Stanford, CA: Stanford University Press.

Inglis, K. S. (1993), 'Entombing Unknown Soldiers: From London and Paris to Baghdad', *History and Memory*, 5 (2): 7–31.

Jelin, E. (2003), *State Repression and the Struggles for Memory*, London: Latin America Bureau.

Joutard, P. (1977), *La légende des camisards: une sensibilité au passé*, Paris: Gallimard.

Judt, T. (2000), 'The Past is Another Country: Myth and Memory in Postwar Europe', in I. Deák, J. T. Gross and T. Judt (eds), *The Politics of Retribution in Europe: World War II and its Aftermath*, 293–323, Princeton: Princeton University Press.

Kansteiner, W. (2002), 'Finding Meaning in Memory: a Methodological Critique of Collective Memory Studies', *History and Theory*, 41 (2): 179–197.

Kattago, S. (2015), 'Introduction: Memory Studies and its Companions', in S. Kattago (ed.), *The Ashgate Research Companion to Memory Studies*, 1–19, Farnham: Ashgate.

Kennedy, R. and Nugent, M. (2016), 'Scales of Memory: Reflections on an Emerging Concept', *Australian Humanities Review*, 59: 61–76.

King, A. (1998), *Memorials of the Great War in Britain: The Symbolism and Politics of Remembrance*, Oxford: Berg.

Klein, K. L. (2000), 'On the Emergence of *Memory* in Historical Discourse', *Representations*, 69: 127–50.

Knittel, S. C. (2014), *The Historical Uncanny: Disability, Ethnicity, and the Politics of Holocaust Memory*, New York: Fordham University Press.

Koselleck, R. (1979), *Vergangene Zukunft: Zur Semantik geschichtlicher Zeit*, Frankfurt am Main: Suhrkamp.

Landsberg, A. (2004), *Prosthetic Memory: The Transformation of American Memory in the Age of Mass Culture*, New York: Columbia University Press.

Leerssen, J. and Rigney, A., eds (2014), *Commemorating Writers in Nineteenth-Century Europe: Nation-Building and Centenary Fever*, Basingstoke: Palgrave Macmillan.

Levy, D. and Sznaider, N., eds (2001), *The Holocaust and Memory in the Global Age*, Philadelphia: Temple University Press.

Leydesdorff, S., Passerini, L. and Thompson, P., eds (1996), *Gender and Memory*, Oxford: Oxford University Press.

Loraux, N. (2001), *The Divided City: On Memory and Forgetting in Ancient Athens*, New York: Zone Books.

Maier, C. S. (1993), 'A Surfeit of Memory? Reflections on History, Memory and Denial', *History and Memory*, 5 (2): 136–52.

Majerus, B. (2014), '*Lieux de mémoire* – a European Transfer Story', in S. Berger and B. Niven (eds), *Writing the History of Memory*, 157–71, London: Bloomsbury.

Mälksoo, M. (2009), 'The Memory Politics of Becoming European: The East European Subalterns and the Collective Memory of Europe', *European Journal of International Relations*, 15 (4): 653–80.

Margalit, A. (2002), *The Ethics of Memory*, Cambridge, MA: Harvard University Press.

Marschall, S. (2010), 'Commemorating the "Trojan Horse" Massacre in Cape Town: The Tension between Vernacular and Official Expressions of Memory', *Visual Studies*, 25 (2): 135–48.

Martin, J.-C. (1989), *La Vendée de la mémoire: 1800–1980*, Paris: Seuil.

Neiger, M., Meyers, O. and Zandberg, E., eds (2011), *On Media Memory*, Basingstoke: Palgrave Macmillan.

Nora, P., ed. (1984–92). *Les lieux de mémoire*, 7 vols, Paris: Gallimard.

Nora, P. (1996), 'General Introduction: Between Memory and History', in P. Nora (ed.), *Realms of Memory*, vol. I: *Conflicts and Divisions*, 1–20, New York: Columbia University Press.

Nora, P. (1998), 'The Era of Commemoration', in P. Nora (ed.), *Realms of Memory*, vol. III: *Symbols*, 609–37, New York: Columbia University Press.

Olick, J. K. (2000), 'Collective Memory: The Two Cultures', *Sociological Theory*, 17: 333–48.

Olick, J. K. (2007), *The Politics of Regret: On Collective Memory and Historical Responsibility*, London and New York: Routledge.

Olick, J. K., and Robbins, J. (1998), 'Social Memory Studies: From "Collective Memory" to the Historical Sociology of Mnemonic Practices', *Annual Review of Sociology*, 24: 105–40.

Olick, J. K., Vinitzky-Seroussi, V. and Levy, D., eds (2011), *The Collective Memory Reader*, Oxford: Oxford University Press.

Onken, E.-C. (2007), 'The Baltic States and Moscow's 9 May Commemoration: Analysing Memory Politics in Europe', *Europe-Asia Studies*, 59 (1): 23–46.

Passerini, L. (2003), 'Memories between Silence and Oblivion', in K. Hodgkin and S. Radstone (eds), *Memory, History, Nation: Contested Pasts*, 238–54, London: Routledge.

Pickering, M. and Keightley, E. (2013), 'Introduction: Methodological Premises and Purposes', in E. Keightley and M. Pickering (eds), *Research Methods in Memory Studies*, 1–9, Edinburgh: Edinburgh University Press.

Popular Memory Group (1982), 'Popular Memory: Theory, Politics, Method', in R. Johnson, G. McLellan, B. Schwartz and D. Sutton (eds), *Making Histories: Studies in History-Writing and Politics*, 205–52, Minneapolis: University of Minnesota Press.

Radstone, S. and Schwarz, B. eds (2010), *Memory: Histories, Theories, Debates*, New York: Fordham University Press.

Reading, A. (2011), 'Memory and Digital Media: Six Dynamics of the Globital Memory Field', in M. Neiger, O. Meyers and E. Zandberg (eds), *On Media Memory*, 241–52, Basingstoke: Palgrave Macmillan.

Reading, A. and Katriel, T., eds (2015), *Cultural Memories of Non-Violent Struggles: Powerful Times*, Basingstoke: Palgrave Macmillan.

Ricœur, P. (2006), 'Memory – History – Forgetting', in J. Rüsen (ed.), *Meaning and Representation in History*, 9–19, Oxford and New York: Berghahn Books.

Ricœur, P. (2000), *La Mémoire, l'histoire, l'oubli*, Paris: Seuil

Rigney, A. (2005), 'Plenitude, Scarcity and the Circulation of Cultural Memory', *Journal of European Studies*, 35 (1): 11–28.

Rigney, A. (2008), 'The Dynamics of Remembrance: Texts between Monumentality and Morphing', in A. Erll and A. Nünning (eds), *Cultural Memory Studies: An International and Interdisciplinary Handbook*, 345–53, Berlin and New York: De Gruyter.

Rigney, A. (2012), *The Afterlives of Walter Scott: Memory on the Move*, Oxford: Oxford University Press.

Rigney, A. (2016), 'Differential Memorabilty and Transnational Activism: Bloody Sunday, 1887–2016', *Australian Humanities Review*, 59: 77–95.

Rigney, A. and Leerssen, J. (2014), 'Introduction: Fanning out from Shakespeare', in J. Leerssen and A. Rigney (eds), *Commemorating Writers in Nineteenth-Century Europe: Nation-Building and Centenary Fever*, 1–23, Basingstoke: Palgrave Macmillan.

Rothberg, M. (2009), *Multidirectional Memory: Remembering the Holocaust in the Age of Decolonization*, Stanford, CA: Stanford University Press.

Rothberg, M. (2011), 'From Gaza to Warsaw: Mapping Multidirectional Memory', *Criticism*, 53 (4): 523–48.

Rothberg, M. (2013), 'Multidirectional Memory and the Implicated Subject: On Sebald and Kentridge', in L. Plate and A. Smelik (eds), *Performing Memory in Art and Popular Culture*, 39–58, New York: Routledge.

Rothberg, M. (2014), 'Multidirectional Memory in Migratory Settings: The Case of Post-Holocaust Germany', in C. De Cesari and A. Rigney (eds), *Transnational Memory: Circulation, Articulation, Scales*, 123–45, Berlin: De Gruyter.

Rousso, H. (1991), *The Vichy Syndrome: History and Memory in France since 1944*, Cambridge, MA: Harvard University Press.

Samuel, R. (1994), *Theatres of Memory*, vol. I: *Past and Present in Contemporary Culture*, 2nd edn, London and New York: Verso.

Savage, K. (1994), 'The Politics of Memory: Black Emancipation and the Civil War Monument', in J. R. Gillis (ed.), *Commemorations: The Politics of National Identity*, 127–39, Princeton: Princeton University Press.

Seraphim, F. (2006), *War Memory and Social Politics in Japan, 1945-2005*, Cambridge, MA: Harvard University Asia Centre.

Spillman, L. (1997), *Nation and Commemoration: Creating National Identities in Australia and the United States*, Cambridge: Cambridge University Press.

Stoler, A. L. (2011), 'Colonial Aphasia: Race and Disabled Histories in France', *Public Culture*, 23 (1): 121–56.

Sturken, M. (1997), *Tangled Memories: The Vietnam War, the AIDS Epidemic, and the Politics of Remembering*, Berkeley: University of California Press.

Sturken, M. (2007), *Tourists of History: Memory, Kitsch and Consumerism from Oklahoma City to Ground Zero*, Durham and London: Duke University Press.

Tamm, M. (2015), 'Introduction: Afterlife of Events: Perspectives on Mnemohistory', in M. Tamm (ed.), *Afterlife of Events: Perspectives on Mnemohistory*, 1–23, Basingstoke: Palgrave Macmillan.

Terdiman, R. (1993), *Present Past: Modernity and the Memory Crisis*, Ithaca, NY: Cornell University Press.

Thomson, A. (2007), 'Four Paradigm Transformations in Oral History', *The Oral History Review*, 34 (1): 49–70.

Thomson, A., Frisch, M. and Hamilton, P. (1994), 'The Memory and History Debates: Some International Perspectives', *Oral History*, 22 (2): 33–43.

Traverso, E. (2016), *Left-Wing Melancholia: Marxism, History, and Memory*, New York: Columbia University Press.

Trouillot, M.-R. (1995), *Silencing the Past: Power and the Production of History*, Boston: Beacon.

Tumblety, J. (2013), 'Introduction: Working with Memory as Source and Subject', in J. Tumblety (ed.), *Memory and History: Understanding Memory as Source and Subject*, 1–16, Abingdon: Routledge.

Valensi, L. (1992), *Fables de la mémoire: la glorieuse bataille des trois rois*, Paris: Seuil.

Van Houts, E. (1999), *Memory and Gender in Medieval Europe, 900–1200*, Basingstoke: Macmillan.

Weinrich, H. (1997), *Lethe: Kunst und Kritik des Vergessens*, Munich: Beck.

Welzer, H., Moller, S. and Tschuggnall, K. (2002), *'Opa war kein Nazi': Nationalsozialismus und Holocaust im Familiengedächtnis*, Frankfurt: Fischer.

Wertsch, J. V. (2002), *Voices of Collective Remembering*, Cambridge: Cambridge University Press.

Wieviorka, A. (2006), 'The Witness in History', *Poetics Today*, 27 (2): 385–97.

Winter, J. M. (1995), *Sites of Memory, Sites of Mourning*, Cambridge: Cambridge University Press.

Winter, J. (2001), 'The Generation of Memory: Reflections on the "Memory Boom" in Contemporary Historical Studies', *Canadian Military History*, 10 (3): 57–66.

Winter, J. and Sivan, E. (1999), 'Setting the Framework', in J. Winter and E. Sivan (eds), *War and Remembrance in the Twentieth Century*, 6–39, Cambridge: Cambridge University Press.

Wood, A. (2013), *The Memory of the People: Custom and Popular Senses of the Past in Early Modern England*, Cambridge: Cambridge University Press.

Woolf, D. (2003), *The Social Circulation of the Past: English Historical Culture 1500–1730*, Oxford: Oxford University Press.

Young, J. (1993), *The Texture of Memory: Holocaust Memorials and Meaning*, New Haven: Yale University Press.

Zerubavel, Y. (1995), *Recovered Roots: Collective Memory and the Making of Israeli National Tradition*, Chicago: University of Chicago Press.

CHAPTER 6
HISTORY OF KNOWLEDGE
Martin Mulsow

A new development

The term 'history of knowledge' is currently used with a variety of meanings which originate in the various directions from which the term has developed. We can say however that many of these directions converge, and that the project of this new discipline or transdisciplinary movement clearly has a unified general direction of travel (Vogel 2004; Völkel 2007; Füssel 2007; Fried and Stolleis 2009). One initial meaning of the term 'history of knowledge' consists in the extension of the accepted practice of the history of science to objects which are not scientific in the narrower sense, for example works of popularization and compilations. More precisely, this extension is not just a broadening of the range of objects of study, but also of types of approach. As with 'science studies', which are consciously interdisciplinary, the history of knowledge is concerned – beyond the distinction between 'internalist' and 'externalist' approaches – with practices, settings, or '*lieux de savoir*' (Jacob 2007, 2011), and with the 'persona' of the scientist or scholar (Park and Daston 2008). This includes even 'scientific errors', as the intention here is no longer to write a history of the progress of true understanding. A particular emphasis within this history of knowledge is that of a cultural history of fundamental scientific concepts such as objectivity, demonstration, error, belief, and proof (Daston and Park 2001; Daston and Galison 2007; Daston 2011). Alongside this, 'orders of knowledge' are studied, that is the classification and presentation of found knowledge (Schützeichel 2007, Chap. 6).

A second use of the term relates to a more recent type of history of information and communications (Brendecke, Friedrich, and Friedrich 2008). If we think of information as the 'raw' form which precedes the 'cooked' form of knowledge (Burke 2000, 2012), questions arise as to how this raw form is obtained and the ways in which it is transformed into genuine knowledge. Harold Cook speaks of an 'information economy' (Cook 2007). Findings concerning trade, travels, questionnaires, and newspapers are related to epistemological researches into the transformations, reconstitutions, and combinations of information as it becomes knowledge (Stagl 2016; Keller 2015).

The third way and quite different way of writing the history of knowledge is as a 'poetics of knowledge' (Vogl 1997; critical: Stiening 2007). This approach, derived from Foucault, is an attempt to view the 'poetic' constitution of knowledge in terms of its articulation in works of art, and in literary texts in particular. Literary and cultural theorists of this type ask whether the free spaces of the realm of the aesthetic may enable alternative thoughts and ways of thinking which are not obligated to discursive claims to truth, and which tend to be excluded in the cultures within which they arise.

Fourthly and finally, the history of knowledge can also be understood – in a way that is hardly separable from the other three tendencies – in terms of an extension of the idea of knowledge to include practical knowledge, social knowledge, artisanal, craft and everyday knowledge, spatio-cartographical knowledge, pictorial and orientational knowledge (Landwehr 2002). This direction is taken primarily by historians who work closely with empirical material. For these historians the intention is to at least qualify the primacy of the social or the political, and to attend to the problems of classification of their objects of study and of their intellectual dimension. Some methods, including serial methods, have been adopted from the history of mentalities, in which it was already a concern to go beyond the purely social.

The research situation is fluid, and has not yet taken on the forms of fixed disciplines, though the first professorial chairs, large-scale projects, or series of books are now trading under this flag.[1] But for many branches of study there now seems to be a real opportunity firstly not simply to contextualize scholarly and scientific knowledge, as has been done up till now, but to bring this knowledge into contact with other *forms of knowledge*, and secondly, to view social, economic, and political processes from the perspective that knowledge has played a role within them which should not be underestimated.

Knowledge?

But what is knowledge, in the sense of the history of knowledge? To a particular person or group of people in the year 1690 we might ascribe for example knowledge of (1) the defeat of the French forces at the siege of Bonn in October 1689, (2) the mineral resources of a particular region, (3) the production of gold, (4) the manner in which one should conduct oneself at the Imperial Court in Vienna, (5) the inauthenticity of the Hermetic texts, (6) the physics of solid bodies. These are quite distinct forms of knowledge. Knowledge item (1) is essentially a discrete item of information which has of course a contextual background (it is only meaningful if one has some idea of the events of the Nine Years' War), but which as such can be expressed in a single statement. By contrast, knowledge item (2) is complex and requires a whole sequence of information on deposits of salt, copper, and silver; their geographical situation; and accessibility to mining. This knowledge can be set out in tables and charts, but can also be obtained from the unwritten knowledge of local miners. Knowledge item (3) is a matter of 'know-how', a mixture of theoretical and operational knowledge which can be gained from years of experimental practice. But here we also encounter a fundamental difficulty of the history of knowledge: our contemporary understanding tells us that it is not possible to produce gold from base metals by any known means. If we are to think of knowledge as being true, justified belief, this was not knowledge, as it was not true and did not, in any practical sense, actually work. Nevertheless, some people around 1690 regarded their technical understanding of alchemy as *knowledge* of how to make gold, and saw their lack of practical success as simply the fault of a variety of external circumstances – the procedure would soon succeed. It would be unsatisfactory for the historian if 'knowledge' of this kind were to be disregarded, and if account were to be taken only of knowledge which we continue to regard as true today. This would be to introduce retrospectively a distinction within the range of beliefs held by people in history – a distinction which did not exist for those people, and which would therefore distort our description of them. As historians, we must therefore abandon the direct criterion of the truth of beliefs (Knoblauch 2010: 359–66), and obliquely categorize as knowledge what was held to be knowledge at the time.

This definition appears to rest on circular reasoning, but it does not. It attenuates the idea of knowledge to something that is not factual, but which merely derives from justifiable beliefs. The difficult question here is: by whom were these beliefs held to be knowledge, to be true? Certainly not solely by the person in question. If for instance it was held, around 1400, to be knowledge that the sun revolves around the earth, this was because this 'knowledge' was embedded in the context of the Ptolemaic-Aristotelian world view which was widely accepted at the time. Our example of gold production is more difficult. Here too there is a broad explanatory context accepted by many at the time, the sulphur-mercury theory of metals, according to which the production of gold must be possible in principle (Principe 2013). Nevertheless, alchemy was controversial on numerous counts, and there were many who rejected its 'knowledge' as obscurantism and fakery, and who engaged its supporters in a 'boundary work' or demarcation dispute over what was and was not legitimate knowledge (Mulsow and Rexroth 2014). So with the formulation, 'what was held to be knowledge at the time', we enter a grey area where we must decide in each individual case whether we should speak of knowledge or merely of individual beliefs.

Another, even more fundamental problem consists in the fact that the classical notion of knowledge as justified true belief no longer holds good in contemporary philosophy. Since the 'Gettier problem', cases have appeared for which the classical definition leads to unsatisfactory results (Baehr 2012; Bonjour and Sosa 2003). There is therefore now a variety of new approaches to the problem of defining knowledge differently, such as through the reliability of the procedure of cognition, or through the epistemic virtues of the person who knows (Zagzebski 1996). These problems do not necessarily impinge on the historian, as they are too specialized to be relevant to his or her aims, but they can stimulate him or her to apply categories such as epistemic virtue to history and to test their productivity and usefulness in relation to particular situations in the past.

But let us continue with our examples of historical forms of knowledge. Knowledge item (4) is social or orientation knowledge (Fuchs and Schulze 2002) that must be learned, and which does not simply consist of rules and background knowledge, but requires also the priming layer of a 'social sense' (Pierre Bourdieu), which allows the actor to assess the situation. This kind of knowledge is also of great interest to the historian, and can give insight into an actor's horizon. Knowledge item (5) is philological, scholarly knowledge which is itself complex and can hardly be reduced to a simple proposition, as it relies, to a far greater extent than the information contained in knowledge item (1), on a web of theoretical insights and assumptions. Finally, knowledge item (6) is complex theoretical knowledge which around 1690 for example was available within the framework of

Cartesian physics, and is therefore hardly 'true' in the sense of contemporary physics, but which for an actor of the time was an unquestionable part of their general education.

We see therefore that it is hardly meaningful to draw up a hard border between information and (complex) knowledge. Rather, the history of information – the history of the collection, propagation, and adoption of facts – is part of the history of knowledge, just as all forms of practical, implicit, and social knowledge are part of this history, numerous theoretical insights being inseparable from types of practice, if not in fact embodied in them. There is an important distinction to be made however between potential and actual knowledge. While actual knowledge is always tied to persons as its carrier, where books, charts, libraries, or archives are concerned we can speak of a potential knowledge, which can be reactivated by actors who read the books or research the archives. Potential and actual knowledge do not by any means necessarily coincide. Although the Spanish at Simancas amassed a huge quantity of knowledge about their possessions in the New World from their informers, they seldom had recourse to this archival knowledge (Brendecke 2009). Archive history must therefore always be complemented with the history of archive use (Friedrich 2013) if it is to form part of the history of knowledge.

Knowledge cultures

The more recent cultural history of knowledge and its practices has developed numerous interesting areas of investigation, only a few of which can be mentioned here (for a more complete survey, see Burke 2016). For example, we can ask questions of scale: is knowledge 'in quantity', involving large amounts of data in the context of more complex organizations, differently structured to knowledge at a smaller scale, where it deals only with individual facts or a small number of people? (Knorr-Cetina 1999) What role is played by the spatial location of knowledge and the mobility of its actors (Roche 2003; Van Damme 2006)? Are there for instance centres and peripheries, and are spaces of power identical with those of knowledge? In the early modern period, universities were after all often intentionally sited not in capital cities or large centres of population, but in the 'pedagogical provinces', somewhat at a remove, where the bustle of business would not disturb the academic calm, and unruly students could not endanger the state. By contrast, the French Enlightenment for example is hardly thinkable without the urban character of the major salons and the speed of communication which existed only in the metropolis. Indeed, could the history of the Enlightenment be written differently, if it were told from the perspective not so much of its content as from that of its conditions of knowledge? (Van Damme 2014) What of the materiality of objects? (Waquet 2015; Smith and Schmidt 2008) Does a dimension of knowledge adhere to them, which would imply that particular attention should be paid to how both natural objects and artefacts were collected, and to how they were circulated? Does even the body and corporeality of the person who knows play its own, often unrecognized, role? (Smith 2004) Lastly, we can ask whether affectivity and emotionality, which have for so long been obscured where the objectivity of understanding is concerned, have an influence on knowledge which can be reconstructed and described.

Common to almost all such questions is that knowledge is always understood here as embedded in a particular situation – embedded in 'knowledge cultures'. But what are knowledge cultures or epistemic cultures? As epistemic cultures in the narrower sense I would point to those social and institutional formations whose primary purpose is the acquisition of knowledge. This could be a laboratory, an informal circle of philosophers perhaps only communicating by letter, or it could be a whole university. Each epistemic culture has specific characteristics and ideals, sometimes its own specific style of thinking (Fleck 2011). In contrast to a pure history of science and the humanities, the term 'history of knowledge' would also apply to a group of spies as an epistemic culture. These actors are also in pursuit of a type of knowledge, and are doing whatever they can to discover certain facts, albeit in this case not scientific or scholarly facts, but politically or economically relevant ones.

As a knowledge culture in the broader sense, one could point by contrast to any larger-scale formation which coheres through close communications, such as a city, a court, or a milieu. Knowledge would be *one* of the various aspects of any such formation, which however we would be considering from the perspective of its knowledge assets and how this knowledge was communicated. This distinction is helpful in detaching the gaze of the history of knowledge from the institutions on which the history of science has long been fixated, in order to break new ground for study.

The broad bandwidth of knowledge

The history of knowledge is able to demonstrate this multiplicity particularly strikingly in those cases where the history of specific knowledge cultures is under examination, in the interleaving and continuity of different forms of knowledge within a single context – as a new direction or programme for research, the history of knowledge is a markedly *integrative* discipline. If it has value, it is precisely in the bringing together of phenomena that have up till now been examined separately. An example of this kind of concentrated investigation, which will be discussed in more detail here, is knowledge at court: the role of knowledge within the households of rulers in the early modern period (Mulsow 2016). Here connections can be made with recent court research, in terms of the analysis of political communication and the description of actual attendances and opportunities for access, rather than the simple defining of the functions of court offices (Hengerer 2004; Schlögl 2004; Haas and Hengerer 2008). Because only in this way can knowledge be localized in concrete situations within this milieu, and its meaning examined. If court research of this kind is connected up with the history of knowledge as the history of intellectual practices, a synchronization of praxeologies comes about: what are the effects of the praxis of court communication on the practices of knowledge (such as documentation and mapping, but also: gaining the upper hand in a dispute over rank, keeping secrets, dissimulation)? Conversely, how do the practices of knowledge affect communication at court? Do exclusive possessors of knowledge have greater opportunities of access to the ruler? Does the archivist and historian come into conflict with the Privy Council, because he wishes to document secret proceedings? To the two components of recent court research and the history of intellectual practices we can add the idea of an 'histoire totale' (Lucien Febvre). A project emerges of an analysis, interleaved and as comprehensive as possible, of flows of information and knowledge at a single court, a history which has the ruler at its centre, but which is by no means focused exclusively on him, taking equal note of the partially independent communications between scholars or between court officials and their institutions. Neither is this a history to be written from the top down, with the ruler instructing the experts on what to research; it is equally a matter of registering the initiatives of the knowledge actors in forwarding their own interests and persuading the ruler or high officials at court to tolerate and finance them. We must assume negotiations between the various actors, and take into account the possibility that some knowledge was able to flourish specifically in 'niches' at court, at a remove from dense networks of communication.

To sketch out the possibilities of a history of knowledge of this kind, I would like to use here the example of Gotha in the 1680s. Gotha was the ducal residence of the small to mid-sized territory of Saxe-Gotha-Altenburg. This territory was established in 1640 through a division of inherited lands and was from the start a 'model state' in terms of modern administration, schooling, social disciplining, and confessionalization, and had high cultural aspirations, as compensation for the loss of electoral rights of the Ernestine branch of the Wettin dynasty in 1547 (Klinger 2002; Albrecht-Birkner 2002; Facius 1933; Westphal 2007). In 1680, under Duke Frederick I and his court officials, the court was in its second generation, and retained politicians and scholars of considerable quality (Hess 1962; Mulsow 2013). The core territories of Saxe-Gotha had however been greatly reduced as a result of the division of the dukedom, in principle on an equal basis, between the seven sons of the first duke, Frederick's father. As the eldest of the sons, Frederick was faced with the task of negotiating with his brothers to build his share of power and territory to the fullest extent. This involved him over the next several years in complex proceedings at the Imperial Aulic Council, eventually leading in 1686 to Imperial assent to the division of the inheritance (Westphal 2002).

Many of the policies pursued by Frederick can be described as markedly entrepreneurial and business-oriented. He sought to meet payments due to his brothers by building up a profitable trade in hiring out his soldiers as 'subsidy troops' (Thiele 2014). Debts owed to him by the emperor for such subsidies also helped to promote his case at the Aulic Council (Westphal 2002: 154–63). At the same time, Frederick made efforts to increase the income from his territorial woodlands by using the ores and mineral resources of the Thuringian Forest in intensive alchemical experimentation. He invested large sums in paying for the services of advisers, hoping to obtain the formula for the production of gold from base metals (Humberg 2005; Mulsow 2014a; Keller 2016). In 1688 Frederick was still speculating over possible gains to be converted to the acquisition of territory – this time involving the risky procedure of going over to the side of the French in the midst of the Nine Years' War. He conducted covert negotiations with

Paris over hiring troops to the French. He confided these plans in person and off the record to his chancellor, Bachoff von Echt, swearing him to silence: 'Only that he should say Nothing of this to no-one.'[2]

Many of these policies are in fact knowledge-based; the 'entrepreneur' depended on information about his territories, about military and legal matters and the functioning of alchemical processes. Timber revenues required accurate surveying of woodlands and mapping of forests (see, in general, Gottschalk 2004; Cooper 2009; Wakefield 2009). Official surveys of the ducal lands had already been made between 1640 and 1660, but more and more concrete information was now being produced and used. Frederick drove on this accumulation of administrative knowledge, which culminated in the compendious record of the *Gotha Diplomatica* of 1715 (Rudolphi 1715). Even though some of this knowledge was initially only potential, and we should not underestimate the extent to which local administrative practices and central record-keeping can diverge (Brakensiek 2010), Frederick nevertheless had concrete plans to make use of it. Historiographic knowledge also flowed into the *Gotha Diplomatica*, and when he incorporated part of the territory of the neighbouring county of Gleichen into Saxe-Gotha, Frederick made use of information unearthed on its history for him by scholars such as Caspar Sagittarius (Sagittarius 1732).[3]

Frederick needed the expertise of his advisers for the alchemical exploitation of the mineral resources of the Thuringian Forest, but he himself studied this arcane knowledge in depth, and together with his court physician Jakob Friedrich Waitz he carried out practical alchemical experiments in person, following procedures set out by his experts (Mulsow 2014a). It was important that this knowledge be kept secret, and it was known in Gotha only to a small and trusted circle; it included practical knowledge, such as how to produce suitable glass vessels, about which Frederick corresponded with various artisans, but also scholarly knowledge which Frederick got via his agents or gathered from manuscripts in the Imperial Library in Vienna, which he had copied, partly in exchange for military assistance in the form of troops supplied to the emperor.[4]

Frederick's trade in subsidy troops also created a requirement for military knowledge (see, in general, Heyn 2015; Wilson 1998). A history of knowledge can attempt to reconstruct the efforts of Frederick and his officials to elicit the going rates in the market for troops – the Duchy was in competition with other states and needed to price its services accordingly. Beyond this, the court needed to acquire practical knowledge of recruitment and training, and of the places where the troops would be stationed, as thousands of men would typically be required within a short period of around three months. For this reason, standing regiments would be supplied 'on loan' and subsequently replenished. In addition, knowledge was required of the countries to which the troops were to be sent.

The need for this knowledge was part of the general need of the various states for an understanding of the world beyond their borders, as supplied by their agents, who acted not only as their extended eyes and ears, but sometimes also their hands. In Paris, Frederick had Baron von Rußwurm and Baron von Schwartzenstein; his agents in Vienna were Tobias Sebastian Praun and intermittently the court councillor, Avemann;

in Amsterdam Job Meyer and others (see Frederick's diaries: Friedrich I. 1998–2003). More than five to ten agents would have been too expensive, but this was considerably more than states even smaller than Frederick's could afford. These agents were highly complex knowledge actors. They were tasked with investigating and reporting on the political situation, sounding out the state of the market in soldiers, buying books, coins and works of art, sourcing alchemical formulations, and arranging the copying of the relevant manuscripts. This complexity appeared differently to the agents themselves. They needed to build up their own information networks, often based on the spoken word, and they frequently worked not only for a single ruler but for several, which could raise questions of loyalty, as every employer preferred exclusive access to the information supplied.

The books, art objects, and coins sent by the agents needed to be examined, listed, and classified at Frederick's Friedenstein Castle residence, but also studied and recorded by experts. Frederick's father had already in his time set up a library and rooms housing artworks, and engaged scholars to take charge of these collections (Eberle 2010). This became a tradition in Gotha, and the further political hopes evaporated of regaining the state's electoral rights and transregional importance, the more emphasis the dukes at Gotha laid on their cultural capital. They had inherited a large part of the documentation of the Wittenberg Reformation, which offered the possibility of converting this potential capital (and potential knowledge) into historical works, such as Seckendorff's *Historia Lutheranismi* and Pfanner's history of the various Imperial Diets that followed the Thirty Years' War (Strauch 2005). The history of the duchy itself and of its dynasty was of course also a subject of research (Sagittarius 1700–1701; Tentzel 1716). The collection of coins at Gotha contributed to the writing of dynastic history as an 'histoire metallique' (Tentzel 1705). From another perspective, the Gotha historian Tentzel used his amicable connections with the medallist Christian Wermuth, and the medals designed by Wermuth with Tentzel's help, to increase his own opportunities for access to the ruler and to suggest reforms to him, such as incorporating the coin collection into the archive.

The historical forms of knowledge were closely related with the expertise in the law which the ruler needed in order to act on a firm legal basis. The genre of the 'discorso' had existed since the Renaissance; these were handwritten historical and legal analyses for princes, intended to provide them with a basis and recommendations for their actions in specific situations (Zwierlein 2006). Friedrich himself made use of the expertise of his archivist Pfanner, who produced for him some ninety handwritten volumes, in which he gives an account of mutual inheritance pacts (*pactum confraternitatis*), rights of succession, and questions of fiefdom and rank affecting neighbouring territories such as Kursachsen, Hessen-Kassel, or Kur-Hannover (Mulsow 2016).[5] A praxeological history of knowledge could investigate how Pfanner compiled these volumes and how he developed systems to orient himself within them. While Frederick's agents functioned as sensory organs for contemporary politics, Pfanner's expertise provided him with perceptions of long-term opportunities and risks relating to the surrounding territories. For example, there were conflicts with the neighbouring interrelated counties of Schwarzburg-Rudolstadt and Schwarzburg-Sondershausen in Arnstadt (Czech 2003). Relations with these counties were strained by the efforts of the Counts to attain membership of the Imperial Diet, efforts which succeeded in 1697 and 1711 respectively. Initially, only the Ernestine dukes had been entitled to maintain an army, but the Schwarzburg counts now claimed this right. Pfanner provided expertise on this both to Frederick and to the counts.

Up to this point we have focused on the knowledge relations between the duke and his experts, but political and epistemic communications at court are extremely multifaceted. What about the 'horizontal' knowledge relationships between different court officials? Social knowledge was required to orient oneself at court successfully and to find niches in which one could pursue one's own interests; individual initiatives are to be found everywhere. The *Historia Lutheranismi* for example would never have been written without Seckendorff's personal initiative, at a time when he was no longer even employed at the Gotha court. But it is also relevant whether the knowledge in question was potentially controversial or damaging, whether it was exclusive, and how things stood with hierarchical relations and competition at court. Waitz, for instance, needed to beware of revealing his knowledge of alchemical experiments to the court theologians, who already regarded with extreme mistrust the duke's apparent wasting of tens of thousands of thalers on 'godless' experiments in natural science. For Bachoff von Echt, concealment of the secret negotiations with France was a matter of life and death. Pfanner embroiled himself in a murderous dispute over rank with the other court historian Tentzel, a dispute sparked by trivialities, but one which was to determine who held sway at court (Pfanner 1696). Gotha was a 'society of those present' (Schlögl 2014), meaning that everyone crossed paths with everyone else almost daily, and was able to exchange information and views with them in person. To enter the presence of the duke was prized by many, but also consciously avoided by others. As editor of a reviewing journal, Tentzel made use of his many 'horizontal' contacts with other members of the international 'republic of letters', and deployed his position in the world of scholarship and in the 'public eye' (Gestrich 1994; Arndt 2013) as symbolic capital at court. This also enabled him to gain independence from court life, as well as making him attractive to other courts.

Caspar Sagittarius got into serious difficulties, risking imprisonment on several occasions when, as 'general Ernestine' historiographer, he attempted to visit the archives of the duke's various brothers and cousins in Coburg and Weimar, all of whom were in dispute with each other (Mulsow 2013). Multiple loyalties proved irreconcilable. In order to gain an overview of complex 'vertical' and 'horizontal' communications of this kind, which were always also epistemic communications, or at least had epistemic relevance, it seems appropriate to develop an idea of knowledge economy which is attuned to balances and compensations, synergies, and conflicts.

Epistemic virtues and epistemic vices

In staking his hopes entirely on alchemy, Frederick I was accused by theologians, though not to his face, of handing large amounts of the state budget over to fraudsters.

This accusation touched on questions of ideals and vanities, but also of the affective priming of epistemic activity and the management of not-knowing. I have indicated that newer approaches in epistemology assign the idea of epistemic virtue, among other ideas, a central role as a guarantor of the objectivity of knowledge. To use this idea for the historical reconstruction of knowledge cultures would entail examining the habitus of actors in terms of their probity, trustworthiness, meticulousness, and love of truth (Daston and Park 2001). These and similar questions can also be asked of others besides scholars and scientists: in our example of the court, we can equally well ask them of cartographers, archivists, or men of letters. But at the same time, our example taken from court research shows that this way of looking at things, more or less prevalent in the Royal Society or at universities, runs into difficulties here. The court was after all seen even at the time as the sphere of dissimulation, patronage, and flattery, that is of 'political' behaviour in the older sense of the word (Biagioli 1993). Just as with clandestine and underground activities, which also required dissimulation, we should consider whether attention to the epistemic virtues should not be complemented by an acknowledgement of the epistemic vices. These would have been forms of habitus which systematically distorted 'true knowledge' and correct results. We touch here on the connection between error and corruption, between misapprehension and social dependency. The difficult – and fascinating – aspect of this is not simply to chalk up the epistemic virtues, alongside trust (Shapin 1994), on the 'good' side of the equation, and the epistemic vices, alongside mistrust, on the 'bad' side, but to understand in a historically adequate way the 'crooked routes' of some actors as necessary 'communicative detours' (Reinhard 2007), which they were obliged to make in order to arrive at their intended destination.

Court Councillor Pfanner, the Gotha archivist, and historian, had the highest standards of historical accuracy, but these were combined with the 'vice' of reclusiveness and uncommunicativeness to an extent which could be described as autistic, as well as a theological 'unreliability' which brought him undesirably close to Catholics and Calvinists – besides his juridical persona, he cultivated a second one in his spare time, in which he wrote books on early Christianity (Mulsow 2015b, 2016). What standards should apply here for a local knowledge culture? The retrospective ones of today, or those of the contemporary employer and commissioner of work? In his epistemically virtuous readiness almost to sacrifice himself for his work on a comprehensive catalogue of types of coin in the ancient world, Andreas Morell, Pfanner's numismatic colleague at the nearby court of Arnstadt, was strongly influenced by the ideals of religious Quietism which he had encountered in Paris, and which propounded a 'pure love' – for God, for truth – in opposition to 'self-love' and self-interest. This led Morell on a 'detour' via the Bastille, in which he was incarcerated, having failed to come to a suitable accommodation with his employers at the French court, who had required of him a 'dependable' subservience (Mulsow, forthcoming).

One question raised by the example of alchemy at the court of Gotha is that of dealing with not knowing. The ruler could not know, but only hope, that his investment in the alchemical philosophers' stone would result in success. Conversely, his external advisers, such as Baron von Gastorff, needed to translate their own not knowing how to make gold into 'specimina' of successful transmutation which would convince the duke – either by treating other metals with fake gold colouring, or by stringing him along with promises and anecdotes. It is interesting that we cannot by any means say in every case that these advisers, if they had been free to speak honestly, would have described themselves as 'not knowing' in relation to transmutation. Rather, this 'dark side of knowledge' (Zwierlein 2016a) can be characterized historically by dismantling the alchemists' beliefs, separating out components of certainty as to alchemical functioning in principle from components of uncertainty (which they kept hidden), as to the concrete action of their processes. This division is detectable in retrospect in many 'formulae' for making gold. It is also visible in the complicated manner in which the advisers entered into their contracts with the ruler, securing funds for themselves to create niches for their 'real' research.

To a large extent, dealing with not knowing had the most relevance to imperialist, colonialist, or precolonialist excursions into distant lands; the further the remove from the European and familiar world, the greater was the ignorance in relation to distances, routes, languages, traditions, and mentalities (Zwierlein 2016b). Frederick I himself harboured no imperialist dreams for Gotha – that would have been ridiculous – but his father did actually equip an expedition to Ethiopia, because one of his court officials, Job Ludolf, happened to be an enthusiastic student of the Ethiopian language. Having met a real Ethiopian, Ludolf had compiled the first reliable Ethiopian grammar (Flemming 1891). The duke scented an opportunity to ingratiate himself with the emperor; his Ethiopian expedition would search for the legendary ruler Prester John and his armies, and find a Christian ally who could exert pressure on the southern flank of the hostile Ottoman Empire.

Our examples show that not only knowledge, but especially knowledge mixed with not-knowing, can have a strong affective aspect (Reckwitz 2012; Bromhall 2017). The greater the vagueness, the more abundant the projective space which is filled with hopes and fears, desires, and feelings of guilt. Affective ambivalences can shape whole cultures, as Simon Schama has shown, and their effects are felt within knowledge cultures too (Schama 1987). When the Dutch bourgeoisie acted out their unease at the extent of their own riches, this resulted in a flowering of knowledge forms concerning abstinence, purity, and transience, which related not just to practical matters, but which also found expression in theological treatises or physical experiments. One can go so far as to claim that affective relationships influence the transfer of knowledge down the generations, for instance within the narrower circle of family history (Mulsow 2012: 276–87). Psychologists speak of 'multigenerational accounting', which operates when for instance someone whose grandfather was an active National Socialist takes up a profession which might make amends for that guilt, even when the existence of the guilt has been communicated to them only unconsciously. The transfer of knowledge can thus sometimes be 'dysfunctional', not conforming to the model of transmission from teacher to student, but taking place obliquely, in a deposition and outdoing of relevant persons in the past. In this way, epistemic vices or virtues sometimes contain an element of intergenerational psychology.

Securing knowledge and the loss of knowledge

The example of Gotha also shows that knowledge can have a very variable status in terms of its chances of being preserved: not all knowledge survives the passage of time. Some knowledge is not fixed in written form, either because as 'know-how' it is only communicated to students verbally (this applies mostly to practical knowledge), or because it belongs to no tradition and there is therefore no interest in passing it on. Many baroque operas and plays of the period, for instance, have been lost – including in Gotha – because the ensemble or company did not have the score or text printed, wishing to retain the sole right of performance and to exclude imitators. Apothecaries and alchemists kept their formulae secret to some extent, because they represented their knowledge capital; they either did not write them down at all, or only in closely guarded manuscripts (Jütte 2015). These manuscripts could then easily be lost at a later stage. We can speak of a 'precarious knowledge' (Mulsow 2012) when knowledge may be extinguished at any time along with its bearer – the living person or the fragile manuscript. Knowledge is only secure when it can be fixed over time by being printed in a book or by institutional stabilization, as in established traditions of teaching and learning.

The category of precarious knowledge becomes central above all in the realm of forbidden knowledge and knowledge which is fought over. The documents of Gotha's military spies in war zones or even only in neighbouring territories are highly charged texts which could be intercepted with fatal consequences, as in the 'Grumbach feud' of the 1560s (Rous 2014). But scholarly texts were also at risk. A graduate of the nearby university at Erfurt, Christian Gottlieb Priber, went to America in the 1730s and joined the Cherokee Indians. He had become radicalized as a lawyer and had developed ideas according to which private property was responsible for the inequalities and injustices in society. He emigrated in order to realize his utopia of an ideal state among the Indians; during these years he wrote a book in which – in a manner comparable to Gottsched and Wolff, but more radical – he set out his own system of natural law and the state. Priber was captured by the English colonial government in 1743, and died in prison two years later; his handwritten book, which he always carried with him, was taken from him and probably destroyed (Naumann 2001). Knowing that he might be imprisoned, Priber had in fact left a copy of his book with some friends, in the hope that it would be taken to Europe and printed, but this did not happen. Priber's political and constitutional ideas on collective property, tolerance, and asylum, enriched by his valuable experiences among the Indians, were lost. These ideas were precarious and endangered knowledge – like those of many other radicals, atheists, freethinkers, and heterodox thinkers.

If we take the totality of carriers of precarious knowledge of this type, who existed not only in the persecuted 'underground' but in all sections and at all levels of society (established academics such as Isaac Newton or Hermann Samuel Reimarus had manuscripts in their desk drawers which they could not have published and whose existence was therefore permanently at risk), we can speak of a 'knowledge precariat', analogous to the current social precariat of the short-term employed on the labour market, a grouping that likewise cuts across established social strata. The counterpart to this idea would be something like a 'knowledge bourgeoisie', the totality of those who are able to secure the future of their knowledge and to disseminate it. This albeit unusual categorization of knowledge on the basis of the criterion of security offers the possibility of bypassing traditional forms of research into for instance the 'Radical Enlightenment', which are based on criteria of content and are therefore always susceptible to the drawbacks of projecting the frameworks of today onto the subject (La Vopa 2009). We can stay closer to the empirical situation, in which it was particularly those carriers of knowledge who touched on 'sore points' in the social consensus who were in danger. In contrast to straightforward censorship research, this view takes in texts which were withheld from the outset and never came to the attention of the censor, as well as texts such as formulae and musical scores, which as locally situated manuscripts did not belong to any of the types of text which were subject to censorship. The materiality of knowledge is also given its due in this approach, recognizing that the material condition of the text as physical object can be decisive, for instance, where a manuscript rots away in an attic, finally becoming illegible.

As with the perspective of epistemic virtues and vices, the approach in terms of precarity of knowledge can be reformulated as a question for research – in this case, how did actors such as freethinkers, spiritualists, or alchemists respond to the threats to their knowledge, of which they were well aware, and what strategies did they develop to preserve it? Such strategies might begin with a denial of epistemic authority, through putting one's own views in the mouths of discussion partners or of authors one wished to rebut; they might continue with the adoption of pseudonyms or the use of misleading titles, and end with the forming of covert networks for clandestine distribution (Cavaillé 2002; Mulsow 2012: 11–57). This approach also implies the necessity of reconstructing, as far as possible, the purely oral dimension of the transmission of knowledge (Waquet 2003). Paradoxically, a further chance of preservation resulted precisely from the rarity of precarious and forbidden knowledge. We find in the seventeenth century and above all in the eighteenth century numerous learned collectors specializing in 'clandestina', 'rarissima', and 'heterodoxa', and who knew where to find a veritable black market in texts of this kind. These collectors saved a wide range of precarious knowledge from oblivion and, however unintentionally, were the means by which it became accessible once again to like-minded heterodox thinkers (Mulsow 2008, 2014b). To remain with the example of Gotha: a large number of heterodox manuscripts are now held in the Gotha library, such as those of the spiritualist Friedrich Breckling. They are there because they were bought up by the ultraorthodox librarian Ernst Salomon Cyprian for use in his campaign against radical Pietism. Other, separatist, readers were able to access these manuscripts.

On the way to a global history of knowledge

Can the history of knowledge find a connection to the contemporary concern with a global history of ideas? Or does the concentration on very concrete knowledge cultures, as sketched out here, tie it too closely to microhistory? A 'global history of knowledge' would always run the risk of becoming diffuse in its grasp as a result of its expansion to a global level, and of losing density to an extent that could not be compensated for (Rothschild 2006). More recent examples have shown however that microhistory can also become global, where for instance very specific persons and themes are followed on their transnational routes (Ghobrial 2014). It is therefore possible to sketch out the opportunities open to a history of knowledge pursuing a globalized agenda in a way similar to the history of science (Renn 2012), art history (Elkins 2006), the history of ideas (Moyn and Sartori 2013), or the history of philology (Pollock, Elman, and Chang 2015). We should always bear in mind that this history of knowledge would be the product of a double expansion: from the history of science and the humanities to the history of knowledge where knowledge is more broadly defined, and from traditional Eurocentric history to a transnational and transcultural history (Mulsow 2017).

Finally, let us draw once again on the example of Gotha, to look for a direction for a project of this kind which would be shielded from the dangers of this double expansion. Between 1684 and 1687, Johann Otto von Helbig was one of the alchemical advisers of Frederick I. As a soldier of the Dutch East India Company he had spent the two years from 1676 to 1678 in Batavia, in what is now known as Jakarta. There, as a member of the circle of the apothecary Andreas Cleyer, and through exchanging ideas with local experts, he had begun to develop further his ideas on natural philosophy, arriving eventually at a new and 'unheard-of' physics (*Introitus in veram atque inauditam physicam*, 1682), which he then peddled around the courts of Europe (Mulsow 2015a). A traditional historiography would be content to describe the effects of Helbig's book in the scientific world of the European baroque, how it was received, and the recognizable influences on it of such figures as Jakob Böhme and Johann Baptist van Helmont. A global history however would use Helbig as a kind of endoscope, to investigate the presence of Indian (there were Persian-speaking Indians from Gujarat in Batavia) and Chinese conceptions of matter and alchemical processes, and from there to trace the spread of these ideas in South-East Asia, and their intertwining with European science. Vera Keller has recently explored the paradoxes inherent in the fact that Helbig corresponded in Europe with a community of Hermeticists who saw themselves as universal in outlook and ideology, while the actual universality, in the sense of globality, of this community derived precisely from the marginal position – from a European perspective – of Helbig in Batavia (Keller 2012). Helbig named the transmutational substance which he had developed in his experiments, and which he transformed into money at the courts of Europe, 'tessa', thereby coining a neologism which (inaudibly to European ears) alludes to the Persian word for saltpetre; in a sense, the cultural translation which was the undertaking of all of his physics was thus semantically contained in a single term.

Of course, with these reflections we are in the area of global history, but we are still within that of the history of science. What further questions would a global history *of knowledge* ask? It would enquire not only into the doctrines, but also, more intensively, into the practices which Helbig encountered in Batavia and which he brought into contact with his own, because the ideas which he took up there could have been founded in practices and ways of dealing with materials which were already thousands of years old, and had left deep traces in the affectivity of the cultures which practised them (Smith 2014). A history of knowledge of this kind would also ask the question of the precarity of the knowledge which was transported to Europe from Asia on trading ships: when substances and instruments belonging to the Chinese practice of moxibustion reached Amsterdam, what really arrived in Europe, and what, in terms of context and background knowledge, had been lost on the way (Cook 2007: 339–77)? A focus on epistemic virtues and vices can also be applied to global contexts like these: Helbig's ideals of virtue, which were intrinsically linked to the practices of an 'adept' of European alchemy, probably encountered other attitudes in the minds of the alchemical experts working in Batavia within the Indian tradition – or encountered Ming Dynasty Chinese conceptions of how practical knowledge should be combined with and related to more general doctrines.

In practice, this transformation of the history of science and the humanities into the history of knowledge has in many cases already taken place, including in the globalized dimension. Nevertheless, the challenges are immense. The routes which led out from contact zones such as Batavia and connected to knowledge from India or China need to be traced precisely, if the researcher is not to become lost in generalities (see, in general, Raj 2007). Conversely, the routes taken by 'brokers' (Schaffer et al. 2009) such as Helbig following their return to Europe should be examined as to how the 'exotic' (Schmidt 2015) and hybridized knowledge brought from Asia to Gotha was taken up there and how its techniques were implemented. Was this knowledge 'pidgin knowledge' (Fischer-Tiné 2013), a theoretical construct formed in distant lands beyond European shores, where certain standards, which would have been applied in experiments conducted in Europe, had to be abandoned for the sake of a harmonization of one's own practices with those of the local population?

The interaction of various kinds of knowledge which we have sketched out as a possible 'total history' for a single European court takes on a different aspect in the case of global history. Where the innovative aspect of a history of knowledge at court was the – hitherto hardly ever achieved – connecting up of administrative knowledge, political knowledge, practical know-how, and scholarly knowledge, in the global context it is the uncovering of 'knowledge paths' which cross-cultural borders, carrying theoretical knowledge embedded in transfers of material goods, local practices, and affective connotations. New paths are however being trodden in both of these areas.

Comment

Lorraine Daston

Martin Mulsow's stimulating chapter on the current state and future prospects of the history of knowledge takes a broad church perspective: the practical know-how of the potter (or the alchemist), the erudition of the bookish scholar, the subtlety of the courtier, the information gathered by questionnaires and travellers, the theories and predictions of the scientist, the secrets of the spy – all of these and more, much more, are grist for the historian's busy mill. Although some of Mulsow's most striking examples of what the history of knowledge could be come from the small but fascinating ducal court of Gotha in the late seventeenth century, both his opening survey of what is currently subsumed under the capacious rubric of the history of knowledge and his concluding reflections on the potential impact of globalized perspectives are panoramic in scope – almost vertiginously so. One of the several pleasures of the chapter is Mulsow's vivid evocation of all that might be included in what he calls 'the broad bandwidth of knowledge'. No *Wunderkammer* was ever so delightfully and miscellaneously over-stuffed. As Mulsow observes (in the section pointedly headed 'Knowledge?', that question mark a challenge flung down), philosophical nostrums such as 'knowledge is true, justified belief' are of little help to the historian in managing this overwhelming variety: 'It would be unsatisfactory for the historian if "knowledge" of this kind [the example is alchemical procedures for making gold] were to be disregarded, and if account were to be taken only of knowledge which we continue to regard as true today'.

Yet even if historians of knowledge shift the responsibility for defining their subject matter to the historical actors, the problem is not solved. In many epochs and cultures, for example, practical knowledge, especially that of low-status groups such as handworkers, peasants, servants, and women, is often not recognized, either semantically or socially, as genuine knowledge. Should the historian follow suit? Moreover, as Mulsow points out in the case of the Gotha court intrigues surrounding the duke's alchemical adventures, what counts as knowledge is often controversial among the historical actors themselves. Even within a single epistemic culture – be it a laboratory of chemists, a network of spies, or a guild of goldsmiths – there are almost always differing views about the validity of claims and the efficacy of methods. Indeed, such divergences are essential to the emergence of novelty within epistemic cultures.

Finally, knowledge, however and by whomever defined, is never a static category, always mutating in response both to internal and external pressures: Renaissance European courts cultivated forms of knowledge, such as engineering and alchemy, marginalized by universities; gardeners of many lands had to learn how to cultivate exotic plants such as potatoes and tulips in new soils and climates (Koerner 1999; Egmond 2010); Chinese emperors employed first Islamic and later Jesuit astronomers as the most expert in their field, but expert in different ways (van Dalen 1997; Hsia 2009); commodities such as porcelain or indigo dye inspired imitators who invented new techniques and products in the process (Berg 2015). Surely a history of knowledge should also attend to the dynamics of the category, as well as to the diversity of its definitions in any given cultural and historical context. Historicism alone will not order the miscellany.

Even after the usual historical strictures against anachronism have been honoured, we are still left with the question, what is the history of knowledge about? Or perhaps more sharply formulated, is there anything that the history of knowledge is *not* about? This is a particularly uncomfortable question for the burgeoning young field of the history of knowledge because it owes a great deal of its current appeal to its come-one-come-all embrace. In contrast to the snobbery of the history of science, traditionally preoccupied with fencing off its subject matter from pseudo-science and drawing boundaries between modern and premodern science or between Western science and the rest or (at least in twentieth-century Anglophone circles) between the two cultures of the sciences and the humanities, the history of knowledge rolled out the welcome mat to the knowledge of bureaucrats, artisans, office-workers, farmers, courtiers, humanists, psychoanalysts, animal keepers, and merchants. To be fair, historians of science of the past twenty-five years have paved the way by purging their definitions of science of anachronisms and focusing on scientific practices such as collecting, experimenting, observing, and note-taking. These latter led historians from the laboratory to the workshop, forge, and kitchen (Smith 2004; Leong 2008); from the observer's notebook to the humanist commonplace book (Blair 2004; Kraemer 2016); from the natural history museum to the cabinet of curiosities (Findlen 1994); from experimental protocols to household recipes (Leong and Rankin 2011; Smith 2016). Core scientific practices such as experiment and observation proved to be entangled with people and sites previously absent in standard accounts of key episodes in the history of science: 'science in context', as the research programme became known.

And therein lay the rub: context, like knowledge, is a potentially infinitely expandable category; which context was relevant for doing the history of science in context depended on which science was under investigation. In the great majority of cases, historians of science have relied on tried-and-true actors and achievements from an older historiography to circumscribe context. This generalization holds even for some of the most innovative studies produced by the science-in-context programme. No one has ever doubted the significance of figures such as Galileo or practices such as experiment in the history of science; to show the importance of the Medici court for Galileo's career (Biagioli 1993) or of alchemy to Isaac Newton's natural philosophy (Dobbs 1991) widened the context of science without exploding it. Narratives were still tethered to the familiar cast of characters and milestones, and context was defined accordingly: stories that began in port city markets or apothecary shops or beer manufacture ended with Francis Bacon or the mechanical equivalent of heat. The studies were often brilliant and the results illuminating; thanks to them, the history of science has become truly historical. But it has so far been spared the acute problems of definition of subject matter and therefore of context that confront the history of knowledge.

As Mulsow remarks, aspirations to create a global history of knowledge sharpen the double challenge of defining subject matter and context. Not only do different cultures at different times understand knowledge in different ways; the circulation of people, ideas, and things over oceans, continents, and millennia raises questions about whether the implicit analytical units of culture and period have any traction in analysing, for example, how knowledge of silk manufacture travelled from China to Italy or telescopic astronomy in the reverse direction. Recent studies of the 'brokers' who connected cultures and commodities reveal the skein of skills – diplomatic, linguistic, economic – required of these habitual go-betweens, who not only transmitted knowledge but also created (and sometimes codified) it (Schaffer et al. 2009). Faced with such teeming variety, Mulsow understandably recommends nominalism to the would-be historian of knowledge: 'So with the formulation, "what was held to be knowledge at the time", we enter a grey area where we must decide in each individual case whether we should speak of knowledge or merely of individual beliefs.'

Prudent though such a policy may be, I confess that I find it unsatisfying. Just as there is no culture without knowledge, there is no culture without an at least implicit systematics of knowledge, starting with an epistemological hierarchy (often intertwined with a social hierarchy) of which kinds of knowledge are more or less valued, by whom, and why. These hierarchies also rank knowers and the epistemic virtues they are expected to display. Even without the existence of epistemic cultures self-consciously dedicated to the pursuit of knowledge, such hierarchies exist. They erect criteria for what counts as knowledge and why – and also which knowledge is worthy of societal support and transmission. Renaissance courts, for example, were not epistemic cultures, though they may have employed a variety of knowledge-seekers, from alchemists to mathematicians to philologists, as well as military engineers, cooks, and huntsmen. But courts did impose criteria for knowledge, criteria sometimes at odds with those imposed by coeval universities: practical efficacy was prized over causal explanation; particulars about the properties of plants and waters over universal generalizations; elegance over erudition. By offering plummy patronage positions to talented men (and a few women) on the make, courts succeeded in shifting the criteria and thereby reshuffling the hierarchy, with remarkable results: court physicians began collecting and comparing observations of individual cases (Pomata 2010); naturalists studied the exotica and exceptions on display in princely *Wunderkammern* (Daston and Park 1998); mathematicians turned to problems of engineering (Valleriani 2010); natural philosophers probed the secrets of alchemy, the court science par excellence (Smith 1994; Nummedal 2007).

Viewed from a more philosophical standpoint, these are the shifts in ideals and practices that created new epistemic values as well as new knowledge: prediction of particular effects (a lowly value previously associated with natural divination and the mechanical arts) merged with explanation by universal causes (a lofty value associated with the liberal arts); experiment and observation (two words rarely found together in medieval texts and still more rarely associated with learned pursuits (Park 2011)) formed a powerful alliance in natural inquiry; the stock of hands-on practical knowledge rose and that of metaphysics plummeted; the pursuit of knowledge became collective among both humanists and naturalists.

This is just one well-studied example – and simply the best known among historians of science – of the dynamism of systems of knowledge, in which new epistemic values topple old ones, rearrange classifications of knowledge, and invert hierarchies of kinds of knowledge and knowers. It is also an example of ferment introduced by cross-cultural encounters brought about by commerce, conquest, and curiosity: new commodities such as the exotic plants that beautified gardens and expanded the apothecary's store of drugs also became new objects of inquiry for botanists, chemists, and physicians (Cook 2007; Boumediene 2016). Analogous transformations of knowledge systems occur in all cultures, although attitudes towards novelty – bane or blessing? – may make them more difficult to detect. Continuity in traditions is both a value and achievement, realized by chains of teaching and transmission that need not be textual, as the mnemonic feats of Indian pandits and the flourishing handicraft lineages in almost every culture testify. 'Lineage' is meant literally here: the role of the family, both biological and cultural (cp. 'alma mater', 'Doktor-Vater'), as the vehicle for the cultivation, transmission, and advance of knowledge of both hand and head well into the modern period. Nor need the knowledge be textual: images and objects and indeed whatever human activities capable of achieving recognized virtuosity also qualify, from exquisite tapestries to heroic horsemanship. Because knowledge systems crystallize in institutions and livelihoods, transformations provoke struggles that force the combatants to make epistemic values explicit. School curricula and incomes reveal the winners: when in 1798 Kant defended the prerogatives of the philosophical faculty against the 'higher' faculties of law, theology, and medicine, he did so against a background of centuries of higher salaries for professors of the latter (Kant 2005).

Historians of knowledge are rightly sensitive to the nuances of cognate words in other languages and epochs. Distinctions such as that between *wissen* and *kennen* in German, or *ars* and *scientia* in Latin, offer valuable clues to the ways in which knowledge hierarchies are articulated and ranked. They also point towards the epistemic values enshrined in these orders: for example, the certainty and universality of *scientia* in medieval Europe versus the utility and progress of *ars*. The same holds in spades for the cognate vocabularies of other cultures and epochs, which have the potential to unsettle the historian's own tacit assumptions about what counts as knowledge.

However, to make a fetish of words might blind historians to analogies that span the knowledge systems of diverse cultures. For example, governing extensive territories, managing resources and technologies, and waging wars may produce similar constellations of planning, record-keeping, risk assessment, and bureaucracy (roughly equivalent to Mulsow's complex of courtly knowledge) that would reward comparative study under the umbrella of the history of knowledge, no matter which words in the relevant languages do or do not single out these competences (Brian 1994; Soll 2009; Brendecke, Friedrich, and Friedrich 2008). Mutatis mutandis, the same might be said of the efflorescence of philological scholarship in many, though by no means all cultures. The paradigms of grammar provide multiple learned traditions with the paradigm of all rigorous knowledge, of systematized regularities so ironclad that even exceptions are classified (Pollock, Elman, and Chang 2015; Grafton and Most 2016). These are no doubt only two of the many subjects that would reward comparative study and provide materials for generalizations that cut across specific linguistic communities.

Why strive for comparisons and generalizations when the particulars of all that is currently subsumed under the ample rubric of the history of knowledge glint so invitingly? Aside from the missed opportunities to discover at least structural affinities among diverse traditions, there is the otherwise insoluble riddle of why some kinds of knowledge travel, both across epochs and cultures (Burke 2016). In the case of diachronic transmission, scholars of classical traditions have long puzzled over why, for example, Indian television productions of the ancient Sanskrit *Ramayana* epic still transfix the nation or why a thorough acquaintance with Thucydides and Livy was considered essential to the training for European male elites well into the nineteenth century. The vast labour required to safeguard the continuity of such traditions across centuries, including manuscript copying and collecting, the establishment and maintenance of libraries, and the unbroken chain of teaching and commentaries, simply deepens the perplexity of how some knowledge transcends time. Long-lived classical traditions, whether religious, philosophical, medical, or mathematical, are as much the cause as the product of cultural continuity. The synchronic question as to why some knowledge crosses cultural boundaries (and much does not) poses analogous challenges to the historian's stock-in-trade of contextual explanations. The comparison with commodities like silk and spices that roam far and wide is strained: exotic wares may be expensive but they are generally easily consumed; in contrast, an exotic philosophical or astronomical text may demand strenuous efforts of translation and study even to be rendered intelligible, much less irresistible.

In both diachronic and synchronic cases of transmission (a word that cries out to be unpacked, as Mulsow notes), it is plausible to assume that the knowledge systems of the host culture already contain some analogue or affinity with the imported knowledge. This is obvious in the case of diachronic classical traditions: the knowledge systems in question have been to a large extent designed to preserve and study a canon. Not so obvious are the mechanisms that refresh an old text for new audiences, starting with that fountain of youth, the much-abused and little-studied commentary. The analogues or affinities that smoothly slot imported knowledge into extant knowledge systems are multiple, from the substantive (e.g. an established discipline of rational theology or art of archery) to the formal (e.g. conducting learned discourse in riddles or disputations). In some cases, what begins as a comparative study of apparently diverse cultural knowledge systems may end as the discovery of a common culture. For example, recent comparative studies of natural knowledge in what used to be the distinct specialties of the history of medieval Latin science and the history of medieval Islamic science have concluded that it would be more accurate to talk of a shared knowledge system that reached from Central Asia to Northern Europe, despite differences of languages and religions (Park 2016; Feldhay and Ragep 2017).

Can the comparative study of knowledge systems give a shape to the still amorphous and expanding field of the history of knowledge? A shape is not a definition: given the difficulties historians of science have encountered in attempting to define their considerably narrower subject matter, it is unlikely that knowledge can be clearly circumscribed by either content or form. Indeed, one of the original attractions of the history of knowledge, especially for historians of science weary of sterile debates about internal versus external approaches, was the absence of any such bold line between knowledge and its contexts. The variety and dynamism of knowledge systems is well adapted to historicist and global approaches; the hierarchies and interactions among their parts and practitioners justifies the name of systems. Such systems are rarely closed and never static. Their omissions – what *cannot* be an object of knowledge – are as distinctive as their positive epistemic hierarchies and values. They cut the channels into which curiosity flows.

Response

Martin Mulsow

Lorraine Daston is quite right to seek to adjust the high-risk course I have steered. I had argued for a history of knowledge as 'histoire totale', as a reconstruction of all of the conceivable forms of knowledge within a given knowledge culture. In response, Daston is justified in asking: would this not lead to a history of knowledge that is arbitrary and formless? She encapsulates her response in the pointed question: what then would *not* be part of the history of knowledge?

The question requires an answer. The concept of knowledge should not go the same way as the concept of culture, which is now so widely seen as discredited by its indiscriminate application – everything is in some way culture. Having become fashionable, the history of knowledge is exposed to the same danger. There is therefore a real need to devise strategies of demarcation and delimitation, to give the idea of knowledge a clear outline.

This is completely in line with my intentions. My understanding of a 'histoire totale' was not a simple piling-up of forms of knowledge, but, of course, a unity in which the individual elements are seen in their relations to each other. This was the intention of my example of the court of a minor ruler: in a situation of this kind there is a complex intercommunication within which the administrative knowledge of a court official, the researches of a historian, and the ruler's collecting activities all relate to each other. As I have said, individual knowledge cultures have specific characteristics and ideals, and a particular style. But Daston is right in her view that this point is still under-defined. So how do the forms of knowledge relate to each other?

She focusses on the point where I say that knowledge is 'what was held to be knowledge at the time', and stress that this is a grey area, in which distinctions must be made in each individual case. Here Daston offers clearer criteria for how one might begin to detect what was held to be knowledge in a particular knowledge culture. Her answer is that there are always specific hierarchies, however implicit, which determine what is and is not knowledge. It could be added: and how highly a particular form of knowledge is valued, while another form is seen as of lesser importance. She says that these hierarchies and priorities (e.g. practical knowledge taking precedence over theoretical knowledge) are revealed most clearly in situations of conflict, although one can also attempt to distil them out from the language used within their contexts.

This clarification is very welcome. If we apply it to my example of the court at Gotha, we can see that quite different priorities prevailed there at different times. At times, knowledge in the natural sciences was valued more highly, while at other times, literary 'knowledge' played a more prominent part, and the latest news from the salons of Paris was sought, via the 'correspondence littéraire'. But how precisely the 'dynamic' of knowledge – a metaphor that would repay analysis – operated in each case between the factual knowledge of the collectors who studied natural history, the measurements and surveys of the engineers, the juridical expertise of the Privy Councillors and the ruler's understanding of the politics of the Empire, can only be established by specific research on the basis of the relevant sources. Perhaps it is overstating the case to speak of 'knowledge systems' here, and less decided expressions should be found to describe the relations between different forms of knowledge.

For there are also points at which the view of the history of knowledge, as taken by historians of science – including Daston's view – differs from my own, which is more the view of the history of knowledge as taken by a historian. The history of science, which has the great merit of making permeable the borders between text and context, between 'internal' and 'external' points of view, has always been able, as Daston stresses, at least to anchor itself in indisputably great figures (such as Galileo) or important practices (such as the experiment) as points of departure, thus ensuring the relevance of the research, whatever the diversions into the detail of the context.

The historian does not have these benchmarks to the same extent. He or she may begin with undoubtedly 'important' knowledge cultures such as that of the court of Rudolf II in Prague, or from central institutions such as the Imperial Chamber Court, but historians are also known for their tendency to rummage in little-known and out-of-the-way places. And not without reason: it is in just such places that the unexpected and less typical dynamics of knowledge can sometimes be found. A small court like that at Gotha clearly functions completely differently as a knowledge culture to a large court like Vienna or Paris. Equally, a less well-known circle of radical regime critics in Wertheim or Altona may have developed quite different hierarchies of knowledge to those of the Academy Leopoldina. The regime critics valued highly whatever was proscribed or suppressed, or that could have subversive effects, and therefore had a canon of knowledge quite different from that of an official institution.

With this I come back to the problem of the idea of 'knowledge systems' for historians of knowledge. The forms of knowledge in Gotha were undoubtedly interrelated, but they probably stood in rather loose relations to each other – one did not always know what another was doing, nor that the findings of both could be meaningfully combined. The priorities of one were not always congruent with those of another. Related to this is the fascinating question of who, within a given knowledge culture, understands the hierarchies and dynamics of different kinds of knowledge. The ruler? This view would be based on an old-fashioned top-down idea of absolutism, the idea of a ruler who sees all. More often it was gifted court councillors who were also scholars or scientists, such as Hiob Ludolf and Veit Ludwig von Seckendorff in Gotha, or Leibniz in Hanover, who had the overview; it was in their minds that most of the threads of administrative knowledge, political planning, learned expertise, and knowledge of the court collections converged.

Minds such as these may also have held the clearest ideas on what counted as knowledge, and what should be excluded from this claim. For a programme of research, this would mean that we should study the systems of preference of selected 'knowledge actors' such as these court officials, as evidenced in their actions, communications, and the notes and records they kept. Seckendorff for instance devised the classification system for the library at Gotha. What does this tell us about what counted as knowledge and what did not?

Lorraine Daston lays particular stress on the difficult question of the transformations of knowledge systems. She points out that it was precisely the shifts in the ideals and practices of knowledge that gave rise to new epistemic values and to new knowledge. These shifts can be hidden and almost invisible, and finely attuned senses are needed to discern the 'lineages' both within and between cultures. Can the historians among the historians of knowledge agree here? Undoubtedly, even when scientific or scholarly knowledge is not involved, transformations of knowledge and shifts in the ideals of knowledge are particularly interesting. Perhaps historians need to loosen a little here the criterion of 'newness' (at least where an aspect of the history of progress is concerned): transformations can offer insights even when they are simply adaptations to a different 'environment', to changes in conditions, such as a change of ruler or a particular economic reform.

And this brings me to the final point of Daston's concentrated and very stimulating remarks. This point concerns the call to give a greater role to comparative studies 'under the umbrella of the history of knowledge'. Yes – absolutely! This is another way in which Daston suggests that the history of knowledge can avoid the danger of losing itself in arbitrary detail. Comparisons make generalizations possible and sharpen awareness of the regularities of knowledge systems, and therefore also of what cannot be classed as knowledge. They also allow historians to recognize which 'slots' exist in particular knowledge cultures, into which elements of other knowledge cultures can be imported and installed. If this 'modelling kit' metaphor of knowledge transfer does not appeal, we can see the affinities between the cultures concerned as forces of attraction: Helbig in Indonesia felt particularly drawn to certain practices and concepts of the indigenous population, of the Indians and of the Chinese, because he had the feeling (it is often no more than this) that they could help him to solve problems within his own system of chemical knowledge.

Transmissions across cultural borders, whether temporal or spatial, are an almost insoluble tangle of contingent factors and less contingent affinities. Nevertheless I agree completely with Daston, that comparative studies of knowledge systems (or loose conglomerates of knowledge) can be a way to guide the history of knowledge out of its 'cabinet of curiosities' condition. It will then be possible to see what could be held to be knowledge at a particular time, who was competent to decide on this question, and in what directions this knowledge could move.

Notes

1. See for example the 'Cultures of Knowledge' project at Oxford University, the programme of the Max Planck Institute for the History of Science in Berlin, the 'Lieux de Savoir' project in France, or the 'Creating a Knowledge Society' project at the NIAS in Amsterdam.
2. Frederick I to his Chancellor Bachoff von Echt, Forschungsbibliothek Gotha, Ch. A. 830, p. 122.
3. Staatsarchiv Gotha: Geheimes Archiv PP I Nr. 1. I owe this information to Rainer Prass.

4. ThStA Gotha Geh. Archiv E XI Nr. 70, fol. 68.
5. The 'Pfannersche Sammlungen': ThHStA Weimar, F 573-F 662; ThStA Gotha, MMM 3 1 Bd. 1–29.

References

Albrecht-Birkner, V. (2002), *Reformation des Lebens: Die Reformen Herzog Ernsts des Frommen von Sachsen-Gotha und ihre Auswirkungen auf Frömmigkeit, Schule und Alltag im ländlichen Raum (1640–1675)*, Leipzig: Evangelische Verlagsanstalt.
Arndt, J. (2013), *Herrschaftskontrolle durch Öffentlichkeit: Die publizistische Darstellung politischer Konflikte im Heiligen Römischen Reich 1648–1750*, Göttingen: Vandenhoek.
Baehr, J. (2012), *The Inquiring Mind: On Intellectual Virtues and Virtue Epistemology*, Oxford: Oxford University Press.
Berg, M. (2015), 'Skill, Craft and Histories of Industrialization in Europe and Asia', *Transactions of the Royal Historical Society*, 24: 127–48.
Biagioli, M. (1993), *Galilei Courtier: The Practice of Science in the Culture of Absolutism*, Chicago: University of Chicago Press.
Blair, A. (2004), 'Note-Taking as an Art of Transmission', *Critical Inquiry*, 31: 85–107.
Bonjour, L. and Sosa, E. (2003), *Epistemic Justification: Internalism vs. Externalism, Foundations vs. Virtues*, Malden, MA: Blackwell.
Boumediene, S. (2016), *La colonisation du savoir: Une histoire des plantes médicinales du 'Nouveau Monde' (1492–1750)*, Vaulx-en-Velin: Les éditions des Mondes à faire.
Brakensiek, S. (2010), 'Verwaltungsgeschichte als Alltagsgeschichte. Zum Finanzgebaren frühneuzeitlicher Amtsträger im Spannungsfeld zwischen Stabsdisziplinierung und Mitunternehmerschaft', in M. Hochedlinger and T. Winkelbauer (eds), *Herrschaftsverdichtung, Staatsbildung, Bürokratisierung. Verfassungs-, Verwaltungs- und Behördengeschichte der Frühen Neuzeit*, 271–90, Vienna and Munich: Böhlau.
Brendecke, A. (2009), *Imperium und Empirie: Funktion des Wissens in der spanischen Kolonialherrschaft*, Cologne: Böhlau.
Brendecke, A., Friedrich, M. and Friedrich, S., eds (2008), *Information in der Frühen Neuzeit: Status, Bestände, Strategien*, Berlin: LIT Verlag.
Brian, E. (1994), *La mesure de l'État: Administrateurs et géomètres au XVIIIe siècle*, Paris: Albin Michel.
Bromhall, S., ed. (2017), *Early Modern Emotions: An Introduction*, London and New York: Routledge.
Burke, P. (2000), *A Social History of Knowledge: From Gutenberg to Diderot*, Cambridge: Polity.
Burke, P. (2012), *A Social History of Knowledge Vol. II: From the Encyclopaedia to Wikipedia*, Cambridge: Polity.
Burke, P. (2016), *What is the History of Knowledge?* Cambridge: Polity.
Cavaillé, J.-P. (2002), *Dis/simulations: Religion, morale et politique au XVIIIe siècle. Jules-César Vanini, François La Mothe Le Vayer, Gabriel Naudé, Louis Machon et Torquato Accetto*, Paris: Champion.
Cook, H. (2007), *Matters of Exchange: Commerce, Medicine, and Science in the Dutch Global Age*, New Haven: Yale University Press.
Cooper, A. (2009), *Inventing the Indigenous: Local Knowledge and Natural History in Early Modern Europe*, Cambridge: Cambridge University Press.
Czech, V. (2003), *Legitimation und Repräsentation: Zum Selbstverständnis thüringisch-sächsischer Reichsgrafen in der frühen Neuzeit*, Berlin: Lukas.

Dalen, B. van and Yabuuti, K. (1997), 'Islamic Astronomy in China During the Yuan and Ming Dynasties', *Historia Scientiarum*, 7: 11–43.

Daston, L. and Park, K. (2001), *Wonders and the Order of Nature*, New York: Zone Books.

Daston, L. and Galison, P. (2007), *Objectivity*, New York: Zone Books.

Daston, L., and Lunbeck, E. eds (2011), *Histories of Scientific Observation*, Chicago: Chicago University Press.

Dobbs, B. J. T. (1991), *The Janus Faces of Genius: The Role of Alchemy in Newton's Thought*, Cambridge: Cambridge University Press.

Eberle, M., ed. (2010), *Die Kunstkammer auf Schloss Friedenstein Gotha*, Gotha: Stiftung Schloss Friedenstein.

Egmond, F. (2010), *The World of Carolus Clusius: Natural History in the Making, 1550–1610*, London: Pickering & Chatto.

Elkins, J., ed. (2006), *Is Art History Global?* New York: Taylor and Francis.

Facius, F. (1933), *Staat, Verwaltung und Wirtschaft in Sachsen=Gotha unter Friedrich II. (1691–1732). Eine Studie zur Geschichte des Barockfürstentums in Thüringen*, Gotha: Engelhardt-Reyher.

Feldhay, R. and Ragep, F. J., eds (2017), *Before Copernicus: The Cultures and Contexts of Scientific Learning in the Fifteenth Century*, Montreal: McGill University Press.

Findlen, P. (1994), *Possessing Nature: Museums, Collecting, and Scientific Culture in Early Modern Italy*, Berkeley: University of California Press.

Fischer-Tiné, H. (2013), *Pidgin-Knowledge: Wissen und Kolonialismus*, Zürich and Berlin: Diaphanes.

Fleck, L. (2011), *Denkstile und Tatsachen*, Berlin: Suhrkamp.

Flemming, J. (1891), *Hiob Ludolf: Ein Beitrag zur Geschichte der orientalischen Philologie*, 2 vols., S.l.

Fried, J. and Stolleis, M., eds (2009), *Wissenskulturen: Über die Erzeugung und Weitergabe von Wissen*, Frankfurt: Campus.

Friedrich I. (1998–2003) = *Friedrich I. von Sachsen-Gotha-Altenburg, Tagebücher von 1667–1677*, eds R. Jacobsen and J. Brandsch, 3 vols, Cologne: Böhlau.

Friedrich, M. (2013), *Die Geburt des Archivs: Eine Wissensgeschichte*, Munich: Oldenbourg.

Fuchs, R.-P. and Schulze, W., eds (2002), *Wahrheit, Wissen, Erinnerung. Zeugenverhörprotokolle als Quellen für soziale Wissensbestände in der Frühen Neuzeit*, Münster: LIT.

Füssel, M. (2007), 'Auf dem Weg zur Wissensgesellschaft: Neue Forschungen zur Kultur des Wissens in der Frühen Neuzeit', *Zeitschrift für Historische Forschung*, 34: 273–89.

Gestrich, A. (1994), *Absolutismus und Öffentlichkeit: Politische Kommunikation in Deutschland zu Beginn des 18. Jahrhunderts*, Göttingen: Vandenhoek.

Ghobrial, J.-P. (2014), 'The Secret Life of Elias of Babylon and the Uses of Global Microhistory', *Past and Present*, 222: 51–93.

Gottschalk, K. (2004), 'Wissen über Land und Leute: Administrative Praktiken und Staatsbildungsprozesse im 18. Jahrhundert', in P. Collin and T. Horstmann (eds), *Das Wissen des Staates: Geschichte, Theorie und Praxis*, 149–74, Baden-Baden: Nomos.

Grafton, A. and Most, G. W., eds (2016), *Canonical Texts and Scholarly Practices: A Global Comparative Approach*, Cambridge: Cambridge University Press.

Haas, S. and Hengerer, M., eds (2008), *Im Schatten der Macht. Kommunikationskulturen in Politik und Verwaltung 1600–1750*, Frankfurt: Campus.

Hengerer, M. (2004), *Kaiserhof und Adel in der Mitte des 17. Jahrhunderts: Eine Kommunikationsgeschichte der Macht in der Vormoderne*, Konstanz: Konstanz University Press, 2004.

Hess, U. (1962), *Geheimer Rat und Kabinett in den ernestinischen Staaten Thüringens: Organisation, Geschäftsgang und Personalgeschichte der obersten Regierungssphäre im Zeitalter des Absolutismus*, Cologne: Böhlau.

Heyn, O. (2015), *Das Militär des Fürstentums Sachsen-Hildburghausen 1680–1806*, Cologne: Böhlau.

Hsia, F. (2009), *Sojourners in a Strange Land: Jesuits and Their Scientific Missions in Late Imperial China*, Chicago: University of Chicago Press.

Humberg, O. (2005), *Der alchemistische Nachlaß Friedrichs I. von Sachsen-Gotha-Altenburg*, Elberfeld: Humberg.

Jacob, C., ed. (2007 and 2011), *Lieux de savoir*, 2 vols so far, Paris: Albin Michel.

Jütte, D. (2015), *The Age of Secercy: Jews, Christians, and the Economy of Secrets, 1400–1800*, New Haven: Yale University Press.

Kant, I. (2005), *Der Streit der Fakultäten*, ed. H. Brandt and P. Giordanetti, Hamburg: Felix Meiner Verlag.

Keller, V. (2012), 'The Centre of Nature: Baron Otto von Hellwig between a Global Network and a Universal Republic', *Early Science and Medicine*, 17: 570–88.

Keller, V. (2015), *Knowledge and the Public Interest, 1575–1725*, Cambridge: Cambridge University Press.

Keller, V. (2016), '"A Political Fiat Lux": Wilhelm von Schroeder (1640–1688) and the Co-Production of Chymical and Political Oeconomy', in S. Richter and G. Garner (eds), *'Eigennutz' und 'gute Ordnung': Ökonomisierungen der Welt im 17. Jahrhundert*, 353–78, Wiesbaden: Harassowitz.

Klinger, A. (2002), *Der Gothaer Fürstenstaat. Herrschaft, Konfession und Dynastie unter Herzog Ernst dem Frommen*, Husum: Matthiesen.

Knoblauch, H. (2010), 'Was ist Wissen?', in H. Knoblauch (ed.), *Wissenssoziologie*, 2nd edn, 359–66, Konstanz: UTB.

Knorr-Cetina, K. (1999), *Epistemic Cultures: How the Sciences Make Knowledge*, Cambridge, MA: Harvard University Press.

Koerner, L. (1999), *Linnaeus: Nature and Nation*, Cambridge, MA: Harvard University Press.

Kraemer, F. (2016), 'Albrecht von Haller as an Enlightened "Reader-Observer"', in A. Cevolini (ed.), *Forgetting Machines: Knowledge Management Evolution in Early Modern Europe*, 224–42, Boston: Brill.

La Vopa, A. (2009), 'A New Intellectual History? Jonathan Israel's Enlightenment', *The Historical Journal*, 52: 717–38.

Landwehr, A. (2002), '"Das Sichtbare sichtbar machen": Annäherungen an "Wissen" als Kategorie historischer Forschung', in A. Landwehr (ed.), *Geschichte(n) der Wirklichkeit. Beiträge zur Sozial- und Kulturgeschichte des Wissens*, 61–89, Augsburg: Wißner.

Leong, E. (2008), 'Making Medicines in the Early Modern Household', *Bulletin of the History of Medicine*, 82: 145–68.

Leong, E. and Rankin, A., eds (2011), *Secrets and Knowledge in Medicine and Science, 1500-1800*, Farnham: Ashgate.

Moyn, S. and Sartori, A., eds (2013), *Global Intellectual History*, New York: Columbia University Press.

Mulsow, M. (2008), 'Die Transmission verbotenen Wissens', in U. J. Schneider (ed.), *Kulturen des Wissens im 18. Jahrhundert*, 61–80, Berlin: De Gruyter.

Mulsow, M. (2012), *Prekäres Wissen: Eine andere Ideengeschichte der Frühen Neuzeit*, Berlin: Suhrkamp.

Mulsow, M. (2013), 'Informalität am Rande des Hofes. Anwesenheitskommunikation unter Gothaer Gelehrten um 1700', *Daphnis: Zeitschrift für Mittlere Deutsche Literatur und Kultur der Frühen Neuzeit*, 42 (2): 595–616.

Mulsow, M. (2014a), 'Philalethes in Deutschland. Alchemische Experimente am Gothaer Hof 1679–1683', in S. Laube and P. Feuerstein-Herz (eds), *Goldenes Wissen: Die Alchemie – Substanzen, Synthesen, Symbolik*, 139–54, Wolfenbüttel: Herzog-August-Bibliothek.

Mulsow, M. (2014b), 'Radikalaufklärung, moderate Aufklärung und die Dynamik der Moderne', in J. Israel and M. Mulsow (eds), *Radikalaufklärung*, 203–33, Berlin: Suhrkamp.

Mulsow, M. (2015a), 'Alchemische Substanzen als fremde Dinge', in B. Neumann (ed.), *Präsenz und Evidenz fremder Dinge im Europa des 18. Jahrhunderts*, 43–72, Göttingen: Wallstein.

Mulsow, M. (2015b), 'Impartiality, Individualisation, and the Historiography of Religion: Tobias Pfanner on the Rituals of the Ancient Church', in B. C. Otto, S. Rau and J. Rüpke (eds), *History and Religion: Narrating a Religious Past*, 257–68, Berlin: De Gruyter.

Mulsow, M. (2016), 'Wissen am Hof. "Gesamternestinische" Gelehrte zwischen Weimar und Gotha um 1700', in F. Bomski, H. T. Seemann and T. Valk (eds), *Mens et Manus: Kunst und Wissenschaft an den Höfen der Ernestiner*, 35–54, Göttingen: Wallstein.

Mulsow, M. (2017), 'A Reference Theory of Globalised Ideas', *Global Intellectual History*, 2: 67–87.

Mulsow, M. (forthcoming), 'Das numismatische Selbst. Epistemische Tugenden eines Münzzeichners', in A. Gelhard and M.-R. Hackler (eds), *Epistemische Tugenden*.

Mulsow, M. and Rexroth, F., eds (2014), *Was als wissenschaftlich gelten darf. Praktiken der Grenzziehung in Gelehrtenmilieus der Vormoderne*, Frankfurt: Campus.

Naumann, U. (2001), *Pribers Paradies: Ein deutscher Utopist in der amerikanischen Wildnis*, Frankfurt: Eichborn.

Nummedal, T. (2007), *Alchemy and Authority in the Holy Roman Empire*, Chicago: University of Chicago Press.

Park, K. (2011), 'Observation in the Margins, 500–1500', in L. Daston and E. Lunbeck (eds), *Histories of Scientific Observation*, 15–44, Chicago: University of Chicago Press.

Park, K. (2016), 'Rethinking the History of Western Science Narrative, Translation, and the Longue Durée', Fetishizing Science conference, Einstein Forum, Potsdam. Available online: http://www.einsteinforum.de/veranstaltungen/rethinking-the-history-of-western-science-narrative-translation-and-the-longue-duree/?lang=en (accessed 2 June 2017).

Park, K. and Daston, L., eds (2008), *Cambridge History of Science, Vol. 3: Early Modern Science*, Cambridge: Cambridge University Press.

Pfanner, T. (1696), *Ad Guil: Ernestum Tentzelium Historicum Saxonicum epistola de confessione styli aliquantulum difficilioris, S.l.*

Pollock, S., Elman, B. A. and Chang, K. K., eds (2015), *World Philology*, Cambridge, MA: Harvard University Press.

Pomata, G. (2010), 'Sharing Cases: The Observationes in Early Modern Medicine', *Early Science and Medicine*, 15: 193–236.

Principe, L. (2013), *The Secrets of Alchemy*, Chicago: University of Chicago Press.

Raj, K. (2007), *Relocating Modern Science: Circulation and the Construction of Knowledge in South Asia and Europe, 1650–1900*, New York: Palgrave Macmillan.

Reckwitz, A. (2012), 'Affective Spaces: A Praxeological Outlook', *Rethinking History*, 16: 241–58.

Reinhard, W. (ed.) (2007), *Krumme Touren: Anthropologie kommunikativer Umwege*, Cologne: Böhlau.

Renn, J., ed. (2012), *The Globalization of Knowledge in History*, Berlin: Open Access.

Roche, D. (2003), *Humeurs vagabondes: De la circulation des hommes et de l'utilité des voyages*, Paris: Fayard.

Rothschild, E. (2006), 'Arcs of Ideas: International History and Intellectual History', in G. Budde, S. Conrad and O. Janz (eds), *Transnationale Geschichte*, 217–26, Göttingen: Vandenhoek.

Rous, A.-S. (2014), *Geheimdiplomatie in Sachsen 1500–1763: Spione - Chiffren - Interzepte.* Unpublished Habilitationsschrift Erfurt.

Rudolphi, F. (1715), *Gotha Diplomatica oder ausführliche Beschreibung des Fürstentums Sachsen-Gotha*, Frankfurt am Main and Leipzig: Benschen.

Sagittarius, C. (1700–1701), *Historia Gothana*, Jena: Bielcke.

Sagittarius, C. (1732), *Gründliche und ausführliche Historie der Grafschaft Gleichen*, Frankfurt: Barrentrapp.

Schaffer, S., Roberts, L., Raj, K. and Delbourgo, J., eds (2009), *The Brokered World. Go-Betweens and Global Intelligence, 1770–1820*, Sagamore Beach, MA: Science History Publications.

Schama, S. (1987), *The Embarrassment of Riches: An Interpretation of Dutch Culture in the Golden Age*, New York: Vintage.

Schlögl, R. (2004), 'Der frühneuzeitliche Hof als Kommunikationsraum. Interaktionstheoretische Perspektiven der Forschung', in F. Becker (ed.), *Geschichte und Systemtheorie: Exemplarische Fallstudien*, 185–225, Frankfurt: Campus.

Schlögl, R. (2014), *Anwesende und Abwesende: Grundriss für eine Gesellschaftsgeschichte der Frühen Neuzeit*, Konstanz: Konstanz University Press.

Schmidt, B. (2015), *Inventing Exoticism: Geography, Globalism, and Europe's Early Modern World*, Philadelphia: University of Pennsylvania Press.

Schützeichel, R., ed. (2007), *Handbuch Wissenssoziologie und Wissensforschung*, Konstanz: Konstanz University Press.

Shapin, S. (1994), *A Social History of Truth: Civility and Science in. Seventeenth-Century England*, Chicago: Chicago University Press.

Smith, P. H. (1994), *The Business of Alchemy: Science and Culture in the Holy Roman Empire*, Princeton: Princeton University Press.

Smith, P. H. (2004), *The Body of the Artisan: Art and Experience in the Scientific Revolution*, Chicago, Chicago University Press.

Smith, P. H. (2014), 'Knowledge in Motion: Following Itineraries of Matter in the Early Modern World', in D. T. Rodgers, B. Raman and H. Reimitz (eds), *Cultures in Motion*, 109–33, Princeton, NJ: Princeton University Press.

Smith, P. H. (2016), 'Historians in the Laboratory: Reconstruction of Renaissance Art and Technology in the Making and Knowing Project', *Art History*, 39: 210–33.

Smith, P. H. and Schmidt, B., eds (2008), *Making Knowledge in Early Modern Europe*, Chicago: University of Chicago Press.

Soll, J. (2009), *The Information Master: Jean-Baptiste Colbert's Secret State Intelligence System*, Ann Arbor: University of Michigan Press.

Stagl, J. (2016), *A History of Curiosity: The Theory of Travel 1550–1800*, London and New York: Routledge.

Stiening, G. (2007), 'Am "Ungrund" oder: Was sind und zu welchem Ende studiert man "Poetologien des Wissens"?', *KulturPoetik*, 2: 234–48.

Strauch, S. (2005), *Veit Ludwig von Seckendorff (1626–1692): Reformation des Lebens – Selbstbestimmung zwischen lutherischer Orthodoxie, Pietismus und Frühaufklärung*, Münster: LIT.

Tentzel, W. E. (1705), *Saxonia Numismatica, Ernestinische Linie*, 3 vols, Gotha: Wermuth.

Tentzel, W. E. (1716), *Supplementum Historiae Gothanae*, Jena: Bielcke.

Thiele, A. (2014), 'The Prince as Military Entrepreneur? Why Smaller Saxon Territories Sent 'Holländische Regimenter' (Dutch Regiments) to the Dutch Republic', in J. Fynn-Paul (ed.), *War, Entrepreneurs, and the State in Europe and the Mediterranean, 1300–1800*, 170–92, Leiden: Brill.

Valleriani, M. (2010), *Galileo Engineer*, London: Springer.

Van Damme, S. (2006), '"The World is too Large": Philosophical Mobility and Urban Space in Seventeenth and Eighteenth-Century Paris', *French Historical Studies*, 29: 379–406.

Van Damme, S. (2014), *À toutes voiles vers la verité: Une autre histoire de la philosophie au temps des Lumières*, Paris: Seuil.

Vogel, J. (2004), 'Von der Wissenschafts- zur Wissensgeschichte: Für eine Historisierung der Wissensgesellschaft', *Geschichte und Gesellschaft*, 30: 639–60.

Vogl, J. (1997), 'Für eine Poetologie des Wissens', in K. Richter et al. (eds), *Die Literatur und die Wissenschaften 1770–1930*, 107–27, Stuttgart: Metzler.

Völkel, M. (2007), "'Lob des Blütenstaubs" oder, musivisches Werk'? Neuerscheinungen auf dem Gebiet der Wissensgeschichte', *Archiv für Kulturgeschichte*, 89 (1): 191–216.

Wakefield, A. (2009), *The Disordered Police State: German Cameralism as Science and Practice*, Chicago: Chicago University Press.

Waquet, F. (2003), *Parler comme un livre: L'oralité et le savoir*, Paris: Albin Michel.

Waquet, F. (2015), *L'ordre matériel du savoir: Comment les savants travaillent XVIe–XXIe siècles*, Paris: CRNS éditions.

Westphal, S. (2002), *Kaiserliche Rechtsprechung und herrschaftliche Stabilisierung: Reichsgerichtsbarkeit in den thüringischen Territorialstaaten 1648–1806*, Cologne: Böhlau.

Westphal, S. (2007), 'Nach dem Verlust der Kurwürde: Die Ausbildung konfessioneller Identität anstelle politischer Macht bei den Ernestinern', in M. Wrede and H. Carl (eds), *Zwischen Schande und Ehre. Erinnerungsbrüche und die Kontinuität des Hauses. Legitimationsmuster und Traditionsverständnis des frühneuzeitlichen Adels in Umbruch und Krise*, 173–92, Mainz: Zabern.

Wilson, P. (1998), *German Armies: War and German Society 1648–1806*, London: UCL Press.

Zagzebski, L. (1996), *Virtues of the Mind: An Inquiry into the Nature of Virtue and the Ethical Foundations of Knowledge*, Cambridge: Cambridge University Press.

Zwierlein, C. (2006), *Discorso und Lex Dei: die Entstehung neuer Denkrahmen im 16. Jahrhundert und die Wahrnehmung der französischen Religionskriege in Italien und Deutschland*, Göttingen: Vandenhoek.

Zwierlein, C., ed. (2016a), *The Dark Side of Knowledge: Histories of Ignorance, 1400 to 1800*, Leiden: Brill.

Zwierlein, C. (2016b), *Imperial Unknowns: The French and British in the Mediterranean, 1650–1750*, Cambridge: Cambridge University Press.

CHAPTER 7
HISTORY OF EMOTIONS
Piroska Nagy

Emotions, a history

Relegated, even omitted from a discipline aiming to give an account of human history mainly by describing institutions and the progress of reason, emotions take centre stage in history today. While twenty years ago such a focus did not exist, the history of emotions, a new approach and domain, has become one of the most dynamic (sub)fields of modern historical research, an institutionally recognized area around which initiatives are blossoming.[1] A late child, the history of emotions is highly self-conscious, producing a continuous discourse on its methodology and epistemology in order to answer the unavoidable questions of research. Indeed, as inquiries on the emotions in history draw on questions raised in the disciplines of psychology and anthropology, sociology and emotion science, such research involves, beyond the regular questions a historian has to face, interdisciplinary and epistemological interrogations. In a context of fulfilment and abundance, where the first overviews are being produced (Plamper 2015; Rosenwein and Cristiani 2017; Boddice 2018),[2] this chapter aims at giving a synthetic image of the history and the debates animating the field.

Before going further, one important question has to be addressed. The term 'emotion', which describes a category that did not exist as such before the nineteenth century, but used here to designate the subfield and the object of our inquiry, is an academic convention, a *meta-category*.[3] It enables us to discuss affective phenomena independently of the indigenous terms and categories, as the cultures historians are dealing with may have very different concepts and conceptions of what we identify as 'emotion' today. In current scientific parlance, 'emotion' is frequently distinguished from 'affect', which has a long past and has recently been used to designate, in part of the literature, a pre-cultural, autonomous, bodily event, which precedes any cognitive operation (Plamper 2015: 225–37; cf. Tomkins 1962–92; Massumi 2002, 2015) – in the same way twelfth-century thinkers of emotion distinguished *passio* (our emotion) from *prepassio* (today's affect) (Boquet 2009). Finally, in France for instance, some prefer to refer to the 'histoire du sensible' or 'histoire des sensibilités', which includes not only the history of the senses and that of (short-term) *émotions* and (long-lasting) *sentiments*, but also the history of imagination and of representations.[4]

While the domain is recent, we must not forget that many earlier historians did consider the role emotions had to play in history – among these thinkers are Jules Michelet, in nineteenth-century France, and the Dutch Johan Huizinga in the first decades of the twentieth century, who are the best known in the field. The list of pioneering historians would be long, including, among other well-known names, those of Norbert Elias (a sociologist), Alain Corbin, Peter Gay, Theodore Zeldin, Jean Delumeau, and Peter N. Stearns. But above all the others, we have to mention the founder of the Annales school, Lucien Febvre, author of a now classical text published in two versions, recognized as a manifesto for the history of emotions, written after his participation in an interdisciplinary conference on 'Sensibility in Man and Nature' held in 1938.[5] Considering the substantial list of forerunners throughout the twentieth century, instead of trying to date its birth, we should rather speak about the sudden re-discovery after a slow, partly invisible growth, of the history of emotions around the year 2000.[6]

While Lucien Febvre's manifesto seems to have been inspired partly by his worries at the rise of Nazism and fascism in Europe, Jan Plamper, similarly, links the abrupt success of the history of emotions in the wake of the millennium to 9/11 (Plamper 2015: 60–7). Indeed, both contexts brought about crucial interrogations in Western civilization concerning the outburst of hatred and violence in human interaction, and the world climate of 2018 continues to keep these questions burning. Yet, beyond the immediate political context and atmosphere, it is necessary to evoke the 'affective turn' or 'emotional turn', affecting in the last decades not only the social and natural sciences, but the whole of contemporary Western societies.[7] Undeniably, emotion has come to qualify intelligence, to motivate ways of living and consuming, and to take part in everyday social exchange, discourse and argument (Illouz 2006, 2008; Prochasson 2008). Whatever one thinks of this turn, the idea itself and the sociological analysis behind it point not only towards contemporary transformations of Western societies but also towards the epistemological reasons explaining the emergence of the interest for historical research in emotions, anchored in the context of the social sciences between the 1980s and the turn of the millennium. Though these questions inspired a series of publications in the last fifteen years, they deserve to be rapidly addressed here, as they may help us map and understand the main epistemological debates and divisions that were, and still are in some cases, working throughout the recent history of the field. These debates and divisions make a strong impact on the methodological issues a historian has to cope with, when turning to emotions (Rosenwein 2002; Boquet and Nagy 2009, 2016a; Deluermoz et al. 2013; Plamper 2015).

Actually, in spite of its success, the epistemological status of the history of emotions is far from being clear today. For some of us, it is part of cultural history[8] – while others would say, history of emotions is related or belongs to neurohistory (Smail 2008, see also Boddice and Smail in this volume). Some would argue that it is part of emotion science, at least for the last century; others, that it has to be classified under the history of science. What, then, is the specificity of the field inside general history, or history *tout court*? Closely related to these epistemological problems, another important question concerns the definition, nature, and status of the emotions a historian has access to, compared to those that psychologists or neuroscientists study. What emotion are we studying the history of? Though they may seem highly theoretical, all these questions involve choices of method, and have an effect on the very ways of practising the history of emotions, which are far from being based on a consensus today.

Sciences and history of emotions

The development of a history of emotions has been closely related to the rise of scientific interest in emotions. The historian's conception of emotions is strongly dependent on their relationship to the scientific context. In other words, the study of emotions remained attached to a psychology (Deluermoz et al. 2013: 155). The history of this relationship has been told more than once,[9] characterized as it has always been by a series of permanent and fertile tensions, from the past century to the present. The most important tension is the one opposing nature to culture, and its corollaries: body/soul, reason/drive – tension presented in the scientific study of emotions that emerged in the late nineteenth century. The two best-known psychological texts on emotion written at the end of the nineteenth century – Darwin's *The Expression of Emotions in Man and Animals* (1872) and William James's essay 'What Is an Emotion?' (1884) – were particularly important for the influence they exerted on later emotion theorists, including Freud and other psychoanalysts. Beyond all their differences, both present a universalistic approach, associating emotions with the body, and ultimately, with the 'animal nature' of man. The originality of James's approach was to understand emotions as the last of a three-sequence process: perception of an exciting fact → bodily manifestations → emotion (James 1884; Plamper 2015: 175–6). According to him, when experiencing a loss, we are sad because we cry, and not the contrary.

The idea of the natural character, or even the animal nature, of emotion was conveyed by the first modern social theorists reflecting on collective emotions. The elaboration of the notion of collective emotions is generally (and erroneously) attributed to the French Gustave Le Bon and Gabriel Tarde, whose works, published around 1900, represent the best-known starting point of twentieth-century reflections on communal emotions and emotions of crowds (Barrows 1981). If the period gives birth to the idea of a collective political consciousness by which a crowd can transform history, the 'psychology of the crowd', a new 'science' emerging between sociology and psychology, was nourished by the sacred terror aroused by the anonymous mob, considered as governed only by emotions escaping the control of reason and common sense. The reactivation of this old anxiety, frequently present from ancient and medieval chronicles up to journalistic accounts of political protests today, can be easily explained by the sociopolitical constitution of an urban working class, in the last decades of the nineteenth century (Boquet and Nagy 2016a). Le Bon's *Psychology of the Crowd* (1895) had a great impact on Freud's conception of communal emotions, for instance. For Sigmund Freud, who explained collective psychology by his theory of the individual psyche, the emotional and irrational nature of the crowd was nourished by the unconscious, since the people or mob colludes, in his view, with the deep part of the psyche, the id (Freud 2005 [1921]; Robert 1974: 81; Moscovici 1981). According to this perspective, collective popular emotion threatened the high values of consciousness and the acquisition of individuality.

In philosophical terms, the interrogation which led to the interest in emotions in the social sciences was rooted, according to Hervé Mazurel, in the joint heritage of three great thinkers of the late nineteenth and the early twentieth century, Marx, Nietzsche, and Freud, whose anti-idealist and anti-essentialist projects contributed significantly to revalue the weight and force of affective life in the determination of human acts and representations (Mazurel 2014; Nagy 2017: 17–18). Thus, the birth of intellectual projects focusing on emotions and sensibility have to be linked to the rupture launched in Western thought by the demystifying hermeneutics of these three 'masters of suspicion', to use a term of Paul Ricœur's. Emotion did not belong to psychologists alone. In this sense, Johan Huizinga's *Autumn of the Middle Ages* (1919 [1965]) was based on a vision of emotions placed on the natural side of the nature/culture tension, as well as the works inspired by him, like the sociologist Norbert Elias' *Civilizing Process* (1939 [2000]), only noticed by the academic community in the 1960s and 1970s. Just as Lucien Febvre, Elias viewed the Middle Ages through the spectacles of Huizinga and, beyond, most probably through ideas from psychologists and psychoanalysts, if not directly from Freud. Their vision of emotions easily explains why the period did not mark the beginning of the research on the history of emotions: since they were considered as natural and ahistorical, there was not much to be said about them in historical terms. If emotions intervened in history, it was the natural side of man that was being expressed.

This vision of emotions – baptized a 'hydraulic vision' by Barbara H. Rosenwein (2002: 834: 'the emotions are like great liquids within each person, heaving and frothing, eager to be let out') – and frequently called the 'myth of passion' (as opposed to reason), following the philosopher Robert Solomon (1993: 77), dominated the approaches to emotions by anthropologists and historians until at least the 1970s. This domination can be explained by the heuristic power of the 'myth of passion', excluding emotions from history, as well as by the influence of the 'civilizing process' of Elias on the community of historians. This model offers the possibility of thinking about the emotional life of a whole society. According to Elias, civilization was understood as the control, sublimation, or suppression of emotions. Following Freud, only the quantity of emotions expressed was observed and considered to change. Feelings as such, their shape and constellation, were not questioned or reflected upon.[10]

Though a growing awareness of emotions can already be perceived from the 1970s both in anthropology and history (Plamper 2015: 90–8), the real shift came only at the end of the decade with the growing importance of the linguistic and the cultural turn, which brought a new, social constructivist vision of emotions. Since the 1980s, a series of anthropological works directly dedicated to emotions were published, in which for the first time, emotions and feelings were considered to differ from one culture to another, not only in their expression, but also in the way they were felt. Michelle Z. Rosaldo's study (1980) on Ilongot headhunting on a little Polynesian atoll, followed by the works of Lila Abu-Lughod (1986) and Catherine A. Lutz (1988), to mention just the most famous ones of this generation, had in common a social constructivist vision of emotion. They consider 'emotional experience … [as] pre-eminently cultural' (Lutz 1988: 5): in some ways, the exact opposite of the approach prescribed by the 'myth of passion'. In 1986, a collective book entitled *The Social Construction of Emotions* was published with the participation of psychologists, anthropologists, historians, and sociologists (Harré 1986). Though one can distinguish between a weak and a strong constructivism – preserving or rejecting the idea of a common basis of emotions in human nature or beyond, as well as that of a metalanguage in which we can speak about different cultures – the consequence, in the series of studies inspired by cultural constructivism, was an interesting discussion of indigenous affective anthropology, trying to understand the way non-Western expressions, terms, and ideas of emotions are shaped and arranged in relation with visions of the human being, body, and mind.

This approach came to challenge Western conceptions of emotion. Historians found themselves in a struggle between the modern idea of the natural character of emotions and historical evidence, which suggested the contrary. Yet, the way historians dealt with emotions changed only gradually. In spite of a rising interest in the topic from the 1970s onward, both in Europe and the New World, within the growing field of cultural history many of the publications of the period were still strongly marked by the 'myth of passion' in the wake of the late success of Norbert Elias's civilizing process. In the 1990s, alongside a similar shift in philosophy and sociology, the attitude of historians started to shift. A series of historical works paid attention to emotions, or emotional expressions – laughter, the kiss, weeping – analysed in their own right and integrated into the social and cultural logic which ordered them. The idea that emotions and their gestures had their own history, in every culture, which did not necessarily obey to the chronology or even the logics of the civilizing process, was slowly gaining ground (see, for example Monsacré 1984; Carré 1993; Le Goff 1989, 1997; Jaeger 1999). In parallel, the idea that not only the expression but also the conceptualization of emotions was different from one culture to another started to spread (Wierzbicka 1997). In this period, though, while research progressed, it was still rare to find historians who would speak about a history of emotions, besides Peter N. Stearns (Stearns and Stearns 1985; but see also Zeldin 1982). In most of these studies, no specific label of a field, or any epistemological or methodological discussion about emotions was included; we can only reconstruct the slow rise of what can be analysed post facto as the emergence of a trend.

The open questioning of the Eliasian 'grand narrative' in history and its vision of emotions as natural and acultural came only with the second manifesto for a history of emotions, that of Barbara H. Rosenwein (2002). Studying thoroughly the ways historians dealt with emotions, her article examines the epistemology underpinning their approach and underlines, for the first time, the links between the psychoanalytic vision of the psyche and the hydraulic vision of emotions; the process of civilization of Elias, the myth of passion, and a teleological vision of progress; finally, Western dualism opposing nature and culture, and thus relegating emotions outside what could be studied in history. In her proposal to overcome the obstacles that prevent taking emotions seriously, Rosenwein associates social constructivism with cognitive psychology. In psychology, views on emotions started to change after the Second World War, probably under the influence of the questions made possible by the psychoanalysts' division of the psyche into three (ego, id, and superego). Especially from the 1960s on, research in clinical psychology, to a great extent linked to research on the brain, led to the elaboration of a new paradigm with a major impact on the history of emotions beginning around 2000 and still noticeable today. According to cognitivists, emotions and cognition are strongly linked, in individual human decisions and activity as well as in social interactions and society. To consider emotions as cognitive and cultural, Rosenwein argues, opens up the possibility for a history of emotions. Emotions as cognitive and cultural: this was exactly the impression anthropologists had during their fieldwork in remote societies. Another fundamental turn Rosenwein proposed, against the 'grand narrative' of Elias, was to consider emotions on a smaller scale than that of societies. Emotional life and expression are, according to her, shared competences proper to social and cultural communities, which have to be contemplated as plural, in a given society. Rosenwein's project was formulated as a coherent one, propelling culturally constructed, cognitive emotions as explored and used by individuals and groups to the forefront of historical research. A new domain was launched: the history of emotions, within which many historians, already working on the topic, entered into dialogue in the next few years.

Present debates: Epistemology and methodology

The last fifteen years have seen the flowering of research in the history of emotions, raising a series of debated issues. After the honeymoon, the improbable marriage of cognitivism and cultural constructivism as the epistemological and methodological basis of a history of emotions became difficult to maintain, as it was founded on two contradictory visions of emotions and anthropologies. Cognitive psychology is based on a universalist vision of man, while cultural constructivism claims a sort of relativism, questioning the existence of emotions common to humankind.

On the one hand, cultural constructivism may seem a convenient method for historians, particularly for those working on remote cultures in space and/or time, as they have to become anthropologists in order to understand the codes in which these cultures expressed themselves. On the other, problems posed by constructivism and more generally by postmodern relativism were already the basis of criticisms in the 1990s. William M. Reddy, a pioneer of the history of emotions, published an article entitled 'Against Constructivism' (Reddy 1997, see also Hacking 2000). While cultural history, usually based on a constructivist paradigm, was expanding in the European academic world, in North America the social sciences and especially the humanities were marked, in the 1990s and 2000s, by a growing dissatisfaction with the programmatically 'logocentric' approaches – that is, the emphasis on language. In this context, emotions as a new topic seemed to present a special interest: they have a living, bodily manifestation, which can neither be denied nor reduced to discourse, and has been considered as neglected or even dismissed in the humanities (Leys 2011: 140; cf. Bynum 1991; Lyon 1995). In cultural studies, as well as in philosophy, art history, and literature, the 'affective turn' of the last decade was partly conducted by those who reacted to postmodern deconstruction, based on language, relativism, and psychoanalysis, by turning towards the bodily basis of emotion, baptized *affect*, which has the advantage, in their view, of offering a new biological basis on which to establish the humanities (Clough 2007; Massumi 2002, 2015).

This new conception of emotion is grounded on 'affect theory', where affect is opposed to an emotion understood as the cultural component of affective phenomena. For instance, the philosopher Brian Massumi considers affect as 'irreducibly bodily and autonomic'. It is an experience prior to language and consciousness, which by consequence does not involve cognitions or beliefs about the world (Massumi 2002: 28, cf. Leys 2011: 437). While this vision of affect, developed in the early 2000s, is in radical opposition to the understanding of emotion as an *appraisal* of the world,[11] it matches well with the views of psychologists and neuroscientists on emotions. In psychology, affect theory was firstly developed by Silvan S. Tomkins in 1962, and shares similarities with the theory of United States' most famous psychologist in the last decades, Paul Ekman. Both distinguish discrete affects or emotions (nine for Tomkins, six and later sixteen for Ekman), which are considered to be universal and natural (Ekman 1972; Tomkins 1962–92).[12] For Tomkins and those inspired by him, affects are bodily, unintentional reactions, a kind of 'affect-programme' located in the brain. Contrary to appraisal theorists, affect theorists see cognition and affect as two separate systems (Leys 2011). These theories of Tomkins and Ekman easily raise objections from historians: Ekman's theory of basic emotions with fixed facial expressions which can be found all over the world leaves no place for cultural variation. Still, the conglomerate of affect theory is deeply coherent with the neuroscientific view of emotions (Leys 2011: 443) and with some recent trends in cognitive psychology (Smail 2008), which have, far too frequently, a leading academic position today.

Besides its universalism, the cognitivist paradigm of emotions, which served as an important aid in rehabilitating emotions as part of history, places historians face to face with a dilemma. Like Odysseus, they are forced to navigate between the Charybdis of over-cognitivizing and rationalizing emotions, and the Scylla of over-naturalizing them. What remains of the core of human experience of emotions as shared and even contagious, of this tremor of the soul strongly linked to the body, if we consider it *totally* rational and natural? A vision of humankind grounded in cognitive science and affective neuroscience raises the danger, already mentioned, of naturalist reductionism: the oblivion of symbolic content, of subjective meaning, of all that creates human mystery and makes societies hold together – which constitutes a large part of historians' material. Such a vision would certainly help to do away with constructivism, relativism, subjectivism, and postmodernism, all at the same time, and this partly explains its success. Even if there has been a cultural and social inflexion to neuro-cognitivism in the last few years, this does not help historians of emotions to work with their evidence, as it leads them to understand human beings and societies as governed by transparent mechanisms, and so to de-subjectivize and de-politicize human constructs (see Lloyd 2007; Reddy 2010; Leys 2011; Mandressi 2011; Deluermoz et al. 2013). With such a definition of emotion we are faced with the problem that either our evidence cannot be understood with the help of the most authoritative sciences studying it, or it does not give us access to what *real* emotion should be, only to its representations, to a discourse on it. This feeling is amplified by the fact that historical evidence gives us access to languages of emotions, but not to the very gestures or physical transformations that emotions may involve: all that we know about past emotions is already mediated by the languages (spoken, of gestures, or iconographic) that we have to decode. From this statement, it is an easy jump to the affirmation that historians can never touch 'real emotion', the natural one, but only a kind of cultural surface. It is through this reasoning that the German medievalist Rüdiger Schnell (2015) wrote a book of 1,000 pages, seeking to demonstrate that a history of emotions is simply not possible.

The position of Schnell poses the question of the very nature of emotion for historians. As we meet them in historical evidence, emotions are deeply 'encoded' with symbolic meaning, which cannot be reduced to bodily states or waves. For historians who seek to pinpoint, describe, and understand the emotional behaviour and the specific codes of a remote society or simply of the documents they study, real questions – *historical questions* – concern human motivations, experiences, and consequences. To be sure, psychology helps us to *reflect on* what people may feel in a certain situation, but it does not *enlighten* us *on the historical meaning* of what people really experienced according to their own worldview, explaining motivation and seeking specific results in their own words – questions that historians try to answer with the aid of their sources. Still, if the success of affective and neuroscience in the humanities can be explained in part by their academic weight and greater respectability, it can also be explained by the inherent difficulties of a historical study of emotion: the unresolved epistemological and methodological questions, the transience of the traces and the consequent frailty of scientific legitimacy. In this situation, many historians coming to the study of emotions are attracted by the enormous literature on the topic not only in the country of psychology, but on the whole continent now known as 'emotion science'.[13] Trying to understand and interpret the sources, they seek a theory that would help them to understand what emotion is. For this reason, historians are tempted to ground their studies on a vision of emotions based on psychology – that is, an epistemology exterior to history. Yet, such an option raises questions: Is there a paradigm of emotion today, which might be common to historians, psychologists, and neuro-scientists? Or, going further in epistemological terms, how far can historians build on, or even link their vision of emotion to science, which has its own paradigms, epistemology, and history?

Curiously enough, a way out of this jungle of epistemological traps consists in doing history. This means, firstly, to behave like historians towards scientific theories and paradigms of emotion, in other words to be aware of their own historicity. Grounding our history of emotions on the scientific paradigm of our day, how could we hope for it to be more 'true' than that of Huizinga, Febvre, and Elias, whose epistemology was based on the hydraulic vision of emotions, strongly linked to the myth of passion? In other words, repeating the error of Febvre or Elias will not help us come to stronger conclusions. On the contrary, we may emphasize the link between the social and political context of postmodern, individualistic societies and the development of interest for emotions on one hand, and the paradigm change conducting to the success of cognitive science and psychology on the other. The culture of postmodernity has emotions as core values, as Anna Wierzbicka (1997) would say.

Doing history, in this case, means reflecting on emotions not on the basis of the worldview of our society – though, as always, contemporary theories may guide us in raising or understanding problems or specific cases in history – but on the basis of the very anthropology and vision of emotions developed by the past societies we study. Indeed, a constant dialogue between their world and ours is absolutely necessary, if only to produce an intelligible discourse. In a sense, a historian facing historical sources has to become a constructivist anthropologist and try to decipher and reconstruct past societies' emotional vocabulary, imagery, and behaviour, inserted as they were in larger social codes. Our sources, firstly texts and iconography, contribute to the production of a cultural discourse on emotions that we want to understand: most frequently, they are our only window on the emotions of a past society. In this case it is not important to discuss if there is, or is not, an emotion 'beyond' our sources; what matters is to understand the limits, functioning, shape, and transformations of the emotions that people of other times lived, described, staged, sought, or fled. The great advantage of this approach is to enable us to appreciate, just like the 1980s anthropologists, the radical otherness of the culture under study, the way their emotions are conceptualized and expressed, all strongly linked to indigenous anthropology and cosmology. This is certainly the less ethnocentric way of studying emotions, granting the greatest importance to the emotional map of a given culture. This method is also the most realistic one, helping us to understand the emotional world of a culture far away in time and space, of which only words and names remain, as Umberto Eco (1980) reminded at the end of the *Name of the Rose:* 'Stat rosa pristina nomine, nomina nuda tenemus.'[14]

Thinking that such an attitude would reduce our field of vision to a plain sequence of signs would oppose the linguistic expression of emotion to its corporeal experience, and forget how far bodily manifestations of emotions are themselves the products of interiorized cultural norms, which give way in a certain form to what is felt; and how far language is inventive in working with bodily signs.[15] Thus, while it is well known that weeping, just like laughter, can be in some cases dissociated from sadness or joy, one can also weep in ritualized situations, or in a deep communion with the divine in medieval Christianity – while laughter can be provoked and nonetheless felt. On the contrary, all the work a historian can do starts with this assumption, according to which historical emotions can be retraced through and between words and bodily signs, words and silence, and the ways in which words and expressions are used.

Working with emotion language: Reading emotions

On this basis, how should one, practically speaking, undertake *any* history of emotions? What methodology does a historian need to employ in order to find historical emotions, 'emotional facts'? What does one have to be aware of, when interpreting them, in order to avoid presumptuous projections and anachronism?

Certainly, whatever position is defended in epistemological terms, the main act founding the history of emotions is *taking emotions seriously*, as *a subject of historical interest*. From then on, two ways of comprehending emotions in history can be clearly distinguished. They represent two ways of questioning emotions, which have chronologically succeeded each other. The first consists of being interested in what emotions, a specific emotion or emotional expression are or were, in a given culture and period. In this case, emotions are seen as a *topic*: the history of shame, of laughter, of weeping, of anger in a given spatio-temporal context becomes the subject of inquiry. The second way of grasping emotions involves trying to understand what the expression or feeling of emotions, an emotional interaction or the eviction of emotions in a given situation, reveals about the way a society functions, or of the concrete relationship or situation at stake. In this second case, the status of emotions is different: it is not so much a topic than *an analytical category*, entering as a piece in the jigsaw puzzle of general history (Deluermoz et al. 2013). These two ways of conceiving emotions may reveal a difference at the epistemological level, though. The first one considers emotions as a category to construct: what emotion as such (e.g. *motus animi*, passion, or *affectus*) was and meant in relation to the body, but also in the web of social relations and representations; what specific emotions (pride, jealousy, or hatred) did and meant at a given moment in a given culture. The second way of considering emotions involves, by definition, a somewhat functionalist attitude towards them, which does not aim at questioning the category 'emotion' as such. For this reason, this method can quite easily be grounded on a universalist or psychological conception of emotions, which marks then its limitation too.

As already noted by Lucien Febvre in his famous article, various sources, written and iconographic, can contain information about emotions. The first and most evident method is to study words, expressions, and idioms relative to emotions: they deliver a great deal of data concerning affective life and the place of emotions or of a given emotion in the culture that uses them. Among others, they inform us on the way a culture or group conceived the production of emotions, related to their anthropology. In this sense, for instance *motus animi* of ancient or medieval Latin clearly refers to the soul – while modern 'emotion', which still holds the idea of motion, does not designate the entity or organ that feels or produces it. Emotion language includes the designation of the emotion as such, of the different kinds of emotion, which can be felt or described, and finally the expressions and metaphors used both to display emotions as well as to designate emotions and their manifestations (Kövecses 2000; Cairns 2016). Gestures like weeping and laughter are not emotions themselves, but they demonstrate emotions which can vary within the same cultural context, and which change to an even greater extent from one culture, and context, to the other. In this sense, the terms describing or naming gestures and unintentional bodily signs have to be included in what is considered as composing the emotional grammar of a culture and a language. The way in which a culture expresses emotions and shapes its norms of emotional control tells us a great deal of its affective anthropology. To these methods based on the study of discourse we can add the grammar of iconography, by which a culture expresses and represents emotions in image and sculpture, and which can be studied either in comparison with texts or in their own right. Both will contain 'names' of emotions (shame, anger, love, etc.) as well as bodily gestures (blushing, trembling, laughing, weeping, etc.), neither of which goes without saying. As several historians working on ancient or medieval societies have shown, a term for an emotion can go through a semantic change when societies change, as the sentiment it designates changes with cultural transformations; in the same way, new emotions arise while others disappear in the course of social and cultural mutations which either validate them or make them inadequate at the end (see Konstan 2016).

The study of emotional language, often criticized as a method that reduces emotions to dry, rational signs and makes emotional history much too disembodied, cannot be used alone. First, it is now frequently enriched by the attention one can pay to the way language enters in dialogue with embodied emotion, in a frequently figurative way (Cairns 2016; Frevert 2011). Secondly, two important questions concern the interpretation of silence, in terms of emotion in a text; and the action of larger social norms, which can govern the way emotional language is used or displayed. Indeed, emotion can be present in a text without being named. Emotional silences constitute a tricky affair for the researcher, as the reasons of silence may be various. They certainly inform us about the emotional norms: either about those, which command the 'encoding', the production of a source, or about the ones described in the text. How do we find and decode emotional silences, in these very frequent cases? The method of *scripts* is commonly used to understand emotional processes or practices. Elaborated by psychologists and appropriated to the study of emotions by the historian Robert Kaster, it consists of analysing culturally codified, longer sequences of interactions with regard to the emotions they provoke and channel, in order to understand the sequence of norms and gestures, eliciting specific emotions. When such a script is at work, it may happen for instance that a given emotion may not even be mentioned, but the members of the cultural community know it is at stake (Kaster 2005: 8; Pancer 2008). This helps to think with the silence of texts. Silences, scripts, and embodied emotions help to change the approach we have of the affective world as historians, focusing not so much on emotional discourse as a theory but on the discourse on emotions as a social practice, and even on emotions as a practice (Eitler and Scheer 2009; Scheer 2012), which helps to see the body, feeling, and manifesting emotions, as integrated within social practices and processes.

To these basic methods we must add a few specific cases, like the study and deciphering of traces of emotions, mostly unintentional, that a historical document can hold. The traces of tears on a manuscript can be those of the author or scribe, but also those of one or more readers, touched by their reading, at any moment of time; it may be the proof that the rhetoric presented in the text to make the reader feel certain emotions was effective. Historians can work with the signs of past emotions on objects, illuminating the society, which produced and/or used them. In this sense, texts, images, or artefacts can be analysed in relation to the emotions they provoked in the past; and historians can pose new questions about the ways in which they themselves interact with the very objects, sources, and topics of their research. Indeed, working on past emotions is particularly prone to provoke emotions; this point is brought to the forefront to an even greater extent for those doing oral history or other forms of the history of the present (Plamper 2015: 276–92; Gammerl 2014). In any case, the emotions that historians meet are not, and can never be, bare facts or given data, but mysterious and complex traces of a culture that need to be deciphered. Even in the case of cultures close to us, a historian has to behave like a cultural anthropologist in the field, trying to reconstruct the webs of meaning in the society under study, including words and gestures, silences and images, which together produce a specific affective constellation characterizing a world.

Tools for historians: Interpreting emotions

In the last twenty years, historians have elaborated a series of tools helping to work with emotions. A first question, already mentioned above, concerns the scale of the emotional culture one takes under study. To the scale of whole societies, as in the time of Huizinga, Elias, or Febvre, many studies add or substitute the scale of smaller emotional communities. When the study of emotions shifted from a sociological model to a psychological one, the temptation was great to substitute collective emotions with those of individuals. The notion of emotional communities can be understood as a sophisticated middle-scale. Elaborated by Rosenwein (2006, 2015), it helps historians to do emotional microhistory. Emotional communities may be large and small: of the scale of a town or village as well as of a looser linguistic community, or one composed of a web of people who, for instance, had the same education or the same master. A second advantage of emotional community as a tool is to translate what could be called emotional competence: the fact that the same person may belong to different communities according to age, education, past and present place of living, social position, and so on – and may share with these various communities different norms and ways of expressing and even feeling emotions. Others like William M. Reddy prefer to speak about emotional regimes, which are for him strongly linked to political regimes, and the norms they enact concerning emotional behaviour. Studying the French Revolution, Reddy associates an emotional regime with the Ancien Régime, another, bringing the authorization of abundant and unbounded emotional expression, with that of the first years of the Revolution until the end of the Jacobine rule, and a new one, much more restrictive, with the Restoration. For him, emotional norms shift with the change of regimes – and excessive emotional suffering enhances the change of emotional and political regimes. In some ways, the notion of emotionology, invented by Carol C. and Peter N. Stearns in the 1980s, is not far from that of emotional regime. This notion involves 'the attitudes or standards that a society, or a definable group within a society, maintains toward basic emotions and their appropriate expression; ways that institutions reflect and encourage these attitudes in human conduct, e.g., courtship practices as expressing the valuation of affect in marriage, or personnel workshops as reflecting the valuation of anger in job relationships' (Stearns and Stearns 1985: 813).

All these conceptual tools aid in dealing with emotional norms, with the dimension of an emotional culture that is certainly the most perceptible and readable in a given society. Indeed, enacting emotions according to, or circumventing norms does frequently involve some kind of change. Emotions as felt, expressed – betrayed or displayed – pop up in the continuum of life as well as in the texture of narration, so that they constitute an event – which provoked the description we read. Emotions viewed as events help historians to explore social and historical change on a human scale. Actually, as their Western name and etymology indicates (Hochner 2016), emotions have to do with movement, action, and interior and social change. We have already envisaged them as a social practice: it is in this direction that we can explore what emotions actually do. After having believed for a long time that people were affected by emotions, historians today are interested in their *agency*, considering that feelings and emotional display intervene in human interaction in various and active ways. Historians have elaborated diverse tools to deal with this active dimension of emotions-as-feelings as well as of emotional displays. It is this aspect of emotions that Reddy baptized an *emotive*, on the model of performative speech acts analysed by J. L. Austin. An emotive statement or expression – though Reddy speaks only about verbal acts, bodily expressions of emotions can be included in his model – both describe what is felt and modifies the interior state of those involved: it changes its world like performatives. As anthropologists have already remarked, expressing and attributing emotions do change the relationship between individuals involved in a scene. Reddy speaks about the 'navigation of feeling', resulting from the exploration of self, which may have self-altering effects, as in the case of emotional conversion, a frequent case in medieval times and texts. Processes, emotions participate in change, both changing themselves and producing change: perspectives that make them an object worthy of the historian's interest (Reddy 2001: 109, 128–9; for cases of emotional conversion, see Boquet and Nagy 2010; Nagy 2017).

*

The trajectory proposed here suggests that the history of emotions definitely belongs to general history. Emotions, as we meet them, must not be essentialized: there is no simple definition to what an emotion is. Working with emotions means a series of questions to answer, which differ according to the period, the document/s or historical problems addressed: they concern the terms, the bodily and cognitive movements involved, the images and concepts used to express them, and, last but not least, the social agency of the emotions represented, described, or prescribed. In order to avoid getting lost in anachronism or ethnocentrism, while seeking the answers to these questions, all references to emotions in a past culture have to be carefully contextualized. At the micro level, one has to work with the specificities of the documents themselves, in relation to an event or scene. At the macro-level, contextualizing means an attempt at understanding and reconstructing a given society's affective anthropology: the constellation of its core values with emotivity, specific emotions, and emotional expressions. Though many monographic studies on emotions have been produced in the last twenty years, such a mapping of emotional cultures, in most cases, still remains to be done. While strictly speaking, the rigour of the historical method suggested here places the history of emotions in the field of cultural history, this does not exclude possibilities for interdisciplinary exploration and creativity. A cultural history of emotions is nourished by anthropology, linguistics and may enter into discussion with sociology as well as with social psychology, and can, at any moment, use the sciences of emotions as heuristic tools. Finally, the history of emotions as a field may be considered as one which is predestined to integrate – better late than never – emotions into history.

Comment

Ute Frevert

First of all, I would like to congratulate Piroska Nagy on having written on the history of emotions in such a delightfully reflective and critical way. She has indeed introduced the reader to major problems and controversies within the field, as much as she has elegantly engaged with questions of epistemology and methodology. Her account of early pioneers and why they failed to have an impact on historiography is as lucid as her perspective on affect theory and her forceful plea to historians to approach the subject as anthropologists rather than as neuroscientists or psychologists.

My commentary is thus not meant as a substantial critique. Instead, I would like to offer a few additional viewpoints and trajectories that might recalibrate some of the challenges currently faced by historians of emotions. My comments focus on three different issues: one, historical background; two, brains and bodies; three, how the history of emotions fares in the wider profession.

Historical background

Why is it that the history of emotions has become such a burgeoning field in the past few years? In 2008, two centres were established, first in Berlin, then in London; in 2011, the Australian Research Council started funding another centre on emotions in Europe between 1100 and 1800. These initiatives and institutions produced and supported numerous lectures, conferences, and publications. Nearly every academic press is eager to launch its own book series; new journals emerge,[16] and older ones are keen to publish special issues. Within the past decade, historians of emotions have made a significant contribution to historiography, and beyond. The media take a great interest in our work, and report on it on a regular basis (which does not happen quite so frequently in other fields of historical research).

Such interest attests to the interrelation between our research and what happens in the non-academic world. It is true, as Piroska Nagy claims, that contemporary Western societies are intensely vested in emotions. They are witnessing a steady stream of emotional references, be it in politics or in the economic sphere. Journalists and political scientists discuss the emotionalization of politics (closely linked to the recent surge of right-wing populism); in economics, emotions have been (re)discovered as important resources for enhancing productivity and consumption. Advertising uses emotions to promote *n'importe quoi*, from cars to cosmetics, salads, and pet food. In a similar vein, the craze about emotional intelligence, introduced by Daniel Goleman's popularizing 1995 bestseller, is all about improving economic success, sales figures, and, ultimately, financial gain.

How, then, do the general interest in emotions and the academic history of emotions interact and inform each other? The question might be answered differently by modern history experts compared with historians of the premodern era. To historians focusing on modern history it is a well-established epistemological practice to borrow one's questions and intellectual curiosities from what can be observed in the present. Historians thus aim at enlightening themselves and their contemporaries as to why certain trends prevail, and what lies in the background. History here plays the role of a critical observer and interpreter, analysing the very logic and semantic politics of the here and now. In contrast to the social sciences, however, it does so by adding historical depth, narrative, and interpretation of current events, debates, and developments.

Having said this, the recent obsession with emotions seems to be part of several historical trends: first, an infatuation with the self and its very identity. This can be traced back to the therapeutic turn of the 1970s and 1980s, which staged the individual as the bearer of feelings that constituted her authentic self. But it also resonates with the neoliberal emphasis on self-optimization that has included, from the very start, emotions as a motivational resource. They not only help the individual person to perform well and ever better; they also offer – second – new opportunities for the economy. Emotions can themselves be commodified and tied to certain goods and services, in the same way that shopping is marketed as a path to happiness. Third, the recent wave of globalization that has been accompanied and popularized by digital media has supported the search for human universals. In this very context, Paul Ekman's (1999) concept of basic emotions has gained new and wider currency. If we believe in a set of emotions common to and recognizable by all mankind, such emotions can serve as a powerful means of promoting communication and cooperation across the world. Even though they are subject to cultural variations, they are said to be universally readable, thus forming strong bonds of mutual connectivity.

The list of circumstances that structurally account for emotions to become centre stage in our contemporary world might be even longer. The extent to which science has been a factor remains an open question. Possibly, the ennoblement of emotions within and through cognitive psychology and neuroscience has helped them gain social acceptance. At the same time, instrumental rationality has widely lost its appeal and proven insufficient in solving the world's manifold problems. Especially where moral dilemmas are concerned, it rarely delivers what it promises. In this respect, emotions are increasingly regarded as providing invaluable guidance and no longer as instigators of chaos – especially since chaos already exists without their doing.

Brains and bodies

Even though we are still unsure as to whether and how the sciences of emotion have contributed to changes in the way we currently view and make use of emotions, they have done a lot to convince us that they have been instrumental. Neuroscientists in particular have been extremely bold and outspoken, and their promises have gained them ever-increasing financial support and institutional funding. Rarely have these promises been fulfilled. Reducing mind, cognition, consciousness, sensation, and emotion to neurobiological processes has crippled the attempt to understand them in their complexity. I would therefore refrain from hailing 'neuro-cognitivism' as the 'most authoritative science' studying emotions. Although neuroscientists still claim such authority, we should not grant it. We should instead give serious consideration to internal criticism, like the concerns voiced by Lisa Feldman Barrett in her recent book *How Emotions Are Made* (2017, see also Leys 2017). According to Barrett, a renowned psychologist and neuroscientist, the 'classical view of emotion' – as being caused by brain circuits that then trigger physical changes inside the body – has to be replaced by what she terms the 'theory of constructed emotion'. This theory invites us to think of emotions as made and not triggered, and their making draws heavily on past experience and cultural knowledge. To historians, such theory is of great significance, since it brings history back into how emotions are created as 'a product of human agreement'. The theory is compatible with cultural historians' predilection for (milder) notions of social constructivism, but it also allows for attention to be given to bodily processes – without, however, re-naturalizing the body and its complicity in creating emotions.

In my view this is one of the toughest challenges for historians researching emotions in former times: historicizing emotions as bodily feelings. It is one thing to acknowledge the body as a crucial site of feelings and sensations (which modern historians sometimes tend to overlook or diminish); it is another to be aware of the body's ability to produce and manipulate feelings. As early as the fifth century, Augustine observed that *motus animi*, the invisible interior movement of the soul, could be enhanced by the moving body. The stirring of the heart that had in fact triggered such exterior movements was in turn intensified by the latter. Nine hundred years later, Thomas Aquinas expressed similar thoughts: signs of humility, such as bending one's knees, did not only express our inner feelings, but also increased our *affectus* to submit to God. Writers of the seventeenth, eighteenth, nineteenth, and twentieth centuries all subscribed to notions of the creative body that did more than render the invisible visible.

So far, so good. But what about change that historians are, or should be, professionally interested in? The concept of a body that both expresses and produces emotions swiftly acquires an alluring quality of timelessness. Quoting Augustine and Pascal, as well as Darwin and Wundt, who all confirmed the concept, might lead us to forget that the human body that they had in mind was not the same. Bodies, too, have a history as cultural historians have taught us, both as 'real' and as imagined entities. The body that Augustine referred to was different from the body that contemporaries have in mind. Work and workout regimes, sports and fashion, cosmetic surgery and hygiene have vastly altered the way modern people perceive their bodies, and that perception transforms the way bodies make themselves felt. Historicizing the body, then, must have consequences for its role in expressing and creating feelings. But how can they be studied?

As usual, we can do no more to be acutely aware of such processes of historicization. Again, we will not have any assistance from our colleagues in psychology or neuroscience. We might instead turn towards anthropologists and learn from them. Moreover we have to read our sources most carefully and listen to the way they describe what is going on inside and outside of the body, what kind of agency they give it, and how they conceive of its relationship with the environment. Neither the human body nor human emotions can bridge the gap between us and our ancestors, or, for this matter, between inhabitants of the modern urban West and villagers in remote areas of India or China.

The house of history

If the history of emotions is part of history – in as much as emotions are, to quote Barrett once again, 'a product of human agreement' – we should worry less about how it relates to neuroscience and more about how it fares among historians. Is it welcomed by the profession, or shunned and marginalized? What promises does it make, what added value is there to be gained by focusing on emotions?

On the one hand, historians of emotions cannot complain about lack of funding or interest. They organize panels at annual professional meetings and get their articles accepted and printed by high-profile journals. In 2015, at the 22nd World Congress of Historians in Jinan (China), where colleagues from all over the globe met to present and discuss their research, 'historicizing emotions' was chosen as one of the four major themes. This testified to the intellectual appeal of the new field, and the topic attracted immense curiosity among those participants (mainly from China) who had never heard of it before.

On the other hand, not every colleague is easily won over. Openly or behind closed doors, many voice their doubts about what historians of emotions have to offer. Does the history of emotions really expand or alter current knowledge, or is it simply old wine in new bottles? Some go even further; to them, the history of emotions is just another culturalist fad that contributes to rendering history utterly irrelevant and promoting its decline. In his recent diatribe against fellow historians who take to 'arcane topics' rather than transmit crucial political and economic knowledge, Niall Ferguson picked out a history of emotions course at his own university in order to prove his point. According to the Harvard professor, such courses are completely 'disconnected from our contemporary concerns' and help to reduce and finally obliterate historians' public influence in explaining and making sense of the world (Ferguson 2016).

Ferguson is wrong on several points. History of emotions classes do resonate with students because they are, as argued above, closely associated with contemporary challenges and experiences. They help undergraduates understand how and why their social, political, and economic environment is putting so much emphasis on performing, manipulating, and instrumentalizing emotions. They teach them about modern subjectivity and the role emotions are supposed to play in an individual's self-fashioning and relationships. Furthermore, they inform them about the reasons and historical circumstances under which such a role has been carved out and popularized. Why should this be less relevant and enlightening than teaching students about the French and American revolutions, or the rise and fall of the rate of economic profits? If the paramount role of historians is to critically educate citizens about their background and how this matters for their identity and politics, a class on the history of emotions is as valuable and elucidating as a lecture on past wars or elections. The profession has long since dropped the claim that history should be mainly about great men making political decisions; with the advent of historical anthropology and cultural history, topics like birth and death, health and illness, sexuality and marriage, food and drink, work and leisure have captured historians' attention. The 'house of history', as David Blackbourn once remarked, has many rooms and can thus host different topics and approaches. Over the years and decades, some may vacate their rooms and pass them on to new inhabitants, others move from small niches to spacious salons, and vice versa.

What is best about this 'house' is that all rooms have unlocked doors, to each side. This, in principle, allows for communication and mutual exchange, for intense debate and learning from one another. For the principle to be turned into practice, however, an open mind, curiosity, and generosity on all sides are required. Newcomers self-evidently have to invite older tenants and explain why their presence makes a difference. Those who already live there and cultivate their scepticism are asked to listen politely, and critically engage with the new residents. To ignore them, or to accuse them of making the whole house crumble, does not constitute constructive behaviour.

Historians of emotions are therefore well advised to reach out to other colleagues and demonstrate what they might gain by the new approach or perspective (I would rather not talk about subfields, as the agricultural metaphor calls up neatly separated territories with sharp boundaries and invisible 'no trespassing' signs). One aspect of such gains concerns a wealth of new topics to be researched. Yet not every historian is interested in discovering new topics. Many content themselves with revisiting classical sites and events, and each anniversary, especially in modern history, sees bookshelves full of new releases, as could be witnessed in 2014 (beginning of the First World War), 2017 (Russian Revolution; US-American entry into the war) and, presumably, in 2018 (end of the war). But even new books on old topics benefit from novel approaches. The diplomatic history of the July crisis of 1914, for example, can be greatly enriched by focusing on the notion of honour and shame and how it was used to legitimize national politics and garner public support. To this very day, many international conflicts and foreign policy decisions have been informed and shaped by the quest for national honour and the fear of being publicly shamed and humiliated. At the same time, honour and shame are by no means ahistorical staples, instead, they have to be problematized and contextualized in any given society in order to grasp their precise meaning and operating range.

Factoring emotions into historical accounts and analysis implies taking them seriously as historical phenomena per se. If this is what Piroska Nagy had in mind when she introduced emotions as an 'analytical category', I would agree with her. Nevertheless I would stress that it is not enough for historians to consider emotions in a 'functionalist' mode, and assume, for instance, that rage and resentment motivated Parisians to storm the Bastille prison in 1789, or Russian citizens to raid St. Petersburg's Winter Palace in 1917. Even if we rightly credit emotions with motivating strength, we should still go deeper into the 'structures of feeling'.[17] We should not pretend to know how rage and resentment actually felt and worked, but explore how participants themselves described their emotions, where they originated, and what they did to them. We should then draw a map of those emotions that were known and labelled at the time, and become aware of their semantics. We should investigate whether speakers attempted to evoke emotions, with what kind of rhetoric, and to what avail. We should, in short, not naturalize, but historicize emotions, as we do with any other object of historical research.

The use of emotions as a tool for analysing historical developments also entails asking questions about change. Unlike anthropologists and social scientists, who investigate people and social order at a given time (usually in the present), historians are by definition concerned with continuities and discontinuities over time. Even if they focus on relatively short periods like the Reformation or the First World War, they do so with a keen interest in the 'before' and the 'after'. But how can we operationalize change in regard to emotions? We can, first, conceive of emotions as active proponents of social and political change. The analysis of emotional styles and how these are cultivated and practised, but also challenged and criticized in institutions such as the family, the military, at the workplace, in schools and universities draws attention to the degree to which such styles undergo changes and in turn influence institutional politics. A case in point is what happened in Western societies during the 1960s and 1970s when liberalization was closely connected to and often instigated by the quest for emotional emancipation and the freedom to explore and follow one's 'true' feelings.

Second, we can see change in the way emotions are mapped. Some emotions that figured prominently in the early modern period became obscure in later times or found themselves pushed to the margins. Others became more salient and were cherished as useful and benevolent, like empathy or trust in our current world. Public and media discourse works as a powerful amplifier. If certain emotions are constantly talked about and praised, while others are neglected and forgotten, there are consequences regarding how and what people actually feel. The words *Groll* (grudge) and *Grimm* (wrath), for instance, have by now completely disappeared from spoken German, and it is highly improbable that people still know the feelings. They might feel rage, anger, and resentment – but no longer the specific *Groll* or *Grimm* that was the topic of eighteenth- and early nineteenth-century stories.

Third, change can also be detected in the manner in which those emotions that have kept their names and appearance on the map are socially framed and contextualized. What has happened to humility over the years, decades, and centuries? Who was and is supposed to show it, towards whom? What kind of body language was and is used to express or heighten it? Under which circumstances could humility flourish, and what made it weaken? We could – and should – ask similar questions about other emotions and thus write well-researched and finely nuanced topical histories of shame, greed, anger, and the like. If these histories pay close attention to context, they can go far beyond the topical. They can become societal histories that use emotions to link subjectivities to social, political, and economic structures and developments. This would, I predict, cause a major stir in the house of history.

Response

Piroska Nagy

I am very thankful to Ute Frevert, who raises a series of thoughtful issues in her very constructive comment. While I agree with most of her points, there remains space for debate.

Frevert underlines the historical conditions of present-day societies that led to the recent obsession with emotions, to use her own words. These conditions, well known today, include the scientific interest in emotions, from the direction of the cognitive neurosciences as well as the humanities. In speaking about the sciences, my aim was to underscore the ways in which they share the historical conditions that they also help shape, as part of an interdependent world. While a scientific discourse, perhaps by its very nature, frequently puts forward the paradigm it defends as if it held an unconditional truth, the job of historians, for their part, is to emphasize the *historicity* of scientific paradigms and their inscription in specific contexts. This larger outlook makes it possible to enhance understanding, as well as dialogue, discussion, and debate in and between the sciences and scientific paradigms. In the light of this, the book of Lisa Feldman Barrett is a most welcome contribution. It shows the great importance of contextualizing, explaining, and endorsing the ongoing changes in neuroscience towards the scientific recognition of the cultural dimension of emotions. This approach has the great advantage of making interdisciplinary discussion possible, and enabling us to go beyond the frequently disappointing exchanges of the last decades between two, incompatible visions of emotions and anthropologies.

A second question raised by Frevert concerns the definition of the history of emotions: whether it is a field of history, an approach, a perspective or an analytical category. She is right to emphasize that, for many of us, it is an approach, a perspective rather than a specific field. Considering it as an analytical category makes it a tool among many. Still, from the larger perspective of the 'house of history', the history of emotions remains widely seen as a specific field, given that many books and articles are published with emotions, or one emotion, in the title, and that we have spent years reflecting on questions of methodology and epistemology specific to what it means to track emotionality in various types of historical sources. The topics that have become common in the past two decades – communities and cultures of feeling, specific emotions like shame, anger, expressions of emotion such as blushing – were difficult to imagine fifty or sixty years ago. Considering our own history, we must not forget how arduous it has been, over the past four decades, to claim intellectual and epistemological legitimacy for this type of historical enquiry, and how important it is to occupy a room in the 'house of history'. These decades can be counted from the pioneering works quoted in my paper above, starting from the end of the 1970s and continuing with a number of interesting works in the mid-1980s. Jacques Le Goff started his great enquiry on laughter in 1988, which produced, alas, very few articles but fertilized historiography.[18] These groundbreaking studies, conducted without the help of present-day, internet-based visibility, generous grants and institutional research programmes, were great intellectual achievements. They made room for the next, more 'interconnected' generation around the turn of the millennium – that of B. H. Rosenwein and W. M. Reddy, who steered the field towards dialogue with contemporary social sciences and with the emerging sciences of emotions. The foundations were thus laid for a *field* called 'history of emotions' which started to ask questions about its own frontiers, and developed its methodology and epistemology. All these scholars, without any great structure to help them, paved the way slowly and patiently in the academic world towards the institutional recognition that crowned the process in the last decade.

Today, independently from academic structures of excellence,[19] and despite persisting conservative challenge, the intellectual and epistemological legitimacy of shedding light on a whole dimension of human existence that was long forgotten is globally recognized. In this context, questioning emotions brings an additional perspective, as noted by Ute Frevert, which may enhance the understanding of historical movements, events and changes. We have to ask, though, what this additional perspective means and what changes it brings to the general view. To answer this question, the active role that emotions play in many human situations and interactions should be underlined. Emotions, intimately linked to movement (be that of the soul, a society, or polity), frequently possess an *agency* which makes them *actors of history*. As W. M. Reddy has already noted, specific practices of emotions enhance change, or help to cope with, react to, or integrate change. In that sense, they intervene regularly in historical processes of transformation. This is what many historians of emotions, working on a variety of topics, have shown over the past twenty years, from medieval weeping to the emotions of common people in the French Revolution.[20]

A third issue that Ute Frevert underlines concerns the strong link between the history of emotions and the history of the body. The history of emotions, as an approach and a field, emerged in connection with that of the body: the history of the senses, of sensibilities, and of other specific fields, all born in the second half of the twentieth century as parts, or children, of a history of *mentalités*. These fields are all akin to what is known today as cultural history. However, while the history of the body developed from the 1980s (exemplified in the groundbreaking works of Peter Brown and Caroline W. Bynum), the history of emotions started to flourish later, and became a distinct field of study around 2000. Both the emergence and the delay were strongly linked to the development of the scientific and societal context. While the kinship between the two fields was evident from the start, a great part of the potential synergy remains unimplemented, as studies on the body have all too easily left emotions aside, and emotions have often been studied without questioning the way emotions are present in, and manifested by, our living bodies. A greater attention to the interrelatedness of body and emotions (as in the study of gestures, rituals, and ceremonies) as well as to body language, both intentional and unintentional, may help us to better understand the links that past cultures made between emotions and the body. In the past century and a half, the kinds of sources that document the involvement of bodies in society have multiplied with the development of photography and film, the increasing practice of oral history, and the growing importance of preserved memoirs, diaries, private correspondences, and other personal narratives. But the further away we dig in the past, the greater the scarcity of traces providing a grasp of the affective dimension of human lives. At this point, we also have to remind ourselves of a particular feature of the history of emotions, especially for earlier periods: namely, that for all the periods preceding modernity, we do not possess any direct records of the emotions of the 'silent crowds' – the majority of women and men who made up societies. We are only given a glimpse of what their emotions *could or should have been*, as considered by the writing elites who produced most of our historical evidence. Before the nineteenth century, if not later, writing a history of emotions 'from below' would be an impossible task to undertake. Also, the descriptions of emotions of common people, made by the literate elites, follow traditional stereotypes that make it risky to trust them.

For similar reasons, what we might call a 'decolonisation' of the history of emotions – doubtless a problematic term – is at once a crucial and extremely difficult task. As we have discussed above, Western anthropologists pioneered the transcribing of indigenous affective anthropologies, and an ever-growing series of books published by specialists of Asia, for instance, speak about Chinese or Indian emotions in various periods of history.[21] However, are there so many historians who deal with the history of emotions, *in* the emerging countries themselves: India,[22] China, Pakistan, Egypt, Togo, or Burkina Faso? And how can they work in an authentic way on a topic with a Western nomenclature, which emerged in the Western social and scientific context? As history-writing as an academic practice functions according to Western norms and criteria, with the tools of a Euro-American, English-dominated conceptual framework and anthropology, *what does it mean*, ultimately, to decolonize the history of emotions? How far is this task possible, beyond working *on* subaltern subjects as an anthropologist, coping with the complex problems of intercultural translation? (Pedwell 2016) How do we deal with the fact that translating indigenous affective anthropology into contemporary Western concepts contributes to dualistic approaches and terminology, and thus helps to sustain the Western domination of thinking?

It is with these crucial questions, which should occupy centre stage in the history of emotions, that I shall stop.

Notes

1. In a chronological order, the project on medieval emotions, 'Les Émotions au Moyen Âge' started in 2005; the Centre for the History of Emotions at Queen Mary, London, and the Max Planck Institut für Bildungsforschung 'History of Emotions' project on early modern to contemporary emotions in 2008; the Australian Research Council Centre of Excellence for the History of Emotions was financed from 2011 to 2017. See also the Amsterdam Centre for Cross-Disciplinary Emotion and Sensory Studies, among others.

2. The last two volumes are still in press at the moment of finishing this article.

3. The term *meta-category* comes from Plamper (2015: 38); on the emergence of the notion of emotion, see Dixon (2003) and Hochner (2016); on the changes of the vocabulary of feeling in the last three centuries, see Frevert (2014).

4. This is the case of Alain Corbin (1998) and the younger historians inspired by him, see Deluermoz et al. (2013) and Mazurel (2014)

5. From the oral communication, Febvre published two slightly different texts in, the *Annales* (Febvre 1941) and, in 1943, in the proceedings of the meeting.

6. See in this sense Boquet and Nagy (2016a). For the list of forerunners, see Huizinga (1965 [1919]); Lefebvre (1932); Bloch (1939); Elias (2000 [1939]); Febvre (1941) for a start; Tenenti (1957); Mandrou (1959, 1961); Zeldin (1973–77, 1982); and Stearns and Stearns (1985); and Gay (1984–98).

7. For two very different uses of these terms, see Clough (2007) and Leys (2011), and a polemic one concerning history, Fossier (2010).

8. See for instance the Annual Conference of the International Society for Cultural History (ISCH), in 2017: ISCH 2017 *Senses, Emotions and the affective Turn: Recent Perspectives and New Challenges in Cultural History*, Umeå, Sweden, 26–29 June, see: https://emotionsandsenses.wordpress.com/2016/11/23/isch-conference-senses-emotions-and-the-affective-turn/ (accessed 1 March 2017).

9. In a chronological order, see Boquet and Nagy (2009); Deluermoz et al. (2013); Mazurel (2014); Plamper (2015); and Boquet and Nagy (2016).

10. See this perception of emotionality in Delumeau (1978), and still in Muchembled (2011) among others; in anthropology, see Briggs (1970).

11. This idea started with one of the renowned ancestors of cognitivist psychology of emotions, Magda Arnold (1960), and was used largely by psychologists and philosophers until the 2000s.

12. See also the webpage of P. Ekman, http://www.paulekman.com (accessed 1 March 2017).

13. See, for a start, the diversity of disciplines contributing to *Emotion Review*, http://journals.sagepub.com/home/emr (accessed 1 March 2017).

14. This hexameter was inspired by a quotation of Bernard of Morlaix (or of Cluny), monk at Cluny under the abbot Peter the Venerable: 'Nunc ubi Regulus aut ubi Romulus aut ubi Remus?/Stat Roma pristina nomine, nomina nuda tenemus.' *De contemptu mundi*, lib. I, v. 951–2 (written c. 1140).

15. For those who build on a universal body, see Cairns (2016). For a mitigated approach, see Kövecses (2000: 139); for a constructivist view of body, see Eitler and Scheer (2009: 290–3).

16. *Passions in Context: International Journal for the History and Theory of Emotions* (since 2010); *Emotions: History, Culture, Society* (since 2017).

17. I borrow this term from Raymond Williams (1977: 128–35), although Williams used it in a rather metaphorical way.

18. His articles, as many of the books concerned, were quoted in my chapter above. Besides these ones, see Vincent-Buffault (1986); linked to Le Goff, see Schmitt (1990); Nagy (2000); Boquet (2005).

19. In a way, just like intellectual legitimacy does not depend on institutional recognition, institutional recognition does not always lead to the foundation of permanent institutes – see for instance the Australian scene, or the EMMA (*Emotions in the Middle Ages*) project in France, the first Francophone research programme on the history of emotions, supported by two institutions for eight years. Without any stable institutional background, the research realized in and around EMMA continues, and are today widely known. See http://emma.hypotheses.org (accessed 17 September 2017) and lastly, Boquet and Nagy (2015).

20. Reddy (2000). In this sense, see the works of Sophie Wahnich (2008); also Nagy (2000).

21. The list would be long to quote. See for instance the audacious comparative history of Reddy (2012); and Pernau et al. (2015) for the problems raised by this kind of enterprise.

22. For a few works 'made in India' in English, see for instance Raychudri (2005); Ray (2001, 2007). I am grateful to Rochona Majumdar for these references.

References

Abu-Lughod, L. (1986), *Veiled Sentiments: Honor and Poetry in a Bedouin Society*, Berkeley and Los Angeles: University of California Press.

Arnold, M. (1960), *Emotion and Personality*, New York: Columbia.

Barrett, L. F. (2017), *How Emotions are Made: The Secret Life of the Brain*, Boston: Houghton Mifflin Harcourt.

Barrows, S. (1981), *Distorting Mirrors. Visions of the Crowd in Late Nineteenth-Century France*, New Haven and London: Yale University Press.

Bloch, M. (1939), *La Société féodale*, Paris: Albin Michel.

Boddice, R. (2018), *The History of Emotions*, Manchester: Manchester University Press.

Boquet, D. (2005), *L'Ordre de l'affect au Moyen Âge. Autour de l'anthropologie affective d'Aelred de Rievaulx*, Caen: Publications du CRAHM.

Boquet, D. (2009), 'Des racines de l'émotion. Les préaffects et le tournant anthropologique du XIIe siècle', in D. Boquet and P. Nagy (eds), *Le Sujet des émotions au Moyen Âge*, 163–86, Paris: Beauchesne.

Boquet, D. and Nagy, P. (2009), 'Pour une histoire des émotions: l'historien face aux questions contemporaines', in D. Boquet and P. Nagy (eds), *Le Sujet des émotions au Moyen Âge*, 15–51, Paris: Beauchesne.

Boquet, D. and Nagy, P. (2010) 'L'efficacité religieuse de l'affectivité dans le *Liber (passus priores)* d'Angèle de Foligno', in D. Alfonsi et M. Vedova (eds), *Il Liber di Angela da Foligno : temi spirituali e mitici. Atti del Convegno internazionale di studio (Foligno, 13-14 novembre 2009)*, 171–201, Spoleto: Centro Italiano di Studi Sull'Alto Medioevo.

Boquet, D. and Nagy, P. (2015), *Sensible Moyen Âge. Une histoire des émotions dans l'Occident médiéval*, Paris: Seuil (forthcoming in English translation: *Medieval Sensibilities. A History of Emotions in the Middle Ages*, Cambridge: Polity Press.)

Boquet, D. and Nagy, P., eds (2016), 'Une histoire intellectuelle des émotions de l'Antiquité à nos jours', *Ateliers du Centre de Recherches Historiques*, 16, available online: https://acrh.revues.org/6720 (accessed 1 March 2017).

Briggs, J. L. (1970), *Never in Anger: Portrait of an Eskimo Family.* Cambridge MA: Harvard University Press.

Bynum, C. W. (1991), *Fragmentation and Redemption: Essays on Gender and the Human Body in Medieval Religion*, New York: Zone Books.

Cairns, D. (2016): 'Mind, Body and Metaphor in Ancient Greek Concepts of Emotion', Ateliers du Centre de Recherche Historique, 16, available online: https://acrh.revues.org/7416 (accessed 1 March 2017).

Carré, Y. (1993), *Le Baiser sur la bouche au Moyen Age: Rites, symboles, mentalités à travers les textes et les images (XIe-XVe siècles)*, Paris: Léopard d'Or.

Clough, P. T (2007), 'Introduction', in P. T. Clough and J. O'Malley Halley (eds), *The Affective Turn: Theorizing the Social*, 1–33, Durham: Duke University Press.

Corbin, A. (1998), 'Histoire et anthropologie sensorielle', in A. Corbin, *Le temps, le désir, l'horreur. Essais sur le XIXe siècle*, 227–41, Paris: Flammarion.

Darwin, C. (1872), *The Expression of the Emotions in Man and Animals*, London: Jon Murray.

Deluermoz, Q., Fureix, E., Mazurel, H., and Oualdi, M. (2013), 'Écrire l'histoire des émotions: de l'objet à la catégorie d'analyse', *Revue d'Histoire du XIXe siècle*, 47: 155–89.

Delumeau, J. (1978), *La Peur en Occident, XIVe-XVIIIe siècles: une cité assiégée*, Paris: Fayard.

Dixon, T. (2003), *From Passions to Emotions. The Creation of a Secular Psychological Category*, Cambridge: Cambridge University Press.

Eco, U. (1980), *Il Nome della Rosa*, Milan: Fabbri-Bompiani.

Eitler, P. and Scheer, M. (2009), 'Emotionengeschichte als Körpergeschichte: Eine heuristische Perspektive auf religiöse Konversionen im 19. und 20. Jahrhundert', *Geschichte und Gesellschaft*, 35 (2): 282–313.

Ekman, P. (1972). 'Universals and Cultural Differences in Facial Expression of Emotion', in J. Cole (ed.), *Nebraska Symposium on Motivation*, 207–83, Lincoln, Nebraska: University of Nebraska Press.

Ekman, P. (1999), 'Basic Emotions', in T. Dalgleish and M. Mower (eds), *Handbook of Cognition and Emotion*, 45–60, Chichester: John Wiley.

Elias, N. (2000), *The Civilizing Process. Sociogenetic and Psychogenetic Investigations*, revised edn, Oxford: Blackwell.

Febvre, L. (1941), 'La sensibilité et l'histoire: Comment reconstituer la vie affective d'autrefois?', *Annales d'histoire sociale*, 3 (1): 5–20.

Ferguson, N. (2016), 'The Decline and Fall of History', available online: https://www.goacta.org/images/download/Ali-Ferguson-Merrill-Speech.pdf (accessed 17 July 2017).

Freud, S. (2005 [1921]), *Massenpsychologie und Ich-Analyse. Die Zukunft einer Illusion*, Frankfurt: Fischer Verlag.

Frevert, U. (2011), *Emotions in History: Lost and Found*, Budapest: Central European University Press.

Frevert, U. (ed.) (2014), *Emotional Lexicons. Continuity and Change in the Vocabulary of Feeling 1700-2000*, Oxford: Oxford University Press.

Fossier, A. (2010), 'Un "emotional turn" en histoire?' *Nonfiction*, available online: http://www.nonfiction.fr/article-3832-un_emotional_turn_en_histoire.htm (accessed 2 March 2017).

Gammerl, B. (2014), 'Transitory Feelings? On Challenges and Trends within the History of Emotions', *Contemporanea*, 17 (2): 335–44.

Gay, P. (1984–98), *The Bourgeois Experience. Victoria to Freud*, 5 vols. Vol. 1: *Education of the Senses*, Oxford: Oxford University Press, 1984; Vol. 2: *The Tender Passion*, Oxford: Oxford University Press, 1986; Vol. 3: *The Cultivation of Hatred*, New York: W. W. Norton, 1993; Vol. 4: *The Naked Heart*, New York: W. W. Norton, 1995; Vol. 5: *Pleasure Wars*, New York: W. W. Norton, 1998.

Hacking, I. (2000), *The Social Construction of What?*, Cambridge, MA: Harvard University Press.

Harré, R. (ed.) (1986), *The Social Construction of Emotions*, Oxford: Blackwell.

Hochner, N. (2016), 'Le corps social à l'origine de l'invention du mot "émotion"', *Ateliers du Centre de Recherches Historiques*, 16, available online: https://acrh.revues.org/7357 (accessed 25 February 2017).

Huizinga, J. (1965), *The Waning of the Middle Ages: A Study of the Forms of Life, thought, and Art in France and the Netherlands in the Fourteenth and Fifteenth Centuries*, Harmondsworth: Penguin Books.

Illouz, E. (2006), *Les sentiments du capitalisme*, Paris: Seuil.

Illouz, E. (2008), *Saving the Modern Soul. Therapy, Emotions, and the Culture of Self-Help*, Berkeley: University of California Press.

Jaeger, C. S. (1999), *Ennobling Love. In Search of a Lost Sensibility*, Philadelphia: Pennsylvania University Press.

James, W. (1884), 'What is Emotion?', *Mind*, 9: 188–205.

Kaster, R. A. (2005), *Emotion, Restraint and Community in Ancient Rome*, Oxford: Oxford University Press.

Konstan, D. J. (2016), 'Their Emotions and Ours: A Single History?', Ateliers du Centre de Recherche Historique, 16, available online: https://acrh.revues.org/6756 (accessed on 25 February 2017).

Kövecses, Z. (2000), *Metaphor and Emotion. Language, Culture, and Body in Human Feeling*, Cambridge: Cambridge University Press.

Le Bon, G. (1895), *Psychologie des foules*, Paris: F. Alcan.

Lefebvre, G. (1932), *La Grande Peur de 1789*, Paris: Armand Colin.

Le Goff, J. (1989), 'Rire au Moyen Âge', *Cahiers du Centre de Recherches Historiques*, 3: 1–14.

Le Goff, J. (1997), 'Une enquête sur le rire', *Annales. Histoire, Sciences Sociales*, 52 (3): 449–55.

Leys, R. (2011), 'The Turn to Affect: A Critique', *Critical Inquiry*, 37 (3): 434–72.

Leys, R. (2017), *The Ascent of Affect: Genealogy and Critique*, Chicago: University of Chicago Press.

Lloyd, G. (2007), *Reflections on the Unity and Diversity of the Human Mind*, Oxford and New York: Oxford University Press.

Lutz, C. (1988), *Unnatural Emotions: Everyday Sentiments on a Micronesian Atoll and Their Challenge to Western Theory*, Chicago: University of Chicago Press.

Lyon, M. (1995), 'Missing Emotion: The Limitation of Cultural Constructionism in the Study of Emotion', *Cultural Anthropology*, 10 (2): 244–63.

Mandressi, R. (2011), 'Le temps profond et le temps perdu. Usages des neurosciences et des sciences cognitives en histoire', *Revue d'histoire des sciences humaines*, 25: 165–202.

Mandrou, R. (1959), 'Pour une histoire de la sensibilité', *Annales. Économies, Sociétés, Civilisations*, 14 (3): 581–8.

Mandrou, R. (1961), *Introduction à la France moderne. Essai de psychologie historique*, Paris: Albin Michel.

Massumi B. (2002), *Parables for the Virtual: Movement, Affect, Sensations*, Durham, NC: Duke University Press.

Massumi B. (2015), *The Politics of Affect*, New York: Polity Press.

Mazurel, H. (2014), 'De la psychologie des profondeurs à l'histoire des sensibilités. Une généalogie intellectuelle', *Vingtième siècle*, 123 (3): 22–38.

Monsacré, H. (1984), *Les larmes d'Achille*, Paris: Albin Michel.

Moscovici, S. (1981), *L'Âge des foules. Un traité historique de psychologie des masses*, Paris: Fayard.

Muchembled, R. (2011), *A History of Violence from the End of the Middle Ages to the Present*, London: Polity Press.

Nagy, P. (2000), *Le don des larmes au Moyen Age. Un instrument spirituel en quête d'institution, Ve–XIIIe siècle*, Paris: Albin Michel.

Nagy, P. (2017), 'The Power of Medieval Emotions and Change. From Theory to the Unexpected Use of Spiritual Texts', in P. Förnegård, E. Kihlman, M. Åkestam, and G. Engwall (eds), *Tears, Sighs and Laughter. Expressions of Emotions in the Middle Age*, 13–39, Stockholm: Kungliga Vitterhets Historie och Antikvitets Akademien.

Pancer, N. (2008), 'Les hontes mérovingiennes: essai de méthodologie et cas de figure', *Rives nord-méditerranéennes*, 31, available online: https://rives.revues.org/2783 (accessed 25 February 2017).

Pedwell, C. (2016), 'De-colonising Empathy: Thinking Affect Transnationally', *Samyukta. A Journal of Gender and Culture*, 16 (1): 27–49.

Pernau, M., Jordheim, H., Bashkin, O., Bailey, C., Benesch, O., Ifversen, J., Kia, M., Majumdar, R., Messner, A. C., Park, M., Saada, E., Singh, M. and Wigen, E. (2015), *Civilizing Emotions: Concepts in Nineteenth-Century Asia and Europe*, Oxford: Oxford University Press.

Plamper, J. (2015), *The History of Emotions: An Introduction*, Oxford: Oxford University Press.

Prochasson, C. (2008), *L'empire des émotions. Les historiens dans la mêlée*, Paris: Demopolis.

Ray, R. (2001), *Exploring Emotional History: Gender, Mentality, and Literature in the Indian Awakening*, New Delhi: Oxford University Press.

Ray, R. (2007), *The Felt Community: Commonality and Mentality Before the Emergence of Indian Nationalism*, New Delhi: Oxford University Press.

Raychudri, T. (2005), *Perceptions, Emotions, Sensibilities: Essays on India's Colonial and Post-colonial Experiences*, New Delhi: Oxford University Press.

Reddy, W. M. (1997), 'Against Constructionism: The Historical Ethnography of Emotions', *Current Anthropology*, 38 (3): 327–51.

Reddy, W. M. (2001), *The Navigation of Feeling: A Framework for the History of Emotions*, Cambridge: Cambridge University Press.

Reddy, W. M. (2010), 'Neuroscience and the Fallacies of Functionalism', *History and Theory*, 49 (3): 412–25.

Reddy, W. M. (2012), *The Making of Romantic Love: Longing and Sexuality in Europe, South Asia and Japan, 900–1200 CE*, Chicago: Chicago University Press.

Robert, M. (1974), *D'Œdipe à Moïse. Freud et la conscience juive*, Paris: Calmann-Lévy.

Rosaldo, M. Z. (1980), *Knowledge and Passion: Ilongot Notions of Self and Social Life*, Cambridge: Cambridge University Press.

Rosenwein, B. H. (2002), 'Worrying about Emotions in History', *American Historical Review*, 107 (3): 821–45.

Rosenwein, B. H. (2006), *Emotional Communities in the Early Middle Ages*, Ithaca and New York: Cornell Univesity Press.

Rosenwein, B. H. (2015), *Generations of Feeling. A History of Emotions, 600–1700*, Cambridge: Cambridge University Press.

Rosenwein, B. H. and Cristiani, R. (2017), *What is the History of Emotions?*, Cambridge: Polity Press.

Scheer, M. (2012), 'Are Emotions a Kind of Practice (and Is That What Makes Them Have a History?). A Bourdieuian Approach to Understanding Emotion', *History and Theory*, 51 (2): 193–220.

Schmitt, J.-C. (1990), *La Raison des gestes dans l'Occident médiéval*, Paris: Gallimard.

Schnell, R. (2015), *Haben Gefühle eine Geschichte? Aporien einer History of Emotions*, Göttingen: Vandenhoeck & Ruprecht.

Smail, D. L. (2008), *On Deep History and the Brain*, Berkeley: California University Press.

Solomon, R. C. (1993), *The Passions. Emotions and the Meaning of Life*, Indianapolis: Hackett.

Stearns, P. N. and Stearns, C. Z. (1985), 'Emotionology: Clarifying the History of Emotions and Emotional Standards', *American Historical Review*, 90 (4): 813–36.

Tenenti, A. (1957), *Il senso della morte e l'amore della vita nel Rinascimento (Francia e Italia)*, Turin: Einaudi.

Tomkins, S. S. (1962–92), *Affect, Imagery, Consciousness*, 4 vols, New York: Springer.

Vincent-Buffault, A. (1986), *Histoire des larmes, XVIIIe–XIXe siècles*, Paris: Rivages.

Wahnich, S. (2008), *La Longue patience du peuple. 1792. La naissance de la République*, Paris: Payot.

Wierzbicka, A (1997), *Understanding Cultures Through Their Key Words: English, Russian, Polish, German, Japanese*, Oxford: Oxford University Press.

Williams, R. (1977), *Marxism and Literature*, Oxford: Oxford University Press.

Zeldin, T. (1973–77), *History of French Passions*, 5 vols, Oxford: Oxford University Press.

Zeldin, T. (1982), 'Personal History and the History of Emotions', *Journal of Social History*, 15 (3): 339–47.

CHAPTER 8
HISTORY OF THINGS
Ivan Gaskell

History *of* things or history *through* things?

Things are traces of the past, however recent or remote. As such, they can offer information and suggest ideas unavailable through written sources. These may not invariably lead directly to large-scale historical revelations, but the nuances and insights they offer can alert historians to issues they might otherwise overlook. These, in turn, can illuminate matters of considerable import in the making of history. Historians can learn about the behaviour of people who use things from those very things themselves. Historians can thereby learn things unavailable by other means.

In this chapter, I first look at some general issues in respect of the practice of history as it relates to tangible things, including whether, and, if so, in what sense, things can be agents. In the second section, I then outline – far from exhaustively – a number of areas of scholarship that fruitfully address the interpretation of the past using tangible things, and discuss what might be a distinction between *objects* and *things*. *Meaning* is a term scholars often use in relation to things. I explain briefly that I focus, rather, on the *point* of things, exemplified by their making and their use – in particular, on this occasion, on their use as items of exchange within and among social groups. I explore some aspects of how things change hands in the third section, before turning in the fourth and final section to my case study. This is an account of how perceiving that a piece of fabric has been mutilated – that a scrap of silk is missing – can lead directly from the consideration of that thing itself to that of large-scale tensions among social groups in a complex society.

This chapter does not so much concern history *of* things as history *through* things. History of things implies two distinct modes. One entails putting things first as the focus of critical investigation. This leads to a practice analogous to the discipline of art history whose practitioners engage artworks as things fit for critical evaluation and explanation (see Kemal and Gaskell 1993). The other is a history of technologies in a broad sense, focusing on the various ways in which humans have adopted, made, and adapted things for purposive activities so that the changes to things themselves take precedence. This includes not only the changing ways of, for instance, spanning bodies of water through ever-developing bridge design, but the gathering and preservation of things in museums.

Histories of things in these two senses have increasingly, though not invariably, entertained an often loosely applied notion of things having what is often termed *agency*. It is important to notice the specific affordances of things that affect and in some cases determine how humans and things behave and change in reciprocal relationships, and not to assume a human–thing relationship that relegates the thing to a purely passive role. However, unless one accepts various non-Euro and some Euro[1] (miraculous or magical) accounts of the capacity – sometimes described as the animacy – of things, we must recognize the ascription of agency to things as catachresis: that is, an attempt to describe an otherwise fugitive phenomenon by metaphorical means. Things – even such things that appear to affect other things directly, such as a magnet that attracts iron filings – are not imbued with agency in any strict Euro philosophical sense, for that sense confines agency per se to distinctively human action. Some philosophers, such as Charles Taylor (1977), though, have drawn a distinction between human and non-human agents thereby acknowledging the possibility of non-human agency in some indistinct sense. Non-philosophical theorists have proposed that some or even all non-human things are agents that can act within networks that can also include humans.[2] If we acknowledge that such descriptions are purely metaphorical, the way is open for some rhetorically effective manoeuvres, but only at the expense of a philosophical precision that itself appears to remain beyond reach. I have therefore chosen to focus on making history *through* things, a choice that puts the people who make and use them at the centre of attention. In doing so, I acknowledge that things may have animate or numinous properties, but not in a Euro material–semiotic or actor–network sense. The property of things that concerns me here is their capacity to mediate human relationships among individuals and social groups across space and time. That capacity is the principal source of their interest for historians.

Some scholarship concerning history and things

Most numerous among those scholars who interpret the past by appealing to material things are archaeologists. Archaeologists appeal to material things, often, but not exclusively. Some would claim that the principal difference between archaeologists and historians is that the former predominantly appeal to things found beneath the surface of the earth or sea and related surface features, whereas historians rely on written texts. Yet historians can also appeal to material things, whether excavated or not. There would seem to be a fuzzy distinction between the practices of history and archaeology, even though the educations of adherents of both disciplines remain largely separate. Although this chapter inevitably takes some archaeological practices into account, it focuses on interpretations that do not depend on formal archaeological techniques and procedures. Nonetheless, some of those who have engaged in historical archaeology, in which the examination of things can often, though not invariably, be conducted in conjunction with the interpretation of documents, have been among the most successful in promoting a distinctively historical approach to material traces of the past. Some of that historical work has been mediated and stimulated by ethnographic scholarship. In North America, unlike in most other parts of the world, the discipline of archaeology is closely linked with that of anthropology. This made it institutionally feasible for scholars with an anthropological education to adopt archaeological procedures leading to a manner of approaching material traces of the past that opened the door to historical enquiry. The single most influential text in this regard is arguably *In Small Things Forgotten: An Archaeology of Early American Life*, by James Deetz ([1977] 1996). If anthropologically inflected archaeology was one disciplinary source of work on the things of the past in North America, folklore studies was another. The folklorist Henry Glassie, whose attention is far from confined to North America, has provided another source of inspiration for those who use material traces of the past to create history, notably in his major study, *Material Culture* (1999).

Routes to the American past have not been confined to traces of settler colonialism in a patriarchal register (most famously, perhaps, New England gravestones of the seventeenth and eighteenth centuries, cf. Deetz 1996: 64–90) but have come to include feminist perspectives, including on Indigenous topics. Prominent examples include Janet Spector's discussion of the roles of women in a Native community in present-day Minnesota, *What This Awl Means* (1993), and Laurier Turgeon's exemplary study tracing the repurposing of metal cooking items by the Indigenous inhabitants of New France (1997). Increasingly, though, there are calls from Indigenous scholars for others not to interfere. Some have emulated such uncompromising advocates of Indigenous values as Vine Deloria, Jr. (Yankton Dakota of the Standing Rock Sioux Nation) whose publications, including *Custer Died for Your Sins* (1969), may not have specifically addressed material things, but who made clear his concern for their cultural significance by his long-term board membership of the National Museum of the American Indian. The growth of Indigenous scholarship on Indigenous things is nowhere stronger than in Aotearoa New Zealand, where activist Māori scholars such as Ngahuia Te Awekotuku (2007) and Paul Tapsell (2015) have set examples. The future of history through things lies as much with Indigenous scholars as with anyone.

Europeans have also engaged in material culture history – some, like David Gaimster, as museum scholars, and others, like Giorgio Riello, within the academy. If Gaimster's catalogue of German stoneware in the British Museum and other London museums far transcends the catalogue genre (1997), Riello has investigated a host of commodities from footwear to cotton (2006, 2013). Riello and others, notably Paula Findlen, have edited collections addressing material things that admirably aim at cosmopolitanism of attention, inviting consideration of things from Indonesia, Japan, and the Ottoman Empire as well as Western Europe (Gerritsen and Riello 2015; Findlen 2012). However, few of the contributing authors are from beyond the homogeneous European and North American world. The incorporation of scholarly voices from elsewhere entails going against the academic grain that predominates in that North Atlantic world.[3] Yet innovative work in material culture history that blurs the boundaries of archaeology and history is being conducted by scholars in many other places, from Central and South America to Asia. For instance, the University of Michigan-trained historian, Uthara Suvrathan, is advancing a new, far-reaching interpretation of long-term political formation in south India that shifts the focus from successive territorially extensive empires of relatively limited duration to the smaller regional polities that constituted them, but that exhibit far greater stability and longevity. Her work is based on archaeological surveys, the study of surviving inscriptions (mostly on copper plates), and colonial maps. The relatively obscure town of Banavasi in the present-day state of Karnataka is her principal case study.[4]

Much work by historians addressing tangible things that does not intersect with archaeology treats things not as rich traces of the past that careful and appropriate examination and analysis using techniques employed by anthropologists and art historians, among others, can elucidate for historical ends, but as mere illustrations entirely subordinate to arguments they derive from written sources. Other kinds of historical enquiry that appear to appeal to tangible things, while often illuminating in their fields, do not usually include sustained attempts to elucidate historical questions much beyond their immediate subject. The genre of collection history, dealing with the epistemological consequences of the European gathering of natural and artificial things first into cabinets of curiosities in the sixteenth and seventeenth centuries, and subsequently into museums of various kinds in the eighteenth and nineteenth centuries, boasts many distinguished studies, but rarely involves close attention to individual things or groups of things in such a way as to illuminate broader historical concerns not directly concerning those collections themselves.

Some make the case that things can be treated as traces of the past even if they only survive – if they can be said to survive at all – as no more than representations in language. An example is inventories of various kinds. Historians who analyse inventories, whether from, for instance, colonial New England or late medieval Mediterranean Europe, can certainly uncover designations and, on occasion, descriptions of material things, their circumstances, and their uses that would otherwise remain inaccessible. Such work – for example, that of Peter Benes (1989) and others in New England, and Daniel Lord Smail (2016) in Marseille and Lucca – can therefore considerably enhance the interpretation of the past, whether in conjunction with surviving tangible things or not.[5] But, invaluable as such work can be, it is not in itself what I mean by history through things.

Far closer to what I have in mind as an instance of making history through material things is the 'Making and Knowing Project' at Columbia University led by Pamela Smith. Ironically, the starting point for Smith and her colleagues is a text: an untitled late sixteenth-century manuscript in the Bibliothèque nationale, Paris, whose author describes a wide variety of processes of making in what would now be designated arts, crafts, and technologies. The scholars engaged in investigating these techniques work in three groups dedicated, first, to mould-making and metal-making; second, colour-making; and third, natural history, practical optics, and medicine. Much of their work involves reconstructing and actually practising the techniques described in the manuscript. The things thus made may be contemporary, but are the result of past processes in which practitioners – then and now – acquire and transmit knowledge by the very acts of making those things. While the progress of the project can be followed on its website, Smith and her colleagues have published several collections on the claims that inform and arise from it (Smith, Meyers, and Cook 2014; Anderson, Dunlop, and Smith 2015).[6]

Some of the authors I have mentioned write of *objects*, some of *things*. Paula Findlen uses both in the title of her edited volume, *Early Modern Things: Objects and Their*

Histories, 1500–1800 (2012). I have written of both, too. Although my fellow authors and I sought to pay attention to the nuanced meanings of the material world in our book, *Tangible Things: Making History through Objects*, we chose to follow convention by using the terms *object* and *thing* interchangeably (Ulrich et al. 2015: 2). However, in this chapter I prefer to write of *things*. But my *things* are not the unbounded things of recent 'thing theory'; that is, linguistically constituted disembodied theoretical entities (Brown 2004). They are the material things of this world that can lead existences independent of human perception or cognition. That we might not know them independent of our perceptual and cognitive processes is no reason to assume that they do not exist in their own right. Further, I use the term *thing* in order to acknowledge that any given thing may have animate or numinous properties, even if dominant Euro opinion does not recognize those properties. That things are materially embodied before they are linguistically distinguished does not mean that they are necessarily exclusively material entities. Many things have immaterial aspects, too. Further, things may be capable of agency in some range of catachrestic – that is, rhetorical – as well as in the aforementioned literal senses. Such objects are *things*.

One might choose to focus on any among a number of aspects and associations of things, including their selection from among the materials of the world, their modification or making, their initial use, and their subsequent uses. I omit all mention of their meaning. Although people ascribe meaning to things – different meanings at different times and in different places – many commentators assume that any given thing has some kind of original meaning that takes precedence over all others. I have sought to query dependence on attempts to ascertain meaning elsewhere, preferring to establish the *point* of any given thing (Gaskell 2006). Here, I hold no more than that the ascription of what I prefer to term *significance* to a thing is but one form of use.

Neither shall I discuss the selection or making of things in my case study in this chapter, though this is not because I consider them unimportant. They are vital, but here I shall focus on use, and specifically on two aspects: continuities and changes in use when a thing changes hands. This is best understood in terms of mutability or instability, though instability does not preclude continuity. Things are unstable in two principal senses. First, their physical constitution changes, whether slowly or swiftly, with or without direct human intervention, deliberately or inadvertently. Things go through a wide variety of material changes, some cyclical (as discussed, for instance, by Michael Thompson 1979) and others arbitrary in a social, if not in a material, sense.[7] The thing in the case study that follows has suffered inadvertent wear and tear, and deliberate alteration amounting to mutilation. Without denying the importance of changes in the material constitution or condition of things, in this chapter I focus on changes in use, which is not a property of things themselves, rather a characteristic of human behaviour in respect of things. Changes of use can entail changes in significance.

Next, I give some examples of consistency and continuity of use of things within coherent social groups even as those things change hands. Then I give an example of a change of use when a thing changes hands between social groups: a single artefact changing hands during the American Civil War. This case study reveals that in some instances social groups between which an item changes hands can share some values and not others. This affects how the groups relate to each other as expressed by things changing hands.

The principal character in my case study is a twenty-two-year-old volunteer lieutenant of artillery from Massachusetts named William W. Carruth. I introduce this case by mentioning not things but a person, yet the thing he used is our portal to the past.

In preparation for turning to my case study, let us consider how things can change hands without changes of use or of significance. These transfers take place within, rather than between, culturally distinct social groups, and reinforce existing use and significance.

Things changing hands: Some distinctions

When on the Northern Plains of North America a medicine bundle changes hands from one Niitsítapi (Blackfoot) man to another by mutual agreement, the transfer concerns a package of material items: various animal or bird skins, claws, or bones, for instance. Yet associated with each of these items is a body of knowledge expressed in song or chant. The new possessor or guardian of the bundle has to learn these expressions of this knowledge perfectly from his predecessor. The bundle also brings with it a number of obligations regarding its proper care. Passing on the medicine bundle is not merely a transfer of a material thing, but of an entire body of knowledge, and an onerous set of obligations. Within the Niitsítapi realm, the material thing cannot be dissociated from its immaterial components, such as chants and obligations, and retain its identity as a medicine bundle. This is not to claim that a medicine bundle is no more than the signifier or embodiment of an abstraction – of a culture. Rather, it has affordances that are specific to its various material properties. A medicine bundle and its associated chants are specific things in their own right, and are, in Bjørnar Olsen's phrase, 'indispensable constituents of the social fabric' that act in the world (Olsen 2010: 37–8). That acknowledged, within the Niitsítapi realm, any such transfer is likely to occur within a framework of shared cultural understanding: the parties to a transfer of guardianship know what is going on, and usually conform.[8] The same can be said of a transfer of a thing with material aspects within any culturally homogeneous society. When I visit a supermarket to get food in New York City, I know to take the items to the register and proffer sufficient cash or my credit or debit card. I know to press certain buttons on a device overseen by the clerk. Again, both parties know what is expected of them, and usually conform.

Exchange in what is generally termed the market may well be the dominant mode of transfer of things in the contemporary world, whether on the small retail scale of the supermarket, or on the world's leading commodity exchanges where contracts in pork bellies, orange juice, and a host of other things, or in instruments derived from them, are traded in dizzying bulk. The art market is different again. Buying a Rembrandt or a Rothko is not like buying a box of breakfast cereal or orange juice futures. The process of identifying the properties of the thing is different in each case. Is the market the only exchange mechanism? Citing ritual gift exchange in any number of settings, anthropologists will confirm that the market is far from the only way in which things change hands. For all its sophistication and variety, it is not necessarily any more culturally complex than other human mechanisms of exchange, such as reciprocal gifting.[9]

All the kinds of transfer of things that I have mentioned so far – Niitsítapi medicine bundles, supermarket groceries, commodity futures, fine art paintings, and reciprocal gifting – occur within single cultural systems in which everyone concerned – those who part with things and those who receive things – know what is going on and know how to conduct themselves. Each kind, of course, admits of misunderstandings or abuse. For instance, I might choose to shoplift in a supermarket, or an art dealer might attempt to pass off forgeries as original works by leading artists.[10] But, generally speaking, these systems work. They can be quite complicated, and no one formal explanation can account for the variety of behaviours they occasion. Can we imagine how complicated things can get when the participants in a transfer of things belong to different societies with different cultural conventions and expectations? Yet those different societies with different cultural conventions need not be as far apart as, say, people of European origin and the Indigenous inhabitants of the Northern Plains of North America who encountered one another as the former moved seemingly inexorably westwards. They can be superficially similar, and even share some ostensibly fundamental values, like the inhabitants of the Northern and Southern sections of the United States during the antebellum years, the Civil War, and Reconstruction in the nineteenth century.

In seeking to cast light on aspects of the transfer of culturally charged material items between societies that have different cultural values, I do not wish to imply that the things changing hands are no more than ciphers or tokens that serve solely to signify those cultural values. Rather, such things are parties to the process of changing hands each with its own set of materially grounded, specific affordances. However, I want to focus not so much on those affordances as on how users accommodate such things on their own culturally specific terms. Even when neither party to an exchange can compel the other, matters are complicated. They become more complex yet, and assume a greater urgency epistemologically, ethically, and aesthetically, when the societies to which the parties concerned belong are likely to develop, or are already in, an unequal power relationship, or are contesting their claims to autonomy or to exercise power by recourse to violent confrontation.

At times, tensions between or among social groups do not lead to outright confrontation, but find accommodation within a single social institution. Some institutions exist solely to promote rivalry among constituent groups as expressed foremost in formal competition, such as sports teams in a league, whether baseball, football, soccer, or hockey, to cite North American examples. Other institutions promote competition among hierarchically conceived units in the belief that their efficiency is thereby increased. An example is the rivalry often found among regiments in the army of a nation state. The latter are the circumstances of my case study, in which military units from different geographical parts of a single polity, serving under the same command, exhibited not only the cooperative behaviour necessary for success – indeed, for survival – but also rivalries and tensions symptomatic of cultural differences among regions or sections that, if not checked, might have threatened the coherence and viability not only of the command, but of the entire polity. The thing I have chosen to discuss in detail changed hands in unusual, even enigmatic, circumstances. I chose this case because it strains the definition of differences between cultural groups, and brings to light tensions that might not otherwise be so vividly apparent. As in my brief examples of things changing hands within cultural groups above, the two groups in this case study – military units – shared certain values as well as professed some differences. Furthermore, I chose this case because it depends on identifying and describing specific properties exhibited by the thing in question. This is a factor that I consider vital to the thorough, as opposed to the superficial, use of things by historians as traces of the past.

One thing that changed hands: A flag

The specific thing to which I appeal to act as the prompt to clarify potentially destructive divisions within a military command and, by extension, an entire polity is found in the collection of the General Artemas Ward House Museum in Shrewsbury, Massachusetts. Major General Ward was a military commander during the Revolutionary War. His namesake descendant gave the property to Harvard University in 1925. Ward family history is, in part, local, but it is also the history of the progress of white American colonial settlement in the eighteenth and nineteenth centuries in personal detail. From that fine-spun thread historians can weave large stories.

Figure 8.1 Guidon of the Sixth Independent Battery, Massachusetts Volunteer Light Artillery, c. 1862, silk, General Artemas Ward House Museum, Shrewsbury, Massachusetts.

The thing that concerns us is a perished US flag (Figure 8.1).[11] It is currently framed and protected under glass. The number of stars in the canton accords with the number of states in the union, thirty-four in this instance. This form was in use only between July 1861 and July 1863. Adam Goodheart has suggested that the proliferation of the popular use of the US flag did not begin until after the opening episode of the Civil War, the bombardment of Fort Sumter in Charleston Harbor in April 1861.[12] Following its surrender, its commandant, Major Robert Anderson, brought the garrison flag with him to New York where it began its career as the focal point of patriotic rallies in northern cities. The flag entered the national imaginary, not only by this means, but by adoption and adaptation. The artist Frederick Edwin Church almost immediately made a painting in oils in which he used the contemporaneous symbolic conventions of landscape painting to produce an image of heavenly patriotism, *Our Banner in the Sky*. This was the basis of a popular edition of lithographic prints, published in New York in June 1861, that sold widely in the North, and an emulative edition of lithographs, published in New York three months later after a painting by William Bauly, *Our Heaven Born Banner* (Figure 8.2).

The flag in the Ward House, though, is clearly no ordinary flag. One edge is indented to form a swallowtail. This form of flag is a guidon, a military flag of the kind associated with a small unit, such as a company or battery. Embroidered on it are 'BATON ROUG[E]', '6th – ', and 'ASS BATY'. The name of the capital of Louisiana is a battle honour, awarded when a military unit has acted with distinction. The '6th' and the letters below it associate it with the 6th Independent Battery, Massachusetts Volunteer Light Artillery. But the disfigured abbreviation presents a puzzle. The 'M' has been deliberately

Figure 8.2 Sarony, Major, and Knapp after William Bauly, *Our Heaven Born Banner*, 1861, chromolithograph, Library of Congress Prints and Photographs Division, Washington, DC.

Figure 8.3 Guidon of the Sixth Independent Battery, Massachusetts Volunteer Light Artillery, c. 1862, silk, General Artemas Ward House Museum, Shrewsbury, Massachusetts (detail).

cut out (Figure 8.3). Why? What is the significance of the new word – 'ASS' – formed by the excision? Was this mutilation a deliberate insult? Regimental flags and battery guidons – colours – symbolized a unit. They were, and remain, the focus of individual unit ritual, and esprit de corps. To lose one in combat was a calamity. Men gave their lives in attempts to retain them. Others died trying to capture them. Unit pride was represented by the aggregation of hard-won battle honours inscribed on the flag – names that each member of the unit could recite with pride.

Who could have been responsible for the deliberate damage to the guidon? Had Confederates seized and mutilated it to humiliate the New England artillerymen? When might a Confederate force have seized the battery's guidon? This puzzle led me from a scrap of missing silk to a threat to the coherence of the Union. It is a puzzle that arises not from consideration of written words of any kind – the things that usually prompt historians – but from the physical properties of a material thing. This is what properly distinguishes history through things from other historical practices. Although remarking on the physical properties of the thing is necessary for the inquiry, such scrutiny is not sufficient. No answer can be adequately disclosed by examination of the thing in question – the mutilated guidon – alone. From the thing we must pass to words used in conjunction with it. Finding an answer to the puzzle means sketching a brief history of the battery from its muster to its arrival in Baton Rouge.

The 6th Independent Battery, Massachusetts Volunteer Light Artillery, was a unit equipped with four six-pounder guns and two rifled cannon. It was part of the contingent raised by Massachusetts lawyer, woollen cloth magnate, and politician Benjamin Butler. It was mustered at Lowell, Massachusetts, in January 1862, and was part of the force commanded by Major General Butler that captured and occupied New Orleans three months later. He remained as military governor. The battery was part of the occupation force attached to the Second Brigade of the Department of the Gulf. The section of the battery commanded by Lieutenant William Carruth subsequently took part in two actions, first, seizing railroad rolling stock at Brashear City, 90 miles west of New Orleans; and, second, at Houma, about 60 miles to the southwest, where civilians had ambushed Union soldiers of the 21st Indiana Volunteer Infantry, killing two. Unable to identify those responsible, Union troops destroyed houses and an outlying plantation to punish the whole town (Winters 1963: 150–1). On both occasions, the section of the battery operated with the 21st Indiana, a collaboration that continued when Lt. Carruth's section of the battery accompanied that regiment on two expeditions up the Red River, capturing two steamboats.[13] In the meantime, the two other sections of the battery under the battery commander Captain Charles Everett had participated in a month-long reconnaissance up the Mississippi to the Confederate stronghold of Vicksburg. The various sections of the battery were reunited in June at Baton Rouge. Further actions led to its first fatal casualty, while others succumbed to sickness. In the words of the official report of the Massachusetts adjutant-general, William Schouler, 'nearly the whole command was prostrated by swamp fever' (*Public Documents of Massachusetts* 1863: 410). Captain Everett departed in late July for New Orleans to procure supplies, leaving the whole battery under the command of Lieutenant Carruth.

The Confederates had designs on Baton Rouge. Confederate Major General John Breckinridge led a force south from Vicksburg. The ironclad ram *Arkansas*, having damaged the Union flotilla of ironclads during her descent of the Yazoo River to Vicksburg, steamed down the Mississippi. There was to be a coordinated attack on Tuesday, 5 August by Breckinridge's two divisions from the east, and by the CSS *Arkansas* on the river to the west. Piecing together what happens in the fog of war is notoriously difficult. This is especially so when the ground is literally covered by fog, as it was on the morning of 5 August. The tension between extremes of order and chaos in human affairs is nowhere greater than on the battlefield. One has to rely on official but self-serving reports written in the immediate aftermath and on first-hand accounts by others, sometimes written long after the events they describe.

The Union troops in Baton Rouge were almost all inexperienced. Some had seen limited action. Others, such as the 7th Vermont, were green. They had no idea of what was about to hit them. Most of Breckinridge's Confederate troops were seasoned veterans. The Confederates attacked from the east, forcing the Union troops to retreat. The Union commander, Brigadier General Thomas Williams, was killed. Colonel Thomas W. Cahill of the 9th Connecticut Infantry took command. He organized a further retreat to defences near the penitentiary where his position could be covered by fire from the Union gunships on the river to the west. Meanwhile, as the CSS *Arkansas* approached, her engines failed as she was preparing to engage the USS *Essex* four miles above the town. Rather than risk her falling into Union hands, the captain fired the crippled vessel (see Smith, Jr. 2011). Without her support, Breckinridge could make no further progress, so he withdrew, leaving the Union forces in control of the town.

What was the role of the Massachusetts 6th Battery? Like other units that day, it was badly under strength, many of its men being sick with fever. The battery was in the thick of the fighting from the outset at about 4.00 am, at times firing canister at advancing Confederates only thirty yards distant. The Massachusetts adjutant-general's report for 1862 states: 'In this action the battery had only between thirty and forty men for duty, and three officers. Out of this number thirteen were killed or wounded. ... In this action the battery fully upheld ... the honor and reputation of the old Commonwealth' (*Public Documents of Massachusetts* 1863: 411).

Lt. Carruth is tactfully guarded in his own immediate post-battle report. He gives a succinct account of how he ordered his battery to fall back along a road onto a line formed by the 14th Maine and one company of the 21st Indiana (Company F, under Captain Francis Noblet). The width of the road allowed only two guns to bear. Carruth continues this part of his report dramatically, implying that his quick action saved the position:

> Three cannoneers were shot dead and 3 more wounded at these guns, leaving only the two sergeants to work them, and had it not been for the bravery of these two sergeants and the gallant conduct of some of Captain Noblet's company who in answer to my appeal came forward and acted as artillerymen, it is probable that the left flank of our whole line would have been turned. (*The War of the Rebellion* 1880–1901: 65)

Let us try to look a little more closely at what, in a subordinate clause, Carruth terms 'my appeal'. An unnamed former soldier of the 21st Indiana gives a vivid account of this incident published just one year after the end of the war. Describing the Confederate attack, he writes:

> At the same time the Rebel batteries opened, first just clearing the tree tops, then a little lower and a little lower, until they began to plough through our ranks. Carruth's battery replied. In return a shell was hurled at him, killing a pair of horses and several men, and throwing his whole command into confusion. With difficulty he held a few men together until the battery was moved back to the camp of the Fourteenth Maine. At this moment company F [21st Indiana] was retreating, fairly beaten off the ground; Carruth rode up to the company and cried, 'For God's sake, Indianians, man a Massachusetts battery which Massachusetts men have deserted!' The appeal was responded to by several of the company, who threw away rifles and ammunition, mounted the horses and manned the guns, while the rest of the company acted as a support. In less than ten minutes the battery that would have destroyed our regiment was silenced. (Anon., 'Eighteen Months of the Twenty-First. – By a Member of the Regiment', in [Merrill] 1866: 562)

The Indianian suggests that only the prompt and heroic response by members of Company F of his regiment, acting in the place of cowardly Massachusetts men who had deserted their posts, had saved the day. As one might imagine, there is no hint of cowardice in any official account of the incident, least of all in Carruth's own.

What the truth of the matter might have been is likely impossible to know. What can be ascertained is that the battery continued to serve in close action, losing a further five men wounded, in addition to the three already killed and three wounded, and one listed as missing (*The War of the Rebellion* 1880–1901: 51). It is just possible that in the single man listed as missing we catch a glimpse of a desertion in the face of the enemy that may have given rise to Carruth's speech as reported by the Indianian, but this can only be pure surmise. We also learn from the Massachusetts adjutant-general's report, published in 1863, that 'the peculiar circumstances under which the battery was recruited necessitated the enlisting of a class of men, many of whom proved physically incapable of enduring a soldier's life, and were consequently discharged' (*Public Documents of Massachusetts* 1863: 411). Running through all accounts of the battle, though, is a consistent pattern of distrust between the regiments of New Englanders and Westerners. It seems likely that the relationship forged earlier in the campaign between the men of the battery and the men of Company F of the 21st Indiana, and between their commanding officers, led to their overcoming that mutual distrust. Their earlier cooperation at Brashear City, Houma, and on the Red River may have disposed Capt. Noblet and the men of Company F to come to the aid of Lt. Carruth and the Massachusetts artillerymen more readily than might otherwise have been the case, just as their earlier shared experiences may have emboldened Lt. Carruth to seek the Indianians' aid.

What forms did the distrust among units take? Both Confederates and some Easterners suspected Western regiments from Indiana, Wisconsin, and Michigan of wavering in their loyalty to the Union. The unnamed member of the 21st Indiana whom we have already seen impugning the valour of the 6th Massachusetts Battery, scouted the advance of the Confederates before first light under cover of fog. He claims to have heard Maj. Gen. Breckinridge encourage his men by saying that 'the Indianians were tired of the war, and would lay down their arms at the first opportunity' ([Merrill] 1866: 561). Such claims were hopeful magnifications of known divisions within Indiana. Like its western neighbour, Illinois, the state was culturally divided between the northern counties that had seen an influx of settlers from New England and other northeastern states, and the southern counties, settled mainly by Southerners from neighbouring Kentucky and Tennessee. The best-known Southern settler in Indiana during the first half of the nineteenth century was Abraham Lincoln, who, as a seven-year-old boy, was brought by his parents from Kentucky to southern Indiana in 1816 (Warren 1959: 11). As Eric Foner (2010: 6) has remarked, 'This region retained much of the cultural flavor of the Upper South' in terms of speech, building styles, settlement patterns, foodways, and family connections. All but the members of one of the ten companies of the 21st Indiana – just over one thousand officers and men – were from west-central and southwestern counties. Capt. Noblet and the men of Company F were nearly all from Martin County, one of the two southernmost Indiana counties represented in the regiment (Faller 2013: 6–8). Whether incomers from Tennessee or Kentucky, or sons of such immigrants, they had far more in common culturally with the Southerners in the Confederate forces facing them than with the New Englanders. Crucially, though, these southern Indianians appear to have identified primarily not as Southerners but as Westerners.

The men of the Western regiments at Baton Rouge enjoyed a bond of shared Western identity and mutual solidarity going back to the organization of the Northwest Territory in 1787 from which were formed the states of Ohio, Indiana, Illinois, Wisconsin, Michigan, and part of Minnesota.[14] They expressed this even during the battle by welcoming one another vociferously when taking adjacent positions. When Brig. Gen. Williams ordered the 6th Michigan to reinforce the right flank of the 21st Indiana, the Indianians gave three cheers, proclaiming their affinity with their fellow Westerners (Faller 2013: 58). Such Westerners could not conceal their contempt for certain error-prone New England troops. The official report of the 21st Indiana departs from customary sobriety and tact to criticize the 7th Vermont. Captain James Grimsley, to whom command of the 21st Indiana fell when all officers senior to him had been killed or wounded, wrote scathingly: 'To add to the danger and desperation of our situation, the Seventh Vermont, from their camp back of us, opened a fire in the direction of all engaged, and which killed many of our own men outright and wounded several more'. He added: 'At the most critical period of the fight, … the Seventh Vermont Regiment, which was ordered by General Williams to support us, refused to do so' (*The War of the Rebellion* 1880–1901: 74). These are very strong accusations in an official report. A board of inquiry exonerated the 7th Vermont, but Maj. Gen. Butler shamed the regiment by ordering that no battle honour for Baton Rouge should be added to its colours (*The War of the Rebellion* 1880–1901: 50). Rumours circulated that Butler had made a scapegoat of the Vermont regiment for political reasons, the state being the least politically powerful represented at Baton Rouge, and his order was subsequently rescinded, but by then damage had been done to its reputation.

In this act of shaming, once again the importance of colours comes to the fore. This brings us back to the guidon in the Ward House Museum, and the puzzle of the missing 'M'. The three Massachusetts batteries were not the only artillery units at Baton Rouge. Among the others was the battery of the 21st Indiana, commanded by Lieutenant James Brown. The itinerant newspaperman, George Harding, then serving as a lieutenant in the 21st Indiana, gave an account of his own experiences during the battle, including being fired on by the 7th Vermont (Harding 1882: 295, 298). Without explaining how it came about, he also reported that, although his own company (Company F) had 'been detached from the battalion to support a section of Everett's battery [6th Massachusetts Battery] in another part of the field', he fell in with Capt. Grimsley's company (Harding 1882: 302). That is, although his company was the one that came to the aid of the 6th Massachusetts Battery following Carruth's appeal, Lt. Harding did not take part in that relief. Of the artillery, he only mentions that the various batteries 'did excellent service. They poured in destructive charges of canister and grape at ranges in distances less than thirty yards'. Among them was what he terms 'our own mule battery', that is, Lt. Brown's battery of the 21st Indiana (Harding 1882: 299). Its guns and limbers were drawn not by biddable horses, as was normal practice, but by stubborn mules. This unusual distinction stood out among regiments wherever the 21st Indiana served, giving rise to the nickname by which the regiment was known. That nickname, borne with pride by the members of the regiment, was the Jackass Regiment.

A likely connection with the guidon now becomes clear. It was not captured and disfigured by Confederates, but likely adapted by the Jackass Regiment to become the colour of the 'ASS BATY'. It was a gesture of regimental pride and – we might say – derisive teasing, presumably executed after the battle honour had been bestowed, but before the colour was returned to the newly promoted Captain Carruth (*Public Documents of Massachusetts* 1863: 411). On 4 July 1863, with the admission of West Virginia to the Union, a guidon with thirty-five stars superseded the one now in the Ward House Museum. It seems reasonable to assume that the old guidon fell to its commanding officer, Capt. Carruth. Colours continued to be things held in the highest esteem by those serving under them. At Baton Rouge, one cause of the disgrace of the 7th Vermont had initially been thought to be its loss of its colours, though this turned out to have been only its camp colour when the Confederates overran its camp. Its regimental colour was saved, though not by the Vermonters, for it was reportedly 'brought off the field by the Massachusetts battery' (*The War of the Rebellion* 1880–1901: 50). Another report specifies that the 6th Michigan, which, as we have seen, had come to the aid of the 21st Indiana, captured the colours of the Confederate 4th Louisiana, 'but', according to the official report of the chief engineer officer on the field, 'only after they had shot down four successive color-bearers' (*The War of the Rebellion* 1880–1901: 51). Colours mattered.

After the Battle of Baton Rouge, Carruth continued to serve with distinction in the Gulf and the James campaigns. At war's end, he entered Harvard Law School, graduating in 1869. He practised law in Boston, and became the first judge of the Municipal Court of Newton, Massachusetts. He died in 1906 and is buried in Mount Auburn Cemetery, Cambridge, where his gravestone reads: 'William Ward Carruth. Minute Man of 1861. Civil War Veteran'. How, though, might the guidon have entered the General Artemas Ward House Museum? Carruth, whose full name, as recorded on his gravestone, was William Ward Carruth, was a member of the Ward family. His mother, Sarah Anne Henshaw Ward, was the daughter of Thomas Walter Ward, sheriff of Worcester County, Massachusetts. In 1831, Sarah Ward married Francis Sumner Carruth, a successful Boston merchant, treasurer of the Boston Lead Company, and an original director of the Safety Fund, subsequently first National Bank of Boston. William Ward Carruth, born in 1840, was the fifth of eight children, three of whom died in infancy (Martyn 1925: 354–5). William Ward Carruth was the first cousin of two Ward brothers who had also served as officers in Massachusetts regiments in the Civil War: Charles Grosvenor Ward, killed at the second Battle of Drewry's Bluff, Virginia, in 1864, and Thomas Walter Ward, III, who survived the war, and moved with his family soon after to homestead in Nebraska. All three officers were great-grandsons of Major General Artemas Ward. Charles and Thomas's sisters, Elizabeth and Harriet, remained unmarried, and lived at the Ward House until their deaths in 1900 and 1909 respectively. They tended it carefully as a memorial to their great-grandfather, the general, turning it into an informal house museum before that term existed. They likely welcomed any Ward family memorabilia. They may especially have welcomed items associated with Maj. Gen. Ward's successors in military service as part of the elaborate preparations for the visit to the house by none other than General of the Army William Tecumseh Sherman in September 1881.[15] This would have been a most suitable occasion for the display of family items associated not only with Maj. Gen. Ward, but with his descendants who had fought in the war for the preservation of the Union.

This is a story of conflict and reconciliation, distrust overcome, and regimental pride in which a symbolic thing that held a similar significance for two distinct cultural groups –

one from urban, industrial eastern Massachusetts, the other from rural, agricultural southern Indiana – changed hands between them. A 'MASS' guidon likely passed into the hands of the 21st Indiana to be returned an 'ASS' guidon. The members of the two units shared values that were not confined to recognizing the symbolic status of a guidon. They were staking their lives on a shared perceived need to preserve the integrity of the Union by force of arms. Yet they differed considerably in others, such as social organization, labour practices, and foodways. In spite of cultural differences, the Indianians assumed that the guidon meant much the same to the Massachusetts men as it did to them. Were this not the case, the modification they presumably made – the removal of the 'M' – would have failed to signify between them. Further, it seems likely that the two groups were able to overcome their cultural differences in part because of the trust built up between them during their time together as a combined and dangerously exposed independent military unit in largely hostile territory at Brashear City, Houma, and on the Red River. As a result, sympathy prevailed.

Close examination of the physical properties of the altered guidon that changed hands twice between two distinct cultural groups reveals it to be an up-until-now unrecognized symbol of the pride of two units that in the heat of battle overcame sectional differences, east and west, that at times could threaten the cohesion of the Union Army. Only by overcoming such sectional differences within that army could the war for the preservation of the Union be won.

The way this guidon changed hands, like innumerable others, reveals aspects of human behaviour in the past otherwise inaccessible to historians. Careful attention to the way things that are often complex, and physically and cognitively unstable, change hands between and among social groups, large or small, is one way of making history through things. This observation has consequences that historians, who are usually wholly dependent on documents, can ignore if they so choose, but only at the expense of accepting unnecessary limitations on the historian's craft. If historians are to use tangible things more than merely illustratively, they have to acquire a range of skills more readily associated with disciplines other than history, including but not confined to anthropology, archaeology, art history, folklore studies, museum studies, religious studies, and sociology. This is far from beyond the competence of historians, for, after all, many have long practised history as a magpie discipline, adapting procedures from these and other fields of study for their own purposes. Therefore, why not acquire the varied skills necessary for the interpretation of tangible things of many kinds, and embrace what those many tangible things can tell us of the past?[16]

Comment

Bjørnar Olsen

Introducing his well-written chapter, Ivan Gaskell pertinently explains why his concern is not so much 'history of things', as suggested by the title, but 'history *through* things'. In other words, a history informed by things, that is, the material remains of past societies, however recent or remote. Such history, he notes, has not played any prominent role in the discipline. Indeed, as Gaskell comments, 'Much work by historians addressing tangible things … treats things not as rich traces of the past … but as mere illustrations entirely subordinate to arguments they derive from written sources'. I find it easy to agree with his observation. Despite some signs of change (see, for example, Trentmann 2009; Gilbert 2017, in addition to Gaskell's references), there has been and still is a profound neglect of things both as an issue for more general historiographic reasoning and as significant sources for historical analyses of the past. In a discipline that likes to pride itself as *the* study of the past, and whose very name is consistently confused with its object of study, Gaskell's criticism and concern for things are thus most welcome and pertinent.

There are, however, also points where I feel we are in less agreement and also issues that I find are missing or not accentuated in Gaskell's chapter. This will of course always to some degree be a matter of preferences and interest but addressing them may hopefully provide some interesting points for discussion. These include general issues related to theory, especially thing theory and the conception of agency, but also more concretely the role things play in Gaskell's own case study. Yet another issue I want to bring to the table is to what extent things can be conceived of as pliable and ready-at-hand sources for historical analyses, or whether their very ontological difference enact a resistance that affect our study and conception of the past?

Theory: Agency and thing theory

Gaskell presents his points of view in an admirably clear manner. Nevertheless, he seems somewhat reluctant to engage in explicit theorizing about his subject matter. This 'avoidance' is visible in his review of scholarship concerning things and history; for example, when the work of James Deetz and Henry Glassie are presented as moulded only through a disciplinary framework (anthropological archaeology and folklore, respectively), without mentioning the crucial theoretical impact from structuralism on their work (e.g. Glassie 1975).

More intriguing, however, is that Gaskell does not expose his own position and the philosophy that grounds it more clearly; not the least since his text nevertheless contains an implicit, though somewhat ambivalent, subtext of theoretical likes and dislikes. At places he flags his distaste for 'thing theory', including those scholars who ascribe agency to things, but at other places he himself articulate viewpoints closely kindred with the positions he otherwise distance himself from. Thus, on the one hand, he emphasizes things' active role and their 'specific affordances … that affect and in some cases determine how humans and things behave and change'. On the other hand, he speaks rhetorically against the idea of ascribing them agency, allegedly because Western philosophy 'confines agency *per se* to distinctively human action', and which thus only can happen 'at the expense of a philosophical precision that itself appears to remain beyond reach'.

The problem with doctrinal statements like this is the taken-for-granted assumption about what Western philosophy and thinking *is*, a pigeonholing that does not allow for different positions and changing epistemologies and ontologies. Quite a few Western philosophers of today would accept – and indeed have proposed – various notions of thing agency (including Michel Serres, Graham Harman, and Levi Bryant, just to mention a few), reflecting perspectives emerging from the ongoing withering of the bifurcated Cartesian ontology. And which also have roots in phenomenological thinking, and more generally in the work of thinkers such as Benjamin, Whitehead, Bergson, and others.

I also find Gaskell's portrayal of 'thing theory' (and theorists) to be all too narrow and unjust, and with a tendency to scapegoat positions. This also acts as a kind of self-positioning through negation, such as when he declares that the things of recent thing theory are just 'linguistically constituted disembodied theoretical entities'. Though there may be a few examples of things being conceived of as linguistically (or rather semiotically) constituted (e.g. Law 1999), far the majority of recent thing theorists would argue fiercely against such a view. In fact, most of them would rather agree with Gaskell's well-expressed point that things 'exist in their own right', and very well, 'independent of human perception or cognition' (see, for example, Barad 2007; Bryant 2011; Morton 2013; Harman 2016). One may only recall Bruno Latour's (1988: 193) famous statement about things-in-themselves and the galloping zebras:

> Things-in-themselves? But they're fine, thank you very much. And how are you? You complain about things that have not been honored by your vision? You feel that these things are lacking the illumination of your consciousness? But if you missed the galloping freedom of the zebras in the savannah this morning, then so much the worse for you; the zebras will not be sorry that you were not there, and in any case you would have tamed, killed, photographed, or studied them. Things in themselves lack nothing, just as Africa did not lack whites before their arrival.

Clearly, how we understand things, how we conceive of their *being* (i.e. ontology), will also affect their epistemological potential as sources to the past. The persistent modern ontological divide for long rendered knowing and interpretation an act of reaching that which is beyond things and data, attending to a presumed extra-material domain devoid of objects and non-humans. Much epistemological and methodological debate in archaeology, such as the question of how to bridge the gap between a static archaeological record and the dynamics of past societies, has been rooted in this bifurcated world. Though Gaskell may be hostile towards it, the current turn towards a more egalitarian or 'flat' ontology has clearly opened for a different take. When no longer treated as epiphenomenal residues of society but as indispensable constituents of the world, societies included, the epistemological status of things *as data* cannot remain unchanged. Gaskell's concern is 'history through things' and I think that concern would have benefited from a clearer exposition of his own take on the ontology and epistemology of things. What we can say, or not say, *through* things largely depend on that.

Small things forgotten?

Let me illustrate this through a rereading of James Deetz's archaeological study of the profound changes that took place in the colonies along the eastern seaboard of North America from the second half of the eighteenth century onwards (Deetz 1977, see Olsen 2010). These changes revealed a clear tendency: the communal, common, and heterogeneous were losing ground to the individual, private, and ordered. For instance, the communal infrastructure of eating was replaced by individual plates and cutlery and by individual chairs for people to sit on around the dinner table. As this took place, congested communal burial grounds were gradually replaced by small, individual family graveyards. Increasingly, houses were symmetrically organized and divided into separate rooms, with public and private spaces separated. Bunks were replaced by beds, clothes became increasingly differentiated, people acquired personal effects, chamber pots, musical instruments, books, and so on. According to Deetz, these material changes reflected an accommodation to a new conception of the world and the individual's place within it, 'an expression of a newly emergent world view characterized by order, control, and balance' (Deetz 1977: 61).

Deetz saw this as an *idea* being carved out and embodied in solid material. He believed that a mental concept of order, individuality, and privacy emerged prior to (and consequently was the cause for) its material realization. Thus, what the diverse material changes really tell us, 'in ways great or small', is about a change in the American way of thinking. This change, Deetz asserts (1977: 127), 'must have been at a very deep level of the Anglo-American mind, since it is so abstract as to manifest itself on the surface in so many different ways. The entire social order must have been similarly affected'. In this scheme, things faithfully execute this change, and as such constitute trustworthy sources to recall it, but are themselves assigned little causality or effects on 'what happened'.

From a more thing-oriented or 'flat' perspective, the emphasis on a 'prior' mental template or worldview becomes far less important than the 'how to'. How could a subject-centred society emerge? How could a new order become effective and stable? How many different types of actors were gathered and mobilized in creating it? Instead of any central hero subjects – human, worldview, mind – we should envisage a regiment of actors: plates, forks, gravestones, humans, houses, chamber pots, garbage pits, and so on acting together. In each settlement these entities joined forces, acting together as entangled assemblages.

While things in Deetz's scheme act as *intermediaries*, which obediently transport meaning without transformation, they may rather be conceived of as *mediators*: as innumerous interactors that transform, translate, distort, and modify (Latour 2005: 39–40). Through processes of delegation and translation forming many and complex hybrid relations, they prescribed new bodily practices and programmes of action, which effectuated and over time stabilized a new social configuration. Any mental conception of the individual, the private, and the pure may as well be seen as the outcome of these programmes rather than their cause. In any event, such conceptions would have been impossible to think and implement without the collaboration of things. Thus, and not without a certain irony, the individual was made possible by the collective work of an army of actors.

History through things?

Explaining his own take on things' role in historical research, Gaskell writes that the property of things that concerns him is 'their capacity to mediate human relationships among individuals and social groups across space and time. That capacity is the principal source of their interest for historians'. While it may be debated which thing capacity is the primary source of interest to historians, this is still a vital concern to many students of material culture. Thus, I was excited to see how this perspective would spell out in Gaskell's case study.

To summarize very briefly, this study deals with rivalries between two units within the Union Army: one from urban, industrial eastern Massachusetts, the other from rural, agricultural southern Indiana, and where the focus of attention is how regimental tension, pride, and distrust were negotiated and overcome through active engagement with things. Or to be more precise, with one symbolic thing, a US military silk flag – that changed hands between them and which itself became altered through these transactions. Passing into the hands of the Indiana men, the M was removed from the embroidered 'MASS' inscription to be returned as an 'ASS' guidon.

Gaskell writes interestingly about how the flag both expressed and negotiated conflicts between the groups, and also how the effectiveness of the mutilation was based on certain shared values. What interests me here, however, is why he chose this particular case to exemplify a more thing-oriented historical approach? Gaskell explains that the case 'strains the definition of differences between cultural groups, and brings to light tensions that might not otherwise be so vividly apparent', and, moreover, asserts that the case was chosen 'because it depends on identifying and describing specific properties exhibited by the thing in question. This is a factor that *I consider vital to the thorough as opposed to the superficial use of things by historians as traces of the past*' (emphasis added). Later he declares that it was 'close examination of the physical properties of the altered guidon' that disclosed its status as a regimental symbol of pride.

My immediate reaction is to what extent was it 'close examination' of the altered flag that revealed this? Or was it rather the case that the encounter with the modified guidon in the Ward House Museum in Shrewsbury, Massachusetts, triggered a curiosity; created a historical enigma that could only be solved through examining historical sources? To an archaeologist close examination of the physical properties would involve technical investigation of the flag, traces of use, how the embroidered letter was removed (carefully or hastily), chemical investigations, and so on. Nothing of this is implied here, and also the emphasis on 'careful attention' to the way things change hands, seems not to necessitate much concern with the actual thing itself and its material affordances.

What Gaskell's case study offers is an exciting, interesting, and alternative account of social interaction between different units of the Union Army. It is clearly *inspired* by the observed museum object but is otherwise entirely based on historical sources. It is texts, not things, that are scrutinized. Even the clue to the only object of attention – the silk guidon – is linguistic, a word embroidered on it – and the removed letter (M). It is thus quite telling when Gaskell acknowledges that 'no answer can be adequately disclosed by examination of the thing in question – the mutilated guidon – alone … . Finding an answer to the puzzle means sketching a brief history of the battery from its muster to its arrival in Baton Rouge'. Thus what we end up with is largely history as conventionally understood and performed.

Gaskell chose a single item for his study and though close archaeological examination likely would have revealed important new insights, the choice may be revealing for some of the differences between a historical and an archaeological approach. Archaeologists work with masses of things, with things soiled and broken, and closely examining the archaeological record involves careful attention to the contexts, characteristics, and identities of these myriads of things. Given Gaskell's vision of a 'history through things' one may speculate how it would have benefited and differed through such an approach. For example, how material from archaeological investigations of the battlefields from the Revolutionary War could have informed his concern with how things mediate relations and differences between social groups and perhaps brought to light 'tensions that might not otherwise be so vividly apparent'? Or would that have turned the case study into something else than history – in other words, making his more restricted choice a disciplinary imperative?

Past through things: Still history?

The comments above relate further to the question about the compatibility of history and things. While often 'ontologized' as *the* past, it is important to keep in mind that history represents only one, albeit in modern thought dominant, mode to conceptualize the past. This is a mode closely associated with and deeply affected by its records (i.e. texts and narratives), and thus, at least traditionally, with linear cultural historical plots. Though things can be domesticated to inform and sustain also such plots, as illustrated by archaeological periodization and chronologically and culturally ordered museum collections (Olsen and Svestad 1994), there is an immanent resistance in things that object to the pace and passing of history. Things persist, many of them, at least, and although ageing and transforming, these ingredients and residues of supposedly ended or replaced pasts stubbornly linger on and gather around us. Just imagine what any place, city, or landscape would have been without the things of the past; a present past still involved in – and constitutive for – all our conducts.

If we take these properties seriously, how would they affect our conception of historical time and succession; of the past itself and the modern conception of it as 'gone'? May it be that things opt for a different past that does not necessarily comply well with the historical project as traditionally understood, and thus the tropes of linearity and continuity, succession and replacement, often associated with it? A past that evidently and always already is both present and chronologically mixed, and which thereby defies modernity and historicism's wished-for ideal of completeness, order, and purified time. This furthermore raises the question whether one just can incorporate things in history (themselves being 'blasted' out of history, as Walter Benjamin claimed) without history itself becoming affected, perhaps even shattered?

This reasoning may seem somewhat off target and irrelevant to the topic of Gaskell's chapter and I should add that this is not any criticism but more a point of general interest that became accentuated by his proposal of 'history through things'. I should also immediately add that archaeologists, despite their concern and care for things, have done little to explore the alternative conceptions of the past strongly suggested by their hybridized material record (Olsen 2012; Nativ 2017). Rather than taking it seriously as an expression of how the past actually gathers in every 'now' or present, we have tended to see it as a distortion of an originally pure historical order supposed to exist beyond and prior to the entangled mess we excavate and which we thus need to restore.

Things' untimely presencing is, however, also in another way reflective of the way their very being differs from that of texts and language. Though the latter are inevitably parts of our society, they are in the world in a very different way than things. While past texts clearly may be more than historical sources and still make an impact on our lives, *past things* make up the world, constituting the omnipresent minutiae of the everyday. They are not here primarily as sources or communicative devices to be consciously interpreted or read; their very being and presence involves all our conducts and also constitutes a ready-to-hand existential reassurance. Strangely, despite the new concern in historiography with 'presentism', 'afterlife', 'mnemohistory', and 'effective history' (e.g. Lorenz 2014; Tamm 2015), this abundant material self-presencing of the past has hardly become a serious matter of concern.

And perhaps the concept of self-presencing is crucial here because the material accumulation and exposure of the past is not driven for the most part by some human-initiated agendas of restoring, selecting, or editing the past. In fact, it happens mostly according to material and natural trajectories that are beyond human control and intervention, and which accordingly also care for the unwanted and stranded, the failed or never-completed undertakings; in short, an unruly heritage that exposes us to an abundance of uncanny and involuntary memories. Gaskell touches upon this when he asserts that things 'can lead existences independent of human perception or cognition', but unfortunately without discussing any possible consequences of such unruliness. His focus is consistently on how things are used and controlled by humans, and above all, how they mediate human relationships among individuals and social groups. But many things have the capacity of escaping human control and stewardship; many of them outlive us. Such released things do not change hands anymore, but rather become 'out of hand' (Pétursdóttir 2014) and disclose unforeseen potentials and abilities to act in their afterlife. Just think of waste, sea-born debris, toxic residues in soil and water. They are no longer mediating relationships between individuals and social groups, but in their releasement enact their own unruly agency. To what extent are these undisciplined things an issue for the historian?

Response

Ivan Gaskell

Before addressing Bjørnar Olsen's comments on my chapter, I should like to mention that we distinguish similarly between *history* and *the past*, or – better yet – *pasts*.[17] The past, also conceivable in the plural, is that which has occurred. This may be partly recoverable in the form of history, the discourse historians make, although, as Olsen notes, 'history, though often confused with the past, represents only one (albeit dominant) way to conceive of the past', a point made eloquently by Raphael Samuel (2012) who described other ways of doing so. Work with tangible things qualifies as a way of addressing the past to make history. My conception of history is 'an articulation of the ever-changing relationship between the present and its pasts' (Gaskell 2013: 41). I believe that Olsen and I agree on this point.

Olsen observes that the survival of things from the past to the present makes that past present. (In using the singular *past* I stipulatively imply the plural.) In perduring, things may undergo exaptation, or adaptation through purposeful modification, as well as other changes often grouped together as the effects of time.[18] Insofar as humans play an indirect role – at most – in at least some of these changes, I agree with Olsen that things can escape human control and stewardship. Some things may never have been directly subject to them. Some accounts of the past accommodate the perdurance and exaptation of such things independent of human existence, be they mountains or molecules. Yet I choose to practice an anthropocentric history in which things that perdure are of interest to the extent that they impinge on human lives.

Olsen's remarks concerning my chapter fall under two headings. The first is a questioning of what he perceives to be my lack of clear commitment to a theoretical position (in particular, my reluctance unreservedly to endorse thing theory and actor network theory). The second is a claim that my case study – the 1861–63 guidon of the 6th Independent Battery, Massachusetts Volunteer Light Artillery – depends on purely textual analysis, rather than on an examination of the thing itself that takes its supposed capacity to act over time into account. I shall address the second of these claims first.

Olsen points out – quite rightly – that in my case study I appeal to texts, including official campaign reports, and eyewitness accounts of combat. Because I focus on the words embroidered upon it, he further claims that I treat the guidon itself not as a material thing but as a text.

When making history from things, I never hesitate to appeal to pertinent texts. Although one can often learn a great deal from the careful scrutiny of the material aspects of a tangible thing, sooner or later – usually sooner – examiners come up against the limits of the warrantable inferences they can draw from a thing alone. To their credit, archaeologists – and Olsen is an archaeologist – spend a great deal of effort ingeniously attempting to overcome the absence or paucity of documentary material related to the things they analyse. However, just as the examination of, say, an orchid herbarium specimen sheet soon reaches the limits of warrantable historical inference, prompting the historian to relate it to documents, so the inspection of the guidon similarly has inherent limitations as a means of making historical claims (see Gaskell 2015). Yet in spite of those limitations, careful scrutiny of a thing itself prior to any appeal to documents can reveal aspects of the past that are not otherwise available.

The salient property of the guidon now is deliberately inflicted damage. That damage may have been to an embroidered text, but the embroidery was an original, integral part of the guidon. This is not to put text first, but to bring silk, needlework, and inferred purposive human action with a cutting instrument – knife or scissors – to the forefront of attention.[19] The entire guidon in its perished and mutilated state, not the mere emendation of 'MASS' to read 'ASS', matters, though that very emendation, in particular, is what prompted my consideration of divisions within a Union military command, and, by extension, of tensions within the Union more generally. This guidon, though, offers what no other trace of these divisions can: the physical trace of a relationship between two small bodies of men, as different from one another as they were similar, forged in the repeated agony of combat.

I chose to explore the ramifications of just this one feature of the guidon, yet a more thorough study would treat other features as equally revealing of human relations. Where did the silk come from? How was it spun, dyed, and woven, and by whom? Are the stitches machine or hand sewn?[20] What place did silk and machine sewing play in the provision of textiles, North and South, during the years of conflict? Can the guidon be said to be imbued with agency in any sense, and, if so, how?

The latter question raises the issues that together I describe above as Olsen's first objection: that I am ambivalent about the ascription of agency to things. I am attracted to modes of explanation that acknowledge – at least initially – the likelihood that all identifiable factors in a relational network can potentially contribute equally to its capacities and that of its parts. However, in accounting for such networks some scholars elide distinctions among what should properly be described as different kinds of actors, whether human, material, or numinous. Without realizing it, some scholars offer explanations for phenomena by ascribing a capacity to an entity by means of catachresis. That is, in the absence of any other means of capturing the capacity in question, they use a metaphor. Yet they fail to recognize this. The ascription of agency to things can be just such a catachresis.

There is a further difficulty in appeals to agency. Much usage of *agency* ignores the variety of actions that one can describe under this term. 'Agency' is a term subject to what W.V.O. Quine calls *semantic ascent* (Quine 1960: 270–6), which gives rise to what Ian Hacking terms *elevator words* (Hacking 1999: 22–4). One of their characteristics is instability of sense.[21] That instability permits imprecise usage as when some thinkers elide the distinctions among the various senses of what is actually not a single predicate but a number of them identically termed, leading to the erroneous assumption that their respective properties are interchangeable. At the very least, agency involving human volition and intention must be accounted distinct from the agency of natural forces, such as the tides, and different again from the agency of the numinous realm, such as that of a deceased ancestor, spirit, or a creator god.

Certain kinds of agency may appear implausible to certain kinds of people. Unlike some who work with Western philosophy, I do not find it especially troubling to hold in my mind simultaneously two or more apparently mutually exclusive, culturally distinct explanations of a set of phenomena denoted as agency. I am not intent on establishing an ontological definition of agency. Further, I resist any notion of multiple ontologies. However, I am fully prepared to work with – and, at times, within – a wide variety of standpoint epistemologies.[22]

Olsen suggests that I do not lay out my theoretical cards plainly. That may be so in large part because I enjoy no unquestioning confidence in any one method or set of explanations. For some scholars, their theory of choice can be so self-evidently true as to be common sense. Most of all, I distrust common sense, and, like Henry David Thoreau (my guide to many puzzles), I would have it that 'my facts shall all be falsehoods to the common sense. I would so state facts that they shall be significant shall be myths or mythologic. Facts which the mind perceived – thoughts which the body thought with these I deal – I too cherish vague and misty forms – vaguest when the cloud at which I gaze is dissipated quite & nought but the skyey depths are seen' (Thoreau 1992: 170–1). Or, as he put it more famously in *Walden*: 'The commonest sense is the sense of men asleep, which they express by snoring' (Thoreau [1854] 1862: 347).

If I were to return to the guidon in a theoretical mode that Bjørnar Olsen may find congenial, I might suggest that it is no less an actor than are the officers and men of the Massachusetts battery or of the Indiana infantry company whose actions I describe; and that, in a certain measure, the guidon brought about its own fate. As a tangible thing, the guidon has prominent immaterial as well as material constituents, for it is invested with the pride of two military units that might readily have led men to sacrifice their lives for it. Furthermore, it is also invested with the pride of the Ward family in whose secular memorial it has assumed its place. Yet I cannot regard it as other than a thing that people have made, used, and continue to use. In stating this, I readily acknowledge that this guidon has acted throughout its existence in accordance with its nature, just as the Zuni twin Ahayu:da figures act according to their nature, and the icon of the *Virgin of Vladimir* acts according to its nature.[23] To describe these locutions as catachreses is not to detract from the role these things have played and might yet play; but the respective capacities of these things differ in kind, and cannot be reduced so as to be accounted for by a single theory. I might wish that the present and its pasts were that tidy, but – to be frank – I don't.

Notes

1. By *Euro* I mean the hegemonic tradition emanating from Europe that has spread worldwide, especially that adhering to communities of colonizers and their settler descendants.

2. The most influential thinker in this respect is the sociologist Bruno Latour (see, for example Latour 2005).

3. I know this only too well from my efforts, with Sarah Anne Carter, often unsuccessful, to include scholars from Africa, Asia, Oceania, and South America in the *Oxford Handbook of History and Material Culture* (Oxford and New York: Oxford University Press, forthcoming).

4. Uthara Suvrathan is preparing a book, 'Persistent Peripheries: Archaeological and Historical Landscapes of an Early City in South India, 3rd c. BCE–18th c. CE.' See also Suvrathan (2014a, b).

5. A selection of early American probate inventories is available, together with examples from the United Kingdom and Jamaica at *Historic Probate Inventories Online*: http://www.angelfire.com/md3/openhearthcooking/aaInventories.html (accessed 2 February 2017).

6. For the website, see *The Making and Knowing Project: Reconstructing the 16th-Century Workshop of BnF Ms. Fr. 640 at Columbia University*: http://www.makingandknowing.org/ (accessed 2 February 2017).

7. I assume that material changes conform to definable laws within a dominant Euro paradigm, though I also acknowledge that other explanations can on occasion be valid, whether miraculous in the Euro sense or as a result of things having the properties of living beings in various other belief systems.

8. For an early appreciation of this phenomenon by a sympathetic, observant, and trusted outsider, see McClintock (1910: 76–112, 251–70, 1935).

9. The Kula exchange system of red shell disc necklaces and white shell armbands in the Massim archipelago east of Papua New Guinea is a well-known example of complex gift exchange, as described by Malinowski (1922), though in recent years market practices have affected some Kula exchanges, which, in any case, are more complex and varied among the communities concerned than Malinowski allowed. See Leach and Leach (1983).

10. Such accusations led to the closure of the long-established New York dealer, Knoedler in 2011. See Gaskell (2013a).

11. Guidon, c. 1862, plain weave silk, General Artemas Ward House Museum, Shrewsbury, Massachusetts (HU3484).

12. Goodheart (2011: 20–2, 179–80). The Fort Sumter flag is one of four designs used between July 1859 and July 1861 which has thirty-three stars, following the admission of Oregon as the thirty-third state.

13. For the official report of the actions, which describes the destruction and depredations at Houma as the units 'having done all that circumstances required', see *Public Document No. 7: Annual Report of the Adjutant-General of the Commonwealth of Massachusetts, with Reports from the Quartermaster-General, Surgeon-General, and Master of Ordnance for the Year Ending December 31, 1862*, in *Public Documents of Massachusetts* (1863: 409–10).

14. Much has been written on the disaffection of parts of the former Northwest Territory, its exacerbation owing to the disruption of trade routes to the south down the Mississippi on which many were economically dependent, support for the anti-war Northern Democrats or 'Copperheads', and the statements both in and out of Congress of Ohio politicians such as Clement L. Vallandigham (tried by a military court for disloyalty in 1863, expelled to the Confederacy from where he sought refuge in Canada until returning to the Union the following year), Alexander Long, and Samuel S. Cox. The creation of an independent republic in the Northwest, a separate section with its own privileges within the Union, or even in association with the Confederacy, were all discussed. See, in the first instance, Weber (2006).

15. General Sherman's visit on Thursday, 8 September 1881, is described in a letter dated 10 September 1881 by Elizabeth Ward to her sister-in-law, Clarinda Clary Ward, wife of Civil War veteran Thomas Walter Ward, III, in Norfolk, Nebraska (in the collection of the General Artemas Ward House Museum, Shrewsbury, Massachusetts, kindly made available by the curator, Paula Lupton).

16. The material on the guidon is the substance of a paper I presented at the annual meeting of the American Historical Association in Denver in January 2017. I should like to thank Laurel Thatcher Ulrich for her invitation to participate, and for her priceless companionship in the course of our explorations with our students of the General Artemas Ward House Museum. I should like to acknowledge the invaluable assistance of the curator of the General Artemas Ward House Museum, Paula Lupton. My thanks also go to the editors of the present volume for invaluable comments on earlier drafts. As always, Jane Whitehead is my inspiration and editor of first resort.

17. I should like to thank Bjørnar Olsen for his thoughtful comments, and also to acknowledge the support for my work by my permanent senior fellowship at the Lichtenberg-Kolleg (Advanced Study Institute in the Humanities and Social Sciences), Georg-August University, Göttingen.

18. 'Exaptation' is a term from evolutionary biology to account for features 'evolved for other uses (or for no function at all), and later "coopted" for their current role' (Gould and Vrba 1982: 6; see, further, Eaton and Gaskell 2009: 252, 260). Material change over time, its aesthetics, and its consequences for the study of the past is the subject of my ongoing collaborative research with A.W. Eaton.

19. Further examination of the guidon at the General Artemas Ward House Museum on 22 August 2017 confirms that the damage to the embroidered lettering was deliberately inflicted with a cutting instrument so as to leave the newly exposed edges uneven. The strokes, whether with knife or scissors, were sufficiently precise to remove the 'M' alone. The guidon is in a severely perished state. It adheres to a non-acid-free board sealed within a glazed, black, simple profile wooden frame. For anyone other than a specialist conservator to remove it from its frame outside of a conservation lab would be the height of irresponsibility, so the kind of tests Olsen recommends have to date remained beyond my reach. The guidon awaits conservation examination and treatment that the senior official responsible for arts and culture at Harvard has assured me she will follow up on and will keep me informed (emails to the author, 28 and 31 August 2017).

20. Laurel Thatcher Ulrich and I have been exploring issues raised by early sewing machines for some time. Most recently, this led to her publication: Ulrich (2017).

21. I repeat this claim from Gaskell (2006: 327) where the term in question is 'meaning'.

22. Feminist philosophers have led the way in recent years in defining standpoint epistemologies, though in part by expanding on questions first raised conspicuously by Robert Hooke in his *Micrographia* (1665).

23. On the Ahayu:da, see Isaac (2011); see, also, on Zuni thought and scholarship, Enote (2015) (Jim Enote is executive director of the A:shiwi A:wan Museum and Heritage Center, Zuni, New Mexico); on the *Virgin of Vladimir*, see Gaskell 2003.

References

Anderson, C., Dunlop, A. and Smith, P. H., eds (2015), *The Matter of Art: Materials, Practices, Cultural Logics, c. 1250–1750*, Manchester: Manchester University Press.

Barad, K. (2007), *Meeting the Universe Halfway: Quantum Physics and the Entanglement of Matter and Meaning*, Durham: Duke University Press.

Benes, P., ed. (1989), *Early American Probate Inventories* (*Dublin Seminar for New England Folklife* 12), Boston: Boston University.

Brown, B., ed., (2004), *Things*, Chicago: University of Chicago Press.

Bryant L. (2011), *The Democracy of Objects*, Ann Arbor: Open Humanities Press.

Deetz, J. (1977), *In Small Things Forgotten: The Archaeology of Early American Life*, New York: Anchor Books.

Deetz, J. (1996), *In Small Things Forgotten: An Archaeology of Early American Life*, revised and expanded edn, New York: Anchor Doubleday.

Deloria, Jr., V. (1969), *Custer Died for your Sins: An Indian Manifesto*, New York: Macmillan.

Eaton, A. W. and Gaskell, I. (2009), 'Do Subaltern Artifacts Belong in Art Museums?', in J. O. Young and C. Brunk (eds), *The Ethics of Cultural Appropriation*, 235–67, Oxford and Malden, MA: Wiley-Blackwell.

Enote, J. (2015), 'Museum Collaboration Manifesto' (2015 International Conference of Indigenous Archives, Libraries, and Museums, Washington, DC): A:shiwi A:wan Museum and Heritage Center, available online: http://ashiwi-museum.org/collaborations/museum-collaboration-manifesto/ (accessed 9 July 2017).

Faller, P. E. (2013), *The Indiana Jackass Regiment in the Civil War: A History of the 21st Infantry/1st Heavy Artillery Regiment, with a Roster*, Jefferson, NC: McFarland & Co.

Findlen, P., ed. (2012), *Early Modern Things: Objects and their Histories, 1500-1800*, New York: Routledge.

Foner, E. (2010), *The Fiery Trial: Abraham Lincoln and American Slavery*, New York and London: W. W. Norton.

Gaimster, D. (1997), *German Stoneware, 1200–1900: Archaeology and Cultural History*, London: British Museum Press.

Gaskell, I. (2003), 'Sacred to Profane and Back Again', in A. McClellan (ed.), *Art and its Publics: Museum Studies at the Millennium*, 149–62, Oxford and Malden, MA: Blackwell.

Gaskell, I. (2006), 'Diptychs – What's the Point?', *Journal of Aesthetics and Art Criticism*, 64: 325–32.

Gaskell, I. (2013), 'Historical Distance, Historical Judgment', in M. S. Phillips, B. Caine and J. A. Thomas (eds), *Rethinking Historical Distance*, 34–44, New York and London: Palgrave Macmillan.

Gaskell, I. (2013a), 'Gallery Charm', *Brooklyn Rail*, April 3, available online: http://www.brooklynrail.org/2013/04/artseen/gallery-charm (accessed 8 October 2016).

Gaskell, I. (2015), 'An Orchid: Say It With Flowers', in L. T. Ulrich, I. Gaskell, S. J. Schechner and S. A. Carter, *Tangible Things: Making History through Objects*, 38–45, Oxford and New York: Oxford University Press.

Gerritsen, A. and Riello, G., eds (2015), *Writing Material Culture History*, London: Bloomsbury.

Gilbert, B. (2017), 'Ideas, Persons, and Objects in the History of Ideas', *Journal of the Philosophy of History*, 1–22, advance online publication: http://booksandjournals.brillonline.com/content/journals/10.1163/18722636-12341371 (accessed 10 September 2017).

Glassie, H. (1975), *Folk Housing in Middle Virginia: A Structural Analysis of Historical Artifacts*, Knoxville: University of Tennessee Press.

Glassie, H. H. (1999), *Material Culture*, Bloomington, IN: Indiana University Press.

Goodheart, A. (2011), *1861: The Civil War Awakening*, New York: Knopf.

Gould, S. J. and Vrba, E. S. (1982), 'Exaptation – A Missing Term in the Science of Form', *Paleobiology*, 8: 4–18.

Hacking, I. (1999), *The Social Construction of What?*, Cambridge, MA: Harvard University Press.

Harding, G. C. (1882), *The Miscellaneous Writings of George C. Harding*, Indianapolis, IN: Carlton & Hollenbeck.

Harman, G. (2016), *Immaterialism: Objects and Social Theory*, Cambridge: Polity Press.

Isaac, G. (2011), 'Whose Idea was This? Museums, Replicas, and the Reproduction of Knowledge', *Current Anthropology*, 52: 211–23.

Kemal, S. and Gaskell, I. (1993), 'Interests, Values, and Explanations', in S. Kemal and I. Gaskell (eds), *Explanation and Value in the Arts*, 1–42, Cambridge and New York: Cambridge University Press.

Latour, B. (1988), *The Pasteurization of France*, transl. A. Sheridan and J. Law, Cambridge, MA: Harvard University Press.

Latour, B. (2005), *Reassembling the Social: An Introduction to Actor-Network-Theory*, Oxford and New York: Oxford University Press.

Law, J. (1999), 'After ANT: Complexity, Naming and Topology', in J. Law and J. Hassard (eds), *Actor Network Theory and After*, 1–14, Oxford: Blackwell.

Leach, J. W. and Leach, E., eds (1983), *The Kula: New Perspectives on Massim Exchange*, Cambridge and New York: Cambridge University Press.

Lorenz, C. (2014), 'Blurred Lines: History, Memory and the Experience of Time', *International Journal for History, Culture and Modernity*, 2 (1): 43–62.

Malinowski, B. (1922), *Argonauts of the Western Pacific: An Account of Native Enterprise and Adventure in the Archipelagoes of Melanesian New Guinea*, London: Routledge; New York: Dutton.

Martyn, C. (1925), *The William Ward Genealogy: The History of the Descendants of William Ward of Sudbury, 1638-1925*, New York: A. Ward.

McClintock, W. (1910), *The Old North Trail; or, Life, Legends, and Religion of the Blackfeet Indians*, London: Macmillan.

McClintock, W. (1935), 'The Blackfoot Beaver Bundle', *Masterkey*, 9.

Merrill, C. (1866), *The Soldier of Indiana in the War for the Union*, Indianapolis, IN: Merrill & Co., Vol. 1.

Morton, T. (2013), *Hyperobjects. Philosophy and Ecology after the End of the World*, Minneapolis: University of Minnesota Press.

Nativ, A. (2017), 'No Compensation Needed: On Archaeology and the Archaeological', *Journal of Archaeological Method and Theory*, 24 (3): 659–75.

Olsen, B. (2010), *In Defense of Things: Archaeology and the Ontology of Objects*, Lanham, MD: Alta Mira Press.

Olsen, B. (2012), 'After Interpretation. Remembering Archaeology', *Current Swedish Archaeology*, 20: 11–34.

Olsen, B. and Svestad, A. (1994), 'Creating Prehistory: Archaeology Museums and the Discourse of Modernism', *Nordisk Museologi*, 1: 3–20.

Pétursdóttir, Þ. (2014), 'Things Out-of-Hand: the Aesthetics of Abandonment', in B. Olsen and Þ. Pétursdóttir (eds), *Ruin Memories: Materialities, Aesthetics and the Archaeology of the Recent Past*, 335–64, London and New York: Routledge.

Public Documents of Massachusetts 1863 = *Public Documents of Massachusetts. Being the Annual Reports of Various Public Officers and Institutions for the Year 1862, Vol. 2 (Nos. 7 to 10)*, Boston: Wright & Potter.

Quine, W. V. O. (1960), *Word and Object*, Cambridge, MA: MIT Press.

Riello, G. (2006), *A Foot in the Past: Consumers, Producers and Footware in the Long Eighteenth Century*, Oxford and New York: Pasold Research Fund/Oxford University Press.

Riello, G. (2013), *Cotton: The Fabric that Made the Modern World*, Cambridge: Cambridge University Press.

Samuel, R. (2012), *Theatres of Memory: Past and Present in Contemporary Culture*, rev. edn, London: Verso.

Smail, D. L. (2016), *Legal Plunder: Households and Debt Collection in Late Medieval Europe*, Cambridge, MA: Harvard University Press.

Smith, Jr., M. J. (2011), *The CSS Arkansas: A Confederate Ironclad on Western Waters*, Jefferson, NC: McFarland.

Smith, P. H., Meyers, A. R.W. and Cook, H. J., eds (2014), *Ways of Making and Knowing: The Material Culture of Empirical Knowledge*, Ann Arbor: University of Michigan Press.

Spector, J. (1993), *What This Awl Means: Feminist Archaeology at a Wahpeton Dakota Village*, St. Paul: Minnesota Historical Society Press.

Suvrathan, U. (2014a), 'Spoiled for Choice? The Sacred Landscapes of Ancient and Early Medieval Banavasi', *South Asian Studies*, 30: 206–29

Suvrathan, U. (2014b), 'Regional Centres and Local Elite: Studying Peripheral Cores in Peninsular India (c. First to Eighteenth Century CE)', *Indian History: Annual Journal of the Archive India Institute*, 1: 89–142.

Tamm, M., ed. (2015), *Afterlife of Events: Perspectives on Mnemohistory*, Basingstoke: Palgrave Macmillan.

Tapsell, P. (2015), 'Te Haupapa', in A. Cooper, L. Paterson and A. Wanhalla (eds), *The Lives of Colonial Objects*, 26–33, Dunedin: Otago University Press.

Taylor, C. (1977), 'What Is Human Agency?', in T. Mischel (ed.), *The Self: Psychological and Philosophical Issues*, 103–35, Totowa, NJ: Rowman & Littlefield.

Te Awekotuku, N., with Nikora, L. W. (2007), *Mau Moko: The World of Māori Tattoo*, Honolulu: University of Hawai'i Press.

The War of the Rebellion 1880–1901 = *The War of the Rebellion: A Compilation of the Official Records of the Union and Confederate Armies. Published under the Direction of the … Secretary of War, Washington: Government Printing Office, ser. 1, vol. 15.*

Thompson, M. (1979), *Rubbish Theory: The Creation and Destruction of Value*, Oxford and New York: Oxford University Press.

Thoreau, H. D. (1862), *Walden; Or Life in the Woods*, Boston: Ticknor and Fields.

Thoreau, H. D. (1992), *Journal*, gen. ed. R. Sattelmeyer, *Vol. 4: 1851–1852*, ed. L. N. Neufeldt and N. C. Simmons, Princeton, NJ: Princeton University Press.

Trentman, F. (2009), 'Materiality in the Future of History. Things, Practices, and Politics', *Journal of British Studies*, 48: 283–307.

Turgeon, L. (1997), 'The Tale of a Kettle: Odyssey of an Intercultural Object', *Ethnohistory*, 44: 1–29.

Ulrich, L. T. (2017), 'An Orphaned Sewing Machine', *Harvard Magazine*, 5 January, available online: http://harvardmagazine.com/2017/01/an-orphaned-sewing-machine (accessed 9 July 2017).

Ulrich, L. T., Gaskell, I., Carter, S. A. and Schechner, S. (2015), *Tangible Things: Making History through Objects*, Oxford and New York: Oxford University Press.

Warren, L. A. (1959), *Lincoln's Youth: Seven to Twenty-One, 1816–1830*, Indianapolis, IN: Indiana Historical Society.

Weber, J. L. (2006), *Copperheads: The Rise and Fall of Lincoln's Opponents in the North*, Oxford and New York: Oxford University Press.

Winters, J. D. (1963), *The Civil War in Louisiana*, Baton Rouge: Louisiana State University Press.

CHAPTER 9
HISTORY OF VISUAL CULTURE
Gil Bartholeyns

If we recall the title chosen by Peter Burke – 'History of Images' – for Ivan Gaskell's (1991) contribution of his edited volume, *New Perspectives on Historical Writing*, the title the editors proposed for this chapter speaks for itself. That *history of images* marked an 'innovation' in relation to art history and the importance historians attach to the image as an object of study.[1] Almost thirty years later, a *history of visual culture* suggests another change. From art to the image and from the image to visual culture; this would appear to be the general schema. The momentum visual culture has acquired in the meantime, however, calls for a new description of the phenomenon that reaches back to before the 1990s.

From art to the image

The title of the art historian Hans Belting's opus magnum, *Bild und Kult* (1993 [1990]), is a fine example of this first shift: 'image' replaces the 'art' and this is no anodyne change. In 1997, Jean-Claude Schmitt (1997) stressed the widespread promotion of the word 'image' and the development of a history of image, based on the art history methods and theories (e.g. Panofsky's iconology, Shapiro's new definition of style, or Francastel's notion of 'figurative thought'). This new appetite of historians for images has developed hand in hand with the increase in their documentary value, both factual and ideological, like two coextensive levels of interpretation: what the image shows and how it shows it; even when it is a so-called naturalistic representation. An image is always an act of image making. It is this 'constructed' dimension, both intentional and involuntary, that leads the historian, as well as the sociologist and the anthropologist, to use the terms visualization and, above all, figuration.

Of course, images have almost always contributed to establishing facts and our understanding of the societies that produced them (Haskell 1993): Herodotus refuted the claims of his informants by observing figurative works; images were the objects of antiquarian specialities such as numismatics long before the establishment of the modern discipline of history. But despite this established tradition of using images as evidence (Burke 2001), visual evidence only really found favour with the modern historian about two generations ago at the most; witness the use of a phrase like 'the invisibility of the visual' by sociologists of science (Fyfe and Law 1987), in a book about the visual production of social difference and power.

History's relatively recent conquest of the visual, which includes the production of investigative images and the viewing of cinema, exhibitions, and comics/graphic novels as forms of writing, is not unique. It is part of a wider movement that has transformed the social sciences into a form of savoir faire (e.g. Becker 1974 and Harper 1988, to cite but two), exemplified by the ethnographic film. This wider movement is attested to by the creation, in 1986, of the review *Visual Sociology*, renamed *Visual Culture* in 2002.

Beginning this overview in an irenic and conciliating manner, generously associating history and art history, is certainly a way of avoiding latent discord. If other narratives are in fact possible, this one presents the advantage of revealing their reciprocal support, even better, a continuum. Thus, the aesthetic dimension of an image is considered an important element of its cultural or political dimension. A masterpiece also possesses a social existence, it is an artefact whose biography can be established (Kopytoff 1986). 'How art become Art' (Pommier 2007) – a process that is part of the general revival of social scientific criticism of their own founding principles and which profoundly changed the direction of specialists' research. They study the emergence of the figure of the artist through the commission, the development of studios, markets, and the 'second market' which, through connoisseurship, gave birth to art history: first as the *Art of Criticism*, in the words of Jonathan Richardson in 1715 (Guichard 2007), then as a historical account.

From the image to visual culture

The method adopted by Michael Baxandall, beginning with *Painting and Experience in Fifteenth-Century Italy* (1972), is exemplary of that social history of art that leads to 'visual culture' as a principle of historical and structural convergence. Baxandall starts off from contracts, accounts, as well as vernacular usages, such as the mind's visualization when praying, to present a general history of the image and perception. Probing the underlying culture is, for him, a necessity as 'a society's visual practices are, in the nature of things, not entirely or even mostly represented in verbal records'. To his mind, forms are partly explained because 'social facts lead to the development of distinctive visual skills and habits: and these visual skills and habits become identifiable elements' in artworks (Baxandall 1972: 109 and preface). The expression 'the period eye', he uses, also clearly suggests the configuration of visual culture as a history.

This dialogic and relation of inclusion are even more active in Svetlana Alpers's masterpiece on Dutch culture in the seventeenth century (Alpers 1983). *The Art of Describing*, Alpers stated in 1996, 'was not a study of the history of Dutch painting, but painting as part of Dutch visual culture … . It aimed to focus on notions surrounding vision (the mechanism of the eye), on image-making devices (the microscope, the camera obscura), and on visual skills (map-making, but also experimenting) as cultural resources related to the practice of painting. This offered the additional benefit of granting painters a seriousness that was appropriately "visual" in nature' (Alpers 1996: 26).

It was through Alpers that Bruno Latour serendipitously gave what some, in hindsight, consider as one of the first definitions of visual culture. Latour claims that scientific modernity is less easily explained by a sudden cerebral modification ('the scientific mind') than by a whole series of 'minor' technical adjustments through which, notably, images became 'immutable mobiles' that let us describe, compare, and virtually transport all the objects in the world – as demonstrated in Alpers's book which, Latour (1986: 9–10) writes 'does not focus on the inscriptions or the pictures but on the simultaneous transformation of science, art, theory of vision, organisation of crafts and economic powers. People often talk of "world views" but this powerful expression is taken metaphorically. ... How a culture sees the *world*, and makes it visible. A new visual culture redefines both what it is to see, and what there is to see.'

Cultures of the visual: Of the eye, the gaze, the *imago*, and the visible

Nevertheless, Alpers uses the term 'visual culture' in a more *historical* sense than Latour, who draws inspiration from it, and also more historical than Baxandall from whom she borrowed it. As Alpers explains (1996: 26), she 'was dealing with a culture in which images, as distinguished from texts, were central to the representation (in the sense of the formulation of knowledge) of the world'. Dutch culture in the seventeenth century was for Alpers a culture of the visual, a culture of the eye, and the gaze. Contrary to Italian art, founded on a textual and narrative culture, the 'Nordic tradition' made an episteme of the visual.

Similarly, Jean-Claude Schmitt (1996) referred to the medieval West as a 'culture of *imago*'. Not only does the image impregnate the theological and anthropological foundations of Christian society – God creates man in his own image, the Son is the image of the Father – but the medieval authors use the term 'imago' in a wider sense. It designates simultaneously these foundations, material depictions, and mental images. The logical consequence for Schmitt was to foster the project of bringing together, like three summits of a dynamic triangle, first the forms taken by the *imagines* over time (icons, reliquary statues, etc.), then the social and cultural evolutions that make the image sway between refusal and adoration (condemnation of idolatry, cult of images, 'the middle way' first favoured in Europe), and finally the subject or subjectivity that visual experiences (contemplation, visions, dreams) and pictures (paintings of those experiences, self-portraits, etc.) helped to shape (Schmitt 2002). Hence, for example, the incarnational paradigm tended to bring the figure out of its representation, making it an active presence, while contemplative posture tended to absorb the spectator in the image.

This 'culture of *imago*', Schmitt's term for European culture's relation to images and the visual for more than ten centuries, implies a series of specific conceptions. According to Augustinian theory, there are three types of vision: the vision of concrete objects, our mental representation, and the intellectual vision of realities that exist beyond all images (Camille 2000). In (approximate) line with classical and medieval scientific theories of the topic (Lindberg 1976), sight is generally considered to be a material and energetic phenomenon, similar to a reciprocal flux between the observer and the thing observed, such that the vision of an object enters the body through the eye, wielding its influence as deeply as on the foetus, for example, depending on the nature of the things the mother sees – pleasant or hideous. This conception also plays a role in the *virtus* of religious images.

The medieval 'imago' implies a theory of the sign and knowledge (every object is a sign of another, the visible points to the invisible). It implies a theory of light (the divine *lux* is not the material *lumen*, to the sensitive *lumina* respond the 'true light' of the revelation), but also the power of ornamentality – rather than mere meaningful representation – by syntactically linking the intermittent domains of the earthly and the divine, the living and the dead, the figurative and the figural. Or indeed an organization of magical–religious space, the rite and ritual objects that constantly pose the question of the visible and the exhibited.

Finally, inherent contradictions and oppositions traverse this culture. The growing materialization of the sacred in the late medieval period (sumptuous reliquaries, animated statues, bleeding images, etc.) is contemporaneous with the development of restrained inner piety (Bynum 2011), a tension that is part of a long-standing and constantly renegotiated polarity between 'god and gold', which we might call spiritual materialism. In another register, the dominant iconology of resemblance is opposed to a 'negative' iconology which postulates that divine and spiritual realities, being 'beyond imagery' and human understanding, cannot be represented or are only expressed accurately, notably in verbal images, by the formless, the monstrous, the unnatural, that is, unlike the idea we usually have of grandeur (Boulnois 2008).

For Georges Didi-Huberman (2007), the *visible* is constantly opposed to the *visual* in speculative and moral thought. The visible is the abundance of effigies, imitation rather than incarnation, representation rather than presence, a display where people indulge in the pleasure of seeing and being seen (theatre and games to those who despise the Roman Empire, liturgy and mass to reformers). The visual 'is what is seen beyond, in the beyond', it is grace, or the becoming of the visible. The pagan is a man of the visible, who settles for what he can see, the Christian is the man of the visual, who reaches beyond appearances.

The longue durée and revisiting

It is worth stressing these aspects in part because they represent a long and significant period, but above all because they must be seen in different ways: some as a template for more 'modern' attitudes; others as the edifice that this same modernity will set out to topple; yet others as false friends, false continuities, for similar effects often have different causes. The historian then is faced with a problem of heterochrony. What is more, English-language visual studies are perhaps less practised in the classification of classical visual cultures than in those of recent times, which I shall address below.

For the period stretching from late Antiquity to the Reformation, visual culture has largely been described on the basis of images, notably religious images. Why? Because they are an object of debate, they challenge institutions and provoke astonishing outbursts of violence. In other words, they left behind multiple sources. From the acceptance of the worship of icons first established in 787 at the Second Council of Nicaea to the *beeldenstorm* of the summer of 1566 in Flanders iconolatry and iconophobia form a rowdy couple. Over the centuries, these confrontations gave rise to a highly complex doctrine of images that affects their nature and the uses to which they are put in the Byzantine and Western worlds respectively.

As has so often been remarked, the image is a central paradigm of Christian culture. 'Man walks in the image', as the psalm says in Augustine's version. But one can just as well start from the visual. The world begins with the separation of light and darkness. The light that makes all things visible is a creation. God 'sees' that everything is good (Genesis 1, 4, and 31). 'Seeing, for You, is doing' (Nicholas of Cusa, 1453). Man, like a sacred effigy, is first moulded, then animated. One follows God when one sees His face inside oneself. God's gaze is very nearly so direct a figure of action as 'the hand of God'. We find the 'God's gaze', for instance, in the Bible (Job 34, 27), but its translation into images occurs much later (Schmidt-Burkhardt 2002) than the hand of God, inspired oratorical flourish by which one visually expresses the Word and judgements (Figure 9.1). Logically enough the divine Eye shines upon the sovereign, who looks in turn upon his

Figure 9.1 'Beware, beware, the Lord sees' (*Cave cave d[omi]n[u]s videt*), can we read in the radiant iris, in the centre of which stands Christ like the pupil of the eye. The circle surrounding the eye represents the deadly sins by daily scenes and the four outer circles represent the four last things (death, judgement, heaven, and hell). Attributed to Hieronymus Bosch, *The Seven Deadly Sins*, c. 1505, oil on wood, 119.5 × 139.5 cm. Museo del Prado, Madrid.

subjects, as in Jean Froone's famous etching of Louis XIV as a child (1640). This eye establishes a 'political optic', just like Thomas Hobbes's *Leviathan* (1651), that biblical monster whose body is here represented as a mass of individuals gazing up towards the mighty crowned head who looks out upon his vast domains (Bredekamp 1999). These topoi signal a history of surveillance that significantly predates the standard history of its techniques and apparatuses.

Not only does God see everything, but he is also the only one who can see into people's hearts, scrutinize their depths, know their secrets, and decide. The Middle Ages see the elaboration of a version of this biblical theme, known as the *occulta cordis*, or doctrine of the opacity of others' souls, in the context of debates surrounding self-mastery and confession. No man, in short, can see into the depths of another, as through a glass. Ideas that identity is unfathomable; the soul, immune to trespass; and spontaneity, to be rejected together form an ethic and model of the person, and social judgements and the critical gaze are weapons of the weak. Richard Sennett (1990) charts 'the modern fear of exposure' in his history of the 'conscience of the eye' in urban society, beginning with the medieval period. Though we have inherited from the Enlightenment an ardour for transparency that experiences of totalitarianism have yet to dampen (Vidler 1992), the citizen's call for transparency when faced with the opacity of power marks a troubling chiasmus with the omniscient god and veiled subject of the Middle Ages.

Historicity in question

Let us recap. The nebulous notion of the image has thus replaced the anachronistic idea of art, and 'visual culture' has been drafted in to describe a total history of images and of the gaze for societies often considered in the *longue durée*, sketching out their moments of ruptures and gradual shifts. But different scholars understand different things by visual culture, and it is often used in extremely extensive ways. For W. J. T. Mitchell (2002), for instance, 'visual culture is the visual construction of the social, not just the social construction of vision', 'even something as broad as the image does not exhaust the field of visuality'. According to the art historian Norman Bryson (2003) 'the study of the structure and operations of visual regimes, and their coercive and normalizing effects, is already one of the defining features of "visual culture" as distinct from traditional art history'.

These declarations of principle are fairly representative: the historical perspective is absent from these statements and the only history deemed worthy of mention is that of disciplinary reshufflings. Historicization, for the most part, is not an end in itself, but merely adds a little depth; it is elaborated in terms provided by the present. Sometimes in straightforward, and most welcome ways, it involves 'genealogies' (of particular visual forms, ideas, or techniques), as when Lev Manovich contrasts the *Language of New Media* (2001) in its recent and older incarnations. Sometimes, however, things are a little more ambitious. It is best to address this 'discursive style' via a particular example.

In *Visual Empire* (2007), Susan Buck-Morss asks why it is so difficult to decapitate power. How is it that popular sovereignty always resurrects 'an aura of quasi-mystical power around the sovereign figure', refusing to make history for itself and accepting the 'state of exception' that only citizens are legitimately entitled to declare? Buck-Morss's response is a series of displacements. First, the sovereign is understood as an icon in the theological sense, then a metaphysical figure that resolves the outstanding neo-Platonic problem of how to articulate ideal and terrestrial forms. Next, the Incarnation is experienced as an image that makes visible the enigmatic relations between believer and godhead, formerly expressed in the Greek term 'economy' (*oikonomía*), to which modern man offers up his idolatrous worship, thereby justifying the use of the term 'iconomy'. Finally, the Roman Empire, that historical *fons* of state sovereignty, shifts with the advent of Christianity into a logic of correspondence: God-Emperor, Church-State, and so on. In a few adroit leaps, the author takes us 'from the Byzantine iconocracy to the modern "empire of the gaze", from patriarchal church management to the global media industry' (Buck-Morss 2007: 182). The past is woven into the narrative in recursive waves, and in almost ahistorical fashion, finally leading the reader not to his ontology of power, but to an ontology of the image as power.

In a world where the regressive method and ahistorical approach of Marc Bloch (which works backwards, asking questions born of another time) have been firmly integrated, such genealogies and histories by analogy are not perhaps an accident. And even less so in an intellectual climate where non-linear and counterfactual history have somehow become reputable, opening up space for invocations, ghosts of the past, temporal contradictions, and, ultimately, for any experience (however distant or remote) so long as it casts light on the present.

Surveillance: A metahistory

In a similar fashion, it is precisely because surveillance elicits such fear in the here and now that it has become an object of historical interest. A sort of inside-out history, an archaeology of the present. The visual field thus comprises the analysis of the different possible combinations of force and gaze, of sight and power, from Foucault's *Discipline and Punish* (1977) to the military drone's survey and destroy (Mirzoeff 2011; Chamayou 2013; Hasian 2016). The disciplinary thought of Jeremy Bentham and his panopticon act as a bridgehead. The very idea of surveillance seems to be born of this new 'technology of power', which Foucault (1980) nonetheless claims is in fact a solution to an older problem, that of the cost of discipline. So this 'starting point' of a history of optical control and security-oriented visibilities is also the product of a series of much older concerns, such as divine and then civil all-seeing, monastic domesticity, penitence as a public discipline rather than as an interior modification of the conscience, the semantic link between disciple and discipline, educational manuals for princes or young girls, sometimes referred to as a Mirror or as Institutions of discipline; the imperious quality of the other's gaze in sixteenth- and seventeenth-century court sociability, or for instance scale models offering a bird's eye view of towns and the countryside used to manage conquered territories, which placed the observer of the miniature city a cannon shot from it. But the most revealing element is perhaps the evolution of a certain vocabulary. Up until the sixteenth century, *surveiller* (to survey) did not mean 'pay attention, observe closely'; instead, *surveille* simply meant 'pre-eve', or the day before the day before, and 'vigilance' meant both insomnia and wakefulness, and vigilance proper. The hardening of the visual meaning only emerges in the seventeenth century and the French term '*surveillance*' only appears in the dictionary of the French Academy a century later in 1798. It is only then that this verb, previously restricted to the *pater familias* or tutor is extended to other domains, notably that of policing. This is not, of course, to suggest that until then there was no surveillance, but the naming of the phenomenon signals a shift in momentum.

As well as being significant in itself, the panopticon has also become something of a historical symbol, emblematic of European societies of the eighteenth and nineteenth centuries where production was organized around unified spatio-temporal units and people shifted from one closed environment to another. These so-called disciplinary societies came on the heels of 'societies of sovereignty' based on the extraction of surplus production rather than on its organization, on the arbitration of life and not its management; the second half of the twentieth century meanwhile is supposedly marked by the rise of 'societies of control' – societies where crisis has struck all the different environments supposed to discipline the individual and where a breakdown of barriers between them signals a shift from the mould of discipline to the modulation of control, from the factory to the company, from periodic to continuous assessment, from enclosure to indebtedness, from a vertical, compartmentalized society to an open, limitless one (Deleuze 1992; Hardt and Negri 2000). And these transformations provoke a series of responses that hystericize the visual field: sousveillance answers surveillance, militant countervisualities (Boidy 2016) answer dominant visual forms, the desire for invisibility answers the abuses of visibility, because to be visible is to be vulnerable (The Invisible Committee, 2009).

The history of the identification of people (from the very first identity documents and arrest warrants issued in the fifteenth century (Groebner 2004) to numerical anthropometry (Caplan and Torpey 2001)) does not sit well with the putative sequence of sovereignty–discipline–control. And surveillance, classically associated with 'disciplinary societies', plays a dominant role in recent forms of governmentality and subjection. This means that surveillance is both a metahistorical question and a contemporary regime (Lyon 1994) that reinstates the categories of sovereignty, discipline, and control in a yet more axiomatic history, and one that is even more the fruit of an unsettled and agitated presentism (Whitaker 1999; Lyon 2003; Monahan 2006); 'surveillance' rather than 'control', precisely because of the visual mediation of practices. Thus, public anonymity and biometric confidentiality are disappearing; we are entering an era of 'invisible images'. This, according to Trevor Paglen (2016), is the most revolutionary aspect of digital images: images both generated and processed by machines in the interests of the market (turning every instant of existence into capital), or in order to punish, as with video-ticketing of offenders managed by private companies using recognition technology and identity databases. Though these changes are rarely the object of explicit 'histories', the number of titles using expressions like 'the end of' or 'the rise' suggest a historical consciousness of change.

Visual culture as visuality

Official genealogies credit Michael Baxandall and Svetlana Alpers with founding visual culture studies, but one could equally give credit to so perspicacious a writer as John Berger (1972, 1980), and his early analyses of 'ways of seeing'. Marshall McLuhan (1964) also discussed 'the visual man' and 'people of visual culture' as a particular attitude (disposition) emerging out of the specialization of the senses and of activities in certain societies, opposed to tactile or kinetic cultures, identifiable in the design of housing for example. Taking Baxandall and Alpers as a starting point, however, is no mere historical convention; it is because historical necessity drove these authors to combine works of art and images into one relational ensemble that we have come to call 'visual culture'.

After a slight interval, that takes us to the cusp of the 1990s, the notion of visuality came to play this overarching role, taking as its starting point not images, but vision or sight. Visuality can mean a great many things: 'visual techniques', 'ways of seeing and being seen' (Mitchell 1995: 542), 'the conditions under which we see' or 'manner of inhabiting gaze' (Havelange 1998), but it always concerns the ways in which culture conditions visual experience. Vision/sight is biological; visuality is a social fact. It can also, therefore, be made into an object of history, and this history has principally been 'an archaeology of the gaze' (Simon 1988, 2003), composed of descriptions of 'regimes' and so 'ruptures'. We can identify two non-exclusive approaches.

On the one hand, the question of the place of sight in the wider economy of the senses is present in almost all historical works. It is a venerable and nice question. Lucien Febvre, imbued with an ideology of progress, considered that until the sixteenth century, man's 'sight was undeveloped', because he had not yet 'isolated it from the other senses' (Febvre 1942: 403, 471). On the other hand, the idea of ways of seeing provides a conceptual framework for both detailed investigations and bold, broader pictures. So for Heidegger (1977 [1938]), perspective and modern science transform the world into an image, a world-picture (*Weltbild*), where nature is represented for its own sake and where the subject is distinct from objects of perception, rather than immerged in them, like the classical or medieval subject.

It is primarily the question of visual modernity that has attracted the attention of historians. In an essay of ongoing heuristic value, Martin Jay (1988) explored the 'scopic regime' of Western modernity, situating its beginnings in the Renaissance. Jay works from the widespread assumption that modernity is centred around sight and its dominant regime identifies with 'Renaissance notions of perspective in the visual arts and Cartesian ideas of subjective rationality in philosophy' (Jay 1988: 4). Perspectival images no longer look at the spectator as he becomes the origin point of what he sees.

This de-eroticization of the gaze, which put differently had previously been qualitative, supposedly contributed to separating the image from its context, making it into the object of the external desire of the bourgeoisie – a desire they sated at its market value. Jay, however, asks whether Cartesian perspectivalism is not in fact less hegemonic than we might suppose and whether other scopic regimes perhaps compete with the terrifying unity of a world objectified by a monocular subject. Indeed, northern European painting depicts a world that overspills the limits of Albertian space, offering us not a subject of sight, but a subjectless sight – in other words, a world indifferent to the position it occupies. For Jay, these qualities anticipate the visuality of photography, which is also a society surface, a fragment of reality, a snapshot of life. The 'baroque' model is, he suggests, another alternative, one that abandons geometric beauty for the irreducible sublime, evidence for illegibility, univocity for plurality, exteriority for the body, transparency for haptic materiality. Ultimately, might it not be the plurality of regimes – (Cartesian) perspectivalism, (Baconian) art of observation, (Leibnizian) proliferation, etc. – that characterizes modern visual culture (Jay 2012)?

Around the same time, Jonathan Crary (1988, 1990) wrote a history of the emergence of a 'modern and heterogeneous regime of vision'. His goal was to break with traditional histories, which postulated a constant progress in the likeness of representation from the Renaissance onwards, or saw in the modernism of the 1870s and 1880s a radical break with this quest for naturalist vision. The camera obscura does indeed seem to be the principle model of human perception in the seventeenth and eighteenth centuries, creating a passive, uninvolved observer, and making observation into the source of rational and empirical knowledge of the world (1990: chap. 2). For Crary, however, it is not towards the end of the nineteenth century, but in the 1820s and 1830s that the real rupture occurs, not in the world of images, but in that of sight. The discovery of the 'physiological observer' then begins to disrupt the status of the visual and of the subject: 'It is a moment when the visible escapes from the timeless incorporeal order of the camera obscura and becomes lodged in another apparatus, ... the human body' (1988: 70); the body becomes a site of truth and so of power. The continuity between subject, sight, and world is broken and the distinction between exterior and interior abolished. The object depends upon the eye. The observer is embodied. Goethe (using the colours that float across the closed eye), Schopenhauer (for whom the sight of a beautiful landscape is also a cerebral phenomenon), Johannes Müller (who asserts that the electrification of the optic nerve generates light), but also so-called consecutive retinal images or even romanticism in a post-Kantian intellectual climate, all push perception towards the realm of the subjective and open up a path towards a manipulable subject. At the very least, the recognition of visual subjectivity is, for Crary, the starting point for a series of inventions (such as the phenakistiscope – literally the 'deceitful view' – the zootrope, the diorama, the kaleidoscope, and the stereoscope) – that play on the eye's strengths and weaknesses and transform the observer into an elementary piece of the apparatus.

Thus the rejection of classicism and artists' search for 'pure perception' or a gaze free from external conventions are, for Crary, the delayed effect of changes that took place half a century earlier in the field of visuality. This historicization could be refined by distinguishing, *qua* models, the darkroom, and perspective. It is not only the human eye that can 'subjectivise' itself. The camera obscura, ultimately displaced by physiological optics, also loses its aura of objectivity, with its inverted image and blurred contours; it even comes to represent 'obscurantist' forces and the fetishism of external things. This is decidedly not the case for perspectival projection, which requires light and offers a form of transparency that though somewhat glacial, remains unequivocal (Damisch 1995).

It is easy to understand why Jonathan Crary, assuming 'techniques of the observer' to be a major historical phenomenon, takes spectacle to be the critical concept of modernity and attention to be a political concept (Crary 1989, 1999, 2013). For Nicholas Mirzoeff, it is visuality itself that acts like a forcefield to identify authoritarian and captivating visual culture. In *The Right to Look* (2011), Mirzoeff undertakes a counterhistory of visuality, understood as a military technique and 'a specific technique of colonial and imperial practice, operating both at "home" and "abroad"' (Mirzoeff 2012: xix). Supremacy depends on the capacity to visualize, and visualization is the organizing principle of both the slave plantation, with its overseer, and fully monitored contemporary public space.

Three histories: Extension of the visible, objectivity, and visibility

The visible was the metaphysical frontier between this life and the afterlife, between human (terrestrial) and divine (celestial) worlds, between ordinary perception and that of the visionary or the initiated. With few exceptions (e.g. Pantin 1995; Aït-Touati 2011), histories of the visible have neglected the transposition or residue of such schemas into scientific thought and practice. We immediately find ourselves at the academies of science, in salons, and presented with images of things and beings too distant, too diminutive, and too furtive to be visible to the 'naked eye'. The heavens are straight away some extraordinary far-off sight, while the devil has become a miasma. Even if in Kepler's *Somnium* (1610), the moon is described thanks to a demon and the hero's mother is a magician, even if photography was immediately supposed to be able to reveal religious *invisibilia*, narratives are still typically 'natural'. This is a narrative of the instruments and techniques that augment the eye's natural capacities or which offer 'views' and so proofs (Sicard 1998), from the telescope to the observation balloon or satellite, by way of chronophotography, prints, or engravings, which are like 'frozen moments'. All the way up to those images that are no longer optic, but a product of calculation: the cosmic or nanometric landscapes that are projections or 'artist's impressions' of non-visual realities. These aesthetic artefacts can be classed with projections of non-existent or virtual things, like the fantasmagoria of magic lanterns (Vermeir 2005). Which is why it may be useful to distinguish *a priori* between *optical instruments* such as the telescope, which are concerned with the observability of beings or things, and *optic instruments* such as the Claude glass (Maillet 2004) or peep box (Figure 9.2). This distinction is broadly kept, and the history of looking glasses has a foot in both camps, as in the seventeenth century it was both a form of recreation, with tinted glass and the multiplying glasses that offered avaricious men a vision of riches, and a compensatory technique (Maillet 2007),

Figure 9.2 Foldable peep box dated 1760, with a magnifying lens 12 cm in diameter and inclined mirror, allowing for the placement of seven layers to create an illusion of depth. Martin Engelbrecht, Augsburg (Germany), 20.2 cm × 22 × 81 cm (closed). Centre national du cinéma et de l'image animée, CNC-AP-11-1119 b. Photo: Stéphane Dabrowski – La Cinémathèque française.

whereas the magnifying glass was exploratory in nature. The same is true of 'better than nature' exotic dioramas, and panoramas, either indoor depictions that gave impression of being elsewhere or mountain sites offering a vision of the wider surroundings (Bigg 2007). The same is true of astronomy's 'spectacular realities' (Schwartz 1998), such as the planetarium (Bigg and Vanhoutte 2017), or of cinema, which was invented both as a sort of marvel (Méliès) and as document (Lumières). Indeed, many instruments are historically determined by their use: stereoscopy, a leisure pursuit in the nineteenth century, was also employed in the medical observation of x-rays.

The diligent reader, however, may be overwhelmed by a sort of myth, a total history of the prodigious extension of the domain of the visible effected by viewing or vision machines (Gleizes and Reynaud 2017). Many studies inadvertently give an impression of a continuous progress of sight and visualization. Paradoxically, it is the realization from the 1990s onwards of the overlap between science, art, technology, and society that is to blame for this overall impression, which more domain-specific knowledge actually protected us from. The study of relations between science and art (Wise 2006; Hentschel 2014) and the transformation of the history of ideas into a history of scientific practice (Schaffer 2014) are the two guiding threads of visual studies of science, where we primarily have the Anglo-Saxons to thank for the 'turn to practice' and primarily the Germans for the aesthetic element.

Scientific images have 'styles' (Bredekamp, Dünkel, and Schneider 2015) and respond to epistemological regimes that are also visual ones. The work of Lorraine Daston and Peter Galison (1992, 2007) perfectly embodies this historiographical evolution by offering a history of objectivity through the imagery of scientific atlases. Prior to the eighteenth century, when the authors' study begins, the dominant visual regime was one of copresence, individualized representation, and authorship of the image (Guichard 2015), alongside a second regime that one might call *curiosa*, with its taste for the monstrous, and the rarity and diversity of specimens. In the beginning of the eighteenth century, there emerged a new regime of 'truth according to nature', where scientists and artists collaborated to master variability through synthetic images, before such aesthetic interventions were rejected in the nineteenth century, in favour of the 'mechanical objectivity' of photography. However, because mechanical recording could never be entirely objective, and because it could never be representative (of, say, variation), it produced two reactions: first, a rejection of the image, as scientists turned to the 'structural objectivity' of logic and mathematics, and second a regime of 'expert judgement', which finally came to dominate in the natural and empirical sciences. This explains the rise of visual sequencing, or Valdemar Firsoff's projection of the moon's surface, generated via the interpretive superposition of images taken from different angles. Science and art are a stormy couple whose relationship moves through distinct phases (Jones and Galison 1998). One doesn't need to overdose on relativism to admit that no solution necessarily renders reality better than any other; merely differently, depending on what one is aiming for. Each connotes a particular 'worldview', insofar as images are stable forms capable of transforming, rather than simply representing, reality.

In the twentieth century, scientific images began increasingly to weaken, or even break with, the indexicality between reality and image: for instance, the first DNA images produced by X-ray crystallography, in 1937, or scanning tunnel microscopy energy profiles. The very first example of this is perhaps Joseph von Fraunhofer's solar spectrum image produced around 1814, which presents a gradation of coloured stripes separated by dark lines identified as the sun's chemical signature (Figure 9.3). In the last two cases, it is no longer about making the invisible visible, but about visualizing the non-visual. These images, which are often subject to artistic intervention, are what Daston and Galison call 'presentations' as opposed to 'representations'. Art and science rekindle their relationship where reality has no image – and where the image determines reality.

Let us now sketch out one final parallel history. The most obvious history of visibility is undoubtedly that of power, of ascendancy, of the social benefits of being visible, of being 'seen'. This is not the same as the history of subjecting visibility discussed above, nor that of the exposition of colonial, female, or monstrous bodies (Courtine 2006), whose voyeurism is the reverse face of the same phenomenon, nor yet that of the excessive media exposure

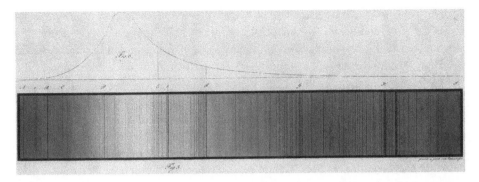

Figure 9.3 Absorption lines (dark lines) in the solar spectrum, now known as Fraunhofer lines. Spectroscopy by Joseph von Fraunhofer, 1814. Deutsches Museum, Munich.

that subjects peoples in crisis to their planned disappearance (Didi-Huberman 2012). For John Thompson (1995, 2005), the traditional visibility of power is one of copresence, the model of which is the public appearance. This form of visibility generates symbols and mises en scène that establish distance as the yardstick of splendour. It is accompanied by a 'publicity of the image'. Louis XIV was a past master in the art of image production (Burke 1992). In the words of Louis Marin (1988: 11), 'representation and power share a common nature ... the representational apparatus transforms force into power'. For Thompson, the classical regime of visibility really emerges with printing and is quite different from the subsequent radio and televisual regime. Representations produce a deferred visibility, whereas the visibility of electronic media is characterized by 'despecialized simultaneity'. The television, in particular, redefines public-capacity *as* visibility and creates a relationship of power predicated on intimacy: political leaders address their public as friends, in an unprecedented form of face-to-face interaction. But this comes at a price: the media, in turn, project forms of visibility that end in scandal and lead to political over-exposure.

Thomas Mathiesen (1997) refers to this visibility of the few to the many as a Synopticon, in contrast with the classic Panopticon where the many are visible to the few. For Mathiesen, the synoptic gaze underpins the normativity of the democratic subject, whereas for Foucault, this was a product of the panoptic gaze. Nathalie Heinich (2012) brings some of these questions into focus in her description of the shift from the celebrity of the Ancien Régime to contemporary visibility, understood as the 'technical production of ubiquity' or the exponential generation of the 'effect of presence'. In Bourdieusian terms, Heinich sees 'visibility as capital'. For her, photography, which links a face to a name and reticularly multiplies the person, is a sort of big bang of this history of social difference as differences of visibility.

If surveillance is the figure of the panopticon (*universal, total*) and celebrity that of the synopticon (*simultaneously, together*), internet combines the two into a 'schizoptic' mode. The mass observer and the mass observed are fused into the same person, but the lived experience of the two states is disassociated. What I am calling the Schizopticon consists in the consensual (because of their duality, but above all because of their disjunctivity) unification of the seer and the seen.

The era of the 'visual turn'

What, for a historian, is the significance of the visual turn simultaneously diagnosed in Germany and the United States in the early 1990s (Mitchell 1992b; Boehm 1994; Moxey 2008; Boehm and Mitchell 2009)? Not a great deal, unless we treat it as a chapter in the history of visual culture. Intellectual emotions dominate this history. A deluge of images drowns reality, a new Babel becomes possible. For the last twenty years, liminal biblical metaphors have been put to work to capture the heights of these sensations and have functioned like a self-fulfilling prophecy in the academic sphere. Some scholars are sincerely troubled, or sincerely pragmatic: young people must be given the means to understand the world they live in because this world is not merely saturated, but also produced by images. There can be no doubt that visual studies emerge out of teaching, in Rochester, Chicago, or Irvine. The development of cinema and particularly television, along with the perceived need to acquire 'visual culture', alongside 'literary culture', made it a matter of pedagogical concern in the 1950s. Kenneth Winetrout's *The New Age of the Visible* (1964) marks one early turning point: 'We live in the age of visible, largely because we are so good at creating the visible ... there has never been anything quite like television which went from initial marketing to saturation in a few short years', but we are still not educating consumers (1964: 46, 49).

The pictorial or iconic turn of the 1990s somehow grounds itself in an event experienced as an ontological modification of reality via 'new' media and 'new' technologies. This is no chimera. Though academics often appeal to social justifications, this is not to imply that even tiresome erudition can account for today's world. The wave of images crashing over us is a figure of sincerity. We can sense this totality if we think of the First Gulf War (1990–91) – a media spectacle that screened for the first time the live destruction of targets. In the wake of 2001, Jean Baudrillard (2002: 19) described the nature of these events as profoundly 'visual': international conflict, which revolves around globalization, is 'so difficult to grasp that it is sometimes necessary to save the idea of war via the performance of spectacular events, such as the Gulf War or the invasion of Afghanistan'. Jonathan Crary explained that at the very time he was writing his history of modern visuality, the 'nature of the visual' was undergoing an even more important transformation than during the Renaissance. He draws particular attention to synthetic images and the analogical rupture that Christine Buci-Glucksmann (2002) glossed as the 'image-flux' and Thomas Golsenne (2015) described as the 'mosaic image'. Some authors, such as Mitchell (1992a), sounded the trumpets of the Apocalypse, predicting the collapse of the truth regime of images (see Gunthert 2015: 17–30). There has, however, been no crisis of the pixel. On the contrary, the digitalization of the visual has even allowed for an accentuation of the existential functions of photography (Bartholeyns 2014, 2015). The post-photographic era has remained confined to the realm of the Cassandra for the straightforward reason that faith in images is not a technical problem. What this example shows is that images and their agency must be addressed from an anthropological standpoint. But we should not get ahead of ourselves.

With the passage of time, we have grown into the habit of considering the visual turn to be a reaction to the importance of linguistic paradigms in the social sciences between the 1960s and the 1980s. But quite the opposite is true. It is the 'linguistic turn', that is the reaction, a brief but perfectly controlled departure from the tracks. It was just at the point of the as-yet-unnamed visual turn that Richard Rorty (1980) and others denounced the specular metaphor that has historically underpinned Western rationality. John Dewey (1929) had already criticized the 'spectator theory' of knowledge. When all is said and done, Rorty's 'mirror-complex' is perhaps one of the signal contributions of critical visual studies. In much the same way as the semiotician Roland Barthes' *Mythologies* (1972) unmasked the ideology at the heart of public spectacle. Twentieth-century thought in general displays a 'denigration of vision' – an antivisual attitude that Martin Jay (1993) described as 'anti-oculocentrism'. Guy Debord (1970), by analysing the spectacle not as a set of images but as a social relationship mediated by images, is a classic example of negative representations of the visual by the very people dedicated to describing its inexorable ascent. Indeed, visual studies are often accused of reintroducing, by the back door, the domination of visuality and a fetishism of the image. The iconic turn is an ironic turn.

With a little distance, then, we can see the visual turn as a broad realignment, that began in the second half of the last century and was accompanied by a self-proclaimed philosophical iconoclasm; but which was also but one visual turn 'among others' that have marked recent history. Sensorial upheaval also occurred in the second half of the nineteenth century (Hamon 2001; Charpy 2015). 'Around 1860–1880, a new frenzy of the image' irrupted into quotidian existence (Foucault 2001: 1575). With his habitual gravity, Walter Benjamin spoke of 'a sphere reserved one hundred percent for images' (Benjamin 1986 [1929]: 191). These quantitative phenomena, which also generate a 'market of the visible' (Szendy 2017), endow Norman Bryson's (2003) logical inversion with anthropological significance: it is not the surfeit of images, but their chronic scarcity, not excess, but insatiable desire that is characteristic of such moments.

Comment

Jean-Claude Schmitt

Gil Bartholeyns has pulled off the tour de force, in my view truly admirably, of reviewing in some twenty pages the state of visual studies today, as well as their emergence and evolution on the international scholarly scene over the past few decades. The bibliography – not a bibliography of convenience which too often reflects merely the technical possibilities of the computer, but a true working bibliography in which every title has been read and contemplated; and the excellence of the comments – occasionally too allusive, but more space should have been allotted to the author for him to be able to do full justice to each work – testify to the breadth and depth of his thought. To the best of my knowledge, his treatment of the subject is unprecedented and will remain a milestone in the long history of social sciences confronted with the question of the 'history of visual culture'. The work of a historian resorting to the characteristic practices of his discipline, this survey concerns in fact *all* the social sciences in *all* (or almost all) the Western world. Because the two striking features of this chapter are that it brilliantly ranges across all – or almost all – domains of study, and it lists all the works published on this issue in all the countries where the subject is topical, principally in Western Europe (first and foremost Germany, France, and Great Britain) and in the United States. The two qualities of interdisciplinary and international research, too rarely combined, deserve to be underscored, too, since linguistic limitations (particularly in English) are wreaking havoc, especially when reinforced by a monodisciplinary bias. Gil Bartholeyns, on the contrary, is a polyglot and has read everything. And even if his information does betray a few lacunae – how could it be otherwise? – the informed reader can easily continue on his own towards Italy and the Spanish-speaking countries.

The tour de force also owes its success to the fact that under the title 'History of visual culture', the author does not juxtapose *two* parallel 'histories', that of academic reflection and that of the place of the 'visual' in the evolution of Western societies. Instead, he continually entwines them in order to make it clear that they are interdependent and it would be impossible to explain the development of an interest for this field of research without getting interested in the transformations (over a time span anything but linear, and without postulating an immediate relation of cause and effect) of all the technical, social, cultural, political systems that, taken together, define 'the visual'. A *double history*, then, but without forced parallelism, so much so that in the author's view it is possible to observe in philosophers, like Richard Rorty, Roland Barthes, Guy Debord, an unprecedented 'denigration of the vision' precisely at the moment when television and advertising flood the whole public domain with images. And conversely, that as a result of the most tangible dissolution of the materiality of the image into the pixels of the numerical image, as well as of the buoyancy of social networks, the questions of the researchers begin to multiply and they are directed to previously unknown paths only remotely related to the traditional scientific disciplines that deal with figurative arts and images.

In the face of such complexity and such apparent contradiction, simplification may prove useful, and the historical scheme sketched by the author can, at least on first acquaintance, help us understand what has been going on over half a century. Broadly speaking, he says, we have passed from *art history* (which, put in a nutshell, addresses artists, studios, style, the dating of works, their aesthetic value, etc.) to a *history of images* (which is no longer employed by the historian for the analysis of images as simple *illustrations* but turns to dealing with *all* the images, not just the most 'beautiful' ones, and strives primarily to understand how they work, what are their uses, their functions in the society, their social effects or 'agency') to arrive, a few years later, at *visual studies* that comprise and surpass previous approaches to bring forth something new and more in sync with the contemporary omnipresence and domination of the 'visual' (and not only the 'visible'). The consequence of this for the researchers is a profound paradigm change, even a reshuffling of priorities: as strikingly formulated by W. J. T. Mitchell and quoted by Gil Bartholeyns, 'visual culture' is not merely 'the social construction of vision', but 'the visual construction of the social'. Thus, what renders the emergence of 'visual studies' legitimate is, in the final analysis, the hypertrophy and tyranny of the 'visual' as a technical, social, economic, political reality that dominates all the aspects of society, insinuating its way into all the interstices of social relations as well as into each individual's intimate retreats: to bring but a few random examples, the omnipresence of the numeric and of 'imagery' in all their forms (in the best of cases, in medical usage); the proliferation of social networks (where virtual image reigns, for instance in Facebook, so aptly named: isn't it precisely on the surface of the 'face' that image and identity meet?); the narcissism of selfies (taken alone, with a friend, at the foot of a monument or in the flattering company of a celebrity, and, most importantly, instantaneously shared and spread on the planetary level) (see Gunthert 2015: 151–70); the political and ethical implications of videosurveillance and espionage of electronic communications (because from a 'sovereign' society under the Ancien Régime we moved on to a 'disciplinary' society in the nineteenth century, with its 'panoptic' universe of encarceration so beloved by Michel Foucault, and finally, in our own times, to a 'society of control' with an unprecedented 'scopic' efficiency); and above all the transformation of citizens affected by deceitful algorithms and 'targeted' advertising images popping up on their PC screens, into consumers enslaved by 'images' and turned, whether they like it or not, into accomplices of the global market (compared to which the State-Leviathan nowadays looks like a puny creature). Thus, without the slightest doubt, we have enough reason to declare and legitimate the advent of a new field of study surpassing the limits of traditional disciplines which continue, however, to nourish their own competences – history, sociology, philosophy, anthropology, psychology, neurobiology, and still others – in service of ever more complex and flexible investigations comprising the three great axes that the author lists at the end: on the one hand, the culturalist axis that emphasizes the ideological and cultural constraints of a given society and on the other, the naturalist axis stressing the psychological and neurobiological conditionings, and in between the two, the anthropological axis, investigating into all the relations that *make up* the society, in a resolutely comparative perspective, taking into account the temporal depth of historical transformations and ultimately by highlighting the resistance to the unique model promoted by the West – since in spite of a rapid and profound standardization of cultural practices, the contradictions and oppositions are manifest. Beneath a superficial conformity, it is probable that China or India, drawing inspiration from their own traditions, will mark down paths alternative to the dominant current of today. A 'connected history' that tracks the contradictions born of the encounter of cultures has a bright future ahead.

The proposed historical approach thus starts from the present. It is intrinsically *regressive*. Whether we like it or not, it is an understanding of the 'visual' and what is at stake there that commits us to explore past centuries and at the same time to go beyond earlier scientific paradigms, like 'art history' or even a 'history of images'. But frankly speaking, isn't history always 'regressive', as Marc Bloch theorized? We wouldn't today be able to write history in the same way as it used to be written 50 or a 100 years ago, because in the meanwhile the world has changed and historians, no matter what period they study, are always and primarily historians of their own times. This, by the way, is the reason why they are sometimes tempted by the self-celebration of new paradigms capable, in their view, of upsetting all commonly accepted conclusions, such as a 'visual turn' that, like its antecedent 'linguistic turn', will bring about a decisive scientific rupture. One must remain level-headed, and I appreciate the moderation of Gil Bartholeyns when he declares that 'intellectual emotions dominate this history. A deluge of images drowns reality, a new Babel becomes possible. For the last twenty years, liminal biblical metaphors have been put to work to capture the heights of these sensations and have functioned like a self-fulfilling prophecy in the academic sphere.' This prudent criticism not devoid of humour does justice to the real history of scientific knowledge that, at least in our domains, never progresses (and by saying 'progresses', I do not imply any advancement) by making 'turns' or untimely leaps. Social sciences and the discipline of history, in particular, evolve as if by capitalization: there are gains and there are losses (how many fruitful ideas have been forgotten that would deserve to be unearthed again?); real paradigm changes are not many, and only rarely are they turbulent: the triumphalist proclamation of whole series of consecutive 'turns' rather caters to mercantile expectations or flatters the researchers' career profiles than proffers a faithful description of the way science advances. I think that the movement proves itself as it advances: even if it is important to build a theory of our scientific practices, it is the combination of complementary approaches – historiography and field – that can protect us, on the one hand, from narrow-minded empiricism, and on the other, from the sand castles of theorizing. Simply a change of vocabulary is not enough to secure the true novelty of ideas.

The 'field', of course, is a field of study that one chooses for oneself and explores and clarifies in one's own manner. It is also a space-time that one compares and links to other historically located space-times, as need arises: I, as a medievalist, have learnt a lot from frequent perusal of the specialists of Greek antiquity, and a place should be made in the bibliography and historical panorama for the works of Jean-Pierre Vernant (2007a [1985] and 2007b [1990]) and the members of his team (Lissarrague 1987, 2013; Frontisi-Ducroux 1991, 1995; see also Schmitt 2001). These works have contributed hugely, both in and outside of France, to paving the tortuous way towards 'visual studies'. For me, at any rate, they proved decisive as to the way in which I learnt to simultaneously consider material and visible images (and notably cultic images), the Christian theology of the image and the dissemblance, and finally the immense domain of the 'imaginary': visions, memories, dreams (Besson and Schmitt 2016). There are, however, many essential components of a historically placed 'visual culture', tackled in their anthropological complexity as if in a permanent dialogue between textual and iconographic documents, on the micro level of the case, the file, the singular experience, and quite as inevitably, on that of a broader general history. This is because, while it is essential to order evidence in series, this must necessarily be preceded by a precise analysis of each image, each text, sometimes even of each word. Let me give here one instance of this, suggested to me by a quote used by Gil Bartholeyns: 'Man walks in the image', from Ps. 39:6. Giacometti's famous 'Walking Man' will come to one's mind! But the Vulgate puts it more precisely: 'Verumtamen in imaginem pertransit homo.' The accusative case, *'in imaginem'*, forbids us from turning the 'image' or the 'shadow' into a static cadre of the human march 'in the image' (*in imagine*): St Jerome in his translation wanted to signify both *movement and destination*: man *tends towards the image*, an expression that we can take to signify his desire to become again that for which he was created *ad imaginem Dei*, 'in the image of God', erasing the 'dissemblance' caused by Original Sin. But even if this is the Christian interpretation of the psalm, its original meaning may have been completely different – rather than an image, the insubstantial 'shadow' was used by the psalmist to describe man's wandering: 'Every human being that walks only a shadow' (Ps. 36:6).

Everyone moving rapidly over their 'field' is incessantly interrupted by such obstacles, preventing them from speeding. A whole set of observations, discontinued and incomplete, of detail are required before we can attempt to connect them so as to imbue the whole with historical meaning. Therefore, I would plead here for an approach at once microhistorical and generalist, which I describe as 'transversal'. It is one that I recently tried out in studying the rhythms – notably iconic and visual rhythms – of medieval society, in the very long duration (Schmitt 2016). It consists in cross-referencing an indefinite number of dossiers considered relevant (like, for example, the Bayeux tapestries or an illuminated psalter) in order to pose them *all* the possible questions and track all the semantic, symbolic, ideological relations that occur to the researcher. Such, in my opinion, is the only means of conciliating the intensity of anthropological questioning with a historical perspective. The 'history of visual culture' will thus become ever more legitimate and recognized.

Response

Gil Bartholeyns

Jean-Claude Schmitt's remark on my use of Ps. 39:6 ('Man walks in the image') is a clear example of the sorts of problems historians are confronted with, and an ideal case for demonstrating the importance of case-by-case, word-for-word microhistorical analysis before moving onto questions of broader meaning. One might continue by noting that 'man walks in the image' is not a translation of the psalm as it appears in the Vulgate, but rather the standard translation of Augustine's version of the psalm: *'in imagine ambulat homo'*. The accusative form of the Vulgate (*'in imaginem'*) cannot be translated as 'in a vain shew/image', but should instead be rendered as 'towards the shew/image', which Augustine underscores by his use of the ablative (*'in imagine'*). With the preposition *in*, the ablative refers to the place man currently is (the state in which he finds oneself), whereas the accusative marks the place (or state) towards which he proceeds. For Augustine, man walks as an image; for Jerome, he tends towards the divine image. Ultimately, the historical meaning of the phrase must be determined by the way it was read in the Middle Ages, and this meaning might well be that of Augustine. Man is thus himself the ambulant image, bringing us back to the original text where man is nothing but a moving shadow (Ps. 39:6).

This level of analysis is all the more important because even those of us who are trained to maintain a critical distance nonetheless tend to address the question of images, and indeed images themselves, on the basis of our own experience, as they appear to speak across time and space. Indeed, this is partly what makes them intriguing, as Schmitt notes when he points to a particular, and for us rather unusual, image from a medieval manuscript and declares it a fascinating example of the ambivalent relationship that the historian maintains with his subject, adding that the figures and gestures depicted on this timeworn page 'move me and provide, across the centuries, an odd sense of proximity' (Schmitt 2017: 136).

Schmitt's comment rightly underscores that the historians broke new ground by 'dealing with *all* the images, not just the most "beautiful" ones'. This is true, but he and I nonetheless concur that the point is not in fact so straightforward. Schmitt also notes the role played by French classical historians in developing an anthropological interrogation of images and visuality, and mentions that historians of ancient Greece helped him to 'anthropologise' his approach to visual culture. Alongside this question of 'democratization', I would also like to address the role of anthropology, because it is here, as I tried to make clear, that we find the true turning point in visual history and the history of images, undertaken since the 1990s.

Certainly, the cardinal contribution of the history of images has perhaps seemed to be the opening up to an ever broader corpus of images and naturally to align visual studies with the evolution of media in the twentieth century. This opening up, however, has been rather relative. Visual studies may address 'popular culture', but they do so via the idea of visuality. Representations typically serve to uncover ideologies of race, class, gender, and species. And the study of non-artistic images is frequently restricted to scientific images, or to ones drawn from the world of design and avant-garde technology. Truly 'low' iconography is rarely explored. James Elkins (2002: 93) remarks on this latent snobbery, or at least the aesthetic partiality of visual studies, but his response to his own mantra of 'most images are not art' is to explore 'informational images', that is, diagrams, schemas, heraldry, and so on (Elkins 2000).

Historians' interest in 'minor images', meanwhile, is not a direct passion. Rather it is the outcome of an overturning of the elitist paradigm and event-driven history that prevailed until the 1960s in favour of an historic paradigm based around the quotidian, the neglected, and the collective. It is, therefore, perhaps a little over-generous to suggest that historians valiantly struggled to 'democratise' images; the underlying intention comes from further afield. Fifteenth-century prints, nineteenth-century postcards, and American pulp magazines are not 'new' objects or indeed necessities: their study helps to understand popular piety, the tourist industry, and the twentieth-century extraterrestrial imaginary. If scholars investigate graffiti, ex-votos, pilgrim badges, misericords, and caricatures, it is the better to drive forward a project of historical anthropology (Bartholeyns, Dittmar, and Jolivet 2008). To pretend otherwise would be to deny their value as historical traces and, for older productions, to ignore the work of folklorists and others investigating what the nineteenth century referred to as 'popular imagery' (Bartholeyns 2016a).

Anthropologising images

If there has been a 'turn' for historians of art, images, and the visual, then it is an *anthropological* one and tied up with the material and performative turns. Though the 'political' is the main horizon of visual studies *qua* new critical theory (Bartholeyns 2016b; Boidy 2017), it is the 'anthropological' that is the lodestar of history. First and foremost, this is a matter of the 'meeting of the history of art and anthropology' (Dufrêne and Taylor 2009). It is also a question of comparative or postcolonial history: Serge Gruzinski's (2001 [1990]) pioneering work on aesthetic cross-fertilization between Europe and the 'New World' played out in debates about idols and the colonization of the Americas with images; William Pietz's (2005) 'genealogy of the problem' of the African fetish; Hans Belting's (2011b) *Florence and Baghdad*, which explores critical thought surrounding images in Islam and the Renaissance's debt to Arab optics; and lastly the European regime of visibility where the female Muslim veil appears as doubly paradoxical insofar as it offends the Western insistence on transparency, but transforms women into images of Islam as the act of veiling draws the gaze to the very thing it veils (Aboudrar 2014).

It is also a question of anthropologists laying claim to the terrain of history. Jack Goody (1997), for instance, understands historical resistance to images as a 'cognitive contradiction' regarding everything that makes that which is absent present, and those things, such as flowers or poetry, that can be seized upon for their lack of 'reality' in moments of crisis. Philippe Descola (2005–11) confronts the Moderns' 'naturalist ontology' with works of art and their classical historiography. Carlo Severi (2017), in the guise of an 'anthropology of visual beliefs', explores the properties (human form, gaze, sonority, etc.) that seem to confer on Western and non-Western objects the status of quasi-persons.

Historians, in turn, have come to address general anthropological questions. Belting (2011a) proposed an anthropology of the image that puts corporeality right back at the centre of iconic and visual processes, via the correlation of image, medium, and body, as people both generate images in themselves and materially project them into the world. Caroline van Eck (2015) also identifies physicality as an animating element of images. Horst Bredekamp (2017) developed a theory of *Bildakt* or 'image acts' (Bartholeyns and Golsenne 2009), thus settling several points of the debate surrounding the 'power of images', understood both as their potential for action and as animated being or bodily substitute in diverse cultural contexts. This anthropologization, having explored the active role of images, is marked by the effort to reinsert them into society: images are addressed as beings capable of having an effect upon the world, rather than primarily as representations susceptible to internal (iconological) analysis. Their effects have come to take precedence over meaning, which is simply one factor of their agency among many. Questions such as 'what do pictures want' (Mitchell 2005), and statements such as 'the object stares back' (Elkins 1996: 70–2), or 'what we see, what sees us' (Didi-Huberman 1992), reflect this tendency to take seriously the fact that the image imposes a relationship.

I would like to use Janet Wolff's (2012) critical essay as a springboard, as the position it adopts allows for a comparison of this anthropology of the image conducted by both anthropologists and historians. Wolff identifies an 'evaporation of the social' and an abandoning of cultural approaches in such disparate developments as the 'turn to affect', the return of phenomenology, the insistence on immediacy and presence, the actor–network theory, the reconfiguration of the human/non-human, nature/culture and subject/object boundaries that she describes as posthumanist theory, and of course neuroaesthetics. Yet it is clear that within this disparate ensemble that Wolff categorizes as a 'new kind of animism', there persists a *culturalist* frontier that she views but darkly, being herself situated at one of its extremities.

Indeed, psychoanalytical, and later cognitivist, explanations of the 'power of the image' (Freedberg 1989) are simply unacceptable for the vast majority of historians, who nonetheless take as a given the fact that artefacts are full social agents, located at the interface of institutions and emotions. People, who demonstrate a natural tendency to develop relationships with objects, are also the condition of their 'power', but this power must be collectively or individually activated. This is how Alfred Gell (1998) resolves the apparent incompatibility of different levels, by linking 'internalist' processes (where subjectivity is attributed to things) and 'externalist' ones, where the agency of an artefact, its 'art', is the product of asocial injunction, as with a religious tradition, or an apparatus of attention.

What we have then is three distinct models: culturalist, anthropological, and naturalist. These are positions, but not ones situated on a continuum moving from purely social explanations to purely sensorial or cognitive ones. Interrogating form, presence, visibility, ornamentation, contact, resemblance, or materiality is a way of anthropologizing one's study. In such approaches, the image and the visual are not dependent on a particular historical situation or brain. There is no need either to refuse (like Wolff) or wish (like Freedberg) to 'primitivize' particular modern attitudes, but instead one can simply empirically note that it is not straightforward to burn a photograph or gouge out the eyes of an image. In 2009, the legal system of France, the constitutionally most secular country on earth, authenticated a belief in magic when it condemned the producers of a 'voodoo' doll of a former president (Favret-Saada 2009). Images that talk or bleed need not be relegated to the 'Middle Ages' or to reduce to 'mere religiosity' pilgrims photographs of the sky taken in the hope of a sighting of the divine (Claverie 2012) or the banal use of digital images in religious practice (Dittmar 2016). Nor, finally, need we – in a rejection of total constructivism or perfect essentialism – fall back upon the basic heteronomy of phenomena and abandon all hope of grasping their 'modalities'. It is precisely the analysis of singularities observed over a period of centuries and in a range of places that, in a Christian context say, allows for the identification of certain recurrent traits of iconic *virtus*, such as the *plastic* salience of the image, the *transit* of a model's 'virtue' via its representation, the effigy's *inhabitation* by its prototype, the ritual *infusion* of potency, the *conductivity* of direct sight, and so on, where some can be related to dogma, others to popular experience, and so forth.

The general situation of debate leaves the historian with an impression of déjà-vu as regards the representativity of the cases found in the sources. One can safely say that a little theoretical deflation (particularly where the conflict seems primarily to stem from the adoption of a particular stance) would do nobody any harm at all. And there is only one way to achieve such an end: back to the field.

Note

1. It is no accident that the chapter was retitled 'Visual history' in the second edition of the volume, in 2001 (Gaskell 2001).

References

Aboudrar, B. N. (2014), *Comment le voile est devenu musulman*, Paris: Flammarion.

Aït-Touati, F. (2011), *Contes de la lune. Essai sur la fiction et la science modernes*, Paris: Gallimard.

Alpers, S. (1983), *The Art of Describing: Dutch Art in the Seventeenth Century*, Chicago: University of Chicago Press.

Alpers, S. (1996), answer to the 'Visual Culture Questionnaire', *October*, 77: 26.

Barthes, R. (1972), *Mythologies*, New York: Hill & Wang.

Bartholeyns, G. (2014), 'The Instant Past. Nostalgia and Digital Retro Photography', in K. Niemeyer (ed.), *Contemporary Nostalgia and Media*, 51–69, Basingstoke: Palgrave Macmillan.

Bartholeyns, G. (2015), 'Rien ne se crée, rien ne se perd, tout se regrette', *Terrain*, 64: 12–33.

Bartholeyns, G. (2016a), 'L'ordre des images', in J. Maeck and M. Steinle (eds), *L'Image d'archives. Une image en devenir*, 21–42, Rennes: Presses universitaires de Rennes.

Bartholeyns, G. (2016b), 'Un bien étrange cousin, les *visual studies*', in G. Bartholeyns (ed.), *Politiques visuelles*, 5–28, Dijon: Les Presses du réel.

Bartholeyns, G., Dittmar, P.-O., and Jolivet, V. (2008), *Image et transgression au Moyen Âge*, Paris: Presses universitaires de France.

Bartholeyns, G. and Golsenne, T. (2009), 'Une théorie des actes d'images', in G. Bartholeyns, A. Dierkens and T. Golsenne (eds), *La Performance des images*, 15–25, Brussels: Editions de l'Université de Bruxelles.

Baudrillard, J. (2002), *L'Esprit du terrorisme*, Paris: Galilée.

Baxandall, M. (1972), *Painting and Experience in Fifteenth-Century Italy: A Primer in the Social History of Pictorial Style*, Oxford: Clarendon Press.

Becker, H. S. (1974), 'Photography and Sociology', *Studies in the Anthropology of Visual Communication*, 1: 3–26.

Belting, H. (1993), *Likeness and Presence: A History of the Image before the Era of Art*, Chicago: University of Chicago Press.

Belting, H. (2011a), *An Anthropology of Images*, Princeton: Princeton University Press.

Belting, H. (2011b), *Florence and Baghdad: Renaissance Art and Arab Science*, Cambridge, MA: Belknap Press.

Benjamin, W. (1986), 'Surrealism: The Last Snapshot of the European Intelligentsia', in his *Reflections*, 177–92, transl. E. Jephcott, New York: Schocken Books.

Berger, J. (1972), *Ways of Seeing*, London: Penguin Books.

Berger, J. (1980), *About Looking*, New York: Pantheon Books.

Besson, G. and Schmitt, J.-C. (2016), *Rêver de soi. Les songes autobiographiques du Moyen Âge*, Toulouse: Anacharsis.

Bigg, C. (2007), 'The Panorama, or La Nature A Coup d'Œil', in E. Fiorentini (ed.), *Observing Nature. Representing Experience: The Osmotic Dynamics of Romanticism 1800–1850*, 73–95, Berlin: Dietrich Reimer Verlag.

Bigg, C. and Vanhoutte, K. (2017), 'Spectacular Astronomy', *Early Popular Visual Culture*, 15 (2): 115–24.

Boehm, G. (1994), 'Die Wiederkehr der Bilder', in G. Boehm (ed.), *Was ist ein Bild?*, 11–38, Munich: Fink.

Boehm, G. and Mitchell, W. J. T. (2009), 'Pictorial versus Iconic Turn: Two Letters', *Culture, Theory & Critique*, 50 (2–3): 103–21.

Boidy, M. (2016), 'Le black bloc, terrain visuel du global', *Terrains/Théories*, 5, available online: http://teth.revues.org/834 (accessed 20 November 2017).

Boidy, M. (2017), *Les études visuelles*, Paris: Presses universitaires de Vincennes.

Boulnois, O. (2008), *Au-delà de l'image. Une archéologie du visuel au Moyen Âge, Ve–XVe siècle*, Paris: Seuil.

Bredekamp, H. (1999), *Thomas Hobbes visuelle Strategien. Der Leviathan: Urbild des modernen Staates. Werkillustrationen und Portraits*, Berlin: Akademie Verlag.

Bredekamp, H. (2017), *Image Act: A Systematic Approach to Visual Agency*, Berlin: De Gruyter.

Bredekamp, H., Dünkel, V. and Schneider, B., eds (2015), *The Technical Image: A History of Styles in Scientific Imagery?* Chicago: University Of Chicago Press.

Bryson, N. (2003), 'Visual Culture and the Dearth of Images', *Journal of Visual Culture*, 2 (2): 229–32.

Buci-Glucksmann, C. (2002), *La Folie du voir. Une esthétique du virtuel*, Paris: Galilée.

Buck-Morss, S. (2007), 'Visual Empire', *Diacritics*, 37 (2–3): 171–98.

Burke, P. (1992), *The Fabrication of Louis XIV*, New Haven: Yale University Press.

Burke, P. (2001), *Eyewitnessing. The Uses of Images as Historical Evidence*, London: Reaktion Books.

Bynum, C. (2011), *Christian Materiality: An Essay on Religion in Late Medieval Europe*, New York: Zone Books.

Camille, M. (2000), 'Before the Gaze. The Internal Senses and Late Medieval Practices of Seeing', in R. S. Nelson (ed.), *Visuality Before and Beyond the Renaissance: Seeing as Others Saw*, 197–223, Cambridge: Cambridge University Press.

Caplan, J. and Torpey, J., eds (2001), *Documenting Individual Identity. The Development of State Practices in the Modern World*, Princeton: Princeton University Press.

Chamayou, G. (2013), *Théorie du drone*, Paris: La fabrique

Charpy, M. (2015), 'Pour portrait. Sur les usages sociaux des figurations de soi au XIXe siècle', in D. Dubuisson and S. Raux (eds), *A perte de vue. Les Nouveaux paradigmes du visuel*, 209–23, Dijon: Les presses du réel.

Claverie, E. (2012), 'Taking Pictures of Supernatural Beings', in B. Latour and P. Weibel (eds), *Iconoclash*, 460–61, Cambridge, MA: MIT Press.

Courtine, J.-J., 'Le Corps Anormal', in A. Corbin, J.-J. Courtine and G. Vigarello (eds), *Histoire du corps, 3. Les mutations du regard. Le XXe siècle*, 209–73, Paris: Seuil.

Crary, J. (1988), 'Modernizing Vision', in H. Foster (ed.), *Vision and Visuality*, 29–51, Seattle: Bay Press.

Crary, J. (1989), 'Spectacle, Attention, Counter-Memory', *October*, 50: 96–107.

Crary, J. (1990), *Techniques of the Observer: On Vision and Modernity in the Nineteenth Century*, Cambridge, MA: MIT Press.

Crary, J. (1999), *Suspensions of Perception: Attention, Spectacle and Modern Culture*, Cambridge, MA: MIT Press

Crary, J. (2013), *24/7: Late Capitalism and the Ends of Sleep*, London: Verso.

Damisch, H. (1995), *The Origin of Perspective*, Cambridge, MA: MIT Press.

Daston, L. and Galison, P. (1992), 'The Image of Objectivity', *Representations*, 40: 81–128.

Daston, L. and Galison, P. (2007), *Objectivity*, New York: Zone Books.

Debord, G. (1970), *The Society of the Spectacle*, Detroit: Black & Red.

Deleuze, G. (1992), 'Postscript on the Societies of Control', *October*, 59: 3–7.

Descola, P. (2005–2011), *Anthropologie de la nature: Modalités de la figuration* and *Ontologies des images*, Collège de France, available online: http://www.college-de-france.fr/site/philippe-descola/resumes.htm (accessed 20 November 2017).

Dewey, J. (1929), *The Quest for Certainty: A Study of the Relation of Knowledge and Action*, New York: Minton Balch & Company.

Didi-Huberman, G. (1992), *Ce que nous voyons, ce qui nous regarde*, Paris: Minuit.

Didi-Huberman, G. (2007), *L'Image ouverte*, Paris: Gallimard.

Didi-Huberman, G. (2012), *Peuples exposés, peuples figurants. L'Œil de l'Histoire, 4*, Paris: Minuit.

Dittmar, P.-O. (2016), 'De la trace à l'apparition, la prière photographique', *Archives des Sciences Sociales des Religions*, 174, 169–90.

Dufrêne, T. and Taylor, A.-C. (2009), 'By Way of Introduction', in T. Dufrêne and A.-C. Taylor (eds), *Cannibalismes disciplinaires. Quand l'histoire de l'art et l'anthropologie se rencontrent*, 15–22, Paris: Musée du quai Branly–INHA.

Eck, C. van (2015), *Art, Agency and Living Presence: From the Animated Image to the Excessive Object*, Leiden: Leiden University Press.

Elkins, J. (1996), *The Object Stares Back: On the Nature of Seeing*, San Diego: Harcourt.

Elkins, J. (1998), *On Pictures and the Words That Fail Them*, Cambridge: Cambridge University Press.

Elkins, J. (2000), *How to Use Your Eyes*, London and New York: Routledge.

Elkins, J. (2001), *The Domain of Images*, Ithaca: Cornell University Press.

Elkins, J. (2002), 'Preface to the Book A Skeptical Introduction to Visual Culture', *Journal of Visual Culture*, 1 (1): 93–9.

Favret-Saada J. (2009), 'On y croit toujours plus qu'on ne croit. Sur le manuel vaudou d'un président', *L'Homme*, 190: 7–26.

Febvre, L. (1942), *Le Problème de la incroyance au XVIe siècle. La religion de Rabelais*, Paris: Albin Michel.

Foucault, M. (1977), *Discipline and Punish: The Birth of the Prison*, New York: Pantheon Books.

Foucault M. (1980), 'The Eye of Power. A conversation with Jean-Pierre Baour and Michelle Perrot', in his *Power/Knowledge. Selected Interviews and Other Writings 1972–1977*, ed. C. Gordon, 147–65, New York: Pantheon Books.

Foucault, M. (2001), 'La peinture photogénique', in his *Dits et écrits, vol. 1*, 1575–83, Paris: Gallimard.

France, C. de (1982), *Cinéma et anthropologie*, Paris: Editions du CNRS.

Freedberg, D. (1989), *The Power of Images: Studies in the History and Theory of Response*, Chicago: University of Chicago Press.

Frontisi-Ducroux, F. (1991), *Le Dieu-masque. Une figure de Dionysos d'Athènes*, Paris and Rome: La Découverte and Ecole française de Rome.

Frontisi-Ducroux, F. (1995), *Du masque au visage. Aspects de l'identité en Grèce ancienne*, Paris: Flammarion.

Fyfe, G. and Law, J. (1987), 'Introduction: One the Invisibility of the Visual', in G. Fyfe and J. Law (eds), *Picturing Power. Visual Depiction and Social Relations*, 1–14, London: Routledge.

Gaskell, I. (1991), 'History of Images', in P. Burke (ed.), *New Perspectives on Historical Writing*, 168–92, Cambridge: Polity Press.

Gaskell, I. (2001), 'Visual History', in P. Burke (ed.), *New Perspectives on Historical Writing*, 2nd rev. edn, 187–217, Cambridge: Polity Press.

Gell, A. (1998), *Art and Agency: An Anthropological Theory*, Oxford: Oxford University Press.

Gleizes, D. and Denis, R. (2017), *Machines à voir. Pour une histoire du regard instrumenté (XVIIe–XIXe siècle). Anthologie*, Lyon: Presses universitaires de Lyon.

Golsenne, T. (2015), 'L'image-mosaïque', in D. Dubuisson and S. Raux (eds), *A perte de vue. Les Nouveaux paradigmes du visuel*, 97–109, Dijon: Les presses du réel.

Goody, J. (1997), *Representations and Contradictions: Ambivalence Towards Images, Theater, Fiction, Relics and Sexuality*, Oxford: Blackwell.

Groebner, V. (2004), *Der Schein der Person. Steckbrief, Ausweis und Kontrolle im Europa des Mittelalters*, Munich: C. H. Beck.

Gruzinski, S. (2001), *Images at War: Mexico From Columbus to Blade Runner (1492–2019)*, Durham: Duke University Press Books.

Guichard, C. (2007), 'Connoisseurship and Artistic Expertise. London and Paris, 1600–1800', in C. Rabier (ed.), *Fields of Expertise. A Comparative History of Expert Procedures in Paris and London, 1600 to Present*, 173–91, Newcastle: Cambridge Scholars Publishing.

Guichard C. (2015), '"D'après nature" ou "chose vue"? Autorité et vérité de l'image scientifique au XVIIIe siècle', in D. Dubuisson and S. Raux (eds), *A perte de vue. Les Nouveaux paradigmes du visuel*, 35–51, Dijon: Les Presses du réel.

Gunthert, A. (2015), *L'Image partagé. La Photographie numérique*, Paris: Editions Textuel.

Hamon, P. (2001), *Imageries. Littérature et image au XIXe siècle*, Paris: José Corti.

Hardt, M. and Negri, A. (2000), *Empire*, Cambridge, MA: Harvard University Press.

Harper, D. (1988), 'Visual Sociology: Expending Sociological Vision', *The American Sociologist*, 19 (1): 54–70.

Hasian, M. Jr. (2016), *Drone Warfare and Lawfare in a Post-Heroic Age*, Tuscaloosa: University of Alabama Press.

Haskell, F. (1993), *History and its Images: Art and the Interpretation of the Past*, Yale: Yale University Press.

Havelange, C. (1998), *De l'Oeil et du Monde. Une histoire du regard au seuil de la modernité*, Paris: Fayard.

Heidegger, M. (1977), 'The Age of World Picture', in his *The Question Concerning Technology and Other Essays*, 115–54, New York: Garlan Publishing.

Heinich N. (2012), *De la visibilité. Excellence et singularité en régime médiatique*, Paris: Gallimard.

Hentschel K. (2014), *Visual Cultures in Science and Technology: A Comparative History*, Oxford: Oxford University Press.

Invisible Committee (The) (2009), *The Coming Insurrection*, Los Angeles: Semiotext(e).

Jay, M. (1988), 'Scopic Regimes of Modernity', in H. Foster (ed.), *Vision and Visuality*, 3–27, Seattle: Bay Press.

Jay, M. (1993), *Downcast Eyes: The Denigration of Vision in Twentieth-Century French Thought*, Berkeley: University of California Press.

Jay, M. (2012), 'Scopic Regimes of Modernity Revisited', in I. Heywood and B. Sandywell (eds), *The Handbook of Visual Culture*, 102–13, London: Berg.

Jones, C. A. and Galison, P. (1998), 'Picturing Science, Porducing Art', in C. A. Jones and P. Galison (eds), *Picturing Science, Porducing Art*, 1–23, New York: Routledge.

Kopytoff, I. (1986), 'The Cultural Biography of Things: Commoditisation as a Process', in A. Appadurai (ed.), *The Social Life of Things*, 64–91, Cambridge: Cambridge University Press.

Latour, B. (1986), 'Visualization and Cognition: Thinking with Eyes and Hands', *Knowledge and Society: Studies in the Sociology of Culture Past and Present*, 6: 1–40.

Lindberg, D. C. (1976), *Theories of Vision. From Al-Kindi to Kepler*, Chicago: University of Chicago Press.

Lissarrague, F. (1987), *Un flot d'images. Une esthétique du banquet grec*, Paris: Adam Birot.
Lissarrague, F. (2013), *La Cité des satyres. Une anthropologie ludique (Athènes, VIe-Ve siècle avant J.-C.)*, Paris: Editions de l'EHESS.
Lyon, D. (1994), *The Electronic Eye: The Rise of Surveillance Society*, Cambridge: Polity Press.
Lyon, D. (2003), *Surveillance after September 11*, Cambridge: Polity Press.
Maillet A. (2004), *The Claude Glass. Use and Meaning of the Black Mirror in Western Art*, New York: Zone Books.
Maillet A. (2007), *Prothèses lunatiques. Les lunettes, de la science aux fantasmes*, Paris: Editions Amsterdam.
Manovich, L. (2001), *The Language of New Media*, Cambridge, MA: The MIT Press.
Marin, L. (1988), *Portrait of the King*, Minneapolis: University of Minnesota Press.
Mathiesen T. (1997), 'The Viewer Society. Michel Foucault's "Panopticon" Revisited', *Theoretical Criminology*, 1(2): 215–34.
McLuhan, M. (1964), *Understanding Media: The Extensions of Man*, New York: McGraw-Hill.
Mirzoeff, N. (2011), *The Right to Look: A Counterhistory of Visuality*, Durham: Duke University Press.
Mirzoeff, N. (2012), 'Introduction: For Critical Visuality Studies', in N. Mirzoeff (ed.), *The Visual Culture Reader*, 3rd edn, xxix–xxxviii, New York: Routledge.
Mitchell, W. J. T. (1992a), *The Reconfigured Eye: Visual Truth in the Post-photographic Era*, Cambridge, MA: MIT Press.
Mitchell, W. J. T. (1992b), 'The Pictorial Turn', *ArtForum*, 5: 11–35.
Mitchell, W. J. T. (1995), 'Interdisciplinarity and Visual Culture', *The Art Bulletin*, 74(4): 540–44.
Mitchell, W. J. T. (2002), 'Showing Seeing: A Critique of Visual Culture', *Journal of Visual Culture*, 1 (2): 165–85.
Mitchell, W. J. T. (2005), *What Do Pictures Want?*, Chicago: University of Chicago Press.
Monahan, T., ed. (2006), *Surveillance and Security: Technological Politics and Power in Everyday Life*, New York: Routledge.
Moxey, K. (2008), 'Visual Studies and the Iconic Turn', *Journal of Visual Culture*, 7 (2): 131–46.
Paglen, T. (2016), 'Invisible Images (Your Pictures Are Looking at You)', *The New Inquiry*, 57, available online: https://thenewinquiry.com/invisible-images-your-pictures-are-looking-at-you (accessed 20 November 2017).
Pantin, I. (1995), *La Poésie du ciel en France dans la seconde moitié du seizième siècle*, Genève: Droz.
Pietz, W. (2005), *Le Fétiche. Généalogie d'un problème*, Paris: Kargo & L'Eclat.
Pommier, E. (2007), *Comment l'art devient l'Art dans l'Italie de la Renaissance*, Paris: Gallimard.
Rorty, R. (1980), *Philosophy and the Mirror of Nature*, Princeton: Princeton University Press.
Schaffer, S. (2014), *La Fabrique des sciences modernes (XVIIe–XIXe siècle)*, Paris: Seuil.
Schmidt-Burkhardt, A. (2002), 'The All-Seer: God's Eye as Proto-surveillance', in T. Levin, U. Frohen and P. Weibel (eds), *Ctrl [Space]: Rhetorics of Surveillance from Bentham to Big Brother*, 17–31, Cambridge, MA: MIT Press.
Schmitt, J.-C. (1996), 'La culture de l'*imago*', *Annales. Histoire, Sciences Sociales*, 51 (1): 3–36.
Schmitt, J.-C. (1997), 'L'historien et les images', in O. G. Oexle (ed.), *Der Blick auf die Bilder. Kunstgeschichte und Geschichte im Gespräch*, 7–51, Göttingen: Wallstein Verlag.
Schmitt, J.-C., ed. (2001), *Eve et Pandora. La création de la femme*, Paris: Gallimard.
Schmitt, J.-C. (2002), *Le Corps des images. Essais sur la culture visuelle au Moyen Âge*, Paris: Gallimard.
Schmitt, J.-C. (2016), *Les Rythmes au Moyen Âge*, Paris: Gallimard.
Schmitt, J.-C. (2017), 'Encounter: Rhythmicity of an Image', *Gesta*, 56 (2): 133–36.
Schwartz, V. (1998), *Spectacular Realities: Early Mass Culture in Fin-de-siècle Paris*, Berkeley: University of California Press.

Sennett, R. (1990), *The Conscience of the Eye: The Design and Social Life of Cities*, New York: W. W. Norton & Company.

Severi, C. (2017), *L'Objet-personne. Une anthropologie de la croyance visuelle*, Paris: Editions Rue d'Ulm, Presses de l'Ecole normale supérieure – Musée du quai Branly.

Sicard, M. (1998), *La Fabrique du regard. Images de science et appareils de vision (XVe–XXe siècle)*, Paris: Odile Jacob.

Simon, G. (1988), *Le Regard, l'être et l'apparence dans l'otique de l'Antiquité*, Paris: Seuil.

Simon, G. (2003), *Archéologie de la vision. L'optique, le corps, la peinture*, Paris: Seuil.

Szendy, P. (2017), *Le Supermarché du visible. Essai d'iconomie*, Paris: Minuit.

Thompson, J. B. (1995), *The Media and Modernity: A Social Theory of the Media*, Cambridge: Polity Press.

Thompson, J. B. (2005), 'The New Visibility', *Theory, Culture & Society*, 22 (6): 31–52.

Vermeir, K. (2005), 'The Magic of the Magic Lantern (1660–1700): On Analogical Demonstration and the Visualization of the Invisible', *British Journal for the History of Science*, 38 (2): 127–59.

Vernant, J.-P. (2007a), *La Mort dans les yeux. Figures de l'Autre en Grèce ancienne*, in J.-P. Vernant, *Oeuvres*, vol. 2, Paris: Seuil, 1473–519.

Vernant, J.-P. (2007b), *Figures, Idoles, Masques*, in J.-P. Vernant, *Oeuvres*, vol. 2, Paris: Seuil, 1521–661.

Vidler, A. (1992), 'Transparency', in his *The Architectural Uncanny. Essays in the Modern Unhomely*, 217–26, Cambridge, MA: MIT Press.

Whitaker, R. (1999), *The End of Privacy: How Total Surveillance is Becoming a Reality*, New York: The New Press.

Winetrout, K. (1964), 'The New Age of the Visible. A Call to Study', *AV Communication Review*, 12 (1): 46–52.

Wise, M. N. (2006), 'Making Visible', *ISIS*, 97 (1): 75–82.

Wolff, J. (2012), 'After Cultural Theory: The Power of Images, the Lure of Immediacy', *Journal of Visual Culture*, 11 (1): 3–19.

CHAPTER 10
DIGITAL HISTORY
Jane Winters

A brief history of digital history

Before digital history there was history and computing (just as before digital humanities there was humanities computing). The beginnings of humanities computing are usually located in the work of the Jesuit priest Father Roberto Busa, who in 1949 began his work to create an *index verborum* for the writings of Thomas Aquinas (Hockey 2004). This endeavour displayed the concern with text that has characterized much work in humanities computing, but was also very clearly an exercise in historical research. Busa was doing what historians have always done, that is, making best use of the available tools and methods to answer particular questions; deploying technology to help him innovate and gain insight into his chosen subject.

Digital history, however, both falls within and is in many ways distinct from the field of digital humanities. Tim Hitchcock colourfully describes digital humanities as 'something of a pantomime horse – with criticism, distant reading[1] and literary theory occupying the front end ... while history, geography and library science are stuck in the rear – doing the hard work of creating new digital resources, and testing new tools' (Hitchcock 2016). Much debate in the digital humanities has focused on the question of whether or not it constitutes a distinct discipline, and this shows no sign of abating. The editors of the recently published *New Companion to Digital Humanities*, for example, note in their preface to the volume that 'it remains debatable whether digital humanities should be regarded as "a discipline in its own right" rather than a set of related methods' (Schreibmann Siemens and Unsworth 2016: xvii). Patrik Svensson, among others, has identified the significance of 'the discursive shift from humanities computing to what is now being termed the digital humanities', arguing that this 'renaming ... brings with it a set of epistemic commitments that are not necessarily congruent with a broad and inclusive notion of the digital humanities' (Svensson 2009: 2). Digital history has largely stood outside these arguments, and the relatively recent reframing of history and computing in these terms has attracted far less discussion. Its practitioners, if such they can be called, are generally more concerned to ally themselves with the historical than the digital, to continue to locate themselves within a particular historical field.

But there is difference and variety, and the development of digital history has not been an uncontested and linear one. There have been stops and starts along the way, falls from grace, shifts in emphasis, recurring problems, and new challenges. The first major initiative in the digital field was the 'Cliometrics Revolution' of the 1960s and 1970s, which developed out of a joint 1957 meeting of the Economic History Association and the National Bureau of Economic Research Conference on Income and Wealth in Williamstown, Massachusetts (Cliometric Society n.d.). The term itself was proposed by the American economist Stanley Reiter and it came to describe a 'movement to "modernize" traditional economic historiography by applying more formal styles of economic analysis and more up-to-date quantitative methods to historical data and methods' (Lyons, Cain, and Williamson 2007: xii). Cliometrics was novel, it was collaborative, and it relied on the availability of large quantities of data, which often had to be newly assembled in ways which were susceptible to computational analysis. But, and this is a phenomenon which has dogged digital history over its short lifetime, the technical and quantitative skills required for this new approach to historical research were alien to many, and the proponents of Cliometrics met with considerable suspicion, even resistance. And it was not just quantification that was the problem, it was the employment of computational techniques and the use of computer-readable data: 'With more and more scholars employing all the tools and techniques, using all the data processing machines, and also those frightening projected scanner devices, which we are told will read documents and books for us, there is still no machine for digesting the sources' (Bridenbaugh 1963: 322). This was a heartfelt plea for the importance of the human, the individual, both as researcher and as object of research.

As might be expected from its North American origins, it took a while for Cliometrics to influence research in the UK, but it began to gain some traction with the work of the Cambridge Group for the History of Population and Social Structure, founded in 1964 by Peter Laslett and Tony Wrigley (Lyons, Cain, and Williamson 2007: 25–6). The 1970s saw wider adoption of the new methods in the UK and the rest of Europe, and there were attempts to make them accessible to the kinds of historians for whom Bridenbaugh feared (Floud 1973). They were, however, to be relatively short-lived, and Cliometrics had begun to fall out of favour by the end of the decade. Not only had it failed to break in to the mainstream of historical research, but there had been a strong reaction against some of its more grandiose claims. It cast a long, and frequently negative shadow: in 1989, for example, it could be stated that 'computers in history are still too frequently found guilty through their association with the bold but fatuous claims made by a handful of irresponsible men and women who claimed that quantification held forth the promise of transforming history from an art into an objective science' (Greenstein and Morgan 1989).

Despite the legacy of Cliometrics, the 1980s would see the rise of what began to be described as history and computing, a more common phraseology than historical computing. In March 1986 a conference was held at the then Westfield College, University of London, 'to attempt to inaugurate an association for historians who used or wished to use computers in their work, whether that work was research or teaching' (Denley and Hopkin 1987: ix). The approach here was immediately more inclusive and welcoming than the rather daunting Cliometrics, with its very high barrier to entry. The volume arising from that conference, and particularly the editors' introduction, admirably sets out the range and scope of the new ways of working, as well as both the hopes for their transformative effect and the degree of caution that had previously been missing. The editors identify four cross-cutting themes emerging from the conference, which still have resonance today: the evolution of computational methods beyond 'quantification and data processing'; the unprecedented opportunity for exchange between historians with very different geographical and chronological focus, who might previously never have encountered each other – an opportunity which extended to those in other disciplines; an awareness of the need for training and for the provision of sufficient technical resource; and finally the very international complexion of history and computing (the conference was attended by delegates from more than nineteen, predominantly European, countries) (Denley and Hopkin 1987: ix–x). There was a real sense of being at the start of something new, with the editors writing that 'this blend of qualitative and quantitative, of insight and deduction, of old-fashioned instinct and modern processing power, offers a rare combination; something of which historians can, for once, be proud' (Denley and Hopkin 1987: x).

The Westfield conference paved the way for the Association for History and Computing (AHC), which was formally established at a second event the following year. Like its initiating conference, the AHC was not just a UK endeavour, but it was largely a product of Western Europe. This is not to say that advances in digital history were not happening elsewhere on the continent. In 1992, for example, a conference was held in Uzhgorod, Ukraine, on 'New Information Technologies in Historical Research and Teaching', which brought together scholars from East and West in order to break down some of the barriers between the two. The published proceedings of this event (Borodkin and Levermann 1993) indicate that the barriers were certainly not those of interest, theory, or methodology but rather of opportunity.

The AHC's commitment to digital pedagogy alongside research was an important focus from the outset, and was reflected in developments elsewhere. These took two main forms, which continue to shape digital history in the early twenty-first century: using emerging technologies to teach more traditional history in the classroom; and training the next generation of digital historians. More interesting for the development of digital history, however, was the concern to equip historians with the knowledge and skills to use computers effectively in their research. One early, and ultimately rather short-lived, initiative was the launching of an MA in Computer Applications for History at the Institute of Historical Research, University of London, in the autumn of 1990 (Institute of Historical Research 1991). The list of approaches and techniques studied in the first course module is instructive for the state of the field in the early 1990s:

> The coding debate; alternative database systems; discipline-specific software; the declarative approach – artificial intelligence and expert systems; record linkage; family reconstruction; simulation and data modelling; communications; standardisation of databases; pictorial analysis; cartographic methods; the publishing of sources and of research; computers and the teaching and presentation of the past. (Institute of Historical Research 1990: 202)

The terminology might be different in some instances (pictorial rather than image analysis, for example), but it is notable how many of these methods and concerns continue to be central for digital history. There was also far less emphasis on text than might be expected, or indeed than might have characterized a course focusing on the digital humanities. Here we find the visual, the geographical, quantitative analysis, and statistical methods, even practical digitization. The connection with Westfield and the AHC is clear from the wide-ranging teaching offering, but more specifically from the personnel involved: two of the initial teams were from the newly formed Queen Mary and Westfield College, Virginia Davis and Peter Denley (Institute of Historical Research 1990: 203).

The new AHC organized workshops and annual international conference, but also launched a journal to showcase the best digital historical research. The first issue of *History and Computing* was published by Oxford University Press in 1989, and the journal ran for just fourteen years until 2002. In 2007 it re-emerged, published by Edinburgh University Press, but this time as a rather different beast, the *International Journal of Humanities and Arts Computing*. There was not, it would seem, sufficient demand for a periodical dealing solely with digital history, rather than with the wider humanities (and arts). And this was not unique either to the European academic environment or to the 1990s, as the journal of the American Association for History and Computing (AAHC), launched almost a decade later in 1998, also ceased publication after only thirteen years. However, as two of the very few publishing venues dedicated to history and computing at an important period in their development, it is not just their fate that is significant but the type of research that they published, and the subtle differences in emphasis.

In his editorial in the first issue of *History and Computing*, R. J. Morris poses the question 'Can an historical journal or magazine be based upon a technology?' His answer is an unqualified 'yes', for two reasons: first, the 'quantity and persistence' of enquiries from colleagues about history and computing suggested that the time was right to address them in a formal venue; but more importantly

this new technology does have an all-pervasive influence on the practice of history. It raises fundamental questions about methods and the evaluation of results. Indeed the very language with which many historians describe their craft has changed as they move from data capture, and databased [*sic*] construction, to record linkage, analysis and output. (Morris 1989: iii)

The editorial emphasizes the need to share knowledge and experience about the new technologies available to researchers, but also picks up on something which had emerged very clearly from the first Westfield conference, that 'the demands of the machine have revealed common issues of methodology and interpretation that range across centuries and continents'. Debate about the capacity of digitally afforded research to address large questions, and the value of such a macro-level approach to history, has been threaded through digital history from the start. The table of contents for this first issue also reflects the mix of the practical and the theoretical that has been another characteristic of digital history.

In the first issue of the *Journal of the Association for History and Computing* by contrast, Jeffrey Barlow's editorial concentrates not so much on research but on the mode of dissemination of that research. He is concerned with the move from print to electronic, from 'P-journal' to 'E-journal' as he describes it (Barlow 1998). The issue itself contains articles primarily on digital pedagogy, as well as on using the web and presenting information electronically. It is much more practical and classroom focused than its UK predecessor, which explicitly foregrounds research.

Differences in approach between North America and Europe can be traced further back too. In the United States, for example, there was a much greater emphasis on the development of digital projects and tools, and on digital history as making a vital (in both senses) contribution to public history. This is perhaps seen most clearly in the work of the Roy Rosenzweig Center for History and New Media (CHNM) at George Mason University, founded in 1994. Cohen and Rosenzweig's (2006) book serves as something of a manifesto for this approach, one which is profoundly shaped by the web. It is part practical guide, part rallying cry for the broadening of communication and debate about history through technology. The vision is a collaborative and participatory one, which expands the definition of historian beyond the university to embrace 'amateur enthusiasts, research scholars, museum curators, documentary filmmakers, historical society administrators, classroom teachers, and history students at all levels' (Cohen and Rosenzweig 2006: 2–3). It foreshadows not so much crowdsourcing as the interaction of academic researchers with 'citizen historians' in an exchange of knowledge and skills.[2] Today, the CHNM website summarizes its work in these terms: 'We create websites and open-source digital tools to preserve and present the past, transform scholarship across the humanities, advance history education and historical understanding, and encourage popular participation in the practice of history.' This is the arena in which digital history most closely intersects with public history.

While Cohen and Rosenzweig (2006) present an overwhelmingly positive view of digital history, like the founders of the AHC they strike a note of caution: 'Doing digital history well entails being aware of the technology's advantages and disadvantages, and how to maximize the former while minimizing the latter.' They identify five areas of particular concern, specifically 'quality, durability, readability, passivity, and inacessibility'. Unlike the AHC's early concerns about overblown claims for computational research, however, these 'dangers' are more connected to the technology itself and the way in which it alters production, but more importantly consumption.

The approach to digital history espoused by the CHNM, which is often strongly connected to libraries and the digitization of special collections, is apparent elsewhere in the United States. Seefeldt and Thomas (2009) link the rise of digital history from the 1990s onwards to the 'communication revolution' brought about by the advent of the web. They acknowledge the theoretical and methodological aspects of digital history, but conclude that 'to do Digital History ... is to digitize the past, certainly, but it is much more than that. It is to create a framework through ... technology for people to experience, read and follow an argument about a major historical problem.' Ideas of production and co-production are also present in this definition – institutions and individuals are working together to put a range of histories online. But it would be wrong to see this emphasis as a solely North American one. The relationship between public and digital history has recently occupied researchers in Italy and the Netherlands. The work of Noiret, for example, quite explicitly links public and digital history (see, among others, Noiret 2015), and even moves towards a quite distinct concept of digital public history. Similarly, Danniau, significantly an officer of the Royal Netherlands Historical Society, reflected on 'the dreams, practices and future for digital media for public history' (Danniau 2013: 118).

It is worth acknowledging here the role of funding, and funding bodies, in the development of digital history, and arguably in some of the focus on projects and tools. From the National Endowment of the Humanities (NEH) in the United States to the Arts and Humanities Research Council (AHRC) in the United Kingdom and the Centre national de la recherche scientifique (CNRS) in France, there have been a range of programmes promoting digital research in the humanities – and digital history has been a major beneficiary of this investment. The AHRC's Resource Enhancement Scheme, for example, which ran from 2000 to 2009, funded 195 projects of which 24 per cent are categorized as medieval and modern history (Dunning 2011). And the scheme had three very specific aims: 'To promote access to and availability of high-value research resources in the arts and humanities'; 'to support the development of high-level finding aids to research resources'; and 'to support the development of generic tools for use in the exploitation of research resources in the arts and humanities'. This is more about digital history as research infrastructure than as a new way of approaching historical research. Many of the projects which received Resource Enhancement funding have gone on to be transformative of the discipline in varying ways, the Old Bailey Proceedings Online being just one obvious example, but that was not the main purpose of the scheme which supported them.

The diversity of digital history

So it would seem that if anything can be said to characterize digital history it is diversity, a willingness to accommodate different methods and approaches and to cross boundaries. But digital history is not as fragmented, even inchoate, as this might suggest. This disparate set of activities can be organized into a number of overlapping categories: communicating history and historical data using digital tools, to fellow researchers, to the public and in a range of classroom settings; working with digital sources, both digitized and born digital; researching the history of the digital itself; and finally, deploying digital tools and methods to explore new ways of conducting historical research, even to ask new kinds of questions.[3]

Communicating history

The first of these brings together the pedagogical concerns of European history and computing and the democratizing impulse so apparent in the North American tradition.

It encompasses a diverse range of activity in widely differing contexts, and crucially, it is not confined to the academy. A simple, but effective example of this kind of digital history is the proliferation of historical figures with a lively and informative, if unlikely, presence on Twitter. Some are more or less parodic, but others represent significant underlying research and have a clear pedagogical as well as entertainment purpose.[4] A step beyond this are the digital exhibitions produced by museums, libraries, and university history departments and research centres. These may be aimed at school children, like the Museum of London's initiative to tell the story of the Great Fire of London using computer games and Minecraft, or present more complex ideas to an older audience, like the Bodleian Libraries' 'Marks of Genius', which explores attitudes to genius as manifested in books and manuscripts in their special collections. Major digital research projects frequently also have their own public engagement strands, which make use of digital technologies to communicate in novel and interesting ways and to reach new audiences.

Historical research has been performed in public, often before a wide audience, throughout most of the twentieth century, but digital tools, and in particular the web and social media, have changed the relationship between the historian and the reader or consumer. In the digital space, history need not be communicated from the top down, but may be shaped from below through interaction and increasingly co-creation (see note 2). There are a multitude of examples to choose from, but I will highlight just two here. First, there is the pioneering work of the Transcribe Bentham project at University College London. Its aim was to engage the public in helping to transcribe the manuscript papers of the eighteenth-century philosopher and reformer Jeremy Bentham, and at the same time to help volunteer transcribers acquire new historical research skills. The project's success is notable, not least because this is far from the most obvious material for a crowdsourcing initiative. The Bentham papers provide a serious challenge for the non-specialist: the content itself is intellectually complex, and there is the added problem of deciphering Bentham's handwriting. But it is this very difficulty, and the willingness of sufficient volunteers to engage with the task, which illustrates the potential of this way of working to alter how we think about the practice of digitally afforded history. At the other end of the spectrum lies a project like England's Past for Everyone (EPE), funded by the UK's Heritage Lottery Foundation from 2005 to 2010. Local history is an area where digital collaboration has proven to be particularly effective, and EPE was an early attempt to harness local knowledge and enthusiasm to create a national digital resource. While the legacy of the project is now largely an analogue one, with books outlasting interactive teaching resources, it too showed what digital history could bring to the study of the local.

Digital history is well suited to public engagement, and to the creation of impact, because more often than not it is at least partially accessible to a diverse and global virtual audience. This is not to emphasize numbers (downloads, visits, unique users), but to think imaginatively about how research enters people's lives online. Individuals and communities may interact with the results of digital history on public transport, in the garden on a summer's evening, or in a range of informal educational contexts. And it is one of the interesting challenges posed by digital history that this immediately takes scholarship beyond the control of its creator(s). There is much future research to be done into how people consume, remix, and reuse the outputs of digital history, and how this in turn influences its focus and development.

Working with digital sources

Perhaps the most reductive definition of digital history is that which defines it purely as research drawing on digital, or more correctly in this context, digitized primary sources. In this view, digital history is using Early English Books Online to research seventeenth-century sermons, or exploring the British Library Newspapers for references to a particular nineteenth-century member of Parliament. There can be no doubt about the transformative effect on historical research of the mass digitization of manuscripts, letters, books, newspapers, government records, diaries, and ephemera that has taken place over the past two decades (Meyer 2011; Tanner and Deegan 2011). To interrogate these materials, to make use of keyword searching, to benefit from carefully structured metadata, to engage (consciously or not) in distant reading (Moretti 2005, 2010) is, of course, to do digital history but it is far from the whole of digital history. The next step along the digital path is to comprehend how these digital objects have been created, how the searchable text has been generated, how much detail might have been lost during the imaging process, how the analogue original relates to its digital surrogate. This deep knowledge of how digitized data is created, and understanding of the human and machine processes involved, is essential if researchers are to move from being relatively passive recipients of digital information to being engaged digital historians. This is the point at which we go beyond simply doing the same kind of research more quickly and on a larger scale – two things incidentally which should not be dismissed – and begin to conceive of new types of research questions. As the history of digital history has shown, this has long been the ultimate aim – and one which can seem perennially unfulfilled.

What if the answer lies in the sources themselves, and specifically in the born-digital data with which historians are just beginning to work – the archived web, social media, emails, government file systems, personal digital archives held on computer hard drives? These sources pose enormous challenges for researchers, but they also have enormous potential. We cannot yet know how valuable they are, or will be to future historians – they are too large, too messy, sometimes simply too unknowable given the tools and methods available to us at present. The archive of UK web space from December 1996 to April 2013, for example, consists of more than 3.5 billion items, approximately 65 terabytes of data. And this will begin to look small: the full .uk domain crawl undertaken by the British Library in 2013 alone is roughly half the size of the data collected for the previous sixteen years, at 1.9 billion items and 30.84 terabytes. Simply harvesting all of this data took seventy days (Webber 2014). It is possible to get some sense of what is in the archive – a full-text search is now available via the British Library's SHINE interface, some derived datasets have been published which provide information about file types, and so on – but this is truly unexplored, and to an extent currently unexplorable territory.

We already have twenty years of the archived web, thanks to the work of the Internet Archive (IA), so for contemporary historians at least this is becoming a primary source which cannot be overlooked. It is hard to imagine how one would write a history of the developed world in the late twentieth and early twenty-first century which did not draw on web archives, which encompass so many different types of information produced by so many different types of content creators. While diversity of approach may make digital history rather hard to pin down, it is a necessary response to something as complex and varied as the archive of the web.

Archives will continue to collect paper records, of course, but what might once have been deposited in hard copy will increasingly only exist in digital form. This is true for government as for other kinds of data. A report produced by The National Archives of the UK notes the number of government departments likely to begin transferring born-digital material for archiving for the first time: 'The data collected indicates that, by 2016, there are expected to be 12 departments scheduled to transfer digital records, with an approximate total of 50 in 2021.' There is a very clear direction of travel here, and one with which historians are going to have to make an accommodation. And as with the archived web, this is very big and very messy data: for example, just 'one department had an email server that contained ½ billion emails' (The National Archives of the UK 2016: 5, 17). The business of government is going digital and historians will have to respond.[5] These questions arise not just for complex and large-scale textual data, but perhaps even more pointedly in relation to the ever-increasing volume of digital video and audio available online, from YouTube channels to podcasts produced by public service broadcasters; archived and emulated video games, like those preserved in the IA's Internet Arcade; software and executable code; digital art; virtual and augmented reality. Digital history, and digital historians, will have to adapt to meet the new theoretical and methodological questions posed by working with these and other data formats yet to be imagined.

The history of the digital

One of these adaptations will have to be a greater understanding of the technological contexts in which this data has emerged. A palaeographer knows how parchment and ink were produced in the thirteenth century, and so too the digital historian will be required to understand how the internet works and how algorithms are constructed. The history of the digital, of the web and associated communication technologies, has only emerged relatively recently as a concern for digital historians rather than for researchers working in the field of media and communications. This is perhaps necessarily the case – the web, after all, only came into being in 1989 – but there is a growing interest in our recent digital past. This can be seen in new research projects like Web90, which is 'Dedicated to French Heritage, Memories and [the] History of the Web in the 90s', and Ian Milligan's groundbreaking work on GeoCities (Milligan 2017); in the advent of new journals like *Internet Histories*, which is 'concerned with research on the cultural, social, political and technological histories of the Internet and associated digital cultures'; and in the publication of the first humanities monographs to deal with the web as history (e.g. Brügger and Schroeder 2017). Historians have never simply worked with text; they have understood how a manuscript has been produced or how a newspaper has been circulated, and what this means for any analysis of its content. The same is true for digital data and the social, cultural, and technical infrastructures which underpin its creation and transmission. To take just one example, historians will need to understand software emulation and what the addition of this intervening access layer means for our interpretation of the 'original' user experience (Anderson, Delve, and Powell 2012). Digital history has yet fully to embrace the potential of oral history in this area – and this is not just about interviewing pioneers in computing and technology, although that is, of course, important, but recording the experiences of people who played computer arcade games in the 1980s or used Facebook in the 2000s.[6] The rapid pace of technological change makes studies of this kind even more imperative.

Breaking new ground?

All of this suggests that the digital historian may be so busy learning new skills, struggling to keep up with new types of data and new types of tools, that they will have little time to do the groundbreaking research that has been the tantalizing promise of digital history from the outset. The range of tools and approaches available is daunting, and on the face of it ever more inaccessible to the majority of historians. It is one thing to learn how to apply the techniques of Geographic Information Systems (GIS), to use cloud-based tools like Voyant to undertake some basic topic modelling, even to learn how to construct simple regular expressions or write a basic Python script; it is quite another to begin to engage with machine learning or to deploy state-of-the-art social network analysis. But this is where the real innovation will be found in the future, in the interdisciplinary spaces between the data and computer sciences and history. This is not the place to rehearse old arguments about whether or not humanities researchers, and historians in particular, should learn to code. As is so often the case, the answer depends on what you would like to achieve, on the time available, and on personal interest and aptitude. What is more important, it seems to me, is to understand the possibilities (and limitations) of computational methods for historical scholarship; to be able to engage in productive dialogue and collaboration with researchers in other disciplines to answer historical questions; and to articulate the contribution of historians to digital research.

This inevitably moves digital history away from the individual towards a more team-based model – the kind of research encouraged by large funding programmes like the European Commission's Horizon 2020 scheme and the Trans-Atlantic Platform Digging into Data Challenge 2016. This is a very different way of working for most historians, but it is beginning to generate results which are suggestive of change not just in the scale but in the type of research that can be carried out. The work of Ruth and Sebastian Ahnert, a historian and physicist respectively, on Tudor letter (and power) networks is striking in its 'application of mathematical and computational techniques developed by scientists working in the field of complex networks' to a corpus of early modern letters. Increasingly typical of this kind of digital history, their research sheds important new light on Protestant networks, but also seeks to demonstrate 'how the discipline of network analysis can transform the way we interact with archives' (Ahnert and Ahnert 2015: 1, 32). Their findings are applicable to a particular early modern context but the method is extensible far beyond that. Other examples of innovation through collaboration include the Digital Panopticon project, which aims not only to investigate the punishment of men and women convicted at the Old Bailey from 1780 to 1925 but to 'develop new and transferable methodologies for understanding and exploiting complex bodies of genealogical, biometric, and criminal justice data'; and Digging into Linked Parliamentary Data, which brought together historians, computational linguists, and computer scientists to explore decades of parliamentary proceedings in three different countries, Canada, the UK, and the Netherlands. In the latter example, something as superficially simple (although in practice very complicated indeed) as securely identifying the gender, constituency, and party of each speaker in parliament, and associating this information with every speech, question, or interruption that they made, has opened up new avenues for linguistic, historical, and political research (Blaxill and Beelen 2016). Digital history is advancing historical research, but it is also shaping and being shaped by equally innovative work in other fields, within and outside the humanities. Innovation is not confined to these large-scale interdisciplinary research projects, but the work that is emerging from such initiatives, and the openness and transparency about tools and methods that they embrace, are seeding the smaller-scale innovation of the future.

It is also the case that innovation in digital history might look strangely familiar, as new technologies revivify old questions and approaches. The spectre of Cliometrics could be found in the bold statements made about Culturomics, and the arguments which swirled around its claims to extend 'the boundaries of rigorous quantitative inquiry to a wide array of new phenomena spanning the social sciences and the humanities' (Michel et al. 2010: 176). Here we go again, it would seem. However, there are very real discussions to be had about the potential of using digital tools and sources to return to the *longue durée*, to explore big history. This is one of the central arguments of *The History Manifesto*, which proposed that access to big data, and the tools with which to analyse it in increasingly sophisticated ways, might 'drive the social sciences towards larger and larger problems, which in history are largely those of world events and institutional development over longer and longer periods and time' (Guldi and Armitage 2015: 88–116). A special issue of the *Low Countries Historical Review* on 'Digital History', published in 2013, similarly includes an article discussing 'Big Data for Global History'. It is framed as demonstrating the 'Transformative Promise of Digital Humanities', but the concerns are demonstrably historical ones (van Eijnatten, Pieters, and Verheul 2013: 55). These arguments are very clearly rooted in digital history's past, with some of the same reasons to show caution, but the discussion has become more nuanced as the technology has advanced. Both the opportunities and the pitfalls are more apparent, and there remains room for a range of different approaches rather than a single all-encompassing quantitative solution. The potential of this kind of digital history, and the more measured claims for what it might be able to achieve, are very well illustrated in a recent study of 150 years' worth of digitized newspapers. In their introduction, the authors distance their research from previous studies 'based almost entirely on counting words, ignoring both semantics and context'. The aim is rather to use big data analysis to identify 'trends and changes, which might otherwise go unnoticed ... enabling a complementary approach with closer investigation by traditional scholars' (Lansdall-Welfare et al. 2017: 457–8).

If 'traditional scholars' are to engage fully with this kind of digital history they are going to have to expand their reading practice, to take in new publishing venues and journals that would never before have caught their attention. Digital history may be found in the pages of leading historical journals, although in truth it is yet to make much headway there, but it may equally be discovered in the *Proceedings of the National Academy of Sciences of the United States of America* or in *Digital Humanities Quarterly*. At present, the outputs of digital history do still generally assume a familiar form – the article or monograph – but that too is changing. The really transformative result of a digital project might be a piece of code, a new ontology, an interactive 3D model of a building, a virtual representation of a battle, or the sonification[7] of historical data. These will always have to be documented and described, and their importance discussed in academic journals, but it is the digital objects themselves that fully embody the research. The structures and assumptions which underpin scholarly communication will inevitably be challenged by these ways of working, by the products of digital history – but digital history can also provide some of the solutions and help to shape the way in which we consume historical research in the twenty-first century.

Conclusion

Digital history is so difficult to encapsulate both because it is still developing and because it quite legitimately means different things to different people in different settings. We have not yet had time to get distance on it, to step back and consider fully what it does and does not allow us to do. Nor has there been sufficient opportunity to evaluate what happens to those kinds of historical research, those kinds of sources, which are not quite so susceptible to digital analysis. It is still early days, but already we are all in a sense digital historians: it is increasingly rare to find a researcher who has never had cause to consult a digitized source; the use of digital secondary sources is now so commonplace as to be unremarked; the process of writing history has been transformed by similarly ubiquitous personal computers and word-processing software. An inclusive understanding of digital history encompasses this full spectrum of activity – historical research is generally digitally afforded – but it also expands to accommodate the historian as data scientist, working with data on an unprecedented scale and making use of the most sophisticated computational techniques currently available. As the pioneers of digital history were at such pains to point out, this is not a revolution in historical practice. It is, however, an opportunity to enhance existing knowledge and method through the use of new digital tools, the interrogation of new kinds of born-digital source, and the development of new, often interdisciplinary, digital approaches. Digital history will undoubtedly look very different ten or even five years from now, but there will also be continuity with the aims of the earliest practitioners to make use of the digital to learn, to teach, to collaborate, and to share. We are just beginning to work out how to start writing the history of the twenty-first century.

Comment

Steve F. Anderson

As I write this, a star-shaped bubble hovers in the margin of my screen, inviting me to explore resources that Google's recommendation engine has identified as potentially relevant to my work. This feature of the 'Google Docs' online writing application dubbed 'Explore' uses a machine intelligence algorithm to make connections between the words on the screen and a collection of dynamically generated online resources. At the moment, these suggestions seem obvious and unhelpful – the Wikipedia entry on Roberto Busa, a link to the Association for the Advancement of Artificial Intelligence, a *New York Times* article on the way linguistic metaphors structure thinking, and so on – but it is not difficult to imagine such a system growing exponentially more valuable the better it gets to know my own writing and that of my field: the links I follow, the sources I cite, the resources I attend to, and those I don't. Perhaps such a system could one day identify conceptual omissions and methodological shortcomings or offer genuine insights and alternative paths of investigation. Even if it is not currently useful, the innocuous but persistent presence of the Explore icon brings with it a subtle acculturation. In time, this may evolve towards an expectation that digital tools for writing would be incomplete without the capacity to recognize and expand the resources at an author's disposal.

All of this takes place in what is commonly known as 'the cloud', a mendacious euphemism for physically remote servers designed and operated by some of the world's richest technology corporations.[8] The purported immateriality of cloud computing makes it easy to imagine its affordances – speed, scale, ubiquity, interconnection – being seamlessly and irrevocably integrated into daily life. As the quality of recommendations suggested by Explore and its successors grows more sophisticated, we may begin to accept their suggestions as a natural part of the way we research and write, maybe even think. These, by extension, will shape the questions we ask about our world, present and past, all of which may ultimately make for scholarship that is better or worse than it was before. We may grow complacent and solipsistic within our scope of research or discover a depth and breadth of resources that would be difficult to access without computational assistance. Similar anxieties – as well as hopes for improvement – have accompanied each generation of technology at its moment of emergence, and predictable cycles of disruption, response, and equilibrium are easy enough to trace back through time.

This example also hints at the merging of human and machine intelligence that is already well under way both inside and outside of academia. Computational affordances for researching and writing are becoming encoded into the technologies available to historians at a level so basic as to barely invite comment. In the conclusion to her chapter 'Digital history', Jane Winters summarizes this state of affairs succinctly: 'Already we are all in a sense digital historians.' This statement exemplifies the author's even-handed survey of digital history that might otherwise veer towards hyperbole. Winters's reflections remain measured as she navigates meticulously between the twin declarations of doom and moral panic that often attend digital intrusions on existing academic fields. In Winters's view, the proliferation of digital tools and methods signifies neither the end of history nor its salvation.

Among Winters's most illuminating framings of digital history is the roughly concurrent rise of the 'digital humanities', an encompassing term that both benefits and suffers from fluid definitional boundaries. Where digital humanities yokes together multiple strategies of computational research and presentation, digital history has been perhaps unfairly anchored to the econometric modelling known as Cliometrics, which enjoyed a brief period of efflorescence in the 1960s and 1970s. Advocates of Cliometrics ultimately eroded their field's long-term viability by understating the limitations of computational analysis, resulting in a backlash that reasserted the primacy of human agency in historiography. While Winters looks hopefully to emerging technologies, she resists claims of newness, noting that 'innovation in digital history might look strangely familiar, as new technologies revivify old questions'. This allows readers to ponder more subtle aspects of the evolving relationship of human and machine intelligence, such as the difference between automation and augmentation.

A revealing example may be found in the work undertaken by the Jesuit priest Father Roberto Busa in the 1950s and 1960s. Winters describes Busa as 'doing what historians have always done, that is, making best use of the available tools and methods to answer particular questions; deploying technology to help him innovate and gain insight into his chosen subject'. Busa's concordance to the works of Thomas Aquinas, known as the *Index Thomisticus*, is among the most widely cited origin myths for the digital humanities, but it should be noted that this lineage better serves some visions of digital humanities than others. The service that IBM provided was essentially that of automating the most labour intensive aspects of processing Busa's meticulously encoded data set. As a historical paradigm, Busa's relationship with IBM was that of a client outsourcing the automatable parts of his research to a technical support team. IBM, in turn, viewed the project as a public relations opportunity at a time when computing was largely confined to business and industrial applications, far from the arts and humanities (see Jones 2016). This client-support model of Busa's *Index Thomisticus* has widely overshadowed competing visions of digital humanities focusing on the capacity of computers to augment human intelligence. Such augmentation takes place in a wide range of computationally enhanced modes of inquiry – examples cited by Winters include GIS-based historical mapping and environmental reconstructions using 3D modelling software – but also expressive possibilities that include the activation of multiple senses, embodiment, affect, interactivity, and so on, a mode of expression that Holly Willis (2015: 74) has termed the 'cinematic humanities'. In contrast, the type of automation offered by IBM – and followed by successive generations of humanities computing technicians – required researchers to reduce their objects of study to computable quantities, a constraint that significantly shaped the type of questions that may be asked.

Winters stops short of advocating the potential – or indeed the responsibility – for historians to participate directly in the design and development of the digital tools that subtend this aspect of their field. Such advocacy originates more natively within adjacent fields such as information science, where the analysis of tools and the development of critical paradigms for designing those tools are of central importance. In 2009 Johanna Drucker argued that 'if humanists are interested in creating in their work with digital technologies – the subjective, inflected, and annotated processes central to humanistic inquiry – they must be committed to designing the digital systems and tools for their future work' (Drucker 2009). I would support Drucker's statement, but as the most powerful tools for digital analysis grow orders of magnitude more complex, it raises practical issues of domain knowledge and the extent to which one trained in the humanities or social sciences is capable of meaningful, direct participation in the design of algorithms.

For her part, Winters notes that 'a palaeographer knows how parchment and ink were produced in the thirteenth century, and so too the digital historian will be required to understand how the internet works and how algorithms are constructed'. I agree with this statement as well, but in practice, the functioning of algorithms – especially those governed by the commercial logics of social media[9] – lies in the domain of proprietary trade secrets at too many commercial enterprises for such information to be readily available to scholars. And this says nothing of their capacity to engage and understand it. So, what is to be done? Winters deftly shifts the debate to the importance of 'understanding of the human and machine processes' underlying digitized history and points to the importance of conceiving new avenues of research, ultimately 'deploying digital tools and methods to explore new ways of conducting historical research, even to ask new kinds of questions'.

Although it seems foundational to the fields of 'humanistic inquiry' referenced by Drucker, prioritizing research questions over methods is not always a given for data-driven research. For pragmatic reasons, it is not uncommon for a digital history project tasked with 'Digging into Data' to proceed from an available data set or particular tool for analysis. Such projects must resist potentially deleterious effects of inverting the preferred sequence of selecting data, tools, and research questions. That is, the availability of 'data' and the tools to analyse it may point to achievable avenues of investigation, but these may or may not be the most urgent research questions to undertake.[10] A more productive sequence prioritizes research questions, which then motivate the collection of data and, if needed, development of tools and protocols for defining, capturing, and analysing it. Likewise, owing to the breadth of digital resources, domain knowledge is often productively supplemented through collaboration. Winters notes the interdependence of fields and investigations facilitated by digital methods. 'Digital history is advancing historical research, but it is also shaping and being shaped by equally innovative work in other fields, within and outside the humanities. Innovation is not confined to these large-scale interdisciplinary research projects, but the work that is emerging from such initiatives, and the openness and transparency about tools and methods that they embrace, are seeding the smaller-scale innovation of the future.' Ideally, there is a bidirectional relationship between the tools and methods for digital research and the potential for impact is broadened by approaches that are fundamentally open, extensible, and interoperable.

Along with recognizing the emergence of digital tools designed explicitly in service of scholarly research, digital historians would be well advised to remain attentive to the potentials of data captured for other purposes – say, commerce or law enforcement – to operate as unintended repositories of historical evidence. The US National Security Agency's metadata collection system known as PRISM and its counterparts in other national contexts are well known for their potential intrusions on privacy, but these are less frequently imagined as resources with historiographical significance. We have seen the power of tools designed for fine-grained analysis of shopping habits and political predispositions when applied to the massive data generated by users of social media networks. Why not apply similar, large-scale analysis to questions of cultural or historical consequence using the evidence gleaned from social behaviours tracked online? Even if we accept the need for temporal distance as a requirement for historical insight, it is still possible to imagine brushing existing data systems against the grain as a tactic to yield historical insight.

Digital history is both a part of daily life now and an ever-receding spectre on the technological horizon. Historians need to be ready for it, as Winters asserts, but also to take seriously the responsibility for developing technically sophisticated understandings of the way these powerful systems will develop in the future, ultimately holding them to the same standards of critical inquiry as their analogue predecessors. Winters follows this logic one step further to ask, 'What if the answer lies in the sources themselves, in the "born digital data" of social networks and the archived web?' Winters here adopts the convention of using biological metaphors to characterize data as something that is 'born' rather than defined and captured through instruments, algorithms, and systems, but her supposition remains worthy of serious consideration. Specifically, Winters refers to 'the potential of using digital tools and sources to return to the *longue durée*, to explore big history'. While evangelists for 'big data' aim to increase their profit margins with narratives of innovation and exception, Winters correctly notes the ebb and flow of micro- and macro-histories, which are as likely to be driven by ethical and political exigency as by advances in technology. At the same time, it must be admitted that the scale of data captured and stored by today's social networks, search providers, government security agencies, and telecommunications industries does not simply represent an amplification of previous tools of information technology. To understand the impact of such systems requires a significantly transformed conception of the relationship between this scale of digital information and its potential impact on the social world. Such questions may be best served by a method that resembles traditional historical research – with its concomitant rigour, scepticism, and ethical and evidentiary standards – but resulting in a mode of output that is adaptable based on the expressive needs of the analysis.

To this end, Winters admits to a refreshing range of unconventional historiographical practices and modes of output: 'The really transformative result of a digital project might be a piece of code, a new ontology, an interactive 3D model of a building, a virtual representation of a battle, or the sonification of historical data. These will always have to be documented and described, and their importance discussed in academic journals, but it is the digital objects themselves that fully embody the research.' This final phrase constitutes one of Winters's most provocative challenges for emerging genres of digital history. Hearkening back to debates related to film and history, it is very different to imagine the tools of digital history as offering mere supplements to conventional history than to imagine them constituting a new historiographical mode in their own right. As Winters suggests, it is as a self-sufficient embodiment at the conjunction of historiographical research and presentation that we find the most provocative possibilities for the future of digital history.

Present-tense accounts – for example, journalism or personal documentation – of events were once characterized as the 'rough draft' of history, awaiting the perspectival shift that accompanies integration into a retrospective historical narrative. Increasingly, history's 'rough draft' may reside in data that is collected, stored, and analysed across multiple spheres of everyday life. But as Lisa Gitelman argued in *Raw Data Is an Oxymoron*, it is precisely the purported objectivity of data that necessitates its most vigorous interrogation. In the book's introduction, she writes, 'At a certain level the collection and management of data may be said to presuppose interpretation … . Events produce and are produced by a sense of history, while data produce and are produced by the operations of knowledge production more broadly' (Gitelman 2013: 3). The emergence of digital tools for capturing, organizing, and analysing data on a massive scale highlights the need for sophisticated critical models for understanding these systems in relation to historical inquiry. Winters's articulation of 'digital objects' that 'fully embody the research' represents an important intervention into contemporary discourses of digital history.

In a culture addicted to – and overwhelmed by – digital information, history's contestation takes place in the design of tools for managing data and in the algorithms created to analyse it as much as in the interpretive narratives of historians, writers, and media makers. It is not just incumbent upon critics of history to understand and critique the functioning of these systems; this is the job of an informed, technologically literate citizenry as well. As access to information continues to be intentionally shaped by the predictive algorithms and echo chambers of social media (which are then available for exploitation by the highest bidder), awareness of the interdependence of ideology, economics, and technology becomes more imperative than ever. At stake in future manifestations of digital history is also the politics of the present. Winters' thoughtful and incisive treatment of the full spectrum of digital historiography – from access-oriented digitized collections to the cascade of digital information in the archived web – represents a necessary step towards a critically engaged, technologically empowered understanding of digital history.

Response

Jane Winters

Steve Anderson begins his thoughtful, and thought-provoking, comment by reflecting on the digital context within which his own research and writing takes place. Stepping back to think about what new (and not so new) digital technologies mean for the practice of history, both now and in the future, is something that we often fail to do: as Anderson notes, 'Computational affordances for researching and writing are becoming encoded into the technologies available to historians at a level so basic as to barely invite comment.' The apparent seamlessness with which digital technologies have been integrated into everyday life, and into all stages of the historical research process – from the first keystroke giving substance to a thought to the final publication of a book or article – is one reason why the very idea of 'digital' history can seem problematic. Why is the qualifier needed if all research, all history, is in some sense digital? Perhaps we will reach a point where referring to digital history seems quaint, a throwback to a time when we were still excited about the advent of each new digital tool, the publication of each newly digitized primary source. But we are not there yet: as Anderson emphasizes, we do not know where digital technologies will lead us – or conversely, how we might be able to shape or transform them for the purposes of historical analysis. Those 'twin declarations of doom and moral panic' are still very much present, alongside expressions of technological utopianism. This tension has been present throughout the short history of digital history, by whichever name it has been known. The response to overblown statements about disaster or transformation should not, however, be indifferent acceptance or the occlusion of the digital. Digital technologies may be affecting all of our daily interactions, both personal and professional, but that does not mean we should not think critically about the specific ways in which they influence how we 'do' history. The nature of digital history may be contested, but for the time being at least the term tells us something about historical research in the early twenty-first century.

Anderson usefully distinguishes between two very different approaches to digital research in humanistic fields: a 'client-support model' which relies on the outsourcing of complex computational work to technicians; and a model in which digital technologies are applied 'to augment human intelligence'. He sees the former as constraining the types of question that can be asked, even if the automation that it has allowed has been transformative in other ways, for example speed and scale. There are interesting implications here too for the skills that historians need to acquire to work in the digital space. Arguably, the large-scale collaborative projects that have produced some of the most interesting digital history in recent years rely precisely on the kind of outsourcing that Anderson views as limiting. They may be conceived as interdisciplinary – and some of the projects that I have described above really deliver on this promise – but there is often a moment of divergence, a hiving off the computational work. Koeser (2015) sums this up as 'Trusting Others to "Do the Math"': she acknowledges that at some stage in the research process this placing of trust in others becomes unavoidable, but it should not be done blindly. As Anderson rightly comments, however, intellectual curiosity and due diligence can only get you so far; and the limits may well be imposed by commercial actors. From Busa's reliance on IBM to the potential of the diverting Google Docs Explore feature, reliance on and partnership with business introduces opacity. Scholarly commitments to transparency and openness hit up against commercial imperatives and intellectual property; our ability to understand and explain is curtailed. This has clear implications for the reproducibility, or even feasibility, of some kinds of research. Data may be only partially released, withdrawn on a whim or simply discarded; tools may be discontinued once they have outlived their commercial usefulness or silently changed in ways which distort research.

While openness is to be applauded, I agree that it is not always an unalloyed good, particularly in an information environment distinguished by inequalities of access. Anderson notes that 'it is not uncommon for a digital history project … to proceed from an available data set or particular tool for analysis'. In this scenario, it is availability which determines the work to be undertaken and not the significance of the research questions. This may lead to an interesting re-flourishing of particular areas of study – in the UK, for example, the publication of the full text of Hansard under an Open Government Licence has facilitated several digital research projects[11] – but the risk of 'inverting the preferred sequence of selecting data, tools and research questions' is undoubtedly real. Historians have always had to work with what is available to them, but in the sense of what has survived rather than what is easiest for them to access and use.

Ease of use, of course, is not just about availability and permissive licensing. Anderson picks up on the problems posed by the sheer scale of the digital data that is already available to researchers, whether it is generated by government or by business. He rightly asserts that this unprecedented volume of information does not require simple 'amplification' of existing tools and methodologies, but a real adjustment in thinking, 'a significantly transformed conception of the relationship between this scale of digital information and its potential impact on the social world'. This is far from an uncritical acceptance of the claims made for 'big data', rather a call for the reconfiguration of humanities research to take account of a dramatically changing landscape. Vast quantities of born-digital data are part of this landscape, and, while it is always important to question terminology, I would argue for the value of 'biological metaphors' here. Data is indeed 'defined and captured through instruments, algorithms and systems', but humans are still very much present – as subjects of data collection, as data collectors/owners, as programmers, as systems administrators. Historians are well placed to remind society about the humans who are present in digital data, with their messy births, lives, and deaths.

Anderson draws on debates about film and history to consider whether it is possible 'to imagine the tools of digital history as constituting a new historiographical mode in their own right', rather than simply facilitating or supplementing 'conventional' research. I share his view that this is a challenge for digital history to explore if it is to remain relevant, a challenge to which it has so far largely failed to rise. His assertion that 'it is as a self-sufficient embodiment at the conjunction of historiographical research and presentation that we find the most provocative possibilities for the future of digital history' asks us to experiment, to risk failure, to move beyond well-established modes of scholarly communication. And I would suggest that the risk should not be left to researchers at the start of their careers, who almost always have more to lose by straying from well-trodden paths.

Finally, Anderson explicitly connects the digital history of the future with the 'politics [and economics] of the present'. If historians of the early twenty-first century fail to get to grips with the full complexity of the digital data ecosystem, he argues, the effects will be felt by their successors. This resonates strongly with my own experience of working with web archivists to inform the ways in which access to their collections will be mediated for humanities researchers. Decisions that are made now will influence how (if) born-digital archives are used in decades to come, and embedding understandings of their creation and collection will be essential. The combination of knowledge and skills required to do this effectively is new, even if it is underpinned by engrained modes of critical thinking and established disciplinary theoretical and methodological approaches.

As digital historians, perhaps the most that we can hope for is that current and emerging historical research practices do not close off new questions, even if we may be sceptical about the possibility of genuine novelty. The best way to achieve this is to embrace plurality and variety, to encourage work across 'the full spectrum of digital historiography', and to be open to collaboration across disciplines and sectors. Maybe ultimately 'digital' will cease to be meaningful in association with historical research, but I do like Anderson's acknowledgement that, while digital history is with us today, it is also 'an ever-receding spectre on the technological horizon'. The digital tools and data that we have now, the digital histories that we are able to write, will not remain static. There may always be a place for digital experimentation at the edges of current historical practice, and it may even continue to be described as digital history.

Notes

1. 'Distant reading', first advanced by Franco Moretti (2010), involves understanding literature not through the in-depth study of individual texts but through the analysis of data at scale. The approach need not, of course, be confined to literary studies.

2. The citizen science movement emerged at the beginning of the twenty-first century, and saw the engagement of large groups of volunteers to solve complex research questions, with each individual contributing at a micro level to the whole (Hand 2010). As this approach has begun to be applied to historical research – Zooniverse, one of the early citizen science initiatives, now lists nine history projects for example – the concept of citizen history, and the citizen historian, has begun to take shape.

3. In preparation for writing this article I conducted a Twitter survey, asking simply 'What does digital history mean to you?' This approach is, of course, entirely unscientific and involves a self-selecting sample, but the responses were nonetheless interesting. While diversity, and even confusion, were on display, most respondents agreed on at least one of these broad headings (Winters 2016).

4. Examples include Samuel Pepys (@samuelpepys), which is tweeting the diaries of Samuel Pepys in 'real time', and John Quincy Adams (@JQAdams_MHS), a project of the

Massachusetts Historical Society to tweet the diary of the US president at the rate of a line a day. This approach has also been taken to the communication of information about historical events, often in connection with major anniversaries. For example, on 1 July 2016, Cambridge University Library 'live tweeted' the first day of the Battle of the Somme as recorded in the diary of Siegfried Sassoon (Dixon 2016).

5. In the UK, for example, the Cabinet Office Technology Transformation programme has resulted in a move to cloud-based working using Google Apps. There are potentially very exciting possibilities for the historian here, such as the opportunity to see the entire production history of a document, but there are also daunting archival, access, and research challenges.

6. It is encouraging to see this beginning to change, for example with the work of Julianne Nyhan and Andrew Flinn (2016) on the history of humanities computing; Cathy Marshall on attitudes to the ownership and reuse of social media (2015 etc.); and the oral history programme of the Computer History Museum, Mountain View, California. It is, however, noteworthy that this research is not being conducted by historians.

7. Sonification involves representing data through sound other than speech. As with more traditional visualization, it can reveal underlying patterns and trends.

8. For an idiosyncratic and richly historicized critique of the ideologies of cloud computing, see Hu (2015).

9. The notion of social media logic is articulated in Van Dijk and Poell (2013).

10. Although not traditionally 'historical', several of the critical visualization projects undertaken by the Cultural Analytics research initiative founded by Lev Manovich exemplify this tendency. For a more nuanced critique, see my subsection 'Analyzing Cultural Analytics' in Anderson (2017).

11. For example, Digging into Linked Parliamentary Data (https://dilipad.history.ac.uk/) and the Hansard Corpus: British Parliament 1803–2005 (http://www.hansard-corpus.org/; part of the SAMUELS project) were both funded in 2014.

References

Ahnert, R. and Ahnert, S. E. (2015), 'Protestant Letter Networks in the Reign of Mary I: A Quantitative Approach', *English Literary History*, 82 (1): 1–33.

Anderson, D., Delve, J. and Powell, V. (2012), 'The Changing Face of the History of Computing: The Role of Emulation in Protecting Our Digital Heritage', in A. Tatnall (ed.), *Reflections on the History of Computing*, 362–84, Berlin and Heidelberg: Springer.

Anderson, S. F. (2017), *Technologies of Vision: The War Between Data and Images*, Cambridge, MA: MIT Press.

Arts and Humanities Research Board (n.d.), 'Guide to the Resource Enhancement Scheme', available online: http://web.archive.org/web/20001006075845/http://www.ahrb.ac.uk/research/enhancement/index.htm (accessed 6 October 2016; captured 28 October 2000).

Barlow, J. G. (1998), 'Editorial: Why an Electronic Journal in History and Computing?', *Journal of the Association of History and Computing*, 1 (1), available online: http://quod.lib.umich.edu/j/jahc/3310410.0001.109/--editorial-statement?rgn=main;view=fulltext (accessed 30 September 2016).

Blaxill, L. and Beelen, K. (2016), 'A Feminized Language of Democracy? The Representation of Women at Westminster since 1945', *Twentieth Century British History*, 27 (3): 412–49.

Bodleian Libraries (2015), 'Marks of Genius: Masterpieces from the Collections of the Bodleian Libraries', available online: http://genius.bodleian.ox.ac.uk/ (accessed 21 December 2016).

Borodkin, L. I. and Levermann, W. (1993), 'Introduction', in L. I. Borodkin and W. Levermann (eds), *History and Computing in Eastern Europe*, 1–5, St. Katharinen [Göttingen]: Max Planck-Institut für Geschichte In Kommission bei Scripta Mercaturae Verlag.

Bridenbaugh, C. (1963), 'The Great Mutation', *American Historical Review*, 68 (2): 315–31.

Brügger, N. and Schroeder, R. (2017), *The Web as History: Using Web Archives to Understand the Past and the Present*, London: UCL Press, available online: https://www.ucl.ac.uk/ucl-press/ browse-books/the-web-as-history (accessed 7 October 2016).

Cliometric Society, 'About the Cliometric Society', available online: http://cliometrics.org/about. htm (accessed 21 July 2016).

Cohen, D. J. and Rosenzweig, R. (2006), *Digital History: A Guide to Gathering, Preserving, and Presenting the Past on the Web*, Philadelphia, PA: University of Pennsylvania Press.

Danniau, F. (2013), 'Public History in a Digital Context: Back to the Future or Back to Basics?', *Low Countries Historical Review*, 128 (4): 118–44.

Denley, P. and Hopkin, D. (1987), 'Introduction', in P. Denley and D. Hopkin (eds), *History and Computing*, ix–x, Manchester: Manchester University Press.

Dixon, J. (2016), 'Live Tweeting the First Day of the Somme from the Diary of Siegfried Sassoon', *Cambridge University Library Special Collections*, available online: https://specialcollections. blog.lib.cam.ac.uk/?p=12810 (accessed 21 December 2016).

Drucker, J. (2009), 'Blind Spots: Humanists must Plan their Digital Future', *The Chronicle of Higher Education*, 3 April, available online: http://www.chronicle.com/article/Blind-Spots/ 9348 (accessed 27 June 2017).

Dunning, A. (2011), *List of Digitisation Projects Funded under UK's AHRC Resource Enhancement Scheme*, available online: http://eprints.rclis.org/17517/ (accessed 21 December 2016).

Floud, R. (1973), *An Introduction to Quantitative Methods for Historians*, Princeton, NJ: Princeton University Press.

Gitelman, L. (2013), *Raw Data is an Oxymoron*, Cambridge, MA: MIT Press.

Greenstein, D. and N. Morgan (1989), 'Software for Historians?', *History and Computing*, 1 (1): 38–41.

Guldi, J. and Armitage, D. (2015), *The History Manifesto*, Cambridge: Cambridge University Press, available online: http://historymanifesto.cambridge.org/ (accessed 26 September 2016).

Hand, E. (2010), 'Citizen Science: People Power', *Nature*, 466, 685–7, available online: http:// www.nature.com/news/2010/100804/full/466685a.html (accessed 6 October 2016).

Hitchcock, T. (2016), 'The Digital Humanities in Three Dimensions', *Historyonics*, available online: http://historyonics.blogspot.co.uk/2016/07/the-digital-humanities-in-three.html (accessed 26 September 2016).

Hockey, S. (2004), 'The History of Humanities Computing', in S. Schreibman, R. Siemens and J. Unsworth (eds), *A Companion to Digital Humanities*, Oxford: Blackwell.

Hu, T.-H. (2015), *A Prehistory of the Cloud*, Cambridge, MA: MIT Press.

Institute of Historical Research (1990), 'M.A. in Computer Applications for History', *Historical Social Research / Historische Sozialforschung*, 15 (4): 201–5, available online: http://www.jstor. org/stable/20754537 (accessed 30 September 2016).

Institute of Historical Research (1991), *Annual Report, 1 August 1990–31 July 1991*, London: Institute of Historical Research.

Jones, S. E. (2016), *Roberto Busa, S. J., and the Emergence of Humanities Computing: The Priest and the Punched Cards*, New York: Routledge.

Koeser, R. S. (2015). 'Trusting Others to "Do the Math"', *Interdisciplinary Science Reviews*, 40 (4): 376–92.

Lansdall-Welfare, T., Sudhahar, S., Thompson, J., Lewis, J, FindMyPast Newspaper Team and Cristianini, N. (2017), 'Content Analysis of 150 Years of British Periodicals', *Proceedings of the National Academy of Sciences of the United States of America*, 114 (4): 457–65.

Lyons, J. S., Cain, L. P. and Williamson, S. H. (2007), 'Introduction: Economic History and Cliometrics', in J. S. Lyons, L. P. Cain and S. H. Williamson (eds), *Reflections on the Cliometrics Revolution: Conversations with Economic Historians*, 1–42, London: Routledge.

Marshall, C. C. and Shipman, F. M. (2015), 'Exploring the Ownership and Persistent Value of Facebook Content', in *Proceedings of the 18th ACM Conference on Computer Supported Cooperative Work and Social Computing*, 712–23, New York: ACM Press.

Meyer, E. T. (2011), *Splashes and Ripples: Synthesizing the Evidence on the Impacts of Digital Resources*, Jisc Report, May 2010, available online: https://papers.ssrn.com/sol3/papers.cfm?abstract_id=1846535 (accessed 21 December 2016).

Michel, J.-B., Shen, Y. K., Aiden, A. P., Veres, A., Gray, M. K., Google Books Team, Pickett, J. P., Hoiberg, D., Clancy, D., Norvig, P., Orwant, J., Pinker, S., Nowak, M. A. and Aiden, E. L. (2010), 'Quantitative Analysis of Culture Using Millions of Digitized Books', *Science*, 331 (6014): 176–82.

Milligan, I. (2017), 'Welcome to the Web: The Online Community of GeoCities and the Early Years of the World Wide Web', in N. Brügger and R. Schroeder (eds), *The Web as History: Using Web Archives to Understand the Past and the Present*, London: UCL Press, available online: https://www.ucl.ac.uk/ucl-press/browse-books/the-web-as-history (accessed 7 October 2016).

Moretti, F. (2005), *Graphs, Maps, Trees: Abstract Models for a Literary History*, London and New York: Verso.

Moretti, F. (2010), *Distant Reading*, London and New York: Verso.

Morris, R. J. (1989), 'Editorial', *History and Computing*, 1 (1), iii–vi.

Noiret, S. (2015), 'Historia digital e historia pública', in J. A. Bresciano and T. Gil (eds), *La historiografía ante el giro digital: reflexiones teóricas y prácticas metodológicas*, 41–76, Montevideo: Ediciones Cruz del Sur.

Nyhane, J. and A. Flinn (2016), *Computation and the Humanities: Towards an Oral History of Digital Humanities*, Cham: Springer Open, available online: http://www.springer.com/us/book/9783319201696 (accessed 27 December 2016).

Schreibmann, S., Siemens, R. and Unsworth, J. (2016), 'Preface', in S. Schreibman, R. Siemens and J. Unsworth (eds), *New Companion to Digital Humanities*, 2nd edn, xvii–xviii, Oxford: Blackwell.

Seefeldt, D. and Thomas, W. G. (2009), 'What is Digital History?', in *Perspectives on History: The Newsmagazine of the American Historical Association*, available online: https://www.historians.org/publications-and-directories/perspectives-on-history/may-2009/intersections-history-and-new-media/what-is-digital-history (accessed 30 September 2016).

Svensson, P. (2009), 'Humanities Computing as Digital Humanities', *Digital Humanities Quarterly*, 3 (3), available online: http://digitalhumanities.org:8081/dhq/vol/3/3/000065/000065.html (accessed 31 December 2016).

Tanner, S. and Deegan, M. (2011), *Inspiring Research, Inspiring Scholarship: The Value and Benefits of Digitised Resources for Learning, Teaching, Research and Enjoyment*, Jisc Report, available online: https://www.kdl.kcl.ac.uk/fileadmin/documents/Inspiring_Research_Inspiring_Scholarship_2011_SimonTanner.pdf (accessed 21 December 2016).

The National Archives of the UK (2016), *The Digital Landscape in Government 2014–15: Business Intelligence Review*, available online: http://www.nationalarchives.gov.uk/documents/digital-landscape-in-government-2014-15.pdf (accessed 22 December 2016).

Van Dijk, J. and Poell, T. (2013), 'Understanding Social Media Logic', *Media and Communication*, 1 (1): 2–15.

Van Eijnatten, J., Pieters, T. and Verheul, J. (2013), 'Big Data for Global History: The Transformative Promise of Digital Humanities', *BMGN – Low Countries Historical Review*, 128 (4): 55–77.

Webber, J. (2014), 'How Big is the UK Web?', *UK Web Archive Blog*, available online: http://britishlibrary.typepad.co.uk/webarchive/2014/06/how-big-is-the-uk-web.html (accessed 22 December 2016).

Willis, H. 2015. 'Writing Images and the Cinematic Humanities', *Visible Language*, 49 (3): 62–77.

Winters, J. (2016), 'What Does "Digital History" Mean to You?' available online https://wakelet.com/wake/755ec944-be79-43f7-8660-bd4b0dc90bcc (accessed 7 October 2016).

CHAPTER 11
NEUROHISTORY
Rob Boddice

Why do practices and experiences have unstable historical meanings and values? The question leads us to the truth of individual perception. Rather than looking for what actually happened, neurohistorians are looking for how things actually *seemed*. In this they share much in common with cultural historians, but neurohistorians make cultural historical claims more concrete. Neuroscientific developments have emphasized the plasticity of the human brain and the dynamic relationship among context, brain, and experience. This insight can be employed by historians to argue that individual or group perceptions are not mere points of view or subjective perspectives on an objective reality, but rather reliable statements of reality as it was experienced. Neurohistorians underwrite social construction with a demonstrable relationship between context and brain.

The pursuit of the history of experience has been given its 'hunting license' (Reddy 2015) by the last ten years of a certain strand of neuroscientific research.[1] It attests to the contingency and the mutability of experience. This chapter will lay out the intellectual and scientific justifications for neurohistory, showing both where it has come from and where it might go, and addressing along the way the refinements that have taken place in its first years of existence. It will, out of necessity, have to dwell on the neuroscientific research that has made neurohistory possible, which, I would guess, is unfamiliar to the vast majority of historians. But this diversion should not be off-putting. I include it to provide neurohistory's guiding compass, not because historians themselves have to be particularly literate in neuroscience, since neurohistory is not, in my estimation, a particularly brain-centred approach to the past.[2] Rather, it is an approach to the past that is cognizant of the evidence for brain plasticity in human development, and of the ways in which context is instrumental in the construction of experience, at a neurochemical level. I will argue that these things change the register of archival interpretation, from metaphor to literalism.

It is fitting that Daniel Lord Smail, the originator of neurohistory, is the respondent for this chapter. Smail pioneered the idea of neurohistory in his 2008 book *On Deep History and the Brain*, introducing historians to the implications of evolution – especially the evolution of human neuroplasticity – and the broad implications of psychotropics – any stimulus that alters the brain's chemistry and with it human perception – for the first time. The project laid out by Smail not only explains how new emotions, experiences, and behaviour might emerge (and disappear), but also the extent to which the neurological complex that lies at the heart of experience is directly hitched to social practices and social institutions. We can no longer think in terms of nature and nurture, but only in terms of bioculture, which is not immune to history, but mutable (see Smail 2014a;

cf. Cooter 2014: 145). This observation radically alters our perception of what humans and human brains are.[3] Though I will address Smail's contribution in due course, I want, at first, to show how, through the history of pain, I came to a neurohistorical understanding of past experience myself, independent of Smail's book. There is value in this, I think, for in this way the whole argument does not stand or fall on Smail's own conception of neurohistory.

Mutable pain and the dynamics of emotion

At the forefront of contemporary pain research I identify four key principles, all of which might sound surprising to the non-expert. (1) Physical injury is not directly correlated with pain intensity, does not determine pain, and might not be painful at all. (2) No two pain experiences are alike: the same person might experience the same stimulus differently at different times in the day; across cultures, classes, ethnicities, and genders, pain experiences are different. There is no universal measure of pain, or a pain standard. (3) The experience of pain in humans is absolutely dependent on affective activation of the brain, without which an injury has no meaning. (4) The same kind of affective activation can occur without any injury at all, suggesting that so-called 'social pain' or 'emotional pain' is, in fact, the same kind of event that we usually ascribe to bodily injury.[4] In consideration especially of points 3 and 4, I have argued (Boddice 2014, 2017) that pain is most usefully considered to be an emotion.

The first two points, which have been confirmed many times over through empirical and controlled studies, suffice to demonstrate that the experience of pain cannot be reduced to a science of sensitivity or of bodily damage. Points 3 and 4, however, lead us to an explanation of *why* human experience is irreducible to mechanical explanations. The key phenomena here help us to understand the brain's role in producing painful experience, which in turn will lead us to generalize further on the neurohistorical implications of brain plasticity.

The first of these phenomena is 'pain asymbolia', a condition marked by an individual's lack of capacity to ascribe meaning to injury or danger. The bare sensory capacity to detect a change in bodily state is present. A person with pain asymbolia might be able to detect compression or heat, for example, but a failure in the affective activation of the brain means that there is no capacity to attach value to compression or heat. Such a person is indifferent to harm and does not react to injury or the potential for injury in ways one might otherwise expect. A broken foot is not protected by a limp. The danger inherent in an onrushing vehicle as someone crosses a street is not detected. The hand being burnt by a flame is not pulled away (Grahek 2007; Wall 2002: 49–51).

The second phenomenon is 'social pain'. Naomi Eisenberger (2003) and her team ran experiments on the impact of the brain on feelings of social exclusion. Participants in a social game who were deliberately excluded were shown to have similar neural affective responses to those who experienced pain from physical injury. The conclusion drawn is that social pain, or emotional pain, is of the same order of phenomenon as painful injury.

Being bullied, ostracized, or bereaved is experientially comparable to bodily injuries that result in pain.

Taking both these strands together, we can conclude that the meaningfulness of pain is derived affectively. In turn this means that the meaning of pain is contextual, for the fear, anxiety, and perception of danger that accompany an injury or a circumstance of social exclusion are based on learnt (cultural) understandings of threat, inclusion, attachment, and so on. Context and attention can radically alter the way a stimulus is evaluated. That is why a stimulus that might look painful is experienced as pleasure, or as nothing at all. There are, for example, many well-documented cases of gun-shot victims who do not realize that they have been shot (Wall 2002: 5–7).

How and why injury does often result in pain holds an illustrative key to understanding neuroplasticity, for it shows how people conceive of themselves as bodies, or how we can say, when something is happening to our bodies, that it is happening to *us*. The essential ingredient to an understanding of how pain, or other sensory experience, works is to disassociate experience with anything intrinsic to objects in the world. No matter what the state of damaged nerves in the periphery of the body, pain is not inherent to this damage. Neuroscientists now understand individuals to have a 'neuromatrix' that produces a 'neurosignature' of the body. This is the 'image' or 'pattern' of the body that is understood as the *self*. The neurosignature is always there and is genetically programmed, but it is also plastic. The neurosignature makes experience out of the sensory information the brain receives from the periphery. This information both feeds and makes the neuromatrix according to a whole raft of variables. Sensory inputs, from the skin, from optic and auditory sources, account for some of these variables. These are intermixed with affects and emotions, made in and through culture and cultural experience. Body parts too have designated meanings or values ascribed to them, as do their organization into gestures, movements, and postures. Many of these movements and positions are themselves responses to cultural prescription and experience. All are processed together in the brain and, in the language of Ronald Melzack (2005), who first imagined the neuromatrix, 'arranged' into a symphonic output that adds up to what we know of as the body-self.

The major significance of this theory is that it gives credence to highly individual experiences of reality that have mystified researchers. Those suffering from phantom limb pain, for example, perplexed physicians for centuries (Price and Twombly 1978; Bourke 2014; Witte 2014). A phantom limb is experienced as present, and sometimes extremely painful, even though the limb in question is missing. This is now understood as a result of a disruption of the neurosignature (Melzack 2005; cf. Vaso et al. 2014). The neuromatrix might command the missing limb to move, a command sent with increasing amplification because there is no modulating response from the periphery. This is often experienced as muscle cramp in the absent limb.

To a person with phantom limb pain, both the experience of the missing limb and the pain in it are real. Treatment involves attempting to modify the neurosignature so as to change that reality. In other words, the solution pertains to brain plasticity. Work in this regard has led to evidence that individuals can purposefully control parts of their brains that have become associated with physical pain. Similar experiments have shown that the brain activity associated with motor functions can be reproduced even without making the associated bodily movement. Under controlled circumstances, neuroscientists are exploring the extent to which they can provide evidence for something we talk about casually all the time: we can control our emotions, our affective responses to sensory stimuli, and the brain activity associated with movement (Zeidan et al. 2012; Cair 2007; deCharms et al. 2004; Haller, Birbaumer, and Veit 2010). Our experience of the world is, to some extent, subject to our autonomous control.

Words, emotions, experience

Current best practice in the clinical setting is to give credibility to the subjectivity of the person in pain. The pain is wherever and whatever the patient says it is. There is no empirical reality of the person's pain beneath this level, irrespective of any mechanical problems that might exist. Treatment does not overlook first-hand testimony and search instead for the underlying mechanics of the problem. Management of pain begins when the sufferer's account of it is first believed. What happens if we apply this principle historically?

To take people at their word about their experience of pain is, in my estimation, to entertain a radical historical revisionism. Whole rafts of myth and metaphor re-emerge as credible reporting. What seem like strange phenomena that we tend to want to explain *away* become strange in a new light and demand that we simply try to *explain*. The ecstatic pain of sixteenth-century Spanish mystic Teresa of Avila; the virtuosity of disciplinary pain and self-flagellation of medieval Catholic orders; the pleasurable pain of Sacher-Masoch; the cosmological acceptance of pain among Hindu or Buddhist ascetics – all these things and many more besides become explicable not as othered curios or cultural glosses on universal and biologically determined psycho-physiological mechanics. If social pain is entertained as *real* pain, then profoundly important histories of social exclusion, or even the fear of social exclusion, also take on an entirely new significance at the level of the history of experience. They become explicable as past historical realities of experience, alien, perhaps, to us, but no less *real* for that. Importantly then, this revisionism is not limited to pain. If it is accepted that the value of pain lies in the contextuality of affective activation, then we might extrapolate that all affective experience is similarly made.

Worlds of pain therefore give way to worlds of emotion and experience in general. The contingency and vicissitudes of experiences of pain suggest the extent to which experience itself is mutable. If we feel safe enough to throw out the old aphorism about pain being the great human universal, then what else might we throw away? This kind of impetus activated the research of Lisa Feldman Barrett (2006a, 2006b; Gendron and Barrett 2009) as she tried to unlock the contingency of emotional experience, against the grain of psychological work that insisted on fixed values for 'basic emotions' and a direct correlation between automatic affects and automatic facial expressions, across time and across cultures.[5] It is no longer the case that we turn to the neurosciences to find out the transhistorical and universal qualities of the brain. On the contrary, we turn to the neurosciences to find out what proportion of the brain's development happens in the world, through culture. Human encounters with each other, with objects and technology, and with spaces and places, all continually write to the brain and help to constitute the meaningfulness of who and what we are.[6] This is particularly important in childhood (and therefore also in the history of childhood), where the objects of play and learning, and the styles and forms of interaction are massively influential on the development of the brain.[7]

In a series of landmark papers, Feldman Barret and her colleagues have demonstrated that there is no universal relationship between facial expressions and affective states, going on to show that facial expressions themselves are tied to languages of expression and reception that help shape experience. Emotion words, in all their myriad linguistic varieties over time and place, are dynamically involved in the formation of our perception of affective states themselves. The same could be said for physical expressions and the whole range of gestures and postures that help us know the emotional context of any situation. Taken together, these are not utterances and movements fixed and determined by an unchanging biology, but practices and vocabularies learnt in context. These neuroscientific insights are confirming both the historical-anthropological theory of 'emotives' developed by William Reddy (1997) and the historical practice theory about emotions put forward by Monique Scheer (2012), both of which explicitly emphasize the historicity of experience.[8] What we say and what we do with our bodies are parts of a process of working out what to feel, how things *are*.

Genetics

It is perhaps counterintuitive that such arguments draw upon evolutionary biology, but that field does play a supporting role in neurohistorical analysis. The key argument from evolutionary theory, for historians, is that evolutionary adaptations that took place through natural selection came bundled with other uses that went beyond the initial reason for the adaptation's selection. Individual examples of this are called 'exaptations'. Culture itself can be considered as such. McGrath (2017: 133) gives the example of recreational sex as an exaptation: procreation would be the evolutionary reason for the selection of traits that make sex part of human life; but, as he points out, recreational sex also 'secures social bonds and reproduces cultural desires', both of which are beyond the natural-selection explanation for sex, but which have themselves become factors in additional selection. The conclusion to be drawn is that culture is a product of evolution and, moreover, becomes a part of the 'natural' world in which further adaptations are selected. The brain, and whatever the brain produces, is not exempt from these forces. McGrath (2017: 133) summarizes as follows: 'For practitioners of neurohistory, the repeated behaviors comprising cultural relations reciprocally influence the brain's plasticity – a process called the "Baldwin effect." Neurons are wired to a social context. Changes in culture take place within and through the brain's continuous evolution.' There is also an essential dynamic to be added here, which is to say that the brain's continuous evolution takes place within and through cultural change. They are each other's cause and effect. This is not to emphasize circularity, but a fundamental *dynamism*.[9]

If cultural relations literally *make* the brain – new synaptic connections are being made in the crucible of everyday interactions – then we cannot presume to understand, *a priori*, what past experience of different cultures was like. We certainly cannot presume that our own experiential register is appropriate for judging how it felt to be an historical actor. Doubt is further enhanced by that neurobiological knowledge that tells us that missing limbs feel present, and by experiments that show how experiences can be processed in the brain even if they are not objectively happening in the world. To compound this further still, we must not only think of human evolution in terms of what is commonly known as 'evolutionary time'. Human life is constantly evolving, at a micro-evolutionary level. Cultural adaptation and innovation, including technological change, radically alters what humans do and how humans interact. Such changes in practice and exchange inevitably effect how the brain develops. We are, in a profound sense, our worlds.

'Genes' are often on people's lips. It is common to speak of genetic programming and of genetic dispositions. How we are is how we are written in our DNA. At best that is a very partial statement. Genetic expression is dependent on a range of factors, chemical and environmental, as well as cultural. There is little evidence that behaviour is genetically programmed. We are not, and certainly our emotions are not, reducible to our DNA.

One could also go further along the genetic route. New research in epigenetics has the potential to impact historiography in profound ways. As geneticists continue to build their understanding about the ways in which the experience of parents can effect gene expression in their offspring, the more alive we become to the possibility of epigenetic history. We are not dealing here with the inheritance of acquired characteristics in a Lamarckian sense, or in the sense of substantial changes in DNA that become heritable. Rather, epigenetics looks at the protein packaging of genetic material, and the effect on gene expression of environmental and experiential impacts on this packaging. We are beginning to understand that extreme experiences, especially prolonged ones, such as famine, warfare, and poverty, can have an effect that is bequeathed to offspring that impacts gene expression and the body's physiological stress reaction (specific findings on the epigenetic inheritance of stress were found by Weaver et al. 2004; Dietz et al. 2011). Though it would be difficult to say exactly how such effects would alter experience at the individual level, we might be able to see signs of them at the societal level, looking at aggregate changes in the ways in which associations are formed and interpreted and experience is mediated and recorded.

As genetics takes a social turn, so historians can turn to it. The history of stress, for example, offers a fruitful avenue of exploration, for the concept has both emotional and physiological connotations, which are necessarily connected. We know that the experience of pain in infancy directly effects the way in which the body handles physiological stress and the production of cortisol, the body's stress hormone, in later life, and that infant pain is correlated with the occurrence of adult anxiety disorders

(Page 2004). The development of the phenotype does not follow a simple computer programme or the determined sequences of genetic code (see, for example, Véron and Peters 2011). Neural and synaptic development in infancy seems to have a significant impact on the way in which stimuli are experienced in later life. A science of touch has demonstrated that infants exposed to the reassuring touch of a parent in early life go on to have decreased risk of anxiety, chronic pain, depression, as well as decreased risk of what might seem like socio-economic diseases, such as heart disease, obesity, and so on (Meany 2001; Weaver et al. 2004; cf. Manning 2007: xi). The dynamic interaction of touch as a meaningful act – a caress, a punch – directly impacts the way the body develops its physiological stress responses. We are being physically made, *constructed*, after birth. And insofar as we are being physically made, we are also being affectively made: the emotions do not exist immaterially, but are part of the development of brain function. How we are expressed as individuals, therefore, has a lot to do with the world in which we find ourselves. Epigenetic influences promise to further develop this study, as we hone the possibilities for biocultural history that has emotions at its heart (see, for example, Cheung and Lau 2005).

Smail's model

If there is an element in Smail's (2008) work that does not sit well with historians, it is his adherence to something so historically 'deep' that, from the perspective of most historians, it sounds like a transhistorical universal. This uneasiness is compounded by Smail's recourse to a basic-emotions model. 'Many of the things we do', he writes, 'are shaped by behavioural predispositions, moods, emotions, and feelings that have a deep evolutionary history.' He argues that things like emotions and pain are 'physiological entities, characteristically located in specific parts of the brain and put there by natural selection', and that they are 'relatively automated' (2008: 113). In what follows I want to show how we can – must – extricate neurohistory from this model although, in so doing, we leave Smail's framework otherwise largely intact.

There are good grounds to object to the idea that emotions and pain, among other things, have been 'put there' by 'nature', and operate basically automatically. Smail himself qualifies all of this in due course, but the looming large of 'nature' and automation suggest a pre-cultural background to the human being, which always begs the question of what a human being without culture is. Smail himself is well aware of the false dichotomy between nature and culture, and yet the tension remains. While Smail is one of the few historians to incorporate genetics into historiographical practice, he walks a fine line when working out exactly where historians should enter the genetic debate. At what point can we say that evolutionary biology is not the principal agent of change, but culture is? That there is a line, is clear enough:

Genes alone are not enough to build deep grammar or a theory of mind in the absence of specific developmental experiences. These developmental experiences are not only environmental; they are also cultural. In this way, culture can actually be wired in the human body. Since cultures change, human psychologies, in principle, can differ greatly from one era to the next. (Smail 2008: 131)

So far so good, but Smail leaves room for concessions in the direction of evolutionary psychology, in the laying down of 'basic fears, urges, and other predispositions'. He insists on a 'universal biological substrate that simply cannot be ignored' (2008: 113–4). Why not? What if we reject reference to this 'universal' entirely? How relevant is it, and how universal can it really be said to be, when the meaning of existence is so culturally bound?

Smail's argument does in fact tend in this direction. In his striving for balance, it is not always clear where a neurohistorian should draw the line between biological, genetic fixity and cultural development. As Smail (2008: 144) says, 'A neurohistorical approach suggests the possibility of significant changes over time in the social distribution of cognitive modules as an effect of cultural, not biological, inheritance'. Insofar as psychologies change from context to context, and insofar as human culture is exaptive, so we can chart the micro-evolutionary history of experience among humans as biocultural beings.

Smail himself leads in this direction, for he points out that 'behaviors that are shaped by predispositions and emotions are often plastic, not hardwired'. And this means that even the 'universal biological substrate' must have its nuances: 'Basic social emotions are almost certainly universal. Nonetheless ... they do different things in different historical cultures' (2008: 114). He goes on to point out, emphatically and rightly, that any 'quest to identify "human nature"' is 'futile', since 'biology and cultural studies are fundamentally congruent' (2008: 125). Yet the problem with this analysis remains one of teleology. For example, starting with a known concept of 'disgust', usually in English, the physiological and gestural signs of this concept are mapped onto other cultures who, when representing similar physiological signs and expression, are said to be 'disgusted', even if the local concept in question is worthy of a rich conceptual analysis of its own and does not bear any contextual or experiential resemblance to 'normative' representations of disgust in Anglophone contexts. To concede that social emotions 'do different things in different historical cultures' makes it meaningless, even an obfuscation, to say that, 'disgust' is nevertheless 'universal', irrespective of its different contexts, signs, and experiences. To quip, 'Same disgust, different object', as Smail does, is to impose a preferred and *a priori* conceptual definition on a physiological process that does not, in fact, need to be so defined (2008: 115). Bare physiology does not carry any meaning and, as we have seen, words do *count*. To identify a physiological process with an emotion itself is confusing if it is then necessary to talk about emotions as dynamic experiences dependent on cultural context.

Larry McGrath (2017) entertains the possibility of a radical rejection of the universal emotion by proposing that the existence of plasticity undermines or contradicts allusions to the universal, and I would tend to agree. Given Smail's emphasis on the vast array of ways in which different cultures can 'exploit' physiological stimuli, it is difficult to see why the basic emotion model is retained. We ought to be able to re-work the following statement of Smail's (2008: 115) to better represent the fact that human nature *is* human culture: 'Given the plasticity of such emotions as disgust, the interaction between universal cognitive or physiological traits and particular historical cultures is never simple'. By simply removing the word 'universal' from this quote, and by adding quotation marks around the word 'disgust', we have a usable appraisal of the problems facing historians of emotion and neurohistorians alike: 'Given the plasticity of such emotions as "disgust", the interaction between cognitive or physiological traits and particular historical cultures is never simple.'

This position also makes for a more consistent approach to the other aspects of Smail's configuration of a neurohistorical agenda. As he says, just because the capacity for a certain physiological state is universal, it doesn't mean that we're all bound to have it. Hormones need receptors in the brain in order to have effect, and the presence of specific receptors often depends on 'development and experience', which in turn depend on 'cultural norms' (2008: 115). Moreover, what one *does* because of a physiological state is not determined by the physiological state. Smail identifies this truth, but seems at first to represent the relationship between physiology and behaviour as a one-way street. 'Human behavioral norms, suitably internalized, allow one to ignore or override the predispositions one may have toward doing things or the emotions experienced while doing them,' Smail states. To exemplify the point he notes (2008: 116), 'Few people cave in, on the spot, to the feelings of lust they might occasionally have toward someone who is not their partner.' True enough. But the modification of behaviour necessarily also modifies the physiological state. The physiological state that is experienced, in context, as lust, might quickly become a source of longing, of shame and guilt, of unrequited love, and of grief. The cascade of experiences related to behavioural modification does not take place against a stable background of physiological lust, and nor can we assume that all of the emotional experiences in this sequence are preceded by their respective physiological indicators. We are always in an emotional two-way street. Smail, in turn, acknowledges this. In fact, it is a guiding principle for neurohistory: 'cultural practices can have profound neurophysiological consequences' (2008: 117).

Neurohistorical practice

Some historians have already begun to explore the possibilities of neurohistory, to some extent following the notion of Edmund Russell (2012: 11) that contemporary brains – and the neuroscientific insights into them – can 'serve as models for those of the past'. Modern brain science provides us insight into what happens to the production and reuptake of neurotransmitters while, for example, surfing the web, or riding a rollercoaster. Cultural practices that are evidently historical do impact our bodies and change our brains. These are psychotropic practices, according to Smail's (2008: 157–89) usage. We might ask: What does a new technology – the printing press, the steam engine, the internet – or new access to a drug – caffeine, alcohol – do to change us at a neurological level, and what are the effects of that change? The printing press, for example, implies new practices of reading, seeing, and touching, as well as new social configurations and new instruments of power (Gertsman 2013); the steam engine implies new practices of work, travel, time-keeping, and even the experience of nervous illness (Caplan 1995); mass media imply new practices of communication, organization, identification: new experiences of reality (Luhmann 2000). The consumption of new chemical compounds in the stuff of food, drink, and drugs implies new social configurations, not only of production and supply, but also of consumption (Hunt 2014; Matuskey 2012). The placebo is one fascinating area of potential neurohistorical inquiry, because we know that in the right conditions the consumption or application of literally *anything* can have a positive analgesic effect, demanding us to look carefully at what precisely constitutes the 'right conditions' (Moscoso 2014; cf. Meissner and Seidel 2012). According to Larry McGrath (2017: 134), 'Examining the shifting landscape of psychotropic practices lies at the heart of neurohistorians' ambition to bring together biology and culture.' But if 'the conditioning of the nervous system [is] the principal means through which institutions are established and extended over long expanses of space and time', then we must also seriously entertain the inverse proposition: that the establishment of new institutions and new practices is the principal means through which the nervous system is conditioned.

Most recently, Julia Bourke (2016) applied neurohistorical methods to anchoristic guidance writing, specifically *De Institutione Inclusarum* (c. 1160) of Aelred of Rievaulx. She views the guide as a 'means' by which an anchorite could pursue 'an emotional aim – that of mystical union, in which the anchorite is subsumed by the divine' (2016: 126). Not unusually, for a neurohistorian, textual practices are analysed for their psychotropic effects: 'All reading shapes a reader's interior world to some extent, whether the reader is aware of this or not.' In this case, 'Devotional reading … is a conscious effort to use the act of reading written text to construct a spiritually significant internal space and to fill that space with useful images and affective states in service of a religious goal' (2016: 126). Here I would add a nuance to this not untypical neurohistorical quest for the interior. If reading practices shape a reader's interior world and if, as we see from medical research into affective pain experience, experience is an output of the brain, then the distance between interiority and exteriority is collapsed. The shaping of the interior world is the shaping of the world. To be subsumed by the divine is not experienced as an entirely interior phenomenon. The divine, in this instance, exists. In particular, effortful production of *caritas* (translated here as 'compassion') is connected to studies on the effortful direction of empathy in contemporary neuroscientific experimentation, with the observation that practice, in both senses (doing and repetition), led to a more 'automatic' response over time (2016: 132).

An emphasis on reading also dominates Cristian Berco's (2016) account of racialization in the Spanish Inquisition, but the reading in question is not of texts but of facial features and of the unstable distance between phenotypical description and ontological status in the perception of skin colour. Berco disrupts ahistorical labelling that would conjoin skin colour and racial category by unfolding the extent to which cognitive perceptions of skin colour were so fluid in early modern Spain. Berco (2016: 59) points us towards a history of 'perceptual culture' that depends precisely upon the mutability of perception confirmed by contemporary neuroscience. The focus is shifted from the objective reality of facial features and their organization (expression) to the perception of those features, which was (is) bound up with expectations for how faces *should* look, and of contingent connections between appearance and status. Such work drives us to the momentariness of experience, orienting the historical gaze to the smallest instant of time and the ripples that flow out from it.

Lynn Hunt's (2009) proposal to recast the French Revolution, probing its distinct experiential phenomena, also depends on analyses of new reading and perceptual practices. She observes (2009: 672) that '*Experience* is not a neutral term'. The self that experiences is not reducible either to a completely incoherent entity, awash in discursive threads and entanglements, or a completely coherent, rational thing. Drawing from neuroscientific accounts of what comprised the self, and the functioning of experience, Hunt cast the historical net anew. The self 'is not a physiological substance', but it is based in 'matter'. The self is 'not simply a discursive effect', but 'an activity'. The brain 'arranges, categorizes, and manages experience, consciously or unconsciously, creating over time the cohesion and continuity that we call identity, which is never fixed and yet is real, not to mention crucial for survival in the world' (2009: 673). She might have gone further. To say that the brain 'arranges, categorizes, and manages experience' is to imply that experience exists out there, to be in some way sorted out by the brain. It would be better to say that the brain itself constructs experience, based on its arrangement, categorization, and management of stimuli from the world. There is no experiential feeling inherent in events, in objects, or in relations. They all have to be made. Hunt pursues a complex relationship of conscious and unconscious, rational and emotional, without quite collapsing these distinctions. A loose reference to 'hardwiring', a reference to something neurologically permanent in the human, the historicity of her argument notwithstanding, allows her to suggest that selves have a universal capacity for 'empathy'.[10] Individuals are not isolated beings, but social ones. What is more, this social essence is inscribed in the biology of individual bodies. McGrath (2017) in particular is critical of the way Hunt dispenses with an emphasis on self-regulation and suggests that neurohistorians in general have jettisoned the role of 'the active contributions of historical actors' in brain activity. They are, he claims, relying on an 'automatic conception of affect' where 'psychotropics generate direct affects via the brain independent of cognitive input'. The risk, he states, is that 'biochemical alteration risks becoming unmoored from the significance that historical actors attribute to their affective experiences' (2017: 6; cf. Hunt 2014).

Hunt's neurohistorical intervention is an explanation of an earlier (2007) work. As Jeremy Burman (2012) has pointed out, Hunt's neurohistorical turn provides the explanatory model for the emergence, in the French Revolution, of 'socially directed individual feeling' en masse: sympathy, in context, or empathy, if the universalism of the analysis is to be given its full political charge. In short, Hunt's argument about the effects of the new literary form of the epistolary novel, which allowed for the practice of emotional projection across social divides and beyond the confines of immediate kinship and community, is explicable by a turn to neurobiology. In Burman's (2012: 89) words, 'The new literary form parasitized an already-existing human capacity and extended it to apply beyond the circle of close relations; that it provided a new way to make felt individual meaning at the social level'. Hence the need, in Hunt's later piece, for the reference to hardwiring. Yet as we have seen, such language carries a large risk of over-extrapolation from a universal biological substrate. If we are truly to set about doing neurohistory in order to find out what it felt like to be an historical actor, hardwiring always presents us the easy option of inferring experience in the past by filtering it through our own in the present, using presentist psychological categories.[11]

Conclusion

What are we really doing when we are doing neurohistory? The end in mind, I would posit, is not a history of the brain, nor a history of the nervous system. Our aim is to find out how experiences felt and what they motivated; to get at how reality seemed. We are looking at experiential 'landscapes', as it were, to reach a better understanding of why societies worked in the ways they did, radically different from one another, and changing over time. In sum, neurohistory is not a 'psychological project', and our neurohistorical gaze is not directed at the 'history from within', but on the realities made by interactions between worlds and within.[12] The neurohistorical insight is to trust that when an historical actor says 'it felt like this', we do not have to translate that into a contemporary psychological figure; we do not have to take it as metaphor. On the contrary, if experience is historical because the brain is bioculturally made, then we must be prepared to risk taking historical actors at their word. To do that, affective statements have to be read in context, against other affective statements, against the languages of the body or gesture, of interaction and intercourse, and against the sensual worlds in which historical actors moved and existed.[13] In this, at the very least, we can follow Hunt (2009: 678): societies and social movements 'must be learned, lived, embodied, and felt within individual selves'.

The neurohistorical approach warns us, fundamentally, that we probably do not know and cannot assume what it was like to be there, in an historical moment. We cannot hope to explain it in *our* terms, according to *our* experiential frame of reference. But we can explain it in the terms of historical actors themselves, in their connected networks of individuals (Burman 2012: 96). We can reconstruct their experiential frame of reference, including those situated practices that would have driven synaptic development and those psychotropic influences that would have washed the historical mind. We can, as Steve Fuller (2014: 109) puts it, immerse ourselves in the 'lifeworld' of past actors. If past experience seems unfamiliar, strange, seemingly implausible, but empirically verifiable, then our powers of historical analysis and explanation promise to expand dramatically.[14]

Comment

Daniel Lord Smail

When I first suggested the idea of a neurohistory some years ago it seemed obvious to me that history could learn something from neuroscience and vice versa. It still seems obvious to me. One of history's great contributions to the human sciences springs from the historian's instinct to suppose that nearly everything in the human world is subject to change. Looking around, it would be easy enough for a casual observer to imagine that things like the nation state, sex roles, and ketchup are timeless givens. The work of history is to show that the modern instantiations of these things, appearances notwithstanding, actually came into being in the past, have present-day forms that are different from those of the past, and will continue to change in the future. Once upon a time, it seemed perfectly obvious that the brain–body system was one of those timeless givens, and therefore uninteresting to practitioners of a discipline concerned only with things that can change. Then came the revolution. Over the last two or three decades, cognitive neuroscience and related fields, by virtue of what they have demonstrated about the plasticity of neurons, receptors, and other features of the central nervous system, have made it possible to add the brain–body system to the list of things that we can usefully historicize.

The brain-body system, in the neurohistorical approach, is a system whose form can change significantly over time even as the components remain stable. The changes to the form are not random; they emerge instead from a complex dance involving the body on the one hand and human society and culture on the other. As individual bodies continuously adapt and respond to their surroundings from one era to the next, the aggregate body, something we can define heuristically as a statistically averaged set of bodily traits characteristic of a sub-population, is different from the aggregate body of eras both before and after. Crucially, the human brain-body system, in its actions and reactions to its cultural surroundings, is not simply passive, like clay in the hands of a potter. Neurohistory instead treats the body as an actor in history. Through interactions with cultural forms and social practices, the body constantly generates unpredictable new patterns or historical trajectories. The body, therefore, is one of the sources of contingency in the human past.

Since *On Deep History and the Brain* was published in 2008, the theoretical resources available for the framing of neurohistory have grown apace. Approaches or bodies of theory including epigenetics, actor–network theory, the history of emotions, microbiomics, and the archaeology of entanglement, some of which have been synthesized in the emerging field known as the new materialism, have transformed the theoretical grounds on which we can base a neurohistorical approach to the past (Coole and Frost 2010; LeCain 2017). Understandably, certain ideas or phrases used in the book no longer sit well with current scholarship. Metaphors such as 'wiring' were inapt even at the time, and although I used the word 'brain' both in the title and in the book, this was a too-convenient shorthand for a much more complex and interesting entity, the brain–body system. From time to time, I have used small thought pieces to make piecemeal adjustments to the basic model (e.g. Smail 2014b). But it is clear that neurohistory is overdue for the kind of theoretical overhaul proposed by Rob Boddice in his contribution.

In this comment, I will summarize some of the highlights of Boddice's own approach to neurohistory and the challenging and interesting revision he proposes, and will use the occasion to amplify or extend some of his important observations. As I shall suggest, the approach he has laid out here runs the risk of removing the keystone that supports the edifice of neurohistory. That keystone consists of a materialist understanding according to which the body is a complex assemblage of electrical impulses and chemicals, all of which influence mood, feeling, emotion, and behaviour. This assemblage, by virtue of its material properties, is susceptible to environmental influences. Recent work has shown that our own microbiome is not the least of these factors (Cryan and Dinan 2012). In this materialist understanding, neurohistory should be seen as a branch of environmental history, allowing the brain–body system to be viewed as a node in a complex entanglement of historical actors. Ultimately, I believe it may be more appropriate to interpret Boddice's model not as a revision to neurohistory so much as a necessary and useful complement that expands the approach to include forms of historical explanation that operate at microhistorical scales.

Boddice has proposed the possibility of reframing neurohistory in a way that will allow it to harmonize with the history of experience and the history of emotion. His approach is designed in part to solve one of the crucial methodological problems associated with neurohistory. Any approach to the past informed by neuroscience runs up against the fact that we cannot actually know anything about the movement of chemicals or the action of synapses in the bodies of actors in the past. Even if we could devise a way to assemble such evidence, perhaps via chemical analyses of bone or tissue, it is difficult to imagine how any of these findings could be meaningful, given the fact that neurohistory treats only with aggregates and never with individuals. What 'evidence' we have, therefore, is rarely more than suggestive, and one is reduced to constructing plausible scenarios or models grounded in very little that any would regard as evidence. The modern evidence generated by neuroscientific research is robust, but extrapolating from this to the past in a simple-minded way would violate the very premise of the approach.

Boddice has offered an intriguing way to skirt this methodological pitfall, namely, by taking experience itself as the subject of analysis. If we proceed from the assumption that human experience is shaped by context, then we can take the changing forms of individual experience as the direct subject of historical inquiry without the need to worry overmuch about whether that change has any measurable material dimension. To use Jeremy Burman's (2014) terminology, we can seek to develop a 'history from within'. Boddice's fascinating discussion of pain offers a useful model of this approach. Pain research in recent years has shown that the relationship between an injury and the experience of pain is not nearly as automatic as the common-sense understanding suggests. Pain can be experienced in very different ways, including (sometimes) not at all. To some degree, individuals are capable of managing their own pain. To the extent that people take their cues from culture, this research suggests that whole cultures may have tools or devices that modify the pain thresholds of those who participate in the culture. Furthermore, cultural norms can associate experiences of pain with stimuli that vary from one society to the next. Given these insights, we can take historical accounts of pain that seemed bizarre or inexplicable to previous historians and treat them as reasonably accurate reports of individual experience.

In an important section, Boddice appropriately locates neurohistory's grounding principle in the understanding that the human brain–body system, far from being fixed or hardwired in some genetic way, is partially open to environmental or developmental influences and permeable to culture. That he chose to label this section 'Genetics' rather than 'Epigenetics' is something of a misdirection, in my view, but the ensuing discussion conveys well why it is that most historians have ceased to use the word 'biology' as if it were synonymous with 'universal', 'unchanging', and 'hardwired'. One of the problems with this syllogism, which used to be widespread, always lay in the fact that this is not what 'biology' means to evolutionary biologists, a group whose opinion on the matter is worth listening to. As conceived by Charles Darwin, evolutionary biology is the science of change. The Darwinian revolution challenged the received idea that species and phenotypes were timeless givens, created by God and incapable of change. The putative distinction between biology and culture, in other words, should never have been framed as the difference between fixity and changeability. It should have been understood instead as a matter of difference at the level of temporal scales, distinguishing the deep time of genetic change from the short time of recent human history.

The difference in temporal scales, of course, is not insignificant. In the last two decades of the twentieth century, some scholars in the fields of sociobiology and evolutionary psychology developed an approach based on the assumption that the human brain and body undergo adaptation over time but at a pace so slow as to be irrelevant for short-term historical analysis. But we now know that this assumption was at best incomplete and perhaps just simply wrong. Fields such as epigenetics have demonstrated how genetic expression itself, in the aggregate, can be turned on and off in response to changing environmental circumstances (in addition to the literature cited by Boddice in his contribution, see Jablonka and Lamb 2014; Niewöhner 2011; Roth et al. 2014; Brooke and Larsen 2014). Scholars working in fields such as dual inheritance theory have argued, moreover, that the genome itself is not the only medium for preserving and transmitting information (Richerson and Boyd 2005). Culture, both animal and human, is another such medium. So, for that matter, is the ecological niche itself, as proposed by the theory of ecological inheritance, an idea that has emerged from the larger field of niche-construction theory (Odling-Smee 2003; Laland, Matthews, and Feldman 2016). As Boddice concludes very appropriately, we now recognize that human life constantly responds to environmental factors on both macro-evolutionary and micro-evolutionary time scales.

Biological adaptation, in short, is not just genetic. It operates in multiple temporalities, using different mechanisms. An example that I find useful describes the adjustments made as an individual travels from lower to higher altitudes. As you ascend, your body copes with the lack of oxygen by panting – a reaction that takes place within a matter of minutes. This is a temporary adjustment. If you remain at a high altitude for a long time, your body's metabolism will gradually adjust – a matter of weeks or months. This adjustment is not remembered in the genome; the memory is coded instead in a different location in the body. Finally, if you and your descendants settle down to live at 10,000 feet, selection pressures may cause your distant descendants to adapt genetically – a matter of generations.

All of these responses operate on different time scales. All of them are 'biological'. From a theoretical perspective, even the oxygen canister and mask that you might bring with you for the ascent is biological, for it has long been understood that behaviour, including learned behaviour, forms part of the repertoire of mechanisms that some organisms use to adjust to changes in life circumstances. To put this differently, the body is indifferent to the mode whereby an adaptation is preserved or remembered, whether through genetic changes or cultural adaptations or anything in between. This understanding of the multiple temporalities of biological response has made it possible for us to think about collapsing the distinction between culture and biology and therefore between history and evolution. This collapsing has been pursued systematically in the post-genomic literature and by an approach known as the extended evolutionary synthesis; both approaches seek to overcome the distinction between culture and biology (Richardson and Stevens 2015; Pigliucci and Müller 2010; Laubichler and Renn 2015).

This understanding shapes my response to Boddice's critique. He declares that we can and must extricate neurohistory from a model in which predispositions, moods, emotions, and feelings are understood to have a deep evolutionary history, and in which certain responses can be theorized as being relatively automated. I have no objection to reworking the language and removing things that are problematic in this formulation; it would violate the very premise of my historical philosophy to imagine that a model first proposed in 2008 should not be allowed to change with the times. Among other things, it makes perfect sense to say, as Boddice has done, that the brain necessarily constructs experience. But in welcoming this move, I will continue to insist that the brain is constructing experience out of embodied changes that arise because of the body's *material* properties. For neurohistory to be interesting, we need to recognize that the body has innate features.

In theorizing this, I have found it increasingly helpful to understand neurohistory as a branch of environmental history (Smail 2012). Over the past half century or so, the relational or interactionist perspective on communication that grew out of cybernetics and system theory has suffused a number of fields of inquiry (Bateson 1972). Among historians, the approach has taken root most explicitly in the field of environmental history. Studies in environmental history take it for granted that humans and the environment are equal players in a complex relationship of give and take (Cronon 1991). Rather than offering a history in which humanity is the only agent in creating change, the field assumes that change emerges unpredictably from this relationship. But this is where the fun begins: for what, exactly, is the range of eligible partners in this complex theoretical dance?[15] In the case of environmental history, the dance partner typically takes the form of water, climate, sources of energy, disease, and so on. But there are others, ranging from material culture and the built environment to books and computers, as proposed by the theory of material engagement (Malafouris 2013).

When neurohistory is reformulated as a branch of environmental history, it allows us to treat the human body, in the aggregate, as one of these actors. As noted earlier, in the post-genomic world of current scholarship, we think of the body as an entity that is relationally produced through complex and ongoing developmental processes. Where history is concerned, the aggregate body responds to changing cultural and environmental factors in much the same way that rivers and water tables have responded to the building of channels and dams or that the atmosphere has responded to rising levels of carbon dioxide. That is to say, it responds contingently, in accordance with some of its innate properties, and it responds in ways that can have long-term, unanticipated consequences for human culture and society.

Examples offering theoretical grounds for this move abound. To take a recent case, rates of violent crime in the United States dropped significantly between 1990 and 2000. The phenomenon was so noticeable that it immediately prompted a number of studies by scholars who sought to explain it. One of the most interesting explanations was offered in 2007 by the economist Jessica Reyes (2007), who suggested that the removal of lead from gasoline between 1975 and 1985 was an important factor in the decline in crime. 'Childhood lead exposure', she argued, 'increases the likelihood of behavioral and cognitive traits such as impulsivity, aggressivity, and low IQ', factors that are in turn associated with criminal behaviour. Reyes was not trying to argue that children's exposure to lead 'caused' any specific act of violence. You cannot say that O. J. Simpson killed his wife because he suffered from lead exposure as a child. Instead, the causal factor that is visible in the data is probabilistic in nature. Being probabilistic, the result is visible only across an entire sub-population. To put this differently, it was a feature of the aggregate body, which, according to the argument, suffered slightly more from lead poisoning than the aggregate body before the introduction and widespread use of unleaded gasoline. Crucially, the effect of the removal of lead on violence, if Reyes is right, has been entirely indirect and contingent. There is nothing in the way that human society operates that could have allowed us to predict in advance that lead poisoning could have rendered people, in the aggregate, slightly more impulsive. In other words, it makes no sense to explain either violence or its decline only in terms of some hardwired propensity towards violence, as Steven Pinker (2011), to take an obvious example, has done.

The probabilistic nature of effects such as lead poisoning is crucial, in my view, for the kind of theoretical overhaul of neurohistory that I hope to see in coming years. In his contribution, Boddice has emphasized the importance of understanding the historical variability of individual experience. This feels right to me. But this is a different kind of neurohistory from the one I conceived, which is concerned only with landscapes of probability and which understood outcomes only in the aggregate.[16] Boddice's model will be more appealing to historians who prefer the particular to the general and are more inclined to study the exception rather than extrapolate the rule. Historical explanation is always particular to the scale at which it is conceptualized. What Boddice has recommended here is a model for doing neurohistory that operates closer to the microhistorical end of the spectrum. Rather than a revision to neurohistory, it might be more useful to see this model as providing a complement to the macrohistorical version, thereby allowing branches of neurohistory to operate across the full spectrum of historical explanation.

Response

Rob Boddice

The overwhelmingly positive outcome of this exchange is the emerging possibility of a meaningful communication between neurohistory as a branch of environmental history (a macrohistorical approach) and neurohistory as a branch of the history of individual experience/emotions (which Smail characterizes as a microhistorical approach). As a caveat, I would add that the history of experience and the history of emotions, even though they tend to lead with individual or tightly located examples, do also contribute to a much broader appreciation of the aggregate of experience. The advantages that have been gained in the history of emotions by thinking about 'emotionology' (Stearns and Stearns 1985) and 'emotional regimes' (Reddy 2001), for example – in short, the kinds of cultural codes for emotional expression that in turn influence and are influenced by emotional experience – speak to broad experiential vistas. They help us understand the ways in which experiences were delimited in cultural terms. Individual cases populate the landscapes we can discern in the general, and it seems to me that what Smail is suggesting is a vital and underappreciated way of mapping that landscape in greater depth and greater detail. Exactly how the relationship between the macro and micro is to work, I shall return to presently.

On the face of it, I do not disagree with Smail that 'the brain is constructing experience out of embodied changes that arise because of the body's *material* properties'. We share, I think, a deep commitment to the historicization of the body. If there is a point of divergence, it may prove to be semantic rather than substantial. Smail says that the 'brain–body system' is 'partially open to environmental or developmental influences and permeable to culture'. It is the word 'partially' that is the sticking point, as well as the insistence that for 'neurohistory to be interesting, we need to recognize that the body has innate features'. I agree that, in a deep historical sense, the body does certain things under certain environmental conditions with a reassuring degree of predictability. To that extent, I also agree that there is a relatively stable materiality of human *stuff*. But since all bodies are always in an environmental and cultural context, then all bodies are, as it were, contextually contingent. And of course, what happens in consequence of a stimulus, in and among bodies in a broader sense, is dependent on the broader 'ecology', to extend Smail's environmental approach, in which bodies are situated. This view does not, I think, plasticize the body out of existence, but it does foreground a good dose of analytical caution when dealing with material continuities and 'innateness'. I think it is difficult to defend 'innateness' while at the same time so strongly emphasizing the body's contingency. The risk, it seems to me, is that 'innate' is too easy to conflate with something 'universal', which, we agree, is not an apt way to characterize human biology. For the same reason, I do not know how one would assess where the limits of openness to environmental or cultural change are to be set. The *stuff* of history of is real *stuff*, no doubt, but it is historical *stuff* all the same.

For my part, the exchange with Smail has confirmed the necessity of revision, not only to the neurohistorical project, but also to the ways in which the history of emotions has engaged (or failed to engage) with it. There is, without any doubt, a clear link between the two approaches, and a sense in which they could unite to their mutual advantage. Yet there is a palpable perception among many historians of emotions that neuroscience adds little to our understanding of emotions in the past, while there is, on the other side, a sense among neurohistorians that the focus on emotions is too limited to that which is conscious, or self-managed, as opposed to those bodily activities that are 'automated'. I therefore end this rejoinder with an indication of the need for revision within the history of emotions/experience, in order that the communication between macro- and micro-history that Smail envisages can take place fluidly. If neurohistory is 'to operate across the full spectrum of historical explanation', it needs to be theoretically consistent.

In my view, the history of emotions must transcend any association with contemporary psychological categories of 'emotion'. The field has a much broader compass than this, setting out to historicize all forms of affective experience that encompass moods, feelings, sentiments, affects, passions, and so on, according to the contextual and linguistic environment of historically specific situations. Part of this concerns the reconstruction of past experiences that have little to do with internal processes at all, but which take place in the dynamics of relationality and interpersonal politics. We are finding new categories of experience in tandem with historical formulations of the self and of society. But partly this also concerns an historicization of that which seems 'automatic' in the body, and which tends to be labelled as 'affect' in today's parlance. To borrow a turn of phrase from the work of Sara Ahmed (2004: 27), conscious and non-conscious affective behaviour happens *as if* automatically in any given setting, because of the cultural conditioning that takes place through dynamic encounters with other people and other things. The example of physiological stress in my chapter here would be a case in point. While the body's stress response is, essentially, automated, the things that trigger a greater production of cortisol are in the world. The objects that cause injury, or the conditions that are associated with chronic pain, or even the typical practices associated with mothering an infant, are all historically contingent. Moreover, what happens in the world because of a cortisol surge in the body are also contingent. In short, when the body undergoes physiological stress that takes it out of a homeostatic state, then the person associated with that body *does* something. It seeks help, a painkiller, a hug, a drink, and so on. These practices are associated with and carried out in the name of emotions and practices that seem to spring up automatically, but which are highly specific. My argument within the history of emotions, partly inspired by Smail's work and in common with the practice theory applied by Monique Scheer (2012), is that we must extend our focus to what emotions *do*, and to understand the embeddedness of affective experience.

In the end, this does not discard the body, but puts it squarely in the world, in the interaction with other bodies and other objects. To pursue one of Smail's examples, about the correlation between a decline in lead exposure and a decline in violent crime, we cannot be entirely satisfied with an appraisal of the aggregate body and probabilistic environmental causes. While the analyses that allow us to use such categories are most valuable, they gain traction only in the context of things like educational practices, access to and emotional attachment to firearms, social policy, policing, and welfare provision. It is true that one could not connect any specific act of violent crime to lead exposure, but it is not immaterial what *type* of violent crime – what *practices* of violent crime – take place in a given probabilistic environment. Put another way, the macrohistorical view does not become particularly useful until and unless we populate it with other particulars of the context, including the specifics of individual experience. This implies that neurohistory, the history of emotions, the history of experience, have to be shared projects, with the macro and the micro being deployed not in parallel, but through a deep appreciation of their entanglement.

Notes

1. Speaking of the brain research of Lisa Feldman Barrett.

2. William Reddy has suggested a cautious but engaged approach, without all historians having to 'immerse themselves'. Quoted in Plamper (2010: 248).

3. Cf. Cooter (2014: 152). Cooter claims that books such as Smail's close down conversations 'about the nature of history … and, ultimately, about what it is to be human'. Though I too reject those parts of Smail's argument that rely on biologism, even a cursory reading of *Deep History* ought to have revealed that Smail was questioning what it means to be human, and the nature of history, in the most fundamental way.

4. The literature to support these observations would comprise a long list, in lieu of which I provide some key texts that summarize these views: MacDonald and Jensen-Campbell (2011); Melzack and Wall (1996); Gatchel et al. (2007); Grahek (2007).

5. There are many varieties of emotional/experiential universalism, from 'affect theory' to 'basic emotions', 'ur-emotions', and 'culture-independent concepts'. See Tomkins and McCarter (1964); Ekman and Friesen (1971); Parrott (2016); Wierzbicka (1999: 25, 35). For an accessible account of Feldman Barrett's reversal of the universalist position, see Fischer (2013).

6. Smail (2014) has offered a case study of the 'unpredictable ways in which cognitive and endocrinological systems have interacted with a changing material environment'. The historical case built by Stephen T. Casper (2014: 132) that casts great doubt on 'proponents of neuroculture [who] claim the brain as their transhistorical object' seems to be misplaced if it is aimed at neurohistory in particular.

7. For a review of historical research in this direction, see Olsen (2016); for reinforcement from developmental psychology, see Pesce et al. (2016).

8. Rather than exhorting that historians catch up 'with the present and its progress' or subscribe to naïve faith in the transparency of this particular 'advance of knowledge', I suggest simply that historians read critically across disciplinary boundaries. I am not, after all, suggesting a transformation of what historians do, but of what questions we ask.

Cf. Stadler (2014: 144). Furthermore, surely if the cross-disciplinary movement comes from the place of a critically minded historicism, that movement is worth taking. Cf. Cooter (2014: 149).

9. Cf. Burman (2012: 91). This article was revised and updated as Burman (2014).

10. There is, in fact, already a rich historiography and theoretical landscape that suggests the mutability and contextuality of empathy. See Young (2011); Lanzoni (2012); Engelen and Röttger-Rössler (2012); and Rameson and Morelli Lieberman (2012).

11. That is precisely what Lucien Febvre (1992: 213) warned against when first advocating for a history of the emotions.

12. Cf. Burman (2014: 81). A side project, of course, is to introduce historicity to neuroscience, and this indeed would put the brain front and centre, although the consequences of doing so for neuroscientific practice remain illusive. Still, as Smail (2014: 113) has pointed out, 'It is important for cognitive neuroscientists to learn how to come to grips with the brain's historicity'.

13. This aspect is, however, very much in accord with Burman (2014: 82).

14. Indeed, the neurohistorical turn can, if taken in this way, serve to undermine the more fundamentalist and transhistorical strand of neurobiology that has concerned historians of emotions and historians of science alike. See Cooter (2014: 147–8).

15. The idea of a 'dance' is a rather inadequate metaphor inasmuch as it suggests the existence of a relationship between two, and only two, actors. In fact, interaction takes place across a complex network of exchanges, where every actor is entangled with a range of other actors (Latour 2005; Hodder 2012).

16. In hindsight, one of the major flaws of *On Deep History and the Brain* (Smail 2008) lies in my failure, at the time, to adequately describe the probabilistic nature of neurohistorical explanations.

References

Ahmed, S. (2004), 'Collective Feelings: Or, The Impressions Left by Others', *Theory, Culture and Society*, 21: 25–42.

Bateson, G. (1972), *Steps to an Ecology of Mind*, San Francisco: Chandler Pub. Co.

Berco, C. (2016), 'Perception and the Mulatto Body in Inquisitorial Spain: A Neurohistory', *Past and Present*, 231: 33–60.

Boddice, R. (2014), 'Hurt Feelings?', in R. Boddice (ed.), *Pain and Emotion in Modern History*, 1–15, Basingstoke: Palgrave Macmillan.

Boddice, R. (2017), *Pain: A Very Short Introduction*, Oxford: Oxford University Press.

Bourke, J. (2014), 'Phantom Suffering: Amputees, Stump Pain and Phantom Sensations in Modern Britain', in R. Boddice (ed.), *Pain and Emotion in Modern History*, 66–89, Basinsgtoke: Palgrave Macmillan.

Bourke, J. (2016), 'An Experiment in "Neurohistory": Reading Emotions in Aelred's *De Institutione Inclusarum* (*Rule for a Recluse*)', *The Journal of Medieval Religious Cultures*, 42: 124–42.

Brooke, J. L. and Larsen, C. S. (2014), 'The Nurture of Nature: Genetics, Epigenetics, and Environment in Human Biohistory', *American Historical Review*, 119 (5): 1500–13.

Burman, J. T. (2012), 'History from Within? Contextualizing the New Neurohistory and Seeking Its Methods', *History of Psychology*, 15: 84–99.

Burman, J. T. (2014), 'Bringing the Brain into History: Behind Hunt's and Smail's Appeals to Neurohistory', in C. Tileagă and J. Byford (eds), *Psychology and History: Interdisciplinary Explorations*, 64–82, Cambridge: Cambridge University Press.

Cair, A. (2007), 'Regulation of Anterior Insular Cortex Using Real-time fMRI', *Neuroimage*, 35: 1238–46.

Caplan, E. M. (1995), 'Trains, Brains, and Sprains: Railway Spine and the Origins of Psychoneuroses', *Bulletin of the History of Medicine*, 69: 387–419.

Casper, S. T. (2014), 'History and Neuroscience: An Integrative Legacy', *Isis*, 105: 123–32.

Cheung, P. and Lau, P. (2005), 'Epigenetic Regulation by Histone Methylation and Histone Variants', *Molecular Endocrinology*, 19: 563–83.

Coole, D. H. and Frost, S., eds (2010), *New Materialisms: Ontology, Agency, and Politics*, Durham, NC: Duke University Press.

Cooter, R. (2014), 'Neural Veils and the Will to Historical Critique: Why Historians of Science Need to Take the Neuro-Turn Seriously', *Isis*, 105: 145–54.

Cronon, W. (1991), *Nature's Metropolis: Chicago and the Great West*, New York: W. W. Norton.

Cryan, J. F. and Dinan, T. G. (2012), 'Mind-altering Microorganisms: The Impact of the Gut Microbiota on Brain and Behaviour', *Nature Reviews Neuroscience*, 13 (10): 701–12.

deCharms, R. C., Christoff, K., Glover, G. H., Pauly, J. M., Whitfield, S. and Gabrieli, J. D. (2004), 'Learned Regulation of Spatially Localized Brain Activation Using Real-time fMRI', *Neuroimage*, 21: 436–43.

Dietz, D. M., Laplant, Q., Watts, E. L., Hodes, G. E., Russo, S. J., Feng, J., Oosting, R. S., Vialou, V. and Nestler, E. J. (2011), 'Paternal Transmission of Stress-Induced Pathologies', *Biological Psychiatry*, 70: 408–14.

Eisenberger, N. I. (2003), 'Does Rejection Hurt? An fMRI Study of Social Exclusion', *Science*, 302: 290–2.

Ekman, P. and Friesen, W. (1971), 'Constants Across Cultures in the Face and Emotion', *Journal of Personality and Social Psychology*, 17: 124–9.

Engelen, E.-M. and Röttger-Rössler, B. (2012), 'Current Disciplinary and Interdisciplinary Debates on Empathy', *Emotion Review*, 4: 3–8.

Febvre, L. (1992) 'Une vue d'ensemble: Histoire et psychologie', in L. Febvre, *Combats pour l'Histoire*, 207–20, Paris: Armand Colin.

Feldman Barrett, L. (2006a), 'Are Emotions Natural Kinds?', *Perspectives on Psychological Science*, 1: 28–58.

Feldman Barrett, L. (2006b), 'Solving the Emotion Paradox: Categorization and the Experience of Emotion', *Personality and Social Psychology Review*, 10: 20–46.

Fischer, S. (2013), 'About Face: Emotions and Facial Expressions May Not Be Related', *Boston Magazine*, July, available online: http://www.bostonmagazine.com/news/article/2013/06/25/emotions-facial-expressions-not-related/ (accessed 12 December 2016).

Fuller, S. (2014), 'Neuroscience, Neurohistory, and the History of Science: A Tale of Two Brain Images', *Isis*, 105: 100–9.

Gatchel, R. J., Peng, Y. B., Peters, M. L., Fuchs, P. N. and Turk, D. C. (2007), 'The Biopsychosocial Approach to Chronic Pain: Scientific Advances and Future Directions', *Psychological Bulletin*, 133: 581–624.

Gendron, M. and Feldman Barrett, L. (2009), 'Reconstructing the Past: A Century of Ideas about Emotion in Psychology', *Emotion Review*, 1: 316–39.

Gertsman, E. (2013), 'Multiple Impressions: Christ in the Winepress and the Semiotics of the Printed Image', *Art History*, 36: 310–37.

Grahek, N. (2007), *Feeling Pain and Being in Pain*, 2nd edn, Cambridge, MA: MIT Press.

Haller, S., Birbaumer, N. and Veit, R. (2010), 'Real-time fMRI Feedback Training may Improve Chronic Tinitus', *European Radiology*, 20: 696–703.

Hodder, I. (2012), *Entangled: An Archaeology of the Relationships Between Humans and Things*, Malden, MA: Wiley-Blackwell.

Hunt, L. (2007), *Inventing Human Rights: A History*, New York: Norton.

Hunt, L. (2009), 'The Experience of Revolution', *French Historical Studies*, 32: 671–8.

Hunt, L. (2014), 'Modernity: Are Modern Times Different?' *Historia Critica*, 54: 107–24.

Jablonka, E. and Lamb, M. J. (2014), *Evolution in Four Dimensions: Genetic, Epigenetic, Behavioral, and Symbolic Variation in the History of Life*, rev. edn, Cambridge, MA: MIT Press.

Laland, K., Matthews, B. and Feldman, M. W. (2016), 'An Introduction to Niche Construction Theory', *Evolutionary Ecology*, 30 (2): 191–202.

Lanzoni, S. (2012), 'Introduction: Emotion and the Science: Varieties of Empathy in Science, Art, and History', *Science in Context*, 25: 287–300.

Latour, B. (2005), *Reassembling the Social: An Introduction to Actor-Network-Theory*, Oxford: Oxford University Press.

Laubichler, M. D. and Renn, J. (2015), 'Extended Evolution: A Conceptual Framework for Integrating Regulatory Networks and Niche Construction', *Journal of Experimental Zoology Part B: Molecular and Developmental Evolution*, 324 (7): 565–77.

LeCain, T. (2017), *The Matter of History: How Things Create the Past*, New York: Cambridge University Press.

Luhmann, N. (2000), *The Reality of the Mass Media*, Stanford, CA: Stanford University Press.

MacDonald, G. and Jensen-Campbell, L. A., eds (2011), *Social Pain: Neuropsychological and Health Implications of Loss and Exclusion*, Washington: American Psychological Association.

Malafouris, L. (2013), *How Things Shape the Mind: A Theory of Material Engagement*, Cambridge, MA: MIT Press.

Manning, E. (2007), *Politics of Touch: Sense, Movement, Sovereignty*, Minneapolis: University of Minnesota Press.

Matuskey, D. (2012), 'Erythroxylum Coca and Its Discontents: A Neurohistorical Case Study of Cocaine, Pleasure, and Empires', in E. Russell (ed.), 'Environment, Culture, and the Brain: New Explorations in Neurohistory', 55–9, *RCC Perspectives*, 6.

McGrath, L. S. (2017), 'History, Affect, and the Neurosciences', *History of Psychology*, 20 (2): 129–47.

Meany, M. (2001), 'Maternal Care, Gene Expression, and the Transmission of Individual Differences in Stress Reactivity Across Generations', *Annual Review of Neuroscience*, 24: 1161–92.

Meissner, K. and Seidel, C. C. (2012) 'The Power of Beliefs: The Concept of Placebo and Placebo Effects in Politics and History', in E. Russell (ed.), 'Environment, Culture, and the Brain: New Explorations in Neurohistory', 27–32, *RCC Perspectives*, 6.

Melzack, R. (2005), 'Evolution of the Neuomatrix Theory of Pain', *Pain Practice*, 5: 85–94.

Melzack, R. and Wall, P. D. (1996), *The Challenge of Pain*, London: Penguin.

Moscoso, J. (2014), 'Exquisite and Lingering Pains: Facing Cancer in Early Modern Europe', in R. Boddice (ed.), *Pain and Emotion in Modern History*, 16–35, Basingstoke: Palgrave Macmillan.

Niewöhner, J. (2011), 'Epigenetics: Embedded Bodies and the Molecularisation of Biography and Milieu', *BioSocieties*, 6 (3): 279–98.

Odling-Smee, F. J. (2003), *Niche Construction: The Neglected Process in Evolution*, Princeton, NJ: Princeton University Press.

Olsen, S. (2016), 'Learning How to Feel Through Play: At the Intersection of the Histories of Play, Childhood and the Emotions', *International Journal of Play*, 5: 323–28.

Page, G. G. (2004), 'Are There Long-Term Consequences of Pain in Newborn or Very Young Infants?', *Journal of Perinatal Education*, 13: 10–7.

Parrott, W. G. (2016), 'Psychological Perspectives on Emotion in Groups', in D. Lemmings, H. Kerr and R. Phiddian (eds), *Passions, Sympathy and Print Culture: Public Opinion and Emotional Authenticity in Eighteenth-century Britain*, 20–46, Basinstoke: Palgrave Macmillan.

Pesce, C., Masci, I., Marchetti, R., Vazou, S., Sääkslahti, A. and Tomporowski, P. D. (2016), 'Deliberate Play and Preparation Jointly Benefit Motor and Cognitive Development: Mediated and Moderated Effects', *Frontiers in Psychology*, 7: 1–18.

Pigliucci, M. and Müller, G. B., eds (2010), *Evolution, the Extended Synthesis*, Cambridge, MA: MIT Press.

Pinker, S. (2011), *The Better Angels of Our Nature: Why Violence Has Declined*, New York: Viking.

Plamper, J. (2010), 'The History of Emotions: An Interview with William Reddy, Barbara Rosenwein, and Peter Stearns', *History and Theory*, 49: 237–65.

Price, D. B. and Twombly, N. J. (1978), *The Phantom Limb Phenomenon: A Medical, Folkloric, and Historical Study: Texts and Translations of 10th to 20th Century Accounts of the Miraculous Restoration of Lost Body Parts*, Washington DC: Georgetown University Press.

Rameson, L. T., Morelli, S. A. and Lieberman, M. D. (2012), 'The Neural Correlates of Empathy: Experience, Automaticity, and Prosocial Behavior', *Journal of Cognitive Neuroscience*, 24: 235–45.

Reddy, W. (1997), 'Against Constructionism: The Historical Ethnography of Emotions', *Current Anthropology*, 38: 327–51.

Reddy, W. (2001), *The Navigation of Feeling: A Framework for the History of Emotions*, Cambridge: Cambridge University Press.

Reddy, W. (2015), Tweet, 4 August, available online: https://twitter.com/WilliamMReddy/status/628542762284154880 (accessed 20 August 2017).

Reyes, J. W. (2007), 'Environmental Policy as Social Policy? The Impact of Childhood Lead Exposure on Crime', *National Bureau of Economic Research*, available online: http://www.nber.org/papers/w13097 (accessed 5 July 2017).

Richardson, S. S. and Stevens, H., eds (2015), *Postgenomics: Perspectives on Biology after the Genome*, Durham, NC: Duke University Press.

Richerson, P. J. and Boyd, R. (2005), *Not by Genes Alone: How Culture Transformed Human Evolution*, Chicago: University of Chicago Press.

Roth, R. A., Brooke, J. L., Larsen, C. S., Russell, E., Harper, K., Scheidel, W., Hunt, L. and Thomas, J. A. (2014), 'Introduction: Roundtable: History Meets Biology', *American Historical Review*, 119 (5): 1492–99.

Russell, E., ed. (2012), 'Environment, Culture, and the Brain: New Explorations in Neurohistory', *RCC Perspectives*, 6.

Scheer, M. (2012), 'Are Emotions a Kind of Practice (and is That What Makes Them Have a History)? A Bourdieuian Approach to Understanding Emotion', *History and Theory*, 51: 193–220.

Smail, D. L. (2008), *On Deep History and the Brain*, Berkeley: University of California Press.

Smail, D. L. (2012), 'Neuroscience and the Dialectics of History', *Análise Social*, 47 (4): 894–909.

Smail, D. L. (2014a), 'Neurohistory in Action: Hoarding and the Human Past', *Isis*, 105: 110–22.

Smail, D. L. (2014b), 'Retour sur On Deep History and the Brain', *Tracés*, 14 (3): 151–63.

Stadler, M. (2014), 'Neurohistory Is Bunk? The Not-So-Deep History of the Postclassical Mind', *Isis*, 105: 133–44.

Stearns, P. N. and Stearns, C. Z. (1985), 'Emotionology: Clarifying the History of Emotions and Emotional Standards', *American Historical Review*, 90: 813–36.

Tomkins, S. S. and McCarter, R. (1964), 'What and Where are the Primary Affects? Some Evidence for a Theory', *Perceptual and Motor Skills*, 18: 119–58.

Vaso, A., Adahan, H. M., Gjika, A., Zahaj, S., Zhurda, T., Vyshka, G. and Devor, M. (2014), 'Peripheral Nervous System Origin of Phantom Limb Pain', *Pain*, 155: 1384–91.

Véron, N. and Peters, A. H. F. M. (2011), 'Tet Proteins in the Limelight', *Nature*, 473: 293–4.

Wall, P. (2002), *Pain: The Science of Suffering*, New York: Columbia University Press.

Weaver, I. C., Cervoni, N., Champagne, F. A., D'Alessio, A. C., Sharma, S., Seckl, J. R., Dymov, S., Szyf, M. and Meaney, M. J. (2004), 'Epigenetic Programming by Maternal Behavior', *Nature Neuroscience*, 7: 847–54.

Wierzbicka, A. (1999), *Emotions Across Languages and Cultures: Diversity and Universals*, Cambridge: Cambridge University Press.

Witte, W. (2014), 'The Emergence of Chronic Pain: Phantom Limbs, Subjective Experience and Pain Management in Post-War West Germany', in R. Boddice (ed.), *Pain and Emotion in Modern History*, 90–110, Basingstoke: Palgrave Macmillan.

Young, A. (2011), 'Empathy, Evolution, and Human Nature', in J. Decety, D. Zahavi and S. Overgaard (eds), *Empathy: From Bench to Bedside*, 21–37, Cambridge, MA: MIT Press.

Zeidan, F., Grant, J. A., Brown, C. A., McHaffie, J. G., and Coghilla, R. C. (2012), 'Mindfulness Meditation-related Pain Relief: Evidence for Unique Brain Mechanisms in the Regulation of Pain', *Neuroscience Letters*, 520: 165–73.

CHAPTER 12
POSTHUMANIST HISTORY
Ewa Domanska

Since the late 1990s, the humanities and social sciences have been going through major changes caused by a decline of poststructuralist influence and the end of postmodernism, symbolically marked by 9/11 (Bachman-Medick 2016). These processes have stimulated the emergence of a field of multidisciplinary knowledge that might be referred to as the non- or post-anthropocentric humanities inspired by a set of variously defined tendencies that can be gathered under the term 'posthumanism' (Hayles 1999; Wolfe 2010; Herbrechter 2013; Braidotti 2013; Nayar 2014). It would be difficult to ignore the fact that both academic journals and conference organizers, as well as the media and popular culture, have shown great interest in questions relating to animals, cyborgs, plants, things, zombies, technological progress, genetic engineering, the medicalization of society and the related issues of the Anthropocene, biopolitics, non-human rights, global warming, natural disasters, and the extinction of species. I would say that, essentially, whenever we encounter the prefixes bio-, eco-, geo-, neuro-, necro-, techno-, and zoo-, we are entering the space of post-anthropocentric humanities which is also associated with such terms as posthumanities[1] and/or biohumanities (Rose 2013; Stotz and Griffiths 2008).

As is so often the case with avant-garde tendencies, history seems to be mainly re-active – meaning, it reacts (usually after around 10–15 years) to theoretical shifts that happened earlier in other disciplines (mainly in anthropology, art history, literary studies, philosophy, or sociology). The end of postmodernism had therefore already been announced in the humanities when historians began to treat it seriously. And it seems that, generally speaking, they are still working through its outcomes (AHR Forum 2012). In textbooks of contemporary historical writing, recent developments in this field come to an end in the 1980s and 1990s and are still associated with classic environmental history, history of mentalities, microhistory, gender history, global history, memory and history, oral history, subaltern history, and visual history, with the occasional mention of more recent interest in counterfactual history, digital history, emotions and history, and transnational history (Partner and Foot 2013; Iggers, Wang, and Mukherjee 2017). However, the current paradigm shift from new humanities (still tied to postmodernism) to post-anthropocentric humanities (informed by posthumanism) has already begun to resonate among historians, who do not ignore this impulse as they did for years in the case of postmodernism (Domanska 2010). There are strong voices arguing that history is already beyond the linguistic turn and that it has passed the phase of narrativism and its fascination with text, discourse, and narrative. These opinions are expressed by Peter Burke, Caroline Walker Bynum, Dipesh Chakrabarty, Dominick LaCapra, Lynn

Hunt, Nancy Partner, Michael Roth, and Gabrielle Spiegel (to name only a few) (Burke 2012; Bynum 2009; Hunt 2014). A growing interest in post-anthropocentric (and/or posthumanist) approaches to animal history, biohistory, environmental history, history of things, the emergence of new subfields such as big history and neurohistory as well as discussions about the Anthropocene and climate change, non-human agency, relations between humans and non-humans, the question of scale and non-anthropocentric conceptions of time (geological time) are all signs of posthumanist marks on the discipline of history. Nor do historians ignore the fact that today, it is not philosophy but biology from which history is learning (AHR Roundtable 2014; Kaiser and Plenge 2014; Rose 2013: 25).

There is no posthumanist history understood as a subfield of historical reflection, even if the term sometimes appears in texts written by non-historians.[2] In this chapter, for heuristic reasons, I will use the term 'posthumanist' as an adjective and treat it as a cross-disciplinary perspective. This move allows me to indicate how in various subfields of history, scholars are affected by the non-anthropocentric mode of thinking that operates in the contemporary humanities and use posthumanism as a productive critical tool and interpretative platform for thinking about the past. Employing various approaches and theories (such as actor–network theory, object-oriented ontology, multispecies theories, relational epistemologies, and new materialisms) allows them to question concepts and ideas that have been used as the bases of historical knowledge: anthropocentrism, Cartesian rationality, agency, identity, individuality, time, space, subject, and power.

What is posthumanism?

It is important to indicate that there is no one coherent trend that might be labelled as posthumanism, just as it is no singular humanism that is often presented as its opposition (Campana and Maisano 2016: 1ff). Posthumanism is more of an intellectual movement associated with various academic icons such as Neil Badmington, Jane Bennett, Rosi Braidotti, Donna Haraway, N. Katherine Hayles, Bruno Latour, Michel Serres, and Cary Wolfe, among others. For example, Rosi Braidotti mentions 'critical posthumanism' with its origins in anti-humanism, 'ecological posthumanism', and 'post-anthropocentric posthumanism', as well as 'the analytic post-humanism of science and technology studies' and 'post-anthropocentric neo-humanism' (Braidotti 2013: 38–49, 78). Recent texts also add terms associated with alternative political projects, such as 'insurgent posthumanism', (Papadopoulos 2010) and related to deep history, such as 'geological posthumanism' (De Bruyn 2013). I will base the considerations that follow on two complementary definitions proposed by Jeff Wallace and by Ivan Callus and Stefan Herbrechter:

Posthumanism is here defined as a critique, both of an essentializing conception of human nature, and of human exceptionalism, and is generally characterized by discourses of the dissolution or blurring of the boundaries of the human, whether conceptual and philosophical (as in the 'decentring' of the human in 20th-century structuralist and poststructuralist thought) or scientific and technological (as in biotechnologies, genetics and cybernetics). (Wallace 2010: 692–3; see also Phillips 2015)

Posthumanism ... may therefore be seen as an attempt to create an interdisciplinary conceptual platform that draws together perspectives and investigations from the arts, the humanities and the sciences in the face of a radical and accelerated questioning of what it means to be human and what the re-imagined end(s) of the human might be. Accordingly, it focuses strongly on the contemporary technological, cultural, social and intellectual challenges to traditional notions of humanity and the institution of the humanities. (Callus and Herbrechter 2012: 250)

The above definitions provide a promising starting point for discussing the roles and status of the particular approach to the past embodied in the academic discipline of history in light of the challenges it faces from posthumanism and the posthumanities.

Any consideration of posthumanism should state from the outset that it has emerged as a response to a question being posed in a new context (namely, the context of technological progress and increasingly prevalent phenomena of the contemporary world, such as poverty, terrorism, migration, repeated acts of mass killings and genocide, environmental damage, and climate change). That question is: What is the human, and what is life? Researchers exploring this issue make the following assumptions: the contemporary world is characterized by accelerated technological progress which in turn brings radical transformation (and enables change) both to the human condition (posthumanists prefer this term to 'human nature') and also to the cultural and natural environment.[3] 'We may be about to enter into a posthuman future,' wrote Francis Fukuyama, noting the dawn of 'the "posthuman" stage of history' (Fukuyama 2002: 7, 217). One outcome of these processes, and particularly of advancements made in biology, neurophysiology, genetic engineering, and prosthetics, is that we are now observing an escalating process of 'cyborgization' and the emergence of the phenomenon known as the posthuman. With this specific figuration of subjectivity, we enter a space of transhumanism that remains anthropocentric. It makes the assumption that humans as a species are in a constant process of becoming and change, while contemporary technology gives us tools to improve the human being to become more than human through biological and technological modification – genetic engineering, nanotechnology, prosthesis, regenerative medicine, psychopharmacology, slowing down the ageing process, morphological freedom, mind uploading, and so on (Bostrom 2003; More and Vita-More 2013). These ideas, which belong to such fields of interest as posthuman disability studies, posthuman soldiers and posthuman warfare, and posthuman sport, might be associated with the history of the (posthuman) future (Baofu 2009). These ideas sometimes surface in works on the history of disability (Singer 2010), military history (Bourke 2014; Coker 2004), and sport history (Butryn 2003) but do not transform historical reflection (at least not yet).

Posthumanists reject the humanistic definition of the human being as the measure of all things and its fixation on the narcissistic, autonomous subject, which – as gender theorists have stressed – has been revealed to be the white, middle-class, European male (anthropocentrism = androcentrism). The object of the posthumanities is therefore not Man but rather *Anthropos and Homo sapiens* (or the human animal) entangled in interspecies and environmental relations. Drawing inspiration from the anti-humanism of Gilles Deleuze, Jacques Derrida, Frantz Fanon, and Michel Foucault[4] and poststructuralist discussions on the end/decline of the human on the one hand, and, on the other, from the achievements of contemporary life sciences, posthumanism contests the European and Christian traditions' vision of the human being as the centre of the universe and at the top of the hierarchy of species ('species chauvinism'). It turns instead towards a conception of the human being as a species that exists in relation with other organic and nonorganic life forms. The human is thus depicted as a specific form of life among other animals, thanks to his possession of consciousness and language, which render him capable of abstract and rational thought and of creating culture and civilization (these being deemed the most complex and developed forms of communal life). Following in the footsteps of biologists (and science fiction authors), posthumanists conceive of humanity as a particular ecosystem: a holobiont (Gilbert, Sapp, and Tauber 2012: 327, 331, 334) that in effect forms a conglomerate (or assemblage) comprising the various species that inhabit it while always remaining engaged in a process of co-creation with other forms of life, as well as with machines and things. As Donna Haraway says, paraphrasing Bruno Latour, 'we have never been human' (Gane 2006: 135–58; Haraway 2008). At least, we have never been the kind of humans envisioned by the humanities' traditional models. This kind of ecological, post-anthropocentric posthumanism is present in animal history and environmental history.

Post-anthropocentrism can be considered fundamental to the posthumanities. The neutralization of the differences between the humanities and social sciences, on the one hand, and the life sciences on the other, is another key trait of the posthumanities. This has stimulated the formation of many bridging disciplines that link, to quote C. P. Snow, the 'two cultures', thus attempting to formulate complementary responses to questions about humanity and life. When it comes to historical research, the relevant bridging disciplines include multispecies history, neurohistory, biohistory, zoohistory, and geohistory (Rudwick 2005) – these are terms already familiar to historical reflection (geohistory, for example, was a concept used by Fernand Braudel). However, turning theory into practice in the context of the posthumanities requires the historian to devise alternative approaches to research, perhaps by formulating new research questions that prompt them to use a new source base (such as big data, landscape, animal 'testimonies'), while also demanding competence (education) in the relevant fields of history and the natural sciences alike.[5]

Historians and posthumanism

Critical posthumanism, often used by historians, does not efface the human being from its field of interest, but rather decentralizes it and problematizes the understandings offered by traditional humanities (and among them, history). As Rafael Capurro (2012: 9) puts it: 'To go beyond humanism(s) does not mean to go against the "*humanum*" but against the fixation on humanness of the human by failing to see the dimension that allows us to transform ourselves and the world.' Dominick LaCapra is one of these historians who perceives anthropocentric history as reductive and presenting a distorted image of the past by setting forth an ideology of speciesism and human exceptionalism. In the book *History and Its Limits: Human, Animal, Violence* (2009), he is not interested in real animals, but in philosophical debates on humanism and 'whether it has always required a radical other ... in the form of some excluded or denigrated category of beings, often other animals or animality itself' (LaCapra 2009: 152). The author reflects on the binary opposition between human and animal and claims that it situates animals in a separate sphere and justifies oppressive and exploitative human practices towards animals (LaCapra 2009: 150, 153). LaCapra also claims:

> For the questioning of a decisive criterion separating the human from the animal or even from the rest of nature has widespread ramifications, even indicating the need for a massive paradigm shift in the relations of the human, the animal, and nature in general. Such a shift would not only mark a turn away from anthropocentrism but also point to the inadequacies of 'rights' discourse, both human and animal. (LaCapra 2009: 189)

Issues of humanism and anthropocentrism resonate in Gabrielle Spiegel's ideas quite differently. Spiegel broaches the core issues circulating in current debates in the academic world – meaning the question already posed by poststructuralist scholars as 'who comes after the subject?' (Connor, Cadava and Nancy 1991). In her presidential address for the American Historical Association in 2008, Spiegel indicated that

> we sense that the hold of poststructuralism and postmodernism on current historiography is diminishing. ... The new historiography doubtless will also require a revised understanding of subjectivity as something more than the discursively constituted 'subject positions' framed in poststructuralist theory, but also something other than a wholly re-centered humanist subject. (Spiegel 2009: 3, 13)

The avant-garde trends in today's humanities and social sciences are not interested in the human unless it is non-human, that is, unless it either lacks something that our culture has deemed a mark of humanity or has a surplus of something that identifies it as being in excess of humanity. The question of what constitutes the mark of humanity and how to measure its degree poses immediate problems. Is it human dignity and free will, articulate speech, a reflective mind, or genotype? Of particular interest are considerations of human subjects deprived of personhood (dehumanized prisoners of camps, the stateless, migrants, those living in extreme poverty), of those who have transcended humanity thanks to biotechnological progress (such as disabled persons who have acquired special abilities through prostheses and transplants), and of the non-dead (corpses and, in popular culture, zombies and vampires). The non-human has become the paradigmatic figure of the contemporary and the guidepost to the future. But the non-humanity of the human subject analysed by scholars working on so-called animality studies (Lundblad 2009) is only the tip of the iceberg. The problem (of which Spiegel is fully aware) is that now, we are asking not 'who comes' but 'what comes' after the subject.

The impact of posthumanism on historians' works is present, for example, in *Postmedieval: A Journal of Medieval Cultural Studies*, which is considered to be one of the most avant-garde periodicals in the humanities. Theme issues cover such topics as the animal turn, cognitive alterities/neuromedievalism, and ecomaterialism, with references to icons of posthumanist thought such as Bennett, Hayles, and Wolfe.[6] Indeed, the impact of posthumanism might be traced most visibly in the fields of animal history and environmental history, which discuss the place of humans in the history of the Earth and human–animal relations (Guerrini 2016).

For example, Ted Steinberg is aware that 'taking into account the independent world of nature should cause us to rethink the meaning of human agency. We need, in short, a less anthropocentric and less arrogant view of the concept' (Steinberg 2002: 819–20). Similarly, Richard D. Foltz claims that history is about interactions and interconnections that cannot be limited to connections between humans since 'many of our most significant historical interactions have been and continue to be with non-humans.' Calling for the integration of environmental history with world history, he claims that 'world history, if done properly – that is expanding the theme of interactions to include *all* actors, not just human ones – is not only good scholarship, it may be vital to saving the planet!' (Foltz 2003: 11, 20, 23).

In the field of postcolonial history, which addresses problems of colonialism, capital, and climate change, Dipesh Chakrabarty reflects on how our understanding of the human changes when it is located within the discussion on global warming. 'Becoming human was for us a matter of becoming a subject' – he wrote, recalling his involvement in the school of subaltern history. 'The critique of the subject was not the same as that performed by Althusserian antihumanism of the 1960s and 70s … . Postcolonial critique of the subject was actually a deeper turning towards the human' (Chakrabarty 2012: 4). But now, in the age of Anthropocene, when humans are seen as geological agents, we need 'nonontological ways of thinking the human' (because collectively, humans form a geophysical force which is a nonontological agency). Chakrabarty obviously falls among the 'survivalists,' as a scholar with a deep admiration for (Enlightened) humanism and its values (freedom, justice, rights). Post-anthropocentric posthumanists would criticize his 'enlightened anthropocentrism'. However, even he claims that '[historians] should think of humans as a form of life and look on human history as part of the history of life … on this planet' (Chakrabarty 2009: 213, 2015).

Similar ideas resonate in the works of historians such as David Christian, Daniel Lord Smail, and Fred Spier, who work on 'deep' and 'big' history and are interested in a longterm timescale and in seeing humans from an evolutionary perspective (Christian 2004; Fernández-Armesto 2009; Spier 2010; Smail 2008; Shryock and Smail 2011). Such an approach is also presented by Libby Robin and Will Steffen, who adopt the tone of a manifesto when they write:

> History-making today no longer needs the crude notion of 'progress' that the anthropocentric agenda for 'peace' demanded in the 1940s. Rather this world history is for the Anthropocene. This is history in the service of human co-operation in the interests of the planet. … World history is not just about past connections in the human community, any more than it is about Earth systems independent of people. In the geological epoch of the Anthropocene, it must be about 'humans and the rest of nature' taken together at scales appropriate to the questions of history. The community of World History is biophysical and human, and the agents of change are physical and social. … The new global history demands thinking on a planetary scale, for the ultimate sake of the planet itself, because the threats are from the unexpected behaviours of fundamentally changed natural systems. … Global change demands a new idea of 'patriotism', a loyalty not to country but to Earth. (Robin and Steffen 2007: 1711–2)

The notion of including history in discussions on the Anthropocene (Mikhail 2016) allows us to think about the past in terms of geological time and on a planetary scale, while attending to the strong interconnectedness and co-dependency between humans and nature and considering history in positive terms of co-operation, co-evolution, and togetherness rather than conflict and competition. These seem to be the typical motives driving posthumanist history as it is outlined above. They are visible in such subfields of history as labour history, the history of cities, and military history.[7] Note how conceptions of citizenship, co-worker, and patriotism (and the political and social systems they inform), so important in history, would change if their subject were not a human but a non-human (animal, cyborg), and not nation or the country but the species and the planet.

Humanist posthumanism

Of course, attempts have been made long ago to shift historians' attention towards research on the climate and environment. For example, Emmanuel Le Roy Ladurie adopted a longue durée perspective and criticized the 'naïve anthropocentrism' of researchers who attached excessive importance to the influence of the climate on migration and economic crises (Le Roy Ladurie 1967: 19). He stated instead that 'the goal of climate history is not to explain human history' (Le Roy Ladurie 1973: 513). On the other hand, he was in favour of 'climate history with a human face', which would investigate how climate change has impacted human living conditions. In Le Roy Ladurie's view, this would constitute an ecological history concerned with climate change not for its own sake, but for the sake of human beings (Le Roy Ladurie 1967: 19, 25–6). What was innovative in his approach, however, was his choice of subject matter, for by exploring the question of 'human ecology', he opened up research perspectives on 'natural history'.

Nevertheless, Le Roy Ladurie's general framework remained loyal to humanism and its privileging of the human.

This example provides a clue as to the posthumanist revalorization of historical reflection. The introduction (or, rather, re-introduction in a new context) of research on animals, plants, things, the environment, climate, and so on is, however, in itself insufficient. It is not a question of producing further fields of interest regarding plants, animals, or ecological matters. What is crucial is the formation of a theoretical interpretive framework that can inspire different research questions and offer alternative interpretations while demanding the construction of new concepts and theories in a situation where existing theory 'lags behind the facts' and an incommensurability emerges between practice and the theories attempting to describe it.[8] As Wolfe claims:

> One can engage in a *humanist* or a *posthumanist* practice of a discipline, and that fact is crucial to what a discipline can contribute to the field of animal studies. For example, just because a historian devotes attention to the topic of nonhuman animals – let's say, the awful plight of horses used in combat operations during World War I – doesn't mean that humanism and anthropocentrism aren't being maintained and reproduced in his or her disciplinary practice ... . So even though – to return to our historian example – your concept of the discipline's external relations to its larger environment is posthumanist in taking seriously the existence of nonhuman subjects and the consequent compulsion to make the discipline respond to the question of nonhuman animals foisted on it by changes in the discipline's environment, your internal disciplinarity may remain humanist through and through. We may now, then – to move toward a conclusion – suggest a more overarching schema in which such a procedure might be called 'humanist posthumanism'. (Wolfe 2010: 124)

I agree with scholars who believe that history ought to be oriented towards the future (although multiple paths lead to an acceptance of this future-oriented perspective, while adopting it leads to various findings). Already in the 1970s, the well-known Polish historian Jan Kieniewicz made a statement that might be taken as the credo of historiography in the posthumanist age: 'The historian who is brave enough to reach into the past, reconstruct it and explain its meaning to the contemporary world must consistently open the way to that which is yet to come. Futurology is a consequence of doing history; it is its quintessence' (Kieniewcz 1975: 173). In a recent article, Kieniewicz (2014: 66, 76) wrote that this prospective character of thinking about the past demands optimism and should, as he goes on to argue, 'break with the conservatism of fear and revive faith in the future'. While his declarations resemble those presented by researchers recognized as representatives of the posthumanities (Braidotti 2010; Massumi 1993), Kieniewicz explicitly describes himself as a humanist focused on the history of humanity who is proud of his (Eurocentric?) civilization, for whom the main challenge is not the environment but the human being. However, he does link the future-oriented perspective to humanism, believing it to be a civic obligation and a desirable trait in researchers (in that it requires them to take responsibility for both the good and bad aspects of the civilization with which they identify) (Kieniewicz 2014: 66–7, 80). Kieniewicz's position is thus close to that of Le Roy Ladurie. Following Wolfe, we might describe this position as 'humanist posthumanism'. This is the prevailing attitude, I would argue, among historians who show interest in avant-garde humanities research.

Animal history as non-anthropocentric history

Historians' cautious opinions on the critique of humanism and on non-anthropocentric visions of the past are understandable. To a large extent, they are a product of the scholar's ideological standpoint, research interests, geographical location, and the generation that he or she represents. Let us compare, then, the approaches of Le Roy Ladurie and Kieniewicz outlined above with the perspective presented by a scholar belonging to the younger generation – Erica Fudge, who works on animals in the early modern period. Like Kieniewicz, she agrees that history should be thought of 'as the project of the past, but *for* the future' (Fudge 2002: 3). Locating the history of animals within this perspective, she describes its role, stating that 'the history of animals is a necessary part of our reconceptualization of ourselves as human' (Fudge 2002: 5). Kieniewicz and Le Roy Ladurie would surely not object to the above claims. Fudge, however, goes further. Stating that history should turn towards anti-humanism, she issues an appeal that resounds with the tone of a manifesto:

> We must abandon the status of the human as it is presented within humanist history. … By refusing humanism, and, implicitly, anthropocentrism, we place ourselves next to the animals, rather than as the users of the animals, and this opens up a new way of imagining the past. … we must write a history which refuses the absolute separation of the species; refuses that which is the silent assumption of humanist history. (Fudge 2002: 15–16)

The full potential of this idea is revealed in concrete research. It is enough to imagine how the history of animals (or, more generally, multispecies history) is changing the face of such sub-disciplines of historical research as labour history or war history. It shows that labour is often based upon collaboration with animals, whose input into production is mentioned but marginalized and therefore, in effect, barely researched (e.g. horses in salt mines, sheepdogs, and oxen used for ploughing). I will not go into animals on battlefields, many of whom not only became companions in war but even drew fame as non-human heroes, such as the well-known canine hero of the First World War Sergeant Stubby, the pigeon G. I. Joe who was awarded the Dickin Medal (the animal equivalent of the Victoria Cross), and Wojtek (or Voytek) the Bear, the Polish Second World War hero. From this perspective, labour and war appear to be a multispecies endeavour based on collaboration between human and non-human participants. Heroism is not an exclusively human attribute.[9] All this, however, is still insufficient. Fudge presents historians with a difficult challenge: she calls on them to transcend the anthropocentrism typical of historical research and to create a project of non-anthropocentric history that contests the traditional conception of humanistic history (see Fudge 2017). This, however, is not the only challenge. According to Wolfe's suggestion outlined above that 'one can engage in a *humanist* or a *posthumanist* practice of a discipline', the challenge is to transcend the aim of 'writing animals into history', which posthumanists consider to be a highly limited objective. Let us explore this question for a moment.

Hilda Kean compares problems associated with writing the history of animals with those that emerged in the context of writing the history of women, marginalized groups, those who were denied a voice by grand history and those associated with 'history from below' in general. The first stage is to recognize these subjects as historical subjects and therefore include them in mainstream historical research. The next stage is to see them as historical agents capable of transforming socio-cultural reality (Swart 2010: 243; see also Fudge 2002: 5–6). The lack of sources created by such 'others' therefore becomes a typical obstacle to writing their history (the lack of sources = lack of history). Kean writes:

> An acknowledgment of the existence of a 'past' – whether considering animals or humans – needs to precede the making of a history. Most working in the field of Animal Studies would not dispute that (at least certain) animals have *past* lives. Whether past lives become 'historical' lives depends not on the subjects themselves – be these animals or humans – but on those writing about them who then choose to construct a history. This is an important distinction. As Daniel Smail has suggested, 'to admit that other animals have no sense of history is a quite different thing from claiming that animals cannot be held within the embrace of history'. ... The issue then is not about agency of the subjects of history as such (in this instance animals) but the choices, agency if you will, of those seeking to transform such actions into history. There is a distinction to be made between events happening in the past in which even the most conservative of historians would agree animals played a role, most obviously in the economy, transport, or warfare and the turning of this subject matter into particular histories that privilege animals. (Kean 2012: 55–60)

The well-known triad – humanity, agency, and resistance – locates the idea of agency within the frame of human (and animal) rights. Employing such interpretive frameworks when writing the history of animals causes us to fall into the same traps we encountered when writing the emancipatory history of the vanquished and the victim – that is, animals are treated as 'others' (as was previously the case with women, black people, the disabled, etc.). Conceiving animals through categories of otherness, thereby comparing them to servants and slaves, is interesting at the level of traditional historiography, whose fundamental objective is to reveal unknown facts from the past (which in itself is something of value). From a theoretical perspective, however, this hardly constitutes a challenge. I therefore agree with Hilda Kean that 'writing animals into history' is insufficient. The interpretive frameworks need to be reworked (Kean 2012: 65).

Animal studies in the posthumanities (and biohumanities) could aid historical research in transcending reductive (with respect to the history of animals) hermeneutics and the anthropocentric perspective (Baratay 2012, 2015). What is innovative about the posthumanities' approach to writing the history of animals in comparison to the ways in which animals have been taken up as a theme in earlier historical research is that, firstly, animal studies are conducted within the alternative theoretical framework offered by the posthumanities, drawing on the work of scholars construed as their leading representatives (Haraway, Latour, Wolfe); secondly, animals are not explored as symbols or as 'tools' used by humans, but are instead investigated as subjects and historical agents with which humans share their world and which co-create that world (Shaw 2013); thirdly, this approach stimulates interest in the animalistic nature of human beings and reminds us that from a biological perspective, the human being is an animal. It is therefore important to explore the ideas and practices that have led to and legitimized the separation of humans from animals, thus producing the idea of human exceptionalism.

Fudge and other researchers engaged in writing the history of animals are aware that such work requires complementary knowledge that combines the humanities and social sciences with research on animal psychology and cognition and zoology, to name but a few fields (Nance 2015). In this way, the history of animals in its future-oriented mode, as described by Fudge, can lead to the formation of anthrozoological knowledge of the past,[10] something that would no longer be a field of the humanities but would belong instead to the biohumanities. Yet even this fails to satisfy avant-garde researchers. In her review of *Beastly Natures* (2010), Sandra S. Swart wrote: 'This anthology has a sub-textual lament that history is written by humans alone' (Swart 2011). In light of what I have outlined above, the following question emerges: Can we imagine knowledge of the past (which I would not limit to history) that would be based on multispecies co-authorship? The question might seem absurd, but this is far from the case for researchers who read the work of primatologists. Sue Savage-Rumbaugh, for example, published an article as co-author along with three chimpanzees.[11] Let us consider, then, whether and how we could achieve 'interspecies competence', to use Fudge's term (2002: 11), not only for thinking about coexistence with animals but also for creating a multispecies knowledge of the past.

Conclusion

What does posthumanism do to history? It reveals the limitations of history as a specific approach to the past. Posthumanism signals a much more important challenge than the tendencies associated with postmodernism indicated here. It challenges the very foundations of history understood as a specific approach to the past developed within the framework of Greco-Roman and Judeo-Christian traditions with their anthropocentric (and even zoocentric) bias, Eurocentrism, geocentrism, and even exclusive human authorship of knowledge building. As Marc Bloch, a classical figure in French historiography, predicted long ago, our civilization has turned its back on history.[12] On the other hand, with the efforts now underway to redefine humanity and the relations between the human and non-human, history understood as human self-knowledge becomes overridingly important (Collingwood 1994: 10) on the condition that it takes a critical view on the affirmation of humanity. Perhaps we need a history that encourages us to be and remain human (existing in relation to posthumans and various non-humans) without making it something egoistic. Such knowledge might face the supremely important task and challenge of demonstrating the possibility of creating and reinforcing a feeling of 'shared humanity' and species solidarity, and of showing what this depends on and how it has changed. Even if posthumanism influences only avant-garde tendencies in historical studies and not a mainstream history, and is already thought of as something limited that we must move beyond,[13] it shows a need for a more 'visionary', future-oriented history that would help to build knowledge of – as Bruno Latour says – 'how to live together' (and in conflict, I would add), 'to compose a world that is not yet common' (Latour 2005: 254, 259, 262; 2009: 2) and prepare us for the future to come, so fundamentally different from the present.

Comment

Dominick LaCapra

I agree with the overall argument and many of the specific points made in Ewa Domanska's well-documented account of the posthumanist turn in the humanities. In history, as she notes, this turn has thus far been rather limited and calls for further informed, critical work.

Domanska helpfully asserts that she intends to 'use the term "posthumanist" as an adjective and treat it as a cross-disciplinary perspective'. She accurately notes that there is no single or dominant form of posthumanist thought but rather a congeries of initiatives and a series of figures taken by many as iconic. An important (I think the most important) strain of posthumanism is not an anti-humanism even though it may well be a non-humanism requiring a robust critique of anthropocentrism and human exceptionalism. Domanska seems to quote with approval certain claims that earlier theoretical currents are now dead, but important dimensions of poststructuralism have both led up to and been integrated into varieties of posthumanism, notably the questioning of essentialism, of totalization, and of human exceptionalism in favour of a stress on decentring and the deconstruction of binary oppositions. Also prominent in poststructuralism has been the contestation of boundaries (including those between disciplines) and the need for a rearticulation of reconceptualized, problematic distinctions in contrast to rigid binaries. Figures mentioned by Domanska, such as Rosi Braidotti and Cary Wolfe, are manifestly indebted to poststructuralism. Braidotti developed strains in Gilles Deleuze and Luce Irigaray (among others), while crucial to Wolfe's project has been an attempt to coordinate the thought of Jacques Derrida with that of Niklas Luhmann's version of systems theory. Derrida was also crucial in the radical questioning of any dichotomy between humans and other animals, notably in works that deserve a place in any bibliography of posthumanism, for example, his *L'animal que donc je suis* (Derrida 2006).[14]

Noteworthy in Domanska's argument is the importance in posthumanism of the issue of the actual, possible, and desirable relations between humans and other animals. Existentially, especially with respect to current practices, this may be the most pressing issue raised by posthumanism, one that should not be obscured by other fascinating problems focused on by thinkers such as Bostrom, Haraway, and Hayles. Indeed the fascination of artificial intelligence, robots, cyborgs, genetic engineering, and the advent of futuristic possibilities (such as a possible takeover of humans by their more inventive inventions) should not obscure the very real and present challenges posed by practices such as factory farming, at times pointless experimentation, sport hunting as a rather unsportsmanlike sport, training animals to perform for human amusement, captivity in zoos, and other questionable practices. In my judgement, the repeated quest for the decisive but elusive criteria that sharply separate the human from 'the' animal and seemingly provide a foundation for human exceptionalism has as a primary motivation the legitimation of unself-questioning human identity and often dubious human uses and abuses of other animals. This quest is the basis for the seemingly endless series of research projects and publications that seek to specify just what the putative differentiating criteria are, criteria that vary over time and space yet seem to converge on a desire to assure human identity and legitimize human exceptionalism with all it is presumed to justify or allow, up to and including the 'sacrifice' of other animals in the service of human or divine interests.

Here I would qualify one comment Domanska makes concerning my own work and then extend it to a more general point. With respect to my book *History and Its Limits: Human, Animal, Violence* (LaCapra 2009), she states that I am 'not interested in real animals, but in philosophical debates on humanism and "whether it has always required a radical other … in the form of some excluded or denigrated category of beings, often other animals or animality itself"'. I would object that, both in this book and in other publications, I write much about treatment in such sites such as experimental labs, factory farms, and elsewhere, and I see the very real question of real animals as something that should not be etherealized by certain philosophical or, more precisely, what I have termed theoreticist orientations (something I find and criticize extensively in Giorgio Agamben).[15]

Concerning the relation between humans and other animals one prominent point is that so-called imaginative literature (as well as film) is an area in which those relations may be explored in particularly insightful ways that have implications for orientations towards real animals – one reason why a posthumanistic historiography should pay more sustained attention to literature and not only to the social or even the biological sciences. A case in point is J. M. Coetzee, notably his important novels *Elizabeth Costello* and *Disgrace*. One might see a crucial relation between what Costello terms the sympathetic imagination and what I treat in terms of transference, empathy, and compassion. In the revisionary understanding of transference I employ, it refers to the mutual implication of self and other. It is not confined to the nonetheless significant parent/child relation or its clinical repetitions or displacements. It characterizes relations with various others (including animals, objects of study, and the past), forming the basis of attraction and repulsion, even empathy, love, and hate. The importance of empathy (as well as antipathy) does not substitute for ethics or politics but may serve as their motivation and, more generally, their necessary supplement. I would add that a warranted critique of anthropocentrism should not be conflated with a dismissal of anthropomorphism. The latter, tested but not dismissed by critical inquiry, can be defended as itself related to imaginative empathy and compassion that bind humans and other animals (see, for example, Daston and Mitman 2005). Emotion and affect in general (including trauma and haunting post-traumatic effects in both humans and other animals) are areas that may deserve greater attention than Domanska allows, and empathy, not conflated with identification but respectful of the difference or alterity of others, is an emotion that is important for any posthumanism and may have a mutually challenging and reinforcing – not an antithetical – relation to critical reason.

A broader problem is whether binary opposition or dichotomous thinking at times arises, however unintentionally, in dimensions of Domanska's own account. I shall quote a passage with which I in good part agree. But I also see in it a binaristic tendency possibly conducive to the separation of critical theory and attentive concern for real animals:

> It is not a question of producing further fields of interest regarding plants, animals or ecological matters. What is crucial is the formation of a theoretical interpretive framework that can inspire different research questions and offer alternative interpretations, while at the same time demanding the construction of new concepts and theories.

It is not enough, as Domanska puts it elsewhere, to write animals or other non-human beings into history. And, despite its difficulty, it is crucial to work towards a theoretical framework that can inspire different research questions and offer alternative interpretations. But is the theoretical perspective itself enough? It would surely be preferable to add the proviso that the search for better theoretical frameworks should not block or substitute for a sustained attentiveness to the existence and conditions of real beings, such as humans and other animals in both mutually beneficial, cooperative relations and in exploitative, abusive, often traumatizing situations such as factory farms or sometimes questionable experiments.

Domanska also writes: 'Today it is not philosophy, but biology, from which history is learning.' But is this not another both/and rather than an either/or issue? And does not much depend on the kind of biology and the extent to which it is informed by a critical–theoretical perspective as well as care and concern for its objects of study? Some evolutionary biology still seeks to place 'man' at its pinnacle and could be seen as a secular displacement of the great chain of being. In any case, it may be ensconced in an ideology that passes unnoticed insofar as it is numbingly objectifying and gives 'us' a privileged position that makes us number one. A much-praised example of the quest for the holy grail that upholds human exceptionalism is Thomas Suddendorf's *The Gap: The Science of What Separates Us From Other Animals* (2013). The term 'science' here should be taken with a large grain of salt. At the very least it would be more accurate to argue that 'gaps' that are geared to demonstrate human uniqueness or exceptionalism are created much more by ideological incentives than by scientific requirements. Science in Suddendorf takes a narrative turn that is now all-too-familiar in history, and he finds that humans are presumably unique in the ability to spin out endless, varied stories and scenarios. We also presumably have an irrepressible desire to share our imaginings with others. I cannot share Suddendorf's debatable, idealizing imaginings and would rather point to the work of another scientist with a strong interest in biology, real animals, and critical self-reflection. In his *Are We Smart Enough to Know How Smart Animals Are?*, Frans de Waal (2016) stresses the various types of intelligence and ability in different animals.[16] Like Darwin, he argues for differences of degree not kind between humans and other animals and observes that 'uniqueness claims typically cycle through four stages: they are repeated over and over, they are challenged by new findings, they hobble toward retirement, and then they are dumped into an ignominious grave' (De Waal 2016: 126). However one eventually constructs the complex configuration of similarities and differences between humans and other animals, the question remains whether differential criteria would validate human uses and abuses of other animals – a question that would have to be addressed not on narrowly scientific (including biological) but on broader critical, ethical, and political grounds.

An area that may well require a prominent place in any posthumanism is that of ideology and its critique. And a prominent form of ideology that has arisen along with posthumanism focuses on the postsecular. Both share the appeal of a seemingly new orientation. They also share the at best thin coherence of the various 'post' orientations that they follow and in significant measure repeat with more or less significant variations. The postsecular is obviously related to religion and to the question of secularization. Religion has typically been a non-humanism in which the human being, even when positioned above the rest of nature, has a subordinate place with respect to higher spiritual powers, which in monotheisms culminate in the theocentric notion of God. In various traditional or indigenous religions (or what have been construed as such), a God-being or totally other, transcendent Other is not a forceful presence if it plays a significant role at all. More important are spirits or spiritual beings that may have a higher status than humans (and often are seen as closer to non-human animals) but are bound up with other beings in ways that impose limits on human assertion and the exploitation of nature, particularly with respect to sacred sites imbued with spiritual forces. In the West, religion has of course persisted despite the rise of secularity, and it has often been an imposing presence whose continuing role has until recently not been sufficiently recognized by those affirming an Enlightenment project, for example, Jürgen Habermas. Yet Habermas has recently been prominent in the attempt to attend, and even grant a certain validity, to religion as a postsecular orientation that may in part be valuable in supplementing the Enlightenment project, which he now thinks has not fully or even sufficiently succeeded (Habermas 2008).

The relation of the postsecular and the religious is vexed, and the former often seems to be a threshold phenomenon, both similar to and different from more traditional religions. Secularization itself took diverse forms. The clearest was the secularization of church property. But, in more contested, less obvious, and more thought-provoking ways, secularization raised the question of the extent to which seemingly secular processes or phenomena are more or less disguised displacements of religion. Many important figures have addressed the question of the extent and ways secular phenomena, notably the sovereign nation state, could be understood as a displacement of the religious, including Karl Löwith, Carl Schmitt, Hans Blumenberg, and Sigmund Freud. Others pursued further this line of inquiry, including Jacques Derrida, notably in terms of a 'hauntology' displacing ontology.[17]

A perplexing issue is whether and how the posthuman is combined with the postsecular or, in apparent contrast, represents an intensification of a secularity hostile to, or in any event decisively different from, religion as well as various forms of spirituality. In the latter eventuality, the posthuman would be oriented towards seeming paradigms of the secular such as natural science, notably biology. Of course there have been postsecular or even religious aspects in, or bound up with, science, including biology, for example, in a figure such as Pierre Teilhard de Chardin who had impeccable scientific credentials and construed divinity as the motivation of the evolutionary process leading to some unknown Omega point or Singularity (see, for example, Teilhard de Chardin 1974). For those who wanted to dispense with God or pointed to His death, the human being might assume a divine or quasi-divine status, for example, in a religion of Reason or of Humanity (prominent in the French Revolution and later in Auguste Comte), in Feuerbach's transformative criticism of Hegel (based on the interiorization by [super] humans of what was presumably alienated and projected onto God), in Durkheim's approximation if not conflation of society and divinity, or more simply in the human assumption of the sovereign position once held by God and divine-right kings.[18] Up to the present day, a familiar phenomenon is the narcissistic, ultra-nationalistic, scapegoating, authoritarian ruler (or 'con man') who takes himself (usually not herself) to be God or God like and has a cult-like following of true believers who may be willing to affirm whatever the ruler or leader puts forth, however ludicrous and contradicted by well-established facts.

To the best of my knowledge, those interested in posthumanism have not generally explored the question of its possible or actual relations with the postsecular. Yet this is a question that warrants inquiry.[19] Indeed the larger problem may well be the complex formed by the posthuman and the postsecular. Even Derrida, arguably a key inspiration for posthumanism, turned in his later career in a direction I would be loath to follow: a messianicity without messianism, involving an affirmation of *une attente sans attente* or waiting without an expectation of arrival – a waiting for what is unexpectedly to come (*à-venir*) but is not identifiable with a given being or state of affairs (see, for example, Caputo 1997; Derrida and Vattimo 1998, esp. 1–78). The allure of an apocalyptic blank utopia is at play in various influential thinkers, for example, Giorgio Agamben and Slavoj Žižek. Žižek supported the election of Donald Trump (as, in their own ways, did many of his supporters) because he saw Trump as the bringer of 'real' change, of something radically different that would shake up the status quo, departing from familiar neo-liberalism and (hope against hope) leading to desired (yet on arrival perhaps not really desirable) transformation.[20]

One finds an apprehension, perhaps a desire, for a big-bang apocalypse or 'singularity' in certain posthumanists (e.g. Nick Bostrom), and it seems at times to have postsecular resonances as an adventitious, radically transformative advent. One may recall Heidegger's quasi-religious invocation of the *Ereignis* and his latter-day, post-Hitler, apocalyptic assertion that only a god can save us. It is unclear just how prevalent an apocalyptic, posthumanist-postsecular view might be, although it readily feeds into evangelical and fundamentalist forms of Christianity that may combine rapacious exploitation of the environment and pious if not sanctimonious other-worldlinesss, even an ecologically threatening end-of-days theology.

I have concluded by raising certain issues that call for discussion with respect to posthumanism, especially the relations between the posthuman and the postsecular. And I would ask how extreme or complete a break with the past and with varieties of humanism and historiography is sought by advocates of posthumanism. I have a critical response to more unguarded apocalyptic tendencies that may even harbour desires to transcend procedures for substantiating assertions – procedures that are necessary to critically check myth making and a wayward idea of 'alternative facts'.[21] But I would remain open-minded concerning other dimensions of the postsecular, especially the idea of a 'sacred' respect and caring for others, understood in terms of a normatively regulated network of relations along with forms of mutual implication linking past, present, and future and involving other animals, other beings, and the environment.

Response

Ewa Domanska

Dominick LaCapra's enriching comments on interconnections between postmodernism, posthumanism, and postsecularism create a stimulating environment for considering human–animal relationships. This is indeed an important, challenging, and broadly discussed aspect of the posthumanist (non-anthropocentric) impact on the discipline of history. Obviously, there is no posthumanism without postmodernism. So when I wrote about 'the end of postmodernism,' I did not mean to suggest the inapplicability or inadequacy of works by postmodern thinkers for the (post)humanities today. I join those scholars who have argued since the 1990s that postmodernism had reached its peak (Ziegler 1993; Simmons and Billig 1994). This does not mean, of course, that these trends are no longer relevant. They are, however, no longer at the centre of discussions taking place around avant-garde tendencies that do not (as was the case with postmodernism) predominate in the humanities, but do constitute its 'front line' and are responsible for stimulating the reconfiguration of research questions, theories, and approaches.

There is an interesting contrast between those scholars who are deeply rooted in critical theory associated with various postmodernist tendencies and organize their posthumanist and/or non-human turn according to these tendencies, and those who use them as a springboard for ideas intended to transcend postmodernism. LaCapra has been and remains a critical thinker, and as far as the question of the human and the animal is concerned, he is interested in examining differences as criteria for justifying human practices in the treatment of animals. He is also interested in interrogating the limitations of 'rights discourse' (LaCapra 2009: 150, 152, 189). Still, when LaCapra claims in the comments above that ideology and critique should have a prominent place in posthumanism, he represents a continuation of an important and typical feature of an engaged humanities and social sciences that is the quest for justice with its transformative aims. In this way, LaCapra might be positioned within a critical posthumanism that still focuses on the problem of in/justice but locates it within the broader context of a more-than-human world.

It goes without saying that such an approach is important for real practices involving the abuse of animal subjects such as those mentioned by LaCapra: laboratory experiments, zoos, circuses, and so on. This approach changes the way we think about and treat animals. As was also the case with women and people of colour, it also encourages us to change our linguistic habits that legitimize, neutralize, and often hide human violence against non-human animals. For example, instead of 'pets,' style guidelines now recommend authors use the term 'companion animals', instead of 'circus elephants', 'elephants kept in circuses', and so on (Freeman and Merskin 2015). My contribution, however, had a different task. As a scholar interested in emerging methods and theories, I try to inquire if and how posthumanism might pose a challenge to history and open a space for the emergence of alternatives to history understood as a specific approach to the past. And indeed, it might, since it offers – as Jasemin B. Ulmer (2017) indicates – various ways of 'thinking with' (air, animals, earth, plants, rocks, water), 'thinking without' (representation, ecology without nature, the world without us) and 'thinking differently' (about data, writing, thinking in terms of more-than-critical or post-critical research) that undermine the basic premises of historical reflection.

I agree with LaCapra that affect, emotions, empathy, and trauma are important for the respectful treatment of others and as such, should remain significant problems of research. But this is again a problem that has already been addressed in critical studies of 'class, race, and gender'. Without dismissing the obvious need to maintain this approach, I would use not (only) critical theory (and hermeneutics) but also comparative ethology and trans-species psychology to advance research in these matters (Bradshaw and Watkins 2006; Bradshaw 2009). I would therefore advocate a complementary approach (humanities and social sciences that complement and supplement life sciences – and vice versa) and focus on comparative studies that analyse similarities between human and non-human animal behaviour (especially related to traumatic events such as hunting, killing, forced relocation, imprisonment, infant lost, etc.). Here, too, I see a challenge for history understood as a specific approach to the past and for historical theory and research governed by a specific understanding of time, space, rationality, telos, progress, sources, and so on (Domanska 2017). A complementary approach would invite historians to examine the possibility of non-linguistic communication (Martinelli 2010) and to conceptualize non-human animal testimonies as historical sources (Zulueta 2015).

LaCapra's important comment indicates an association between posthumanism and postsecularism (Graham 2016). Indeed, it is quite surprising, given the vast literature on the subject, that the postsecular turn, sometimes labelled as a turn to religion or theological turn (also partly rooted in the postmodernist interest in religion and theology), is hardly noticed by historians (Megill 2013). I do agree with LaCapra that cross-sections of postsecularism and posthumanism open up possibilities for researching questions of anthropocentrism (and anthropomorphism), human and non-human bonds, and relations with nature and the planet. Together with life and earth sciences, eco- or green theology, animal theology (Linzey 2007), and creaturely theology (Moore 2014) as practised within monotheistic religions, this approach not only illuminates the problems mentioned above but also – as in the case of anthropology and sociology – changes how a discipline is practised (Fountain 2013; McLennan 2007). Besides, the posthumanist interest in the (nonintentional) agency of things, object-oriented ontologies and vitalist materialism exposes the history of material culture to fresh air (Schouwenburg 2015), allowing us to rethink our inquiry into, for example, 'premodern sacred things' (Gayk and Malo 2014; Ioannides 2013).

As LaCapra points out, the postsecular turn also revives an interest in various forms of spirituality. Here, it is worth mentioning the recent interest in new animism (and new totemism) observed across various fields and approaches (thing studies as practised in anthropology and archaeology, ecology of matter, the popularity of Amerindian perspectivism, political animism, non-human personhood, etc.) (Harvey 2013). In this context, indigenous knowledges are recognized not so much as the subject of anthropological research but, rather, as a platform for building an alternative understanding of the subject, community, the sacred, time, space, and relations with non-humans (Domanska 2015). For example, indigenous ideas of plant sensing that have been confirmed by plant neurobiology (Chamovitz 2012; see also Pierotti 2010) also help to bridge the humanities, social sciences, life science and indigenous knowledges, and at the same time suggest a need to decolonialize history.

While historians have used a genealogical method in their search for signs of posthumanism in the past (Campana and Maisano 2016), there is a distinctive feature of this tendency that LaCapra seems to underestimate in his effort to recuperate it for critical theory and a presentist approach to posthumanism. Posthumanism is an anticipatory paradigm; it manifests what Fredric Jameson calls 'a revival of futurity' (2010: 42–3) – a revival of future-oriented thinking (utopian and dystopian) that presupposes imagination, prefiguration, speculation, and wonder. Often optimistically, it advocates affirmative ethics and politics (Braidotti 2010, 2014) and promotes 'potential history' (Azoulay 2013). This kind of history encourages scholars to explore unrealized potential in the past in an attempt to reveal what conditions must be created to allow people to become accustomed to each other and to show how they might coexist, even in conditions of conflict. I see this utopian aspect of posthumanism in its search for new (bio-, inter- or multispecies) forms of sociality, collectivity, and community as a crucial aspect of a prefigurative, holistic knowledge of the past.

Notes

Acknowledgements: I am grateful to Paul Vickers for translating parts of this chapter into English and to Eliza Cushman Rose for proofreading.

1. The concept of the posthumanities was popularized by the University of Minnesota Press *Posthumanities* publication series that has been edited by Cary Wolfe since 2007 (see https://www.upress.umn.edu/book-division/series/posthumanities – accessed 11 February 2017).

2. For example, in the article 'The Future of History: Posthumanist Entrepreneurial Storytelling, Global Warming, and Global Capitalism', the authors refer to Dipesh Chakrabarty's works on climate change and use the term 'posthumanist history' to indicate transgressing a divide between natural and human history and treating humans not only as cultural and social agents but also as 'geological agents'. Boje and Saylors (2016: 200); see also Chakrabarty (2016).

3. Posthumanists oppose the dualism of culture and nature, so in order to stress their co-dependence they often use the term 'nature-culture' (Latour 1993: 7, 96, 105–9) or 'natureculture' (Haraway 2004: 63–124; 295–320).

4. Michel Foucault's anti-humanism is well known. He claimed that 'man is only a recent invention, a figure not yet two centuries old, a new wrinkle in our knowledge, and that he will disappear again as soon as that knowledge has discovered a new form' (Foucault 2005: xxv). See also Derrida (1969). The poststructuralist origins of posthumanism are illustrated in the anthology of anti-humanists texts ed. by Badmington (2000).

5. From the perspective of these avant-garde tendencies, the concept of a global world is becoming increasingly oppressive, while planetary identification backed by the ideas of transculturalism becomes increasingly compelling. Even if Gísli Pálsson et al. (2013: 5–6) claim that 'so far there are no "planetary humanities,"' they indicate a strong need for innovative projects related to the Anthropocene's emphasis on the coupling of human society and earth systems. See also Worster (1988).

6. *Postmedieval: A Journal of Medieval Cultural Studies*. Theme Issues: The Animal Turn, vol. 2, no, 1, 2011; Cognitive Alterities/Neuromedievalism, vol. 3, no. 3, 2012, Ecomaterialism, vol. 4, no. 1, 2013.

7. A historical approach to urban animals and the 'anthrozootic city' along with various forms of collaboration between humans and animals are present in articles by David Gary Shaw, Scott A. Miltenberger, and Andrew McEwen published in *The Historical Animal*, ed. by Susan Nance (2015).

8. I am referring here to Imre Lakatos (1978: 5–6), who wrote, 'Where theory lags behind the facts, we are dealing with miserable degenerating research programmes. … In a progressive research programme, theory leads to the discovery of hitherto unknown novel facts. In degenerating programmes, however, theories are fabricated only in order to accommodate known facts.'

9. There is a wealth of literature on this subject, although it primarily consists of publications that are typical examples of 'writing animals into history'. For example, on soldier animals,

see Le Chene (1994); Cooper (1983); Hediger (2013); Karunanithy (2008); Kistler (2006); and Orr (2014).

10. Robert Delort presented this postulate already in his 1984 book *Les animaux ont une histoire* (Delort 1984). At the time, however, historians were still not prepared to make more daring incursions into the territory of the study of nature and thus overcome the anthropocentric paradigm. See also Hurn (2010: 27).

11. I refer to the research of primatologists and to an article published in a scientific periodical that was coauthored by chimpanzees (specifically bonobo, the so-called pygmy chimpanzee (*Pan paniscus*)). See Savage-Rumbaugh et al. (2007).

12. 'Without doubt, civilizations may change. It is not in itself inconceivable that ours may, one day, turn away from history, and historians would do well to reflect upon its possibility' Bloch (1992: 5).

13. Doubts about the potential of posthumanism are expressed by Callus and Herbrechter (2012: 249), who asked if 'posthumanism is sufficiently radical in its rethinking of subjectivity?' Haraway claims that she became interested in companion species and stopped using the term posthumanism since it had been appropriated by transhumanist technoenhancement (Gene 2006: 140).

14. English transl. D. Wills (with the necessary loss of one meaning of 'suis' as 'follow' or 'track') as *The Animal That Therefore I Am* (2008). See also Derrida (2009) and (2011).

15. This dimension of the book, including its critique of 'theoreticism', is clearly seen and well analysed in the essay review by Allan Megill (2013).

16. De Waal offers a general survey of recent scientific tendencies in animal studies. He also demonstrates the potential extent of bonding, respect, and affection between humans and the animals with whom they interact. He strives for a non-anthropocentric perspective that opens onto an array of similarities and differences that resist reduction to simple oppositions subordinated to the quest for decisively differential criteria separating the human from other animals. See also De Waal (2016) on anthropomorphism, esp. pp. 24–6, and on empathy, pp. 132–3.

17. Somewhat hyperbolically, Freud wrote to Wilhelm Fliess: 'By the way, what have you to say to the suggestion that the whole of my brand new theory of the primary origins of hysteria is already familiar and has been published a hundred times over, though several centuries ago? Do you remember my always saying that the medieval theory of possession, that held by ecclesiastical courts, was identical with our theory of a foreign body and the splitting of consciousness?' (Freud 1957: 90). See also LaCapra (1994), chap. 6, 'The Return of the Historically Repressed'.

18. On Durkheim and his predecessors, notably with respect to the secular and the religious, see LaCapra ([1972] 2001), esp. chap. 6, 'The Sacred and Society'.

19. See, however, Hurlbut and Tirosch-Samuelson (2016), esp. chap. 2, 'Manifestations of the Posthuman in the Postsecular Imagination', by Elaine Graham.

20. On Žižek, see, for example, *Vice News* (30 November 2016), available online: https://news.vice.com/story/far-left-philosopher-slavoj-zizek-explains-why-he-suppored-trump-over-clinton (accessed 27 February 2017).

21. See LaCapra (2007); in the same volume, see Domanska (2007). I would not invalidate carefully framed alternative or 'as-if' histories or provocative narratives informed by warrantable assertions about what indeed occurred in the past.

References

AHR Forum (2012), 'AHR Forum: Historiographic 'Turn' in Critical Perspective', *American Historical Review*, 117 (3): 698–813.

AHR Roundtable (2014), 'AHR Roundtable: History Meets Biology, *American Historical Review*, 118 (5): 1492–1629.

Azoulay, A. (2013), 'Potential History: Thinking through Violence', *Critical Inquiry*, 39 (3): 548–74.

Bachmann-Medick, D. (2016), *Cultural Turns: New Orientations in the Study of Culture*, trans. A. Blauhut, Berlin: De Gruyter.

Badmington, N., ed. (2000), *Posthumanism*, Basingstoke: Palgrave Macmillan.

Baratay, É. (2012), *Point de vue animal. Une autre version de l'histoire*. Paris: Seuil.

Baratay, É. (2015), 'Building an Animal History', trans. S. Posthumus, in L. Mackenzie and S. Posthumus (eds), *French Thinking about Animals*, 3–14, East Lansing: Michigan State University Press.

Baofu, P. (2009), *The Future of Post-Human History: A Preface to a New Theory of Universality*, Newcastle upon Tyne: Cambridge Scholars.

Bloch, M. (1992), *The Historian's Craft*, trans. P. Putnam, Manchester: Manchester University Press.

Boje, D. M. and Saylors, R. (2016), 'The Future of History: Posthumanist Entrepreneurial Storytelling, Global Warming, and Global Capitalism', in R. Mir, H. Willmott and M. Greenwood (eds), *The Routledge Companion to Philosophy in Organization Studies*, 197–205, New York: Routledge.

Bostrom, N. (2003), 'Transhumanist Values', available online: http://www.nickbostrom.com/ethics/values.html (accessed 12 February 2017)

Bourke, J. (2014), 'Killing in a Posthuman World: The Philosophy and Practice of Critical Military History', in B. Blaagaard and I. van der Tuin (eds), *The Subject of Rosi Braidotti*, 29–46, London: Bloomsbury.

Bradshaw, G. A. (2009), *Elephants on the Edge: What Animals Teach Us About Humanity*, New Haven: Yale University Press.

Bradshaw, G. A. and Watkins, M. (2006), 'Trans-Species Psychology: Theory and Praxis', *Psyche & Nature*, 75: 69–94.

Braidotti, R. (2010), 'Powers of Affirmation: Response to Lisa Baraitser, Patrick Hanafin and Clare Hemmings', *Subjectivity*, 3 (2): 140–8.

Braidotti, R. (2013), *The Posthuman*, Cambridge: Polity Press.

Braidotti, R. (2014), 'Conclusion: The Residual Spirituality in Critical Theory: A Case for Affirmative Postsecular Politics', in R. Braidotti, B. Blaagaard, T. de Graauw and E. Midden (eds), *Transformations of Religion and the Public Sphere*, 249–72, Basinsgtoke: Palgrave Macmillan.

Burke, P. (2012), 'Cultural History and its Neighbors', *Culture & History Digital Journal*, 1 (1), available online: http://dx.doi.org/10.3989/chdj.2012.006 (accessed 12 February 2017).

Butryn, T. M. (2003), 'Posthuman Podiums: Cyborg Narratives of Elite Track and Field Athletes', *Sociology of Sport Journal*, 20 (11): 17–39.

Bynum, C. W. (2009), 'Perspectives, Connections & Objects: What Happening in History Now?', *Daedalus*, 138 (1): 71–86.

Callus, I., Herbrechter, S. (2012), 'Introduction: Posthumanist subjectivities, or, coming after the subject', *Subjectivity*, 5 (3): 241–64.

Campana, J. and Maisano, S., eds (2016), *Renaissance Posthumanism*, New York, NY: Fordham University Press.

Capurro, R. (2012), 'Beyond Humanisms', *Journal of New Frontiers of Spatial Concepts*, 4: 1–12.

Caputo, J. D. (1997), *The Prayers and Tears of Jacques Derrida: Religion without Religion*, Bloomington, IN: Indiana University Press.

Chakrabarty, D. (2009), 'The Climate of History: Four Thesis', *Critical Inquiry*, 35 (2): 197–222.

Chakrabarty, D. (2012), 'Postcolonial Studies and the Challenge of Climate Change', *New Literary History*, 43 (1): 1–18.

Chakrabarty, D. (2015), *The Human Condition in the Anthropocene*. The Tanner Lectures in Human Values delivered at Yale University, 18–19 February 2015; available on line: https://tannerlectures.utah.edu/Chakrabarty%20manuscript.pdf (accessed 18 April 2017).

Chakrabarty, D. (2016), 'Humanities in the Anthropocene: The Crisis of an Enduring Kantian Fable', *New Literary History*, 47 (2/3): 377–97.

Chamovitz, D. (2012), *What a Plant Knows: A Field Guide to the Senses*, New York: Scientific American / Farrar, Straus and Giroux.

Christian, D. (2004), *Maps of Time. An Introduction to Big History*, Berkeley: University of California Press.

Coker, C. (2004), *The Future of War: The Re-Enchantment of War in the Twenty-First Century*, Oxford: Blackwell.

Collingwood, R.G. (1994), The Idea of History, Oxford and New York: Oxford University Press.

Connor, P., Cadava, E. and Nancy, J.-L., eds (1991), *Who Comes After the Subject?* New York: Routledge.

Cooper, J. (1983), *Animals in War*, London: Heinemann.

Daston, L. and Mitman, G., eds (2005), *Thinking with Animals: New Perspectives on Anthropomorphism*, New York: Columbia University Press.

De Bruyn, B. (2013), 'Earlier is Impossible. Deep Time and Geological Posthumanism in Dutch Fiction', *Journal of Dutch Literature*, 4 (2): 68–91.

De Waal, F. (2016), *Are We Smart Enough to Know How Smart Animals Are?* New York: W. W. Norton & Co.

Delort, R. (1984), *Les Animaux ont une histoire*, Paris: Seuil.

Derrida, J. (1969), 'The Ends of Man', trans. A. Bass, *Philosophy and Phenomenological Research*, 30 (1): 31–57.

Derrida, J. (2006), *L'animal que donc je suis*, ed. M.-L. Mallet, Paris: Editions Galilée.

Derrida, J. (2008), *The Animal That Therefore I Am*, transl. D. Wills, New York: Fordham University Press.

Derrida, J. (2009), *The Beast and the Sovereign, vol. I (The Seminars of Jacques Derrida)*, transl. G. Bennington, Chicago: University of Chicago Press.

Derrida, J. (2011), *The Beast & the Sovereign, vol. II (The Seminars of Jacques Derrida)*, transl. G. Bennington, Chicago: University of Chicago Press.

Derrida, J. and Vattimo, G., eds (1998), *Religion*, Stanford: Stanford University Press.

Domanska, E. (2007), 'Historiographical Criticism: A Manifesto', in K. Jenkins, S. Morgan, and A. Munslow (eds), *Manifestos for History*, 197–204, London and New York: Routledge.

Domanska, E. (2010), 'Beyond Anthropocentrism in Historical Studies', *Historein*, 10: 118–30.

Domanska, E. (2015), 'Ecological Humanities', *Teksty Drugie/Second Texts*, 1: 186–210.

Domanska, E. (2017), 'Animal History', *History and Theory*, 56 (2): 267–87.

Fernández-Armesto, F. (2009), 'History beyond History: New Adventurers on the Frontiers of Traditional Historiography', *Comparative Studies in Society and History*, 51 (1): 212–9.

Foltz, R. C. (2003), 'Does Nature Have Historical Agency? World History, Environmental History, and How Historians Can Help Save the Planet', *The History Teacher*, 37 (1): 9–28.

Foucault, M. (2005), *The Order of Things. An Archaeology of the Human Sciences*, London and New York: Routledge.

Fountain, P. (2013), 'Toward a Post-Secular Anthropology', *The Australian Journal of Anthropology*, 24: 310–28.

Freeman, C. P.; Merskin, D. (2015), 'Respectful Representation. An Animal Issues Style Guide for All Media Practitioners', in N. Almiron, M. Cole, and C. P. Freeman (eds), *Critical Animal and Media Studies: Communication for Nonhuman Animal Advocacy*, 205–20, New York: Routledge.

Freud, S. (1957), *The Origins of Psychoanalysis: Letters, Drafts, and Notes to Wilhelm Fliess, 1887–1902*, Garden City, NY: Doubleday.

Fudge, E. (2002), 'A Left-Handed Blow: Writing the History of Animals', in N. Rothfels (ed.), *Representing Animals*, 3–18, Bloomington, IN: Indiana University Press.

Fudge, E. (2017), 'What Was It Like to Be a Cow? History and Animal Studies', in L. Kalof (ed.), *The Oxford Handbook of Animal Studies*, 258–78, Oxford: Oxford University Press.

Fukuyama, F. (2002), *Our Posthuman Future. Consequences of the Biotechnology Revolution*, New York: Farrar, Straus and Giroux.

Gane, N. (2006), 'When We Have Never Been Human, What Is to Be Done? Interview with Donna Haraway', *Theory, Culture & Society*, 23 (7–8): 135–58.

Gayk, S. and Robyn, M. (2014), 'The Sacred Object', *Journal of Medieval and Early Modern Studies*, 44 (3): 457–67.

Gilbert, S. F., Sapp, J. and Tauber, A. I. (2012), 'A Symbiotic View of Life: We Have Never Been Individuals', *The Quarterly Review of Biology*, 87 (4): 325–41.

Graham, E. (2016), 'Manifestations of the Posthuman in the Postsecular Imagination', in B. Hurlbut and H. Tirosh-Samuelson (eds), *Perfecting Human Futures: Transhuman Visions and Technological Imaginations*, 51–72, Dordrecht: Springer

Guerrini, A. (2016), 'Deep History, Evolutionary History, and Animals in the Anthropocene', in B. Bovenkerk and J. Keulartz (eds.), *Animal Ethics in the Age of Humans*, 25–37, Berlin: Springer.

Habermas, J. (2008), 'Notes on a Postsecular Society (18 June 2008)', available online: http://www.signandsight.com/features/1714.html (accessed 27 February 2017).

Haraway, D. (2004), *The Haraway Reader*, New York and London: Routledge.

Haraway, D. (2008), *When Species Meet*, Minneapolis: University of Minnesota Press.

Harvey, G., ed. (2013), *The Handbook of Contemporary Animism*, Durham: Acumen Publishing.

Hayles, K. N. (1999), *How We Became Posthuman*, Chicago: University of Chicago Press.

Hediger, R., ed. (2013), *Animals and War: Studies of Europe and North America*, Leiden and Boston: E.J. Brill.

Herbrechter, S. (2013), *Posthumanism. A Critical Analysis*, London: Bloomsbury Academic.

Hunt, L. (2014), *Writing History in the Global Era*, New York and London: W.W. Norton & Company.

Hurlbut, J. B. and Tirosch-Samuelson, H., eds (2016), *Transhuman Visions and Technological Imaginations*, Wiesbaden: Springer VS.

Hurn, S. (2010), 'What's in a Name? Anthrozoology, Human-Animal Studies, Animal Studies or Something Else? A Comment on Caplan', *Anthropology Today*, 26 (3): 27–8.

Iggers, G. G., Wang, Q. E. and Mukherjee, S., eds (2017), *A Global History of Modern Historiography*, 2nd edn, London and New York: Routledge.

Ioannides, G. (2013), 'Vibrant Sacralities and Nonhuman Animacies: The Matter of New Materialism and Material Religion', *Journal for the Academic Study of Religion*, 26 (3): 234–53.

Jameson, F. (2010), 'Utopia as Method, or the Uses of the Future,' in M. D. Gordin, H. Tilley and P. Gyan (eds), *Utopia/Dystopia: Conditions of Historical Possibility*, 21–44, Princeton, NJ: Princeton University Press.

Kaiser, M. I. and Plenge, D. (2014), 'Introduction: Points of Contact Between Biology and History', in M. I. Kaiser, O. R. Scholz, D. Plenge, and A. Hüttemann (eds), *Explanation in the Special Sciences: The Case of Biology and History*, 1–23, Dordrecht: Springer.

Karunanithy, D. (2008), *Dogs of War: Canine Use in Warfare from Ancient Egypt to the 19th Century*, London: Yarak Publishing.

Kean, H. (2012), 'Challenges for Historians Writing Animal–Human History: What Is Really Enough?', *Anthrozoös*, 25 (supplement): 57–72.

Kieniewicz, J. (1975), *Kerala od równowagi do zacofania* [Kerala from Equilibrium to Backwardness], Warszawa: Wydawnictwo Uniwersytetu Warszawskiego.

Kieniewicz, J. (2014), 'Ekohistoryk wobec wyzwań przyszłości' [Ecohistorians and Future Challenges], *Przegląd Humanistyczny*, 1: 65–80.

Kistler, J. M. (2006), *War Elephants*, Westport, Conn.: Praeger.

LaCapra, D. (1994), *Representing the Holocaust: History, Theory, Trauma*, Ithaca: Cornell University Press.

LaCapra, D. (2001), *Emile Durkheim: Sociologist and Philosopher*, Aurora, CO: The Davies Group.

LaCapra, D. (2007), 'Rethinking History and Resisting Apocalypse', in K. Jenkins, S. Morgan, and A. Munslow (eds), *Manifestos for History*, 160–78, London and New York: Routledge.

LaCapra D. (2009), *History and Its Limits: Human, Animal, Violence*, Ithaca: Cornell University Press.

Lakatos, I. (1978), *The Methodology of the Scientific Research Programmes. Philosophical Papers, vol. 1*, ed. J. Worrall and G. Currie, Cambridge: Cambridge University Press.

Latour, B. (1993), *We Have Never Been Modern*, trans. C. Porter, Cambridge, MA: Harvard University Press.

Latour, B. (2005), *Reassembling the Social. An Introduction to Actor-Network-Theory*, Oxford: Oxford University Press.

Latour, B. (2009), 'Perspectivism: "Type" or "Bomb"', *Anthropology Today*, 25 (2): 1–2.

Le Chene, E. (1994), *Silent Heroes: The Bravery and Devotion of Animals in War*, London: Souvenir Press.

Le Roy Ladurie, E. (1967), *Histoire du climat depuis l'an mil*, Paris: Flammarion.

Le Roy Ladurie, E. (1973), *Le territoire de l'historien*, vol. 1, Paris: Gallimard.

Linzey, A. (2007), *Creatures of the Same God: Explorations in Animal Theology*, Winchester: Winchester University Press.

Lundblad, M. (2009), 'From Animal to Animality Studies', *PMLA*, 124 (2): 496–502.

Martinelli, D. (2010), *A Critical Companion to Zoosemiotics: People, Paths, Ideas*, Dordrecht: Springer.

Massumi, B. (1993), *The Politics of Everyday Fear*, Minneapolis: University of Minnesota Press.

McLennan, G. (2007), 'Towards Postsecular Sociology?', *Sociology*, 41 (5): 857–70.

Megill, A. (2013), 'History, Theoreticism, and the Limits of 'the Postsecular'', *History and Theory*, 52: 110–29.

Mikhail, A. (2016), 'Enlightenment Anthropocene', *Eighteenth-Century Studies*, 49 (2): 211–31.

More, M. and Vita-More, N., eds (2013), *The Transhumanist Reader: Classical and Contemporary Essays on the Science, Technology, and Philosophy of the Human Future*, Oxford: Wiley-Blackwell.

Moore, S. D., ed. (2014), *Divinanimality: Animal Theory, Creaturely Theology*, New York: Fordham University Press.

Nance, S., ed. (2015), *The Historical Animal*, Syracuse, New York: Syracuse University Press.

Nayar, P. (2014), *Posthumanism*, Cambridge: Polity Press.

Orr, A. (2014), *Wojtek the Bear: Polish War Hero*, Edinburgh: Birlinn.

Pálsson, G., Szerszynski, B., Sörlin, S., Marks, J., Avril, B., Crumley, C., Hackmann, H., Holm, P., Ingram, J., Kirman, A., Pardo Buendía, M. and Weehuizen, R. (2013), 'Reconceptualizing the 'Anthropos' in the Anthropocene: Integrating the Social Sciences and Humanities in Global Environmental Change Research', *Environmental Science & Policy*, 28: 3–13.

Papadopoulos, D. (2010), 'Insurgent Posthumanism. The State of Things', *Ephemera: Theory & Politics in Organization*, 10 (2): 134–51.

Partner, N. and Foot S., eds (2013), *The SAGE Handbook of Historical Theory*, London: SAGE.

Phillips, D. (2015), 'Posthumanism, Environmental History, and Narratives of Collapse', *Interdisciplinary Studies in Literature and Environment*, 22 (1): 63–79.

Pierotti, R. (2010), *Indigenous Knowledge, Ecology, and Evolutionary Biology*, New York: Routledge.

Robin, L. and Steffen, W. (2007), 'History for the Anthropocene', *History Compass*, 5 (5): 1694–719.

Rose, N. (2013), 'The Human Sciences in a Biological Age', *Theory, Culture, Society*, 30 (1): 3–34.

Rudwick, M. J. S. (2005), *Bursting the Limits of Time: The Reconstruction of Geohistory in the Age of Revolution*, Chicago and London: The University of Chicago Press.

Savage-Rumbaugh, S., Wamba, K., Wamba, P. and Wamba, N. (2007), 'Welfere of Apes in Captive Environments: Comments On, and by, a Specific Group of Apes', *Journal of Applied Animal Welfare Science*, 10 (1): 7–19.

Schouwenburg, H. (2015), 'Back to the Future? History, Material Culture and New Materialism', *International Journal for History, Culture and Modernity*, 3 (1): 59–72.

Shaw, D. G. (2013), 'The Torturer's Horse: Agency and Animals in History', *History and Theory*, Theme Issue 52: 146–67.

Shryock, A. and Smail, D. L., eds (2011), *Deep History: The Architecture of Past and Present*, Berkeley: University of California Press.

Simons, H. W. and Billig, M., eds (1994), *After Postmodernism: Reconstructing Ideology Critique*, London: Sage.

Singer, J. (2010), 'Toward a Transhuman Model of Medieval Disability', *Postmedieval*, 1: 173–79.

Smail, D. L. (2008), *On Deep History and the Brain*, Berkeley: University of California Press.

Spiegel, G. M. (2009), 'The Task of the Historian', *American Historical Review*, 114 (1): 1–14.

Spier, F. (2010), *Big History: History and the Future of Humanity*, Oxford and Malden, MA: Wiley-Blackwell.

Steinberg, T. (2002), 'Down to Earth: Nature, Agency, and Power in History', *American Historical Review*, 107 (3): 798–820.

Stotz, K. and Griffiths, P. E. (2008), 'Biohumanities: Rethinking the Relationship Between Bioscience, Philosophy, and History of Science, and Society', *The Quarterly of Biology*, 83 (1): 37–45.

Suddendorf, T. (2013), *The Gap: The Science of What Separates Us From Other Animals*, New York: Basic Books.

Swart, S. S. (2011), 'Historians and Other Animals', review of Brantz, Dorothee, ed., *Beastly Natures: Animals, Humans, and the Study of History*. H-Environment, H-Net Reviews, available online: http://www.h-net.org/reviews/showrev.php?id=31301 (accessed 17 February 2017).

Swart, S. S. (2010), "The World the Horses Made': A South African Case Study of Writing Animals into Social History', *International Review of Social History*, 55 (2): 241–63.

Teilhard de Chardin, P. (1974), *Christianity and Evolution*, transl. R. Hague, New York: Harvest.

Ulmer, J. B. (2017), 'Posthumanism as Research Methodology: Inquiry in the Anthropocene', *International Journal of Qualitative Studies in Education*, 30 (9), 832–48.

Wallace, J. (2010), 'Literature and Posthumanism', *Literature Compass*, 7 (8): 692–701.

Wolfe, C. (2010), *What is Posthumanism?* Minneapolis: University of Minnesota Press.

Worster, D. (1988), 'The Vulnerable Earth: Toward a Planetary History', in D. Worster (ed.), *The Ends of the Earth: Perspectives on Modern Environmental History*, 3–20, Cambridge: Cambridge University Press.

Ziegler, H., ed. (1993), *The End of Postmodernism: New directions. Proceedings of the First Stuttgart Seminar in Cultural Studies, 04.08.–18.08. 1991*, Stuttgart: M & P, Verlag für Wissenschaft und Forschung.

Zulueta, C. C. (2015), 'Nonhuman Animal Testimonies: A Natural History in the First Person?', in S. Nance (ed.), *The Historical Animal*, 118–30, Syracuse: Syracuse University Press.

CONCLUSION
Peter Burke

Today, students of history, old and young, are confronted with a great variety of approaches to the past, a much greater variety than in 1960 (say) or even 1990. It is an exciting situation but also a bewildering one. Hence the need for guides such as *Debating New Approaches to History*. It is the latest in a series of books taking stock of attempts to innovate, to modify the long tradition of historical thought and writing.

The most celebrated of these attempts is probably the historical 'revolution' associated with Leopold von Ranke, a revolution in method that emphasized the value as historical sources of 'records' preserved in archives at the expense of the 'chronicles' written by contemporaries. Ranke's *Critique of Modern Historians* (1824) emphasized the unreliability of chronicles and memoirs, while his later histories of Prussia, England, the Popes, and so on offered models for new narratives of political history.

A succession of new histories

Nearly a century after Ranke's manifesto, in the United States in the early twentieth century, a movement under the banner of the 'New History' criticized the followers of Ranke for their narrow concentration on political history and argued that 'history includes every trace and vestige of everything that man has done or thought since first he appeared on the earth'. As for method, 'the New History will avail itself of all those discoveries that are being made about mankind by anthropologists, economists, psychologists and sociologists' (Robinson 1912). This movement had relatively little success, perhaps because the First World War directed the attention of historians, like other people, back to politics.

Over sixty years later, when the American 'New History' was no longer new, it was the turn of the French to discuss 'new problems', 'new approaches', and 'new objects' in historical thought and writing. This ambitious programme was presented by Jacques Le Goff in three volumes that he edited with Pierre Nora in 1974 (Le Goff and Nora 1974). Four years later, it was summarized in a single encyclopaedic volume intended for a wider public, once again edited by Le Goff (1978) and entitled *La nouvelle histoire* ('The New History'). The volume included (together with shorter articles) essays on the history of the long term, the history of structures, historical anthropology, the history of mentalities, the history of material culture, 'immediate history' (better known in English as 'the history of the present'), the history of 'marginal' groups such as beggars and Gypsies, the history of the collective imagination and a study of the relation between the new history and Marxism. The authors of all four collective volumes came from the third generation of the so-called 'Annales school' (named after the path-breaking journal *Annales*, founded in 1929). The aims of this group of historians were close to those of the

American New Historians, although the Annales school was more successful than their predecessors had been in putting these ideals into practice (Burke 2015).

A few years after the French, similar initiatives were taken in the Anglophone world. At the end of the 1980s, a group of American historians launched what they called the 'New Cultural History' (Hunt 1989). They were sympathetic to the *Annales* movement and invited one of the French group, Roger Chartier, to write in their collective manifesto, but they were also inspired by the cultural Marxism of Edward Thompson and by the new style of North American anthropology, especially the work of Clifford Geertz, who advocated the replacement of the traditional functional analysis of cultures by what he called their interpretation or 'thick description'. Some of them also drew on the ideas of Michel Foucault (O'Brien 1989).

Two years after the publication of *The New Cultural History* (1989), a collective volume published in Britain presented 'new perspectives on historical writing' (Burke 1991). It included essays on history from below, women's history, overseas history, microhistory, oral history, the history of reading, the history of images, a new history of political thought, the history of the body, and finally a new history of events, part of the so-called 'revival of narrative'. The approaches described in the American and British volumes overlapped: contributors to both discussed the work of Edward Thompson and Clifford Geertz, for instance, as well as the history of the body and the history of images.

Today, the approaches just mentioned can no longer be described as 'new'. The debate has moved on and so the volume that you are now reading is very different from its predecessors. For one thing, it is much more of an international project, with authors from ten different countries. Again, comparing *Debating New Approaches* with *New Perspectives*, we see that 'Women's History' has been replaced by 'Gender History', taking account of recent research on masculinity, while 'Overseas History' has been divided into 'Global' and 'Postcolonial' history. Instead of the 'History of Images' you will find both the 'History of Things' (by the same author) and the 'History of Visual Culture'. Instead of 'The History of Political Thought', offered as an example of intellectual history, you will find 'The History of Knowledge'.

However, no fewer than six topics have no parallel in the earlier volumes: 'Environmental History' (which only made an appearance in the second edition of *New Perspectives*); 'History of Memory'; 'History of Emotions'; 'Digital History'; 'Neurohistory'; and 'Posthumanist History'. In a metaphor that has become increasingly popular, these topics may be described as the result of six different intellectual 'turns', following the earlier linguistic, cultural, visual, and global turns. The dizzying number of intellectual turns in the last generation makes stocktaking volumes such as this one increasingly necessary (Bachmann-Medick 2016).[1]

Explaining innovations

It is not difficult to explain the rise of at least some of these new topics. As Marek Tamm suggests in the introduction to this volume, in the history of historical thought, new approaches to the past have generally been inspired by changes in the present. Frederick Jackson Turner, himself a trailblazer of a new approach, the history of frontiers, once wrote, 'Each age writes the history of the past anew with reference to the conditions uppermost in its own time' (Turner 1891). I can only agree, although it is worth adding that historians respond not only to these conditions but also to debates about them.

Today it is obvious enough, for instance, that anxiety about global warming underlies the current enthusiasm for environmental history, while digital history and neurohistory only became conceivable after the digital revolution and the rise of neuroscience. Again, global history is a response to globalization and the history of things to consumer society, while the turn from intellectual history to the history of knowledge has been inspired by discussions of today's 'knowledge economy' or 'knowledge society'.

The relatively sudden appearance of other approaches to the past is not so easy to explain. Hegel once remarked that 'the owl of Minerva spreads its wings only with the falling of the dusk' – in other words, that historians become interested in a given phenomenon when it is in danger of disappearing. For example, the rise of the history of the book in the late twentieth century coincided with the decline of the book as a medium of communication. Perhaps we should be alarmed by the recent increase of interest in the history of memory and the history of emotions.

Fortunately, other explanations for these trends are possible. New approaches to history are linked not only to the 'conditions uppermost' in the world at a given time but also, within the academic microcosm, to new approaches to neighbouring disciplines. Environmental history, for instance, is only a part of a larger intellectual package, environmental studies. The history of knowledge is linked to the sociology, the anthropology, the politics, and even the economics of knowledge. In similar fashion, historians of memory and the emotions share their interest with colleagues in other disciplines, especially psychology. Posthumanist history too forms part of an intellectual package, linked to philosophical discussions of animal rights (Singer 1975), for instance, as well as discussions of the 'agency' of things by both anthropologists (Gell 1998) and archaeologists (Dobres and Robb 2000).

Alternative chapters

There was obviously a case for including other debates in this volume, omitted for lack of space and not for lack of interest. If this had been a two-volume work, I should have voted for chapters on the history of the senses, for instance; the history of space; the history of networks; the history of losers; the history of ethnicities; the social history of language; Public History; 'Connected History'; 'Big History'; and finally, the history of the long term, the complementary opposite of the 'microhistory' that provoked such lively discussions a generation ago. Incidentally, new variants of that approach continue to emerge, notably attempts to link the local with the global (Magnússon 2017). Again, the history of the book, or history of reading, discussed in *New Perspectives* by Robert Darnton, is developing in new directions (Raven 2018).

1. Like the emotions, and connected with it, the senses, or sensibility, have attracted increasing attention from historians in the last few years, as a recent six-volume synthesis testifies (Classen 2014; cf. Jütte 2005; Smith 2007). The interest in the history of sight, or the gaze, was joined by the history of sound (or 'soundscapes'), the history of smell, and finally the history of touch and taste.

2. The so-called 'spatial turn' in history and some related disciplines goes back at least as far as the publications of Michel Foucault on the clinic and the prison in the 1960s and 1970s, but the attention paid to space by historians is still growing. In France, the collective *Lieux de mémoire* (Nora 1984–92) was succeeded by the even more ambitious (but still unfinished) *Lieux de savoir* (Jacob 2007–11). Historians of science focus on observatories and laboratories, historians of historiography on archives and libraries, and historians of riot and revolt on the streets and squares where so many of these collective actions took place (Bravo and D'Amico 2017).

3. It is no surprise to find that in an age of 'networking', historians (following the lead of anthropologists and sociologists) have discovered the importance of networks, held together by personal encounters, by writing letters, and now by e-mail, and transmitting information, ideas, and also objects ranging from coins to dried plants and stuffed animals. A recent study, for instance, examines the network of the natural historian and collector Hans Sloane (Delbourgo 2017). In so doing, this study and others like it encourage us to view what were traditionally considered individual achievements as collective ones. So does the 'history of constellations' (Mulsow and Stamm 2005), concerned with the creativity of small groups of individuals. A well-documented example is the group of friends who formed the Lunar Society in Birmingham in the late eighteenth century (Uglow 2002), to exchange information and debate ideas.

4. It has often been said that history has been written by the victors. This is not altogether true – a glance at the histories of the American Civil War provides an impressive array of counter-examples – but it is only recently that losers have become the focus of a number of studies (Schivelbusch 2003; García de Cortazar 2006; Sandage 2005; Macleod 2008; Barczewski 2016).[2] They mark a reaction against the 'triumphalism' of so many accounts of the past, which make the victory of one group over another seem inevitable. The focus on losers is a natural development from 'history from below', and there would also appear to be a connection between the history of failure and virtual history, another topic in which interest has recently grown (Ferguson 1997). After all, both kinds of history are concerned with possible paths that were not actually taken. Some individuals who never fulfilled the 'great expectations' of their contemporaries have become the subject of monographs (Pallares-Burke 2012), while biographies of successful individuals devote increasing attention to the paths that they did not take.

5. The history of ethnicity, despite its topicality in an age of massive immigration, is taken more seriously by anthropologists (Tonkin, McDonald, and Chapman

1989) than by historians and more seriously by historians in the Americas than in Europe (but see Panayi 2000). In the United States, there have been many studies of 'blackness' and some on 'whiteness' from a cultural point of view (Kolchin 2002). In Latin America, the history of the indigenous peoples has attracted much attention. However, anyone entering the field faces the problem that the term 'ethnicity', which has often been used as a 'politically correct' substitute for 'race', resists definition. In practice, many historians shy away from the 'R' word, although they continue to discuss racism, race prejudice, and even race relations. They treat ethnic groups simply as examples of cultures or subcultures, although these groups often view themselves as united by descent as well as by traditions. Even in a country in which interbreeding makes it unusually difficult to distinguish groups on the basis of skin colour or other physical characteristics, Afro-Brazilians are increasingly identifying themselves as 'black'.

One way to deal with the problem of definition might be to focus on immigration, a topic on which some valuable studies have been published in recent years, including the ways in which newcomers are perceived and received, or their willingness or unwillingness to adapt themselves to their new culture. Another option might be to discuss ethnicity as part of the cultural construction or 'invention' of identity or identities.

A chapter of this kind would already have been an appropriate choice in 1989 or 1991, but the topic still attracts innovative studies. Speaking of identities in the plural allows the old topic of nationalism to be approached in a different way and also places the emphasis on individual choice, notably the way in which individuals have multiple identities (national, local, religious, professional, sexual, and so on) and present themselves in different ways, switching identities (Sollors 1989) according to the situations in which they find themselves.

6. Language is an important sign of identity, as current attempts to revive 'dying' languages such as Scottish Gaelic make very clear. It is surely no accident that social and cultural historians have become increasingly interested in both subjects at a time when identity politics, including the politics of language, is a current topic of conflict as well as debate. Sociolinguists have often pointed out that individuals engage in 'code-switching', speaking different languages, or different varieties of the same language, in different situations, accommodating their speech to their listeners or even to the subject of conversation (Bullock and Toribio 2009). Today, there is increasing convergence between what the linguists call 'historical sociolinguistics' (Hernández-Campoy and Conde-Silvestre 2012), while historians prefer 'the social history of language' (Burke and Porter 1987).

7. 'Public History' is difficult to define, since most history, even 'secret history', is written for the public (Sayer 2015). An imprecise description might be 'history written by trained historians who work outside the academic world, whether in government, museums, heritage, the media (especially television), or as freelance

writers'. Public history is not a euphemism for 'popular history', since some public historians carry out original research. An alternative name for this form of history is 'applied history', on the model of applied economics, geography and psychology. Once again, the name is not a happy one, since some uses of history, for example to legitimate national or imperial expansion or authoritarian regimes, are not to be recommended.

In any case, the rise of this approach in the 1970s, together with its institutionalization in the National Council on Public History, the journal *The Public Historian* and master's courses in many universities, all in the United States, marks, paradoxically enough, a recognition that the analysis and the presentation of the past are not monopolies of universities, that words are not the only medium in which ideas about the past can be communicated and that exhibitions, films, and presentations on television also have important contributions to make. One famous example is the documentary miniseries on the American Civil War directed by Ken Burns and broadcast in the United States in 1990.

8. Practitioners of 'connected history' such as Sanjay Subrahmanyam (1997) have criticized scholars involved with 'area studies' for assuming that the areas they study, Southeast Asia, for instance, are uniform, timeless, and separated from the rest of the world, ignoring connections that are visible as early as the sixteenth century, if not before. As for *histoire croisée*, a phrase that is sometimes translated as 'entangled history', it refers to a variety of connected history that developed in France out of the criticisms of two earlier approaches to the past, comparative history and the history of 'cultural transfers', in other words the movement of artefacts or ideas from one culture to another (Werner and Zimmermann 2006).

One of the criticisms of comparative history is that the binary opposition between similarities and differences, and also between the entities (usually nations) that are compared, assumes an Olympian viewpoint rather than admitting that historians themselves belong to nations, classes, genders, and so on. It is also argued that processes of change rather than static political or social systems should be the focus of analysis. In the case of transfers, and of the cultural encounters in which they take place, the 'entangled' historians have pointed out that the donor culture as well as the receiving culture is changed by this process, so that it would be better to think in terms not of simple transfer but rather of processes of cultural exchange and circulation. One might add to these processes that of 'cultural translation', a useful metaphor used first in anthropology (Beidelman 1971) and then in history and cultural studies (Bassnett 1998), to describe the conscious process of adapting items from one culture to make them fit for purpose in another.

9. As for Big History, discussed in the introduction to this volume, it was placed firmly on the historiographical map by a former historian of Russia, David

Christian, whose book, appropriately entitled *Maps of Time*, began with the Big Bang, nearly fourteen billion years ago, rather than with the invention of writing (once held to mark the frontier between history and 'prehistory') or even the rise of *Homo Sapiens* (Christian 2004; Brown 2012). Big History has received a good deal of publicity, thanks in particular to its challenge to the kind of history taught in the traditional school curriculum. An International Big History Association was founded in 2010 and a Big History Project, supported by Bill Gates, was launched the following year, to teach the subject in the United States, Australia and, it is hoped, all over the world. Linked to Big History is Deep History, launched by Daniel Lord Smail (above, 4–5; Smail 2008; Shryock and Smail 2011). It is concerned with the history of humans (thus including what is traditionally known as 'prehistory'). Inspired by neuroscience (discussed in Chapter 11) Smail is particularly interested in changes in the human brain, whether in the short term (by taking certain drugs, for instance), and in the long term of evolution, but the deep approach has spread to the history of the body, language, food, and other topics.

10. Historians who confine themselves, like the majority of the profession, to the last few thousand years, are also turning away from events or even short-term processes to the study of trends over the long term, usually hundreds of years (Armitage and Guldi 2015, discussed above, 5). This turn is in fact a return, since the French historians associated with *Annales*, especially one of their leaders, Fernand Braudel, were already emphasizing the importance of the long term in the 1950s, and thanks to them, even Anglophone participants in the current debate use the French phrase 'longue durée'. However, there is an important difference between the two phases of the debate. Thanks to the digital revolution, historians are better equipped to analyse 'big data' than they used to be at a time when mainframe computers were the size of small houses and information had to be punched onto cards (Guldi and Armitage 2014: 88–116).

History among the social sciences

Braudel thought of the study of the longue durée as a multidisciplinary approach that would unite history with economics, sociology, geography, and other social sciences. Today, economists, sociologists, geographers, and others are indeed making contributions to this study. Indeed, most of the new approaches discussed in this volume, far from being a monopoly of historians, are shared with colleagues in other disciplines in the humanities and social sciences (archaeology, sociology, geography, anthropology, literature, art, philosophy). I wrote 'shared with' rather than 'in common with' since both formal and informal collaboration between individuals in different disciplines is becoming increasingly common.

The new approaches are increasingly shared with natural scientists as well. Historians of the environment have to become acquainted with a number of scientific disciplines – geology, for instance, climatology, and botany. Historians of the emotions and the senses engage in conversation with experimental psychologists and neuroscientists. Whereas, a generation ago, historians were particularly close to sociologists and anthropologists, today they are beginning to talk to and work with biologists, as new terms such as 'biohistory' remind us, like 'sociobiology', 'bioethics', 'biopolitics', and even 'bioeconomics'.

Biohistory, for instance, was the subject of a debate that was published in the *American Historical Review* in 2014. An evolutionary view of the past, popular in the nineteenth century but rejected in the twentieth, has returned in the twenty-first century in new forms. Thus the historical sociologist Gary Runciman (2009) discusses (and distinguishes) 'cultural and social selection', equivalent to, but far from identical with, natural selection. For his part, the historian Edmund Russell emphasizes what he calls 'co-evolution', in other words the 'process in which populations of different species evolve repeatedly in response to each other' (Russell 2014: 1515; cf. Russell 2011), returning us to the non-human history discussed earlier in this volume.

These dialogues between disciplines would have been inconceivable before the relatively recent trends in philosophy and science that reject the traditional divisions between mind and body, nature and culture (Chapter 12) and even between the body and its environment (Le Cain 2017).

At a time when anxiety over the fragmentation of knowledge is often expressed, such collaborative work is encouraging. However, like other good things, it has its price. On the positive side, it is no longer unusual for different groups of historians to talk to and even work with colleagues in at least one of the disciplines mentioned in the previous paragraph. On the negative side, these groups are in danger of losing touch with their colleagues in the large and increasingly diverse discipline of history itself. The danger is all the greater when new approaches are institutionalized in the form of fields (territories warning off trespassers) or sub-disciplines with their own centres, professorships, societies, journals, and so on.

What is needed is a synthesis of these new approaches, since all of them are parts of what the French call *histoire totale*, not in the sense of an account of the past in all its details, which is obviously impossible, but an integrated account that finds a place for every kind of activity and for the connections between them. Some steps towards integration have already been taken. Network analysis has been employed in intellectual history and also in political history, to study political patrons and clients in 'the network state', while the history of the environment has been extended to the history of war (Keller 2016).

Whether we shall see such a synthesis achieved, only the future will reveal. Looking further into the future, we might ask ourselves the question: What would a volume equivalent to this one look like if it were to be published in (say) 2040 or 2050? How different would it be from the book in your hands, or before your eyes on a screen? What changes in the world would underlie the contrast between the two volumes?

Notes

1. Among them, the affective (or emotional), anthropological, biological, bodily, cognitive, cultural, dialogical, environmental, ethnic, global, informational, interpretative, linguistic, material, memory, narrative, non-human, normative, ontological, performative, phenomenological, postmodern, practice, pragmatic, quantitative, social, spatial, technological, translational, transnational, and visual turns.

2. Historians of Latin America were among the pioneers, including Miguel León-Portilla, *La visión de los vencidos* (1959) and Nathan Wachtel, *La vision des vaincus* (1971).

References

Armitage, D., and Guldi, J. (2015), 'The Return of the *Longue Durée*: An Anglo-American perspective', *Annales. Histoire Sciences Sociales*, 70, English edn: 219–47.

Bachmann-Medick, D. (2016), *Cultural Turns: New Orientations in the Study of Culture*, Berlin: De Gruyter.

Barczewski, S. (2016), *Heroic Failure and the British*, New Haven: Yale University Press.

Bassnett, S. (1998), 'The Translation Turn in Cultural Studies', in S. Bassnett and A. Lefevere (eds), *Constructing Cultures*, 123–40, Clevedon, PA: Multilingual Matters.

Beidelman, T. O. (1971), *The Translation of Culture*, London: Routledge.

Bravo, P. and D'Amico, J. C., eds (2017), *Territoires, lieux et espaces de la révolte, XIVe-XVIIIe siècles*, Dijon: Éditions universitaires.

Brown, C. S. (2012), *Big History: From the Big Bang to the Present*, 2nd edn, New York: New Press.

Bullock, B. and Toribio, A., eds (2009), *The Cambridge Handbook of Linguistic Code-Switching*, Cambridge: Cambridge University Press.

Burke, P., ed. (1991), *New Perspectives on Historical Writing*, Cambridge: Polity Press.

Burke, P. (2015) *The French Historical Revolution: the Annales School, 1989–2014*, Cambridge: Polity Press.

Burke, P. and Porter, R., eds (1987), *The Social History of Language*, Cambridge: Cambridge University Press.

Christian, D. (2004), *Maps of Time: An Introduction to Big History*, Berkeley, CA: University of California Press.

Classen, C., ed. (2014), *A Cultural History of the Senses*, 6 vols, London: Bloomsbury.

Delbourgo, J. (2017), *Collecting the World: The Life and Curiosity of Hans Sloane*, Cambridge, MA: Harvard University Press.

Dobres, M.-A. and Robb, J. E., eds (2000), *Agency in Archaeology*, London: Routledge.

Ferguson, N., ed. (1997), *Virtual History: Alternatives and Counterfactuals*, London: Picador.

García de Cortázar, F. (2006), *Los perdedores de la Historia de España*, Barcelone: Planeta.

Gell, A. (1998), *Art and Agency: An Anthropological Theory*, Oxford: Oxford University Press.

Guldi, J. and Armitage, D. (2014), *The History Manifesto*, Cambridge: Cambridge University Press.

Hernández-Campoy, J. M. and Conde-Silvestre, J. C., eds (2012), *The Handbook of Historical Sociolinguistics*, Oxford: Wiley Blackwell.

Hunt, L., ed. (1989), *The New Cultural History*, Berkeley: University of California Press.

Jacob, C., ed. (2007–11), *Lieux de savoir*, Paris: Albin Michel.

Jütte, R. (2005), *A History of the Senses*, Cambridge: Polity Press.

Keller, T. (2016), 'Aux marges écologique de la belligerence. Vers une histoire environnementale globale de la Première Guerre mondiale', *Annales. Histoire, Sciences Sociales*, 71: 65–85.

Kolchin, P. (2002), 'Whiteness Studies: The New History of Race in America', *Journal of American History*, 89: 154–73.

LeCain, T. (2017), *The Matter of History: How Things Create the Past*, Cambridge: Cambridge University Press.

Le Goff, J., ed. (1978), *La nouvelle histoire*, Paris: Retz.

Le Goff, J. and Nora, P., eds (1974), *Faire de l'histoire*, 3 vols, Paris: Gallimard.

León-Portilla, M. (1959), *La visión de los vencidos*, México: Universidad Nacional Autónoma.

Macleod, J., ed. (2008), *Defeat and Memory: Cultural Histories of Military Defeat in the Modern Era*, Basingstoke: Palgrave.

Magnússon, S. G. (2017), 'Far-reaching Microhistory: The Use of Microhistrical Perspective in a Globalized World', *Rethinking History*, 21: 312–41.

Mulsow, M. and Stamm, M., eds (2005), *Konstellationsforschung*, Frankfurt: Suhrkamp.

Nora, P., ed. (1984–92), *Lieux de mémoire*, 7 vols, Paris: Gallimard.

O'Brien, P. (1989), 'Michel Foucault's History of Culture', in L. Hunt (ed.), *New Cultural History*, 25–46, Berkeley: University of California Press.

Pallares-Burke, M. L. (2012), *O Triunfo do Fracasso: Rüdiger Bilden, o amigo esquecido do Gilberto Freyre*, São Paulo: UNESP.

Panayi, P. (2000), *An Ethnic History of Europe since 1945: Nations, States and Minorities*, Harlow: Longman.

Raven, J. (2018), *What is the History of the Book?* Cambridge: Polity Press.

Robinson, J. H. (1912), *The New History*, New York: Macmillan.

Runciman, W. G. (2009), *The Theory of Cultural and Social Selection*, Cambridge: Cambridge University Press.

Russell, E. (2011), *Evolutionary History: Uniting History and Biology to Understand Life on Earth*, New York: Cambridge University Press.

Russell, E. (2014), 'Coevolutionary History', *American Historical Review*, 119: 1514–28.

Sandage, S. (2005), *Born Losers: A History of Failure in America*, Cambridge, MA: Harvard University Press.

Sayer, F. (2015), *Public History: A Practical Guide*, London: Bloomsbury.

Schivelbusch, W. (2003), *The Culture of Defeat*, London: Granta.

Shryock, A. and Smail, D. L., eds (2011), *Deep History: The Architecture of Past and Present*, Berkeley: University of California Press.

Singer, P. (1975), *Animal Liberation: A New Ethics for Our Treatment of Animals*, New York: New York Review.

Smail, D. L. (2008), *Deep History and the Brain*, Berkeley: University of California Press.

Smith, M. M. (2007), *Sensory History*, Oxford: Berg.

Sollors, W., ed. (1989), *The Invention of Ethnicity*, New York: Oxford University Press.

Subrahmanyam, S. (1997), 'Connected Histories: Notes Towards a Reconfiguration of Early Modern Eurasia', *Modern Asian Studies*, 31: 735–62.

Tonkin, E., McDonald, M. and Chapman, M., eds (1989), *History and Ethnicity*, London: Routledge.

Turner, F. J. (1891) 'The Significance of History', available online: http://teachingamericanhistory. org/library/document/the-significance-of-history/ (accessed 29 November 2017).

Uglow, J. (2002), *The Lunar Men: Five Friends Whose Curiosity Changed the World*, London: Faber and Faber.

Wachtel, N. (1971), *La vision des vaincus*, Paris: Gallimard.

Werner, M. and Zimmermann, B. (2006), 'Beyond Comparison: Histoire Croisée and the Challenge of Reflexivity', *History and Theory*, 45: 30–50.

INDEX

Index

Index

Index

Index